Defending
Israel

Also by Alan Dershowitz

Defending Israel

Against Hamas and
Its Radical Left Enablers

Alan Dershowitz

Hot Books

This book is dedicated to an endangered species:
liberal supporters of Israel—"ken yirbu"

Contents

Defending
Israel

Introduction to the
Paperback Edition

The barbarous attack by Hamas against innocent Israeli civilians on October 7, 2023 was the worst assault on Jewish people since the end of the Holocaust. But the attack itself was not nearly as significant as the reaction to it, especially by young people on the left. Immediately after the attack, and before Israel fired a single shot in response, many people across the world placed the entire blame for these rapes, beheadings, tortures, and kidnappings on Israel. It only got worse after Israel responded and exercised its right and responsibility to destroy the group that committed these atrocities.

In the original introduction to *Defending Israel*, I worried that "Israel's future is at great risk because of diminishing support from young people—soon to be our leaders—especially on the hard left." When I offered this dire prediction in 2019, I had no idea how much worse it would become in such a few short years.

This "blame Israel and the Jews" response to terrorist attacks is part of a long-standing pattern that I have documented in my previous books including *Defending Israel*. Hamas and other terrorist groups understand and exploit this pattern: they attack Israeli civilians, knowing that Israel will respond; Israel does respond, killing civilians who are used as human shills by Hamas; much of the world blames Israel for its response while forgetting the original terrorism or the human shields; and Hamas ends up benefitting from its deliberate, unprovoked, and unlawful attack on civilians. Because it benefits from this deliberate pattern, Hamas repeats the attacks, causing the deaths of both Israeli and Palestinian civilians. Yet despite the obviousness of this despicable tactic by Hamas, much of the world continues to point the blame at its victim—Israel.

The events surrounding the attack on October 7, constituted a repetition of this pattern, but with far greater viciousness on the part of Hamas terrorists. The international reaction to Israel's victimization uncovered deep-seated antisemitism, often disguised as anti-Zionism within large sections of the population. It is a wake-up call that should alert the world to increasing Jew hatred that will almost certainly result in even greater violence against the Jewish people and its nation-state.

But like Kristallnacht eighty-five years ago, which should have warned the world about the impending Holocaust, much of the world is sleeping through this wake-up call. We cannot ignore the lessons of history lest we repeat it. That's why I have authorized the re-release of my book *Defending Israel*. Today more than ever Israel needs to be defended from existential threats that come not only from its neighboring enemies, especially Iran and its surrogates, but also from Jew haters throughout the world, especially among young "woke" progressives of the hard left. I hope my writing provides the defenders of Israel with historical, moral, legal, and other ammunition with which to help wage the just war on behalf of the nation-state of the Jewish people—a battle I have been waging for more than sixty years as described in this book.

Introduction

The Endless Battle

Anti-Zionism and Anti-Semitism on the Rise

FOR LIFELONG SUPPORTERS of Israel, like me, this is the best of times. The nation-state of the Jewish people has never been stronger—militarily, economically, scientifically, diplomatically.

But Israel's future is at grave risk because of diminishing support from young people—soon to be our leaders—especially on the left.

Anti-Semitism, often disguised as anti-Zionism, is on the rise throughout the world. A recent *New York Times* headline read "Anti-Semitism Is Back, from the Left, Right, and Islamist Extremes. Why?" Its answer, in large part, focused on the Israeli government as "a point of divergence from the different strands of contemporary anti-Semitism."[1]

The sources of this bigotry vary—from newly elected members of Congress to rioters in Charlottesville, Yellow Vests in Paris, feminists in Chicago, gay rights activists in San Francisco, violent Muslim extremists in Sweden, radical university professors, supporters of boycotting Israeli products, academics and artists, and students taken with identity politics and "intersectionality." But its effect is the same: a growing opposition to the legitimacy of Israel as the nation-state of the Jewish people and a diminution of its bipartisan support. For many supporters of Israel, that is the core of "the second great mutation of antisemitism in modern times."[2]

In much of Europe, where anti-Semitism on both the hard left and hard right is increasing, Israel has become a wedge issue, sharply dividing left from right. It is possible, indeed likely, that unless current trends can be changed, this dynamic will cross the Atlantic and infect our body politic, even more virulently than it has today. The refusal of leading Democratic presidential candidates to accept invitations to speak at the American Israel Public Affairs Committee (AIPAC), the leading lobby group for Israel, which followed by several years the absence of several prominent Democratic legislative leaders at Prime Minister Benjamin Netanyahu's speech on Iran before a joint session of Congress, reflects a troubling movement within the Democratic Party away from support for Israel. At the same time, Republican support for Israel, especially among evangelical Christians, has strengthened. Israel is thus becoming a wedge in the United States as well—dividing many Democrats from Republicans and dividing Democrats among themselves.

This change has created new conflicts over party allegiances for many supporters of Israel, especially among liberal Jews who have historically voted for Democrats. They continue to favor the social policies of the Democrats—a woman's right to choose, gay rights, gun control, environmental protection, separation of church and state, a liberal Supreme Court—but they feel discomfort over the movement of some Democrats, especially among the young and radical elements of the party, away from support for Israel. This growing discomfort has not yet resulted in a discernable shift in party affiliation among most Jews—in part because the leader of the Republican Party is the very controversial President Donald Trump—but it is causing deep concern about the future of bipartisan support for Israel.

If the drift away from bipartisan support for Israel is not reversed, it will pose real dangers to Israel's security. Today Israel remains capable of defending itself from all external threats, with or without material support from the United States. But it is impossible to assess the impact on Israel's security in the event that an American government hostile to Israel came to power.

It is a goal of this book to try to influence, in a positive direction, this discernable drift away from bipartisan support for the Middle East's only democracy and America's most reliable ally. It is a daunting task, but a crucial one to help secure Israel's future.

I begin this task by telling the great adventure story of Israel's establishment—really, re-establishment—as the nation-state of the Jewish people, and of my long, sometimes challenging, relationship with this ever-changing democracy.

The nation-state of the Jewish people traces its origins to antiquity, but its modern history begins with a tiny, militarily weak, economically impoverished new state that was populated largely by Holocaust survivors, refugees from Muslim countries and long-time residents of Jewish Palestine. It was beloved throughout the world, except by its Arab neighbors. But now that it has become an economic, scientific and military superpower, it is regarded by many as a pariah. Like the Jewish people themselves throughout the ages, the nation-state of the Jewish people has become the victim of its own success. From the Book of Exodus,[3] to the Megillah of Esther,[4] through the "golden age" of Muslim–Jewish relations, to Weimar Germany, to revolutionary Russia, Jewish self-empowerment and success have resulted in reaction, enmity and sometimes catastrophe.

As Israel grows stronger, we are seeing it treated in many quarters as a colonial, imperialist, hegemonic occupier and bully. David has become Goliath as Israel's military arsenal has developed from "slingshots" (literally weapons contrived from surplus parts) into nuclear weapons and high-tech cyber measures and countermeasures, and its intelligence agency is considered among the most respected and feared in the world. It is as if much of the world loves weak and persecuted Jews but is fearful and jealous of strong and successful Jews who defy some old stereotypes (the Jew as nebbish and victim) while reifying others (the Jews as all-powerful controllers of the world and victors). Israel has become the Jew among nations—the object of disproportionate attention, excessive criticism and sometimes excessive praise. More is expected of the Jewish nation, just as more has always been expected of the Jewish people. British rabbi Lionel Blue once quipped that "Jews are just like everyone else, only more so."[5] Bishop Desmond Tutu put it more seriously and critically: "Whether Jews like it or not, they are a peculiar people. They can't hope to be judged by the same standards which are used for other people."[6] The same can be said of the nation of the Jewish people, which is subjected to a discriminatory double standard of judgment by Tutu and so many others.

Israel today is the most condemned nation in world. It is also more criticized now than ever before in its history. Some of this criticism is warranted, and it even comes from Israelis and American Jews who love Israel. I myself have taken issue with some of Israel's policies.[7] But the degree of condemnation and demonization is all out of proportion to what is warranted. Strong as it has become, Israel faces continuing threats to its security and very existence—from Iran, which has vowed its destruction; to Hezbollah, which has tens of thousands of sophisticated rockets aimed at its cities; to Hamas, which fires primitive rockets and firebombs across the border; to the United Nations, which condemns Israel more than all the other nations of the world combined; to campuses, which target only Israel with BDS (boycott, divestment and sanctions) and false claims of "apartheid" and even "genocide." No country faced with comparable threats can boast a better record of human rights, a higher regard for the rule of law or greater efforts to reduce civilian casualties.[8] Nor has any country in history contributed so much to humankind—medically, scientifically, environmentally, academically, culturally—in so short a time as has Israel in its relatively brief existence as an independent state. Yet, it is tiny Israel—with a land mass the size of New Jersey and a population similar to that of Papua, New Guinea—that is the focus of most of the world's protests.

Throughout my life, I have been defending Israel against demonization, delegitimization and double standards. In the beginning, it was against some of my Orthodox elementary school rabbis who did not believe in the religious justification for a Jewish state until the Messiah arrived, and certainly not in the legitimacy of the secular socialist state that David Ben-Gurion declared in 1948. In Zionist summer camp, it was against hard-left zealots like Noam Chomsky, who believed in a single secular state. Later in high school, it was against right-wing extremists, such as Meir Kahane, who believed that the Jewish state must encompass all of biblical Israel.

After the 1967 war, it was against the likes of Daniel Berrigan, who described Israel as a racist criminal entity. Then it was against right-wingers who supported annexing the entire West Bank and opposed the two-state solution. After that, it was against Jimmy Carter, who characterized Israel's control over the West Bank as "apartheid."[9] Then it was against Cornel West, who has accused Israel of being a colonialist state.[10] Now it is against the boycott, divestments and sanctions (BDS) tactic, the intersectionality movement[11] and efforts by hard-left professors and students to demonize and isolate Israel and treat it the way apartheid South Africa was treated.[12]

Although I have no actual lawyer/client relationship with Israel, I have been called "Israel's single most visible defender" and "the Jewish state's lead attorney in the court of public opinion."[13] I take this role seriously, but because I have no formal legal relationship with Israel, I am free to criticize its policies when I disagree with them. Notwithstanding such occasional criticism, I still defend Israel's right to be wrong about specific issues, as all democracies have that right, without delegitimizing it as the nation-state of the Jewish people. Israel is the only country whose very existence is challenged because of disagreements with particular policies it pursues.

In this book, I tell the story of my lifelong relationship with my self-appointed "client." To say that defending Israel in the court of public opinion has become increasingly challenging is to understate the reality. I try to explain—without in any way justifying—this change.

Because the story of my own passionate, if sometimes stormy, relationship with Israel also began in 1948, and because it is reactive to Israel's story, I combine both in this narrative.

The intensity of my own role in defending Israel has varied inversely with Israel's popularity around the world, and especially on university campuses, where I have spent nearly all of my life—more than 60 years. As disproportionate and undeserved demonization of Israel has increased exponentially, so too have my time and efforts—to the point that I now devote a majority of my professional priorities to defending Israel and its supporters. This will continue as long as Israel is unjustly attacked and I have the energy to respond to false accusations with credible defenses. In this book, I defend Israel, though not all of its policies, by truthfully telling its story: its successes, its failures, its virtues, its vices. I have lived by the principle that the best response to falsehood is truth, not censorship. I apply that principle to my defense of Israel in every forum in which it is unjustly attacked. I also tell my story: my defenses; the attacks against me; my changing views and tactics. Our stories are closely related.

The story of Israel can be told in numerous ways. It can be seen through the eyes of its pioneers, chalutzim, some of whom were my relatives, who left Europe in the late nineteenth and early twentieth centuries and made aliya to the promised land; through the eyes of European Jews who escaped or survived the Holocaust and found a new home in Israel; through the eyes of Sephardic Jews who were forced to leave Muslim countries in which their ancestors had lived for millennia; through the eyes of young Israelis who defend their country against wars and terrorism, often at the cost of their lives and limbs—as was the case with two of my cousins, one of whom was killed and the other left as a paraplegic; through the eyes of Israel's prime ministers, most of whom I have known, some more intimately than others; through the eyes of American presidents, several of whom have sought my advice over the years with regard to the Middle East; through the eyes of Israel's raucous political system, its frenzied media competition and its harsh ideological divisions, as manifested by two elections in close proximity in 2019. It can also be seen through the eyes of its current Arab population, many of whose relatives and friends were displaced—others of whom were left on their own—by the numerous wars waged against the Jewish population; through the eyes of Palestinian political and religious leaders, several of whom I have met over the years; through the eyes of its most virulent critics, many of whom I have debated and confronted.

I myself have seen Israel, through my own eyes as an American liberal Zionist, who was brought up as a modern Orthodox Jew and came of age as a more secular, but still traditional, agnostic who questions everything and everyone, even himself.

In this book, I narrate the challenging relationship between the nation-state of the Jewish people and myself, one of its most zealous, if sometimes critical, defenders. It is not a straightforward narrative, because the history of modern Israel is anything but straightforward, but I will try my best to present a coherent and objective account, as seen through my own eyes. I begin with my memories of the establishment of Israel as the nation-state of the Jewish people when I was a 10-year-old child in Brooklyn.

1

From Palestine to Israel

My Earliest Memories of Zionism

THERE WAS NEVER a time that Israel was not a part of my consciousness. But in 1948, when David Ben-Gurion declared the reestablishment of a nation-state for the Jewish people in Eretz Yisrael (the Ancient land of Israel), it became my passion. I was turning 10, and my parents sent me to a Hebrew-speaking Zionist summer camp, called Camp Massad, in the Pocono Mountains of Pennsylvania, where we followed, with deep concern and interest, the news of the War of Independence in which all the surrounding Arab nations attacked the new state. That was more than 70 years ago, and my passion—and concern—has never abated, though the nature and degree of my involvement have changed dramatically over these many decades.

I grew up in a religious Zionist home, attended religious Zionist schools and summer camps, sang Zionist songs, and recited Zionist prayers. Every home in our modern Orthodox Jewish Brooklyn neighborhood of Boro Park had a JNF (Jewish National Fund) "pushka" (charity box) with a map of Jewish Palestine on its blue-and-white metal surface. In the early years, before Israel became a nation, the charity was for purchasing and developing land for Jewish communities in what was to become Israel.[1] (I even have a collection of JNF boxes going back well before the establishment of the state. They show the increasing purchases of land over time.) Much of the land was bought from distant land speculators in Syria and other locations and from local Arab landowners seeking to profit from the high prices offered by the JNF.[2]

David Ben-Gurion, then the head of the Jewish Agency (the pre-state "government"), was sensitive with regard to maintaining good relations with local Arabs.[3]

In elementary school—Yeshiva Etz Chaim (Tree of Life)—we sang "Hatikvah," which was the Zionist anthem of hope, before it became Israel's national anthem. I can still remember the original words, "L'shuv L'Eretz Avoseinu" (to return to the land of our fathers), which we sang until Israel declared statehood. These words of longing and hope were then changed to words of aspiration and determination: "Li' Yot am chofshi b'artzeinu" (to be a free nation in our land).

The lyric was different but the music was the same.

Even our social athletic clubs (they were called SACs), in which we played street games like stickball, punch ball, stoop ball and ringa-levio, had Zionist names. Mine was the Palmach, which was the for-ward strike force of the Haganah, which became the Israel Defense Forces (IDF) after the establishment of Israel. Our club "song" was the battle hymn of the Palmach, which we sang in Hebrew: "rishonim Tamid anachnu Tamid, anu anu Hapalmach" ("We are always the first; we are the Palmach"). (Years later, at a charity event in Los Angeles, I learned that Vidal Sassoon had been a Palmach fighter, and so we re-galed the crowed with an off-tune duet of the battle hymn.) The very idea of a Jewish army capable of protecting Jews was thrilling to young Jews in a neighborhood that included many Holocaust survivors who had lacked any protection.

Several months before Israel's establishment, we had watched the vote of the United Nations to partition British Mandatory Palestine into two states for two people: one for the Jews, one for the Arabs. The Jews immediately, if reluctantly, accepted the partition. The Arabs rejected it. (I own an original edition of the newspaper *Haaretz* that contains a report on the partition as the crucial step to statehood, as well as an original of the newspaper *Hamashkif* announcing the establishment of the state.) There was dancing in the streets. A school assembly celebrated the prelude to statehood by dancing the hora and offering prayers. Among the people I knew, there was no dissent or even doubt.[4] We were all overjoyed.

But joy soon turned to concern, fear and distress when the surrounding armies attacked Israel immediately upon its establishment. Distress turned to tragedy when the son of one of my mother's friends was killed. Moshe Perlstein had been studying at Hebrew University under the G.I. Bill of Rights when the fighting broke out, and he volunteered to join the Haganah. His death brought the war to our neighborhood. Our group of 10-year-old Zionists all imagined ourselves volunteering to fight for Israel's survival when we came of age. Our school raised money to buy a jeep that was shipped to Israel. Before being sent abroad, it was proudly displayed in the driveway of our school.

I attended Camp Massad during the summer of 1948, while the War of Independence was raging (we played sports there using Hebrew words; a "strike" was a "shkia"—literally, a mistake). The Zionists had resurrected the Hebrew language of the Bible and prayer into a vibrant, modern language suitable to the new nation. We were eager to learn Israeli Hebrew, and we did at Camp Massad. Our bunks and divisions were named after areas of Israel (Degania, Emek, Galil). All the counselors were fervent Zionists, even our division head, a 20-year-old student named Noam Chomsky, who was active in Hashomer Hatzair, the "guardians of the young," a left-wing Zionist group. Though Chomsky supported, in theory, a binational secular state, he was not opposed in practice to the state declared by Ben-Gurion. Every day during mealtimes, we heard reports in Hebrew of the progress of the war, and several Israeli counselors left camp to return home to defend their newly born country.

After the long, bitter war, where Israel prevailed, an armistice was declared under which Israel gained additional territory.[5] But victory came with a heavy price. The new nation lost 1 percent of its population, including many civilians who were murdered in cold blood.[6] Among the dead were young men and women who had survived the Holocaust, some volunteers from Europe and America—including Colonel Mickey Marcus, a World War II hero, who became Israel's first modern general and was the subject of the film *Cast a Giant Shadow* starring Kirk Douglas—and many chalutzim.

My uncle Albert (whose nickname was "Itchie"), my father's second youngest brother, stowed away on a ship to Israel in order to help defend the new nation. (He paid the fare several years later when he could afford to.) He eventually became an ultra-Orthodox head of a yeshiva in Bnei Brak and a religious opponent of political Zionism, though he continued to love the people of Israel. His youngest brother, Zecharia, a doctor of psychology, was to follow him several years later, changing his name from the Europeanized Dershowitz (originally Derschovitz) to the Hebraized Dor Shav (the generation that returned). At this writing, he is still living in Jerusalem and remains active in Israeli and Jewish causes.

Another one of my father's brothers had been a captain in the U.S. Army, and he proudly collected guns from his military colleagues to send to Israel. I remember my uncle showing me a Luger confiscated from a German POW that would now be used to protect Jews rather than kill them.

Both my father's and my mother's families had strong connections to Israel. In the early 1930s, my mother's father, Naftuli Ringel, traveled to Palestine to see if he could make a living and bring his family there. He bought a small piece of land on which he hoped to build a home near what is now Ben Gurion Airport. He returned to Brooklyn several months later, brokenhearted, with the realization that he could not make aliya with his wife and six children. He brought back several small sacks of earth from Rachel's Tomb, which he wanted to be buried with. I have one of these sacks in my home as a remembrance of my grandfather's visit to Eretz Yisrael before it was the State of Israel. (When I told this story to a leading political figure in Israel, he generously replied, "If your grandfather had made aliya, you would probably have my job today.")

My father's father was active in rescuing Jews from the Holocaust, some of whom settled in Israel. He obtained false affidavits from neighbors, promising "jobs"—including rabbis, cantors and other religious functionary positions—to unqualified people for nonexistent synagogues. The last such refugee to leave boarded the ship shortly before Hitler invaded Poland. One relative was trapped and couldn't leave, so my grandfather sent my unmarried uncle with his American passport to find her, "marry" her and bring her to safety in America. He did, and then he fell in love with her on the boat and they married in a real wedding upon their arrival in New York. Many of these refugees became prominent Americans, including one who served as chairman of the Columbia University Engineering Department; another became a rabbi in a large Los Angeles synagogue. Hence my natural sympathy for opening our gates to refugees—even illegal ones in extreme situations. (One of my favorite comic shticks was by the Russian-Jewish comedian Yakov Smirnoff, who would stand by the Statue of Liberty thanking her for rescuing him and his family from Soviet tyranny. Then, as he leaves, he turns to Ms. Liberty and shouts, "Now please keep the rest of those damn immigrants out!")

My parents and grandparents belonged to organizations that supported Israel—such as Mizrachi and Hadassah—and they contributed to Israeli charities despite their limited means. Everyone I knew did. My grandmother Ringel had a JNF pushka next to the party-line telephone; everyone who made a call was required to deposit a nickel into it for tzedakah (charity) for the poor Jews of Eretz Yisrael.

I grew up with an uncomplicated love of Israel, and support for its success, as a given. No one questioned it. No one had any doubts or qualms about the righteousness of our cause. To us, Israel was always in the right, and its Arab enemies were always in the wrong. The

Arab war against the Jews of Palestine and then Israel was a continuation of the Nazi war against the Jews of Europe. In fact, several notorious Nazi war criminals had received asylum in Egypt and other Arab countries and were helping them develop weapons systems with which to destroy Israel.

We all believed that if there had been an Israel in the 1930s and early 1940s, millions of Jews—who were trapped in Europe by Britain's immoral policy of strictly limiting Jewish immigration into its mandate and America's bigoted policies that denied visas to Jews seeking refuge from the Holocaust—could have been saved from the Holocaust.

David Ben-Gurion, who personified the new Israel, was the hero (although some, particularly the rabbis, didn't approve of his secularism and socialism). The Arab leaders—from Haj Amin al-Husseini to Gamal Abdel Nasser—were the villains. They were easy to hate because of their association with Nazism, communism, anti-Semitism and other despised ideologies.

They were calling for genocide against the Jewish population of Israel: "Drive the Jews into the sea." The issues were black and white: good versus evil, democracy pitted against tyranny, religious tolerance instead of intolerance, life versus death. The Bible commands, "I have set before you life and death . . . therefore choose life" (Deuteronomy 30:19, KJV). We chose life. It was an easy choice, especially in the shadow of the six million deaths during the Holocaust.

It was also easy to choose Israel because of who else was supporting the new nation-state of the Jewish people—and who was opposing it. Israel was a liberal cause, a leftist cause, a progressive cause, a Democratic cause, a labor union cause, a woman's cause, an academic cause, an African American cause—a cause that all good people, as we defined good, were supporting. Pete Seeger included Israeli folk songs in his popular repertory of working-class music. Left-wing Hollywood types raised funds for the embattled nation. Frank Sinatra helped to smuggle arms to the newly emerging state. Liberal college students spent their summer vacations volunteering in kibbutzim. Later, Martin Luther King and Robert Kennedy would champion Israel.

No one accused Israel of being a "colonialist" project, as some absurdly do today. Whose "colony" could it be? Certainly not that of the British, against whom they had fought for independence, or the Poles, Ukrainians or Russians, whose pogroms they had escaped from. Moreover, unlike the majority populations of America, New Zealand and Australia, Jews were among the aboriginal people of what became Israel. They were returning to their ancient homeland from which they had been forcibly exiled, not colonizing new lands in which they had no roots. The Jews of Palestine and then Israel were the vanguards of the national liberation movement of the Jewish people—a bulwark against colonialism, a liberal oasis amid a reactionary desert.[7] The Israelis were the heroes. Those who would destroy the new state were the villains.

No one questioned Israel's legitimacy. Its birth certificate was based on legal rules and documents: The Balfour Declaration of 1917, the San Remo Resolution of 1920, the League of Nations' Mandate for Palestine of 1922, the Anglo-American Treaty of 1924, and the UN Partition Plan of 1947. Israel was created by the pen, though it had to defend itself by the sword. This was no accident, since most of Israel's founders—Theodor Herzl, David Ben-Gurion, Menachem Begin, Ze'ev Jabotinsky and Yitzhak Shamir—had been trained as lawyers.

Nor did anyone—even Israel's most strident enemies—ever characterize the new nation with words such as "genocidal" or "apartheid," or hold it guilty of "ethnic cleansing" or "colonialism." Genocide is what happened *to* the Jews, not what the Jews had done to others. Apartheid was the denial of all rights to the black population of South Africa, not the equal rights guaranteed to Arab citizens of Israel. Ethnic cleansing was what the Soviet Union did to Konigsberg or the Allies did in Sudetenland, not the complex population exchange that occurred when Jewish residents of Muslim countries were forced to leave places they had lived for thousands of years, and when some Arab residents of the new Israel fled during the Arab-initiated fighting and were not allowed to return. Only bad people engaged in genocide, apartheid and ethnic cleansing, and Israelis were good people.

My family was both liberal and Zionist. Our political heroes were FDR, Harry Truman, Adlai Stevenson, Hubert Humphrey, Robert Wagner, Jacob Javits and Fiorello La Guardia. They were also modern Orthodox Jews who saw no conflict between their religious orthodoxy and their political liberalism, or between their Zionism and their progressive values.

We were centrist liberals who hated Joseph McCarthy and Roy Cohn, but we also despised Stalin and the American Communist Party. No "red diaper babies" in our family. We were taught that Jews were often caught between the black and the red—the black of fascism and the red of communism. We suffered under extremism and thrived under centrist liberalism, hence our centrist liberalism. We supported desegregation, opposed capital punishment, and contributed to the ACLU and NAACP, as well as to the Jewish National Fund. We knew that certain colleges, corporations and neighborhoods didn't welcome Jews, blacks, Catholics and other non-WASPs, but we also understood that these forms of "polite" bigotry were the last gasp of a dying WASP aristocracy. We were not particularly sensitive to discrimination against gays or women, but neither would we have consciously engaged in overt discrimination against any group.

We generally voted for Democrats, but sometimes we backed liberal Republicans (especially if they were Jewish) like Jacob Javits. We were proud to be called "liberals," the ones who cared about others and about preserving liberties. The Conservatives, on the other hand, were selfish, ungenerous and unconcerned about the rights of others.

We marched for civil rights, against blacklists and against the death penalty. We signed petitions against executing Julius and Ethel Rosenberg, though my parents feared that my name on such petitions would give me a "permanent record" as a communist sympathizer. We had doubts about the Korean War, and when we got a bit older, we opposed the Vietnam War. We saw no contradiction between our opposition to America's unjustified foreign military adventures and Israel's need to defend itself against violent neighbors dedicated to its destruction.

Our heroes all supported the establishment of a nation-state for the Jewish people, especially since the Holocaust (a term we didn't yet know) had seen the murder and relocation of so many European Jews, survivors of which were living in displaced persons camps with no country—until Israel was established—willing to take them in. We applauded the law of return by which Israel opened its doors to every Jew in need of asylum. We watched with pride as David Ben-Gurion, Chaim Weitzmann and later Abba Eban made the liberal case for a national homeland for the Jews.

Those who opposed the creation of Israel—the Arab and Muslim countries, some American State Department officials, segments of the British establishment, and European neo-Nazis—were perceived, quite correctly, as reactionary and anti-Jewish. The leaders of the new nation-state of the Jewish people were perceived, also correctly, as progressive and heroic. Still, they had to make the case for Israel against those—including the popular George Marshall, who was secretary of state when the United States recognized Israel—who were arguing that the new Western-oriented nation would destabilize the Middle East. The pro-Israel side prevailed in the court of public opinion—at least for the moment.

There were right-wing elements within Israel, but we took no positions on the internal disagreements between the left and right in Israeli politics. The Israeli right—personified by Menachem Begin—was relatively powerless. The Israeli left—personified by David Ben-Gurion—was in power. All Israeli leaders, regardless of their politics, were our heroes. To be sure, there were a few young right-wing zealots who hated Ben-Gurion and adored Begin and his late mentor, Ze'ev Jabotinsky, but they were on the margin. Among them was a young Zionist—a few years my senior—named Meir Kahane, who attended the same high school I did, where we both served on the debating team. We were later to become ideological opponents, though I also defended his right to express his contrarian—some would say anti-Muslim—views. (I had an Israeli cousin who had served in the Irgun with Menachem Begin and was on the Irgun ship *Altalena* when Ben-Gurion's forces opened fire on it. Till the day he died, he referred to Israel's first prime minister as "David F—ing Ben-Gurion.")

There were also some zealots on the left who considered Begin and Jabotinsky to be fascists and who wanted Israel to be closer to the Soviet Union. Among those was Noam Chomsky, who I first met in summer camp. We, too, became ideological opponents, though I defended his right to oppose—sometimes by questionable means—the Vietnam War.

For most of us, who stood near the center, there was no conflict between our domestic political views and our Zionism. Zionism was seen as a liberal program—the national liberation movement of the Jewish people. Some of the other "countries" in the region—such as Jordan, Iraq, Saudi Arabia and the Gulf states—had been artificially constructed by colonial powers, such as France and Great Britain. These colonial powers selected the artificial kings, princes and dictators to rule their colonies. Other countries such as Egypt and Iran were surrogates of the Soviet Union or the United States—pawns in the Cold War. Israel was an independent democracy, struggling for its survival in a hostile geographic location in which Jews had lived for thousands of years. In its modern incarnation, it had been built by hard-working chalutzim, many of whom lived on kibbutzim and moshavim (agricultural collectives). Young men and women from all over the world—Jews and non-Jews—volunteered to work on the collectives to make the deserts bloom. We praised the draining of the swamps and the destruction of habitats where malaria-carrying mosquitoes thrived, unaware that anti-Israel environmentalists would complain decades later that Israel had tampered with "natural wetlands."

The leading American proponents of the nation-state of the Jewish people—such as Supreme Court justices Louis Brandeis and Felix Frankfurter, Rabbi Stephen S. Wise, Emma Lazarus and Henrietta Szold—were paragons of centrist liberalism. My generation of "religious "Zionists" forgave the secular bent of Israel's leaders. We supported the compromise Ben-Gurion struck with the rabbis, whereby the chief rabbinate assumed control over religious issues, such as marriage, divorce and conversion. (The number of Chassidic and ultra-Orthodox Jews was very small back then, and few expected it to increase so dramatically—and with it the power of the chief rabbinate over all Israelis and even non-Israeli Jews, a development now threatening Israel's democracy and its relationship with diaspora Jews.)

Even the hard left, including many communists, supported Zionism and the establishment of Israel, which they saw as a democratic-socialist island amid a sea of repressive Arab monarchies and tyrannies. Both the United States and the Soviet Union immediately recognized Israel, and Czechoslovakia (then under the control of the Soviet Union) provided arms for the Israeli army. The screenplay for the popular film *Exodus*—based on the equally popular book by Leon Uris—was written by Dalton Trumbo, a writer who had been blacklisted for his alleged membership in the Communist Party. It glorified the establishment of Israel and demonized Israel's Arab enemies.

In the post–World War II period, many new nations emerged from colonialism, basing themselves on national liberation movements. Transfers of populations predicated on ethnicity and religion were accepted as a reasonable price to be paid for stability and homogeneity.[8] For example, the partition of India and Pakistan following the end of Great Britain's colonial rule over a united India resulted in a massive transfer of populations and the creation of millions of refugees.[9]

Israel, established as the national liberation movement of the Jewish people, was accepted by the left, by anticolonialists and by most of the world.[10]

Israel's American opponents were reactionary, often anti-Semitic State Department bureaucrats (some of whom were the same ones who stopped Jews from entering the United States during the Holocaust), oil barons, political isolationists and some "establishment" German Jews. The "good guys" supported Israel; the "bad guys" opposed it. There was no cognitive dissonance between, or discomfort over, our liberal American values and our Jewish nationalistic aspirations.

Electoral choices were easy for liberal Zionists: vote for liberal Democrats like Adlai Stevenson who supported Israel, and vote against Republicans like Dwight Eisenhower who did not. In general, the left and the Democratic Party were more supportive of Israel than the right and the Republicans.

Oh, how things have changed over the past half century! Today, Israel's most fervent enemies are on the hard left, including many Jews. For them "Zionism" is a dirty word, often equated with "fascism," "colonialism," "imperialism," "apartheid," "genocide," even "Nazism." Many on the "soft left"—the kind of centrist liberals with whom I grew up—now also have a disdain for Israel. They cloak that general disdain with claims of opposition to specific Israeli policies or politicians, but polls show that their negative attitude toward the nation-state of the Jewish people often transcends specific policies or particular leaders.[11] This is especially true of younger liberals who were not alive when Israel struggled for its survival in the 1940s, 1950s, 1960s and the early part of the 1970s. It is now Conservatives and Republicans—including many on the Christian right—who are Israel's most fervent supporters. Some on the hard right—such as Pat Buchanan, Richard Spencer and David Duke—are as anti-Zionist as they are anti-Semitic, but they represent a far smaller proportion of the right than the growing proportion of anti-Israel extremists of the left. This shift does create cognitive dissonance for many liberal

Zionists, who support the Democratic Party's domestic agenda but tend to agree more with Republican policies toward Israel.

I will tell the story of this change in the chapters to come, as well as how it impacted my advocacy for Israel. It is sufficient here to note the contrast between my coming of age during a period of near universal support for Israel, and the coming of age of my grandchildren at a more challenging time.

Part of the reason why attitudes toward Israel have changed is the word "Palestine." When I was growing up, the "Palestine" was synonymous with the "Eretz Yisrael." The Jews who lived there were called Palestinian Jews. Immanuel Kant referred to European Jews as "Palestinians living among us."[12] The Jewish newspaper published in Jerusalem was called the *Palestine Post* (now the *Jerusalem Post*). The support group for the Hebrew University was called Palestine Friends of the Hebrew University. When Frank Sinatra performed a concert in the Hollywood Bowl in support of a Jewish state, it was called the "Action for Palestine" rally. I have an old record of "Palestinian Folk Songs" from before the establishment of Israel. They are of course Zionist songs about *Eretz Yisrael*. The Jewish National Fund raised money for Palestine. I own an old JNF charity box that says, "Made in Eretz-Israel (Palestine)." I also own an even older German tzedakah box for "Juden in Palestina." We contributed to the Jews of Palestine. Palestine was a positive name—a Jewish name—among American Zionists.

The area that was named Palestina by the Romans and was, before 1948, the British Mandatory territory of Palestine, belonged as much to its Jewish population as to its Arab one. To Jews, it was always Eretz Yisrael (the land of Israel) or Tziyon (Zion). No one, least of all the Arabs who lived in Palestine, called the local Arab population "Palestinians." Palestine was a geographic concept, not an ethnic or nationalistic one. Indeed, it was a somewhat artificial geographic area, whose boundaries were determined as much by political as by topographic considerations. The ethnic makeup of the geographic areas that came to be known as Palestine consisted of Arabs—both Muslim and Christian—and Jews, along with some Armenians, Druze, Baha'i, German colonists and assorted others. The Arab residents of this area were no more "Palestinian" than were the Jewish residents who lived in Eretz Yisrael. My friend Tzvi Groner's father—who was born in Hebron on the West Bank—referred to himself as "Palestinian" and had a Jordanian passport. Of course, he and all other Jewish Palestinians—some of whose ancestors had lived in Hebron and other Jewish areas of Yehuda and Shomron for generations—were ethnically cleansed from the Jordanian West Bank as soon as Israel became a state.

When the leader of the local Arabs, the Grand Mufti of Jerusalem Haj Amin al-Husseini, testified before the Peel Commission in 1937, he complained about the "detachment of Palestine from the body of other Arab territories," suggesting that the Arabs who lived in Palestine had no distinct national or ethnic character—they were part of the great Arab nation. He didn't want a separate Palestinian state for the Arabs. He simply did not want there to be a state or homeland for Jews anywhere in the region.[13]

Recall, as well, that what is now the nation of Jordan was also part of the original British mandate over what was called Palestine. It was cut out of the mandate in 1920[14] and called Trans-Jordan. It comprises a majority of the original Palestine Mandate and its population was composed largely of Palestinian Arabs. Jordan was truly a "colonial" project, as were the artificial nations of Iraq, Syria, Saudi Arabia and the Gulf states, which were created in the aftermath of the First World War by colonial cartographers sitting in Europe with drafting pens.

Jordan's population still consists of a majority of Palestinian Arabs who have been ruled by the Hashemite clan, a ruling royal family originally from Saudi Arabia.[15]

Many now call themselves Palestinians. The Jews of what is now Israel also referred to themselves as Palestinians—Palestinian Jews who lived in Eretz Yisrael to be sure, in contrast to Palestinian Arabs or just Arabs.

The point is that the local Arabs have now—beginning in the mid-1960s—coopted the word "Palestinian," so as to suggest that *they* are the only rightful residents of Palestine and that the Jewish residents of what is now Israel and has always been Eretz Yisrael are interlopers—or colonialists, imperialists or conquerors. Most ironically, the Jews of what was part of Palestine and is now Israel are sometimes even called "crusaders," out of historical ignorance of the tragic reality that Jews were among those brutally murdered by Christian crusaders in the eleventh and twelfth centuries.[16]

When the United Nations voted to partition Palestine into "independent Arab and Jewish states"—two states for two peoples—the name Israel was never mentioned, nor was the word "Palestinians."[17] Each group could choose to name its state as it pleased. Had the new nation-state of the Jewish people called itself "Jewish Palestine," instead of Israel, the optics would be quite different. But now, the newly named Palestinians—who used to be called Palestinian Arabs, or just Arabs—have laid claim to the name "Palestinian," and to the sympathy that comes with it, for having been displaced from their homeland, Palestine, by the interloping Jews.

The reality is that both Jews and Arabs lived in Roman-named Palestine—Eretz Yisrael—when the United Nations divided it into two areas in order to facilitate the establishment of two states for two peoples: the Jews of Palestine and the Arabs of Palestine. The area allocated to the Jewish state contained a majority of Jews, and there were hundreds of thousands of additional Jews waiting in displaced person camps in Europe and detention centers on Cyprus to be allowed to join family members the moment Israel declared statehood and opened its gates to Jewish survivors. There were also Jews who had lived—some for generations—in the part of mandatory Palestine that was allocated by the United Nations to become an Arab state. These Jews were forced to leave their homes and move to the Jewish state, while Arab residents of the Jewish area were welcome to remain—until Israel was attacked from both within and without. If the Arab states had not attempted to destroy the nation-state of the Jewish people at its birth, the Arab residents of Israel would have been allowed to remain in their homes, where many did remain. Indeed, today there are more Arab citizens of Israel than the total population of Arabs who lived in Palestine-Israel at the time of the partition.[18] So much for ethnic cleansing.

To this day, the leaders of the Palestinian authority refuse to recognize the concept of two states for two peoples, both of whom are indigenous to Palestine. They adamantly refuse to recognize Israel as the nation-state of one of these people: namely, the Jewish people. I know because I have put this question—Will you recognize Israel as the nation-state of the Jewish people?—personally to Mohammad Abbas. He has said no. As we will see, this refusal lies at the core of the ongoing conflict.

The anti-Israel Arab argument is as simple as it is simplistic and ahistorical: we are *the* Palestinians; Palestine is a geographic entity that extends from the (Jordan) river to the (Mediterranean) sea; the Palestinian Arab people rightfully own *all* of Palestine; therefore, there is no room for a Jewish State in any of historic and geographic Palestine. The fallacy is clear, if one substitutes history for labels: the geographic area was Eretz Yisrael before the Romans renamed it Palestina; it has always been populated by both Jews and Arabs who can both lay claim to being called Palestinians; it was only after the United Nations recommended a partition of Palestine into two states for two peoples that local Arab leaders began calling their people Palestinians; this change of labels did not change history or morality; it did not suddenly entitle the local population to *all* of Palestine, in violation of the United Nations Partition Plan, just because they now call themselves *The* Palestinians. The Jewish residents of Palestine—many of whom can trace their roots in the area further back in time than local Arabs—are as Palestinian as the Arab residents are. The geographic area rightfully belongs to both peoples; hence the case for the two-state solution, based on the United Nations partition of Palestine—Eretz Yisrael—into two states for two peoples.[19]

Had the Arab residents of Palestine—and their leaders—accepted the UN proposal of two states for two peoples, today's Palestinians would have a much larger state than any they can realistically hope to get. There would be no refugee problem, no occupation, no Israeli settlements and no continuous warfare. Tens of thousands of lives would have been saved, terrorism would not have become a primary tactic of asymmetrical warfare, and the economic situation of Palestinian Arabs would be far better than it currently is. To be sure, there might still have been conflicts between the Jewish and Arab states, but these conflicts would not have been over whether there should be a state of Israel and a state of Palestine. The entire fault for these continuing problems lies squarely at the feet of the Palestinian leadership, which wanted not to have a Jewish state at all more than they wanted a state of their own. Many moderate Palestinians and academics today recognize this reality and blame their past leaders for refusing to accept the UN partition.[20]

Even after the Palestinian Arabs—and other Arab countries—rejected the UN proposal and waged war against Israel, there was still an opportunity for the Palestinian Arabs to have a state of their own. The war of 1948 ended with an armistice and agreed-upon boundaries. These boundaries gave the Palestinian Arabs control over the entire West Bank and the Gaza Strip (now known as the pre-1967 armistice lines). Nothing, least of all Israel, would have stopped the Palestinians from declaring statehood in their territory. But they did not, and the Jordanian government occupied the West Bank, while the Egyptian government occupied the Gaza Strip. It was these governments, not the Israeli government, that prevented the Palestinian Arabs from establishing a Palestinian state in these large areas.

Nor were these occupations benign. During this period, many Palestinians left the occupied West Bank and Gaza Strip and became part of the "Palestinian diaspora." They were subjected to mistreatment and a double standard in many Arab countries. But the international community didn't care that Arabs were occupying the lands of other Arabs and denying them basic liberties. There were no campus demonstrations, no boycotts, no UN resolutions. These began only after Jews and their nation-state took over the preexisting occupation in a defensive war. The focus of these protests was not on *how* the Palestinians were being mistreated but on *who* was mistreating them.

The Palestinian Arabs were left in a terrible situation, not so much as a result of Israeli actions but largely because of actions and inactions by their own leaders and the leaders of other Arab countries. They could have been integrated into the populations of the West Bank and Gaza instead of being corralled into refugee camps as a way to keep hatred festering.

Many leading Palestinian intellectuals—such as Sari Nusseibeh— have criticized the Palestinian Arab leaders who rejected statehood for the Arabs of Palestine just because they didn't want statehood for the Jews of Palestine.[21] As Abba Eban once put it, "The Arabs never miss an opportunity to miss an opportunity." This quip, made in 1973, proved prescient, as Palestinian leaders missed opportunities for statehood in 2000–2001 and 2008, as we will see in subsequent chapters.

But let's return to my youth, when Israel was first established. Back then, there were no subtle issues with regard to the precise terms of Palestinian or Arab recognition of Israel. The Arab position was clear from the outset. As all the Arab nations unambiguously put it in 1967, "No recognition, no negotiation, no peace." That was the grand mufti's position in 1937 as well—before he became a collaborator with Hitler and an advocate of a different "final solution" to the "Jewish problem." The goal of the Arab leaders was the military destruction of Israel by Arab armies and/or terrorists. The Israeli position was clear as well: defend itself bravely against Hitler's successors. We were not aware of Israel's imperfections or questionable military actions. These only became public years later, when Israel's

"New Historians" took a hard look at what Israel had done to win its War of Independence.[22]

On the basis of what we knew back then, it was easy to choose sides in this conflict between good and evil. All good people chose the side of Israel.

It's fair to say that in 1948, we took Israel's side for granted. Israel had enemies, but they were external. We worried about Israel's survival—militarily and economically. But we didn't worry about defending Israel against delegitimization or demonization by political or ideological enemies. We did not obsess over Israel. It was in our consciousness, but as youngsters coming of age in postwar Brooklyn, we were more concerned with the fate of our beloved Dodgers (who regularly lost to the hated Yankees), with the success of our high school basketball teams (I was a substitute on mine, and once guarded Ralph Lipschitz—later Ralph Lauren—in Madison Square Garden) and with the girls who wouldn't go out with us unless we told them we were planning to become doctors (or at least dentists).

We were ordinary lower-middle-class kids, looking forward to doing better than our hardworking parents and immigrant grandparents. Our Zionism was an uncontroversial part of our psychic and ideological makeup. Life was easy. Conflicts were rare, and what few there were didn't involve Israel.

In subsequent chapters, I tell the story of how all this changed over the next 70 years, as much of the world (especially many on the left and in academia, of which I was a part) turned against Israel and uncritically adopted as a litmus test for progressivism the Palestinian cause—or more precisely the anti-Israel cause because no one seemed to care about the Palestinians when they were denied statehood and oppressed by non-Israelis, namely Jordan and Egypt. This development poses an existential, if not immediate, threat to Israel. It is not immediate because those at the forefront of this change are still a minority of our nation as a whole, but they may represent the future of the Democratic Party and thus challenge the long tradition for bipartisan support for Israel. American support for Israel, regardless of which party is in power, is essential to the continuous success of the nation-state of the Jewish people.

The challenge to bipartisan support for Israel has been gradual, with some dramatic moments, such as the Six-Day War, the Yom Kippur War, the rescue at Entebbe, the election of Menachem Begin, the Camp David Accords with Egypt, the destruction of Iraq's nuclear reactor, Israel's invasion of Lebanon, the Palestinian intifadas, the rejected peace offers by Israel, the boycott tactic against Israel, the election of Benjamin Netanyahu, President Barack Obama's Iran Deal, and President Donald Trump's recognition of Jerusalem as Israel's capital and the Golan Heights as Israeli sovereign territory. These events had a considerable impact on attitudes toward Israel, and on the nature of my defense of that ever-embattled country.

2

Israel's Quiet Period— and Mine

THE NEARLY TWO decades between Israel's War of Independence and its next war of survival in June 1967 were relatively quiet. The new nation was busy absorbing Jewish immigrants from the displaced person camps of Europe and from Muslim nations that were making it impossible for their Jewish residents—many of whom could trace their ancestry in these areas back thousands of years—to remain in the lands of their birth.[1] The Jewish refugees were part of what amounted to an exchange of populations, not so different from the one that occurred when Pakistan separated from India and millions of Indian Muslims were relocated to Pakistan while millions of Hindus and Sikhs were forced to leave Pakistan and move to India.[2] There were other massive population exchanges following World War II in addition to the one in the Middle East.[3] Approximately three-quarters of a million Jews left Muslim countries—many without a choice—and a roughly equal number of Arabs left Israel, some voluntarily, others by force. The Palestinians call the events that led to this transfer the "nakba," or catastrophe, but it was largely a self-inflicted wound, resulting from the decision to wage war against the new nation-state of the Jewish people. Had the leaders of the Arabs in Palestine accepted the UN partition, there would have been no refugee problem, as some Palestinian leaders have recently acknowledged.[4]

The European and Sephardic refugees came to Israel with few material possessions. The survivors of the Holocaust had lost everything, in terms of both family and fortune. The Sephardic refugees from Muslim countries were forced to leave their fortunes—and there were some who left considerable wealth behind—to the nations from which they were being evicted.

Despite the fact that these immigrants were all Jews, and therefore entitled to become Israeli citizens under the Law of Return, they had little in common. They spoke different languages, followed somewhat different religious rituals, and had enormous disparity in educational, cultural and economic backgrounds. They came from nearly every country in Europe and the Middle East, ranging from Germany to Yemen, Russia to Iraq, Romania to Egypt, France to Turkey, Lithuania to Morocco, Hungary to Tunisia, and Poland to Algeria.

They all had to learn Hebrew, a language that had been revived by early Europeans who had made aliya in the late nineteenth century and who turned it from an ancient language of prayer and scripture into a vibrant modern language of day-to-day conversation and contemporary literature.[5] The Sephardic Jews of Palestine, who had lived in Jerusalem, Safed and other historically Jewish cities, already spoke Hebrew, but most of the other olim did not. They also had to learn how to make a living and grow the struggling agriculture-based local economy—few of these refugees had any experience in agriculture—into a gross national product that supported a population that had more than tripled in the years between the establishment of Israel and the Six-Day War.

The Law of Return[6]—one of the first laws enacted by the Knesset, Israel's parliament—was a response to the tragic reality that millions of Jews could have been saved if the nations of the world had opened their doors to Jews seeking to escape Hitler. But even the United States, Canada and other liberal democracies that had been founded by immigrants shut their doors and ports. Recall the tragic case of the *St. Louis*, the ship filled with refugees from Nazi Germany seeking asylum, which was turned away from every port in the Western

Hemisphere. The ship and its passengers were forced to return to Germany, where many of the asylum-seekers were eventually murdered. A prominent public figure—Lavra Delano Houghteling, a cousin of President Roosevelt—reflected the views of many American bigots when she opposed the admission of Jewish children, saying: "20,000 charming children would all too soon grow into 20,000 ugly adults." The Canadian minister of absorption said, in reference to Jewish immigration, that even "none is too many."[7] Under the Law of Return, there would always be one country that would never close its doors to Jews in need of rescue and relocation. There was little controversy back then regarding the Law of Return in the immediate aftermath of the Holocaust, but now there are those who see this law as racist. Many other countries, with no history of genocide and exclusion, have similar laws that are not subject to similar criticism. This is yet another example of the double standard applied to the nation-state of the Jewish people.

My family experienced firsthand the poverty of the new nation. We had relatives who were struggling to make a living in Tel Aviv, Jerusalem and B'nai Brak. My father and mother sent money, second-hand clothing and other necessities to our Israeli relatives, on both sides of our family, who were having a hard time. Our synagogue conducted appeals to support the olim chadashim—the new immigrants. And, of course, every Jewish home had at least one pushka for the Jewish National Fund, and for organisations that collected money for poor and sick Israelis, for yeshivot (Jewish religious schools) and for the Haganah (the Israeli Defense Forces, IDF). When my own children were young in the mid-1960s, they went trick-or-treating not for UNICEF (of which we were vaguely suspicious, even back then, because of its association with the biased United Nations) but for Israel. And neighbors—non-Jewish and Jewish alike—willingly gave to Israel because they admired the young new nation.

Indeed the entire world, with the exception of the Arab nations, seemed to admire plucky Israel. Non-Jewish teenagers from Scandinavia, Germany, France and other European countries volunteered to pick oranges on the kibbutzim, which were seen as cutting-edge socialist collectives. Academics studied this new approach to agriculture, family and living. Israel was the "Sara Lee" of nations. (Remember the cake commercial, "Nobody doesn't like Sara Lee.") Even Iran and Turkey, both non-Arab Muslim countries, worked with Israel, militarily and economically.

Israel was seen as weak, both militarily and economically, and it posed no danger to anyone. Sure, it had to defend its civilians against fedayeen terrorist attacks primarily from Jordan and Egypt, as well as from Syria and Lebanon. The fedayeen were Palestinian terrorists who crossed the borders into Israel to attack civilian targets. These attacks were encouraged and often facilitated by the Arab nations surrounding Israel. The fedayeen were later incorporated into the Egyptian and Jordanian armies, and then into the Palestine Liberation Organization (PLO), which was founded as a terrorist organization in 1964, years before Israel captured and occupied the West Bank and Gaza Strip.[8] The expressed goal of the PLO was the destruction of the Jewish state that existed within the pre-1967 armistice lines.[9] Few criticized Israel's self-defense tactics, though historians now report that some were quite brutal: Israel occasionally responded to terrorist attacks that targeted Israeli civilians with tit-for-tat reprisals against Jordanian and Egyptian civilian targets.

Israel was never more popular and never less controversial than in the eight years between 1948 and 1956. It was also never weaker and more vulnerable. Its economy was in shambles with rampant inflation. They told a joke back then—which in light of subsequent events isn't funny—that reflects the Israeli situation in the 1950s. There were very long lines at Israeli banks to withdraw money and spend it before inflation made it worthless. At one Tel Aviv bank, the line was so long that a furious customer shouted, "I'm sick of standing on line. I'm going to shoot Ben-Gurion." Two hours later, he came back and stood at the end of the line that had barely moved. The others asked why he had come back to this line, to which he replied: "The line to shoot Ben-Gurion was even longer."

During that period, I remained supportive of Israel. Everyone did. But I didn't have to prioritize my defense of the nation-state of the Jewish people, because no one we knew or cared much about was attacking or criticizing it. To be sure, there were controversies, but they were not about Israel's right to exist or its foreign policies. The controversies were largely domestic: Were the rabbis securing too much power in the increasingly secular nation? Were there downsides to the kibbutz movement? Was Ben-Gurion's utopic model of an agriculture-based economy (similar to the model Jefferson proposed and Hamilton opposed) viable in the second half of the twentieth century? (Israel, under prime ministers Shimon Peres and Benjamin Netanyahu, was to shift its economy from oranges to Apples—and other technological innovations.) Was there too much sexual freedom—we called it "promiscuity"—in Israel? (As teenage boys, we wanted to go there and see for ourselves, but we couldn't afford it.) Was Ben-Gurion becoming a tyrant, having served as Israel's only prime minister? Was Israel too close to the Soviet Union and not close enough to the United States? Should Menachem Begin and Yitzhak Shamir, who were both the heads of terrorist organizations during the pre-state period, be allowed to serve in the Knesset as members of the opposition, where, someday in the not too distant future, they hoped to become the leaders of the country?

This last question deeply divided my friends and family. There were some who idealized Jewish terrorists while condemning Arab terrorists. There were others who believed that all terrorism was wrong and that no one with a history of terrorism should be allowed to govern. I was in the latter category, but I also believed that the passage of time could turn a terrorist into a statesman. Obviously, a majority of Israelis agreed and elected both Begin and Shamir to the prime ministership several decades after the establishment of Israel and the creation of a united IDF.

These and other questions were interesting to us, as young Zionists, but the rest of the world didn't seem to care much about Israel, except to support its struggle for military and economic security.

During my high school and early college years, I was consumed with other passions: opposition to McCarthyism; support for racial equality; getting Adlai Stevenson elected president; the Brooklyn Dodgers' first ever World Series win in 1955 (I own Don Zimmer's ring from that series); and bringing football back to Brooklyn College.

I was always a contentious kid attracted to controversies—in school, in summer camp, in my neighborhood—and to defending the underdog. Israel was neither controversial nor perceived as the underdog. So I focused on other issues while still maintaining an interest in Israel. This interest led me to attend a thickly accented speech by David Ben-Gurion, several speeches by British-accented Abba Eban, and wrestling matches by Rafael Halperin, Israel's champion and a symbol of the new Israeli—bronze, ripped and athletic. In 1952, Abba Eban was elected vice president of the UN General Assembly—a feat no Israeli could come close to replicating today.

Hovering in the background was the constant military threat against Israel by those Arab countries committed to its destruction. The illegitimate leaders of those countries—illegitimate because they were either placed in their hereditary positions by colonial powers or attained them by bloody coups d'état—threatened to "throw the Jews into the sea," distracting from their own domestic difficulties. Chief among those who threatened Israel was Egypt under its young new leader Gamal Abdel Nasser, who had helped to overthrow King Farouk in 1952. Nasser's ambition was to rule over a United Arab Nation that would include all the Sunni Muslim countries in the region. These countries—which included Syria, Jordan and Iraq—had little in common beyond language, religion and a desire to rid the region of its "Jewish interlopers."

Egypt already had the strongest and largest army in the region. Now the Soviet Union was beginning to deliver massive supplies of modern weapons to Egypt—including state-of-the-art jets, tanks and munitions—that would guarantee them both qualitative and quantitative military superiority over Israel. The United States, at the time, was refusing to supply arms to Israel, which was getting its weapons primarily from France.[10]

The combination of Egyptian threats to destroy Israel and the increasing supply of Soviet arms that would make this threat viable caused the Israeli general staff to consider a preventive attack on the Egyptian army. The flow of Soviet arms was beginning but had not yet reached the point of no return—when an attack against Egypt would have been unsuccessful. The legality of a "preventive" as distinguished from a "preemptive" attack was questionable under international law.[11] The former occurs before there is an actual or planned attack from the other side. For example, had the British and French attacked the growing German military machine in the mid-1930s in order to prevent it from becoming the most powerful army in Europe (in violation of the Versailles Treaty at the close of World War I), that attack—which might have saved 50 million lives—would have been deemed "preventive" and thus of questionable legality. On the other hand, Israel's later attack against Egypt and Syria that began the Six-Day War in 1967 was deemed "preemptive" because Egyptian forces were massed near Israel's border in what looked like preparation for an imminent attack against Israel. The consensus of international law scholars—as reflected in law review articles, books and academic conferences—was that a preemptive attack was lawful, but a preventive attack was generally not.[12] (International law, in the early years of Israel's existence, generally was balanced when it came to the Arab–Israeli conflict. More recently, it has been weaponized by hard-left academics against Israel.)

In 1956, Israel did not fear an *imminent* attack, but it reasonably feared an *eventual* attack from an enemy that would be capable of destroying it if it were allowed to become massively armed with modern Soviet weaponry (the buildup of Germany's military power in the 1930s was clearly part of Israel's collective memory). Any attack on Egypt would be preventive, rather than preemptive, unless Egypt committed a casus belli—an act of war, as defined by international law—against Israel.

A casus belli need not include an actual military attack. It could include other acts of war, such as the blocking of international shipping lanes to the commercial vehicles of the enemy country. And this is precisely what Egypt did when it nationalized the Suez Canal and prevented Israel from using this vital waterway. It had also blocked the Straits of Tiran, thereby denying Israeli access to the Gulf of Aqaba and its port in Eilat.[13] These acts of economic warfare, backed by military power, constituted casus bellis and entitled Israel to respond militarily.[14]

Accordingly, any military action by Israel would be neither entirely preventive nor preemptive. It would be reactive and, therefore, lawful, even if the primary object was to prevent Egypt from attaining military superiority that would enable it, at a future time, to destroy the new state.

France and England, on the other hand, had not been the object of any casus belli. Their ships were free to sail through the canal and the straits. These colonial nations were fearful of losing their influence in the Middle East if the canal were to be successfully nationalized and wrested from their control by Egypt.

The three countries, for somewhat different reasons, decided to attack Egypt to regain control over the canal, to open the straits to Israeli shipping and to set back Egypt's growing military superiority. It is doubtful that these decisions were influenced, to any substantial degree, by international law; rather, they seemed motivated by self-interest. Historically, most such decisions are indeed based on self-interest, and international law, which is quite malleable, is employed as an after-the-fact justification for or defense of the decisions. What the late secretary of state Dean Acheson once said applied more to Israel than to France or Great Britain: "The survival of states is not a matter of law."[15]

On October 29, 1956, Israeli forces invaded the Sinai by air, land and sea, capturing key strategic positions, such as the Mitla Pass and Sharm el-Sheikh, as well as the Gaza Strip. Two days later, French and British forces joined the battle with a massive bombing campaign. Nasser responded by sinking 40 ships in the Suez Canal, blocking all shipping.[16]

By the end of the Suez Crisis, Egypt's entire air force had been destroyed, along with much of its tank and armored forces. Israel also captured one of its major naval vessels that was shelling Haifa. The Straits of Tiran were opened to Israeli shipping, while the Suez Canal remained closed to all shipping for months. Israel suffered many more casualties (172) than did the French (10) or British (16). Egyptian casualties were far greater though impossible to quantify, with estimates ranging from 1,000 to 3,000 soldiers and as many as 1,000 civilians, mostly from the British bombing campaign and street fighting.[17]

The war was unpopular in Britain and led to the downfall of the Anthony Eden Labour government and the weakening of the French government. President Eisenhower was widely praised around the world for helping to bring it to an end, though many supporters of Israel thought he acted too hastily, denying Israel the opportunity to degrade the Egyptian military further. His actions, which were perceived as one-sidedly against Israel, confirmed the view of my family and friends that they were right in supporting Adlai Stevenson and that the Democratic Party was the pro-Israel party—the Republicans not so much.

I was in my second year at Brooklyn College during the Suez Crisis and active in school politics, beginning my run to become president of the student body (on a platform that included bringing varsity football back and getting more free parking). I wrote op-eds and letters on a variety of subjects. I don't remember whether this Suez situation was among them, but I do remember debating a hard-left critic of Israel's invasion, which I supported, as did all my friends and colleagues. "If Israel decided they had to attack, there must have been good reason, because Israel is a good country that does the right thing." That was our mindset. It wasn't quite "Israel, right or wrong." It was, "Israel is always right, and its enemies are always wrong." This, it turns out, is closer to the truth than its opposite even today: if Israel does it, it must be wrong—which today's anti-Israel zealots espouse. (It is a striking parallel to an old Polish proverb: if there is something wrong in the world, the Jews must be behind it.) Consider, for example, "pinkwashing"—the bigoted term that espouses the absurd view that Israel is good to gays only to whitewash—pinkwash—how bad they are to Palestinians.[18] More on this in subsequent chapters.

We were not thoughtful or nuanced in our defense of Israel back in the mid-1950s and early 1960s because there was no need for thought or nuance. To us, and to most Americans, the issues were black and white, and no reasonable person believed that Israel was a bad country that did bad things.

Following the cease-fire that ended the Suez Crisis, things quieted down again for a period between 1956 and 1966, during which I completed college—having been elected president of the student body and captain of the debate team, which never debated any issue relating to Israel because there was no controversy. We debated capital punishment (I was against it), recognition of "Red China" (I was for it), whether 18-year-olds should have the right to vote (I was for it), and socialized medicine (I was for it).

I also completed Yale Law School, where I was first in my class and served as editor in chief of the *Yale Law Journal* (again, without editing any articles relating to noncontroversial Israel). Despite these accomplishments, I was turned down by all 32 Wall Street law firms to which I applied.

Near the end of my first year in law school, David Ben-Gurion announced the capture by Israeli Mossad agents of Adolf Eichmann, the Nazi fugitive who had overseen the "final solution" to the "Jewish Question." His abduction from Argentina clearly violated international law, and Israel was condemned by diplomats around the world.

But the daring escapade and the decision to put the mass murderer on trial in Israel was applauded by many Americans, Europeans and, of course, Israelis. I was thrilled to see this notorious Nazi being brought to justice in Israel, where he would be prosecuted by Jewish lawyers and tried by Jewish judges. He was defended by a German lawyer. Not only would Eichmann be on trial in the Jerusalem courtroom, but the Israeli judicial system would also be on trial in the court of public opinion.

I was offered my first opportunity to visit Israel to observe the Eichmann trial. One of my favorite law school professors was Telford Taylor, who had served as the chief prosecutor at the Nuremberg Trials, where he replaced Supreme Court justice Robert Jackson. One of the radio networks had asked Taylor to go to Jerusalem and offer ongoing commentary on the trial. Taylor asked me to go with him as his assistant. I was dying to go, but I had just been elected editor in chief of the *Yale Law Journal*, a great honor and responsibility—and also a path to a Supreme Court clerkship. Reluctantly, I had to decline Taylor's offer. Instead, I listened faithfully to his insightful observations about the remarkable trial. When he returned, we discussed it at length, including whether the death penalty was appropriate (I thought not). Among the things he told me was that Hannah Arendt, who became famous for *Eichmann in Jerusalem: A Report on the Banality of Evil*, her polemical account of the Eichmann trial, was hardly ever in the courtroom. She came to Jerusalem with her mind made up in an effort to prove her predetermined thesis regarding both the banality of evil—the bureaucratization of mass murder—and the evil of Zionist leaders during the Holocaust. The facts that the trial disclosed—that Adolf Eichmann was far from banal and that Nazism was supported by some of Germany's most brilliant and nonbanal minds, including Martin Heidegger, who had been Arendt's lover before the war and remained her friend even after the Holocaust—were not included in her book because they undercut her thesis.[19]

I remained close to Telford Taylor—we traveled to the Soviet

Union and Israel together a decade and a half later, when we worked on behalf of Soviet Jewish dissidents and refuseniks. But I've always had some regret about not accepting the opportunity to observe one of the most significant historical events of my lifetime.

In the summer between law school and my first clerkship, I went south to train as an NAACP legal observer during the civil rights movement. The training took place at Howard, a historically black university in Washington, DC. Following several days of training by experienced NAACP lawyers, we were sent south to observe and report on marches, demonstrations and other forms of protest. It was an eye-opening and distressing experience, as I saw firsthand the kind of racism I had only studied in school: segregated bathrooms, lunch counters and schools. This was several years before the brutal murders of three civil rights workers and others seeking justice, so I did not experience or see the violence that was to ensue, but I saw enough to assure a lifetime commitment to civil rights and equality.

Following law school, I was fortunate to clerk for two Jewish judges who were both ardent liberals and Zionists. The first was Chief Judge David Bazelon of the United States Court of Appeals for the District of Columbia. He counted among his closest friends the Israeli ambassador to the United States, Avraham Harman, as well as other Zionist leaders and Jewish legislators, such as Senators Abraham Ribicoff, Jacob Javits and Richard Neuberger. These important supporters of Israel, who voted for pro-Israel legislation and pressed the Kennedy administration to increase its support for the nation-state of the Jewish people, were frequent lunch guests in his chambers, and I was always invited to join (though not to speak unless spoken to).

The attorney general was Bobby Kennedy, with whom the law clerks had lunch in the courthouse. I was selected to pick him up at the Justice Department and walk him to the judges' dining room. He regaled us with fascinating stories of the months he spent in Israel as a journalist for a Boston newspaper during the War of Independence.[20] He loved Israel, Israelis and American Jews—who loved him in return, despite his father's somewhat questionable history during the run-up to World War II[21] and his early support for McCarthyism. During the walk back, the attorney general urged me to come work at the Justice Department after my clerkships.

My year with Judge Bazelon solidified my belief—if it even needed solidification—that one could be a liberal American patriot and a strong supporter of Israel, with no conflict. That belief was strengthened further by my second clerkship with Justice Arthur Goldberg, who had just replaced Felix Frankfurter (another fervent Zionist, though not a very good Jew, especially during the Holocaust).[22]

Goldberg and his wife Dorothy had grown up in Midwestern Zionist circles. They were active in both labor and Zionist causes, and their annual Seder combined labor songs, Zionist songs and a small amount of actual prayer. Among their close friends growing up was a Zionist from Milwaukee named Goldie Meyerson (nee, Mabovitch), who later changed her name to Golda Meir and became the first female leader of a nation who was not the wife or daughter of a male leader. (I would later meet and interview her.) Goldberg, too, had lunches with visiting Israeli dignitaries and leading American Zionists, to which I was always invited.

My two years of clerking strengthened both my liberalism and my Zionism and prepared me for my dual career as a Harvard professor and Israeli advocate. During those years there was little controversy regarding liberalism or Israel. All my friends were both liberals, which meant they supported racial equality, freedom of speech and other center-left positions, and Zionists, which meant they supported Israel's right to exist as the nation-state of the Jewish people. President John F. Kennedy was not as enthusiastic about Israel as his brother Bobby (or his other brother Teddy, with whom I later worked closely). But nor was he as critical of Israel as President Eisenhower, who strongly opposed Israel's military actions in Egypt during the Suez Crisis. Lyndon Johnson, who was then vice president, was among the most pro-Israel politicians in history. I recall Justice Goldberg telling me about a visit by liberal senator Hubert Humphrey to Israel, during which he could hear fighter jets in the distance. Humphrey asked his guide whether the jets "were ours or theirs." By "ours," he meant Israel's. Everyone in the early 1960s was on Israel's side in its never-ending battles with Arab countries that refused to accept a Jewish state.

This simplistic view was to prevail until Israel's victory in the 1967 Six-Day War, after which everything began to change.

3

Six-Day War

The Making of an Israel Defender

SOME CRITICS DIVIDE Jewish supporters of Israel into two groups: those who only began to love Israel after they could take pride in its dramatic victory in the Six-Day War, and those who actively supported Israel before that glorious victory. I fall into the latter category. I began my "second career"—as a defender of Israel in the court of public opinion—during the run-up to the June 1967 war, when it looked like Israel might be destroyed by the combined armed forces of Egypt, Syria, Jordan and other Arab nations.

The year 1967 was also one in which the Harvard Law School faculty would vote on whether to promote me from assistant professor without tenure to full professor with lifetime tenure. I had begun as an assistant professor in 1964, just before turning 26. I had been a popular and successful teacher and had written several articles on criminal law, and I also coauthored with Jay Katz and Joseph Goldstein a case book on *Psychoanalysis, Psychiatry and the Law*.[1] But I was only 28 years old, and no one so young had ever been granted tenure at Harvard Law School. My lack of legal experience—I had never really practiced law—was also a negative factor. Because the tenure process is so secretive and because the tradition at the time forbade any effort by a candidate to seek support or even to inquire whether a senior professor was for or against them, I was in the dark about my prospects, though I believed they were promising.

It was against this background that I began my so-called second career.

Tensions between Israel and its neighbors had increased between the end of 1966 and May 1967, during which time terrorists raided Israel from Egypt, Jordan and Syria. Israel's subsequent reprisals had generated support within the Arab world for a military attack against the Jewish state. Egypt's Gamal Abdel Nasser declared that the national goal of his country was "the eradication of Israel." His state-controlled media called for Israel to be "wiped off the map," and he demanded "Israel's death and annihilation." Syria's defense minister called for a "war of annihilation."[2] Yemen's foreign minister said, "We want war. War is the only way to settle the problem of Israel."[3] And the then chairman of the PLO—Ahmad Shukeiri—threatened to "destroy Israel and its inhabitants, and as for the survivors, if there are any, the boats are ready to deport them."[4] This was before Israel replaced Jordan and Egypt as occupiers of the West Bank and Gaza Strip. For these Arab leaders, *all* of Israel—Tel Aviv, West Jerusalem, Rishon Leziyon—was "occupied" by Jews. Their goal was to end these "occupations" and rid the entire "Zionist entity" of its Jewish population by military conquest.

Having grown up amid survivors of the Holocaust, we took those threats literally and seriously. We knew from the 1956 Suez Crisis that Israel had a good army, but we also knew that the Egyptian, Syrian and Jordanian armies had been strengthened over the years. As King Hussein of Jordan—later a peace partner with Israel, but at the time an implacable foe—put it in the run-up to the Six-Day War, "All of the Arab armies now surround Israel. The UAR [Egypt], Iraq, Syria, Jordan, Yemen, Lebanon, Algeria, Sudan and Kuwait. . . . There is no difference between one Arab army and another."

We were frightened for Israel. War seemed inevitable, especially after Nasser once again blocked the Straits of Tiran from Israeli shipping—an act of war that Israel could not accept—and demanded that the UN peacekeepers, who had been positioned in the Sinai as part of the cease-fire that ended the Suez Crisis, be removed. The removal of these peacekeepers meant that the massive Egyptian army could be positioned near Israel's border, ready to strike nearby civilian targets at any time. Not only was Israel's existence as the nation-state of the Jewish people at risk, but the lives of its citizens were also in danger. Arabs were threatening another Holocaust, just 22 years after the end of World War II.

I became energized. Now Israel was the underdog. It was time for me to become one of its public defenders, at least at Harvard, where I had some visibility. I helped to organize a group of faculty supporters for Israel, which eventually evolved into a permanent monthly lunch group of Jewish faculty who were willing to identify as Zionists. I was the only law school faculty member who regularly attended.

I organized students both at the law school and throughout the rest of the university, some of whom went to Israel to help when exams ended in May. I brought together Israeli visiting professors and scholars to help educate us about the realities on the ground. Among the scholars that I worked with were two who became lifelong friends: Aharon Barak and Yitzhak Zamir, who both became deans of the Hebrew University Law School, attorneys general and justices of the Israel Supreme Court. I solicited financial contributions for Israel from colleagues. Professor Livingston Hall, an elderly Brahmin, gave me $1,000 in cash and said, "Make sure this goes directly to the Israeli army." It did. I personally delivered it to an Israeli military attaché.

I also became acquainted with a young Canadian lawyer named Irwin Cotler, whom I met when he was a graduate student at Yale Law School. Irwin went on to become a distinguished law professor, a human rights activist and eventually the Canadian attorney general and minister of justice. We became lifelong friends and colleagues, later working together on freeing Soviet Jews from communist oppression. Our friendship began in earnest during the run-up to the Six-Day War.

When the war broke out, I actually thought about volunteering to go to Israel to help, but the Israeli counsel general wisely advised that I would be of more help remaining in Cambridge and garnering support for Israel.

Support for Israel was not controversial, even among the left-wing faculty (with the exception of Professor Roger Fisher, who was an early supporter of the Palestinian cause, and, of course, Noam Chomsky, now emiritus professor at MIT and an outspoken radical, who rarely, if ever, supported any Israeli action). I was active in the anti–Vietnam War movement and other liberal causes, but even many antiwar activists tended to support Israel's right to defend itself. It wasn't my principled support for Israel that raised any hackles. It was my very *public* advocacy for the Jewish state that caused concern. Professor Paul Bator cautioned me not to "wear my Jewishness on my sleeve." He meant well, being one of my supporters for tenure, but he honestly believed that being too openly Jewish could hurt my chances. I politely thanked him and told him that Harvard would have to accept or reject me for who I was and that I would remain a public supporter of Israel. This was not too courageous or foolhardy on my part, since I already had tenure offers from Stanford, Chicago, Columbia, Yale and New York University, though I preferred to remain in Cambridge, where my kids were in school.

In the end, I received tenure at Harvard and continued to be a very public supporter of Israel, even as that stance became more controversial and unpopular.

When the war began on June 5, 1967, I gathered with a group of my faculty friends and colleagues—including Marty Peretz, who was soon to become the publisher of the *New Republic*; Michael Walzer, an eminent political theorist; Robert Nozick, one of the world's most distinguished philosophers; and Dick Wurtman, an MIT scientist who pioneered research on melatonin—to watch and wait. Our main source of "inside information" was Professor Nadav Safran, an Egypt-born Israeli, who was teaching government at Harvard. Safran had fought for the Haganah in Israel's War of Independence and had sources in the Israeli military and intelligence community. (Unbeknown to us, Safran also worked with the CIA, receiving funding for conferences and books.) He provided us information before it had been made public.

By the second day of fighting, we knew that the Israeli air force had destroyed the Egyptian air force on the ground. Safran told us that Jordan would soon be attacking Israel, because King Hussein felt he would be humiliated among his peers and subjects if he stayed out of this fight. In the months before the war, he had criticized Nasser for not helping Jordan respond to Israeli cross-border attacks in retaliation for fedayeen terrorist raids against Israeli civilians. He had accused Nasser of hiding "behind the skirts" of the UN peacekeepers. So now he felt obliged to lend his powerful Jordanian legion to the fight. Safran told us that the battle with Jordan would cost many more Israeli lives than the attacks against Egypt and Syria. He was right. Because King Hussein later made peace with Israel, he received a pass from many contemporary historians on his early warmongering and support for terrorism, as well as for the killing of Palestinians during Black September.[5] I later met King Hussein in his palace in Amman. He could not have been friendlier or more anxious to maintain a peaceful relationship with Israel. But in 1967, the king was anything but friendly toward the nation-state of the Jewish people. Despite his subsequent peacemaking, he has the blood of many Israelis, Palestinians and Jordanians on his hands. He also bears considerable responsibility for Israel's half-century occupation of the West Bank, which Israel would not have captured if Hussein had not attacked.

Our Israeli colleagues rushed back to join their military units, arriving in time to participate in the final stages of the short but decisive war. When it was over, we celebrated the victory, joyously, joining many American Jews who had hitherto remained silent but who were now basking in the pride of the Israeli military victory. Nearly everyone—Jews and non-Jews—was overjoyed by the outcome. Even antiwar activists praised Israel for the tiny number of civilian deaths that resulted from the IDF's surgical precision in zeroing in on military targets. It was a time of great joy and pride for Israel, as tourists flocked to see the newly liberated areas—including the Western Wall, Jewish Quarter and Mount Scopus—that had been closed to Jews during Jordan's two-decade-long occupation of these historic religious historic and nationalistic sites.

A joke being told in the United States during these heady days reflected our positive attitude toward Israel and Israelis: A group of American-Jewish tourists is at a Tel Aviv nightclub. They applaud the acrobat and magician, but then an Israeli comedian begins to tell jokes in Hebrew. One of the tourists laughs loudly at his punch line. His friend says, "But you don't understand a word of Hebrew, so how do you know he's funny?" The laughing tourist replies, "He's an Israeli, so I trust him. He must be funny!" That was then.

Soon after the war ended, Justice Arthur Goldberg, who had left the Supreme Court to become the U.S. ambassador to the United Nations, asked for my help. The French (who had earlier been one of Israel's major weapons suppliers—as well as suppliers of components for their nuclear program—but who by then had turned against Israel under the leadership of Charles de Gaulle) and Russians (who broke diplomatic relations with Israel during the Six-Day War) were working on an important Security Council resolution that would, in effect, serve as a peace treaty and roadmap for the future of the Arab–Israeli conflict. Goldberg wanted to be sure it would be fair and not endanger Israel's future. He asked me to come to New York City to be a sounding board and help with his proposed wording.

The thrust of the resulting resolution—which famously became known as "Resolution 242"—was land for peace: Israel would return land captured from Arab countries in exchange for peace and recognition. There were, however, several sticking points on which Goldberg was working. The first was how much "land" for how much "peace." Israel was unwilling to return to the pre-1967 borders, which made it extremely vulnerable to attack—only 10 miles wide at its narrowest point, and its north and south could easily be cut off.[6] It also didn't want to see Syrian troops once again on the Golan Heights, from which they had fired munitions into the Israeli civilian areas below. The Arab states were unwilling to make peace in exchange for anything except Israel's complete destruction. From August 29 to September 1, 1967, eight Arab heads of state, along with Palestinian leaders, met in Khartoum and issued a joint statement declaring, "No peace with Israel, no recognition of Israel, no negotiations with it." Israeli leaders had been—in Moshe Dayan's words—"Waiting for a telephone call" from Arab leaders. Israel promised to be "unbelievably generous in working out peace terms," in Abba Eban's words. Instead of the phone call, they got "the three no's," as the Khartoum Declaration came to be called. As Eban later put it, this was the first war in history in which "the victors sued for peace and the vanquished called for unconditional surrender."[7]

Despite this categorical Arab rejection of the land-for-peace formula, the Security Council moved forward in its efforts to come up with a fair resolution that would be approved unanimously, especially by its permanent members, each of which is granted veto power.

Goldberg worked tirelessly to come up with a consensus formula, but the French and Russians insisted that Israel had to return *all* of the captured land in its lawful defense war. They claimed that no country should be allowed to hold on to land captured during a war, even a defensive war. But following World War II, as well as other wars, nations were not required to return land captured during wars. Territorial adjustments were the rule rather than the exception in postwar diplomacy.[8]

The United States, Great Britain and Israel (which is not a member of the Security Council) wanted a resolution that allowed Israel to maintain control over areas necessary to its security. They did not want to force Israel to return to its vulnerable borders, which Eban had characterized as "the Auschwitz lines." There was an impasse, but Goldberg—who had been a brilliant and successful labor negotiator and had settled many strikes—refused to give up. Finally, he and Hugh Foot, Lord Caradon and Great Britain's UN ambassador, came up with a compromise they hoped would be acceptable to the French and Russians: the French version of the resolution would call for Israel—in exchange for peace—to withdraw from "des territoires." This suggests, without expressly stating, that Israel was expected to withdraw from *all* the territories it captured. The English version calls for Israel to withdraw from "territories"—no *the*. All the negotiations were conducted in English, and the vote was on the English version. This led Goldberg to argue that the resolution left it open for Israel to make *some* border changes necessary to achieve "secure and recognized boundaries," as called for in other parts of the resolution.

I helped Goldberg draft a statement explaining the compromise: "The notable omissions in regard to withdrawal are the words 'the' or 'all' and [any reference to] 'the June 5, 1967 lines.' The Resolution speaks of withdrawal from occupied territories without defining the extent of withdrawal."

This issue has still not been resolved more than half a century after the compromise. One reason it hasn't is that the resolution does not require Israel to give up one inch of captured territories *unless* it receives in return "termination of all claims or states of belligerency and respect for and acknowledgement of the sovereignty, territorial integrity and political independence of every state in the area and their right to live in peace within secure and recognized boundaries free from threats or acts of force." The Arab states refused to comply with the quid pro quo set out in Resolution 242. When Egypt later agreed to these terms in 1979, Israel returned *all* the Egyptian areas captured during the war.[9] And when Jordan made peace in 1994, Israel gave back *all* the areas claimed by Jordan, but not the West Bank, which Jordan had ceded to the Palestinian Authority. Neither the Palestinians nor the PLO was referenced in the Security Council's resolution, which dealt only with states.

Although I worked alongside Goldberg in his efforts to achieve compromise, I can't take any credit for the outcome. I can take some credit for one aspect of Resolution 242, which calls for a "just settlement of the refugee problem." This was the resolution's only reference to Palestinians, though not by name. The Soviet ambassador tried to amend it to refer explicitly to Palestinian refugees, but that amendment was defeated, and Justice Goldberg later observed that "a notable omission in 242 is any reference to Palestinians. [The language of the Resolution] 'presumably refers both to Arab and Jewish refugees, for about an equal number of each abandoned their homes as a result of several wars . . .'"[10]

I helped persuade Goldberg to frame the refugee provision so that it could be interpreted to include the Jewish refugees from Muslim countries. Half a century later, neither refugee problem has been solved, but the wording of the resolution permits Jewish refugees to be included in any discussion or "just settlement of the refugee problem."

Following the acceptance of Security Council Resolution 242, I continued to work informally with Ambassador Goldberg, after he left the United Nations, on Israeli issues, legal cases (including the famous Curt Flood case, which led to the end of the notorious "reserve clause" in major league baseball, and the appeal in the Dr. Benjamin Spock anti-Vietnam case) and his unsuccessful campaign for governor of New York. (My colleague on that campaign was another former Goldberg law clerk, Stephen Breyer, now Justice Breyer.)

My support for Israel remained largely behind the scenes between 1967 and 1970, during which time I became a public media advocate for the nation-state of the Jewish people.

4

The PR War on
Israel Begins

THE YEAR 1968 was the height of controversy surrounding the Vietnam War. Hundreds of thousands of American protestors gathered in New York's Central Park and on the Washington Mall. Faculty members canceled classes in some universities, while students in other universities walked out of classes. Early in the following year, President Lyndon Johnson would announce that he would not run for reelection. Although I supported the right of protestors to miss classes, I decided to take a more positive approach, organizing and teaching the first course on the legal issues surrounding the Vietnam War. The course received widespread media attention, with prominently featured stories in the *New York Times, Time* magazine and other media.[1] Antiwar lawyers, who were contemplating lawsuits against the war, sat in on the class. I was interviewed on radio and TV about the legal issues, including whether the Constitution authorized the president to wage war without congressional authorization and whether some of the means used to conduct the war—including napalm, fire bombings and assassinations—were lawful under international law.

At about the same time, I played a small consulting role in the defense of the alleged antiwar conspirators in the Dr. Benjamin Spock case. Justice Goldberg had agreed to argue the appeal for the

Reverend William Sloane Coffin Jr., who was convicted along with Dr. Spock, Mitchell Goodman and Michael Ferber of conspiring to counsel evasion of the Vietnam draft. I had met Reverend Coffin at Yale when I was a student, and I admired him. I recall that Noam Chomsky, who was an acquaintance at the time, was furious that he had been left out of the indictment, as he considered himself *the* leading antiwar activist. He complained to our mutual friend Leonard Boudin that he had been as radical as the indicted defendants were— as he had incited students to refuse to serve—and asked rhetorically, "What do I have to do to get arrested?" Although I personally disagreed with some of the tactics employed by war resisters, I believed that they were entitled to a zealous defense.

Goldberg won the appeal, and no one went to prison.

Shortly thereafter, I played a more significant role in the trial and appeal of the Chicago Seven, which grew out of antiwar demonstrations during the 1968 Democratic Convention in Chicago. The Chicago Seven case, with its wild shenanigans directed at Judge Julius Hoffman, had been a widely watched political trial involving some of the most prominent antiwar activists. The lead defense lawyer, William Kunstler—a radical lawyer who famously said that he only defended people he "loved"—had been held in contempt and sentenced to prison. He asked me to help write the appellate brief. I responded, "But I don't love you." He came back with, "I love you, so that's good enough." We won the appeal.[2]

One of the defendants at the trial was Abbie Hoffman, who reportedly made some crude remark about how his "Jew lawyers" cared more about Israel than about the United States. It wasn't clear whether he was referring to me or to another Jewish lawyer named Morton Stavis. (He certainly wasn't referring to Kunstler, who cared little for either Israel or the United States), but I called him out in a private letter, to which he responded with a two-page handwritten note that included the following:

I never made a remark about my "Jewish Lawyers." I might
have spoken more positively about the PLO but I would never
make an anti-Semitic juxtaposition such as you think you heard.
If you read my current auto-biography you will see I flaunt my
"Jewishness" at every turn of the road.

It was the first time I had heard a Jew speak positively about the PLO, which, at the time, was an open and avowed terrorist organization that was hijacking airplanes, murdering Jewish children and American diplomats, blowing up synagogues and urging the destruction of the Jewish state.

Israel had not yet built settlements in the territories it had captured during the Six-Day War. The PLO regarded all of Israel as an illegal settlement and called for its destruction by force and violence. Yet Abbie Hoffman—and, as I would later learn, other radical leftists—supported the PLO and opposed Israel's existence as a matter of principle. I never dreamed at the time that this root-and-branch rejection of Israel's right to exist would soon spread from extremists on the radical left to more mainstream academic leftists, and even to some young liberals, in America and Europe.

At about the same time, I became active in the campaign to abolish the death penalty. I had long opposed capital punishment, having written a letter to the editor of the *Washington Post* while in law school opposing the execution of Adolf Eichmann by Israel.[3] I had also drafted a dissent for Justice Goldberg while I was a law clerk, suggesting that the death penalty violated the constitutional prohibition against cruel and unusual punishment.[4] The focus of the campaign was on the racial disparity in the administration of capital punishment.[5] Justice Goldberg and I jointly authored an influential *Harvard Law Review* article titled "Declaring the Death Penalty Unconstitutional."[6] I also litigated First Amendment cases involving antiwar and anti-segregation demonstrators, as well as films such as

I Am Curious Yellow and *Deep Throat*, which were alleged to violate the obscenity laws.[7] *Newsweek* described me as America's "most peripatetic civil liberties lawyer and one of its most distinguished defenders of individual rights."[8]

It was against this background in liberal law and politics that I was asked in the spring of 1970 to make my debut as a public defender of Israel on national television. In 1970, Egypt and Israel were involved in a war of attrition, with many deaths on both sides. The conflict also became part of the Cold War between the Soviet Union and the United States. Proposals for an overarching resolution to the conflict were being offered around the world. One such proposal—which favored the Arab side—had been offered by the American Friends Service Committee, a Quaker group that had shown considerable bias against Israel. PBS was then running a program called *The Advocates* in a prime-time Sunday-evening slot, on which issues of the day were debated by lawyers, academics and public officials. Its founder and executive producer was my colleague, Roger Fisher, who was the only Harvard Law professor to my knowledge who supported the Arab side of the Israeli–Arab conflict. By today's standards, Fisher was a moderate supporter of the Palestinian cause—he did not believe that Israel was an illegitimate state—but in 1970 any support for the Palestinians was unusual.

Fisher supported the Quaker proposals and decided to do a two-part show—the first in the program's history—on the conflict. It would be a broad-based debate format and would be titled "The Middle-East: Where Do We Go from Here?" A specific question it raised was "whether the United States should give more or less military support to the State of Israel." The episode, which was widely watched, would win a Peabody Award.

I had previously been selected as an advocate or witness for the liberal side of several other questions—such as the death penalty and pretrial preventive detention—so it was natural for me to be asked to advocate for the liberal—that is Israeli—side of the questions presented for debate on this show. Fisher would advocate for the Arabs, which was then the conservative position.

My advocacy for Israel required that I travel there to interview Prime Minister Golda Meir, Defense Minister Moshe Dayan, Foreign Minister Abba Eban, General Yitzhak Rabin, Jerusalem mayor Teddy Kollek and other Israeli public officials and military leaders. I had never been to Israel because I couldn't afford the travel expenses, but PBS was paying for everything.

When I told Justice Goldberg that I would be seeing Prime Minister Meir, he said, "You have to bring Goldie a carton of Lucky Strikes unfiltered cigarettes as a gift from me and Dorothy. She loves them, but her security people don't let her have them." This was before I had any inkling of the carcinogenic effects of cigarettes, so I agreed to try to smuggle the contraband to the prime minister.

I was excited about my first visit to the Holy Land, and especially that, as a 31-year-old rookie "TV journalist," I would be getting to meet and interview the great women and men of Israel. This trip to Israel—my first of nearly 100—would be a transformative event in my life and in my defense of Israel.

The advocate against Israel, Roger Fisher, who was also the executive producer, was an admirer of the American Friends Services Committee, a political arm of the Quaker religion that had turned against Israel and had published a one-sided pro-Arab pamphlet. The Quakers had a significant religious presence in Arab countries and virtually none in Israel.

Fisher would get to sit in on my interviews, but I couldn't sit in on his interviews with Egypt's Nasser and Jordan's Hussein, since neither country would allow me to enter their territory because I was a Jew. This gave Fisher an unfair advantage, but there was nothing I could do other than register my protest, because he was running the show.

I flew to Israel with the director of my segment, a young lawyer named Mark Cohen (also excluded from entering the Arab countries), and we checked in to the American Colony Hotel, which was run by

Arabs in the recently captured East Jerusalem. (Fisher had selected the hotel because he felt more comfortable there than in Jewish Jerusalem.) It was an elegant place, pockmarked with bullet holes from the battles that had taken place three years earlier in and around its structures. The food was marvelous, especially the weekend buffets of dozens of locally made Arab dishes.

I was now ready to visit Prime Minister Golda Meir. I wore baggy pants, scotch taping the carton of Lucky Strikes to my calf, and made it through security to an informal, private meeting before we began taping. When I was alone with the prime minister, I produced the hidden treasure and silently handed it to her. She kissed me and immediately speculated, "From Art and Dotty?" I confirmed her suspicion and told her that I had worked with Goldberg as a law clerk and on the Security Council resolution. She replied, "God sent Arthur to the UN at the right time." I quipped, "I read that you were an atheist." She laughed and said, "Sometimes I believe that things are *bashert*"—the Hebrew Yiddish word for predestined. She invited me to her residence for homemade chicken soup. I was shocked to see the run-down state of the prime minister's residence. Israel was indeed a poor country in those days. (Although Israel has gotten richer, the condition of the prime minister's residence hasn't changed that much, except for enhanced security.)

When we began our formal recorded interview, with Fisher present, I asked the prime minister to make the case for American support of Israel, and she answered brilliantly, displaying her love for both of the countries she had lived in. (She had little love for the Ukraine, where she was born, and remembered her father boarding up the door to their home to protect it against a threatened pogrom.) Golda had been educated in the United States and made aliya when she was 23, after her marriage to Morris Meyerson, a sign painter and fervent socialist. They joined a kibbutz but shortly thereafter moved to Jerusalem, where she became active in labor politics.

Her love for both Israel and America came through in every answer. So did her legendary toughness. Ben-Gurion had once told his cabinet that only one of them had "balls," pointing to Golda. She insisted that Israel would never return to its insecure pre-1967 boundaries but that everything else was subject to negotiation. She also insisted that the Arab states had to acknowledge the legitimacy of "an independent Israel state" with which they were prepared to "live in peace."

Golda gave me a letter of introduction attesting to my love of Israel that opened doors with other government officials. Meanwhile, an Israeli-Arab lawyer, who represented accused terrorists, gave me a letter that attested to my support of the human rights of and due process for Palestinians. I worried about giving the wrong letter to the wrong people!

Following my interview with Prime Minister Meir, I met with Shimon Peres. Shimon, with whom I later formed a close friendship, was a young man on the way up. He had been a Ben-Gurion protégé and had held various posts in the Defense Ministry and other offices. Now, at age 46, he was about to be appointed minister of transportation and communications. But his expertise and experience were in arms acquisitions from European nations, including the components for nuclear weapons (which Israel still doesn't publicly acknowledge it possesses). He had just written a book titled *David's Sling: The Arming of Israel*.[9] The David referred, of course, to the biblical King David, who as a youth had defeated the giant Goliath with a slingshot. But it also paid homage to another brave David—Ben-Gurion—who had tasked Peres with acquiring arms for the new state.

Peres was cultured and charming. We talked about art, music, restaurants and films. He told me that he thought Picasso's Blue Period was his best and observed that French was the language of diplomacy because it was so vague. He recommended an Italian restaurant, whose atmosphere was elegant but whose food turned out to be mediocre. He boasted of being related to the American actress Lauren Bacall, who shared his original birth name, Perske (or Perski). He was also down-to-earth. He was a man of war and weapons who wanted nothing more than to turn the swords he had acquired into plowshares. His personal vision for Israel's future was different from his mentor's vision. Although he spent his early years—after making aliya at age 11—at a kibbutz working as a shepherd, he saw Israel's future not as a self-sufficient agricultural society but as a nation that would use its most important natural resource as the basis for world-class technological innovation. That resource was the creativity of its citizens. The second most important resource a nation must possess is water, he told me, bemoaning Israel's limited supply.

My interview with Peres focused mainly on the need for the United States to provide military assistance to Israel. He predicted renewed fighting with Egypt and the need to deter Arab aggression by increasing Israel's qualitative military superiority over the combined Arab armies. A strong Israel will not attack its neighbors, he argued, but a weak Israel will be attacked by those neighbors. The best assurance of peace in the region is an overwhelmingly strong Israel. He did not, of course, mention Israel's nuclear weapons, which he had helped to develop, but he talked proudly of its growing naval and air power and its reliance on technology and intelligence. He made a powerful case for our side of the debate question regarding American military support for Israel.

Peres had a real impact on my own thinking concerning Israel. I came away from our meeting with renewed confidence in my view that a militarily powerful Israel provided the best chance not just for Israel's own security but also for peace in the region. It is a position from which I have never deviated. Nor did I then, or do I now, believe that my support for a militarily powerful Israel is inconsistent with my opposition to the Vietnam or Iraq War. A militarily weak Israel would face immediate threats of annihilation, whereas neither Vietnam nor Iraq posed any comparable threats to American security. As Prime Minister Benjamin Netanyahu was later to put it, "If the Arabs put down their weapons today, there would be no more violence. If the Jews put down their weapons today, there would be no more Israel."

Abba Eban—who had been one of my heroes ever since my father and I watched him on television make the case for Israel—was his usual eloquent self. But in person, he was less charming than he was on TV or from the lectern. He rarely made eye contact with me, looking off into the distance as if he were lecturing to an audience. His remarks appeared scripted, as if he was repeating by rote what he had said many times. Nonetheless, he made brilliant arguments—in the broadest strokes—that we could and did use effectively to make our case during the live debate.

Yitzhak Rabin was the opposite of Abba Eban. He looked straight into your soul with his piercing eyes. His focus, as a military leader turned diplomat, was on assuring that Israel's new borders would prevent future attacks from being successful. While Eban was in the clouds discussing broad philosophical issues, Rabin was in the weeds focusing on practical problems Israel faced in the imminent future.

I interviewed several other Israeli generals who were stationed in the West Bank and police officials who were responsible for preventing domestic terrorism. I also visited several cities in the West Bank, which was quiet. Israel had not yet built civilian settlements in the captured territories, and we were able to sit at cafés in Hebron and other West Bank cities, including Jericho, Bethlehem and Ramallah, and drink delicious coffee with local Arabs. At the time, the West Bank—which most Israelis refer to by the biblical names Yehuda and Shomron—was sparsely populated, with primitive roads. It was beautiful and bucolic. Little did I suspect how contentious and bloody it would become.

I climbed Masada, the high desert fortress from which Jews in the first century held off the Roman legions until it was evident that they would be captured and enslaved. Choosing death over slavery, they committed mass suicide. One of Israel's slogans was, "Never again will Masada fall."

While in Israel, I renewed my friendship with the academics—now professors and soon to be attorneys general and justices—who I had met while they were visiting scholars at Harvard. I also met my Israeli relatives, nearly all of whom were Orthodox, ranging from ultra to modern. Several high school classmates had settled in Israel after completing their education in the United States, and I looked them up. One was a doctor, another a lawyer, a third a professor, and others were in business. The businessmen told me how to end up with a "small fortune" in Israel: "Come with a large fortune."

Although I was only making about $25,000 a year as a young full professor—a very decent salary in those days—my Israeli counterparts were making far less and needed to work at second jobs or receive assistance from abroad. In short, Israel was a "second world" economy whose citizens—many of them brilliant and highly educated—had "first world" aspirations and spending habits. It was a prescription for disaster unless Israel could change the direction of its economy. Nearly every Israeli I interviewed reaffirmed the need for economic change and growth. Part of the problem was the extraordinarily high percentage of the GNP needed to acquire weapons from abroad, which could only be bought with hard currency. Israel had a nascent arms industry, but it was mostly for domestic consumption. Its balance of trade, especially with regard to arms, was seriously out of whack. David Ben-Gurion had built an economy geared to an agrarian state with kibbutzim and moshavim. Its socialism and strong labor unions fed the many poor immigrants who flooded the country after the British barriers were eliminated. But a self-sufficient agrarian Israel could not support the military budget necessary to defend it, nor the lifestyles of those who might emigrate to the United States or Europe if the economy did not improve.

I also visited the Gaza Strip and dined in several excellent restaurants in Khan Yunis and Gaza City. The strip was crowded and bustling, and several of the Arabs I met expressed relief that it was no longer being occupied by the Egyptians. Israeli soldiers mingled with the local population without apparent conflict. I found myself sympathetic to the Arabs of the West Bank and Gaza and especially to the families separated by the creation of refugees during the 1948 and 1967 wars.

But the sad state of the economy—despite being enhanced by contributions from American and European Jews—was not Israel's biggest or most imminent problem. The prospect of renewed warfare consumed the attention of Israeli leaders. Although Peres had been prescient in predicting renewed fighting with Egypt, and although there were continuing military confrontations in the Sinai and other areas (an Israeli cousin of mine, a young poet and an only child of Holocaust survivors, was killed during this war of attrition while serving in the IDF), most Israelis were still giddy over their victory in the Six-Day War. A sense of invulnerability was omnipresent, and tourism and immigration increased.

I came back to America after several weeks with a renewed sense of pride, ready to take on Roger Fisher in the live *Advocates* debate, armed with excerpts from the video interviews I had conducted that we would use as virtual "witnesses" in making the case for Israel.

The two shows were broadcast from PBS studios in Los Angeles, with live audiences. The narrow topic—"Should the U.S. give less or more military support to the State of Israel?"—quickly broadened into "The case against and the case for Israel." It was the first time I really had a chance to formulate and present the case I would be making over the next half a century. I read widely, prepared carefully and practiced repeatedly for my debut as "Israel's lead lawyer in the court of public opinion,"[10] as I would later be dubbed.

Fisher began his argument against U.S. military support for Israel in an eminently reasonable fashion:

The case I want to put to you tonight is the United States should give less military support to Israel. As I put this case, I ask your tolerance. I ask you to listen to what I'm saying with an open mind. Many Americans, particularly American Jews, naturally feel a deep, emotional commitment to Israel and the defense of that place. In this state of mind, you're likely to hear criticism of present policies of Israel as justification of all past Arab actions. The American Friends Service Committee has just produced a report on the Middle East. I agree with two phrases: "There is blame enough for all," and "There are no devils and no angels in the Middle East."

The real question is not the past but where do we go from here? During this hour I will present four things which Israel ought to do and which I believe the United States ought to urge Israel to do and use such military leverage as we have in that direction.

Fisher then laid out his proposals:

With respect to the Palestinian refugees, Israel should begin admitting them to the West Bank and to Israel itself. With respect to the neighboring Arab states, Israel should make a firm commitment of its willingness to withdraw its forces as part of a package settlement. With respect to military matters, Israel should abandon the policy of escalatory retaliation—two eyes for an eye. With respect to negotiations, Israel should be prepared to sit down with indirect talks, not insisting that the first talks be face-to-face.

He called President Nasser and King Hussein as his key witnesses. Nasser began with a straight-out lie, ignoring the "three no's" at Khartoum:

All arrangements for peace which were included in the Security Council we agreed about. There was no agreement from Israel in principle about the word "withdrawal" from the Arab

*occupied territories. [Note that he didn't say "Palestinian"
territories.] So we are sure that Israel doesn't want peace but wants
expansions. So we want President Nixon to use his influence
with Israel and get from them a promise or a word that they are
ready to withdraw from all the occupied territories and they are
ready to solve the problem of the refugees according to the United
Nations resolution.*

Hussein testified similarly:

*If they continue to occupy the territory they have occupied since
June of 1967; if they continue to attack the Arab homeland,
giving them more Phantoms certainly it's not going to help the
move toward resolution at all and, in fact, is encouraging the
further deterioration of the situation toward a climax and could
jeopardize world peace.*

I would have loved to cross-examine both Nasser and Hussein,
but neither was in the studio, so I had to be satisfied with cross-
examining Fisher:

*Mr. Fisher, aren't you aware that President Nasser and King
Hussein speak in one language to their people and say one thing
and speak very differently to the American public as they've
been doing for years? For example, as recently as March 27,
1969, Nasser reiterated the Khartoum Resolution. "We
have declared our principles. No negotiations, no peace, no
relinquishing of one inch of Arab land, and no bargaining
over Palestinian rights. These are our principles. We shall
never give them up."*

I then showed a clip of Hussein talking to his people in Arabic,
with his words translated as follows:

*Kill the Jews wherever you find them. Kill them with your hands,
with your nails, with your teeth.*

The audience gasped. They had never before heard the suave, gentle, smiling king of Jordan speak in such genocidal terms.

After completing my virtual cross-examination of Fisher's witnesses, it was my turn to present my affirmative case. I adopted a multifaceted approach. On the narrow issue of U.S. military support for Israel, I argued along Peres's lines that a strong Israel is the best road to peace:

> *The United States should supply more military support to Israel,
> a country that merely wants to live in peace. The Arab belligerents,
> armed to the teeth by Soviet weapons, and now even pilots, are
> determined to destroy Israel as soon as they are strong enough
> to do so. They reject the UN cease-fire which Israel accepts. The
> interests of world peace and of the United States are best served
> by keeping the peace-seeking country—Israel—strong enough
> to discourage miscalculations by those who want war. For the
> United States now to impose a one-sided arms embargo against
> Israel would be for it to take sides against a small democracy
> threatened by external force.*

With regard to the issue of Palestinian refugees, although I sympathized with their plight, I placed the blame squarely where it belonged—at the feet of Arab leaders:

> *To understand this refugee problem, we must go back to 1947
> when the United Nations partitioned Palestine into two separate
> states. The Jews were given a small area in which they constituted
> a majority of the population. The remainder was to become a
> Palestinian state. Therefore, under the United Nations decision,
> every Palestinian could have lived either as a part of an Arab*

majority in a Palestinian state or part of an Arab minority in Israel—if the Arab countries had not attacked Israel, and if Jordan had not annexed Arab Palestine. Moreover, on the very day that the Arabs declared war against the new state, the Grand Mufti of Jerusalem appealed to the Palestinians to leave their homes. The secretary of the Palestine higher command himself conceded that the refugees are a direct consequence of the unanimous policy of the Arab states.

While the Arab leaders were telling their people to leave their homes, what were Israeli authorities saying? They were telling them to remain. In Haifa, for example, the Jewish Workers Council issued the following plea: "Do not fear. Do not move out. In this city, yours and ours, the gates are open for work for life and peace." It is a tragedy that most of the Palestinians left. But it must be understood that they were not seeking refuge from oppression at the hands of Israel. They had a choice. They could have stayed. They were not refugees in the same sense that the survivors of Hitler's extermination camps were refugees. Those who fled from Nazi Germany had no choice but to die or to seek refuge.

I compared the plight of Jewish refugees from the Holocaust with Palestinian refugees from Israel. I played film clips showing how many countries in the world had turned away Jews fleeing the Holocaust, and then a clip showing Golda Meir describing what Israel had done to Jewish refugees after the war: "We brought our people here."

I asked whether "the Arab states [can] say the same about their people?" It was a rhetorical question, one that I proceeded to answer:

The Arab countries put them in camps instead of taking them into the numerous Arab homelands with a common culture, language and religion. For example, Palestine had for years been regarded as southern Syria. In 1951, Syria had wanted more population. It arranged to have half a million Egyptians come and settle. Yet when the United Nations asked Syria to accept 80,000 Palestinian refugees, they flatly refused. This and other similar refusals led a research team in Europe to conclude that the existence of the refugees were the fault of the inhuman policy of the Arabs for the purpose of maintaining a menacing population on the frontier with Israel.

I argued that the "existence of a refugee becomes a refugee problem only if political considerations are permitted to outweigh human considerations." I pointed to post-partition Pakistan and postwar Germany as examples of countries that had resettled millions of refugees, from India and Sudetenland respectively. I then showed that more than 700,000 Jews were forced to leave Arab countries where their ancestors had been living for hundreds if not thousands of years. They, too, were resettled in Israel. Indeed, the number of Arabs that left Israel was approximately the same as the number of Jews who were expelled from Arab countries.

I had learned a great deal about the refugee issues—both Palestinian and Jewish—from my work with Justice Goldberg at the UN, and I made use of this knowledge in the debate, arguing that "what happened in the Mideast, therefore, can be understood as a legitimate exchange of land and population. There is, therefore, no moral imperative on Israel to take back large numbers of refugees 20 years after they left."

As to the broad question, "Where do we go from here?" I argued in favor of a two-state solution (being one of the first to do so). I was much criticized by both Israelis and American Jews for supporting a state for the Arab residents of Mandatory Palestine, but I was advocating nothing different from what the United Nations partition plan had proposed: two states for two peoples.

I called as a live hostile witness a leader of the Palestinian terrorist group Al Fatah to make the point that Palestinian leadership would rather there *not* be a Jewish state, and that they wanted this *more* than they wanted a Palestinian state living alongside Israel:

DERSHOWITZ: *Didn't Jordan annex the Palestinian state? If not for Jordan's invasion against Israel, couldn't you have been living in Palestine? Could not [the Palestinians] have all gone to Palestine which was set aside by [the United] Nations, established a state and lived there?*

. . .

OMAR: *That was not their intention because they want to create a state in all of Palestine.*

DERSHOWITZ: *So what you're doing is you're fighting now, you're killing in order to get land.*

OMAR: *The Zionists are the only ones who impose this war on us by coming and colonizing our country, by using weapons of mass destruction . . .*

DERSHOWITZ: *They used the United Nations, is that a weapon of mass destruction?*

We then had the following exchange:

DERSHOWITZ: *Could I live in an Arab state today? I mean live, not be hanged in Baghdad.*

OMAR: *There are immigration laws which if you want to come and live in our countries should have to apply, immigration laws . . .*

DERSHOWITZ: *Immigration laws? They wouldn't even let me in to visit to interview Hussein or Nasser . . .*

Following my cross-examination of Omar, I described my discussion with Abba Eban:

DERSHOWITZ: *I asked the foreign minister if an independent Palestinian state on the West Bank would be consistent with Israel's security. He did not rule it out.*

On the issue of borders, I relied on General Rabin:

*YITZHAK RABIN: The Golan Heights topographically were
in control over one-third of Israel. And Syria exploited their
topographical advantage and opened fire whenever they wanted.
The brutal attack on children exemplifies what's going on
along the Lebanese border. If buses of children run now along
the former Syrian border, there is no danger that such an
eventuality would occur.*

Rabin then turned to the West Bank:

*On the morning of the fifth of June, 1967, when the Jordanians
opened fire and moved their forces, we warned them twice but
the Jordanians decided to go into the war. They were capable of
shelling Tel Aviv because of the short distance from Jordan. 60
to 70 percent of the Israeli population were within the range of
the Arab guns. I believe it's about 10 percent now. To give up at
the present the cease-fire lines which gives us a military capacity
to defend ourselves effectively without the need to mobilize our
forces would be almost like committing suicide.*

I then referred to a conversation I had with Ambassador Goldberg
on Security Council Resolution 242:

*I spoke personally to the United States ambassador to the
United Nations who participated in the drafting of this—the
Honorable Arthur Goldberg—he told me of the days of debate
that went into this phraseology and that it means unequivocally
that Israel is not committed to returning all the territories but is
committed and the U.S. is committed to permitting it to make
territorial adjustments necessary for its security. And that is
Israel's position and that is the United States position.*

Finally, I summed up my case:

The war in the Middle East will stop any time the Arabs want it to stop. Israel has reiterated its unconditional willingness to comply with the cease-fire if the Arabs will only stop shooting. Indeed, General Dayan recently said, "The government is ready to reestablish an unconditional and unlimited cease-fire even if this will enable Egypt to reorganize and put up SAM-3 missile sites." But the Arabs persist in seeking a military solution rather than a negotiated settlement. Mr. Fisher said that the initiative for peace lies with Israel. If only this were true. All objective people know that Israel will do almost anything for peace. The initiative lies as it has since 1948 with the Arabs in general and with Nasser in particular. The United States must not blackmail Israel into jeopardizing its security. Should Israel ever lose a war, we can understand what it would face by reading from the Jordanian military document captured during the 1967 war. The orders: destroy the agricultural village of Matzah and kill all its inhabitants.

Fisher was given the last word:

There's a very tough problem in the Middle East. It's not sure peace can be made. The sides as we have heard fell violently about the situation and are prepared to fight. Israel is prepared now to drop heavy bombs on Egypt, well beyond the Sinai, to reduce the possible risk that Russians might be able to get missiles there to help defend Egypt, which is undercutting their ability to inflict unlimited destruction on Egypt later. The Russians have put nothing there except defense equipment.

The problem is not should the United States rally to Israel's support in a hard-pressed fight. The question is, shall we take sides with an overwhelming military superiority now on the Israeli side, shall we take sides or shall we be the peacemakers?

The debate was now over and the viewing audience was asked to vote by mail. The tally was overwhelmingly in favor of Israel: 41,241 to 4,103—more than 10–1 in our favor. It was a sign of the times. The times would soon change, but many of the arguments would remain the same. Israel wanted a peace with secure borders. The Arab countries did not want a nation-state of the Jewish people anywhere in the Middle East. The facts would change, especially with regard to Israeli settlements in the West Bank, which would complicate the quest for a peaceful resolution. But Israel also evacuated settlements they built in the Gaza Strip in an effort to secure peace. So there were no insuperable barriers if the will for peace was present on all sides.

I was now ready to make the case for Israel to anyone who listened, having been energized and educated by my role in *The Advocates* debate.

Several years after this first *Advocates* program on Israel, there would be another one, in which a young Israeli named Ben Natai would reiterate some of the arguments I had made and add new ones. I had met "Ben" several years earlier, when he was an MIT student named Benjamin Netanyahu. We have remained friends since, despite our sometime political differences.

5

Chomsky Attacks Israel on Civil Liberties

IN MID-1970, at the time of *The Advocates* debate, Israel was still supported by the vast majority of Americans and Europeans. Its annexation of Jerusalem and the Golan Heights and its occupation of the West Bank and Gaza Strip were viewed as necessary to secure Israel's security and reduce the likelihood of renewed warfare. Israel had not yet embarked on its policy of settling Israeli civilians in enclaves in the occupied territories. The occupations were military in nature, which were common when an enemy was defeated in a defensive war. (For example, the United States occupied Germany and Japan after World War II.)[1] The Arab leadership had a different view and resisted the occupation with terrorism, both from the occupied territories as well as from within Israel proper. This same Arab leadership had also resisted with violence the very existence of Israel within its pre-1967 borders, and indeed within its pre-1949 partition borders. Israel responded to Arab violence with harsh measures, including the employment of preventive detention against Israeli Arabs and Palestinians it suspected of terrorism but against whom it could not prove their suspicions in a court of law. This led to accusations that Israel was violating the civil liberties of Palestinians.

I decided to spend the summer of 1970 in Israel studying these accusations from the perspective of a pro-Israel advocate of civil liberties. I had written against the use of preventive detention in my own country, and I doubted I could be convinced that it was justified anywhere. I quickly applied for and received a small Ford Foundation grant, and I packed up my family and took off for Israel only a few weeks after I returned from my first trip.

To study this controversial issue, I traveled across Israel, the West Bank and the Gaza Strip, interviewing former and present detainees, lawyers, generals and politicians. Most left-wing Israelis favored preventive detention (or what they called "administrative detention") as a necessary evil in the war against terrorism.

The one political figure who strongly opposed it was Menachem Begin, the former head of the Irgun Zvai Leumi, a paramilitary group outlawed by the British as a terrorist gang during the pre-state period. When I met him in the lunchroom of the Knesset, he was the leader of the right-wing opposition, a hardliner. But he was also a fervent civil libertarian. Indeed, his party's name was Herut—liberty. Begin was a true libertarian philosophically, though a "hawk" when it came to defending Israel militarily. During our lengthy discussion, Begin—who was proud of his training as a lawyer—reminded me that the Knesset had never enacted a preventive detention law; the Israeli authorities were using British Mandatory law, which authorized the detention of any person whose confinement was "necessary" for "securing the public safety."

Begin told me that under this open-ended law, many of his Irgun colleagues had been detained for long periods of time with no due process or real opportunity to prove their innocence. "We should not be doing what they did to us," he insisted.

I spoke to other Israeli officials who believed Israel had no choice but to detain suspected terrorists. Meir Shamgar, who was then the attorney general of Israel, had previously served as advocate general of the Israel Defense Forces and would eventually serve with distinction as the president of the Supreme Court of Israel. He had seen the issue from all sides. As a young man, he had served in the Irgun and had himself been subjected to preventive detention for several years.

When we met, Shamgar explained to me how his emotions pushed him against the use of preventive detention, but his recent experience with Palestinian terrorism pushed him to differ with his former leaders' categorical rejection of its use in all cases. He explained why he believed it was sometimes necessary. He told me about cases in which reliable undercover sources planted within terrorist groups had informed the Shin Bet of impending terriorist attacks (the Shin Bet is the Israeli version of the FBI, whose job it was to ensure Israel's security from domestic danger, such as stopping the bombing of a local supermarket; the Mossad dealt with foreign threats). The suspected terrorist would be detained, but the only admissible evidence against him would be the testimony of the undercover source. If the source were called as a witness in an open trial, his cover would be blown and he could no longer provide lifesaving information. Also, he and his family might be killed. Nor could his information be provided to the court by the person to whom he relayed it; that would be hearsay, inadmissible in a criminal trial. But such hearsay, if deemed reliable and confirmed by other information, could form the basis for a detention order. It was a compromise with due process, but a necessary one according to Shamgar and other Israeli officials.

I visited several detention centers (the letter from Golda got me in), and I interviewed a number of Arab detainees (the other letter from the Arab lawyer got them to talk to me). They all claimed innocence, but I was later given the hearsay evidence against them that seemed convincing. One former detainee, however, a Palestinian lawyer named Sabri Jaris, made a strong case for his innocence. His brother was a Fatah terrorist in Lebanon, and Sabri was suspected of harboring him and a truckload of explosives and detonators that the Shin Bet had found. His brother had escaped, and Sabri was detained to prevent him from harboring or assisting his terrorist brother in committing future terrorist acts. I thought that was a stretch, and I told that to the authorities who had already released him but placed him under travel restrictions. Shortly after I interviewed him, Jaris escaped to Lebanon, where he became an official of Fatah but never himself engaged in any act of terrorism (as far as the Israelis know).

After studying the issue in detail—and comparing Israel's use of preventive detention to what British and Americans have done during wartime—I came to the following conclusion in a report that was published:

> *Having attempted to place the problem in context, I am, of course, entitled to my own personal views. I fully understand the arguments in favor of preventive detention as it is presently practiced in Israel; I am convinced that it is not being abused and that every effort in good faith is being made to apply it only to persons who have engaged in terroristic activities and are likely to continue to be so engaged. I am impressed with the tiny number of Israeli citizens actually detained. And I appreciate, of course, the danger that Israel faces from terrorism. Nonetheless, I personally favor repeal of the Emergency Defense Regulations and particularly of the preventive-detention provision. Nor is there any paradox in understanding the reasons behind a law in recognizing that it has been fairly applied, and yet, at the same time, in favoring its repeal. Although the potential for abuse has not materialized, abuse is inherent in the nature of detention laws of the kind now on the books in Israel. Such laws, in the words of Justice Robert Jackson, "lie about like a loaded weapon."*

I then proposed alternative ways of dealing with the prevention of terrorism:

> *If Israel feels that it cannot live with the normal rules of evidence in cases of suspected terrorists, then the Knesset should*

enact special rules of evidence for a narrowly circumscribed
category of cases during carefully defined periods of emergency.
All other safeguards should be provided, as in ordinary cases.
In the last analysis, such a system might result in the release of
some who are now detained. It is in the nature of any judicial
system that in order to prevent confinement of the innocent,
it might release the guilty. And those released might engage in
acts of terrorism. But risks to safety have always been the price
a society must pay for its liberty. Israel knows that well. By
detaining only 15 of its 300,000 Arab citizens, Israel today is
taking considerable risks. Indeed, what the world must come to
realize is that no country throughout recorded history has ever
exposed its wartime population to so much risk in the interest of
civil liberties.

My analysis of Israel's approach to preventive detention reflected
the approach I was taking toward the nation-state of the Jewish people:
I would try hard to understand the compromises it felt it had to make
with civil liberties—perhaps I would even give it the benefit of the
doubt—but I would not hold back from criticizing Israel when criticism
was warranted.

My report, a version of which was published in *Commentary* magazine,
elicited criticism from both sides. Some Israelis accused me of
not understanding the dangers they faced from terrorism and why it
was necessary to use every available tactic—preventive detention, enhanced
interrogation, paid informers, targeted killings—to prevent
terrorism. Some civil libertarians, both in Israel and in the United
States, accused me of going easy on Israel and not being sufficiently
critical. Among the latter was Noam Chomsky, who challenged me
to a public debate on the issues of the Israeli–Palestinian conflict and
of civil liberties in Israel.

Today, Noam Chomsky is—and was even back then—one
of the most influential professors in the world, owing primarily to

his innovative, if controversial, theories of linguistics. He has been ranked as the most influential academic in the world. He proudly acknowledges that he "uses" his academic status to "make noise": "Since I was known professionally, I thought it was worth exploiting for a better purpose."[2] That "better" purpose has turned him into an all-knowing political guru, though his views on nonlinguistic issues tend to be more ideological than scholarly. His writing is opaque, often bordering on the incomprehensible. On several occasions when I have seen students carrying one of his political screeds, I have asked to look at it. Invariably the bookmark or bent page is near the beginning. I then inquire how much they have actually read and they admit, with embarrassment, that it's hard to get past the introductory pages. I suspect that Chomsky holds the world's record for the highest ratio of books bought to actually read from beginning to end.

Chomsky is a better speaker than he is a writer, but his speeches are polemical rather than analytic. They are sprinkled with phrases such as "there is no dispute about," or "everyone acknowledges," or "it is incontrovertible." These "argument stoppers" generally serve as preludes to both hotly disputed and flat-out false factual assertions. I recall him saying in one debate that it was "incontrovertible that Israel rejected Security Council Resolution 242, while the Arabs accepted it." When I read out loud the documentary evidence that proved that the exact opposite was true, he simply ignored the proof and repeated his "incontrovertible" assertion. That is his style, and his followers, of which there are many, regard him as a prophet who cannot be wrong.

Chomsky had emerged as a leading critic of American involvement in Vietnam, a war he regarded as one of imperialist aggression. We were introduced shortly after I arrived at Harvard in 1964 by Leonard Boudin, a great lawyer whose practice centered on representing people of the left, ranging from Fidel Castro to Dr. Benjamin Spock. I liked Noam, because he has a quick intellect and a strong passion. He is not fun to be with, however, because he has no sense of humor and little tolerance for opposing views, which he often characterizes as "unintelligent," "stupid" or "uninformed." He has called me "not very bright" and "strongly opposed to civil liberties." The first characterization is perhaps debatable. The second is flatly untrue.

His views on Israel in those days were typical of the Zionist left. He was affiliated with Hashomer Hatzair, near the extreme left of Israel's many ideological factions. He wished that the mandate had never been divided into two areas, one for the Jewish and the other for an Arab state. His preference was for a secular, binational, socialist state. But Israel had declared statehood, and the Jordanians and Egyptians had denied the Palestinians statehood by dividing the Arab portions of the mandate, with Jordan occupying the West Bank and Egypt occupying the Gaza Strip. That was the reality on the ground, and Chomsky had to deal with that messy reality. His support for the Palestinian cause had been quoted by Roger Fisher in his opening statement during *The Advocates* debate:

> *In America, there is little willingness to face the fact that*
> *Palestinians . . . have suffered a monstrous historical injustice.*
> *That worse injustice was done to Jews in the past is no reason for*
> *us to overlook the present plight of the Palestinians.*

His rabid hatred for the Jewish state was not yet manifest, and so when we were invited to debate in the early 1970s, I agreed, expecting a serious intellectual exchange of ideas with a fellow progressive. Our political views were quite far apart, even back then: I was a liberal Democrat and he was a radical socialist (or anarchist). Our views on Vietnam were somewhat similar—although his were more extreme—but our views on Israel, as I would learn during the debate, were quite far apart.

The debate—the first of several—was conducted in a large Boston church with a live audience of several hundred pro- and anti-Israel supporters. There were cheers and boos as well as a few shouted interruptions. But for the most part, the debate was civil.

Chomsky's basic position was that all of the British mandate over Palestine—what is now Israel and the West Bank—should be a single binational secular state. (No mention was made of the Gaza Strip.) He proposed two models for successful binational states: Yugoslavia and Lebanon. (He did not mention India-Pakistan before it was divided into two independent nations.) Yugoslavia, which was an assortment of ethnic and religious enclaves cobbled together and kept artificially unified by the charisma of Josip Broz Tito, was torn apart by bloody conflict after his death and ended up becoming several separate nations. Lebanon, which had managed for a time to divide political authority between its Muslim majority and Christian minority, also blew up in a bloody civil war that resulted in a mass exodus of its Christian population. It is now under the military control of Hezbollah, an Iranian-controlled terrorist group.

Neither Yugoslavia nor Lebanon—both failed states—is a positive model for Israel and the West Bank. Nor are there any other successful "one-state" solutions to comparable conflicts.

In my opening statement, I argued for a two-state solution with territorial border adjustments to strengthen Israel's security. Israel had not yet embarked on its controversial policy of building civilian settlements in the captured territories, so this issue did not arise. (When it did, in 1973, I strongly opposed that policy.) My plan called for Israel to annex a small percentage of the unpopulated or minimally populated areas of the West Bank and the Gaza Strip as buffers against future attacks. It should then gradually reduce and ultimately end its military presence in the West Bank and Gaza as soon as all hostilities and threats of hostilities ended and the Arab countries agreed to comply with the terms of Security Council Resolution 242. Implicit in my proposal was that Israel would not build civilian settlements in the areas it was prepared to return in exchange for peace.

My proposal was a variation on the Allon Plan, formulated by Israeli general Yigal Allon, which would have annexed parts of the Jordan Valley and other areas necessary for Israel's security and returned the remainder to Jordan in exchange for peace.

This is what I said about Chomsky's one-state scheme in our 1973 debate:

> *Putting aside the motivations behind such a proposal when it is made by the Palestinian organizations, why do not considerations of self-determination and community control favor two separate states: one Jewish and one Arab? Isn't it better for people of common background to control their own life, culture, and destiny (if they so choose), than to bring together in an artificial way people who have shown no ability to live united in peace.*

The audience overwhelmingly preferred my proposal to Chomsky's, although some thought both were too generous to the losing side of the Six-Day War. A small number of hard leftists favored Chomsky's proposal for a single state.

This was to be the first of several debates between Chomsky and me. This one ended in a friendly manner, with each of us respecting the other's perspective while agreeing to disagree about the optimal solution to the vexing problems. We continued to correspond by mail. In December 1970, I wrote to him complaining about a comparison one of his left-wing colleagues had made between Israel's wars of self-defense and America's war against North Vietnam. Here is his cordial response:

> *Dear Alan,*
> *I agree with you that comparisons between Israel and, say, North Vietnam are likely to be dubious, but not exactly for the reasons you give. North Vietnam was a backward peasant society, which has been under bitter attack and has received very little aid. Recall that in 1954, Bernard Fall predicted with "certainty" that North Vietnam would either suffer a disastrous*

*famine or would become a Chinese colony if the US succeeded
in cutting it off from the south. I needn't comment on what
has happened in recent years. Israel, in contrast, was settled in
the first instance by educated Westerners and has received, by a
large margin, the greatest per capita aid of any country in the
world. It is the most advanced country in the region, by a vast
margin, and also the strongest military power. It does certainly
face potential dangers, but they can obviously not be compared
by those faced by North Vietnam.*
Best, Noam

It was a perfectly reasonable and friendly response. Our subsequent interactions were not as friendly, as the hard left moved from the kind of criticism of Israel's policies leveled by Fisher on *The Advocates* and by Chomsky in our initial debate to delegitimation of Israel as the nation-state of the Jewish people.

My personal break with Chomsky came in 1973, when he supported a professor named Israel Shahak, who had characterized Israel as a "racist society," akin to Hitler's Germany. Shahak was a brilliant Israeli professor of chemistry, who, like Chomsky, was widely respected for his scientific accomplishments. But he was also widely reviled—except by Israel haters—for his comparisons of Israel to Nazi Germany. Recall that this was prior to Israel creating its controversial civilian settlements in the territories it had captured in the Six-Day War.

In an article in the *Boston Globe*, Chomsky called Shahak a civil libertarian. I wrote a letter to the editor disagreeing with him:

*Let no one believe that Shahak is a civil libertarian. He is the
furthest thing from it. A civil libertarian defends the rights of
those with whom he disagrees as vehemently as those with whom
he agrees (consider, for example, the American Civil Liberties
Union's frequent defense of Nazis and right wingers). Shahak*

has never defended the rights of those with whom he disagrees politically; nor has he ever attacked the practices of those with whom he agrees politically. He is about as much of a civil libertarian as are Communists who defend only the rights of other Communists, or Ku Klux Klanners who only defend the rights of other Klanners.[3]

The very best proof of Israel's commitment to liberty is that it permits hate-mongers such as Shahak—and other Israeli-Arab critics of Israel—to travel through the world on Israeli passports spewing forth their venom. Can one think of any Arab country that would permit a Jewish critic publicly to attack its regime?

Chomsky responded that Shahak was a civil libertarian as well as a "man of honor and principle who needs no lessons from Alan Dershowitz or anyone else on what it means to be a civil libertarian."

Dershowitz has chosen to distort beyond recognition what Shahak has said and done to vilify him as a "hate-monger" who "spews forth (his) venom" against Israel. His resort to such tactics and his refusal to consider the actual evidence that Shahak has presented speaks for itself, I am afraid.

I responded:

I was not surprised at the belligerent tone of Noam Chomsky's response to my letter regarding Israel Shahak. Though Chomsky and I have been allies in numerous cases, I have seen over the years that Chomsky will stop at nothing in attacking those who support Israel or in defending those who attack it.

Chomsky disputes my statement that Shahak defends the civil liberties only of those with whom he agrees politically. I again challenge Chomsky to cite me instances where Shahak has ever supported the rights of those who disagreed with his anti-Zionist

political views. . . . Why did [Shahak] refuse to condemn the
execution of Jews in Iraq or the oppression of Jews in the Soviet
Union? I am afraid that both Shahak and Chomsky do need
lessons on what it means to be a civil libertarian.

Finally *The Globe* decided to end this unusual exchange of letters
on its editorial page and Chomsky got the last word:

Dr. Shahak, acting with courage and honor, [has] produced
substantial evidence on violations of human and civil rights by
the Israeli government, avoiding no relevant instances to my
knowledge. Apparently unable to refute the facts, Dershowitz
has chosen to defame the man, in a manner which is as familiar
as it is deplorable.[4]

From that point on my interactions with Chomsky became more
belligerent, as he and others pushed the hard left toward delegitimizing Israel. Our friendship would further deteriorate when, several years
later, he signed a petition in support of an anti-Semitic Holocaust denier named Robert Faurisson, who had published a book denying that
six million Jews had been murdered by gas, bullets and forced starvation.[5] Faurisson claimed that *The Diary of Anne Frank* was a hoax.
He accused the Jews and Israel of exploiting the alleged Holocaust
for financial gain. Chomsky characterized Faurisson's lies as historical
"findings"—that there were no gas chambers or systematic killing of
Jews—based on "extensive historical research."[6] He described Faurisson as "a sort of relatively apolitical liberal." Chomsky also denied that
there were "anti-Semitic implications" in denying the Holocaust:

I see no anti-Semitic implications in denial of the existence
of gas chambers or even denial of the Holocaust. Nor would
there be anti-Semitic implication, per se, in the claim that the
Holocaust (whether one believes it took place or not) is being

exploited viciously so by apologists for Israeli repression and violence. I see no hint of anti-Semite implications in Faurisson's work. [Emphasis added][7]

I responded in a letter to the *Boston Globe*:

While some may regard Chomsky as an eminent linguist, he does not understand the most obvious implications in Faurisson's collective condemnation of the Jewish people as liars. . . . Failure to recognize the anti-Semitic implication of Holocaust denial is like saying there would be no racist implications in a claim that African-Americans enjoyed slavery, or no sexist implication in a statement that women wanted to be raped. The Holocaust is the central historical event of modern Jewish history. Efforts to deny or minimize it are the current tools of the anti-Semite and neo-Nazi. Not surprising both Faurisson and Chomsky are frequently quoted with approval by those hatemongers.

Chomsky's actions in defending the substance *of Faurisson's bigoted remarks against valid charges of anti-Semitism—as distinguished from defending Faurisson's right to publish such pernicious drivel—disqualify Chomsky from being considered an honorable defender of the "underdog" [as he had claimed]. The victims of the Holocaust, not its deniers, are the underdogs.*[8]

For me and many other liberal Jews, that was the last straw. At a time of increasing Holocaust denial or minimization—by Arab leaders, neo-Nazis and even some on the hard left—the idea that the most influential academic in the world would validate Faurisson's deliberate lies as "findings" based on "extensive historical research" was beyond comprehension. It was also beyond comprehension that Chomsky would allow Faurisson to use an essay he had written as an introduction to his anti-Semitic screed.[9] As a result of his getting in bed with this Holocaust denier, Chomsky became a pariah in the

Jewish community. This turned him even more ferociously against Israel. Indeed, it is likely that the nearly universal condemnation by the Jewish community of Chomsky for his role in helping to legitimate Holocaust denial pushed him over the edge when it came to Israel and its supporters. From that point on, it was hard to have a rational discussion with Chomsky on these issues.

Notwithstanding our growing animosity, I continued to debate Chomsky over the years,[10] even as his anti-Israel (and anti-American) views became more and more strident. Indeed, increasing extremism on both sides was squeezing the center and making nuanced discussion more difficult. The growth of the hard right and the settler movement in Israel contributed to this polarization. I was strongly opposed to the settler movement, believing it would make the two-state solutions more difficult. I must admit that I enjoyed sparring with Chomsky and others on both the hard left and hard right. I recall getting a call from Ted Kennedy before the Easter-Passover season in which he teased me:

"Al"—he was the only person who always called me Al—"you're enjoying kicking Chomsky's ass too much. You should cut it out for Lent."

Since Jews don't observe Lent, I kept up my criticism of Chomsky and others.

I also opposed turning the issue into a religious conflict over biblical claims to "Judea" and "Samaria." Both settler and biblical movements, which overlapped, tended to attract zealots for whom pragmatic compromise—so necessary to a two-state solution—was anathema.

Among the most extreme views on the biblical and settler hard right were those of Rabbi Meir Kahane, the leader of the Jewish Defense League, who I would later debate. But first, I was called on to serve as defense counsel for one of his followers.

Around the same time that I was becoming deeply committed to the defense of Israel—through my visits to Israel, appearances on

The Advocates, and debates with Chomsky—another transformative event was developing in my career and my life.

The Jewish Defense League was growing in popularity among some young Jews, especially in Brooklyn and Queens. Founded by Rabbi Kahane as a Jewish self-defense organization, it morphed into a confrontational group that threatened and employed violent means to secure its (often positive) ends. Its violent actions were universally condemned by traditional Jewish leaders—and by me and my friends. We supported the goals of the JDL, especially its advocacy for the oppressed Jews of the Soviet Union, but we despised its violent means.

A family friend and Boro Park neighbor was being accused of murdering a wealthy young woman who had been working as an assistant to the world-famous impresario Sol Hurok. The family friend, Sheldon Seigel, had been recruited by Rabbi Meir Kahane to join the Jewish Defense League.

I despised the violent means used by the JDL, but when a mutual friend asked me to defend Seigel—who was facing a possible death sentence—I felt I had no choice, based on my lifelong commitment to representing even the most despised people accused of crimes. I had represented non-Jews accused of violent crimes, so I saw no principle that would incline me to turn down a Jew—and someone whose family I know.

Seigel was accused of being the "engineer" who had made the smoke bomb that had been planted in Hurok's office, an action intended to be a protest against Hurok for bringing in talent from the Soviet Union as part of a cultural exchange program. "Bullets for ballerinas and bombs for balalaikas" was their slogan, along with "every Jew a 22 [caliber rifle]."

The smoke bomb was designed to frighten and cause panic, but not to kill. Tragically, its smoke in the enclosed area suffocated Iris Kones, a young Jewish woman from an extraordinarily wealthy family who were major contributors to Harvard, among other institutions. Seigel was charged with felony murder, because planting the smoke bomb, regardless of the lack of intent to kill, was a felony, and any death, even an accidental one, resulting from a felony is murder.

My pro bono representation of Seigel on constitutional grounds—the evidence against him came largely from an illegal wiretap—created difficulty for me at Harvard. The victim's relatives threatened to cut off all contributions to Harvard Law School unless I stopped representing Seigel or was fired by the law school. The dean called me in to tell me how "expensive" I was becoming, but that it was worth it. I persisted, and after months of litigation, the team I assembled won a total victory.[11] It was my first big win in a highly publicized case, and it helped establish my national reputation as a winning appellate lawyer at the age of 34.

My involvement in the JDL and Soviet Jewry cases brought me into close contact with the movement to help Soviet Jewry. I was convinced there were better ways to confront this important issue than through the violent means adopted by the JDL. I had read Elie Wiesel's book *The Jews of Silence*, which detailed the plight of the Soviet Jews who were being discriminated against and denied exit permits to Israel. I met with Elie, who urged me to travel to the Soviet Union to defend refuseniks—Jews who were refused exit permits—some of whom were facing imprisonment in the Gulag for protesting their unfair treatment. Two Jewish men were facing the death penalty for trying to steal a small airplane and fly several refuseniks to Sweden.

I helped assemble a team of international lawyers to go to the Soviet Union in an effort to save the lives and liberty of these brave refuseniks. I believe that there, but for the grace of God and the choices my great grandparents made to come to America in the nineteenth century, might go I.

The team was headed by my former professor Telford Taylor, who knew the Soviet chief prosecutor and chief justice from his days as a Nuremberg prosecutor. We traveled to the Soviet Union in 1974 to meet our clients and then to Israel to interview witnesses who had managed to emigrate. In the end, we helped to save the lives of the two refuseniks who had been sentenced to death and to secure the freedom of several who were facing imprisonment or were already in prison.[12]

I subsequently worked with Irwin Cotler to free the Soviet Union's most prominent refusenik prisoner, Anatoly Sharansky, who had been falsely accused of spying for the United States.[13] I helped persuade President Jimmy Carter to make an unprecedented and categorical denial that Sharansky had ever spied for the United States. This resulted in the death penalty being taken off the table, but Sharansky was sentenced to a long term of imprisonment. I then helped to arrange an exchange of prisoners, which resulted in Sharansky's release, after he had served eight years in the Gulag. We met shortly after he crossed the Glienicke Bridge to freedom, and he threw his arms around me and recited the Jewish Prayer, "Baruch Matir Asurim," blessed are those who help free the imprisoned. Despite the fact that I represented him without charge, that blessing was the most meaningful fee I ever earned. "Natan," as he is now called, made aliya upon his release from the Gulag and became one of Israel's most important moral and political leaders.[14]

My involvement in the JDL and Soviet Jewry cases was transformative in my career and my life. Now I was a full-time advocate for Israel, for Soviet Jewry and for the Jewish people—as well as for the liberal domestic causes to which I had devoted so much of my young life.

I also worked with Senator Ted Kennedy and other political leaders on broader diplomatic, legislative, economic and legal efforts to open the gates of the Soviet Union to the nearly two million Jews who were ultimately allowed to emigrate to Israel, the United States and Europe. It was one of the greatest human rights accomplishments in modern history, and the part of my career that I am most proud of.[15]

But these causes—or at least many of those who supported them— were coming into conflict, as it became more difficult to be a liberal supporter of Israel.

6

The Hard Left Denies Israel's Right to Exist

ON THE MORNING of October 6, 1973—Yom Kippur—the Egyptian and Syrian armed forces attacked Israel. Although intelligence sources warned of an imminent attack, the Israeli military was caught off guard. Some Israeli generals had called for a preemptive attack against the enemy air forces, but Prime Minister Golda Meir refused, citing a warning from Henry Kissinger that if Israel once again preemptively attacked—as it had done in 1967—it would not receive any military support from the United States: "Not so much as a nail." At the time, Kissinger was effectively running American foreign and military policy because President Nixon was in the process of being removed from office.

The result of not preempting was an enormous casualty rate among Israeli soldiers in the first days of the war.

Many people around the world, not just Jews, were quite properly shocked that the attack had come on the holiest day of the Jewish calendar. Ironically, it would have been worse had the attack come on a busy weekday rather than on Yom Kippur, a day when the roads were empty and mobilization of reserves from synagogues and homes was facilitated.

Casualties were also high among Egyptian and Syrian soldiers. Before the war Anwar Sadat—who had replaced Nasser upon his death in 1970—had said he was willing to "sacrifice a million Egyptian soldiers" to recover the barren Sinai from Israel.

The fighting was ferocious, both in the Sinai and on the Golan Heights. The Syrian front was far more dangerous for Israel, because the Syrian army was in close proximity to Israeli civilian population centers—and the Syrians made no distinction between combatants and noncombatants.

On the second day of the war—when things were going very badly for Israel—Moshe Dayan reportedly said that "the Third Temple" was in danger because "the fight is over the entire land of Israel," as the Arabs intended "to conquer Israel, to eliminate the Jews." He reportedly suggested to the prime minister that Israel demonstrate its nuclear capacity by detonating an atomic bomb over an unpopulated area. Meir reportedly rejected the idea.[1] Although Israel has never publicly confirmed that it possesses a nuclear arsenal, everyone, especially the Arab countries, knew of its existence. They also knew that Israel had pledged never to be the first Middle East country to deploy a nuclear weapon (if it had one). Dayan wanted Syria and Egypt to see that Israel would break that pledge if its very survival was at stake. Meir wanted to maintain the pledge.

My Jewish friends and colleagues were at Harvard Hillel Yom Kippur services as the war unfolded. Our intelligence source, Professor Nadav Safran, provided a glum assessment. Everyone was shocked that the vaunted Israeli military could be caught so off guard. Prayers were offered for Israeli soldiers. Congregants hid transistor radios in their tallit (prayer shawl) bags. News reports were continually updated.

In the end, Israeli forces counterattacked and won the day. Only a United States–imposed cease-fire prevented Israel from destroying the Egyptian army, which its forces had encircled, with the help of a bold move by General Sharon. But the Israeli casualty rates were too high for a small country, and Golda Meir was soon replaced as prime minister by Yitzhak Rabin, a military hero–turned–peace advocate, who I had met three years earlier.

More importantly, Israel's self-confidence was shaken. This was not a clear military victory like the one six years earlier. Egypt and Syria celebrated the many casualties they had inflicted on Israel and the temporary regaining of captured land they had achieved in the first days of the war. When I subsequently visited Egypt in 1988, I was shown the museum that commemorated Egypt's "victory" over "the Zionist entity" during the "Ramadan war," so named by Egypt because their attack was during their holiest month. For Egypt, even small, symbolic victories are worthy of celebration, even if the ultimate result was a humiliating military defeat.

More than 2,500 Israeli soldiers were killed in the 19-day war, and more than 7,500 were injured. Total deaths among Arab soldiers amounted to more than 15,000, with as many as 35,000 wounded. Nearly 10,000 Arab soldiers were taken prisoner and quickly returned. Hundreds of Israeli POWs were tortured and murdered with their hands tied behind their backs. Documents discovered by Israeli troops during the war showed that Egyptian general Saad el-Shazly had distributed written orders to kill Israeli soldiers even after they surrendered. These deliberate and systematic violations of the Geneva Convention were ignored by the United Nations and the international community.

The biggest impact of the Yom Kippur War was that it demonstrated to Israelis and Arabs alike that Israel was not invincible. It had won this time, but it paid a high price. Next time, or the time after, it could actually lose. Everyone understood that no matter how many times Israel won, if it ever lost a single war, that would be the end of "the Third Temple."

It was against the background of this tragic war that the first major attack by a prominent American against the very legitimacy of Israel as the nation-state of the Jewish people took place. It came from an antiwar Catholic priest who I had once helped defend. His name was Daniel Berrigan, perhaps not a household name today, but back in the early 1970s he was one of the most prominent and charismatic figures in the antiwar movement. Left-wing attorney Leonard Boudin (whose daughter Kathy was convicted of murder after she joined the Weather Underground) had sought my advice when he defended Berrigan in 1971 against criminal charges growing out of his antiwar activities.

I had met Berrigan and been taken by his warmth and charm. Many Jewish, pro-Israel, antiwar liberals were similarly impressed by him. We were therefore shocked when, within weeks of the country's near annihilation at the hands of genocidal Arab armies, he published an anti-Israel screed, which many, including myself, thought crossed the line into anti-Semitism.

In a speech delivered on October 19, 1973, and published widely,[2] the Reverend Daniel Berrigan, S.J., described Israel as "a criminal Jewish community" that has committed "crimes against humanity," has "created slaves" and has espoused "racism . . . aimed at proving its racial superiority to the people it has crushed." It is logical, Berrigan declared, that "racist ideology, which brought the destruction of the Jewish communities at the hands of the Nazis, should now be employed by the state of Israel . . ."

Not content with attacking the Jewish state in these inflammatory terms, Reverend Berrigan also chastised the "Jewish people," who he described as "so proud" and so "endowed with intelligence," as being collectively guilty of numerous sins and crimes. American Jews were the special focus of Berrigan's attack, because they "have in the main given their acquiescence or their support to the Nixon ethos." The American Jewish community's leadership was "fervent in support of Nixon," who was thereby enabled "to mute the horrific facts of the Vietnam war in light of Jewish concern for Israel." This led to the supposed "fact" that "in Nixon's first term alone some six million Southeast Asians had been maimed, bombed, displaced, tortured, imprisoned or killed." Berrigan refers to the iconic figure of six million as "one of those peculiar facts which must be called free-floating; it was a statistic, it did not signify."

He concludes with a veiled threat both to American Jews and to Israel:

To put the matter brutally, many American Jewish leaders were capable of ignoring the Asian holocaust in favor of economic and military aid to Israel. Those of us who resisted the war had to live with that fact. The fate of the Vietnamese was as unimportant to the Zionists in our midst as was the state of the Palestinians. [Again collective guilt: I'm a Zionist who cared greatly about the fate of the Vietnamese as well as the Palestinians, as did many other Zionists.] But I venture to suggest that it is not merely we, nor the Vietnamese, who must live with that fact. So must Israel. So must the American Jews.

I was outraged by Berrigan's bigoted and mendacious words, especially since they had come from an ally in the antiwar movement. These kinds of attacks from the hard left are common today, but they were unheard of back in 1973. I had no idea where this bigotry came from, since Berrigan had worked so closely over the years with so many Jewish lawyers, war resisters and civil rights activists. Some suggested that it reflected his theological views, but I saw no evidence of that. Whatever his motives, I feared that his words could have widespread influence among his many admirers on the left, so I felt I had to respond. I called my friend Leonard Boudin, who was his lawyer and friend. He had no idea that Berrigan felt that way or would publicly express such views. I told Leonard that I would be attacking his client. He said I should do what I had to do, but he couldn't become involved. I understood.

I then wrote and circulated the following public petition to the Harvard faculty and to every liberal I knew:

We are a group of Americans of all faiths and of diverse views on the Arab–Israeli conflict. Many of us have supported the Reverend Berrigan in his activities against the Vietnam War. Some of us have even defended the Reverend Berrigan and his colleagues before courts of law. We have different views on many issues of the day. But we are unanimous in our condemnation—indeed a strong word would be more appropriate—of the thoughts expressed in the Berrigan speech of October 19th. These irresponsible and blatantly inaccurate charges call for no substantive response. They speak for themselves as evidence of either the author's abysmal ignorance or his malice toward the Jewish people. The rhetoric—especially the suggestion of the collective guilt of the Jewish people for which Israel is to be made to pay—is tragically reminiscent of a bygone age. We call on all persons of good will—whatever their political views—to join us in condemning this bigoted attack on the Jewish people.

The response was overwhelming, with hundreds of people from every background signing on to my letter. Chomsky, of course, took Berrigan's side and attacked his critics for creating a "fabrication." Sadly, my old friend and client Bill Kunstler wrote a counter letter agreeing with Berrigan. But Kunstler's main lawyer Morton Stavis—who was far to the left of me and closer to Berrigan and Kunstler on most issues—joined my campaign to discredit Berrigan. He wrote his own heartfelt eight-page, single-spaced critique of his old friend and political ally, which included the following:

Firstly, moving as I do within New Left circles, I am quite accustomed to the fact that many of my colleagues and associates have views with respect to the State of Israel with which I strongly disagree. But some of the formulations which you employed are quite beyond moral disagreement and should not have been employed. I refer to language and rhetoric which is far from the truth and which has the effect of generating blind hostility rather than thoughtful consideration. I mention two examples:

"It is . . . logical, too, that racist ideology, which brought the destruction of the Jewish community at the hands of the Nazis, should now be employed by the State of Israel."

"American Jews—must live with the brutal fact that many American Jewish leaders were capable of ignoring the Asian Holocaust in favor of economic and military aid to Israel."

Aside from the factual inaccuracies of these statements [for example, the vast majority of Jews voted against Nixon and did not support the Vietnam War], the first of these formulations becomes the foundation for charging Israel with Hitlerism; the second can be the foundation for a far-ranging escalation of anti-Semitism in this country.

I suggest that a person of your sense of moral leadership ought to be making speeches to Arabs and Jews alike, telling them that they have to accept each other, that they have to live in peace.

Berrigan had crossed a line that even most hard-left critics of Israel would not cross—at least not yet. He did not back down. Instead he escalated his hateful and mendacious attacks on Israel and American Jews, becoming a full-fledged anti-Semite, repeatedly and collectively attacking "the Jews," "the Jewish Community," "Jewish Leaders" and "the Jewish People." (His language was subsequently emulated by another anti-Semitic cleric, Bishop Desmond Tutu.) Berrigan's bigotry did not stop some of his many followers—including hard-left Jews—from joining his campaign to demonize and delegitimize Israel. It was the beginning of an escalating war between liberal supporters of Israel (which included many who were critical of some Israeli policies) and hard-left delegitimizors of the nation-state of the Jewish people.

The Berrigan–Kunstler–Chomsky attacks were also the opening

salvo of my personal war with the hard left over Israel. My next target was the National Lawyers Guild.[3]

In the 1960s, I had worked closely with the Lawyers Guild on civil liberties issues, such as opposition to the death penalty, racial discrimination and criminal justice reform. But my collaboration with the Guild was to change rather quickly in the early 1970s when it was taken over by anti-American and anti-Israel extremists, most of them not lawyers.

The National Lawyers Guild was established in 1937 as an antidote to the American Bar Association, which was then fighting the New Deal, excluding black lawyers from membership and opposing the labor movement. The original Guild was an amalgam of Roosevelt liberals, CIO labor leaders, black civil rights lawyers and radicals of assorted affiliations and persuasions. Its membership over the years had included such distinguished lawyers as Thurgood Marshall, Ferdinand Pecora, Paul O'Dwyer, Louis Boudin (Leonard's uncle) and William Hastie. During its early years, splits developed between the anti-Communist liberals and the radicals. But the Guild survived and accomplished much good on the domestic front, which included an excellent record of providing legal assistance to the civil rights, labor and antiwar movements.

However, in the late 1960s and early 1970s, at the height of the antiwar movement, the Guild began to be taken over by younger, more militant lawyers from the New Left. Among their pet causes were Fidel Castro and the plight of Palestinians under what was called Zionist Occupation. As George Coak, an admiring Guild historian and a former editor of the monthly *Guild News*, described it, "At the Boulder (Colorado) Convention in 1971 the young veterans of the anti-war movement found they had the Guild in their own hands, and many older members withdrew from active membership. Legal workers [paraprofessionals and support staff] and jailhouse lawyers were admitted to membership." Law students were also admitted, thus strengthening the hold of the young radicals but replacing the percentage of actual lawyers in the Guild to less than half. The Guild no longer considered itself an alternative bar association but rather the prime organizer of "radical legal people" and the legal arm of "the American radical left."

Many of the longtime members of the Guild and even some of its founders, who sympathized with the sufferings of Palestinian refugees, were nonetheless outraged at the decision by the younger radicals to use the Guild as the legal propaganda arm of the Palestine Liberation Organization, which was then considered a terrorist organization. One founding member put it this way: "There is a group within the Guild which is absolutely determined to make the Guild a propaganda voice of the PLO. [T]hey are fostering splits and divisions within the Guild which threatens it very existence."

Earlier in its history, when it was a liberal organization, the Guild had supported the Jewish struggle for national liberation. It had opposed the American arms embargo against the new state. But after joining forces with the International Association of Democratic Lawyers, a communist front organization that, like the Soviet Union, refused to recognize the legitimacy of Israel, it turned more and more against the Jewish state and more and more in favor of Palestinian terrorism. As a long-term observer of the Guild put it,

Basically, you had a situation where a bunch of Third World types wanted to ensure that the Jews in the Guild—and the Jews were almost certainly a majority—would be forced to eat crow, to choose sides. The guild changed dramatically in the 1960s and early 1970s when the veterans of the early days were displaced by the veterans of campus unrest who had gone from SDS to law schools around the country. They're angry, and rigid, and there's no better test of their control of the Guild than forcing the old timers to grovel, and there's no better evidence of their own militance—

if they're Jews—than toadying up to the PLO. Endorsing the
PLO has become a litmus test for Jewish radicals.

The Guild decided to send observers to the trials of accused Palestinian terrorists and to have them report back. One of the observers included in his report the following disclaimer: "I am opposed, on political as well as humanitarian grounds, to terrorism as means of achieving political change." But since the disclaimer expressly contradicted the approval of terrorism by the PLO and the International Association of Democratic Lawyers, the Guild leadership simply decided to excise it from the final report.

In the original report, the observer properly criticized Israel for "interrogating [the alleged terrorist] without the presence of counsel," but added the important caveat that he (the observer) was "personally familiar with this procedure in the socialist countries of Eastern Europe." Rather than risk the wrath of communist lawyers in these countries, the Guild leadership decided to delete this comparison.

The Guild's unwillingness to criticize "the socialist countries of Eastern Europe" was dramatically manifested in an exchange I had with Professor John Quigley, the national vice president of the Guild. After learning that the Guild had decided to send an observer to the trial in Israel, I telephoned Quigley and requested that the Guild also send an observer to the Soviet trial of Anatoly Sharansky. It was the belief of several experts on Soviet law that a request by the Guild to send an observer to the Sharansky trial could have a decided impact on Soviet actions, since the Soviet Union has a close relationship with the International Association of Democratic Lawyers and its constituent members. Professor Quigley was extremely candid in his response: he told me that he doubted the Guild would be willing to send an observer to a Soviet trial, since the "reality" of the situation was that a considerable number of the Guild members approved of the Soviet Union and would not want to criticize a Soviet judicial proceeding.

I wrote articles and made speeches exposing the hypocrisy and bias of the National Lawyers Guild. Many old members and some new ones resigned in protest. But the Guild persisted in its move away from its long-standing commitment to civil liberties and liberalism and toward following the Soviet line with regard to Israel, a line of increased nonrecognition and of no diplomatic relations. Even after the fall of the Soviet Union in 1989 and Russia's subsequent recognition of Israel, the Guild maintained its hard-left delegitimization of, and double standard toward, the Middle East's only democracy.

Members of the Guild also began to infiltrate the American Civil Liberties Union in an effort to turn it from a neutral defender of the civil liberties of all Americans to an advocate for agenda-driven left-wing causes. It succeeded in some areas of the country more than in others, to a point where today it has all but abandoned its original nonpartisan mission. More on this later—but now back to the mid-1970s.

On November 10, 1975, while Israel was still governed by the liberal Yitzhak Rabin and the Labor Party—and before it embarked on its controversial settlement policy—the General Assembly of the United Nations voted overwhelmingly to declare the national liberation movement of the Jewish people to be "a form of racism and racial discrimination." The vote was 72 in favor, 35 opposed and 32 abstaining. (This vote led Abba Eban to quip that if Algeria introduced a United Nations resolution declaring the world to be flat and accusing Israel of flattening it, it would win by a vote of 72 in favor, 35 opposed and 32 abstaining.)

The immediate effect of the vote was to encourage the banning and blacklisting of Israeli and other Zionist speakers on many university campuses, which had "antiracist" platform restrictions. But the significance of the vote went beyond its impact on campus speech. It was a reflection of a worldwide demonization of Israel, led by the Soviet Union, its hard-left followers throughout the West, and the Arab and Muslim world. It was now "legitimate" and "lawful" to single out the nation-state of the Jewish people for international condemnations as a pariah entity.[4] Israel was now in a category of only two nations: apartheid South Africa and the democratic nation-state of the Jewish people.

Matters only got worse when Menachem Begin became Israel's first conservative prime minister in 1977. Until then, David Ben-Gurion and his protégés in the left Labor Party had ruled Israel, while Begin and his right-wing party had been the opposition. The fact that Israel was governed by left-wing socialists and liberals did not stop hard left anti-Israel bigots like Berrigan from demonizing Israel as a fascist regime. Begin's surprise victory turned many American liberals and labor supporters against the Israeli government, and some even against the State of Israel. This significant change, which has endured to this day with several interstitial Labor governments, made the defense of Israel in left-wing circles increasingly difficult, despite the worldwide reality that many democracies have been governed in recent decades by conservative leaders, such as Margaret Thatcher, Ronald Reagan and Angela Merkel.

The election of Begin created some cognitive dissonance for many American Jews like myself and many of my friends and colleagues, who are both liberals and Zionists. We have had to confront this conflict over many years now, and it may well continue into the foreseeable future.

7

Likud and the Liberals

Israel Moves to the Right

I WAS IN Israel the night Menachem Begin was elected prime minister, watching the election returns at the house of my dear friend Yitzhak Zamir, who was then the dean of the Hebrew University Law School. (He would subsequently become attorney general and a justice of the Supreme Court.) The other guests were all liberal academics, lawyers and businesspeople who always voted for the Labor Party. They found it hard to believe that the liberal socialist Israel with which they grew up would now be led by a right-wing former leader of the Irgun, or Etzel, as it was called in Israel. (Several years later, I was with some of the same people when the uncompromising radical Meir Kahane was elected to the Knesset. The shock was even greater.)

I, too, was surprised at the election of Begin, because as an American I thought that the dramatic rescue of the hostages at Entebbe the previous year had solidified support for the Labor coalition, which was in power at the time. Prime Minister Rabin had ordered the operation—led by Yonatan Netanyahu, Benjamin's older brother, and a student at Harvard, who was killed during the rescue—that captured the imagination of the world. The daring raid did much to elevate Israel's prestige around the world. Several movies have been based on it. But Rabin was forced to resign several months later when my old friend Aharon Barak, who was then attorney general, charged his wife with hiding an illegal bank account in the United States.

Rabin's forced resignation marked the beginning of a disturbing development wherein numerous elected Israeli officials have been serially investigated, prosecuted and removed from office. Some were guilty and deserved to be prosecuted, while the guilt of others has been questionable. More on this later.

Rabin was replaced by acting prime minister Shimon Peres, who was not nearly as popular as Rabin. Begin's party won more seats in the 1977 election than Labor and was able to form a hardline government. Continuing threats against Israel, both external (from Egypt, Syria and Iraq) and internal (terrorist attacks by the PLO and other even more radically violent groups) may have inclined some Israelis to give up on peace and demand more hawkish policies, such as annexing the West Bank. My friends watching the election returns believed that Begin's ascension to the prime ministership would set back efforts to achieve peace. Many American Jews agreed, and Begin's election began a period in which the Israeli right would frequently find itself in power, further alienating liberal American Jews.

It turned out, of course, that Begin was able to do what no other prime minister had done: make a peace treaty with Egypt. The credit for that achievement must be shared among several leaders, and there is still disagreement about how to allocate the credit. But Begin played an important role in this peace process. So did President Carter, who was the president least sympathetic to Israel since Eisenhower. But to his credit, he brought Begin and Anwar Sadat to the bargaining table, and the rest is history. Several books have told the story of Camp David, the best of which is *President Carter: The White House Years* by my former student and my friend Stuart Eizenstat, who was there, working side by side with President Carter.

Begin was also responsible for one of Israel's most courageous, if controversial, military actions: the bombing of Iraq's Osirak nuclear reactor in 1981. "Operation Opera," as it was called, ended Iraq's nuclear program. It was criticized by President Reagan, who was generally supportive of Israel, and it resulted in a unanimous condemnation by the Security Council. I supported the Israeli action, especially because it was accomplished with minimal casualties—10 Iraqi soldiers and one French civilian, who was not supposed to be at the reactor on that weekend afternoon.

Begin justified his decision to destroy the reactor before it became "hot" by stating that Israel could never bomb a populated Iraqi city in retaliation for a nuclear attack on Israel. As survivors of the Holocaust, Israelis could never "contemplate bombing [when] . . . tens of thousands of innocent residents would have been hurt."[1] Its only recourse was prevention, rather than retaliatory deterrence. I later wrote a legal analysis—contained in my book *Preemption: A Knife That Cuts Both Ways*—justifying the preventive attack.

Critics accused Israel, which has numerous nuclear weapons, of hypocrisy in attacking Iraq's nuclear weapons program. But Israel has said it would never use its nuclear arsenal aggressively, whereas if Iraq—and now Iran—were to develop a nuclear weapon, there would be every reason to worry that they would try to use it against Israel, despite the near certainty of nuclear reprisal by Israel with devastating consequences.

A decade later, when Iraq invaded Kuwait and then fired Scud missiles at Israeli cities, the world came to appreciate the necessity of destroying Saddam Hussein's nuclear facility, which by 1991 might well have been able to develop nuclear-tipped missiles to attack Israeli population centers. At the time, Dick Cheney, the American secretary of defense, commended the Israeli action as "outstanding" because it "made our job much easier in Desert Storm."[2] That assessment may well be an understatement: if Iraq had nuclear weapons when it invaded Kuwait, they might still be there! The United States would have been reluctant to send troops to a battle zone facing nuclear weapons. Witness the current North Korean standoff.

But not all of Prime Minister Begin's military actions have been vindicated by history. Israel's invasion of Lebanon in 1982 (called

"Operation Peace for Galilee") is now widely regarded as a strategic mistake.

In the eyes of many—not just myself—Israel was morally and legally justified in its initial foray into Lebanon in order to stop terrorist attacks against its civilians. The Palestinian Liberation Organization had moved its terrorist bases into southern Lebanon, from which they were crossing the border and murdering Israeli civilians. The immediate cause of the invasion, however, took place many miles away in London, where terrorists tried to kill, and succeeded in seriously wounding, Israel's ambassador to Great Britain, an act regarded by Prime Minister Begin as a casus belli, justifying a military response. The goal of the operation was to rid southern Lebanon of PLO terrorists, reduce the influence of Syria in Lebanon, and install a pro-Israel Christian government under the leadership of Bachir Gemayel.

In the end, after brutal battles with many casualties, Israel succeeded in its short-term goal of getting the PLO out of southern Lebanon—they were allowed to move en masse to Tripoli, where they remained until 1983. But over the longer term, the vacuum created by the departure of the Sunni PLO was filled by the new, more dangerous, Shia terrorist group Hezbollah (Army of God). It is more dangerous partly because it is motivated by unappeasable religious fanaticism as opposed to being a secular national liberation movement, and partly because it is a surrogate for Israel's strongest enemy, Iran, which funds, arms and directs it. Within a few years, Hezbollah would rule all of southern Lebanon as a virtual mini-state, bristling with Iranian-supplied missiles. This outcome must be counted as a strategic error on Begin's part.

In addition, Israel suffered enduring damage to its moral standing throughout the world—not to mention among Israelis themselves—for its role in the infamous Sabra and Shatila massacre of hundreds of Palestinian civilians by Phalangist militia members. The Phalangists were a Christian-Lebanese anti-PLO party, whose leader, Bachir

Gemayel, was willing to make peace with Israel. He had just been elected president of Lebanon when he was assassinated along with 26 others in a massive bombing at Phalange headquarters.[3] The assassins were believed to be Palestinian militants, since other Phalangist leaders had been similarly assassinated for their willingness to make peace with Israel. Among the victims were the family and fiancée of Elie Hobeika, a prominent Phalangist leader. Hobeika subsequently organized a gang of several hundred young Phalangists, called the "young men," to take revenge against Palestinians for the assassination of President Gemayel. This revenge took the form of a massacre of Palestinians—mostly civilians—in the Shatila refugee camp and the adjoining Sabra neighborhood.

Though no Israeli soldiers participated in the killings, the Kahan Commission—established by Israel to investigate the massacre—led by Yitzhak Kahan, the president of the Supreme Court, concluded that the Israeli military was "indirectly responsible for not stopping it" and that Defense Minister Ariel Sharon was personally responsible "for ignoring the danger of bloodshed and revenge."[4] Sharon was forced to resign as defense minister. His political career did not revive for several years. Meanwhile the Sabra and Shatila massacre became a black mark on Israel's moral standing in the world and a rallying cry for its enemies.

The Lebanon War itself, with its indecisive and morally costly outcome, was Israel's first unpopular war at home, generating massive protests. It was also unpopular among many of Israel's supporters around the world, because it did not seem as necessary to protect Israel's security as previous wars had been. Its controversial nature fueled harsh criticism across the international political spectrum and provided moral ammunition to Israel's enemies, coming as it did at a time of increasing efforts by the hard left to delegitimize the nation-state of the Jewish people.

I could not, and did not, defend all of Israel's actions in Lebanon, especially its role in the Sabra and Shatila massacre. But I did defend Israel against the disproportionate condemnation it was receiving from the international left, which refused to condemn the PLO for provoking Israel into invading Lebanon by its terrorist acts on foreign soil.

It was shortly after the Sabra and Shatila massacre that my own life was threatened by anti-Israel extremists. It was the first such threat I had received—but it would not be the last.

The establishment of the Kahan Commission stimulated me to write an op-ed for the *New York Times* in 1982 calling for the establishment of a second commission to investigate the role of the PLO in general, and its leader Yasser Arafat in particular, in the raft of synagogue shootings and bombings that were plaguing the Jews of Europe.[5] Synagogues and other Jewish institutions in Rome, Paris, Antwerp and Brussels had been attacked. The Rome attack killed a two-year-old child and injured 37 civilians. Dozens of men, women and children were killed and injured in other attacks, including a group of Jewish children waiting for a school bus to take them to a Jewish summer camp. The most lethal attack had been on an elementary school in Ma'alot, Israel, where Palestinian terrorists took 105 children hostage, 22 of whom were killed and 68 injured.

These attacks reminded me of the infamous 1963 bombing of the 16th Street Baptist Church in Birmingham, Alabama, by the Ku Klux Klan during the civil rights movement, resulting in four African American children killed and 22 others injured. The hard left justifiably condemned the KKK killings, but it was silent when the PLO killed innocent Jews in much greater numbers. To the contrary, more and more countries were beginning to "recognize" the PLO as a legitimate political organization, including its violent attacks on Israeli and Jewish civilians as a legitimate form of "resistance." For its part, the PLO and Arafat denied complicity in the murder of Jewish children and other civilians, despite their bloody fingerprints being all over these terrorist attacks.

The hard left, as usual, gave Arafat a pass on his personal involvement in the murder of innocent civilians as well as on his refusal to condemn terrorism. As is all too typical of the hard left, they tolerate all manner of human rights violations by anti-Israel and anti-American tyrants while railing against even the most minor deviations from perfection by Western democracies.

In my *Times* article, I pointed out that the world had demanded an investigation by Israel following Sabra and Shatila and asked, "Why is there no similar demand for an inquiry by the PLO into its own possible complicity in the recent spate of synagogue killings?" It was a rhetorical question, as my op-ed made clear:

> *Some will surely say that it is unrealistic to expect the PLO to conduct a full and open inquiry into possible responsibility for the synagogue killings. If the PLO refused, then its host countries— those who give it sanctuary, diplomatic status and other forms of recognition—should conduct their own inquiries. Countries such as Italy and France, where the atrocities occurred, should subpoena—indeed demand—relevant information from the P.L.O. If the P.L.O. refused to comply with the valid investigative laws of a host country, its office should be closed and its officials expelled.*
>
> *If, on the other hand, the P.L.O. cooperated with the investigation and was shown to have had no connection with the synagogue killings, it would establish the bona fides of its recent condemnation of terrorism directed against Jewish religious targets. This would certainly go a long way toward enhancing its claim to political recognition.*
>
> *The very fact that a call for a P.L.O. commission of inquiry seems unrealistic demonstrates the hypocrisy of those members of the international community who have been bestowing on the P.L.O.—and its leader—the benefits of recognition without demanding the responsibilities of recognition.*

Neither the PLO nor its host countries conducted any investigations. The PLO continued to kill innocent children, while more and

more countries—as well as the Vatican and other religious groups—
gave it recognition and treated its leader like a statesman rather than
the mass murderer he was. This only incentivized the PLO and other
terrorist organizations to increase their reliance on terrorism as the
means to achieve their aims rather than on negotiation and compromise.

This perverse phenomenon led me to write a book titled *Why Terrorism Works*, which argued that the reason terrorism was increasing
as a tactic of choice is *because* it works.[6] Because it worked for the
PLO—gaining them more recognition—it was used more frequently
and with more deadly results. In the *New York Times* op-ed, I called
for putting Yasser Arafat on trial, documenting his personal role in
ordering terrorist attacks against American, Israeli and European targets over a 30-year period.

The most immediate consequence of my initial op-ed was a serious threat on my life by PLO supporters. A Harvard graduate student
from North Africa came to my office one afternoon, shaking with fear.
He asked to close the door and he began to whisper: "They're planning to kill you."

I asked, "Who?"

"My two roommates," he answered. "You can't tell them I told
you."

"Why do they want to kill me?"

"Because of what you wrote about Arafat."

"Are they serious?"

"Absolutely. They have a plan. They have been watching you. They
know where you park your car and what time you leave the office.
They are planning to stage a 'robbery,' and stab you to death. They
have the knives."

"When?"

"This week."

"Did they tell you?"

"No, I overheard them from my bedroom."

"Is anyone else involved?"

"No, I don't think so. Just them."

I promised not to disclose his name, although it seemed clear the roommates would figure out who had betrayed their plot. As soon as he left, I called the Harvard police, who notified the FBI. The students were arrested and confessed to discussing my murder, but they denied having an actual plan or making a final decision. They were immediately deported, and I was told to report anything suspicious to the FBI.

Several years later, the FBI informed me that a neo-Nazi "lawyer" named Matthew Hale had put out a "hit" against me and that I required 24/7 FBI protection for at least a few weeks. To this day, I need police protection when I speak on university campuses.[7]

But it was not the threat of violence against me personally that caused me the greatest concern. It was the growing support for the PLO and the increasing efforts to delegitimize Israel. Both sides of the debate were becoming more extreme and more uncompromising.

Bipartisan support for Israel was still strong, but some on the hard right, led by hard-right political operative, columnist, TV commentator, and sometime presidential candidate Pat Buchanan, were turning against Israel, while some on the hard left, let by Berrigan and Chomsky, were solidifying their long-standing opposition to the nation-state of the Jewish people. In the years to come, the conflict between the Palestinians and Israel would play out less on the battlefield of the Middle East and more on the campuses and in the media of the United States and Europe.

8

Debating Extremists
Left and Right

Vanessa Redgrave and Meir Kahane

DURING THE 1980S, as extreme positions came to the fore on both sides of the Israel debate, I decided to engage with those who held these dangerous viewpoints, not only on behalf of Israel and Jewish interests but on behalf of liberalism itself. Even then, many on the anti-Israel hard left were challenging fundamental principles of free speech and civil liberties. At the same time, hard-right Israelis and their American supporters seemed more and more open to illiberal and even antidemocratic tendencies. As a liberal defender of Israel, but not of its illiberal policies, I felt a responsibility to make the centrist liberal case for Israel's right to exist as the nation-state of the Jewish people and to defend its citizens from both internal and external threats.

Of most immediate concern was the vociferous campaign by members of the international left to legitimate Palestinian terrorism and to delegitimize Israel in the minds of centrist liberals, especially among students. The most prominent leader of this effort was Vanessa Redgrave, the world-famous actor, who was also a member of the Workers Revolutionary Party, a radical British communist organization.[1]

Redgrave was not merely a "supporter of the PLO," like some other Western entertainment figures and celebrities; she was an active propagandist for the organization, which was then engaged in terrorism.

She attended training sessions at their camps, from which terrorist attacks were staged, and called for the total destruction of Israel ("I don't think there is room for a State of Israel."[2]) She was involved in the production of several short films—reminiscent of the ones made by Nazi film director Leni Riefenstahl—extolling the coming destruction of the Jewish state, and she was filmed at a PLO camp dancing while holding a Kalashnikov above her head, an image that was circulated around the world.

Redgrave herself described her role as "active in the struggle for the victory of the Palestinian Revolution," and she pledged to assist the PLO "in every possible way." She opposed the two-state solution to the Israel-Palestinian conflict, supporting instead a military solution under which the nation-state of the Jewish people would be destroyed.[3]

It was not surprising, therefore, that when the Boston Symphony Orchestra hired her in 1982 to narrate several performances of Stravinsky's opera-oratorio *Oedipus Rex*, many of the musicians protested that choice.[4] Some suggested that they would exercise their own freedom of association by refusing to perform with a PLO collaborator who justified the potential assassination of artists. Board members feared that the controversy might reduce contributions to the financially shaky orchestra. There was some concern about disruptions of the performances by the Jewish Defense League or other protestors.

In the end, the orchestra decided to cancel the performances. They offered to pay Ms. Redgrave the $31,000 she would have received if the show had gone on. Ms. Redgrave declined the offer and sued the orchestra for breach of contract and violation of her civil rights. She sought $5 million in damages, claiming that she had been effectively "blacklisted" and that she could no longer find appropriate work as a result of the cancellation.

The orchestra responded that Ms. Redgrave had, in fact, earned more money since the cancellation than before it, and that if anyone had refused to hire her, it was because she had used her art to serve the political ends of terrorism.

They also proved that Ms. Redgrave herself had turned down roles—such as the wife of Soviet dissident Andrei Sakharov in an HBO production—because she believed the film might hurt the cause of communism.

Despite my strong opposition to everything Redgrave stood for, I condemned the decision to cancel her performance. In doing so, I was joined by Lillian Hellman, the Screen Actors Guild and other artists and organizations. But, in addition to supporting her right to perform, I also supported the right of musicians to refuse to perform with her. I wrote that if I were a member of the Boston Symphony Orchestra, I would refuse to be associated in any way with her, "not because of her beliefs, but because of her collaboration with and participation in" the murderous activities of a terrorist group that targeted Jewish men, women and children. I cited the case of the great Metropolitan Opera tenor Richard Tucker, who refused to perform under the baton of conductors who had been Nazi collaborators. Tucker was applauded for his principled stand, and so should the Boston Symphony players who did not want to perform with a collaborator and supporter of terrorism. I took the position that the "musicians should have been allowed not to play, but the concert should still have gone on," with substitute musicians or a smaller orchestra.

Redgrave, of course, used the lawsuit as an opportunity to rail against "blacklisting" and "McCarthyism." I turned her complaints against her by pointing out that she herself had advocated the blacklisting of Israeli musicians. Several years earlier, she had offered a resolution to the British Actors Union demanding that they blacklist Israeli artists and boycott Israeli audiences. The resolution included an ultimatum that "all members working in Israel (must) terminate their contracts and refuse all work in Israel." (So much for the sanctity of contracts!) Several years later, she justified as "entirely correct" the blacklisting of Zionist speakers at British universities. And she praised the proposed assassination of Israeli artists, because they "may well have been enlisted to do the work" of the Zionists.

In the American context, Redgrave cloaked herself in the First Amendment and decried the return of McCarthyism. But in England, she was very much at the forefront of preventing those with whom she disagreed from speaking. She also supported the PLO policy of assassinating West Bank Arabs who expressed views contrary to the PLO. If assassination is the ultimate form of censorship—as George Bernard Shaw once wrote—then Redgrave supported a brand of deadly blacklisting that even Joseph McCarthy never practiced. Were her pernicious political party to come to power, it would make McCarthyism seem mild.

Vanessa Redgrave does not believe in the right of free speech for everyone—only for those with whom she agrees. But I believe in the right of free speech for everyone—even hypocrites who collaborate with murderers. By my principles and those of many civil libertarians who share them, I believe that the Boston Symphony Orchestra was wrong to cancel Redgrave's performance. By Redgrave's "principles," the symphony was absolutely correct in its actions.[5]

Accordingly, at a press conference on April 29, 1982, I issued a challenge to Redgrave to debate me on the issues of blacklisting, as well as on the merits and demerits of her views and activities with regard to terrorism. I believed strongly not only in the right for people like Redgrave to hold and express their odious opinions but also in their duty to defend them publicly. She responded that she could not debate me because the Workers Revolutionary Party does not allow her to say anything that has not been approved in advance by its central committee.

What occurred next was reported in the *Christian Science Monitor*:

Alan Dershowitz—the Harvard law professor and noted "devil's advocate" who champions the unpopular and unfriendly in court—was sitting in a restaurant with his

*children recently when he saw a flier headlined, "Boston
Against Blacklisting."*

*"I immediately wanted to attend this benefit. I'm against
blacklisting," Professor Dershowitz commented later. "Then I
saw who it was for. It was for Vanessa Redgrave."*

*So Dershowitz stood outside the theater, handing out fliers
of his own, alleging that Miss Redgrave supports blacklists in
England.*

I then wrote an op-ed for a Boston newspaper explaining why I
leafleted the event:

*I've been preaching about the First Amendment for most of my
adult life. So, I went out on the street and practiced what I'd
been preaching. There I stood, at the entrance of the Boston
Shakespeare Company, handing out leaflets I had printed up at
my house and reproduced on my small home copying machine.
The event was a fundraiser for an organization called the Anti-
Blacklisting Defense Fund.*

*Now why in the world would I be leafleting an anti-
blacklisting fundraiser? My own views on blacklisting have
always been unequivocal: I'm against it. The reason I was there
is because the event was a thinly disguised fundraiser for Vanessa
Redgrave—who is suing the Boston Symphony orchestra for
blacklisting her, but who is herself in favor of blacklisting and
has proposed her own blacklist of certain artists. I thought that
it was important for the public to know the facts about Ms.
Redgrave's own attitude toward blacklisting artists whose politics
differ from her own.*

My leaflet provided these facts to those attending the anti-
blacklisting fund-raiser and urged them to ask Ms. Redgrave to "explain her hypocrisy." Several members of the audience were surprised

to learn of her views on blacklisting Israeli artists. Others said they knew of Ms. Redgrave's selective condemnation of blacklisting but didn't care, because—as one woman put it—"anything is fair in the war against Zionism."

Redgrave won her contractual suit against the Boston Symphony Orchestra, receiving minimal damages, but lost her suit alleging violation of her civil rights. She also lost big in the court of public opinion, as her hypocrisy regarding blacklisting and her active support for terrorist violence were exposed for all to see.

Unfortunately, what was then a fringe position of the extreme left regarding the boycotting of Israeli artists and academics has since become a mainstream view among many on the left. As I will show in subsequent chapters, the BDS (boycott, divest, sanction) tactic has become pervasive on campuses, along with efforts to silence opponents of this and other anti-Israel activities, such as anti-apartheid week.

Vanessa Redgrave refused to debate our fundamental disagreements over Israel and blacklisting, but Rabbi Meir Kahane—with whom I also had deep, but very different, disagreements regarding Israel—was eager to debate me.

Kahane had founded the Jewish Defense League in the United States, but its violence—even in the service of good causes, such as Soviet Jewry and protection of vulnerable Jews against anti-Semitic violence—alienated mainstream American Jews. The violent acts committed by his followers included bombings and shootings, though none had proved fatal until the accidental death of Iris Kones in the Sol Hurok office. Because of the distain of most American Jews for his methods, Kahane felt he and his organization had no future here. So he and some followers moved to the West Bank, where he formed a right-wing political party named Kach, which was accused of racism for its anti-Arab policies and actions, including violence. He traveled often to the United States to raise money and to preach his extremist views.

Kahane was eager for a mainstream platform because (unlike Vanessa Redgrave) he was in fact being blacklisted by Jewish organizations, universities and other institutions. These institutions refused to give him a platform because they regarded his views as racist, anti-peace and pro-violence. They did not want mainstream Jewish organizations to be in any way associated with his views or those of the JDL. Even Israel had banned his political party from running for the Knesset on the grounds that it was a racist party.

In my speeches and columns, I opposed this ban, and the Supreme Court of Israel overturned it because it was not authorized by law. The Knesset subsequently passed a law prohibiting racist parties from running, and Kahane's party was denied a place on the ballot.

Kahane, though he had support among some hard-right Jews, was a pariah to mainstream Jews, none of whom would engage or debate him. So when Avi Weiss, the liberal Orthodox rabbi of the Hebrew Institute of Riverdale, New York, proposed a debate between us, there was enormous pressure on me from mainstream Jewish leaders to decline.

But having challenged Vanessa Redgrave—whose views and actions were by any standard far more despicable than Kahane's—I decided that I could not turn down the challenge to debate him. (Both Redgrave and Kahane would of course reject any comparison between their views and actions.)

Here is how the *New York Times* reported on the event:

Nearly 1,000 people crowded into the Hebrew Institute of Riverdale, in the Bronx, to hear the three-hour debate. There were some mild hisses and boos, but the audience was generally polite. Outside in the rain, a handful of pickets carried signs calling Rabbi Kahane a racist.

I began my presentation with an explanation of why I was willing to debate Rabbi Kahane:[6]

I am debating Rabbi Meir Kahane because too few blacks debated and responded to Reverend Jackson and Louis Farrakhan. I am debating Rabbi Kahane because virtually no Arabs are willing to debate Yasser Arafat. I think it is imperative that the world understand not only that the vast majority of Jews repudiate Rabbi Kahane's views but also WHY we repudiate those views. I am here as well to demonstrate my unalterable opposition to those Jews—Israeli and American—who seek to silence Rabbi Kahane. I recall, very vividly, spending election night in Israel with a group of some of Israel's most distinguished lawyers and judges. As soon as the ballots were counted and Rabbi Kahane's seat in the Knesset was announced, these distinguished, well-educated people, sat around that room deciding how to silence Rabbi Kahane who had been democratically elected to one of the most democratic Houses of Parliament in the world. Some said let's make it a crime to say what he believes, and such legislation has been drafted. Others said do not let him take his seat in the Knesset. Some said take away his immunity. Others said strip him of his Israeli and his American citizenship. Deport him. Blacklist him.

The democratic response to Rabbi Kahane is to answer him, to compete with him in the marketplace of ideas, to persuade people to reject his ideas on their merits and demerits. The democratic answer to bad speech and offensive speech is not censorship or blacklisting but rather more speech, more debate, better ideas.

I just finished, this weekend, trying to resolve my ambivalences about the speech of a terrible enemy of Israel, a woman named Vanessa Redgrave, who has been blacklisted by several organizations and who was not allowed to perform by the Boston Symphony Orchestra. My response to that was both to support her right to speak but then to challenge her to a debate on the merits of her abominable views toward Israel. She declined that debate because her party forbids her to debate. I am debating Rabbi Kahane because I want to upgrade the quality of the debate, to stop the kind of name-calling and personalization that has characterized so much of the attack on Rabbi Kahane. I am here because I disapprove of guilt by analogy, because I disapprove of efforts to show that he is just like Nazis who deported Jews, and who professed racial purity laws and conducted Kristallnachts. These analogies constitute an insult to the memory of the six million.

There is enough wrong with Rabbi Kahane's views without confusing them with the views of others who are also wrong. I want to find out here precisely what Rabbi Kahane's views are, and I want to try to answer them on their merits.

Kahane was not impressed by my free-speech argument. He insisted, "The greatest of tragedies is not that there are those who call me names, but there are those who would grant me the right to speak because they would also grant the right of speech to Yasser Arafat. That is the greatest tragedy—that Jews are unable to understand the difference between a Farrakhan and an Arafat and a Redgrave on one hand and Rabbi Meir Kahane on the other hand."

I understood the difference, but the First Amendment doesn't accept such distinctions.

Following these preliminary remarks, we moved to the substance of our disagreements. The first question put to us by Rabbi Weiss focused on Kahane's plan to evict, expel and transfer every Arab citizen of Israel. Kahane tried to defend his illegal idea:

First, no Arab in Israel wants to live in a Jewish state. And anyone who thinks so has contempt for the Arabs. The State of Israel was created as the Jewish state and so it is declared in the Declaration of Independence. What Arab wants to live in a Jewish state? The fact that Arabs don't rise up now is only because they're afraid.

Secondly, the question arises: assuming that the Arabs have become saints. Say, I accept that they all become saints. And they sit down, democratically, and they reproduce saints. I don't want to live under a majority of Arab saints. I didn't leave this country to live in Israel to live as a minority under anyone, saint or devil, whatever. So the question that I ask of people who are upset at the things that I say is: What is your answer to the voting question? Do the Arabs have a right to become a majority, democratically, peacefully, in the State of Israel? And when they do, you can bet that the Law of Return, which today applies only to Jews, will not apply to Jews but to Arabs. Do the Arabs have the right, yes or no? If the answer is yes, that's fine, you're democrats, not Zionists. If the answer is no, then you're Kahane.

I replied:

It's dangerous enough when Rabbi Kahane purports to speak on behalf of Jews, but when he also purports to know what is on the minds of the Arabs, we really do have a problem. If Arabs choose, for whatever reasons—economic reasons, political reasons, reasons of geography, reasons of convenience—to remain Israeli citizens, that's what they will remain. And Meir Kahane will not be able to and should not be able to expel or deport valid citizens of Israel.

When Israel was established, those who established it—from Theodor Herzl to Weizmann to Ben-Gurion—realized Zionism was a challenge. It is a great challenge to keep the Jewish state Jewish and democratic. Rabbi Kahane would throw up his hands and say there is no room for democracy. There is nothing Jewish about democracy. I beg to differ. The vast majority of Jews in this world support both Zionism and democracy. The false dichotomy that Rabbi Kahane is seeking to impose on us is not correct, and the ultimate implications of his dangerous views are, once the Arabs are expelled from Israel, then Jews who do not fit Rabbi Kahane's particularistic definition of his kind of

*Jew will also be expelled. And I further challenge Meir Kahane
with this question: The vast majority of Jews in Israel today are
not Orthodox Jews, and yet Israel is a Jewish State. What would
you do under your principles to the vast majority of Jews who
dispute your approach?*

Kahane did not respond. Rabbi Weiss then asked me the obvious
follow-up question: "Are you, Professor Dershowitz, prepared to accept the workings of democracy if those workings result in a state
that is no longer a Jewish State?"

I replied:

*You have just stated the challenge of twenty-first-century
Zionism. I do not shrink from that challenge. I do not think
most Israelis shrink from that challenge. To say that we
understand the challenge is not to say that we can anticipate
all the factors that will eventually lead to a solution to the
problem. I can only repeat what David Ben-Gurion's answer
was, what Golda Meir's answer was, what Chaim Weizmann's
and Theodor Herzl's answer was: "We must struggle to preserve
the Jewish character of the State of Israel." We must encourage
aliya [emigration to Israel]. We must open the doors of Soviet
Jewry and of Syrian Jewry and of Ethiopian Jewry. We must do
things to encourage demographic changes that will insure that
Israel remains a Jewish state.*

*Under no circumstances may we accept the false choice being
put to us. The choice about being a Jewish undemocratic state
where the minority prevails or a non-Jewish democratic state
where the majority prevails. We will not, we must not, allow
that false dichotomy ever to face us. If and when the time comes,
if through all efforts by Israelis there is no way of resolving the
issue, it will not be resolved by the rhetoric of Meir Kahane. It
will not be resolved by the answers of Alan Dershowitz. It will*

*be resolved by the people of Israel through the processes which
they have chosen, through the processes which elected Meir Kahane
to the Knesset, through the processes which allow Meir Kahane
to speak freely in Israel where he would not be allowed to speak
in almost every other country in the world. The democratic
processes, the civil libertarian processes, the freedom processes, the
very legal processes that Rabbi Kahane both uses and condemns.*

Rabbi Weiss then asked me about Judea and Samaria: "How important are our biblical and religious-legal rights to Judea and Samaria? Isn't the retention of the area critical to Israeli security? . . . If Israel has a biblical, legal and security right to Judea and Samaria, why not exercise that right immediately?"

I responded:

*I do think that Israel has a biblical claim to the West Bank.
I also think the Arabs have a biblical claim to the West Bank.
I also think there are Christian biblical claims to Jerusalem. I
do not believe that in the modern world we should try to resolve
disputes over conflicting biblical claims by warfare. I do not
want to see the world, once again, in a war over conflicting
biblical claims, because there is no room for compromise when
one invokes the name of the Bible [and says] not only am I right,
but I alone am right.*

*What I believe is that Israel should not, under any
circumstances, compromise its security needs and its need to keep
Arab enemies away from its large cities. I do not favor the return
to the pre-1967 borders. I generally agree with the Allon Plan.
I generally agree with what I think the vast majority of Israelis
agree with and that is the willingness to make some territorial
compromise in exchange for assurances of peace.*

*I know this will not be a popular position. The wise,
thoughtful, reasoning compromise position almost never is. But*

*it is a position which, deep in my heart, I am convinced will
strengthen Israel, will secure Israel, will make Israel able to cope
with the twenty-first century in both a democratic way and a
Jewish way.*

We then turned to the divisive issue of the role of religion in Israel. Rabbi Weiss asked Kahane whether he "envisions Israel as a
theocratic state governed by the Laws of the Torah." In responding,
Kahane purported to speak for all Orthodox Jews:

*Clearly there should not be one Orthodox Jew in the world that
would not want a theocratic state. Putting it better, there should
not be one religious Jew who would not want a state which is
mandated by the Torah. . . . The Torah mandates a coercion
because that is what God wants. . . . Is there one Orthodox
rabbi that would not [want a theocracy]? Our ultimate aim
must be to create a Torah state. If Israel will not be a Torah state,
then God forbid, the Almighty will bring down upon us the
punishment that he warned about in a Bible that is as applicable
in 1984 as it was in the year 84.*

I replied:

*I believe in Zionism as a principle of choice, of opportunity, of
challenge. Rabbi Kahane sees Zionism as a principle of compulsion,
of separatism, of exclusion. There is no way of debating or
arguing with someone who thinks all that is right is on his side
and he speaks in the name of God. Until God speaks to us in
much clearer ways, we, as human beings, will have to resolve
these disputes among ourselves.*

We were then asked to summarize our views of what it means to
be a Jew and a Zionist. I presented not only my own view but also

what I believed were the views of the vast majority of American Jews who rejected Kahane's false choice between Judaism and liberals.

I have the right to tell you, Rabbi Kahane, there is another Judaism that rejects your negative values. There is a Judaism which is positive. There is a Judaism which is embracing. There is Judaism of Rabbi Hillel that reaches out and gives the best of what we stand for to our children. There is a Judaism that does not require our kids to choose between a neo-fascist philosophy and a democratic philosophy in order to be a Jew. I want my children to revere the memory of Martin Luther King. I want my children to cry bitter tears if again we experience Japanese Americans being placed in concentration camps. To discriminate against anyone is to discriminate against everyone. The moral choice is also the pragmatic choice. To choose to defend the rights of others is to choose to have others defend our rights.

You'll remember the German theologian who said, "When they came for the Jews, I didn't say anything because I wasn't a Jew; when they came for the Communists, I didn't say anything because I wasn't a Communist; when they came for the gays I didn't say anything because I wasn't a gay; and then when they came for me and there was no one left to speak."

Rabbi Kahane did not agree: "I don't know what is Judaism and what is Dershowitzism. If one decides for himself what is Judaism, that is not Judaism."

Rabbi Weiss then asked us both to comment on our backgrounds:

In many ways you share backgrounds. Both of you attended Yeshiva University High School. Since that time, you have diverged so remarkably in your paths. Today you personify different views within the Jewish spectrum. What motivated you and who motivated you most to travel the paths you did?

I replied first:

I grew up in a household where my father, of blessed memory, always talked about defending the underdog, always talked about standing up for those who were least able to stand up for themselves. He always drew from the deepest Jewish values. My grandparents before them, my mother who is here tonight, has always seen much more clearly and with much greater Jewish vision than Rabbi Kahane. The rejection of simpleminded solutions, the necessity of obeying the commandments that when you live in a country, you obey the laws of that country, that you be a good patriotic American citizen and at the same time accept the best of Jewish tradition. . . .

The challenge of life is to define one's own goals, one's own needs. I offer my program to you. I offer it to you as a choice. I didn't tell you to accept my program in the name of anybody else or anything else. I ask you to consider it. I ask you to consider Rabbi Kahane's programs. I ask you to consider seriously the good parts of what he has to offer, because I think Rabbi Kahane has, certainly early in his life, made remarkable contributions to Jewish self-defense. The defending of Jews by walkie-talkies, by billy clubs, by phoning the police, by recourse to all appropriate needs. I only wish it hadn't sunk into the day that a bomb was planted in Sol Hurok's office causing the meaningless empty death of a Jewish woman. I only wish we hadn't come to the day when rabbis, in the name of Halacha, claim that it is appropriate to kill innocent people.

I continue to hope and pray that all of you will define your Americanism, define your Judaism, take the best out of each, and reject that which you feel uncomfortable with. In the end, the values for which we as a people have struggled for thousands and thousands of years will not be solved overnight by a false prophet. You will solve them, the people of Israel will solve them.

Rabbi Kahane replied:

*I think that at the very least on this point, I agree with my
friend and my fellow alumnus from BTA.*

*My family was certainly the influence on my life. And my
father, of blessed memory, a great Talmid Chacham [sage] was a
Jewish activist . . .*

*My opponent is a product of America, a smattering of
Jewishness. I tell you, I appeal to you—time is running out for
you living here in America—go home, go home to Israel. And in
Israel live the life of a Jew.*

*Simpleminded solutions are usually rejected by professors.
I have greater faith in the Sephardic Jew in Israel who sees my
solution as the answer because he doesn't come out of Cambridge.
He lived under Arabs. He knows what Arabs are. He never
again wants to live under Arabs. Don't be put off by such
clichés as, "It's a simpleminded thing." Sometimes simpleminded
answers are quite good and quite correct. Sometimes not. Be
good Jews, be observant Jews, accept the yoke of heaven, the
religious way.*

The debate was concluded. There was no vote on who won.

We debated several more times. I doubt we persuaded each other
of very much. But I continued to defend his right to speak. The last
time we spoke was three days before he was assassinated in November
1990. He was scheduled to speak at Brandeis University, but his
speech was canceled at the last minute, allegedly because of security
concerns. He asked me to call the Brandeis authorities and threaten
to sue. I did and he made his speech. The next speech he gave was in
New York City, where a Muslim terrorist shot him dead. That terrorist had a list of other prominent Zionists who he was planning to as-
sassinate. I was informed that I was on the list. Ten years later, Meir's
son, Binyamin Ze'ev Kahane, was murdered by Palestinian terrorists

on the West Bank. Meir Kahane's political party is now a shadow of its former self.

Time has not been kind to Kahane's brand of Jewish fundamentalism. It did produce Baruch Goldstein, the racist Jewish zealot, who, in 1994, murdered 29 Palestinian Muslims praying at the Cave of the Patriarchs. But he is the exception that proves the rule. Jews have mainly stayed true to their centrist liberal and conservative principles despite the constant fissures for extremists on both sides to abandon them. In 2019, a great controversy erupted both in Israel and throughout the Jewish world when Prime Minister Netanyahu arranged for an extremist right-wing party called Otzma Yehudit, which was reminiscent of Kahane's Kach Party, to merge with a mainstream religious Zionist party, thereby giving it the kind of legitimacy Kahane never had. I joined in the criticism of this dangerous move.

My confrontations with Redgrave and Kahane personified my developing positions with regard to Israel and its critics. I would defend Israel, though not all of its policies. But I would also defend the right of those who demonized Israel—even those who sought its destruction—to express their hateful views. My mother, who was very smart, couldn't accept this cognitive dissonance: "Either you're for Israel or you're against. Don't give me your fancy Harvard talk about free speech. The people you're defending hate us. They want to kill us. They would never defend your right to speech."

She spoke for a lot of people, but I have always defended the rights of those with whom I disagree: from the Nazis marching through Skokie to pornographers, to Redgrave and Kahane. As I told Kahane, "I cannot defend you without also defending the Redgraves of the world. Otherwise, people will think that I'm defending you only because I agree with you. If I were to defend the free speech right only of people I agree with, I would be home watching TV."

My principles have been tested on several occasions. Two years after the Redgrave and Kahane events, the Harvard Law School Forum invited a representative of the PLO to make the case against

Israel. I was asked to make the case for Israel. It was to be the first debate at Harvard involving a leader of the PLO.

I was looking forward to a lively debate. But the State Department refused to grant him a visa. I joined the ACLU in challenging the visa denial. I supported the the right of Harvard students to hear views I despised. Representatives of the Israeli Foreign Ministry were furious at me because they had worked hard to exclude him, but I placed my commitment to free speech above any loyalty to Israel. I would decide for myself, as a private citizen, who to debate and where. A university was the perfect place for such an encounter.

In 2004 when Yasser Arafat died, Palestinian students wanted to have a memorial service at which they raised the Palestinian Authority flag in Harvard Yard. The university refused permission on the ground that it only allowed the flags of countries to be flown from the mast in Harvard Yard. The Palestinian students came to me to defend their freedom of expression. I agreed to challenge the Harvard Policy, but advised them that if they were to be given permission to raise the flag, I would be there handing out leaflets telling the truth about Arafat's murderous background and how he turned down a generous peace offer that would have given the Palestinians a state. We won. They flew the flag. And I handed out leaflets describing Arafat's death as "[u]ntimely—because if he had just died five years earlier, the Palestinians might have a state." The flag and the leaflets were the perfect symbols of the marketplace of ideas at Harvard.

I have drawn the line, however, at debating Holocaust deniers. I had refused to cross this red line for several reasons. First, no rational person can actually believe that there were no gas chambers, no mobile killing units, and no systematic Nazi plan to kill the Jews of Europe. Holocaust deniers are liars and anti-Semites.

Second, to subject the Holocaust to debate—to make its existence a debatable issue—is to demean the memory of the six million who died and the survivors. But to refuse an invitation to debate the Holocaust is to give ammunition to deniers. So in 1991, when I was invited by Bradley Smith—a notorious denier who placed ads in the university newspapers challenging professors to debate—I accepted on one condition: it had to be part of a series of debates. These debates would include the following subjects: the earth is flat; men didn't land on the moon; Elvis is still alive; and the Holocaust didn't happen. It is in that kooky company that Holocaust denial belongs. He turned me down.

In the years following, I had dozens of debates—live and in print—on Israel, both with people to the right of me, like Norman Podhoretz, Pat Buchanan, Dennis Prager and Shmuley Boteach, and to the left of me, like Cornel West, Peter Beinart, Jeremy Ben-Ami, Leonard Fein and Peter Tatchell. I was supposed to debate Professor Edward Said on the hard-left radio show *Democracy Now!*, but at the last minute its biased host, Amy Goodman, pulled a bait and switch and substituted Norman Finkelstein, a failed and discredited academic, who had been fired from several universities.

I also had dozens of invitations to speak about Israel on university campuses and at charitable events. None was more impactful on my personal life than an invitation in 1982 to speak at a Jewish singles brunch in Newton, Massachusetts, sponsored by the Combined Jewish Philanthropies of Boston. My topic was Israel and human rights. Partway through the speech, I spotted a beautiful woman in the audience. I couldn't keep my eyes off her, and as soon as my talk was over, I pushed my way through the crowd and got her name. When I got home, I looked up Carolyn Cohen in the phone book (remember phone books?). There were five Carolyn Cohens in the Boston area. I called the first and asked her to dinner. She told me she couldn't leave the nursing home. The second asked if she could bring her husband. I reached my Carolyn on the third try, and we went to dinner that night—and nearly every night since. So my debates and speeches about Israel paid off, at least for me.

At the same time that I was debating American intellectuals, on both the right and the left, I was criticizing Israel's policies with regard to the building of civilian settlements on the West Bank.

In 1979, I joined 59 other prominent American Jewish figures—including the Nobel Prize winner Saul Bellow, the conductor Leonard Bernstein, the literary critic Alfred Kazin, and the academics Leonard Fein, Martin Peretz, Michael Walzer and Jerome Wiesner—in expressing our "distress" over the building of new Israeli towns on the West Bank that "require the expropriation of Arab land unrelated to Israeli security needs."[7] We suggested that this policy was "morally unacceptable, and perilous for the democratic character of the Jewish State."

The letter was written publicly to Prime Minister Begin, who responded (also publicly) that Jews had an absolute right to live anywhere in "the land of our forefathers," including the West Bank, and that the "right of our people is inseparably bound with the needs and demands of our vital national security"[8]—a highly questionable assertion.

Our letter raised a storm of protests in both Israel and the United States. The inclusion of my name in a *New York Times* report on the controversy caused the rabbi in my parents' Orthodox synagogue—the one in which I grew up and was bar mitzvahed—to call me and the other signers "traitors" to Israel and the Jewish community. But nearly all the signers were staunch Zionists; there were no Chomskys on the list. We honestly believed, and I still believe, that building civilian settlements on the West Bank and in the Gaza Strip was harmful to Israel's moral standing and did not contribute to its security.

I could not then and cannot now defend this policy, though I do not believe it is *the* major barrier to a peaceful two-state solution. The fact that Israel unilaterally abandoned all of its civilian settlements in the Gaza Strip in 2005 and that the vast majority of its West Bank settlers now live in "settlement blocks" close to the Green Line—land that can be swapped for equivalent land in Israel—makes it clear that the primary barrier is the unwillingness of the Palestinians to make the kinds of negotiated compromises that are necessary to reach an agreement. (More on this later.)

My criticism of civilian settlements was not my only point of conflict with the Begin government. I was skeptical about the war in Lebanon, especially after Sabra and Shatila, though I was reluctant to publicly criticize Israeli security and military decisions. But I could not, and did not, defend every military action Israel took. I also could not, and did not, defend every compromise Israel felt it had to make with civil liberties in the name of fighting terrorism, just as I could not, and did not, defend every military decision or compromise the United States made.

I joined then-professor Ruth Bader Ginsberg and several other liberals in supporting the Israeli equivalent of the ACLU—the Association for Civil Rights in Israel—which challenged in court Israel's compromises with civil liberties, and generally won.

My position on Israel guaranteed me enemies on both the right and the left. Right-wing Zionists despised my support for a two-state solution and my opposition to Israel's policies on civilian settlements. They also opposed my willingness to defend the civil liberties and free-speech rights of Israel haters. Left-wing anti-Zionists despised my support for a nation-state of the Jewish people and for Israel's right to defend itself against terrorism and other forms of aggression. The divisions grew even sharper as many on the center left moved further toward the hard left, and many on the center right moved further to the hard right. The center, where I had located myself (center left in my case), was shrinking, and that movement toward extremes made reasoned, nuanced discourse more difficult.

In an effort to maintain centrist support for Israel among law school students and faculty, I worked with several of my students to establish the Harvard Jewish Law Students Association. There was criticism from some faculty members: "Why do you want an all Jewish club at HLS?" they asked. There were already African American and women's law student's associations, but Jews were thought to be different. We believed, however, that the growing opposition to Israel necessitated a collective response. There were other issues as well, including a growing interest in Jewish law and concerns that Jewish applicants were not being treated fairly by some admissions committees. The *Harvard Law School Record* reported:

> *The group's advisor is Criminal Law Professor Alan M. Dershowitz, whom Berlin called the "inspiration" behind the organization. Dershowitz spoke at the organizational meeting emphasizing the need for a group such as this. Dershowitz said that he encouraged the formation of the group to serve as an inspiration to law students and lawyers here and elsewhere. He said groups around the United States have begun to organize by ethnic association, and that historically Jews have been concerned with the rights of all minorities. He said Jews should continue to follow this concern while not neglecting their own legal rights.*

Concern about Harvard's admission policies led to the famous "bagel exchange" that occurred when Dr. Chase N. Peterson, then dean of admissions at Harvard, addressed a group of Jewish faculty members suspicious that Harvard had decided to reduce the number of Jews it would admit. Peterson averred that there was no particular "docket" or area of the country whose quota of admissions had been reduced. Rather, he said, it was "the doughnuts around the big cities" that were not "as successful with the Harvard Admissions Committee as they used to be . . ." He said that "now we have to be terribly hard on people with good grades from the good suburban high schools, good, solid, clean-nosed kids who really don't have enough else going for them." The doughnuts, said Peterson, included such areas as Westchester County and Long Island, suburban New Jersey and Shaker Heights, Ohio. When he described these areas to the Jewish faculty members, the *Crimson* reports, one stood up and said, "Dr. Peterson, those aren't doughnuts, they're bagels."

Our association was open to anyone interested in Jewish and Israeli issues, but naturally it attracted Jewish students from all backgrounds and ideologies. I was its first faculty advisor. The idea spread quickly, and by 1983 we convened the first National Jewish Law School Student Network conference with representatives from 20 law schools. I was the speaker at the first conference. Today nearly every law school has a branch.

Several years later, I helped to organize the first Chabad at Harvard, under the direction of Rabbi Hirschy Zarchi. Chabad is a branch of Orthodox Judaism, sometimes called Lubavitch, which conducts outreach to Jews of all religious and nonreligious persuasions. Its motto is that at Chabad, "every Jew is family." There are now dozens of Chabads, in every major university. They have become centers of pro-Israel advocacy through the United States. I myself am no longer Orthodox—though I continue to attend services in an Orthodox synagogue—but I have deep admiration for those who keep the tradition, especially when they are not judgmental about those of us who express our Jewishness differently.

At the same time that academic and public attitudes among the chattering classes were moving away from the center, both the Israeli and U.S. governments were moving toward center-left positions with the election of Yitzhak Rabin as prime minister and Bill Clinton as president.

9

Oslo and the Murder of Rabin

1992 WAS A good year for centrist liberalism. Yitzhak Rabin was elected to replace Yitzhak Shamir, and Bill Clinton was elected to replace George H. W. Bush. The negotiations that led to the Oslo Accords were about to begin. The first violent intifada, which had caused more than 2,000 deaths, was coming to an end. The prospects for a peaceful resolution of the conflict were looking brighter than ever. Both President Clinton and Prime Minister Rabin were determined to break the deadlock. Even Yasser Arafat seemed closer to accepting a compromise resolution than ever before.

I had met Bill Clinton during the summer of 1994, when I invited him to attend Rosh Hashanah services on Martha's Vineyard, where he was vacationing with his family. He accepted and invited my wife, my son Elon, and me to join him and Hillary for dinner after services. After that, we had numerous meals and drinks with them and other guests—including at the White House—during his presidency. I had met Yitzchak Rabin when he was still a general and on numerous occasions thereafter, both in Israel and in the United States.

In 1993, the Oslo Accords were signed after months of secret talks between Israel and the PLO. Although the Oslo Accords left many issues, such as the status of Jerusalem, unresolved, they provided for mutual recognition between the Palestinian Authority and Israel and an ongoing process that would produce an agreed-upon two-state solution and the resolution of key issues.[1] The famous handshake at the White House was seen around the world. It showed that Rabin—who correctly regarded Arafat as a cold-blooded murderer of Jewish men, women and children—was willing to make compromises, both moral and political, that could resolve the age-old conflict over the Holy Land.

But these positive developments did not have any discernable positive impact on Israel's acceptance among hard-left academics around the world. To the contrary, as Israel offered compromises in the interests of peace, the efforts by the hard left to demonize, delegitimize and isolate Israel only increased.[2] This perverse dynamic—demonstrating that the hard-left opposition was not to Israel's policies but rather to its very existence—has continued to this day.

The early to mid-1990s were busy times for me professionally. A few years earlier, I had won the Claus von Bülow case, and my son Elon had produced an Academy Award–winning film called *Reversal of Fortune*, starring Jeremy Irons (who won the Oscar for Best Actor), Glenn Close (who played Sonny von Bülow) and Ron Silver (who played me). I had also published the *New York Times* number-one bestseller *Chutzpah*. These developments brought me a considerable amount of media attention. As a result, I was retained to represent Leona Helmsley, Michael Milken, Mike Tyson, O.J. Simpson, Mia Farrow, Jim Bakker and other high-visibility clients. Despite my busy schedule of classes and cases, I continued to devote a considerable portion of my time to defending Israel in the court of public opinion.

As the demonization of the nation-state of the Jewish people increased around the world, particularly among the hard left and academics, my involvement increased. Israel remained, and remains, a priority in my professional and private life, despite—perhaps because of—the increasingly difficult challenges faced by liberal supporters of Israel.

Radical leftists chose to downplay Rabin's effort to make peace and instead focused on Israel's imperfections, while ignoring or excusing the crimes of the Palestinian leadership. Anti-Israel groups conducted "apartheid week" events, demanded divestment from Israeli companies and companies that did business with Israel, and shouted down pro-Israel speakers in an effort to prevent their views from being heard.

On November 4, 1995, Israel—and the world—suffered a cataclysmic loss with the assassination of Prime Minister Yitzhak Rabin at a peace rally in Tel Aviv. His assassin was an Orthodox Jew named Yigal Amir, a hyper-nationalist, and an opponent of Rabin's peace efforts.

The impact of this murder on Israel is incalculable. It is the Israeli analogue to the assassination of Abraham Lincoln 130 years earlier. Both killings changed the course of history, for the worse.

The crime impacted me personally in several distinct ways. Eight days before Rabin was killed, Israel's ambassador to the United States had asked me to meet with the prime minister when he was scheduled to speak in Boston later that month. I asked the ambassador what the subject of the meeting would be, and he told me that the prime minister was deeply concerned about the increasingly virulent level of rhetoric in Israel and the fact that certain fringe religious and political figures were advocating violence against government officials. He wanted to discuss whether there were ways of constraining the level of vitriol without infringing on the right of free speech.

I agreed to meet with Rabin and wrote the appointment in my calendar. I also did some research on Israeli law in preparation for the meeting. But it was not to be. Rabin was murdered a week before his scheduled trip to Boston. I could never erase the scheduled meeting from my appointment book or from my mind.

Then a week after the murder, on a Sunday morning, family members of the accused killer knocked on the door of my home, with no appointment, and asked me to represent Amir. I met with them, and they told me that Amir had in fact pulled the trigger, but that he was legally innocent, because the killing was justified under the Jewish law of rodef—a concept akin to preventive or anticipatory self-defense, or defense of others. This concept, which derives from a biblical passage as interpreted by Jewish sages, including Maimonides, authorizes the killing of a person who is about to do great harm to the community.[3] They told me that their relative believed Rabin was about to make a peace with the Palestinians that involved giving back "sacred" land captured by Israel during the Six-Day War. He also believed that this would endanger the lives of Israelis, and so he set out to stop it by killing the rodef who was, in his view, endangering his land and people.

The trial of Rabin's killer promised to be among the most interesting of my career and among the most important in the history of the Jewish state. Although the crime did not carry the death penalty (Israel has abolished the death penalty except for the Nazi genocide against the Jewish people, under which Adolf Eichmann was hanged), the case fit many of the criteria I generally consider in taking a case. It was challenging and historically significant—but I decided not to take it.

The reason was that it involved the kind of political defense that I abhor. If every citizen had the right to decide who was a rodef deserving of death, there would be anarchy. The "rule of personal politics" would replace the rule of law. The rodef defense was not, in my view, a legitimate legal defense, and I, as a lawyer, was not obligated to present it.

I had a more personal reason as well for turning down this case. I deeply admired Rabin, and I supported his efforts to make peace. We had known each other for a long time, though not well, and he had consulted with me regarding several issues. Indeed, he was seeking my advice on the very issue that may have led to this death.

Standing next to Rabin when the fatal bullets were fired was the man who would succeed him as prime minister, my friend Shimon

Peres. He represented an approach to the peace process that was essentially similar to that of Rabin, but he lacked Rabin's popular appeal. So within a year, he was defeated by the younger, more charismatic and more conservative Benjamin Netanyahu, who was also a close personal friend. My early acquaintance with Bibi had ripened into a warm friendship during his tenure as Israel's representative to the United Nations. We have maintained this friendship until today, despite our differences over Israel's settlement policies and other issues, including his apparent willingness to work with the racist Otzma Party.

It was widely predicted that Peres would win the election. In the run-up to the vote, I was asked to speak at the policy conference of the American Israel Public Affairs Committee (AIPAC). Many in that organization, like many in Israel, were moving to the right, so I went out of my way to ask my audience to commit themselves to supporting whichever candidate and party won the election, believing at the time that Peres would win. There was some grumbling from right-wing members, who also expected Peres to win, but most accepted that AIPAC should not take sides in Israeli domestic politics.

Netanyahu won a narrow victory and was able to form a government that lasted for three years, until he was defeated by Ehud Barak in 1999. Netanyahu's election was influenced by the immigration into Israel of nearly a million Soviet Jews in the previous several years. This amazing influx of many highly talented Jews was the epitome of the Zionist dream: to ingather persecuted Jews into the nation-state of the Jewish people. I had worked hard—politically, diplomatically and legally—to help open the exit door for Soviet Jews, and I was proud of the small role I had played in that historic event—including direct advocacy to Soviet leader Mikhail Gorbachev in the Kremlin—that helped to turn Israel into a "startup nation." But not surprisingly, it also moved the Israeli electorate to the right. When people have been as brutally repressed as Soviet Jews had been by communism, it was only natural for them to be suspicious of left-wing parties and more comfortable with a conservative like Netanyahu.

In a subsequent debate between Peter Beinart, the former editor of the *New Republic* and a vocal critic of Israel, and myself, Beinart began by saying how much he admired me for the work I had done to help Soviet Jews immigrate to Israel. Then, in the same breath, he condemned me for supporting Israel as it moved to the right. I pointed out the obvious contradiction in his two statements. It is the very fact that a million Soviet Jews immigrated to Israel that moved Israeli politics to the right. I asked him whether he would want to deport or disenfranchise the million Soviet Jews so that Israel could move back to its traditional left-wing orientation. He laughed, but he failed to respond to my deeper point: that Israel is a democracy in which the majority view prevails. It is also a Zionist country, which includes as one of its primary goals to serve as a place of refuge for repressed Jews, such as those who had suffered discrimination in the Soviet Union. Zionism, a sanctuary for repressed Jews, and liberalism do not always work in tandem, especially when Zionist ingathering of endangered Jews results in a greater number of illiberal voters. Many of the Jews who fled communist oppression are naturally averse to the left, but their children and grandchildren may well move closer to the center and even to the left. That is what happened to Cuban refugees in Florida, and there are indications that it may be happening to former Soviet Jews in Israel. For those of us who would like to see Israel move leftward, our only options are to educate and persuade the younger generation, not to bemoan the political movement rightward by survivors of Soviet repression.

Netanyahu understood this post-Soviet dynamic and used it to his advantage. There were other reasons as well—both domestic and international—for Netanyahu's victory, but this new demographic reality was among them. So was his personal charisma and sharp political instincts. Netanyahu's surprise victory energized right-wing support for Israel in the United States, while at the same time energizing hard-left opposition to the Israeli government. Clinton was still the U.S. president, and he had mixed feelings toward the new prime minister. I discussed Clinton's fraught relationship with the newly elected prime minister and encouraged Clinton to keep an open mind despite his early reservations. For Clinton, Yitzhak Rabin, and his successor Shimon Peres, represented the true Israel. He identified much more with the heavily accented Rabin and Peres than with his perfectly accented contemporary Netanyahu. I was friendly with both of them, and my friendship was used by both, especially when the relationship became testy.

I was in Israel for the spring semester of 1996 doing research for a book when Netanyahu was elected. He invited me and my wife and daughter to his office on a Friday afternoon. We stood outside of the King David Hotel trying to hail a cab, but all the cabdrivers were heading home for the Shabbat weekend. It looked like we might be late for our appointment with the prime minister. Suddenly, a car pulled up. It was the mayor of Jerusalem, Ehud Olmert, who was driving around his city to make sure all the trash had been collected before Shabbat. He shouted to me, "Alan, you'll never get a cab on a Friday afternoon. Where do you need to go?" I told him, and he agreed to drive us there. As I got into his car, a cabdriver pulled over, shouting, "Hey, mayor, I don't try to run Jerusalem, why are you trying to be a cabdriver? Stop taking business from me." I gave the driver $10, and he drove away, but not before giving the mayor the finger.

When I got to the prime minister's office, we schmoozed and took some pictures. Then Bibi invited me to his secure private office. "There's been something I have been wanting to ask you," he said. I expected him to solicit my advice on some critical security or political issue. He put his arm around me and whispered in my ear, "So, did O.J. do it?" I was taken aback, but I quickly responded, "Well, there's been a question I've been wanting to ask you, Mr. Prime Minister: Does Israel have nuclear weapons?" Bibi looked at me sternly and said, "You know I can't answer your question." I looked back at him and said, "Aha! And you know I can't answer your question." Bibi understood, and we both laughed.

Netanyahu had campaigned against the Oslo Accords and taken a harder line than his predecessors did on the peace process, and especially on the occupation and settlement building. He regarded himself as a center-right pragmatist who wanted peace, but only if Israel's security was not compromised. His coalition partners included some who were considerably to his right, especially with regard to the West Bank settlements. The new prime minister surprised the world, and disappointed his hard-right supporters, when he signed the Hebron Protocol with Yasser Arafat, just months after taking office. The protocol ceded control of over 80 percent of Hebron—the holiest biblical city in the Torah and the burial place of Jewish patriarchs and matriarchs—to the Palestinian Authority. It also called for the rollback of Israeli troops in other areas of the West Bank. Beyond its specific changes, it reflected a more positive approach by Netanyahu to the peace process, despite opposition by a significant number of his own cabinet (7 out of 18). President Clinton strongly supported the Hebron Accord, but he opposed the continued expansion of settlements on the West Bank, on the Gaza Strip and in East Jerusalem.

This tension within the Netanyahu government and between Bibi and Bill Clinton characterized much of his first term as prime minister. (He would be elected to a second term in 2009, after a decade out of office.) I recall a dinner on Martha's Vineyard with the president and Mrs. Clinton and several other couples at the home of a mutual friend shortly after Netanyahu's first election. Our host, who was Jewish, was railing against Netanyahu's apparent unwillingness to move the peace process forward. I began to answer him, when Clinton said, "Let me take this."

The president, who had a somewhat tenuous personal relationship with Netanyahu, especially compared to his close friendship for and admiration of his predecessors Rabin and Peres, explained to our host how difficult it was for Israeli prime ministers to get anything done: "My cabinet has to carry out my wishes. If they disagree and refuse, they're gone. My cabinet is on my side. They support me. They want me to succeed. In Israel, every member of Bibi's cabinet has his or her own political agenda. They are rivals. They want to replace Bibi. They are perfectly willing not only to stab him in the back, but in the front—in full view of the world. It is a cabinet of convenience—a coalition cabinet that holds the sword of Damocles over the current government, because if a few of them quit, the government fails. So Bibi's hands are tied by his far-right coalition members."

Our host then asked the president, "We give Israel so much assistance, can't you just tell Netanyahu to make peace with the Palestinians?"

The President smiled and replied, "It's relatively easy with Jordan and Egypt. I can call the king and president and they can usually get it done. But when I call the Israeli prime minister and ask him to do something, he says, 'I have to get the approval of the security cabinet, the large cabinet, the Knesset and then sometimes the Supreme Court. We have to do polling. I'll try my best.'"

"The problem with Israel," the president said emphatically, "is that it's a democracy, damn it!" We all laughed and even the belligerent host shook his head, as if to say, "OK, now I understand."

Clinton was right. Unlike the Arab states, where the leaders can do the bidding of the United States if they choose to, Israel is a democracy whose leader must follow the will of its citizens. But it's also a democracy with a deeply flawed structure, at least when it comes to getting things done. The coalition system of governance allows a small minority to hold the majority hostage to its extreme demands, especially when these demands are *not* to do things that the majority would like to see done. The minority in a coalition government has veto power over many actions of the prime minister and his party, even if these actions reflect the will of a majority or plurality of the citizens.

Because of my close relationship with both Netanyahu and Clinton, I played an informal role in advising them and in facilitating communications between them. When Bibi made his first official visit to the United States during the Clinton presidency, he made the mistake of meeting with the Reverend Jerry Falwell, the founder of the Moral Majority and a virulent critic of President and Mrs. Clinton. Falwell was pushing a video titled *The Clinton Chronicles* that falsely portrayed the Clintons as drug dealers and murderers. The Clintons were furious that Netanyahu had begun his U.S. visit at a Falwell event. The event had been added at the last minute on the recommendation of Israel's ambassador Eliyahu Ben-Elissar, who was not familiar with American politics or the Falwell–Clinton animosity. All he knew was that Falwell represented Evangelical Christians, who were quickly becoming a dominant factor in the Republican Party's increasingly vocal support for Israel in general and for Netanyahu in particular. This factor did not alleviate the anger felt by the Clintons about the Falwell meeting. Bibi asked me to convey to the Clintons that he intended no disrespect for the president or his wife. I communicated this message and others in the months to come.

During his first term, Netanyahu was prevented by his coalition from taking any giant steps that might have moved the peace process forward, such as placing restrictions on settlement building. But Netanyahu did not place impassable barriers in the way of a two-state solution either. Indeed, I think it is fair to say that Netanyahu's first term—especially his signing of the Hebron Accord—helped pave the way toward the Camp David proposals of 2000–2001, put forward by his successor Ehud Barak. But it was Barak's electoral victory over Netanyahu that set the stage for the most generous peace offer the Palestinians would receive up to that time.

10

Clinton and Barak

Palestinians Reject Peace, and the Birth of BDS

THE ELECTION OF Ehud Barak—a war hero/peacemaker in the mold of Yitzhak Rabin—boded well for a continuation of the process that had begun with the Oslo Accords. Barak had served with distinction in an antiterrorist unit of the IDF, famously dressing as a woman in a 1973 raid into Lebanon that killed several key terrorists. He was later promoted to chief of staff of the IDF. When he retired, he waited the prescribed time period before entering politics as a member of the Labor Party. He was elected prime minister in July 1999, while President Clinton still had a year and a half left in his second term. Clinton's impeachment process had ended months earlier, and the president was determined to use his remaining months to secure a deal between Israel and the Palestinians. His first term had begun with the Oslo Accord that created a process designed to lead to a final status agreement. It would be fitting to end his second term with the Holy Grail that had eluded past presidents: a two-state solution to the century-old conflict that would cement his foreign policy legacy.

I had worked behind the scenes with Clinton's legal team, as well as with the president himself, on the Starr investigation, the impeachment and the Senate vote. I had also written a book—*Sexual McCarthyism*—and had appeared on television defending Clinton. So I had the president's ear, and I used it to make the case both for Israel and for an agreement that assured Israel's security.

I also tried, unsuccessfully, to get the president to commute the life imprisonment sentence of Jonathan Pollard, who had pleaded guilty to spying for Israel. I tell the full story of my involvement in the Pollard case in my book *Chutzpah*. Briefly, Pollard had worked for U.S. Navy Intelligence and provided Israel with intelligence material that he believed was necessary to its defense but that was being withheld by the Defense Department. He agreed to plead guilty and cooperate fully in exchange for a promise that the government would not seek life imprisonment, but the prosecutor and the secretary of defense, Caspar Weinberger, broke that promise. I urged Clinton on several occasions throughout his eight years in office to commute the sentence. Clinton wanted to commute the sentence to time served, but the CIA chief, George Tenet, threatened to resign in protest if he did. So, much to my regret, he didn't.

Bill Clinton loved Israel. His attachment to the nation-state of the Jewish people was deeply emotional, as well as intellectual. He told me how his Baptist minister had instilled in him a love of Israel and the Jewish people from an early age. He had enormous respect and affection for Yitzhak Rabin, whose death had a deep impact on him. When he bid Rabin farewell at his funeral in Jerusalem with the Hebrew words "Shalom chaver"—"Farewell and peace my friend"— his emotions were captured by the cameras for all to see. He had persuaded his friend to take the politically risky course of shaking hands with Yasser Arafat on the White House lawn when the Oslo Accords were signed. These accords, which were controversial both in Israel and among American Jews, laid the foundation for a two-state solution by recognizing the Palestinian Authority and its right to limited self-governance in areas of the occupied territories. Rabin's agreement to these controversial provisions, punctuated by his handshake with the man who was responsible for the murder of so many Jews, became an emotional issue in the next election. There were some who believed that it was the handshake with a mass murderer who had called for Israel's destruction that sealed Rabin's fate. But it was also this handshake that held out the hope that enemies could put the bloody past behind them and build a peaceful future. Time was short, though, because Barak assumed the office of prime minister just six months or so before the 2000 presidential campaign season would consume the attention of America and 15 months before Clinton would become a lame-duck president.

Clinton and Barak worked hard to bring the parties together. Clinton pressed Barak to make concessions, and Barak—using an acquaintance of mine to poll the reactions of Israeli citizens to proposed compromises—agreed to offer Arafat nearly everything he was seeking. Though there is some dispute as to precisely what was offered and when, no one disagrees that the offer included statehood for the Palestinians on more than 90 percent of the West Bank and the entire Gaza Strip.[1] Although some Palestinian supporters have denied this, President Clinton and those who participated in the negotiations have confirmed the basic outline of the various offers.

Unbeknownst to Clinton and Barak, a prominent American was working behind the scenes to undercut their peace efforts. He was warning Arafat that if he accepted the Clinton–Barak offers, he would surely be assassinated. The American who was advising Arafat to reject the American–Israeli offer was none other than former president Jimmy Carter.

Carter wanted the credit for solving the Israeli–Palestinian conflict. Indeed, he made the following boast to the *New York Times*: "Had I been elected to a second term with the prestige and authority and influence and reputation I had in the region, we could have moved to a final solution."[2]

Carter had no love for Israel and Israeli leaders, blaming them and them alone for the ongoing conflict. When Arafat finally rejected the generous Clinton–Barak peace offers, Carter mendaciously claimed that it was Barak, not Arafat, who walked away from the negotiations. Carter, who was not there, was willing to take the word of Arafat—a serial liar—over the word of Dennis Ross, a seasoned diplomat who had worked on Middle East issues for several administrations, was there and later wrote a detailed account of the negotiations that contradicted Carter's placing the blame on Israel.[3] By blaming Israel and Israel alone for the failure, Carter also contradicted Arab leaders, such as Prince Bandar of Saudi Arabia, who had told Arafat, "I hope you remember, Sir, what I told you. If we lose this opportunity, it is not going to be a tragedy, [it] is going to be a crime."[4] When Arafat rejected the offer without even making a counteroffer, Bandar called Arafat's rejection "a crime against the Palestinians—in fact against the entire region."[5]

Carter's interference with efforts by the sitting U.S. president to achieve a peaceful resolution, as well as siding with Arafat over Clinton, reflected his strong bias against Israel. This bias was long-standing and pervasive, manifesting itself in many of his actions, beginning with a meeting he had with Golda Meir when he scolded her for Israel's "secular" culture and warned that "Israel was punished whenever its leaders turned away from devout worship of God."[6] He had nothing good to say about other Israeli leaders, though he praised Arafat, Syrian dictator Hafez al-Assad and other tyrannical and terrorist Arab leaders. When Carter visited the Middle East in 2008, he made a point to lay a wreath at Arafat's grave, but he did not visit Rabin's grave or those of Arafat's many Jewish victims.

I was not aware of these biases when I campaigned for Carter in 1976 or even when he helped bring Begin and Sadat to Camp David. The real extent of his anti-Israel feelings did not become public until his pernicious role in the Clinton–Barak peace process became known.

I had met Carter in early 1976, when he sent me a handwritten note telling me that he was "impressed with [my] ideas on crime and punishment," which I had expressed in a recent *New York Times Magazine* article. He asked for my help with "other ideas" that would be very valuable to [him]" in his campaign. A "cc" on the bottom of the page to "Stu" indicated that he had sent a copy to Stuart Eizenstat, his chief domestic assistant. Stu, my former student, was a committed Jew and a strong supporter of Israel, but his role in the Carter administration was primarily domestic. He did play a positive role in the Camp David Accords, and has since written an excellent book about the Carter presidency in all its complexity.[7]

After Carter wrote his letter to me, Stuart called and told me that Carter was coming to speak at Harvard and wanted to meet me. I agreed.

I liked the gracious Southerner and consented to work on his campaign. In June of that year, *Newsweek* ran a cover story on "Carter's game plan" that included a page on "the Carter brain trust." I was featured in that story, with my photograph (beard, long hair, and aviator glasses) and a report that I was a key part of the brain trust and a member of Carter's "task force on criminal justice." Following Carter's election and inauguration, my name was included on several lists of lawyers the president was considering for Supreme Court appointments if any vacancies were to occur. (None did.)

When Anatoly (later Natan) Sharansky was arrested in the Soviet Union in March 1977 and charged with spying for the United Sates, I went to the White House to urge Carter to formally deny that Sharansky had spied for us. I, along with Professor Irwin Cotler, was representing Sharansky as part of my decade-long defense of many Soviet dissidents and refuseniks. Stuart advised me that it would be difficult, since no president ever admits or denies that anyone is an American spy. But after considerable efforts on Stuart's part and mine, President Carter agreed to issue an unprecedented denial, saying that he was "completely convinced" that Sharansky was innocent—a denial that may have saved Sharansky's life. Eventually Sharansky was released from the Gulag, due to the combined efforts of his wife, Avital, his lawyers, and pressure from the United States and Israel. Sharansky arrived in Israel to a hero's welcome and soon became a political and moral leader, much admired by American presidents and Israeli prime ministers alike.

Several years after meeting Carter, I closely followed the Camp David meetings between Israeli prime minister Menachem Begin and Egyptian leader Anwar Sadat. My friend Aharon Barak was Israel's chief legal advisor at the talks, Stuart was an important advisor to Carter, and another former Harvard Law student, Osama El-Baz, was one of the leaders of the Egyptian negotiating team. Once peace was finally achieved, I was invited to the White House ceremony on March 26, 1979.

Despite Carter's success in helping to bring about peace between Israel and Egypt, I campaigned for Senator Ted Kennedy when he decided to challenge Carter for the 1980 presidential nomination. I had served as a lawyer during the Chappaquiddick investigation after he had driven off a bridge, which resulted in the death of Mary Jo Kopechne, and we had become friends. I traveled on the campaign trail with Ted and his wife at the time and made speeches for him. When he lost to Carter in the primaries, I campaigned for Carter's reelection, which he lost to Ronald Reagan. I did not see Carter for several years after that until he wrote his controversial book titled *Palestine: Peace Not Apartheid*. More about that later (but now back to the Clinton–Barak peace efforts).

For whatever reason, Arafat decided to reject the generous peace offers. He did not offer counterproposals or explain why he was turning down the opportunity for statehood for his people. He simply walked away and immediately initiated a second intifada, in which thousands of Israelis and Palestinians were killed. Arafat employed the pretext that Ariel Sharon had visited the Temple Mount, but proof has since emerged that the intifada was carefully planned well before Sharon provided the phony excuse to start the bloodshed. Arafat did not give back the Nobel Peace Prize he had been awarded for signing the Oslo Accords and rejecting terrorism.

At the same time that the Israeli government was offering the Palestinians a state and Arafat was committing "a crime against the Palestinians" by rejecting Ehud Barak's generous offer, anti-Israel activists were plotting the economic destruction of the nation-state of the Jewish people through the bigoted tactic of boycotts, divestments and sanctions. This plot, called BDS, was hatched at an anti-Semitic hate fest in Durban, South Africa, in 2001. Its grandparents on one side were the Nazis who organized the boycott of Jewish businesses, academics and artists in the 1930s. Its grandparents on the other side were the Muslim leaders who organized the Arab boycott of all Israeli and Jewish commerce in the years following the establishment of Israel. Its parents are the contemporary bigots who only single out Israel for boycott and seek to use BDS to end the existence of the world's only nation-state for the Jewish people.

The illegitimate birth of this tactic reflects the anti-Semitic goal of its founders and leaders: to isolate, delegitimize and ultimately destroy the state of Israel and replace it with another Muslim-Arab state. Anyone who supports BDS is thus complicit—knowingly or out of willful blindness—in the world's oldest bigotry.

The goal of the so-called "Durban strategy" was to turn Israel into a pariah state. Based on the inapt South African paradigm, it provided the blueprint for the ensuing boycott of Israel by falsifying parallels between the former's apartheid regime and Israel's territorial dispute with the Palestinians. As a result, calls for "anti-apartheid boycotts" became the battle cry of the broad Israel boycott strategy. The apartheid analogy is absurd on its face and refuted by the facts on the ground: Israeli Arabs—even Palestinians on the West Bank—have more rights and benefits than Palestinians in any other country.

The countries, entities and NGOs participating in the UN conference accused Israel of racism, apartheid, genocide and creating a holocaust. Led by Yasser Arafat and his nephew, Nasser al-Kidwa, the Palestinian UN delegation—in conjunction with Western NGOs and nations belonging to the Organisation of Islamic Cooperation—oversaw the conference's final declaration of principles. It stated:

[We] call upon the international community to impose a policy
of complete and total isolation of Israel as an Apartheid state
as in the case of South Africa which means the imposition of
mandatory and comprehensive sanctions and embargoes, the full
cessation of all links (diplomatic, economic, social, aid, military
cooperation and training) between all states and Israel.

In the highly anti-Semitic milieu of the Durban Conference, U.S. secretary of state Colin Powell ordered the American delegation to stage a walkout. This was his reason:

Today I have instructed our representatives at the World
Conference Against Racism to return home. . . . I know that you
do not combat racism by conferences that produce declarations
containing hateful language, some of which is a throwback to
the days of "Zionism equals racism"; or supports the idea that we
have made too much of the Holocaust; or suggests that apartheid
exists in Israel; or that singles out only one country in the
world—Israel—for censure and abuse.[8]

Congressman Tom Lantos, the only Holocaust survivor to have served in the U.S. Congress, was a U.S. delegate at the Durban Conference. Writing about the blatant anti-Semitism he witnessed there, Congressman Lantos said,

Another ring in the Durban circus was the NGO forum . . . the
forum quickly became stacked with Palestinian and fundamentalist
Arab groups. Each day, these groups organized anti-Israeli and
anti-Semitic rallies around the meetings, attracting thousands.
One flyer, which was widely distributed, showed a photograph
of Hitler and the question "What if I had won?" The answer:
"There would be NO Israel . . ." An accredited NGO, the Arab

Lawyers Union, distributed a booklet filled with anti-Semitic caricatures frighteningly like those seen in the Nazi hate literature printed in the 1930s. Jewish leaders and I who were in Durban were shocked at this blatant display of anti-Semitism. For me, having experienced the horrors of the Holocaust first hand, this was the most sickening and unabashed display of hate for Jews I had seen since the Nazi period.[9]

In the wake of these "gains" made at the Durban conference, Qatari-born, Israeli-educated Omar Barghouti cofounded the Palestinian Campaign for the Academic and Cultural Boycott of Israel (PACBI) in April 2004, which was tasked with "overseeing the academic and cultural boycott aspects of BDS."[10]

The movement was formally launched in July 2005—just as Israel was ending its military occupation of Gaza and uprooting all of its settlements there—and was endorsed by over 170 Palestinian political parties, organizations, trade unions and movements.[11]

Since 2004, Barghouti—who himself received his advanced degree at Tel Aviv University (a fact that flies in the face of his claim of a state-sponsored system of apartheid in Israel)—has been the key driving force behind the global BDS campaign. It is ironic that the leading advocate of a worldwide boycott of Israel—who has said that "all Israeli academics" are members of the "occupation reserve army"—was himself unwilling to disrupt his own education and boycott the "Zionist" institution from which he received his higher education.[12]

Central to Barghouti's tactic has been the engagement of European governments, NGOs and grassroots organizations, as well as university campuses across the United States, in order to push the BDS campaign and grow its support base. As part of his overarching tactic of equating the global BDS campaign with the anti-apartheid movement in South Africa, Barghouti also formed a strategic "alliance" with South African human rights and anti-apartheid activist Archbishop

Desmond Tutu. Like Barghouti, Archbishop Tutu has a sordid history of demonizing Jews and their nation-state.[13]

As we will see later, I was invited to debate Barghouti at Oxford Union, but the founder of BDS refused to debate me because, according to his criteria, I—as an American Jewish supporter of Israel—am subject to his boycott. He also refused to join me in a discussion sponsored by the Young Presidents' Organization (YPO), insisting that he conclude his presentation first so that it would not be seen as a debate, discussion or encounter with me. His bigoted boycott is also directed against non-Israeli Jews, such as the singer Matisyahu—but not (at least according to some leaders of BDS) against Israeli Arabs.[14] In other words, this is a religious, not a national, boycott. That is anti-Semitism, pure and simple. BDS has increasingly been a hotbed of anti-Semitic activity and regrouped bigots of all stripes who feel comfortable with the language used by its leaders.

It is abundantly clear that Barghouti is against the existence of Israel as the nation-state of the Jewish people in any form. He confirmed this in a 2008 column when he declared,

> *It was born out of ethnic cleansing and the destruction of the indigenous Palestinian society, Israel is the state that built and is fully responsible for maintaining the illegal Jewish colonies. Why should anyone punish the settlements and not Israel? This hardly makes any sense, politically speaking . . . why should European civil society that fought apartheid in South Africa accept apartheid in Israel as normal, tolerable or unquestionable? Holocaust guilt cannot morally justify European complicity in prolonging the suffering, bloodshed and decades-old injustice that Israel has visited upon Palestinians and Arabs in general, using the Nazi genocide as pretext.[15]*

Barghouti neglects to mention the role of the Palestinian leadership during the 1930s and 1940s, who had formed an alliance with the Nazi regime in general and Adolf Hitler in particular. The Grand Mufti of Jerusalem, Haj Amin Al-Husseini, collaborated with the Nazis to prevent Jewish refugees from seeking sanctuary in what became Israel. He was instrumental in having Jews, who were on their way out of Europe, sent to death camps. After the war, he was declared a war criminal for recruiting thousands of Muslim Yugoslavs to murder Jews in Croatia and Hungary. Despite his Nazi collaboration—or perhaps because of it—he became and remained a hero to most Palestinians, many of whom hung his picture in their homes. He helped design an Arab fez adorned with a Swastika that his Palestinian followers wore (I saw that fez in a private collection of Nazi-Arab memorabilia). Following the Holocaust, Al-Husseini received asylum in Egypt, where he organized other German Nazis to help in efforts to destroy Israel.[16] So "Holocaust guilt" among the Palestinian leadership was an entirely appropriate factor to consider—though certainly not the only one—in supporting the establishment of two states for two peoples in mandatory Palestine.

Proponents of the boycott against Israel call their bigoted campaign "the BDS Movement." But in reality, there is no such thing. A "movement" suggests universality, such as the feminist movement, the gay rights movement and the environmental movement. If there were a BDS movement that sought to achieve equality, justice and freedom, it would rank every nation on earth by reference to two overriding criteria:

1. the seriousness and pervasiveness of its violation of basic human rights to equality, justice and freedom;
2. the inaccessibility of the victims to judicial, media and political relief.

A true movement would then prioritize its protest activities—its boycotts, divestments and sanctions—according to the universal mantra of all true human rights movements: namely "the worst first."

It would not pick only one country, point out its imperfections, and focus ALL of its protest activities on that one country to the exclusion of all others. Ranked according to the universal criteria outlined above, the list of countries with horrible human rights records and little or no access to relief would be quite long. It would include North Korea, Iran, Cuba, China, Zimbabwe, Myanmar, Belarus, Russia, Turkey, Saudi Arabia, Pakistan, the Philippines, Venezuela and Kuwait, among many others. Israel would be near the very bottom of any objective list, ranking behind every Arab, Muslim, African and Asian country, as well as several Eastern European countries.

No reasonable person, including many supporters of BDS, would dispute this assessment. Even Peter Tatchell, a supporter of BDS whom I debated at Oxford Union in 2015, acknowledged this when he wrote,

> *While I oppose Israel's occupation, I find it strange that some people condemn Israel while remaining silent about these other equally or more oppressive occupations. Many of Israel's critics are also silent about neighboring Arab dictatorships. And where are the protests and calls for boycotts against the tyrannies of Saudi Arabia, Iran, Burma, Zimbabwe, North Korea, Uzbekistan, Bahrain, Syria and elsewhere? Why the double standards?*

Indeed, the only nation subjected to the so-called BDS "movement" is the nation-state of the Jewish people. When only Muslim states were subject to the Trump administration's travel ban, the left was outraged. Why is there no similar outrage at subjecting only the nation-state of the Jewish people to BDS? Many of those who most loudly support boycotting Israel demand that we end boycotts of Cuba, Iran, North Korea and other tyrannical regimes. How can they justify this double standard? There is something very wrong with that picture.[17]

From its very beginning, I have taken a lead in opposing BDS. I have written dozens of columns, delivered hundreds of speeches, debated numerous supporters of BDS, consulted with lawyers who have litigated against BDS, advised legislators who have proposed statutory bans against BDS, spoken to university administrators who oppose student and faculty BDS initiatives, supported political candidates who have campaigned against BDS, encouraged alumni donors who want to pressure their universities against accepting BDS, purchased products that have been targets of BDS, invested in financial companies that have resisted demands to divest from Israeli companies, and counseled students who are confused about the issue. I have also urged artists and entertainers to go out of their way to perform in Israel. One great musician, the pianist Evgeny Kissin, has gone even further. Although he does not live in Israel, Kissin—who I count as a friend—became an Israeli citizen in protest against the boycotting of Israeli artists. Now, anyone who subscribes to that bigoted boycott will not have the pleasure of hearing Kissin play.

In 2014, I wrote an article, which has been widely republished and circulated, for *Haaretz*, outlining the "ten reasons why BDS is immoral and hinders peace."[18]

> 1. ***BDS immorally imposes the entire blame for the continuing Israeli occupation and settlement policy on the Israelis.*** *It refuses to acknowledge the historical reality that on at least three occasions, Israel offered to end the occupation and on all three occasions, the Palestinian leadership, supported by its people, refused to accept these offers. There were no BDS threats against those who rejected Israel's peace offers. Under these circumstances, it is immoral to impose blame only on Israel and to direct a BDS movement only against the nation-state of the Jewish people that has thrice offered to end the occupation in exchange for peace.*

2. *The current BDS tactic, especially in Europe and on some American university campuses, emboldens the Palestinians to reject compromise solutions to the conflict.* *Some within the Palestinian leadership have told me that the longer they hold out against making peace, the more powerful will be the BDS movement against Israel. Why not wait until BDS strengthens their bargaining position so that they won't have to compromise by giving up the right of return, by agreeing to a demilitarized state, and by making other concessions that are necessary to peace but difficult for some Palestinians to accept? BDS is making a peaceful resolution harder.*

3. *BDS is immoral because its leaders will never be satisfied with the kind of two-state solution that is acceptable to Israel.* *Many of its leaders do not believe in the concept of Israel as the nation-state of the Jewish people.*

4. *BDS is immoral because it violates the core principle of human rights: namely, "the worst first."* *Israel is among the freest and most democratic nations in the world. It is certainly the freest and most democratic nation in the Middle East. Its Arab citizens enjoy more rights than Arabs anywhere else in the world. Yet Israel is the only country in the world today being threatened with BDS. When a sanction is directed against only a state with one of the best records of human rights, and that nation happens to be the state of the Jewish people, the suspicion of bigotry must be considered.*

5. *BDS is immoral because it would hurt the wrong people.* *It would hurt Palestinian workers who will lose their jobs if economic sanctions are directed against firms*

that employ them. It would hurt artists and academics, many of whom are the strongest voices for peace and an end to the occupation. It would hurt those suffering from illnesses all around the world who would be helped by Israeli medicine and the collaboration between Israeli scientists and other scientists. It would hurt the high tech industry around the world because Israel contributes disproportionally to the development of such life-enhancing technology.

6. **BDS is immoral because it would encourage Iran**—*the world's leading facilitator of international terrorism*—*to unleash its surrogates, such as Hezbollah and Hamas, against Israel, in the expectation that if Israel were to respond to rocket attacks, the pressure for BDS against Israel would increase, as it did when Israel responded to thousands of rockets from Gaza in 2008–2009.*

7. **BDS is immoral because it focuses the world's attention away from far greater injustices, including genocide.** *By focusing disproportionately on Israel, the human rights community pays disproportionately less attention to the other occupations, such as those by China, Russia, and Turkey, and to other humanitarian disasters such as that occurring in Syria.*

8. **BDS is immoral because it promotes false views regarding the nation-state of the Jewish people, exaggerates its flaws and thereby promotes a new variation on the world's oldest prejudice, namely anti-Semitism.** *It is not surprising therefore that BDS is featured on neo-Nazi, Holocaust denial, and other overtly anti-Semitic websites and is promoted by some of the world's most notorious haters such as David Duke.*

9. **BDS is immoral because it reflects and encourages a double standard of judgment and response regarding human rights violations.** *By demanding more of Israel, the nation-state of the Jewish people, it expects less of other states, people, cultures, and religions, thereby reifying a form of colonial racism and reverse bigotry that hurts the victims of human rights violations inflicted by others.*

10. **BDS will never achieve its goals.** *Neither the Israeli government nor the Israeli people will ever capitulate to the extortionate means implicit in BDS. They will not and should not make important decisions regarding national security and the safety of their citizens on the basis of immoral threats. Moreover, were Israel to compromise its security in the face of such threats, the result would be more wars, more death, and more suffering.*

In 2018, I published a book titled *The Case Against BDS: Why Singling Out Israel for Boycott Is Anti-Semitic and Anti-Peace.* In it, I urge students and others to use their moral voices to demand that both the Israeli government and the Palestinian Authority accept a compromise peace that assures the security of Israel and the viability of a peaceful and democratic Palestinian state. I urge that the way forward should not be by immoral extortionate threats that do more harm than good but by negotiations, compromise and goodwill.

We are winning the war against BDS on campuses, insofar as no mainstream university has boycotted or divested from Israel. But the goals of BDS go beyond these specific outcomes. They include poisoning the minds of students with false accounts of Israel's "apartheid," "genocide" and other sins. (More on this to come.) It is for that reason that I decided to write *The Case for Israel.*

At about the time the Clinton–Barak peace offer was being rejected and the second intifada and BDS weapons were being aimed at Israel, a Harvard student came to see me during the 10 days of Repentance between Rosh Hashanah and Yom Kippur, when Jews are supposed to seek forgiveness for sins of commission and omission. The student asked me to forgive him for his sin of omission in failing to stand up for Israel when his professors or fellow students unjustly condemned the Jewish state. He told me that he was quite knowledgeable about the Israeli–Palestinian conflict, having spent a gap year in Israel and having also attended a Zionist high school. I asked him why he didn't stand up for Israel, and he replied sheepishly, "If I'm perceived as a supporter of Israel, I won't get dates. It's not cool to be a Zionist."

My immediate response was humorous. "Why don't we start a campaign: Support Israel—Date a Zionist Tonight?" He didn't laugh. It was becoming a serious issue on campus. Students were reluctant to stand up for Israel, some out of fear of losing popularity, others out of lack of the knowledge necessary to rebut the growing anti-Israel rhetoric. It was already becoming clear to me that college campuses would become one of the front lines in the war for public opinion on the question of Israel. Moreover, a number of pernicious myths had grown up around the Arab–Israeli conflict, some of them due to ignorance and others promulgated knowingly by anti-Israel activists and propagandists.

The Case for Israel therefore grew out of my desire to write an accessible primer on the core issues in this debate. My target audience was university students, and I arranged with my publisher to make copies available at a reduced cost for them. I was pleasantly surprised when the book not only became a campus bestseller but also landed on the *New York Times* bestseller list for general audiences.

The format of the book was simple and accessible. Each of its 32 short chapters begins with an accusation against Israel commonly made on campuses and in hard-left media. The accusation is followed by a paragraph describing and quoting the accusers. Then comes a paragraph summarizing "the reality." Finally, several pages document "the proof" of the reality.

For example, chapter 5 begins with the following accusation: "While the Arabs were willing to share Palestine with the Jews, the Jews wanted the entire country for themselves." The accuser was Edward Said, a prominent anti-Israel Columbia University professor who, at the time, had considerable influence over faculty and students. I then disproved the accusation with documentary and other historical evidence. It was important to disprove the myths and lies promulgated by Said and other respectable academics, who were using their respectability and popularity on campus to make the case against Israel, based largely on false information. I believed then, and I believe now, that the proper response to false information is competition in the marketplace of ideas rather than attempts to censor the falsehoods. For the most part, truth tends to prevail in the marketplace, if there is hard evidence to support it.

Other accusers included Noam Chomsky, Norman Finkelstein and other hard leftists who accused Israel of apartheid, Nazism and other sins.

Because of its simple format, *The Case for Israel* became a bestseller and an accessible "bible" for defenders of Israel, who would carry it around and turn to the relevant chapters whenever a false accusation was leveled against the Jewish state. I am proud to say that it had a significant impact on campuses, empowering pro-Israel students to respond to the increasingly shrill and mendacious accusations being directed at Israel.

I spoke about the book on numerous campuses. The response from students was very heartening, despite the protests that accompanied my appearances. Perhaps the most gratifying response came from a young man named Kasim Hafeez. Here is his story in his own words:

Growing up in the Muslim community in the UK I was exposed to materials and opinions at best condemning Israel, painting Jews as usurpers and murderers, and at worse calling for the wholesale destruction of the "Zionist Entity" and all Jews.

My father [was even] more brazen in his hatred, boasting of how Adolf Hitler was a hero, his only failing being that he didn't kill enough Jews.

[One day] I found myself in the Israel and Palestine section of a local bookstore and picked up a copy of Alan Dershowitz's The Case for Israel. *Given my worldview, the Jews and Americans controlled the media, so after a brief look at the back, I scoffed thinking "vile Zionist propaganda."*

As I read Dershowitzs' arguments and deconstruction of many lies I saw as unquestionable truths, I searched despairingly for counterarguments, but found more hollow rhetoric that I'd believed for many years. I felt a real crisis of conscience, and thus began a period of unbiased research. Up until that point I had not been exposed to anything remotely positive about Israel.

Now I didn't know what to believe. I'd blindly followed others for so long, yet here I was questioning whether I had been wrong. I reached a point where I felt that I had no other choice but to see Israel for myself, only that way I'd really know the truth. At the risk of sounding cliché, it was a life-changing visit.

I did not encounter an apartheid racist state, but rather, quite the opposite. I was confronted by synagogues, mosques and churches, by Jews and Arabs living together, by minorities playing huge parts in all areas of Israeli life, from the military to the judiciary. It was shocking and eye opening. This wasn't the evil Zionist Israel that I had been told about.

After much soul searching, I knew what I had once believed was wrong. I had been confronted with the truth and had to accept it.

I had to stand with Israel, with this tiny nation, free,

democratic, making huge strides in medicine, research and development, yet the victim of the same lies and hatred that nearly consumed me. . . .

This isn't about religion and politics; it's about the truth.

I'm proud of having played a small part in Hafeez's search for the truth. Several other erstwhile anti-Israel activists told me that my book had changed their minds as well.

The Case for Israel made me a popular speaker on campuses throughout the United States and around the world. I felt a deep responsibility to make the centrist-liberal case for Israel in as many forums as possible. This endeavor took considerable time and effort, but despite my full-time teaching schedule and part-time legal practice, I prioritized my advocacy for Israel because of my strong feelings about the unfairness of the attacks on Israel. There was another reason why pro-Israel campus groups invited me to speak: on many campuses, there were no professors who were willing to make the case for Israel—even the centrist two-state solution case. I was the default choice. It was shocking to me that on campuses with a significant number of Jewish faculty, not a single professor was willing to stand up for Israel. Some of these silent scholars supported Israel in private, but they refused to become publicly identified with Zionism. I should not have been surprised, since even tenured professors are rarely willing to challenge hard-left "political correctness" lest they alienate colleagues and students.

This lack of public support for Israel among university faculty reflects a broader phenomenon. The anti-Israel faculty on most campuses are better organized and more willing to speak out than the pro-Israel faculty. They also present a more united front and a singular program: the end of Israel as the nation-state of the Jewish people and the illegitimacy of Zionism as a national liberation movement. The pro-Israel faculty are deeply divided, from the J Street left to the pro-settlement right. Moreover, many fear reprisals from their better-organized anti-Israel colleagues and students. And their fear is understandable, if not commendable. Being perceived as a Zionist carries with it, on many campuses, risks of unpopularity, lower student evaluations and other consequences, as I will document below. But tenured professors who privately support Israel—without supporting all of its policies—should show more courage in expressing their pro-Israel views, not in the classroom, where the expression of political preferences has no proper place, but in the public square.

The risks to professors were substantial even during the period when Prime Minister Ehud Barak was offering the Palestinians a state. They became even greater when Barak, the candidate of the left-leaning Labor Party, was defeated for reelection by the right-wing coalition headed by Ariel Sharon.

An anti-Semitic pro-Palestinian propaganda poster featuring a caricature of Dershowitz.

‣ Dershowitz family photo, summer 1950.
Alan is wearing the Palmach shirt.

▾ Family portrait at Yom Kippur with
Justice Goldberg and Mrs. Goldberg.

President Clinton and the First Lady attend Rosh Hashanah services on Martha's Vineyard with the Dershowitz family, 1994.

▲ Dershowitz (and son
Elon) showing Prime
Minister Netanyahu one of
Dershowitz's books at the
Prime Minister's Residence,
2010.

▸ Dershowitz, Elie Wiesel and
his wife, and Sara Netanyahu
in the front row for Prime
Minister Netanyahu's speech
to Congress, March 3, 2015.

Dershowitz interviewing Golda Meir for *The Advocates*, 1970.

Dershowitz discussing Iran with President Obama and his Middle East team, 2012.

‣ Dershowitz with his wife Carolyn on a camel at the Pyramids.

‣ Dershowitz outside the gates at Terezín.

▲ Dershowitz being led away after declaring he planned to challenge Iranian President Mahmoud Ahmadinejad about his views on the Holocaust and Israel minutes before the meeting between Swiss President Hans-Rudolf Merz and the Iranian president in Geneva, Switzerland, on April 19, 2009. *(Reuters)*

▼ Dershowitz meets with Israeli Prime Minister Shimon Peres.

11

Sharon and Bush

Partners in the War on Terror

YASSER ARAFAT'S REJECTION of Ehud Barak's peace offer, followed by the bloody second intifada, considerably weakened the Israeli peace camp. Most Israelis no longer believed that Arafat was a potential peace partner. Many now believed that signing the Oslo Accords had been a mistake and that Israel needed to protect itself from terrorism and other threats by showing strength. They wanted a government headed by a prime minister who projected toughness and self-determination. No one fit this bill better than General Ariel Sharon, Israel's most famous military hero, whose only flaw was that he was too tough: he had been removed from his post as minister of defense for his indirect responsibility in not preventing the Phalangist massacres at Sabra and Shatila back in 1982.

Sharon's fame and infamy as a military genius was known throughout Israel. His exploits were the stuff of novels and films: how he disobeyed orders during the Yom Kippur War and surrounded and trapped the Egyptian army; how he disobeyed orders in Lebanon and had his troops move more deeply into that country; how, as a young soldier, he had conducted retaliatory raids in response to terrorist attacks on Israeli civilians; how he had done nothing to stop the Phalangist massacres in Sabra and Shatila. After leaving military service, he became an equally controversial political leader, and he soon helped form the Kadima Party, which was more to the center than his former party, Likud, which he had left.[1]

"To every thing there is a season," wrote the author of Ecclesiastes. And this was the season for Sharon, the warrior. No one expected him to suddenly become a man of peace or to compromise. But as with Begin and Egypt, Sharon surprised the world by calling for a Palestinian entity on the West Bank and by endorsing the roadmap for peace proposed by the United States, Russia and the European Union. His biggest surprise took the form of Israel's unilateral withdrawal from the Gaza Strip in 2005.

Sharon dismantled all the Jewish settlements in the Gaza Strip, over the strong objection of their nearly 9,000 residents. He also ended the military occupation there, removing every soldier and military base. Although the Israeli Defense Forces maintained security control over the air, sea and land borders to prevent terrorism, the residents of the Gaza Strip were free to create a "Singapore on the Mediterranean." They could have used hothouses and agricultural equipment left behind by Israel, as well as the financial support they received from Europe, Arab states and the United Nations to create a thriving economy.[2] Instead, they voted for Hamas, then murdered or expelled Palestinian Authority functionaries before turning the Gaza Strip into a launching pad for thousands of rockets, dozens of terror tunnels, hundreds of incendiary kites and other cross-border attacks on the civilian residents of cities and towns in close proximity.[3]

Sharon's decision to leave the Gaza Strip unilaterally, without any peace deal with the Palestinians, was intended to be a first step in a more general unilateral approach to separating Israel from the Palestinians. Four Jewish settlements in the northern West Bank were also dismantled. The building of a long security barrier separating Israel from the West Bank, which began before Sharon took office, accelerated under his watch. Although its major purpose was to prevent the infiltration of terrorists, the wall's route was seen by many as a new unilaterally imposed "boundary" between Israel and the Palestinian entity from which Israel would disengage. It was also seen as part of the overall process of separation that could lead to a de facto two-state solution.

The entire enterprise of unilateral disengagement was extremely controversial both within Israel and among the Palestinian leadership. Pro-settlement Israelis were furious at Sharon's decision to dismantle existing settlements. Some security-minded Israelis were understandably concerned that ending the military occupation of the Gaza Strip would make the border areas more vulnerable to rocket attacks. Many Israelis were upset that Israel was getting nothing in return for these concessions.

Nor did Israel receive the praise it rightfully deserved. Despite taking these risks for peace, efforts to isolate and demonize Israel—through BDS, UN resolutions and demonstrations—only increased. There was no correlation between Israel's positive actions on the one hand and the condemnation it received on the other, especially from the hard left. The security barrier on the West Bank—which was mostly a sophisticated electronic fence, with solid walls placed in areas from which rifle shots were aimed at Israeli civilians—was called an apartheid wall, despite the reality that it dramatically reduced terrorist attacks and saved lives on both sides.

The absence of a positive response to Sharon's unilateral steps only made them—and him—more controversial, especially among the Israeli right, which accused him of becoming a traitor to their cause. But his support among centrist Israelis increased as he responded vigorously to continuing terrorist attacks while at the same time seeking to disengage from the Palestinians. Sharon maintained a positive relationship with President George W. Bush despite his opposition to the U.S. invasion of Iraq.

The controversy hit home in 2005 when I received an honorary doctorate from Bar-Ilan University.[4] My uncle Zecharia, my father's youngest and only living brother, believes that Israel has the right to build settlements in all of the historical areas that are part of the Jewish patrimony, and he was furious at Sharon for withdrawing from some areas. He had attended all the prior ceremonies at which I had been honored, but he refused to attend this one because of the prime minister's decision to attend. He only came to the reception, after Sharon had flown off in his helicopter.

I met privately with Sharon just before the stroke that disabled him in 2006 and ended his prime ministership. We discussed his unilateral approach, and he asked me my opinion. I told him that I completely supported the dismantling of the settlements, since I had opposed their establishment in the first place. He told me that he had favored the settlements from the beginning—especially those in areas he regarded as essential to Israel's security—but he felt the time had come to separate from the Palestinians and that dismantling some of the non-security-related settlements was necessary to secure this separation. He showed me a map and pointed to several areas in the West Bank in which he intended to dismantle more settlements. The map made it clear, at least to me, that he viewed the security barrier as serving two purposes: prevention of terrorism and a rough boundary for unilateral disengagement.

Before I met Sharon, I didn't expect to like him. He struck me, from a distance, as arrogant and difficult. He had a reputation for ignoring or circumventing the orders of higher-ups, which he had done during the Yom Kippur War and the First Lebanon War. In some important respects, his character conformed to some Israeli stereotypes: much like the sabra, Israel's national fruit, Sharon was prickly on the outside, but sweet on the inside. Until we met in person, I had only seen the outside.

Sharon had a reputation for being brusque and arrogant. In person, at least to me, he was warm and personable. At first, he talked down to me, as if reading from a scripted briefing he had given many times to prominent Jewish visitors from abroad. But I politely interjected, reminding him that I had written several books and numerous articles on what he was telling me. "Can we get to tachlis?" I asked, using a Yiddish term that roughly suggests, "Cut the B.S. and let's get to the point." He laughed and replied, "Good, I like tachlis." We proceeded to have a good substantive discussion of the merits and demerits of unilateral steps designed to create de facto separation on Israel's terms, without the need for negotiation with or agreement from the Palestinians. "I would love to make a mutual deal, like we did with Egypt and Jordan," he said, "but the Palestinian leadership is weak, and they cannot say yes. It may be easier for them to passively accept my unilateral acts than for them to affirmatively agree to them, even if they get less."

It was an interesting perspective, one I had not heard previously. I wasn't sure whether time would prove it right or wrong, but I was not in a position to argue with a man who knew the Palestinian leadership much better than I did.

We had one more conversation before his stroke. One Friday afternoon, I was visiting a group of friends in Tel Aviv who gathered every week for tea, vodka and political conversation—a so-called "parliament." I had been scheduled to meet again with Sharon that day, but his lawyer had canceled the meeting because I was representing an Israeli businessman who was a potential witness in the ongoing investigation of the prime minister and his sons for financial corruption. The lawyer thought it would be a bad idea for us to meet while the investigation was in progress, even though we would be discussing other issues. I agreed.

Just before the Sabbath began, the phone of one of the men attending the parliament rang. He spoke in Hebrew and then handed the phone to me: "Someone wants to speak to you." "Who?" I asked. "A friend," he replied. I took the phone and heard the familiar raspy voice of the prime minister: "Shalom. This is the man you're not supposed to talk to, just calling to wish you Shabbat Shalom." With that, he hung up. It was the last time we spoke.

When he suffered his stroke, Christian Evangelist Pat Robertson—a fellow Yale Law School graduate, who had interviewed me for his show on several occasions—declared that it was God punishing Sharon for abandoning the Gaza Strip and parts of the West Bank. Most of the rest of the world saw Sharon's stroke as a tragedy that might have prevented further withdrawals and further steps toward some sort of rapprochement.

Like Israel itself, Sharon's legacy is somewhat mixed. His military tactics helped Israel during the Yom Kippur War but hurt Israel in Lebanon. Before he became prime minister, his politics—especially his aggressive support for settlements—made the quest for peace more difficult. But when he ascended to the prime ministership, his decision to end the Gaza occupation and withdraw from settlements there gave the Palestinians an opportunity to secure the benefits of self-rule—an opportunity they frittered away by abandoning peace and turning instead to Hamas and terrorism. Sharon was (along with Shimon Peres) the last of the founding generation of Israelis. He will have a positive place in Israel's complicated and ever-changing history.

12

Olmert Attacks Syrian Nuclear Reactor, Offers Peace

Deputy Prime Minister Ehud Olmert became acting prime minister after Sharon's debilitating stroke. Olmert, who I first met when he was the popular mayor of Jerusalem, helped found the Kadima Party with Sharon and served as the prime minister's second in command. After serving as acting prime minister, he led his Kadima Party to an electoral victory before assuming the role of prime minister for nearly three years, a role he held until he stepped down as a result of the investigation that ultimately led to his conviction and imprisonment on charges of corruption. But his three-year term was among the most consequential in Israel's history.

Perhaps the most significant act undertaken by Olmert was the successful attack on a nuclear reactor being built by North Korea in Syria. Olmert, who had a close relationship with President George Bush, had suggested that the United States bomb the reactor, but Bush refused and told Olmert not to do it, suggesting tough diplomacy instead. But Olmert decided that the facility had to be destroyed—and it was, in a precision bombing raid named "Orchard" on September 6, 2007.

There were no public outcries from Syria or North Korea, because neither wanted to acknowledge the reactor's existence. Israel, too, remained silent about what it had done.

Intelligence sources have reported that the air strike was assisted by Special Forces on the ground that pinpointed the target, and by Israel's electronic warfare system that had infiltrated Syria's air defenses and fed them false information while Israeli fighter jets were in the air.

Just imagine how different and even more deadly the subsequent Syrian civil war would have been if Hafez al-Assad had possessed sophisticated nuclear weapons instead of the chemical barrel bombs he used on his own people. Despite President Bush having urged Olmert not to bomb the Syrian facility, the United States came to appreciate that he had done the right thing and had potentially saved many lives. This was especially true when, several years later, ISIS captured the area where Syria had been preparing to create a nuclear arsenal.[1]

In March 2018, Israeli censors finally allowed the government to acknowledge publicly what everyone knew: that the Israeli air force had destroyed the Syrian reactor. A few days later, I conducted the first English-language interview with Olmert about his decision and its implementation.

The interview was part of an Israeli TV show I moderated each week via Skype, titled *One on One with Alan Dershowitz*, in which I ask and answer questions with Israeli guests. The producer is Danny Grossman, a former top gun in both the U.S. and Israeli air force. Danny is also my go-to guy in Israel, arranging all my interviews and visits when I make my frequent trips there. He has been an indispensable associate and friend.

In this interview, Olmert—also an old friend—was candid in assessing the risks Israel faced and proud of the role he had played in protecting Israel from a Syrian nuclear threat. He credited his close personal relationship with President Bush for the positive U.S. response when the attack was a fait accompli. I too knew President

Bush despite my legal role against him in the Florida recount case, representing voters in Palm Beach County who were arguing that the so-called butterfly ballot had caused them inadvertently to cast their vote for a candidate for whom they did not intend to vote. We first met through our mutual friendship with Anatoly Sharansky. Bush wrote me a lengthy handwritten letter about our mutual friend, which included the following:

> *Like you, I care deeply about human dignity and justice. Thanks as well for representing Natan. When I was in Europe, I saw a copy of his book* [The Case for Democracy] *on the desk of the P.M. of Slovakia, was questioned about it at the E.U., and know it was referenced in European press on my trip. Truth is powerful.*
>
> *Best Regards,*
> *George Bush*

I spent some time with President Bush in Israel when we were both there celebrating Israel's sixtieth birthday in 2008. During that visit, Sharansky, Vaclav Havel and I were on a panel discussing human rights. Afterward, we all got into an elevator with Mikhail Gorbachev. I had previously met Gorbachev in the Soviet Union when I was there defending dissidents. He pointed at me and said, "You're the big-shot lawyer who tried to get these people out of prison. You did a good job, but I did a better job. I'm the one who got them out." Havel then turned to Gorbachev and asked, "Why didn't you get us out sooner?," to which Gorbachev replied, "I'm not that good."

Not all of Olmert's military decisions were as successful and un-controversial as Operation Orchard. The 34-day Lebanon War, which began on July 12, 2006, and ended with a UN-brokered cease-fire on August 14, 2006, was started by a Hezbollah incursion into

Israel during which three Israeli soldiers were killed and two kidnapped. Several more were killed in a failed attempt to rescue the kidnapped soldiers.[2]

Israel then launched air attacks and a ground invasion, and Hezbollah fired thousands more rockets at Israeli civilian targets, killing and injuring many. Israel, which regarded Hezbollah as the real power in Lebanon, attacked parts of the Lebanese infrastructure, including its international airport, which—like other Lebanese structures—had mixed military-civilian use and were thus legitimate military targets. In the end, thousands of Lebanese and Israeli civilians were temporarily displaced. As usual, the number and proportion of Lebanese civilians and fighters were hotly disputed—because Hezbollah fighters were civilians by night and terrorists by day—but a total of approximately 1,000 Lebanese were killed. For Israel, 121 soldiers and 46 civilians were killed, with more than 4,000 civilians injured.

The indecisive military outcome was unpopular in Israel and led to protests and the establishment of a commission—headed by retired justice Eliyahu Winograd—that deemed the war as a "missed opportunity" without "a defined military victory." In my interview with Olmert, I raised this issue, and he told me that he believed the war had accomplished what he had set out to do: deter further incursions into Israel from Lebanon.

The international reaction—especially in the media and on campuses—was critical, focusing on the Lebanese civilian casualties and damage to the infrastructure.

While I could not defend everything that Israel had done—or the wisdom of Israel's full-scale response to a cross-border raid by Hezbollah—I did try to explain why there were so many more Lebanese than Israeli civilian casualties. Israel goes to great effort and expense to protect its civilian population, constructing shelters and underground medical facilities, whereas Hezbollah deliberately uses Lebanese civilians as human shields to protect its fighters. Moreover, Hezbollah uses civilian structures—homes, hospitals, schools, shops—as launching places for its rockets. Israeli video footage, obtained for me by Danny, vividly showed how Hezbollah would place mobile launchers in civilian garages and other spaces, exit those spaces to fire the missiles and then retreat to them. Israel tried to avoid unnecessarily destroying civilian structures, but under the law of war, mixed-use structures were legitimate targets as long as reasonable efforts were made to minimize civilian casualties. But for most of the media[3] and on campuses, the body count was all that mattered, even if Hezbollah deliberately conducted its asymmetrical warfare so as to maximize the disparity between Lebanese civilian casualties and those of Israel.

I have pointed out in my writings that the media, and sometimes even academics, misunderstand the legal concept of *proportionality*. No nation is required by international law to limit its military actions to proportionate responses to enemy aggression. It may respond with disproportionate force as long as that force is directed at *military* targets. The legal requirement of proportionality relates to the use of military force that may result in *civilian* casualties. International law requires that when civilian deaths or injuries are contemplated in an attack against legitimate military targets, such anticipated civilian casualties should be proportional to the value of the military objectives sought. For example, if the leaders of a dangerous terrorist cell were hiding in a civilian building, it would be permissible to target those leaders, even if it was anticipated that a small number of civilians might be killed or wounded. But if one terrorist was hiding in a hospital or school, it would not be permissible to risk the lives of patients or students to target that one terrorist.

When Israel invaded the Gaza Strip in 2008, following an increase in Hamas rocket attacks on Israeli civilian targets, there were claims of disproportionality. "Operation Cast Lead," as it was called, began on December 27, 2008, and ended three weeks later. It led to the notorious *Goldstone Report* in September 2009. The report was commissioned by the United Nations Commission on Human Rights.[4] The commission was widely discredited because its members and chairpersons included some of the worst human rights offenders in the world, such as Iran, Syria, Belarus, China, Russia, Venezuela, Cuba, Saudi Arabia and Iraq. In order to lend credibility to the report it commissioned on Gaza, it appointed Richard Goldstone to be its chairman. It was a cynical, if brilliant, choice. Goldstone was a prominent Jew from South Africa, much of whose family lived in Israel. He had served as a judge during the apartheid period in South Africa, but had redeemed himself by his commitment to human rights following Nelson Mandela's assumption to the presidency of South Africa. But Goldstone was also ambitious to achieve status within the UN structure.

I wrote a 50-page[5] rebuttal to that error-filled report, which contributed to Richard Goldstone's decision to retract its most damning conclusions.

According to the report, Israel used the more than 8,000 rocket attacks on its civilians merely as a *pretext*, an *excuse*, a *cover* for the real purpose of Operation Cast Lead, which was to target innocent Palestinian civilians—children, women, the elderly—for death. The report said that this criminal objective was explicitly decided upon by the highest levels of the Israeli government and military and constituted a deliberate and willful war crime. The report found these serious charges "to be firmly-based in fact" and had "no doubt" of their truth, but it cited no credible evidence that actually supported its questionable conclusions.

The same *Goldstone Report*, in contrast, concluded that Hamas was not guilty of deliberately and willfully using the civilian population as human shields. It found "no evidence" that Hamas fighters "engaged in combat in civilian dress," "no evidence" that Palestinian combatants "mingled with the civilian population with the intention of shielding themselves from attack," and no support for the claim that mosques were used to store weapons.

The report was demonstrably wrong about both of these critical conclusions. The hard evidence conclusively proved that the exact opposite was true, namely that (1) Israel did not have a policy of targeting innocent civilians for death—indeed, the IDF went to unprecedented lengths to minimize civilian casualties, including phoning, leafleting and firing nonlethal warning "bombs" to advise civilians to leave buildings that were being targeted—and (2) that Hamas did have a deliberate policy of having its combatants dress in civilian clothing, fire their rockets from densely populated areas, use civilians a human shields and store weapons in mosques.[6]

What is even more telling than its erroneous conclusions, however, was its deliberately skewed methodology, particularly the manner in which it used and evaluated similar evidence very differently, depending on whether it favored the Hamas or Israeli side.

I wrote a detailed analysis of the Goldstone methodology, which is available online.[7] It was sent to the secretary general for inclusion in critiques of the *Goldstone Report* received by the United Nations. This analysis documents the distortions, misuses of evidence and bias of the report and those who wrote it. It demonstrates that the evidence relied on by the report, as well as the publicly available evidence it deliberately chose to ignore, disproves its own conclusions.

The central issue that distinguished the conclusions the *Goldstone Report* reached regarding Israel, on the one hand, and Hamas, on the other, is intentionality. The report credits the most serious accusations against Israel, namely that the killing of civilians was intentional and deliberately planned at the highest levels. The report also discredits the most serious accusations made against Hamas, namely that their combatants wore civilian clothing to shield themselves from attack, mingled among the civilian populations and used civilians as human shields intentionally. These issues are, of course, closely related.

If it were to turn out that there was no evidence that Hamas ever operated from civilian areas, and that the IDF knew this, then the allegations that the IDF, by firing into civilian areas, deliberately intended to kill Palestinian civilians would be strengthened. But if it were to turn out that the IDF reasonably believed that Hamas fighters were deliberately using civilians as shields, then this fact would weaken the claim that the IDF had no military purpose in firing into civilian areas. Moreover, if Hamas did use human shields, then the deaths of Palestinian civilians would be more justly attributable to Hamas than to Israel.

Since intentionality, or lack thereof, was so important to the report's conclusions, it would seem essential that the report would apply the same evidentiary standards, rules and criteria in determining the intent of Israel and in determining the intent of Hamas.

Yet a careful review of the report made it crystal clear that its writers applied totally different standards, rules and criteria in evaluating the intent of the parties to the conflict. The report resolved all doubts against Israel in concluding that its leaders intended to kill civilians, while resolving all doubts in favor of Hamas in concluding that it did not intend to use Palestinian civilians as human shields.

Moreover, when it had precisely the same sort of evidence in relation to both sides—for example, statements by leaders prior to the commencement of the operation—it attributed significant weight to the Israel statements while entirely discounting comparable Hamas statements. This sort of evidentiary bias, though subtle, permeates the entire report.

In addition to the statements of leaders, which are treated so differently, the report takes a completely different view regarding the inferring of intent from action. When it comes to Israel, the report repeatedly looks to results, and from those results, it infers that they must have been intended. But when it comes to Hamas, it refuses to draw inferences regarding intent from results. For example, it acknowledges that some combatants wore civilian clothes, and it offers no reasonable explanation for why this would be so other than to mingle indistinguishably among civilians. Yet it refuses to infer intent from these actions. Highly relevant to the report's conclusion that militants did not intend for their actions to shield themselves from counterattack is that the Goldstone investigators—who included Goldstone himself and several professional Israel bashers—were "unable to make any determination on the general allegations that Palestinian armed groups used mosques for military purposes," "did not find any evidence to support the allegations that hospital facilities were used by the Gaza authorities or by Palestinian armed groups to shield military activities," did not find evidence "that ambulances were used to transport combatants or for other military purposes," and did not find "that Palestinian armed groups engaged in combat activities from United Nations facilities that were used as shelters during the military operations." There is, however, hard evidence—including videos and photographs—that Hamas did operate in mosques and near hospitals and schools.

When the report was dealing with Israeli intentions, it relied on highly questionable circumstantial inferences: since Israel's rockets are relatively accurate, the fact that some hit civilians led to the inference that they were intentionally targeted rather than accidently hit, despite the universally accepted reality that in the fog of war, the most sophisticated weapons sometimes hit unintended targets. But when the report considered Hamas, it ignored the circumstantial evidence, even though it was much stronger in suggesting intent. It is beyond obvious that militants fire rockets from the vicinity of mosques or hospitals not because it is easier to launch rockets near community institutions, but only because of the special protections afforded to hospitals and religious centers in war.

The report—commissioned by an organization with a long history of anti-Israel bigotry and written by biased "experts" with limited experience—was one-sided and wrong in its fundamental conclusions. This should not be surprising since conclusions can be no better than the methodology employed, and the methodology employed in this report was fundamentally flawed. It was as if two different people, with different evidentiary standards, were tasked with writing the report: one the Israel portion and the other the Hamas portion. But it was Richard Goldstone, its chairman, who was fully responsible.

In op-eds and media appearances, I challenged Goldstone to explain the evidentiary bias that is so obviously reflected in the report. I said that the burden was on him to justify the very different methodologies used to arrive at the report's conclusions regarding the intentions of Israel and the intentions of Hamas. I argued that failure to assume that burden would constitute an implicit admission that the conclusions reached in the *Goldstone Report* were not worthy of consideration by people of goodwill.

A debate was arranged by students at Fordham Law School, where Goldstone was a visiting professor. He was invited to defend his report, but he was a no-show, claiming some excuse. So I placed his report on the chair that had been reserved for him and "debated" *it*! I invited students and faculty in the audience to take his side during the question period, but none did.

I had been on friendly terms with Richard Goldstone—I was not a close friend but an admiring colleague—until he signed the report. My criticism of the report, and of him for signing it, were so deep that our friendship could not survive the dispute. I questioned not only his "findings" but his motivations as well. I saw him as an opportunist who placed his ambitions above his commitment to truth. To advance in the world of international diplomacy and law, especially within the structure of the United Nations, a Jew had to lean over backward—in this case doing triple somersaults—to prove the absence of any pro-Israel leanings. In performing these contortions, Goldstone scored points with the UN bureaucracy, but he lost the respect of many of his colleagues, even some who were critical of Israeli actions in Gaza. No reasonable, objective observer could accept the two major conclusions of the *Goldstone Report*: that there was evidence that the Israeli military deliberately targeted civilians in an effort to kill as many innocent noncombatants as possible, and that there was no evidence that Hamas terrorists used

Gaza civilians as human shields. Not only was there *no* evidence that the former proposition was true, but there was substantial evidence that it was false. Consider the very different conclusion drawn by Colonel Richard Kemp, the former commander of British Forces in Afghanistan: "I don't think there has ever been a time in the history of warfare when an army has made more efforts to reduce civilian casualties and deaths of innocent people than the IDF is doing today in Gaza."[8]

The evidence that Hamas used civilians as human shields was overwhelming and indisputable, including admissions—indeed proud proclamations—by Hamas officials describing human shields as martyrs. According to a translation by the Middle East Media Research Institute, on February 29, 2008, Fathi Hamad, a Hamas member of the Palestinian Legislative Council, stated,

> *For the Palestinian people, death has become an industry, at which women excel, and so do all the people living on this land. The elderly excel at this, and so do the mujahideen and the children. This is why they have formed human shields of the women, the children, the elderly, and the mujahideen, in order to challenge the Zionist bombing machine. It is as if they were saying to the Zionist enemy: "We desire death like you desire life."*

There were also videos of Hamas rockets being fired from civilian homes, schools and hospitals, as well as photographic evidence of civilian buildings used as storage facilities for rockets and other weapons.

When the war was over, I wrote a book defending Israel's actions, entitled *The Case for Moral Clarity: Israel, Hamas and Gaza*. Its cover was a cartoon depicting an armed Israeli soldier standing *in front* of a baby carriage to protect the baby and a Hamas fighter standing *behind* a baby carriage, using the baby to protect himself as he fired rockets at Israeli civilians. It made my point more powerfully than any words. And it undercut the conclusions of the *Goldstone Report* more powerfully than any argument.

Eventually, Richard Goldstone disassociated himself from the report's conclusion, but not before it falsely persuaded so many people that Israel bore primary responsibility for the deaths in Gaza.

The wars in Lebanon and Gaza were not Prime Minister Olmert's only problems. His term ended ingloriously with his resignation, forced by the criminal charges he faced.[9] He was accused of corruption for alleged actions he took before he became prime minister. His resignation was not only a personal tragedy but also a tragedy for Israel, the Palestinians and the prospects for peace. Shortly before he resigned, he had offered the Palestinians a deal even better than the one criminally rejected by Yasser Arafat seven years earlier.[10] Although President Mahmoud Abbas had sufficient time to accept the offer, he did not. Nor did he formally reject it. When Olmert was replaced by Netanyahu, the deal was no longer on the table.

I visited Ehud Olmert in prison. I was allowed the visit because I had informally advised his lawyer, who was appealing the conviction. It was devastating to see this great man who I knew and admired for more than two decades in a prison cell. (In Israel, when you ask for a politician's cell number, it isn't always for his phone!)

I was taken to Olmert by a young guard, who I was told was an Israeli Druze. I was quite shocked to see the former prime minister of the nation-state of the Jewish people being ordered around by a young Druze man. Although the Druze, in general, are loyal to Israel and serve in its military, they are closer in ethnicity to Israel's Arabs than to its Jewish population. I guess I should not have been surprised, since the panel that convicted Moshe Katsav, Israel's former president, of sexual crimes included an Israeli Arab. So much for any claim of apartheid.

I spent several hours discussing the political situation with Olmert. He is not a fan of Prime Minister Benjamin Netanyahu, but he wished him well in his efforts to govern a country with millions of prime ministers, generals and opinionated know-it-alls, from taxi drivers to prison guards.

13

Obama and Netanyahu Disagree on Iran and Jerusalem

In 2008, Barack Obama, who I had known as a law student, was elected president of the United States. When he was a student, his mentor was Professor Charles Ogletree, an African American colleague and brilliant criminal lawyer. Obama would visit Ogletree's office, which was in the same suite as mine. Charles was often late for appointments because he ran a clinical program that sometimes ran over. So Obama, garbed in his signature leather jacket, would wait for him, and we chatted while he waited. I liked him and saw his obvious leadership qualities and intelligence.

I was therefore deeply gratified by his later emergence in national politics as a dynamic young figure in the Democratic Party. I naturally couldn't vote for him when he ran for the Senate in Illinois, but I campaigned for him. When he ran for president in 2008, I supported Hillary Clinton, who I knew much better, in the primaries. But after he won the nomination, I campaigned enthusiastically for him in the general election.

My support for this young, relatively unknown candidate—whose record on Israel was sparse—instigated a firestorm of criticism from right-wing Zionists, and even from some concerned centrists. I felt it necessary to explain and justify my support for Obama over Senator John McCain from an American liberal and Zionist perspective.

First, I much favored Obama's policies on issues unrelated to Israel, such as the Supreme Court, the rights of women and gay people, separation of church and state, as well as the economy and environment. But I also preferred Obama to McCain on the issue of Israel. The reason is that I thought it would be better for Israel to have a liberal supporter in the White House than to have a conservative supporter. I believed that Obama's views on Israel would have a greater impact on young people, on Europe, on the media and on others who tend to identify with the liberal perspective. Although centrist liberals in general tend to support Israel, I acknowledged that support from the left seemed to be weakening as support from the right strengthened. I hoped that the election of Barack Obama—a liberal supporter of Israel—would enhance Israel's position among wavering liberals.[1]

During his first term, Obama supported Israel in a variety of important ways. He helped Israel militarily by funding the "iron dome," a sophisticated anti-rocket technology; supporting Israel's defensive incursion into Lebanon; opposing the *Goldstone Report*; increasing financial aid to the IDF and preventing the United Nations from passing one-sided resolutions against Israel. But he strongly—more strongly than his predecessors—opposed Israel's settlement expansion. This put him in conflict with many, though not all, Jewish supporters.

It also put him in conflict with Benjamin Netanyahu, whose second term as prime minister coincided with Obama's presidency.

I continued to support Obama because I, too, was critical of settlement expansion by the Netanyahu government, but other Jewish leaders began to waiver in their support. To deal with Jewish criticism, Obama counted on J Street—a new left-leaning organization that labeled itself "pro-Israel and pro-peace."

J Street was founded near the end of Prime Minister Olmert's term by Jeremy Ben-Ami—a left-leaning Democrat. But it increased its profile considerably when Netanyahu became prime minister. J Street initially saw its role as siding with Obama and giving him Jewish "cover" in his confrontations with Netanyahu regarding settlements and the peace process. Over time, and in an effort to build a base on the hard left of the Jewish community, J Street took anti-Israel positions that even Obama could not support. The *Goldstone Report* was one such issue: J Street brought Richard Goldstone to the Capitol to present his outrageously false conclusions to members of Congress.

But generally J Street toed the Obama line on divisive issues, such as the Iran deal and the Security Council resolution declaring Jerusalem's historically Jewish areas—such as the Western Wall, the Jewish Quarter and the access roads to Hebrew University and Hadassah Hospital—to be "illegally occupied" by Israel.

With regard to Iran, I came face to face with Ahmadinejad. In 2009, I traveled to Geneva to protest a meeting of the UN Human Rights Council, which had invited Mahmoud Ahmadinejad, the Holocaust-denying president of Iran, to deliver the key address. My wife and I were having a drink in the lobby of our hotel when Ahmadinejad and his entourage paraded through. I approached one of his handlers, introduced myself, and told him that I challenged the president to a debate about the Holocaust. His handler asked, "Where, at Harvard?" I replied, "No, the debate should be at Auschwitz; that's where the evidence is." He said he would communicate my offer to the president, who, he told me, was on the way to a press conference. I went and tried to ask Ahmadinejad directly whether he would debate me. I was immediately hauled off by the Swiss police, removed from the hotel and told I would not be allowed to return "for security reasons." I insisted that "security reasons" did not justify protecting the president from a hostile question. I called someone I knew in the Obama administration, who phoned the U.S. consulate in Geneva, and I was allowed back into the hotel with an apology. The photograph of me being removed from the hotel was flashed around the world with the following caption:

> *Harvard Law professor Alan Dershowitz is led away after declaring he planned to challenge Iranian President Mahmoud Ahmadinejad about his views on the Holocaust and Israel minutes before a meeting between President Hans-Rudolf Merz and the Iranian president in Geneva, Switzerland, on April 19, 2009.*[2]

We were not allowed into the chamber where Ahmadinejad was speaking so I led a march into the chamber. Several delegations were absent, and we took their seats. As soon as Ahmadinejad denied the Holocaust, which he did near the beginning of his speech, I stood up and shouted "Shame!" and walked out, passing directly in front of his lectern. Many others walked out as well, including several European delegations. Ahmadinejad's talk was a fiasco, and was reported as such by the media. He had made a fool of himself—with our help.

In 2010, the "human rights" conference was in New York at the UN headquarters. I delivered the following words:

> *One important reason why there is no peace in the Middle East can be summarized tragically in two letters, UN. The building dedicated in theory to peace has facilitated terrorism, stood idly by genocide, given a platform to Holocaust deniers, and disincentivized the Palestinians from negotiating a two-state solution . . . How dare states such as Saudi Arabia, Cuba, Venezuela, Zimbabwe, Iran, Bahrain, Syria, Belarus, and other tyrannies too numerous to mention lecture Israel about human rights? How dare states such as Turkey, that have attacked their own Kurdish minorities and Armenian minorities, and Russia, which has attacked its own Chechnyan minority . . . lecture Israel about peace?*

Is there no sense of shame . . . ? Has the word hypocrisy lost
all meaning . . . ? Does no one recognize the need for a single,
neutral standard of human rights? Have human rights now
become the permanent weapon of choice for those who practice
human wrongs? For shame. For shame.

Shortly after Benjamin Netanyahu was elected to his second term as prime minister, he made me an offer that gave me an existential identity crisis. He urged me to become Israel's ambassador to the United Nations. He said that I was the only person about whom there was a consensus within his security cabinet. I was honored beyond belief to be asked to serve in this important role. Nothing would have given me more personal or professional pleasure than to stand in the well of the United Nations and defend the nation-state of the Jewish people against the defamation and blood libels that are spewed out daily in that chamber of hatred against Israel. My father always taught me to stand up for the underdog, and there is no bigger underdog than Israel at the United Nations, where every year more resolutions are directed against this tiny democracy than all the other countries of the world together. I had written several books and articles on the subject, and I welcomed the enormous responsibility of becoming the spokesperson against anti-Israel bigotry at the United Nations. But as soon as the offer was made, I knew deep in my heart that I would reluctantly have to decline it.

For me, an American Jew, to become the official UN representative of another country would raise the specter of "dual loyalty," a charge frequently made by Israel haters against American Jews who support Israel. At the time, it did not appear that there would ever be any conflicts over the positions of the United States and Israel at the United Nations, because the United States almost always voted with Israel. It would later turn out that during Obama's second term, such conflicts did arise, especially with regard to Iran and the Security Council resolution. But even if there were no actual conflicts, the perception that an American Jew had switched sides and was representing the nation-state of the Jewish people would have given solace to those who have long claimed that American Jews have more loyalty to Israel than to the United States. I explained all this to Netanyahu, but he persisted and asked me to come to Israel and give him the opportunity to change my mind.

I flew to Israel and had a long dinner with the prime minister. He offered compelling arguments as to why my presence in the United Nations would be good for Israel, for the United States, for world Jewry, for American Jews and for peace. He also argued that I should not turn down the job because of what anti-Israel bigots would think and say. "They will think and say it even if you don't take the job." Netanyahu is an extremely persuasive man. But in the end, I persuaded him that I could better serve our mutual interests by retaining my role as an independent and liberal defender of Israel. He reluctantly accepted my decision, but he asked me if I were willing to take on another job. I asked him what it was. He said, "I need you to be Israel's unofficial ambassador to the Jews of America, especially the young ones. America's political support for Israel is every bit as important as its military support, and the two are, of course, related. Please help keep American Jews supportive of our small country." I promised I would, and he gave me a big hug—the first time he had ever shown such physical affection during the many decades that we had known each other.

Even as I walked back to my hotel, I was uncertain whether I had done the right thing. Intellectually, I was satisfied with my decision, but emotionally it left a big question mark. I knew I would be missing a great deal by turning down this unique opportunity. Fortunately, the man Netanyahu picked instead of me—Ron Prosor—performed brilliantly at the United Nations and served his country with great distinction. Israel certainly did not suffer from my decision. But declining the offer did not diminish my advocacy. I traveled around the world making the liberal case for Israel, especially when the IDF was criticized for defending their civilians against terrorist attacks.

On June 13, 2014, the commander of the southern region for the Israel Security Agency (ISA), together with the commander of the Gaza Division of the Israel Defense Forces (IDF), took me into a Hamas tunnel that had recently been discovered by a Bedouin tracker who served in the IDF. The tunnel was a concrete bunker that extended several miles from its entrance in the Gaza Strip to its exit near an Israeli kibbutz kindergarten.

The tunnel had one purpose: to allow Hamas death squads to kill and kidnap Israelis. The commander told me that Israeli intelligence had identified more than two dozen additional tunnel entrances in the Gaza Strip. They had been identified by the large amounts of earth being removed to dig them. Although Israeli intelligence knew where these entrances were, they could not order an attack from the air, because the openings were built into civilian structures such as mosques, schools, hospitals and private homes. Nor could Israel identify their underground routes from Gaza into Israel, or their intended exit points. Israeli scientists and military experts had spent millions of dollars in an effort to develop technologies that could find these tunnels that were as deep as a hundred feet beneath the earth, but they had not succeeded in finding a complete solution to this problem.[3] The planned exits from these tunnels—each had several—were also a Hamas secret, hidden deep in the ground and incapable of being discovered by Israel until the Hamas fighters emerged. At that point it would be too late to prevent the death squads from doing their damage.

I was taken into the tunnel and saw the technological innovations: tracks on which small trains could transport kidnapped Israelis back to Gaza; telephone and electrical lines; crevices beneath schools and other civilian targets that could hold explosives; and smaller offshoot tunnels leading from the main tube to numerous exit points from which fighters could simultaneously emerge from different places. Building these tunnels cost Hamas a small fortune, which came from funds that could have been used to educate, employ and heal the residents of Gaza. It also cost a considerable number of lives and limbs, resulting from frequent accidents that occurred during the dangerous task of excavation and construction. But Hamas's priority was death rather than life.

As soon as I went down into the tunnel, I realized that Israel would have no choice but to take military action to destroy them. Israel had a technological response—though imperfect—to Hamas rockets. Its Iron Dome missile defense system was capable of destroying approximately 85 percent of Hamas rockets fired at its population centers.[4] Moreover, it could attack rocket launchers from the air with sophisticated GPS-guided bombs. But it had no complete technological answer—at least not yet—to these terror tunnels.

At the time, the media reported that Hamas was possibly planning a Rosh Hashanah massacre during which hundreds of terrorists would simultaneously emerge from dozens of tunnels and slaughter hundreds, if not thousands, of Israeli civilians and soldiers.[5] If this report had been true, as many in Israel believed it was, the Rosh Hashanah massacre would have been the equivalent of a hundred 9/11s in the United States. Even if it was an exaggeration, the tunnels certainly provided Hamas with the capability of wreaking havoc on Israeli citizens. There were other reports as well of planned attacks through the tunnels. As one resident of Sderot put it, "We used to look up to the sky in fear, but now we are looking down at the ground."[6]

To me, the only questions were when Israel would act, how it would act, whether it would be successful, and what the consequences would be. Could any nation tolerate this kind of threat to its citizens? Has any nation in history ever allowed tunnels to be dug under its border that would permit death squads to operate against its people?

I discussed these issues with Prime Minister Netanyahu at his home several days later, and it became clear that the Israeli government had been concerned about the security threats posed by these terror tunnels ever since one had been used to kidnap the young soldier Gilad Shalit and kill two of his compatriots.

Ironically, it was while we were in the tunnel that we learned that three Israeli high school students had been kidnapped. Their kidnapping and subsequent murder was the beginning of what turned into Operation Protective Edge, which ended with the destruction of most of the tunnels by special IDF explosive units.

Israel was widely condemned for its military operations in Gaza, with little concern expressed for those Israeli civilians whose lives had been placed in danger by those deadly tunnels.

In a book called *Terror Tunnels: The Case for Israel's Just War Against Hamas*, I made the case that Israel was justified—legally, morally, diplomatically and politically—in responding to the dangers posed by the tunnels and the rocket attacks that preceded and followed their discovery. I also explained why so many of the media, academia, the international community and the general public seemed to blind themselves to the dangers posed by Hamas and blamed Israel for actions they would demand their own governments take were they faced with comparable threats.

The "blame Israel" reaction has serious consequences, not only for Israel but also for the people of Gaza, and for the democratic world in general. Blaming Israel only encourages Hamas to repeat its "dead baby strategy" and other terrorist groups to emulate it. The strategy operates as follows: Hamas attacks Israel either by rockets or through tunnels, thereby forcing Israel to respond to protect its citizens. Because Hamas fires its rockets and digs its tunnels from densely populated civilian areas rather than from the many open areas of the Gaza Strip, the inevitable result is that a significant number of Palestinian civilians are killed. Hamas encourages this result, because it knows the media will focus more on the photographs of dead babies than on the cause of their death: namely, the decision by Hamas to use these babies and other civilians as human shields. Hamas quickly produces the dead babies to be shown around the world while at the same time preventing the media from showing its rocket launchers and tunnels in densely populated areas. The world is outraged at the dead civilians and blames Israel for killing them. This only emboldens Hamas to repeat its strategy following short cease-fires, during which they re-arm and regroup.

In 2018 and 2019, Hamas sent thousands of civilians, including young children and mothers carrying babies, to the fence adjoining Israeli population centers. Their goal was to break down the fence and attack Israeli civilians. Inevitably, some Palestinian children were killed and injured. The media responded precisely as Hamas intended.

I tried to warn the world—in my book and media appearances—that unless Hamas's dead baby strategy is denounced and stopped by the international community, the media, the academy and good people of all religions, ethnicities and nationalities, it will be "coming soon to a theater near you." Hamas repeatedly employs this despicable and unlawful strategy because it works. It works because despite the material losses Hamas suffers in its repeated military encounters with Israel, it always wins the public relations war, the legal war, the academic war and the war for the naïve hearts if not always wise minds of young people. And if it is indeed winning these wars—if its dead baby strategy is working—why not repeat it every few years? That's why cease-fires between Israel and Hamas always entail Israel "ceasing" and Hamas "firing"—perhaps not immediately, but inevitably. And if it works for Hamas, why shouldn't other terrorist groups, like ISIS and Boko Haram, adapt this strategy to their own nefarious goals? The United States is also blamed—to a lesser extent than is Israel—when its military, despite efforts to minimize civilian casualties, produces them anyway because their enemies employ human shields as well.

The only way to end this cycle of death is to expose the dead baby strategy for what it is—a double war crime whose ultimate victims are civilian children, women and men.

I had, and have, only one weapon in this ongoing war: my words. During the course of Operation Protective Edge, I tried to make the case for Israel's just war against Hamas's double war crime strategy. I wrote more than two dozen op-eds, participated in several debates and television interviews, and spoke to numerous audiences. My goal was to show that Israel's military actions in defense of its citizens have been just and that they have been conducted in a just manner. They are no less just than the military actions being conducted by the United States and its allies against ISIS, al-Qaeda, and other terrorist groups. And they have been carried out at least as justly, with a lower percentage of civilian-to-combatant casualties.

Yet Israel has been unjustly condemned from too many corners, thus encouraging Hamas to continue its despicable and unlawful strategy. I argued that for the sake of justice and peace, the world must stop applying a double standard to the nation-state of the Jewish people.

Books and op-eds are comparatively weak instruments for affecting the course of international affairs. Nevertheless, I believe that my advocacy—and that of others such as Bret Stephens, Irwin Cotler and the late Elie Wiesel—for Israel's military response to the Hamas terror tunnels helped to sway general public opinion in favor of Israel. So did the Obama administration's lack of criticism of Israel's military actions before, during and after Operation Protective Edge.

It was for that reason, among others, that I was inclined to support Obama's quest for reelection in 2012, though I had some doubts about his policy with regard to Iran.

In the spring of 2012, I was in Israel. The U.S. election was beginning, and Iran was rattling its weapons. My wife and I were having dinner at a Georgian restaurant and bar in Tel Aviv when my cell phone rang. The restaurant, which was filled with young émigrés from the former Soviet Union, was noisy and raucous, with vodka-inebriated patrons dancing and singing. I could hardly make out what the caller was saying, but I did hear the words "White House" and "president." I walked outside, where the overflow crowd was still loud but I could hear the caller repeating that the president wanted to talk to me. I told her that I couldn't hear clearly from where I was, but that I would be back in my hotel in half an hour. Could the president call me then? Her tone of voice suggested that she was not used to being asked to have the president try again, but she told me he would.

We raced back to our hotel and the president called. He inquired as to whether I had met with the prime minister and I told him I had. He asked me what the most important issues on Netanyahu's mind were, and I replied,

"Number one is Iran."

He followed up, "What's number two?"

I replied "Iran," and continued: "If you want to know what number three is, it's Iran. So is number four, five, six."

"I get the point," he said with a slight laugh. "Can you come see me in the Oval Office, when you get back, to discuss Iran? I want to tell you what we're doing."

We then schmoozed for a few minutes about how much he had enjoyed his visit to Israel and whether my wife was having a good time.

A few weeks later, I was sitting alone with the president in the Oval Office, engaged in a serious discussion about Iran, sanctions, containment, prevention and preemption. Prime Minister Netanyahu was expressing concern to anyone who would listen about Iran's nuclear weapons ambitions. There was talk of a possible deal, but it was light on specifics. I expressed my concerns to the president. He replied: "Alan, you've known me for a long time, and you know I don't bluff. You can count on what I'm telling you. I will never allow Iran to develop a nuclear arsenal, no matter what it takes. My policy is not 'containment' of a nuclear Iran, it's prevention."

I told him that I wasn't worried about Iran developing or acquiring a nuclear bomb during his watch. What worried me was that they could spin enough centrifuges to be ready to transition from civilian to military use in the near future, when his term was over. Obama assured me that both the United States and Israel had sufficient intelligence on the ground and cyber capabilities to make sure that didn't happen. He also said that the sanctions then in place would disincentivize the mullahs from challenging his policies, and that the international community had enough leverage to make a good deal with the Iranian regime, if the Iranians were prepared to negotiate in good faith.

I expressed my own skepticism and relayed the even greater skepticism I had heard from Netanyahu. He said he understood. "There is no perfect solution," he acknowledged, referring to the experience of prior administrations with North Korea. "But we won't allow Iran to become North Korea. I will not take the military options off the table as a last resort, but I will try not to have to use it."

I reminded him of the wise statement that George Washington—whose portrait was in full view—had made about how the best way of avoiding war is to be prepared to wage it. He assured me, "We are prepared, but we are also prepared to negotiate, to sanction and to take other actions."

He then looked me straight in the eye and said, "I want you to know, and I want your friend Bibi to know, I have Israel's back and I will always have Israel's back. You can count on that."

I wasn't sure what to make of his commitment. Many American Jewish and Israeli leaders were growing suspicious of Obama in relation to Israel. They worried that in a second term he would care more about his legacy, of which a deal with Iran would be a prime component, than about Israel's security down the road. I knew that he wanted me to assure these leaders that they could trust him in his final four years.

I had several more White House (and Martha's Vineyard) discussions with President Obama and his staff—especially Ben Rhodes, as well as soon-to-be secretary of state John Kerry, an old friend—in the run-up to the 2012 election and thereafter.

I was comforted by the knowledge that the man in charge of

keeping the pressure on Iran through sanctions was David Cohen, who was then undersecretary of the treasury for terrorism and financial intelligence and who would soon become deputy director of the CIA. David was a childhood and law school friend of my younger son Jamin. I had mentored David while he was in law school and in his first jobs. I knew that he had positive views regarding Israel and was a tough negotiator who was committed to preventing Iran from acquiring a nuclear arsenal. We might disagree about the means necessary to achieve that result, but not on the result itself.

The deal that was eventually struck not only disappointed me, it outraged Prime Minister Netanyahu, virtually all Israelis, many Americans and a significant number of senators and House members. David Cohen believed it was a good, if not perfect, deal that would keep Iran from developing a nuclear arsenal for a considerable number of years. Because the president could not get enough votes to make it a binding treaty, or even an act of Congress, he had to settle for an executive order that could be rescinded by any future president (which is in fact what happened). In exchange for lifting sanctions and billions of dollars in cash, Iran promised to stop spinning centrifuges for a limited number of years. At the end of that period, the agreement did not prevent Iran from spinning enough centrifuges to develop a nuclear arsenal.

When President Obama assured me that he had Israel's back and that he would never allow Iran to develop a nuclear arsenal, he may have believed what he was saying. In light of what actually happened, there are three possibilities: The first is that he actually believed it then, believed it when he signed the deal and still believes it now. If that is the case, then he apparently assumed—in a way that could only be called arrogant—that he knew more about Israel's security than the Israeli officials whose job it is to protect Israel. The second possibility is that he believed it then, but was persuaded by Secretary of State John Kerry and other strong advocates of the deal to change his mind. The third is that despite his assurances to me that he never bluffs, he was, in fact, telling me what he knew I wanted to hear in order to ensure my support among American Jews for his reelection. I don't know which of these possibilities is true, but I do know that none of them makes me feel comfortable about having endorsed and campaigned for him in 2012.

I went to Florida to persuade Jewish voters that they could trust Obama. Obama's invitation to meet with me may have grown out of the skepticism I expressed in op eds and his desire to persuade me he could be trusted on Iran. It worked—at least it did then.

I wrote additional op-eds defending the Obama administration's Iran policy:

> It has taken containment off the table and kept the military option on the table. Everyone hopes that the military option will not have to be employed since it would entail considerable loss of life, especially among Israeli civilians who would be targeted by Hezbollah rockets fired in retaliation against any attack on Iran.
>
> But the best way to avoid the need for military action is for the Iranian mullahs to believe that the United States will never allow them to develop nuclear weapons. If they believe that reality then the pain of the sanctions will pressure them to give up their nuclear ambitions. President Obama has clearly stated that he is not bluffing when he says that his administration will never allow Iran to develop nuclear weapons.

Just months earlier I had expressed skepticism about Obama's policy toward Iran in the *Wall Street Journal*, warning that he would be remembered as the Neville Chamberlain of the twenty-first century if he did not stop Iran from developing a nuclear arsenal.[7] I reminded my readers that Chamberlain had done great things for British citizens during the Depression, but history remembers him only for his failure to confront Hitler. "That is his enduring legacy." I warned Obama that "history will not treat kindly" any leader who allows Iran to develop nuclear weapons.[8]

Despite my strong concerns about Obama's Iran policy, I felt comfortable endorsing him for reelection, based in part on his record up to then with regard to Israel's military actions and his firm assurances to me.

The first event that caused me to reconsider my endorsement was the way Obama and several Democratic senators and members of Congress treated the invitation by the Speaker of the House to Prime Minister Netanyahu to address a joint session of Congress about the Iran deal. Generally such invitations are approved in advance by the president, but Obama did not want the highly articulate and knowledgeable Netanyahu to persuade members of Congress to oppose a deal with Iran. He was furious with Netanyahu for appealing directly to Congress. I was told that Obama urged Democratic senators and congressmen and -women to boycott the talk, which several said they would do.

In the *Wall Street Journal*, I made the constitutional case for the power of the legislative branch to invite foreign leaders disagreeing with the presidential decision. I then argued that one should walk out on tyrants, bigots and radical extremists like the United States did when Iran's Mahmoud Ahmadinejad denied the Holocaust and called for Israel's destruction at the United Nations. To use such an extreme tactic against our closest ally, and the Middle East's only democracy, is not only insulting to Israel's prime minister, but it puts Israel in a category in which it does not belong.

I called several of my friends who had indicated they would boycott Netanyahu's speech and urged them to change their minds. "Would you boycott a speech by Putin or Castro?" I asked. They said no, but they insisted that this was different, because the invitation from the Speaker was partisan. I agreed that this was different because Netanyahu was the democratically elected prime minister of an American ally. I changed several minds, the most important of which was that of Congressman Charles Rangel, the head of the Congressional Black Caucus. *Every* member of the Black Caucus had announced that they would boycott Netanyahu's speech because they thought Netanyahu disrespected the first African American president by accepting Boehner's invitation against Obama's wishes. The action risked becoming a "Black-Jewish" split, with ongoing consequences. Rangel agreed and announced that he would attend the talk.

The Center for Public Integrity reported it as follows: "Thank super lawyer Alan Dershowitz—at least in part—for Rep. Charlie Rangel, D-N.Y. suddenly reversing his decision to skip Prime Minister Benjamin Netanyahu's contentious March 3 address to Congress."

Netanyahu made a powerful speech pointing to the dangers of a nuclear Iran. He received, quite deservedly, standing ovations from both sides of the aisle, which reportedly angered Obama even more.

After the talk, Congressman Rangel thanked me for changing his mind: "I learned a lot from Bibi's talk," he told me. Kenneth Bialkin, a major Jewish leader, also thanked me "for performing a service to the entire Jewish community and African American community, because if Rangel had not changed his mind . . . there would have been a very big backlash . . ."

But I could not persuade Senators Elizabeth Warren and Al Franken, who saw the invitation to Netanyahu as partisan. I told them both that this was a red line for me, and that I would no longer contribute to their campaigns or to the campaigns of any other Democrat who showed such disrespect toward the prime minister of Israel. This was the first, but unfortunately not the last, time mainstream Democrats, who were my friends, would break with the long tradition of bipartisan support for Israel.

I was invited by Bibi to sit next to his wife and Elie Wiesel in the front row of the House gallery for his talk. It was an extraordinary speech that electrified Congress and helped persuade a majority of both Houses to oppose the deal.[9] But Obama decided to circumvent Congress, and although the deal had all the hallmarks of a treaty, he signed it as an executive agreement. This meant that it was subject to abrogation by any future president, without any input from Congress.

As I had done several times before, I decided to write a polemical book about the agreement, titled *The Case Against the Iran Deal: How Can We Stop Iran from Getting Nukes?* I knew that Obama would sign the deal, but I wanted to lay out the arguments against it in the event that a future president—who at the time I believed would be Hillary Clinton—might decide to strengthen its provisions. I ended with a constructive proposal that could prevent Iran from becoming a nuclear power without the United States abrogating the deal (which I knew Hillary Clinton would never do as president):

> *Congress now has the power to improve this bad deal in a way that reduces the changes that Iran will obtain a nuclear arsenal. The key lies in the words of the deal itself. . . . In both the preface and the preamble and general provisions, the following commitment is made: "Iran reaffirms that under no circumstances will Iran ever seek, develop or acquire any nuclear weapons" [emphasis added]. This noteworthy provision is rarely mentioned by supporters of the agreement.*
>
> *Congress should now enact legislation declaring that this reaffirmation is an integral part of the agreement and represents the policy of the United States. It is too late to change the words of the deal, but it is not too late for Congress to insist that Iran comply fully with its provisions.*
>
> *In order to ensure that the entirety of the agreement is carried out, including that reaffirmation, Congress should adopt the proposal made by Thomas L. Friedman on 22 July 2015 and by myself on 5 September 2013. To quote Friedman: "Congress should pass a resolution authorizing this and future presidents*

to use force to prevent Iran from ever becoming a nuclear weapons
state. . . . Iran must know now that the U.S. president is
authorized to destroy without warning or negotiation—any
attempt by Tehran to build a bomb."[10]

Neither Netanyahu nor Obama were happy with my position on the deal. Netanyahu thought I wasn't being tough enough, while Obama thought I was being too tough.

My opposition caused Obama and his national security team to become angry with me. Prior to this, he had invited me to several White House events, including his annual Chanukah celebration. On the day of one such celebration, I was in the Oval Office with Obama when my cell phone rang. The president gave me a look as if to say, you should leave your phone outside when you're in the Oval. I told him I was expecting a call from my grandson telling me whether he had gotten into Harvard. The president told me to take it. Lyle did get in, and the president and vice president sent their congratulations to him, with Biden adding, "But he should go to the University of Delaware. It's a better school."

President Obama also invited my wife and me to the small state dinner at which he bestowed the Medal of Freedom on our old friend Shimon Peres. Other guests included Vice President Biden, Secretary of State Clinton and her husband, Senator John Kerry, Elie and Marion Wiesel. Itzhak Perlman entertained us with beautiful violin music.

Shimon, who always called me "professor Chutzpah," was then close to 90 years old. He spoke of his wish to see peace with the Palestinians during his lifetime. Obama, in a jovial mood, pointed to Shimon's son-in-law, who was also his doctor, and said, "Shimon you are free to go back to Israel when this dinner is over, but your doctor stays here in the White House to take care of me. I want to have your energy and determination when I turn 90."

The only speeches were by the two presidents. The rest of the evening consisted of table-hopping among old friends, exchanging stories, proposals for peace and gossip. The Iran situation figured in virtually every discussion. No one seemed thrilled with it, but most supported it, perhaps out of loyalty to the president. There was considerable goodwill between Shimon Peres's Israel and Barack Obama's America. But Peres's Israel was not Bibi Netanyahu's, and this was the last time during the Obama administration that such goodwill toward Israel would be seen.

President Obama also sent me a very friendly handwritten note on my 75th birthday, wishing me "many more years of adocacy, mischief and great fun!" and ending with his "warm regards."

But following my "advocacy" against his deal—which he perhaps regarded as a bit too much "mischief"—he showed his anger in petty ways, such as disinviting me from the annual Chanukah party. (In contrast, President George W. Bush invited me, despite my strong opposition to his candidacy and to the Iraq war, not to mention my role as one of Vice President Gore's lawyers in *Bush v. Gore*.) Obama also disinvited other Jewish leaders who had opposed the deal.

I didn't care about the childish revenge Obama took against me and other Americans, but I cared deeply about the game-changing revenge he took against Prime Minister Netanyahu and the nation-state of the Jewish people.

In the weeks before the end of his presidency, Barack Obama engineered a Security Council resolution that perniciously changed the status of Jewish Jerusalem. The resolution declared, in effect, that the Western Wall (Judaism's holiest site), the Jewish quarter (in which Jews had lived for thousands of years) and the access roads to Hebrew University (built before Israel became a state and open to all residents of Israel and the West Bank) were illegally occupied by Israel and a "flagrant violation under international law."

This historic and legally flawed conclusion was never before supported by the United States. It was opposed by Congress, the American people and even many within the Obama administration. But

Obama was determined to wreak revenge as he was leaving office on Prime Minister Netanyahu for daring to challenge him on the Iran Deal. Not only did Obama order his representative to the United Nations—Samantha Power, also my former student—not to veto the resolution (which Power was apparently prepared to do), he actually worked behind the scenes to encourage its passage, even when several Security Council members tried to postpone or withdraw it. Although the United States didn't vote for the resolution—it cast a meaningless absention—it pressured several countries that had doubt to vote for it.

I wrote a scathing attack on Obama for changing long-standing American policy in order to exact revenge on Netanyahu and tie the hands of his successors. I urged the next president to immediately and officially recognize Jerusalem as Israel's capital and move its embassy there, arguing that such a move would "dramatically demonstrate that the United States does not accept the Judenrein effects of this bigoted resolution on historic Jewish areas of Jerusalem which are now forbidden to Jews."[11]

My public denunciation of Obama's role in enacting the Security Council resolution was the last straw for both of us. It cooled my long-standing friendship with him. He had broken his promise to me and to the American public. Yes, he did have "Israel's back"—but he painted a target on it and fired a weapon at it as he was leaving office.

It's impossible to know for sure whether Obama's parting shot was directed only against Netanyahu personally or whether it reflected a deeper antagonism against Israel that Obama had kept under the surface until his final weeks in office. I don't know which is worse.

It would be up to the next president to try to undo the damage Obama had peevishly inflicted on Israel and its prime minister.

14

Trump and Netanyahu Agree on Iran and Jerusalem

IN THE 2016 election, I strongly supported Hillary Clinton, who I had known for many years, over Donald Trump, who I had met briefly several times. As a liberal Democrat, I favored Clinton's domestic policies on choice, gay marriage, gun control, environmental policies, taxation and other issues. Because of my family history with regard to immigration—especially my grandfather's role in saving relatives from the Holocaust—I was strongly opposed to Trump's campaign promise to build a wall on the Mexican border. I trusted Clinton on foreign policy, despite the fact that she had served as secretary of state to a president with whom I largely disagreed on foreign policy decisions. I had discussed Iran and Syria with her and was satisfied that her approach would be somewhat different from Obama's.

I was not surprised by Trump's election, having written several months before—when Clinton was ahead in the polls by double digits—that Trump might win, for reasons similar to why Brexit had won and why so many hyper-nationalists and populists were doing well in European elections. I thought that Trump understood this trend, and how it applied to the United States, more clearly than Clinton did.

Not long after his victory, President Trump approached me while I was having dinner with some mutual friends at his Palm Beach hotel. He said that he knew I was a friend of Bibi Netanyahu's and that he wanted to discuss the Israeli–Palestinian issue with me. We had a serious talk that was followed by an invitation to the White House to continue the conversation with Jared Kushner, his son-in-law and senior advisor, and Jason Greenblatt, who was a key player in devising a strategy and plan for reducing the Israeli–Palestinian conflict.

Among the issues we discussed were Trump's campaign promise to recognize Jerusalem as Israel's capital and to move the U.S. embassy there as soon as he was sworn in. I favored the move, but I originally thought it would be better to finalize it as part of a peace deal in coordination with America's other Middle East allies. But after Obama's insidious resolution, I publicly urged the incoming president to restore the status quo by recognizing Jerusalem as Israel's capital immediately. I wrote articles to this effect and spoke to President Trump about it personally.

The Security Council resolution, which declared that "any changes to the 4 June 1967 lines, including with regard to Jerusalem," have "no legal validity," meant, among other things, that Israel's decision to build a plaza for prayer at the Western Wall constituted, in the words of the text, a "flagrant violation of international law." This resolution was, therefore, not limited to settlements in the West Bank, as the Obama administration later claimed. It applied equally to the very heart of Israel.

Before June 4, 1967, Jews were forbidden from praying at the Western Wall, Judaism's holiest site. They were forbidden to attend classes at the Hebrew University at Mt. Scopus, which had been opened in 1925; they could not seek medical care at the Hadassah Hospital on Mt. Scopus, which had treated Jews and Arabs alike for many years; and they could not live in the Jewish Quarter of Jerusalem, where their forbearers had built homes and synagogues for thousands of years.

These judenrein (no Jews allowed) prohibitions were enacted by Jordan, which had captured these Jewish areas during Israel's War of Independence in 1948 and had illegally occupied the entire West Bank, an area that the United Nations had set aside for an Arab state.

When the Jordanian government occupied these historic Jewish sites, they destroyed all the remnants of Judaism, including synagogues, schools and cemeteries, whose headstones they used for urinals. Between 1948 and 1967, the United Nations did not offer a single resolution condemning this Jordanian occupation and cultural devastation of historically Jewish Jerusalem.

When Israel retook these areas in a defensive war against Jordan—which Jordan had started by shelling civilian homes in West Jerusalem—and opened them up as places where Jews could pray, study, receive medical treatment and live, the United States took the official position that it would not recognize Israel's legitimate claims to any part of Jerusalem, even Jewish West Jerusalem, which had been part of Israel since it came into existence as a state and which housed its parliament, Supreme Court, prime minister's residence and president's house. It stated that the status of Jerusalem, including the newly liberated Jewish areas, would be left open to final negotiations and that the status quo would remain in place. That is the official rationale for why the United States refused to recognize any part of Jerusalem, including West Jerusalem, as part of Israel. That is why the United States refused to allow an American citizen born in any part of Jerusalem to put the words "Jerusalem, Israel" on his or her passport as their place of birth.

But even that ahistoric status quo was changed with President Obama's unjustified decision not to veto the Security Council resolution. At the time, it was not known that Obama was discreetly pushing for the passage of the resolution, so it was expected that it would be vetoed, as the U.S. has vetoed all prior Security Council resolutions that were one-sidedly anti-Israel. The United Nations all of a sudden determined that, subject to any further negotiations and agreements, the Jewish areas of Jerusalem recaptured from Jordan in 1967 are not part of Israel. Instead, they were territories being illegally occupied by Israel, and any building in these areas—including places for prayer at the Western Wall, access roads to Mt. Scopus, and synagogues in the historic Jewish Quarter—constitute "a flagrant violation under international law." If that indeed was the new status quo, then what incentives would the Palestinians have to enter negotiations? And if they were to do so, they could use these Jewish areas to extort unreasonable concessions from Israel, for which these now "illegally occupied" areas were sacred and non-negotiable.

President Obama's refusal to veto this one-sided resolution was a deliberate ploy to tie the hands of his successors, the consequence of which was to make it far more difficult for his successors to encourage the Palestinians to accept Israel's offer to negotiate with no preconditions. No future president can undo this pernicious agreement, since a veto not cast can never be retroactively cast. And a resolution once enacted cannot be rescinded unless there is a majority vote against it, with no veto by any of its permanent members, which include Russia and China, who would be sure to veto any attempt to undo this resolution.

The prior refusal of the United States to recognize Jerusalem as Israel's capital was based on the notion that nothing should be done to change the status quo of that city, holy to three religions. But the Security Council resolution did exactly that by declaring Israel's de facto presence on these Jewish holy sites to be a "flagrant violation under international law" that "the U.N. will not recognize."

Since virtually everyone in the international community acknowledges that any reasonable peace would recognize Israel's legitimate claims to these and other areas in Jerusalem, there was no reason to make criminals out of every Jew or Israeli who sets foot on these historically Jewish areas. (Ironically, President Obama prayed at the "illegally occupied" Western Wall.) I urged President Trump to recognize Jerusalem as Israel's capitol because such a decision would help to restore the appropriate balance. It would demonstrate that the United States does not accept the judenrein effects of this bigoted resolution. I told him it would be right to untie his own hands and undo the damage wrought by his predecessor.

Some have argued that the United States should not recognize Jerusalem because it will stimulate violence by Arab terrorists. No

American decision should ever be influenced by the threat of violence. Terrorists should not have a veto over American policy. If the United States were to give in to the threat of violence, it would only incentivize others to threaten violence in response to any peace plan.

It is true that on the day the United States moved its embassy to Jerusalem, Hamas engineered massive protests at the Gaza fence, including efforts by terrorists to cross into Israel to kill and kidnap Israeli civilians. I had been near the fence just days earlier, and I was in Jerusalem itself on the day of the move. It was clear that these preplanned actions by Hamas were not in response to the U.S. decision to move the embassy to Jerusalem, since Hamas did not recognize Tel Aviv as part of Israel. The embassy move provided a convenient excuse for Hamas to do what it was already planning to do.

Trump did the right thing by undoing the wrong that Obama had done at the end of his presidency. Yet many left-wing Democrats—even some who had opposed President Obama's decision to push the anti-Israel resolution through the Security Council and who had urged Obama to move the embassy to Jerusalem—thoughtlessly condemned the move without providing coherent arguments. For them, it was enough that it was President Trump who ordered the relocation of the embassy. If the same action had been taken by a President Hillary Clinton, or even by a President Mitt Romney, it would have been greeted with joy and approval. But because it was taken by President Trump, it was viewed by most Democrats, including many Jewish supporters of Israel, as the reckless act of an impulsive man who was blind to the nuances of Middle East diplomacy.

Toward the end of 2017, I was invited by the emir of Qatar to meet with him in Doha, to discuss among other things improving relations with Israel. Having read that Qatar funds terrorist organizations such as Hamas and the Muslim Brotherhood, I was skeptical, but I decided to research the issues surrounding the relationship between Qatar and these extremist groups. As I read more widely on the subject and spoke to experts in the United States and Israel, as well as to government officials in both countries, more nuances and complexities began to emerge.

There was a growing conflict between Qatar on the one hand and Saudi Arabia and the United Arab Emirates (UAE) on the other. This conflict eventuated in an embargo against Qatar by those two countries. The embargo included a blockade of Qatar's flights and shipping, as well as a denial of food shipments and trade between the countries, thus preventing family members who lived in Qatar from attending weddings, funerals and other family events.

My research revealed conflicting factual claims by each side, particularly relating to the funding of terrorism and commercial dealings with Iran. There were also conflicting claims with regard to government-funded television, such as Al Jazeera, Al Arabiya and other media. I had no way of resolving these conflicting claims without hearing all sides of the issues and seeing for myself. I decided, therefore, to accept the emir's invitation. I would ask hard questions and subject all answers to independent confirmation.

I had another reason for making the trip to Doha. Whenever people wanted to boycott Israel, I would urge them to go to Israel, see what is going on, and decide for themselves. I resolved to apply the same criteria to myself: go to Qatar and then make up my mind.

The issue of Al Jazeera and other government-funded media presented a particularly complex issue for me, as a lifelong defender of freedom of the press. Al Jazeera is a government-controlled medium (as are all media in the Middle East other than in Israel) based in Qatar that publishes both in Arabic and English. The English version tends to be somewhat balanced, but the Arabic version tends to be rabidly anti-Israel. The Saudis and Emirates were demanding that Qatar "shut down" Al Jazeera, especially following its support for the Arab Spring in 2010. I could not support such a demand, though I strongly disagreed with much of what was broadcast on Al Jazeera, as well as on Saudi-funded Al Arabiya.

My meeting with the emir was cordial. I asked him to press Hamas to return the bodies of Israeli soldiers who had been killed in Gaza. He said he would try. We discussed many other issues regarding Israel, with inconclusive results.

In May 2018, I agreed to deliver a lecture on the issue of government-sponsored media at the Northwestern University campus in Doha. Several American universities have well-funded campuses in Qatar, taught largely by American professors and attended largely by Arab students. I knew I would confront a hostile audience mainly composed of Qatari undergraduates raised on anti-Israel propaganda. Although my talk was not about Israel—it was about relations between the media, law and government in both democracies and theocracies—students shouted "Zionist go home," "No Zionists in Qatar," as they unfurled a Palestinian flag, marched in front of me and conducted a walkout. The professor who had introduced me whispered, "Tell them you're not a Zionist and that you support a Palestinian State." I stood up and said. "I'm a proud Zionist, and I support two states for two people." I invited the protestors to stay and ask me hard questions about the Israeli–Palestinian issue, but they left and I gave my talk—discussing the complexity of governmental relationships with critical, often hostile, media—to the remaining students and faculty. The questions were respectful and thoughtful.

I believe strongly in dialogue and engagement even with one's enemies, and certainly with leaders who seem willing to listen to constructive ideas and perhaps to change their ways. I wondered why the opposition to my visits by some American Jews had become so strident, emotional and personal. I learned that some of my critics had financial and other ties to the Saudis and Emirates, and that one of them had begged to be invited to travel to Qatar to meet the emir but had been turned down. Whatever the reasons, there was no cause to question my motives, or those of the supporters of Israel who were seeking dialogue with Qatar. As I write these words, the U.S. government is seeking the support of its peace plan from all the Gulf countries. It is a work in progress.

In April 2018, I was invited to spend two days in the White House consulting and advising on the proposed peace plan. My prearranged visit took place—by complete coincidence—on the day that Special Counsel Robert Mueller and federal prosecutors from New York conducted a search and seizure on the offices of President Trump's personal lawyer Michael Cohen. This led to speculation by the media and others that the Israel issue was a "cover" for a secret meeting for me to give Trump legal advice. As Professor Richard Painter, a Minnesota Democrat who was running for nomination as senator on an impeach-Trump platform, put it in a tweet, "Complete B.S. Alan Dersh does not know anything about the Middle-East. This [meeting] was probably about DOJ's criminal investigation and perhaps firing Robert Mueller." I tweeted in reply that I had written numerous books about the Israel–Palestine conflict and that Trump was the fourth president I had advised on the Middle East. But paranoid and uninformed tweeters and commentators like Painter persisted in their ignorant conspiracy theories.

During my two days at the White House, I proposed ideas regarding the refugee issue, the settlements, Jerusalem and how to get the Sunni Arabs to agree to a plan. I also provided insights into the political realities in Israel, based on my knowledge of the players. I told them about a dinner I recently attended in Washington at the home of a prominent Jewish leader with Palestinian president Mahmoud Abbas and his chief negotiator, Saeb Erekat. I had met them both on several previous occasions and had persuaded Abbas to sign in agreement an op-ed I had written proposing a basis for renewing negotiations. I brought the signed op-ed to Netanyahu in the hope that both sides could agree to sit down and talk. I also gave both Abbas and Netanyahu copies of my old friend Larry David's "Palestinian Chicken" episode from *Curb Your Enthusiasm*, suggesting they watch it together. They both laughed, but no negotiations began.

During the Washington dinner, Abbas asked me to "call [my] friend Bibi and tell him to declare once and for all that he unequivocally accepts the two-state solution." I told him that I had already heard Bibi make such a declaration at Bar-Ilan University. He replied, "But he seems to be backing away." I told him I would make the call if he, Abbas, would declare that he recognizes Israel as "the nation-state of the Jewish people." He said he could never recognize Israel as "a Jewish state," because that would deny the right of return to the Palestinian diaspora and deny equal rights to Israeli Arabs. I told him that by not recognizing the nation-state of the Jewish people while demanding a Palestinian state, he was rejecting the UN partition plan that called for two states for two people. He smiled and said, "It is what it is." I asked him if he could accept Israel as "the nation-state of the Jewish people," rather than as a "Jewish state." He said that might be easier to swallow, but he was not ready to do that either. "Would you ever be willing to do that as part of a negotiated peace?" I asked. "Anything is possible," he said, receiving a dirty look from Erekat, who is believed to be less willing to compromise than his boss is.

My two days in the White House were informative and constructive. I spent hours with Jared Kushner, Jason Greenblatt and several staff people tossing ideas back and forth. They knew that my relationships with Israeli leaders, especially Prime Minister Netanyahu, went back many decades, and they appreciated my insights into their personalities, ideologies and political realities. We all understood that coming up with a plan that was acceptable to both sides—and to the other Sunni Arab countries—is a daunting, some say impossible, task. I will never give up or stop trying to help as an advisor and in other ways, regardless of who is president.

After my first day of work on the plan, the president invited me to have dinner with him and three other people in the White House residence. Trump then invited me to accompany him to the Lincoln Bedroom, where he showed me the original version of the Gettysburg Address. He sat down on Lincoln's bed and asked me to join him. We discussed Lincoln, the Middle East and some mutual friends.

The dinner with the president was private and was supposed to remain confidential to avoid speculation about whether he was asking me to become his lawyer. But it was leaked to Maggie Haberman of the *New York Times*. I don't know who leaked it—some speculated that it was President Trump himself—but my phone log was quickly filled with media calls inquiring whether I had been asked to be his lawyer. Without answering that question—which would be inappropriate—I issued a statement saying that I wanted to maintain my independence and ability to comment, objectively and in a nonpartisan way, on the civil liberties issues being raised by the Mueller investigation.

It was, and is, important to me that people understand that I am not a Trump "supporter." I supported, contributed money to, campaigned for and voted for Hillary Clinton. As a liberal Democrat, I oppose many of Trump's policies, including his approach to immigration, gay and transgender rights, choice regarding abortion, taxation, medical care, gun control, separation of church and state and judicial appointments. I have spoken out against these policies loudly and clearly. I have been particularly critical of his immigration policies, especially his zero-tolerance policy that separated children from parents.[1] But I will not allow my disagreements with President Trump to silence my criticisms of the Mueller investigation and of efforts to criminalize the president's exercise of his constitutional authority. I have already written three books on this issue, and I appear regularly on TV and write op-eds discussing similar legal issues, as I would if Hillary Clinton had been elected and Republican partisans were trying to impeach her and "lock her up" for noncriminal acts. The publisher of my book *The Case Against Impeaching Trump* produced two alternate covers: one with "The Case Against Impeaching Clinton" written on it, which I would have written if Hillary had been elected, and a plain brown wrapper cover for *The Case Against Impeaching Trump* that people on Martha's Vineyard could read without being shunned for their purported Trump support.

My predictions regarding the Mueller Report have proved to be largely accurate: I predicted that the contents of the report would be "devastating" politically, but exculpatory legally, and that President Trump would not be impeached and removed because the evidence would not establish any impeachable "high crimes and misdemeanors," as required by the Constitution. The predictions of many pundits who I debated on CNN, MSNBC, ABC and Fox have proved, on the other hand, to be inaccurate. This is not because I am any smarter than they are; it is because I do not substitute wishful thinking for objective legal analysis.

As I did with President Bill Clinton, I serve as an informal conduit between Trump and the prime minister of Israel, and I have conveyed several messages back and forth on a confidential basis.

Will President Trump be good or bad for Israel? Only time will tell. His decision to move the U.S. embassy to Jerusalem was popular among most Israelis and was only minimally criticized by most Sunni countries. The Palestinians were furious. His subsequent decision to recognize Israel's sovereignty over the Golan Heights, which Israel formally annexed in 1981, was also quite popular with Israelis and produced little reaction from neighboring Arab states. Trump's general support for the nation-state of the Jewish people, and the individuals he has put in positions of responsibility relating to the Middle East, bode far better for Israel and for peace than those of his predecessor.

Will the Israeli government be able to accept a peace plan proposed by President Trump? That, too, is uncertain. Netanyahu faces a criminal proceeding that has made his political survival more dependent on coalition members to his far right, who might well oppose a two-state solution that requires giving up land and ending the building of new settlements. I am confident that Bibi himself, if he remained prime minister, would support a two-state solution that did not compromise Israel's security and that allowed the major settlement blocks to become part of Israel in exchange for an equivalent amount of Israeli land being ceded to a Palestinian state.

I speak to Bibi regularly, and I have written critically of the investigation and the proposed prosecution against him, which focus on gifts he received from friends and questionable deals with the media he allegedly discussed.[2] My fear is that if President Trump comes up with a peace plan that Bibi likes but his coalition partners do not, it may be impossible for him to accept it without risking his political position. If he were to lose an election, his replacement might well be to his right, thus making peace more difficult. Were Israel to reject a Trump peace plan, Trump would not take that lightly. Trump does not readily accept rejection of his ideas, especially because he believes Israel "owes" him as a result of the embassy and Golan decisions. That is why I have privately urged Netanyahu's most important right-wing coalition partners to put statesmanship before politics and accept a peace plan that may require "painful compromises," as Bibi has put it, so long as they do not weaken Israel's security.

In May of 2019, I met alone with Prime Minister Netanyahu in his home for more than two hours. We discussed, as we always do, a range of issues relating to U.S.–Israeli relations, including the peace plan. I came away from the meeting encouraged. But shortly thereafter, he failed to form a government and a new election was scheduled. Then, at the end of June, Jared Kushner unveiled the economic portion of the peace plan, which the Palestinians immediately rejected, despite the enormous benefits it would provide to the Palestinian people. They have refused even to negotiate or offer suggestions to improve the plan.

The Trump plan undoubtedly contains elements that bolster Israel's security, while at the same time increasing Palestinian autonomy and economic viability. It is a good plan that should be accepted by Israel, the Palestinian Authority, the Sunni Arab states and the international community. No one ever lost money betting against peace between the Israelis and their neighbors, largely because the Palestinian leadership has never "missed an opportunity to miss an opportunity." But if they forego this one, as they did in 1948, 2001 and 2008, they will have no one except themselves to blame for the lack of progress toward a resolution of the conflict.

The New Anti-Semitism

Taking the Fight to Campus and Congress

THERE IS NOTHING really new about the "new" anti-Semitism. It is the old wine of Jew-hatred bottled under a new label of anti-Zionism and "intersectionality."

There have been several distinct but sometimes overlapping types of anti-Semitism over time.

The first is traditional right-wing fascist Jew hatred that has traditionally included theological, racial, economic, social, personal and cultural aspects. This type has decreased since the end of World War II, but it rears its ugly and violent head from time to time, as it recently did in Pittsburgh, Charlottesville and near San Diego. We are seeing a resurgence of this today in Greece, Hungary, Austria, Poland and other European countries with rising right-wing parties, some of which are anti-Muslim in addition to anti-Jewish.

The second is Muslim anti-Semitism. Just as not all European nationalists are anti-Semitic, not all Muslims suffer from this malady either. But far too many do. It is wrong to assume that only Muslims who manifest Jew hatred through violence harbor anti-Semitic views. Recent polls show an extraordinarily high incidence of anti-Semitism—hatred of Jews as individuals, as a group and as a religion—throughout North Africa, the Middle East and Muslim areas in Europe.[1] This hatred manifests itself not only in words but often in deeds, such as taunting Jews who wear kippot, vandalizing

Jewish institutions and directing occasional violence at individual Jews. Among a small number of extremists, it also results in the kind of deadly violence we have seen in Paris, Brussels and other parts of Europe. Several decades ago, it manifested itself in attacks on synagogues by Palestinian terrorists, some of whom were operating on behalf of the Palestine Liberation Organization.

Third, there is hard-left anti-Semitism. Although this goes back in time to Voltaire, Marx, Stalin and others, the new anti-Semitism is different in that it often disguises itself as anti-Zionism. This bigotry is seen in the double standard imposed on everything Jewish, especially the nation-state of the Jewish people. It is also reflected in blaming "Jewish power" and the "pushiness" of Jews in demanding support for Israel.

The ultimate form of this pathology is the absurd comparison made by some extreme leftists between the extermination policies of the Nazis and Israel's efforts to defend itself against terrorist rockets, tunnels, suicide bombers and other threats to its civilians. Comparing Israel's actions to those of the Nazis is a not-so-subtle version of Holocaust denial. Because if what the Nazis really did was what Israel is now doing, there could not have been a Holocaust or an attempt at genocide against the Jewish people. A variation on this perverse theme is apartheid denial: by accusing Israel—which accords equal rights to all its citizens—of apartheid, these haters deny the horrors of actual apartheid, which was so much more terrible than anything Israel has ever done.

Fourth, and most dangerous, is eliminationist anti-Zionism and anti-Semitism of the kind advocated by the leaders of Iran, Hezbollah, Hamas and the Islamic State. Listen to Hezbollah leader Hassan Nasrallah: "If [the Jews] all gather in Israel, it will save us the trouble of going after them worldwide," or, "If we search the entire world for a person more cowardly, despicable, weak and feeble in psyche, mind, ideology and religion, we would not find anyone like the Jew. Notice I didn't say the Israeli."

These variations on the theme of anti-Semitism have several elements in common. First, those who subscribe to them tend to engage in some form of Holocaust denial, minimization, glorification or comparative victimization. Second, they exaggerate Jewish power, money and influence. Third, they seek the delegitimization and demonization of Israel as the nation-state of the Jewish people. Fourth, they impose a double standard on all things Jewish. Finally, they nearly all deny that they are anti-Semites who hate all Jews. They claim that their hatred is directed against Israel and Jews who support the nation-state of the Jewish people.

This common core of the "new" anti-Semitism—we love the Jews, it's only their nation-state that we hate—is pervasive among many European political, media, cultural and academic leaders. Polls among Germans showed that a significant number of the children, grandchildren and great-grandchildren of Nazi supporters didn't want to hear about Nazi atrocities, but they believed what Israel was doing to the Palestinians was comparable to what the Nazis had done to the Jews.

This then is the European problem of anti-Semitism that many European leaders are unwilling to confront, because they have a built-in excuse! It's Israel's fault—if only Israel would do the right thing with regard to the Palestinians, the problem would be solved.

Tragically, it won't be solved, because the reality is that hatred of Israel is not the cause of anti-Semitism. Rather, it is the reverse: anti-Semitism is a primary cause of hatred for the nation-state of the Jewish people.

The university campus has become an important battlefield for the new anti-Semitism, as well as a platform for efforts to end bipartisan support for Israel. Current students are future leaders. This is already becoming evident by the election to Congress of several young leftists who want to end the long-standing bipartisan support for Israel.

Just as classic anti-Semitism has gone through different historical phases, so too have the continuing efforts to destroy the nation-state of the Jewish people. The initial phase—from 1948 to

1973—manifested itself through military attacks from Arab armies, especially Egypt, Syria and Jordan. Although this effort came close to succeeding in the Yom Kippur War, it ultimately failed, and its failure was reflected in peace treaties with Egypt and Jordan as well as an informal cold peace with Syria. The second phase—which began even before Israel's Declaration of Independence and continues to some degree even today—is the attempt to destroy or at least weaken Israel through persistent terrorism. The height of this campaign began with the first intifada, started in 1987, in which approximately 150 Israelis, mostly civilians, and 1,000 Palestinians, including many civilians, were killed.[2] It ended with the termination of the second intifada between 2000 and 2005, in which more than 1,000 Israelis, mostly civilians, and more than 3,000 Palestinians, including many civilians, were killed.

The deaths and injuries alone do not tell the whole story of these terrorist campaigns. They changed life both in Israel and in the Palestinian areas. The second intifada ended shortly after Arafat's death. No coincidence. Although terrorism persists, it has been reduced considerably by the security barriers—mostly high-tech electronic fences—that Israel has erected along its borders. Current terrorism emanates primarily from Gaza in the form of rockets, incendiary kites, terror tunnels and other cross-border attacks, which Israel has managed to control through technological superiority, with its Iron Dome defense, anti-tunnel technology and drones.

The third phase in Palestinian efforts to destroy, or at least delegitimize, Israel is much more subtle and difficult to counter by traditional defense tactics. It is directed at the future leaders of the United States and Western Europe, who are now university students. It has taken the form of campaigns to boycott, divest and sanction (BDS) Israel and *only* Israel, to have the international community treat Israel as an apartheid pariah state in the way South Africa was treated, to turn students and faculty against the nation-state of the Jewish people and, most disturbingly, to end the American tradition of bipartisan support for Israel and to turn the Democratic Party into the kind of anti-Israel party that the Labour Party has become in Great Britain.

When I taught first-year criminal law students on their first day at Harvard Law School, they would look at each other and see 150 frightened young women and men anxious about being subjected to the rigorous questioning of the Socratic Method. I would see something different: a future president of the United States; a future editor of the *New York Times*; a future chief justice; a future managing partner of Goldman Sachs; a future king of Saudi Arabia; a future secretary general of the United Nations.

Those are the kinds of future leaders that Harvard and other elite universities teach. And many of those future leaders are being "taught"—propagandized—by hard-left professors who express their extreme anti-Israel views as "truths," both in the classroom and outside of it.

Anti-Israel advocacy among hard-left professors has been common since the mid-1970s, following the break in relations between the Soviet Union and Israel as well as Berrigan's anti-Zionist and anti-Semitic screed. Until recently, this one-sidedly anti-Israel position was limited to a relatively small number of radical students and a larger number of vocal radical professors, who were still a minority in most faculties. But during the last several years, this phenomenon has spread to mainstream students and faculty—not all, but many—through what is called "intersectionality."

Intersectionality is a radical academic construct that argues that all forms of oppression are inexorably linked—capitalism, colonialism, imperialism, racism, anti-Islamism, heterosexualism and, of course, Zionism—and that the oppressors of all victimized groups are essentially the same. This pseudo-academic "theory," which has no empirical or scientific basis, resonates on campuses where "identity politics" have often replaced individual merit. Indeed, the very concept of "meritocracy" has become a "politically incorrect" equivalent of all the above "isms." The villains of identity politics are the "privileged classes," which include white, heterosexual, male students and faculty. The most targeted privileged group on many campuses are Jewish students, especially those who support Israel and who are "accused" of Zionism.

In 2017, at the University of Illinois, flyers were plastered around campus calling for the "end of Jewish privilege." The flyer stated in bold letters that "ending white privilege starts with ending Jewish privilege." The posters had outlines of silhouettes with Stars of David printed on their chests and an arrow pointing to them with the accompanying caption: "the 1%." Although some of the posters identified Black Lives Matter as sponsors, it isn't clear whether they were distributed by extreme right-wing groups using hard-left anti-Semitic tropes or by hard-left anti-Semites. In some respects, it doesn't really matter because many on the hard right and hard left share a disdain for Jews, their nation-state and so called "Jewish privilege." Klansman David Duke, Nation of Islam leader Louis Farrakhan, the former Republican presidential candidate Pat Buchanan, the co-chairwoman of the Women's March, Linda Sarsour, and the darling of the progressive wing of the Democratic Party, Congresswoman Ilhan Omar, have much in common when it comes to Zionism, anti-Zionism and anti-Semitism. That is why Duke has praised Omar, a Muslim woman, despite his long history of anti-Muslim bigotry.

At Hunter College, it was clear who was condemning "the Zionist Administration" for raising tuition and other evils. It was also clear that "Zionist" was a euphemism—a politically correct cover—for "Jew," since the president of Hunter was Jewish. I don't know whether she was a Zionist, and it doesn't really matter, since raising tuition at Hunter was not part of any Zionist plot. That anti-Semitic statement was signed by students for Justice in Palestine in 10 New York City colleges—all with substantial Jewish enrollment. The bigoted statement was intended to link the "victims" of a tuition rise in New York with the "victim" of "oppressions" in Gaza.[3] Quite a stretch, unless you believe that "Zionists" are behind all the evils in the world, as Professor Hamid Dabashi of Columbia tweeted: "Every dirty treacherous ugly and pernicious act happening in the world just wait for a few days and the ugly name of 'Israel' will pup [pop up] . . ."

The same bigoted professor recently compared Israel with ISIS, tweeting that the "murderous thugs" of the jihadist group "conquered parts of Syria and declared a 'caliphate.'" He continued, "Their IS-RAELI counterparts meanwhile conquered parts of Syria and declared it part of their Zionist settler colony . . . The only difference: ISIS does not have a platoon of clean shaven and well coiffured [sic] columnists at the *New York Times* propagating the cause of the terrorist outfit as the Zionists columnists do on a regular basis."[4]

The linking of unrelated "victimizations," despite their tenuous connections, is reflective of a broader trend in hard-left politics, whereby increasingly radical activists demand that the demonization of "Zionism"—often used as a euphemism for Jews—be included, indeed featured, in the package of causes that must be embraced by anyone claiming the label of "progressive." Lumping seemingly disparate groups under the "umbrella of oppression" leads to the forming of alliances between causes that, at best, have nothing to do with each other and, at worst, are averse to one another's stated mission. Their only common feature is that in order to join them, one must demonize the nation-state of the Jewish people and its national liberation movement.

The following are among many examples of radical leftists conflating unrelated grievances: the linking of our government's handling of the Flint water crisis to the "severe" water crisis in Gaza; the shooting of black men by policemen in America to the shooting of terrorists in Gaza; the denial of healthcare to patients with preexisting conditions in America to the terrible conditions in Gaza hospitals caused by Hamas diverting resources from healthcare to rockets and tunnels; the discrimination against LGBTQ people in America to the discrimination against Palestinians on the West Bank.

During a recent interview on PBS, Jonathan Haidt—social psychologist and professor of ethical leadership at New York University's Stern School of Business—said this about the conflation of various left-wing causes under the banner of intersectionality:

> *There is a good kind of identity politics, which is, you know, if black people are being denied rights, let's fight for their rights. But there is a bad kind, which is to train students, train young people to say let's divide everybody up by their race, gender, other categories. We'll assign them moral merit based on their level of privilege. Okay, now let's look at everything through this lens. Palestinians are the victims. So therefore, they are the good and the Jews or the Israelis are the bad. All social problems get reduced to this simple framework.*

The essence of anti-Semitism is the bigoted claim that if there is a problem, then Jews must be its cause. And not just some Jews, but "the Jews" as a collectivity. This presumption of collective action, and collective guilt, always marks the sometimes subtle shift from legitimate criticism of individual actions by Jews to anti-Semitic conspiracy theory. In the Middle Ages, "the Jews" were blamed for the bubonic plague. The Nazis later blamed "the Jews" for Germany's economic collapse after World War I. Today, many hard-left activists explicitly or implicitly blame "the Jews" and "the Zionists" for many of the evils of the world, including climate change.[5] British Labour parliamentarians—and former cabinet member Clare Short—blamed Israel for "undermin[ing] the international community's reaction to global warming" and for causing the "bitter division and violence in the world." She has said that Israel may one day be the cause of the world ending. We Jews have so much power! I'm reminded of the old joke of two Jews in the early 1930s sitting in a Viennese café reading newspapers—one is reading a Yiddish paper, the other a Nazi paper. The first turns to the second and asks, "Why are you reading that Nazi rag?" The second replies, "When I used to read the

Yiddish paper, all I would see was pogroms, Jews starving and other bad news. Now I read in the Nazi paper how Jews are all powerful and control the world. I prefer the good news!"

Jewish students on many campuses are excluded from joining "progressive" groups unless they pass the intersectionality purity test: they must renounce Zionism and support for Israel. Rabbi Susan Talve, a longtime activist on race issues in the St. Louis area, was told that her advocacy for Israel was incompatible with the objectives of Black Lives Matter: "Solidarity from Ferguson to Palestine has become a central tenet of the movement," she was informed, because "Israel and U.S. state oppression are deeply interconnected." Similarly, a student who attended a Black Lives Matter rally at Northwestern University was told, "You support Israel, so you cannot also support us."

Supporters of the LGBTQ community in Israel learned this lesson when BDS activists, together with a local Black Lives Matter chapter, broke up a gay pride event because it featured a presentation by an Israeli group. The protestors claimed that the event organizers had engaged in "pinkwashing" the Israeli occupation by showing solidarity with the Israeli LGBTQ community. Pinkwashing is the claim that Israel, which has one of the best records with regard to LGBTQ issues, only supports the rights of LGBTQ individuals as a cover—a whitewash with a pink hue—for its terrible treatment of Palestinians. Under this absurd theory, whenever Israel does anything good, it must have an evil hidden motive.

Members of the National Women's Studies Association (NWSA) who also support Israel have been similarly excluded. When that organization voted to endorse BDS, one anti-Israel activist explained, "What is significant about this particular resolution is the rationale: one cannot call themselves a feminist . . . without taking a stand on what is happening in Palestine." Apparently, one can call oneself a feminist without taking a stand on Syria, Russia, China, Saudi Arabia, Turkey, Venezuela, Belarus and other nations that grossly violate human rights, including women's rights. According to Linda Sarsour, one can even be a feminist while expressing sexist views—such as calling for Ayaan Hirsi Ali and other female critics of her views to have "their vaginas [taken] away'"—but not while supporting the only country in the Middle East where women have equal rights with men.

Jewish participants at the Chicago "Dyke March"—a parade geared toward that city's lesbian community—were told to leave the parade because their flag, which had a Star of David printed on top of the LGBTQ rainbow flag, "made people feel unsafe." ("Unsafe" is the current weaponized mantra of the hard left.) They were also told that the march was supposed to be "anti-Zionist" and "pro-Palestinian," so Zionists were not welcome.

The International Women's Strike recently published its platform, which singles out Israel from among all the countries in the world for special condemnation. The platform demands the "decolonization" of Palestine and the dismantling of all "walls, from prison walls to border walls, from Mexico to Palestine." No mention was made of the walls that imprison gays in Iran, dissidents in China, feminists in Gaza or Kurds in Turkey. Only the walls erected by the United States and Israel.

Criticizing Israel's settlement and occupation policies is fair game. But singling out Israel for "decolonization" when it has repeatedly offered to end the occupation and to create a Palestinian state on the West Bank and Gaza, and when other countries continue to colonize, can be explained in no other way than its detractors applying a double standard to Jews and their state.

Palestinian-American activist Linda Sarsour, who helped organize the Women's March on Washington in January, responded in *The Nation* to criticism of the anti-Israel plank appearing in a feminist platform:

> *When you talk about feminism you're talking about the rights of all women and their families to live in dignity, peace, and security. It's about giving women access to health care and other basic*

rights. And Israel is a country that continues to occupy territories in Palestine, has people under siege at checkpoints—we have women who have babies on checkpoints because they're not able to get to hospitals [in time]. It just doesn't make any sense for someone to say, "Is there room for people who support the state of Israel and do not criticize it in the movement?" There can't be in feminism. You either stand up for the rights of all women, including Palestinians, or none. There's just no way around it.

Sarsour was responding directly to an op-ed published by Emily Shire in the *New York Times*, in which she asked why women must choose between their Zionism and feminism. The op-ed included the following:

My prime concern is not that people hold this view of Israel. Rather, I find it troubling that embracing such a view is considered an essential part of an event that is supposed to unite feminists. I am happy to debate Middle East politics or listen to critiques of Israeli politics. But why should criticism of Israel be key to feminism?

There is nothing wrong with feminists demanding healthcare for Palestinian women, as long as they also demand healthcare for the women of other countries that deny such care to women. But to single out only women allegedly denied healthcare by the nation-state of the Jewish people—which provides better healthcare to Arabs than any Arab country—is not feminism. It is anti-Semitism.

This type of repressive ideological packaging has left progressive Jews and liberal supporters of Israel in an increasingly uncomfortable position. On the one hand, they care deeply about causes such as women's rights, criminal justice reform, income inequality, environmental protection and LGBTQ rights. On the other, they find themselves excluded from the groups that advance those very causes, because, as Jewish progressives, while they are often critical of specific Israeli policies regarding settlements and the occupation, they refuse to renounce Zionism as a national liberation movement of the Jewish people.

For hard-left activists, this sort of nuanced position is impossible to accept. Their hostility toward Israel does not stem from any particular Israeli actions or policies. Even if Israel were to withdraw from the West Bank, destroy the security barrier and recognize Hamas as a legitimate political organization, it would still not be enough. For those radicals, it is not what Israel *does*; it is about what Israel *is*: the nation-state of the Jewish people, or, to use hard-left terminology, an imperialistic apartheid and genocidal colonialist enterprise. The Black Lives Matter policy platform offers a perfect example of such extreme rhetoric: it states that U.S. military and economic support for Israel makes American citizens complicit in "the genocide taking place against the Palestinian people." I have supported the *concept* of black lives mattering as much as white lives, but I cannot and will not support an *organization* that maliciously has accused Israel of genocide for defending its citizens from terrorism and military attacks. Regardless of how much good BLM may do to reduce police misconduct against African Americans, there must be zero tolerance for the kind of anti-Semitism reflected in their platform. Black lives do matter, but so do Jewish lives.

Intersectionality—which was prominently featured in posters at the 2016 Democratic Convention—has been particularly pronounced on college campuses, where a host of academic groups have passed resolutions in favor of BDS. Many of these organizations have also endorsed the Palestinian Campaign for the Academic and Cultural Boycott of Israel (PACBI), which encourages participants to engage in McCarthyist blacklisting of Israeli academic institutions and to oppose all "normalization" activities, which seek to bring Israelis and Palestinians together in seeking peace.

Intersectionality groups—representing women, African Americans, LGBTQ and other disenfranchised people—are gaining influence on campuses throughout the world. Students want to be aligned with "progressive" causes, and they are being told—falsely—that they cannot be true progressives unless they renounce Israel and Zionism. That is why, in recent years, I have felt a special obligation as a *liberal* supporter of the nation-state of the Jewish people and of its national liberation movement to speak in defense of Israel and Zionism on university campuses around both the country and the world.

Accordingly, I have accepted invitations to speak at Yale, Princeton, Columbia, Penn, Johns Hopkins, Colgate, Barnard, Ohio State, the University of Michigan, Michigan State, the University of Florida, the University of Miami, Fordham, the University of Massachusetts, MIT, Boston University, Northeastern, Emory, the College of Charleston, New York University, Cardozo Law School, Brooklyn College, Hunter College, Oxford University, Syracuse University, Hofstra, Liberty, Elon, Pepperdine, Yeshiva, Georgetown, George Washington, Brandeis, Franklin and Marshall, Nova, Hampshire, Duquesne, Gratz, Lafayette, Boston College, Baruch, the University of London, Lyden University, the Technion, Tel Aviv University, Northwestern University, Stanford, Berkeley, UCLA, the University of California at Irvine, McGill University, the University of Toronto, the University of Cape Town, Charles University in Prague, Beijing University and, of course, Harvard. I have also spoken at several high schools and prep schools, including in South Africa and Australia.

Whenever I receive an invitation to speak at a university, I ask the sponsors why they don't invite one of their own professors to make the case for Israel. Often they tell me that there is not a single professor on their campus willing to risk the wrath of anti-Israel colleagues and students. They worry that their evaluations will suffer or that other negative consequences will ensue. Some are prepared to support Israel privately, but not publicly. Courage is not an attribute of most professors, at least when it comes to taking on the powerful anti-Israel forces at many universities. There are some exceptions, but they are all too rare.

Despite the fact that I make the liberal case for a two-state solution and the end of Israeli settlement, I am almost always the object of protests, walkouts and efforts to silence me. On occasion, armed guards are needed to protect me from physical threats.

There have only been two successful efforts by universities to ban or silence me. The first was by the University of Cape Town in South Africa in 2011. Years earlier, I was banned by apartheid South Africa from delivering an anti-apartheid talk at the University of Witwatersrand (WITS) in Johannesburg. The South African consul general would not grant me a visa unless I showed them my speech in advance. I refused. They refused. And I never gave the speech.

In 2011, the University of Cape Town invited me to give a talk. When I arrived, I was greeted by the following headline in the *Cape Times*: "Dershowitz is not welcome here: Harvard Professor Campaigned against Desmond Tutu." The article was in the form of an open letter signed by left-wing anti-Israel academics, lawyers, judges and others, several of whom were Jewish. Its subheadline was accurate: I had written critically of Bishop Tutu for his virulent anti-Zionism, which had morphed into anti-Semitism.

During the struggle against apartheid in South Africa, Tutu emerged as an international paragon, a religious and moral leader often compared with MLK, but since the end of apartheid his bigoted views on Jews, and Israel in particular, have come to the fore.

I argued in op-eds and speeches that Bishop Tutu was no mere anti-Zionist (though Martin Luther King long ago recognized that anti-Zionism often serves as a cover for deeper anti-Jewish bigotry). He minimized the suffering of those murdered in the Holocaust by asserting that "the gas chambers" made for "a neater death" than did apartheid. In other words, Palestinians, who in his view are the victims of "Israeli apartheid," have suffered *more* than the victims of the Nazi Holocaust. He complained of "the Jewish Monopoly of the Holocaust" and demanded that its victims must "forgive the Nazis," while he himself refuses to forgive the "Jewish people" for "persecute[ing] others."[6] This kind of argument is always a telltale sign insofar as it holds the Jewish people collectively responsible for the actions of Israel. Even the German populace that generally supported Nazism was not held responsible for the crimes of the Nazi regime.

Tutu asserted that Zionism has "very many parallels with racism," thus echoing the notorious and discredited "Zionism equals racism" resolution passed by the General Assembly of the United Nations and subsequently rescinded. Without being specific, Tutu accused the Jews of Israel of doing "things that even apartheid South Africa had not done." He said that "the Jews thought they had a monopoly of God—Jesus was angry that they could shut out other human beings"—and that Jews were "opposed to" his God and have been "fighting against" him. He claimed that his God sides with Palestinians, who he compares to the Israelites under bondage in Egypt, and he has sought to explain, if not justify, how Israeli actions lead directly to suicide bombings and other forms of terrorism. He implied that Israel might someday consider as an option "to perpetrate genocide and exterminate all Palestinians."

He complained that Americans "are scared . . . to say it's wrong because the Jewish lobby is powerful—very powerful." He accused Jews—not Israel—of exhibiting "an arrogance—the arrogance of power because Jews are a powerful lobby in this land, and all kinds of people woo their support."

He compared Israel to Hitler's Germany, Stalin's Soviet Union and apartheid South Africa, saying that they too were once "very powerful" but eventually "bit the dust," as will "unjust" Israel.

He denied that Israel is a "civilized democracy" and singled out Israel—one of the world's most open democracies—as a nation guilty of "censorship of their media." He has urged the Cape Town Opera to refuse to perform *Porgy and Bess* in Tel Aviv and has called for a total cultural boycott of Jewish Israel, while encouraging performers to visit the most repressive regimes in the world.

He has been far more vocal about Israel's imperfections than about the genocides in Rwanda, Darfur and Cambodia. He has repeatedly condemned Israel's occupation of the West Bank without mentioning the many other occupations in the world today. When confronted with his double standard against Jews, he justified it on theological grounds: "Whether Jews like it or not, they are a peculiar people. They can't ever hope to be judged by the same standards which are used for other people." There is a name for non-Jews who hold Jews to a double standard: it is anti-Semite.

Tutu has acknowledged that he has frequently been accused of anti-Semitism, to which he has offered two responses: "Tough luck," and, "My dentist's name is Dr. Cohen." Most disturbingly, Tutu seems to be gleeful about singling out Jews for special condemnation. He seems to enjoy making cruel comments about Jews, Israel, the Holocaust and Zionism.

I stand by criticism of Bishop Tutu, and I'm proud of having the courage to go after a Nobel Prize–winning icon, including in South Africa, where he is generally revered. I wish others would tell the truth about Tutu's sordid history with Jews while at the same time applauding his anti-apartheid activities. There must be zero tolerance for anti-Semitism and other bigotry, regardless of its source. But when the source is someone as influential as Bishop Tutu is, both in South Africa and throughout the world, it is especially important to tell the truth about his anti-Jewish bigotry.

As a result of my writings against this South African icon, the University of Cape Town canceled the talk I was invited to give. Their phony excuse: there was too little interest. My talk was then moved to another venue not far from the campus: more than 1,000 people attended.

The second successful effort to silence me took place in 2009 at the University of Massachusetts–Boston campus. I was invited by student groups to give a talk advocating a two-state solution to the Israeli–Palestinian conflict.

Halfway through my talk, a group of students led by an anti-Israel

Jewish professor began to shout me down and drown me out with boos and chants. I welcome sporadic booing, directed at particular points with which the booers disagree. This was not that. It was a concerted effort to drown me out and prevent the other students from hearing my points.

This is a common tactic on the student left these days, known as deplatforming. In this case, the strategy worked. Instead of shutting down those who sought to censor me, the moderator—a high-ranking official of the university—called an end to the event, not allowing me to finish my presentation. It was a victory for censorship and a defeat for the First Amendment and the very idea of the university itself as a forum for the exchange of ideas and open debate.

I could have sued the university, because it is a public school governed by the First Amendment, but I decided not to for two reasons. First, I had already completed a substantial portion of my presentation when I was shut down; and second, the moderator claimed he stopped the event for my "safety," since the booers were rowdy and threatening. Although the safety issue was almost certainly a pretext, it would have made it more difficult to prevail. I could have been asked, on cross-examination, if I had ever been threatened with violence for my views on the Middle East, and I would have had to say that I had been. I would also have had to say that in several of my university talks, armed guards were either on the stage or nearby in order to protect me from threatened or feared violence.

There were two attempts at campuses of the University of California—also a public school—to ban or silence me. Both failed. The first was much like the one that succeeded at the University of Massachusetts. It took place on the Irvine campus, where again student groups invited me to make the case for Israel.

The large auditorium was filled with students who appeared to fall into three categories. To the left of the lectern were 100 or so students carrying pro-Israel signs, some wearing kippot. To the right were approximately the same number of students carrying pro-Palestinian and anti-Israel signs, some wearing the green colors of Palestine. In the middle, there were several hundred students who did not take sides. They were there to listen and learn. This self-selected seating arrangement, with pro- and anti-Israel groups sitting on different sides of the room, was becoming more common on campuses.

I began by asking the pro-Israel students how many of them would accept the two-state solution, with a nonviolent Palestinian state on the West Bank. Nearly every hand went up.

I then asked the pro-Palestinian students how many of them would accept Israel, if it ended the occupation and settlements and accepted the two-state solution. There was rumbling and discussion, but in the end, not a single hand went up.

I looked to the center of the auditorium, where students who did not align themselves with either side were listening with interest, and said,

> *This is not a dispute between pro-Israel and pro-Palestinian advocates. It's a dispute between pro-Israel and anti-Israel students. The pro-Israel students are also pro-Palestine. They support a Palestinian state, as I do. The pro-Palestinian students seem not to want an Israeli state, even if there is also a Palestinian state.*

I was applauded by many of the center students. My little exercise had neatly illustrated the difference between the two sides and also undermined the claims of pro-Palestinian activitists that they are not opposed to the existence of Israel.

When I began my substantive talk, several of the pro-Palestinian students tried to shout me down, by persistent booing, chanting and screaming. But this time the moderator, who was prepared to deal with the disruption, asked the police to remove the disrupters. I was able to complete my talk, and I received a standing ovation from most of the students.

Shortly after my talk, Michael Oren—an Israeli historian who was then serving as his country's ambassador to the United States—was invited to speak about Israel in the same auditorium. A group of students from the Muslim Student Union set out to prevent him from speaking. They did not try to hide their intention. Here is how the dean of the Law School described it:

> *The Muslim student Union orchestrated a concerted effort to disrupt the speech. One student after another stood and shouted so that the ambassador could not be heard. Each student was taken away by the police only to be replaced by another doing the same thing.*

The students were disciplined by the university for their actions, though the nature and degree of the discipline has been kept confidential. Campus sources have characterized it as a "slap on the wrist." After learning of the careful planning that went into the concerted effort to prevent Oren from speaking and the subsequent cover-up, District Attorney Tony Rackauckas courageously filed misdemeanor charges against those who were arrested.

The decision resulted in an outcry by radicals, many of whom favor censorship of pro-Israel speakers. In a letter to the DA signed by many well-known anti-Israel zealots, the incident was described as merely a protest rather than a determined effort to silence the speaker.

The fact that radical anti-Israel zealots would view censorship of a pro-Israel speaker as a form of legitimate "protest" comes as no surprise. But the fact that the letter of support was signed by two leaders of the American Civil Liberties Union shocked many people. I have been a supporter of the ACLU for half a century, and I was a national board member. I supported the right of Nazis to march through Skokie, and I defended the right of the most virulent anti-Israel speakers to participate in the marketplace of ideas. The ACLU policy has always been to oppose concerted efforts to prevent speakers from delivering their remarks. While sporadic heckling and jeering that merely demonstrates opposition to the content of the remarks is constitutionally protected, the ACLU has always condemned systematic efforts to prevent speakers from delivering their talk—except apparently, when the speaker is pro-Israel.

After being criticized for supporting censorship, one of the ACLU leaders sought to justify his signing of the letter with the following logic: "The district attorney's action will undoubtedly intimidate students . . . and discourage them from engaging in any controversial speech or protest for fear of criminal charges."

In fact, the opposite is true. Letting these students off would only encourage other students around the nation—and the world—to continue with efforts to prevent pro-Israel speakers from delivering their speeches and opinions. The ACLU should support a clear line between occasional heckling and outright censorship. It should not support concerted efforts to silence speakers. In the end, the offending students were successfully prosecuted and given suspended sentences.

The next effort to ban me took the form of a legal barrier when I was invited by Jewish student groups to give a talk at Berkeley in 2018. The Berkeley campus had been roiled by controversies about speakers invited by conservative groups and efforts by extreme leftist groups, such as Antifa, to stop them from speaking. In response, Berkeley enacted a new rule requiring eight weeks prior notice before anyone could speak at a campus event, *unless* an official invitation came from a university department.

On its face, this rule seemed content-neutral, since it applied equally to liberals and conservatives, pro-Israel or anti-Israel speakers. But in practice, it was anything but neutral. University departments at Berkeley routinely invited left-wing and anti-Israel speakers but not conservative or pro-Israel speakers. (This was common around the country, which I learned firsthand when the political science department at my alma mater Brooklyn College officially sponsored anti-Israel speakers but refused to sponsor me.) So the effect of the rule—whether intended or unintended, and many believed it was intended—was to allow left-wing and anti-Israel speakers *immediate* access to students (as well as the official imprimatur of university departments) while requiring conservative or pro-Israel speakers to go through hoops and *wait* eight weeks, which often meant that, before any talk could be arranged, the semester would be over (as it would have been if I had had to wait eight weeks).

When I was invited, the Jewish groups asked several departments to sponsor my talk. None would, though several had recently sponsored anti-Israel speakers.

Because Berkeley is such a large and influential campus, I decided to sue the university for violating my First Amendment rights, as well as those of the students who wanted to hear me. As soon as I announced my intention to sue, the dean of the Law School extended me an invitation, thus negating the suit.

My talk on the two-state solution was protested and leafleted by radical students. I invited the protestors to come and listen, promising to take their critical questions first and to take no friendly questions until I had answered all the critical ones. They refused and walked out. The speech was well received by the audience, but not by the school newspaper's editorial cartoonist, who did not attend but drew an anti-Semitic caricature of me. Here is how it was described by a student who wrote a letter to the newspaper:

> In the cartoon, Dershowitz is depicted with a hooked nose and
> a body of a large amorphous black sphere. His exaggerated head
> and contorted legs and hands evoke images of a spider. The
> rhetoric of Jews as "invasive" insects in society, trying to take
> over resources and power, had long been used to justify violence,
> persecution and murder. The two elements of the cartoon, with
> Dershowitz's face in the front and the black body in the back,
> plays into the anti-Semitic trope of Jews as shape-shifting,
> sub-human entities using deception and trickery in order to

advance their own agendas. This rhetoric is nowhere more common than in Nazi propaganda, and can be traced far beyond WWII in European and American media.

In another letter to the editor, the university's chancellor, Carol Christ, wrote the following:

Your recent editorial cartoon targeting Alan Dershowitz was offensive, appalling and deeply disappointing. I condemn its publication. Are you aware that its anti-Semitic imagery connects directly to the centuries-old "blood libel" that falsely accused Jews of engaging in ritual murder? I cannot recall anything similar in the Daily Cal, *and I call on the paper's editors to reflect on whether they would sanction a similar assault on other ethnic or religious groups. We cannot build a campus community where everyone feels safe, respected and welcome if hatred and the perpetuation of harmful stereotypes become an acceptable part of our discourse.*

It was shocking to me that this vile caricature—which would fit comfortably in a Nazi or white nationalist publication—was published in "the official paper of record of the City of Berkeley" (according to the editor). The cartoon resembles the grotesque anti-Semitic blood libel propaganda splashed across *Der Stürmer* in the 1930s, which depicted Jews drinking the blood of Gentile children. Canards about Jews as predators—prominently promulgated by the tsarist forgery, the *Protocols of the Elders of Zion*—were anti-Semitic back then and are still anti-Semitic today, whether espoused by the extreme left or the extreme right.

Moreover, the anti-Semitic cartoon was printed in reaction to a speech in which I advocated a Palestinian state, an end to the occupation, and principles in opposition to Israeli settlement policies. It's hard to imagine a position more favorable to Palestinian claims and aspirations. Apparently, even this is not enough to warrant a hearing from radical activists.

Nonetheless, just as I have long defended the rights of Nazis to march in Skokie and elsewhere, I defend the right of hard-left bigots to produce this sort of anti-Semitic material, despite it being hate speech. Those who condemn hate speech when it comes from the right should also speak up when hate speech comes from the left. The silence from those on the left is steeped in hypocrisy. It reflects the old adage: free speech for me but not for thee.

The best response to bigotry is the opposite of censorship: it is exposure and shaming in the court of public opinion. I opposed removing the offensive cartoon, as some suggested. I wanted it to be widely circulated for all to see and criticize. It was not removed.

Writing in the *Daily Cal*, students from a pro-Israel organization at Berkeley did just that: they debunked the claim that the cartoonist and the student paper editors at the *Daily Cal* could not have known that this cartoon was steeped in traditional anti-Semitic stereotyping, considering its deep roots in European, and even American, publications.

The students also wrote about the "pain" the anti-Semitic cartoon had caused them:

> *To a Jewish student on this campus, seeing this cartoon in the* Daily Cal *is a reminder that we are not always welcome in the spaces we call home.*
>
> . . .
>
> *Telling Jews that we can or cannot define what is offensive to us, because of our status as privileged minority in the United States, is anti-Semitic.*

Some students also pointed to the swastika that had defaced my picture on a poster outside Berkeley Law School as evidence of a pervasive anti-Semitism disguised as anti-Zionism on that campus. A poster for my talk at Johns Hopkins was similarly defaced: someone drew a Hitler-type moustache on my lip.

Sadly, though not surprisingly, the *Jewish Forward*—a century-old Jewish publication that had become a megaphone for anti-Israel bigotry under the editor at the time—denied that the imagery was anti-Semitic and justified its publication:

> *The mere appearance of blood near a Jew is not a blood libel. The State of Israel has an army, and that army sometimes kills Palestinians, including women and children. When you prick those people, I am told, they bleed. It is perverse to demand of artists that they represent actual, real Israeli violence without blood, just because European Christians invented a fake accusation.*

The *Forward* also argued that the cartoon was a legitimate criticism of my talk. But the cartoonist admitted that he didn't hear my talk. Nor did the *Daily Cal* report on it.

I doubt the *Forward* would publish an op-ed that justified comparable images of women, blacks or gays. But for them, Jews and Zionists are fair game for bigotry.

When the Columbia University chapter of Amnesty International invited me to deliver a talk on human rights in the Middle East, I immediately accepted. As a supporter of the two-state solution and an opponent of many of Israel's settlement decisions, I regard myself as a moderate on these issues.

That was apparently too much for the national office of Amnesty International. They demanded that their Columbia chapter disinvite me. They did not want their members to hear my perspective on these issues.

Their excuse was two old and out-of-context quotes suggesting that I favored torture and collective punishment. The truth is that I am adamantly opposed to both. I have written nuanced academic articles on the subject of torture warrants as a way of minimizing the evils of torture,[7] and I have written vehemently against the use of collective punishment of innocent people—whether by means of the boycott movement against all Israelis or the use of collective punishment against Palestinians. I do favor holding those who facilitate terrorism responsible for their own actions.[8]

As an outspoken Zionist who supports Israel's right to exist as the nation-state of the Jewish people, I have been sharply critical of Amnesty's one-sided approach to the Israeli–Palestinian conflict. For example, I wrote an article criticizing Amnesty's report on honor killings in the West Bank. An honor killing occurs when a woman has been raped and her family then kills her because of the shame her victimization has brought on them. Despite massive evidence to the contrary, Amnesty mendaciously claimed that honor killings had increased in the West Bank since the Israeli occupation and that the fault for this increase in Arab men killing Arab women somehow lay with Israel. The reality is that there are far fewer honor killings in the West Bank than there are in adjoining Jordan, which is not under Israeli occupation, and that the number of such killings in the West Bank has been reduced dramatically during the Israeli occupation. But facts apparently mean little when Israel is involved.[9]

The national office of Amnesty International did not want their members to hear my views on Israel or my criticisms of their organization. This is despite the fact that I was a strong supporter in its early days, before it became so one-sided and began supporting BDS against only Israel. They were afraid to have their Jewish members at Columbia hear the truth. They feared an open marketplace of ideas, so they tried to shut me down by denying the right of their Columbia chapter to sponsor my talk.

Fortunately, another Columbia student group immediately invited me to speak, and some members of Columbia Amnesty, to their credit, came to listen. They asked me hard questions, which I tried to answer with facts and logic. Some agreed with me, while others disagreed. That is the nature of open dialogue, which Amnesty International claims to champion—except when it comes to their own organization.[10]

When I was invited to debate in favor of the motion "Is BDS Wrong?" at the Oxford Union in 2015, I fully expected to lose the vote of the hundreds of students and faculty members of the oldest debating society in the world. "Israel always loses at Oxford," I was warned by colleagues who had debated other Israel-related issues. Nonetheless, I decided to participate. BDS was quickly gaining support throughout Europe and in the United States, and I saw this debate, which would be widely covered and available on the internet, as an opportunity to change some minds.

I proposed as my opponent Omar Barghouti, the Qatar-born, Israeli-educated, cofounder and spokesperson of the BDS campaign, whom I had many times attacked in print, but he refused to debate me. The Union then selected Noura Erakat, a Palestinian American human rights attorney who has been a vocal supporter of BDS.

When she backed out at the last minute, I began to get suspicious. Was the BDS organization boycotting me? After all, BDS advocates have called for "common sense" academic boycotts against individuals who they feel are too vocal in their support for Israel, in addition to a blanket boycott of all Israeli academic institutions.

After speaking with the organizers of the debate at Oxford, I concluded that I was in fact being boycotted.

The Union then selected Peter Tatchell, a distinguished and popular British human rights activist, who has participated in 30 Union debates, most of which he has won. Tatchell accepted. The debate was held in the beautiful, wood-paneled, old auditorium that had featured debates over the years by many world leaders. The overflow crowd reflected the widespread interest in the issue.

I knew I was in for a difficult time, especially when most of the questions from the students seemed hostile toward Israel, though polite. Mr. Tatchell's main argument was that BDS was a nonviolent form of protest against Israel's occupation and settlement policies that mirrored the boycott campaign against apartheid South Africa and followed the principles of Mahatma Gandhi and Martin Luther King. He was articulate in arguing that boycott tactics generally were a nonviolent alternative to war and terrorism.

I argued that BDS was not an alternative to war but rather an alternative to peaceful negotiations by the Palestinian leadership. This is because the BDS campaign is firmly opposed to the two-state solution. Barghouti confirmed as much when he wrote and said, "Definitely, most definitely, we oppose a Jewish state in any part of Palestine." Thus, I argued that the BDS campaign makes it more difficult for the Palestinian leadership to accept the kind of painful compromise that both sides must agree to if there is to be a negotiated resolution.

Many liberal activists such as Mr. Tatchell—whose advocacy on behalf of LGBTQ rights I greatly admire—have made common cause with BDS, hoping to pressure Israel to end the occupation and afford greater self-determination to Palestinians in the West Bank. They seem to believe that a campaign advocating nonviolent tactics is the best way to achieve a lasting peace. But BDS itself is radically opposed to any negotiated settlement.

Mr. Tatchell and many pro-BDS academics also feel that Israel has committed human rights violations both in the occupation of the West Bank and in its prosecution of the armed conflict in Gaza. So, I issued the following challenge to the audience and to any opponent: name a single country in the history of the world that faces threats comparable to those faced by Israel but has a better record of human rights, of compliance with the rule of law and of seeking to minimize civilian casualties.

I invited the audience members to shout out the name of a country.

Complete silence. Finally, someone shouted "Iceland," and everyone laughed.

In the end, our case against BDS won by a significant majority.

Our side won not because of the comparative skill of the debaters—Tatchell was superb—but because I was able to expose the moral weakness of the BDS campaign itself.

Whenever I am protested at universities, I am accused of having denied Norman Finkelstein his academic freedom. Finkelstein was a popular anti-Israel speaker who traveled the country accusing Israel of being worse than Nazi Germany. Protestors hand out leaflets claiming that I was instrumental in getting Finkelstein fired from DePaul University, which had denied him tenure. The claim was that I opposed him because he had attacked my book *The Case for Israel*. Here is what happened.

As soon as *The Case for Israel* hit the bestseller lists in 2003, Noam Chomsky tasked his acolyte Finkelstein with attacking it, as Chomsky had tasked him with attacking other pro-Israel books. Finkelstein then claimed in his writing and public appearances, quite absurdly, that I hadn't even written or read the book. The implication was that some Israeli intelligence agency wrote it and had me sign it. The problem for him is that I don't type or use a computer, so every word of the text was handwritten by me—and I still have the original, handwritten manuscript. He then falsely claimed that I had plagiarized it.[11]

My first reaction was to ignore the attack, as I generally ignore the numerous made-up stories about me that are common on neo-Nazi and Holocaust-denial websites. For example, a story on a conspiracy website Rense had accused me of murdering my first wife. It had "photographs" of her and my children, but those depicted were not my family members. Those in the image had stereotypical Jewish faces with long noses and other "Jewish" characteristics. After receiving complaints, the site changed it, but it kept the accusations that I had beaten my first wife, causing her to be hospitalized. Of course, there was no truth to anything in the article, which can still be found on the internet. Back to the false accusations of plagiarism, I realized its underlying purpose was not so much directed at me as it was at young, untenured academics who might consider writing or speaking in support of Israel. Its goal was to send a powerful message to such academics that if you write in support of Israel, you, too, may be accused of plagiarism and fraud. Finkelstein and Chomsky knew they couldn't destroy me because I have the means to fight back, but they could deter others who lack such means. For an untenured assistant professor to be accused of such dishonesty could be an academic death sentence, even if the accusation was baseless. As Churchill once quipped, "A lie makes its way halfway around the world before the truth can get its pants on." And Churchill said this before the advent of the internet. Today a lie makes its way completely around the world, and the truth—which is often less interesting than the lie—makes it to the bottom of a Google search.

My response took two forms: one defensive and the other offensive. I asked Harvard to investigate the phony plagiarism charge, which they did and concluded it had absolutely no basis. Then I went after Finkelstein.

I decided that the best weapon to use against Finkelstein was his own words. Accordingly, I compiled and circulated a list of some of Finkelstein's most absurd statements about Israel and the alleged "international Jewish conspiracy" that supports Israel. I made my list available for distribution to pro-Israel activists on campuses at which Finkelstein was speaking.

Finkelstein has claimed that Israel's human rights record is worse than that of the Nazis. "[I] can't imagine why Israel's apologists would be offended by a comparison with the Gestapo." He said that Israel's human rights record is "interchangeable with Iraq's" when it was ruled by Saddam Hussein. He supports Hezbollah, an anti-Semitic terrorist group whose goal is to destroy Israel and commit genocide against the world's Jews, and which has repeatedly launched rocket attacks against Israel from its bases in Lebanon. "The honorable thing now is to show solidarity with Hezbollah as the U.S. and Israel target it for liquidation. Indeed, looking back, my chief regret is that I wasn't even more forceful in publicly defending Hezbollah against terrorist intimidation and attack." He also supported Gaddafi's Libya: "Libya had nothing to do with it [the blowing up of Pan Am 103, for which Libya has acknowledged responsibility] but they are playing along." He seemed to justify bin Laden's terrorism against the United States by saying, "We deserve the problem on our hands because some things bin Laden says are true."

Finkelstein has further argued that the international Jewish conspiracy is responsible for a raft of books and films that advance awareness of the Holocaust, including Steven Spielberg's movie *Schindler's List*, Leon Uris's book *Exodus*, Andrew Lloyd Webber's musical *Cats*, and the NBC series *Holocaust*. In Finkelstein's own words,

> *Who profits [from the movie]? Basically, there are two beneficiaries from the dogma: American Jews and the American administration.*
>
> *The name of the character [in Uris's novel* Exodus*] is Ari Ben Canaan because Ari is the diminutive for Aryan. It is the whole admiration for this blond haired, blue eyed type.*
>
> *In 1978, NBC produced the series* Holocaust. *Do you believe it was a coincidence, 1978? Just at this time, when peace negotiations between Israel and Egypt took place in Camp David?*

Nor are seemingly innocent productions above suspicion, such as Andrew Lloyd Webber's blockbuster musical *Cats*, based loosely on the book by T.S. Eliot (himself a notorious anti-Semite): "Some people think that *Cats* is a code word for K-A-T-Z, Katz."[12]

Finkelstein has also demeaned Holocaust survivors:

> *I'm not exaggerating when I say that one out of three Jews you stop in the street in New York will claim to be a survivor.*
>
> *"If everyone who claims to be a survivor actually is one," my mother used to exclaim, "Who did Hitler kill then?"*

According to the *Guardian*, "Finkelstein says . . . that most 'survivors' are bogus."

Along with these incriminating statements, I circulated a list of what other serious scholars had said about Finkelstein's writing, beginning with Peter Novick, the prominent University of Chicago historian who Finkelstein said had inspired him:

> *As concerns particular assertions made by Finkelstein . . . ,*
> *the appropriate response is not (exhilarating) "debate" but*
> *(tedious) examination of his footnotes. Such an examination*
> *reveals that many of those assertions are pure invention. . . .*
> *No facts alleged by Finkelstein should be assumed to be really*
> *facts, no quotation in his book [about the Holocaust] should*
> *be assumed to be accurate, without taking the time to carefully*
> *compare his claims with the sources he cites. Finkelstein's book*
> *is trash.*

The *New York Times* review of Finkelstein's book by the distinguished Brown University professor Omer Bartov characterized it as

> *a novel variation on the anti-Semitic forgery, "The Protocols of*
> *the Elders of Zion." There is also something indecent about it,*
> *something juvenile, self-righteous, arrogant and stupid.*
> *This book is, in a word, an ideological fanatic's view . . . by*
> *a writer so reckless and ruthless in his attacks. . . . [His theory*
> *is] both irrational and insidious. . . . An international Jewish*
> *conspiracy verges on paranoia and would serve anti-Semites.*

Finally, I showed how Finkelstein's work is relied on by neo-Nazis, citing the distinguished writer Gabriel Schoenfeld: "Crackpot ideas, some of them mirrored almost verbatim in the propaganda put out by neo-Nazis around the world."

As a result of my decision to fight back against Finkelstein's attack, I received a letter from Patrick Callahan, one of Finkelstein's colleagues in the DePaul political science department and its former chairman. Finkelstein was being considered for tenure at the time. Callahan invited me to submit a letter documenting "the clearest and most egregious instances of [intellectual] dishonesty on Finkelstein's part." This is part of what I wrote:

> *I would like to point out from the outside that the ugly and false assertions that I will discuss below are not incidental to Finkelstein's purported scholarship; they are his purported scholarship. Finkelstein's entire literary catalogue is one preposterous and discredited ad hominem attack after another. By his own admission, he has conducted no original research, has never been published in a reputable scientific journal, and has made no contributions to our collective historical knowledge . . . although he claims to be a "forensic scholar," he limits his defamations to one ideological group and never applies his so-called "forensic" tools to his own work or to those who share his ideological perspective. . . . That is not forensic scholarship; it is propaganda.*

After discussing his utter lack of any real scholarship, I focused on one particular article he had written about me titled "Should Alan Dershowitz Target Himself for Assassination?"[13] Finkelstein had collaborated with an artist to create a pornographic cartoon of me, masturbating in ecstasy as I watched Israeli soldiers murder Palestinian children. The cartoon aptly represented the content of Finkelstein's article, which accused me of being a "moral pervert." He called me a Nazi, saying that I subscribe to "Nazi ideology," and then he compared me to Nazi propagandist Julius Streicher.

I then proceeded to document a series of made-up quotations used by Finkelstein—quotes that simply didn't exist. These alone should have disqualified him from serious consideration at any university.

In the end, DePaul denied him tenure and fired him. This led Chomsky to escalate his attacks on me, calling me, in his writings and speech, a "maniac," a "supporter of atrocities" and a "passionate opponent of civil rights."

Finkelstein now travels the world—paid in part by Arab sources—attacking Israel, Jews, the United States, DePaul University and me. He visited Lebanon to show solidarity with Hezbollah, the terrorist group that killed hundreds of U.S. soldiers, Jewish children in Argentina and Israeli civilians. As a result of that trip, Israeli authorities prevented him from entering Israel—a decision that I publicly criticized. Lacking the academic imprimatur of a university, his hateful message is fading in the marketplace of ideas, although he still remains popular among left-wing extremists.

The line between extreme anti-Zionism and anti-Semitism often gets blurred, especially when the writer or speaker is Jewish, as Finkelstein and Chomsky are. Their hatred of all things Jewish is as old as Judaism itself. It defies rational, political or moral explanation and demands recourse to psychology. For those of us who are proud of being Jewish, though critical of some aspects of our faith, some of our co-religionists and some Israeli policies, these self-haters are particularly troubling because they give rise to a variation of the argument ad hominem—the fallacy of judging the merit of discourse or an argument by the person who is making it. I call the "self-hating Jew" variant of this fallacy the "argument by ethnic identification." It goes this way: "See, Chomsky is a Jew and if *he* admits that Israel is an Apartheid state, it must be so." It's an absurd argument, but commonly made by Israel-bashers.

Most anti-Zionist Jews try hard to distinguish between hatred of Israel and hatred of the Jewish people. But in the case of Gilad Atzmon—who was not only born Jewish but also Israeli—there is nothing blurry about the line he had crossed.

Atzmon has no academic credentials, but his popularity as a jazz musician has made him a popular anti-Israel speaker on campuses around the world.

In his book *The Wandering Who?* he boasts about "drawing many of my insights from a man who . . . was an anti-Semite as well as a radical misogynist" and a hater of "almost everything that fails to be Aryan masculinity." He declares himself a "proud, self-hating Jew," writes with "contempt" of "the Jew in me," and describes himself as "a strong opponent of . . . Jewishness." His writings, both online and in his book, brim with classic anti-Semitic motifs that are borrowed from Nazi publications.

Throughout his writings, Atzmon argues that Jews "do try to seek to control the world."

Atzmon expanded on this theme in *The Wandering Who?*, repeatedly conflating "the Jews" and "the Zionists." He has made the following claims:

- Calling the credit crunch "The Zio-punch," he says it was not "a Jewish conspiracy" because "it was all in the open."
- Paul Wolfowitz, Rahm Emanuel and other members of "the Jewish elite" remain abroad instead of moving to "Zion" because they "have proved far more effective for the Zionist cause by staying where they are."
- That Jews are evil and a menace to humanity.
- "With Fagin and Shylock in mind Israeli barbarism and organ trafficking seem to be just other events in an endless hellish continuum."
- "The Homo Zionicus quickly became a mass murderer, detached from any recognized form of ethical thinking and engaged in a colossal crime against humanity."
- If Iran and Israel fight a nuclear war that kills tens of millions of people, "some may be bold enough to argue that 'Hitler might have been right after all.'"
- Children should be allowed to question, as he did, "how the teacher could know that these accusations of Jews making Matza out of young Goyim's blood were indeed empty or groundless."

- "The Holocaust religion is probably as old as the Jews themselves."
- The history of Jewish persecution is a myth, and if there was any persecution the Jews brought it on themselves.
- "[I]n order to promote Zionist interests, Israel must generate significant anti-Jewish sentiment. Cruelty against Palestinian civilians is a favorite Israeli means of achieving this aim."
- "Jews may have managed to drop their God, but they have maintained goy-hating and racist ideologies at the heart of their newly emerging secular political identity. This explains why some Talmudic goy-hating elements have been transformed within the Zionist discourse into genocidal practices."
- The "Judaic God" described in Deuteronomy 6:10–12 "is an evil deity, who leads his people to plunder, robbery and theft." Atzmon explains that "Israel and Zionism . . . have instituted the plunder premised by the Hebrew God in the Judaic Holy Scriptures."
- The moral of the Book of Esther is that Jews "had better infiltrate the corridors of power" if they wish to survive.

Finally, Atzmon repeatedly declares that Israel is worse than the Nazis, and he has actually "apologized" to the Nazis for having earlier compared them to Israel:

Too many of us including me tend to equate Israel to Nazi Germany. Rather often I myself join others and argue that Israelis are the Nazis of our time. I want to take this opportunity to amend my statement Israelis are not the Nazis of our time and the Nazis were not the Israelis of their time. Israel, is in fact far worse than Nazi Germany.

In light of this manifestly unhinged bigotry, it should come as no surprise that even some of the most hardcore anti-Israel activists have shunned Atzmon out of fear that his naked anti-Semitism will discredit their cause. Tony Greenstein, a self-styled "anti-Zionist," denounced *The Wandering Who?* as "a poisonous anti-Semitic tome." Sue Blackwell, who co-wrote the Association of University Teachers' motion to boycott Israeli universities in 2005, removed all links to Atzmon from her website. Socialist Worker, a website that frequently refers to Israeli "apartheid" and publishes articles with titles such as "Israel's Murderous Violence," removed an interview with Atzmon and called the evidence of Atzmon's anti-Semitism "damning." At least ten authors associated with *The Wandering Who?*'s leftist publisher have called on it to distance itself from Atzmon's views, explaining that the "thrust of Atzmon's work is to normalize and legitimize anti-Semitism."

Hardcore neo-Nazis, racists, anti-Semites and Holocaust deniers, on the other hand, have happily counted Atzmon as one of their own. David Duke, America's premier white supremacist, has posted more than a dozen of Atzmon's articles on his website, praising the author for "writ[ing] such fine articles exposing the evil of Zionism and Jewish supremacism." Israel Shamir, a Holocaust denier—who has said that "we must deny the concept of Holocaust without doubt and hesitation," argued that Jews ritually murdered Christian children for their blood, and proclaimed that "the rule of the Elders of Zion is already upon us"—refers to Atzmon as a "good friend" and calls him one of "the shining stars of the battle" against "the Jewish alliance."

But neither Atzmon's well-established reputation for anti-Semitism nor the copious anti-Semitic filth that fills *The Wandering Who?* has deterred Professors John Mearsheimer and Richard Falk from actively endorsing Atzmon's work.[14]

Mearsheimer, the Harrison Distinguished Service Professor of Political Science at the University of Chicago and a member of the American Academy of Arts and Sciences, calls *The Wandering Who?* a "fascinating" book that "should be read widely by Jews and non-Jews alike." Falk, Milbank Professor of International Law and Practice Emeritus at Princeton University and United Nations special rapporteur on "human rights in the Palestinian territories," calls *The Wandering Who?* an "absorbing and moving" book that everyone who "care[s] about real peace" should "not only read, but reflect upon and discuss widely."

Falk's endorsement appears prominently on the cover of Atzmon's book. Mearsheimer's endorsement is featured on its first page. These professors are not merely defending Atzmon's right to publish such a book, they are endorsing its content and urging their colleagues, students and others to read and "reflect upon" the views expressed by Atzmon. One wonders which portions of this bigoted screed Professors Mearsheimer and Falk believe their students and others "should" read and "discuss widely." Mearsheimer has defended his endorsement against attacks by me and others by questioning whether his critics have even read Atzmon's book. Well, I've read every word of it, as well as many of Atzmon's blog posts. No one who has read this material could escape the conclusion that Atzmon freely admits: his writings cross the line from anti-Zionism to crass anti-Semitism.

Yet a number of other prominent academics have defended Atzmon and his endorsers. Brian Leiter, the Llewellyn Professor of Jurisprudence at the University of Chicago Law School, dismissed the reaction to the book and to Mearsheimer's "straightforward" endorsement as "hysterical" and not "advanc[ing] honest intellectual discourse," though he acknowledges not having read Atzmon's book.

On the basis of having perused one brief interview with Atzmon, Leiter was nonetheless prepared to defend him against charges that he is an anti-Semite or a Holocaust denier. He should read the book before leaping to Atzmon's defense.

These endorsements of Atzmon's book are the best evidence yet that academic discourse is beginning to cross a red line, and this crossing must be exposed, rebutted and rejected in the marketplace of ideas and in the academy. Further evidence of this trend appeared recently on Atzmon's website, where he announces that he has been invited to "give a talk on ethics at the Trondheim University" in Norway despite his utter lack of credentials to discuss "ethics." This is the same university whose faculty refused to invite me to speak about the Arab–Israeli conflict when I gave several lectures in Norway in 2011 because Norman Finkelstein had already covered the subject!

I wrote op-eds challenging Professors Mearsheimer, Falk and Leiter to a public debate about why they have endorsed and said such positive things about such a hateful and anti-Semitic book by such a bigoted and dishonest writer. None of them responded.

Efforts by the hard left to demonize Israel and to isolate its Jewish supporters are beginning to spread to high schools, both private and public. The most extreme case occurred in 2012 at the Friends Seminary, a high school in New York City, which invited Atzmon to be a featured performer at a celebration of Martin Luther King.

It is not as if Friends Seminary was unfamiliar with Atzmon's anti-Semitic rants. Atzmon was previously invited to make a guest appearance in a class, and one of his essays was distributed to the students. The essay came from his website, which is replete with anti-Semitic "insights."

When I heard about this bizarre invitation, I wrote the following letter to the school's headmaster:

> *Your school is now legitimating anti-Semitism by inviting a self-described Jew hater, Gilad Atzmon, to participate in events at the school. This sends a powerful message to your students, and to other students around the world, that Atzmon's views are legitimate and an appropriate subject for discussion in academic circles.*
>
> *If you believe these views are appropriately discussed, considered and possibly accepted by your students, then you are doing the right thing by associating your school with the man who expressed them. If not, then you are doing a terrible disservice to your students and to the values for which the Friends School purports to stand.*

I cannot overemphasize how serious this matter is. Legitimating the oldest form of bigotry is a moral and academic sin. I cannot remain silent in the face of complicity with bigotry. Nor should you.

The headmaster did not respond, and Atzmon performed to honor a man—Martin Luther King—who despised anti-Semitism and would have been appalled by Atzmon's hateful words. Students cheered his performance and conversed with him.

I cannot imagine an overtly homophobic, sexist or racist musician being invited by any group in any way associated with Friends even if he was being invited because of his "musical accomplishments." (I hear that David Duke, the white supremacist, plays a mean saxophone. In a post, Atzmon said he would be willing to play alongside Duke. What a duet!)

Atzmon is famous (really, infamous) not because he is a distinguished musician but because he is a notorious anti-Semite whose blogs are featured on neo-Nazi websites all over the world. He never would have been invited but for his well-publicized bigotry.

Friends Seminary is well known for inviting artists whose politics and ideology are consistent with the values of the school. Indeed, the poster advertising his appearance included a description of him as a "writer" and "political activist."

The Friends Seminary, like other elite schools around the country, teaches our future leaders. Many Friends schools around the country have espoused strongly anti-Israel policies for years. The Friends Seminary in New York itself has a rabidly anti-Israel history teacher on its faculty who propagandizes his students against Israel in the classroom and who has a picture of Anne Frank wearing a Palestinian headdress on his website. The school has taken students on trips to the Middle East that present a one-sided perspective. Now they have crossed the line from preaching anti-Zionism to tolerating anti-Semitism. Parents, who complained to me, are afraid to complain to the headmaster out of fear that it would affect their children's college prospects.

The teaching and promoting of anti-Israel extremism that often morphs into anti-Semitism is an increasingly disturbing and dangerous phenomenon on many campuses around the world. Academic freedom requires that schools permit teachers to express bigoted views outside of the classroom.

Students and alumni claimed that anti-Semitic tweets by Columbia professor Hamid Dabashi created a "hostile environment," but because these statements were not made in the classroom, they were regarded as protected free speech. I support this freedom to be bigoted in public as long as the school applies the same standard to all forms of bigotry.

Students in a classroom, on the other hand, are a captive audience who are graded and recommended by teachers. Students, too, have academic freedom, which includes their right to express political views different from those of their teachers without suffering adverse consequences. Yet another Columbia professor reportedly refused to allow a student from Israel to speak in his class unless he first acknowledged that the Israeli army committed war crimes. Such censorship not only created a hostile environment but also clearly violated the student's right of academic freedom. Yet, Columbia did nothing about this professor's misuse of his classroom.

When academic departments—such as Brooklyn College's political science department and many departments at Berkeley and other universities—officially sponsor anti-Israel speakers and events but refuse to sponsor pro-Israel speakers and events, this double standard sends a frightening message to pro-Israel students: that their academic department has an official position different from theirs, and that this difference may influence their evaluations. This, too, raises concern about the academic freedom of students.

Universities, as institutions, must be scrupulously neutral with regard to controversial political issues about which students reasonably disagree. So must academic departments. The issue concerning individual teachers is more complex, requiring distinctions between in-class academic lectures and outside-of-class speeches or writings.

Whatever policies universities adopt with regard to teachers must pass "the shoe on the other foot" test: whatever a left-wing professor is permitted to say, write or do must be the same for a right-wing professor. Whatever the rules are for anti-Israel advocates must be identical for pro-Israel advocates.

Too few schools—colleges, universities or high schools—pass that test today.

One university that did take action against a bigoted professor was the University of Michigan, which disciplined and warned a professor who had agreed to recommend one of his students to a semester-aboard program, but when he found out that this student wanted to spend the semester studying in Israel, he refused to write the recommendation on the ground that it violated his commitment to BDS against Israel.

The battle being waged against the legitimacy of Israel on campuses threatens the future of the nation-state of the Jewish people. Israel has devised defenses—imperfect perhaps, but largely effective—against war, terrorism and even the threat of an Iranian nuclear attack. But neither the Israeli government nor its supporters around the world have come up with effective defenses against the massive propaganda campaign being directed against the crucial bipartisan support that is essential for Israel to maintain its military superiority, its international standing and its legitimacy as the nation-state of the Jewish people. Already, we are seeing erosion in support among the left wing of the Democratic Party.

The election to Congress of several young anti-Israel representatives in the 2018 election is only the latest manifestation of a decade-long trend in diminution of support for Israel among left-wing Democrats.

Congress now includes two Muslim women for the first time, a positive development. Unfortunately, both of these congresswomen, Ilhan Omar from Minnesota and Rashida Tlaib from Michigan, are supporters of BDS, as is the new darling of the hard left, Alexandria Ocasio-Cortez from New York.

On a panel on the Israeli–Palestinian conflict, Somali-born congresswoman Omar, who is now also a member of the Foreign Affairs Committee, said, "I want to talk about the political influence in this country that says it is okay to push for allegiance to a foreign country," essentially accusing American Jews of dual loyalty.

Not surprisingly, David Duke—the neo-Nazi Klansman—came out in support of Omar, calling her "the most important member of Congress" because of her "defiance to ZOG."[15] Those initials stand for "Zionist Occupied Government," which is Duke's description of the U.S. government. The anti-Semitic hard left and neo-Nazi hard right agree when it comes to Zionism and alleged Jewish influence.

After more of Omar's history of anti-Semitic remarks were revealed, House Democrats planned to vote on a resolution condemning anti-Semitism. The resolution was initially intended to be a rebuke of Omar. The text of the resolution, while not directly mentioning Omar, says that "the House of Representatives rejects the perpetuation of anti-Semitic stereotypes in the United States and around the world, including the pernicious myth of dual loyalty and foreign allegiance, especially in the context of support for the United States–Israel alliance." However, when the Black Caucus and Congressional Progressive Caucus questioned the Democratic leadership about why Omar was singled out when other minority groups felt they were under constant attack "in the age of Trump," the Democrats broadened the scope of the resolution and included text to condemn hateful expressions of "intolerance" against African Americans, Native Americans, Muslims, Hindus, Sikhs, immigrants and other people of color.

Contrast this with the reaction by the hard left to those who have suggested changing "Black Lives Matter" to "All Lives Matter." They called broadening the scope "offensive" and "racist."

As Donna Brazile, the former interim chair of the DNC, wrote, "Those who are experiencing the pain and trauma of the black experience in this country don't want their rallying cry to be watered down with a generic feel-good catchphrase." And yet, a "watered down" res-olution with "generic feel-good catchphrases" should satisfy Ameri-can Jews who feel more and more alienated by some leaders of the Democratic Party, who embrace radical identity politics and have a blind spot when it comes to Jewish issues.

Many centrist Democrats could not support Black Lives Matter because its leadership accused Israel of genocide. Others could not sup-port the organizers behind the historic Women's March because its radical leaders called the virulent anti-Semite Louis Farrakhan the "greatest of all time." When Farrakhan was seated next to Bill Clin-ton at Aretha Franklin's memorial service, I wrote,

> *Liberals need to make unequivocally clear that the Democratic*
> *Party tent will never be big enough for anti-Semites and*
> *anti-Americans like Farrakhan, just as Republicans need to do*
> *the same with sympathizers of the alt-right. There are not "good*
> *people" on the side of anti-Semitism, any more than there are*
> *"good people" on the side of white supremacy.*
>
> *There is no place for a double standard when it comes to*
> *antisemitism. Black antisemitism should not get a pass on account*
> *of the oppression suffered by so many African Americans. Neither*
> *should "progressive" tolerance of antisemitism of the kind shown*
> *by Bernie Sanders backing Jeremy Corbyn, the anti-Semite*
> *leader of the British Labour Party who may well become the*
> *next prime minister of America's closest ally.*

And yet, many prominent members of the new progressive wing within the Democratic Party, such as Keith Ellison and Maxine Waters, have had close ties to Farrakhan, and too many within the Democratic leadership are unwilling to condemn and oust these anti-Semites from their ranks.[16]

Just as Republicans have a special obligation to condemn anti-Semitism and anti-Muslim attitudes from the far right, so too have

Democrats a special obligation to condemn anti-Semitism on the left, especially as anti-Semitism is on the rise worldwide.

The same is true of many in the media, especially on talk shows and social media that appeal to young viewers, many of whom do not read newspapers and thus get their "information" from these shows and websites. When Congresswoman Rashida Tlaib suggested that her Palestinian ancestors had "g[iven] up their livelihood, their human dignity to provide a safe haven for Jews" who survived the Holocaust, there was understandable criticism of her perversion of history. The Palestinian leadership had, in fact, done everything in its power to deny Jewish victims of the Holocaust "safe Haven." Their leader, Amin al-Husseini, had collaborated with Hitler to prevent Jews from leaving Nazi-occupied Europe and finding safe haven in Palestine. Once Israel was established, Palestinians attacked it in an effort to prevent Holocaust survivors from entering Israel. Yet when Tlaib was interviewed on several talk shows and on social media, she was not confronted with the truthful history of Palestinian opposition to giving safe haven to Holocaust survivors. Instead, she was thrown softball questions and her untruthful responses were greeted with applause from uninformed studio audiences, thus helping to mainstream her anti-Jewish bigotry, and her revisionist and false history.

Not enough is being done to marginalize these anti-Israel Democrats. But in early 2019, a group of prominent present and former Democratic lawmakers—some Jews, some not—was formed to counter what the *New York Times* reported was "alarm" about "the party's drift from the long-standing alignment with Israel" and the "rising skepticism on the left toward the Jewish State."[17] The group calling itself "the Democratic Majority for Israel" includes former Michigan governor (and my former student) Jennifer Granholm, former secretary of housing Henry Cisneros, Congressmen Hakeem Jeffries and Eliot Engel, Democratic operatives Ann Lewis and Mark Mellman and others. They will be supporting "candidates in 2020 who stand unwaveringly" with Israel.

These and other efforts—political, academic, economic, diplomatic, moral—must be deployed in opposition to those who would weaken bipartisan support for Israel. Supporters of Israel should never be reluctant to use U.S. power in the interest of justice. Despite its military strength, Israel remains the underdog in a world dominated by anti-Israel nations, as reflected by the repeated votes of the United Nations. It is in danger of losing the future as greater numbers of young, minority and left-wing people turn against Israel. The anti-Israel forces remain Goliath to Israel's David. The struggle to secure Israel's future must begin on the campuses, but it must not end there. The most powerful weapon in the court of public opinion—truth— must be deployed in every forum where lies are told in an effort to delegitimize the nation-state of the Jewish people. No attempt should be made to censor these lies or those who purvey them. Instead, they must be confronted, debated, corrected and discredited, as I have repeatedly tried to do. I hope to continue to participate in that important effort as long as I have the strength and capacity to speak truth to power. But efforts are underway to try to silence my voice on Israel. An extreme anti-Israel website called Mondoweiss decided to repeat a totally false and thoroughly disproved allegation of sexual misconduct by a woman I had never even met expressly in order to silence me. Here is what it said:

> We have picked up news about the sexual allegations against Dershowitz because Dershowitz is such an outspoken supporter of Israel and the matter has inevitably affected his influence in the foreign policy arena.

It doesn't matter to Israel haters whether the allegations are completely disproved, struck, withdrawn, mistaken and made up—as they were in this case—as long as it negatively impacts my ability to defend Israel. I will continue to fight back against these and other anti-Israel motivated defamations.

Conclusion

Israel—The Next 70 Years

I COMPLETED THE first draft of this memoir 70 years after I first became passionate about the nation-state of the Jewish people, and then began to think about the next 70 years. I decided to travel to Israel for perhaps the 100th time in the last half-century. My pleasure was greatly enhanced by bringing my grandson with me. Lyle, who had recently graduated from college and would soon start medical school, had never been to Israel. Three years earlier I had established this "tradition" by bringing my granddaughter, Lori, to Israel shortly after she graduated. (She, too, is in medical school.) It had been the first trip for her as well.

It was both fascinating and educational for me to see how differently this generation of young people perceives Israel. For them, Israel was not a poor nation, living simply off agriculture and scrounging for weapons with which to defend itself against the mighty armies committed to its destruction that surrounded it. For my grandchildren, Israel is an economic and military superpower, a startup nation whose technological innovations are the envy of the world. Gleaming skyscrapers had replaced the run-down British colonial buildings I witnessed when I first visited Israel. To be sure, my grandchildren knew from having attended college that Israel was also a pariah nation among many on the hard left, especially in academia. They came to Israel with the skepticism that characterizes many millennials raised in secular households and who attended elite colleges. They came to see for themselves and decide for themselves. They knew that their grandfather was a zealous advocate for Israel, though critical of its settlement and occupation policies. They didn't want to be influenced by my ideas, and I know them well enough to understand that any attempt to influence them would backfire.

During my trip with my grandson, we attended the opening of the new U.S. embassy that had just relocated from Tel Aviv to Jerusalem. My grandson had mixed reactions to that event, because it appeared at times like a Republican campaign rally attended primarily by Orthodox Jews, Christian fundamentalists and other assorted right-wingers. Former senator Joe Lieberman and I were the only prominent Democrats seated in places of honor near the front. The event itself was historic, and Lyle understood that he was a witness to both history and controversy. Following the event, we had long and serious conversations about its significance.

That was the only somewhat political event we attended during the 10-day visit. I met with Prime Minister Netanyahu, as I always do when I travel to Israel, but Lyle preferred to wander the streets of Tel Aviv rather than meet my friend Bibi. When I told the prime minister of my grandson's preference, he laughed and said, "Smart kid. I would love to be walking the streets of Tel Aviv myself."

We covered the length and breadth of the tiny country, which Lyle found hard to believe was approximately the size of New Jersey. We were taken inside a terror tunnel built by Hamas under the fence separating Gaza from Israel. We went to a military command center where young female soldiers were each assigned to monitor several hundred yards of the border fence. We discussed with military commanders the options the army has in trying to prevent infiltrators from crossing the border and threatening the Israeli civilians. We both wondered why Israel could not do a better job of avoiding civilian casualties. The commanders explained that they had tried to use sonar devices, teargas, power hoses, rubber bullets and foul-smelling chemicals. None of these nonlethal tactics succeeded in keeping potential terrorists armed with Molotov cocktails, guns and knives from breaking through the fence and attacking nearby civilian targets. Hamas had provided any potential lynch mob with Google Maps coordinates showing the fastest routes from the fence to Jewish kibbutzim, schools and daycare centers. We still wondered whether Israel could do a better job, though we were not as certain that there were viable alternatives.

From the south, we traveled north to the Golan Heights and Israel's border with Syria, Lebanon and Jordan. We flew over the Golan Heights in a helicopter piloted by a former IDF air force officer. At the border fence, we were briefed by the head of the northern command. While we were being briefed, we could see puffs of smoke in the distance and hear the sound of rockets. A few days earlier, these rockets and missiles were aimed at Israel by Iranian forces, but Israel had retaliated and destroyed most of the Iranian rocket launchers. So we were not in danger. But the Iron Dome, which had destroyed the rockets that had crossed into Israel, was visible just yards away from where we were briefed, with its multiple rockets aimed in the direction of Syria in the event that any new missiles approached Israeli territory. We understood why Israel could never turn the Golan Heights over to Syria, who would once again use it as a launching pad for rockets targeting Israeli civilians. It would be as if a nation at war returned a battleship captured from its enemy. (I used this analogy in advocating U.S. recognition of Israel's annexation of the Golan Heights to President Trump.)

We were then taken by my associate Danny Grossman—who had been in both the U.S. and Israeli air forces—to an air force base where Lyle was permitted to "fly" an F15 simulator. He was told he would make a great pilot. When I tried the simulator, I was told to keep my day job. We were then shown a fleet of Israeli drones capable of surveillance as well as bombing. We met with young pilots Lyle's age who flew on missions every day. We were told that there are now more Israeli women flying combat missions in the Israeli air force than there are Saudi women driving cars (although this may now be changing). Lyle had interesting talks with his contemporaries about what it means to risk one's life to protect one's nation and its civilians. Lyle was deeply impressed with the commitment of these pilots, many of whom were active in the peace movement in their spare time. These are warriors who understand the price of war and the benefits of peace.

Lyle loved Jerusalem, especially the juxtaposition of ancient and modern. We went into the tunnels under the Western Wall, and Lyle went through the tunnels in the ancient city of David. We walked through the shuk and along the Via Dolorosa into the Church of the Holy Sepulchre, home to different Christian faiths. We ascended the Temple Mount, where Lyle was forced to put on a "dress" to cover his shorts. We walked up to but not into the two great Muslim holy places: the Al-Aqsa Mosque and the Dome of the Rock. We saw a replica of what the Jewish temple may have looked like when it stood proudly on the Temple Mount.

Lyle is not at all religious, having been raised in a completely secular household. But he was moved by the display of faith evident to anyone who ascends the Temple Mount and then descends to the plaza adjoining the Western Wall. We left notes in the wall, knowing full well that they would never be read. It's a tradition, and traditions have a power of their own regardless of one's belief, disbelief or agnosticism. (I subsequently wrote an op-ed "Confessing" to committing a "war crime" by putting a note in the "unlawfully occupied" Western Wall.)

One of the highlights of our visit was a trip on the back of an ambucycle of United Hatzalah, an Israeli medical rescue organization. By using these ambucycles—high-tech motorcycles that serve as mobile first-responder ambulances—this organization manages to reach anywhere in Israel in about 90 seconds. Its volunteer first-responders speed all over Israel, including the West Bank. Its volunteers include Orthodox Jewish men and women, Christians, secular Jews and Muslims, and everyone else who forms part of the Israeli mosaic. It is an amazing organization, and I have even helped contribute an ambucycle to it. We went to the tech center and watched as accidents showed up on the screen and the nearest volunteers were directed to the victims. It's a perfect marriage of Israel's commitment to high technology and the saving of lives.

Lyle and I ascended Masada, the mountaintop retreat of the remnants of the Jewish community in the first century CE that was destroyed by the Romans. When I first ascended in 1970, it took three hours to hike up the winding road in 100-degree temperature. This time it took five minutes in a funicular. But the impact was still powerful as we saw how the Jews struggled to survive and then chose death over slavery and rape. I bought Lyle a Masada medal with the iconic message that Masada will never fall again—that the nation-state of the Jewish people will never again be put in the position of having to choose between death and slavery.

We visited the Holocaust Museum, which documents an era in which Jews didn't have that choice. Even those who were slaves were murdered. Even those who had converted to Christianity were gassed. Even those who were too young to know they were Jews were subjected to genocide. Lyle was deeply moved by the feeling of helplessness that forced Jews into ghettos and then into extermination camps or death marches. We discussed our own family, many of whom were murdered by the Nazis, including a 17-year-old girl and her 15-year-old brother. I told Lyle the story of my grandfather—his great-great-grandfather—Louis Dershowitz, related briefly in chapter 1, who helped rescue 29 members of our family by securing affidavits, mostly false, from neighbors offering them nonexistent "jobs." They had tried to get visas, but they were rebuffed, like so many other Jews, by the anti-Semitic policies of Roosevelt's State Department. So my grandfather, who lived in the Williamsburg section of Brooklyn, went to neighbors and told them that each of their basements would now become synagogues and they would sign affidavits falsely stating that their "synagogue" needed a rabbi, cantor, sexton, rebetzin, mohel or other religious functionary.

In this way, my grandfather managed to get visas for 28 out of 29 family members who left Czechoslovakia just before the Nazis entered and murdered its Jewish population. But one relative, a teenage girl who was studying the violin in Poland, was left behind. My family wouldn't give up on her, and so my grandfather sent his oldest unmarried son, Milton, into the belly of the beast, Nazi-occupied Poland, to "marry" young Anna. They performed a fake marriage, and they were able to get her out of Poland with his American passport (recall that the United States was not yet at war with Germany). While on the ship returning to America, my uncle actually fell in love with Anna, and they were married shortly after they reached the Statue of Liberty.

Lyle was deeply impressed by the bravery, illegal as it was, of his great-great-grandfather. I could see that Lyle—like his great-great-grandfather, his grandparents and his parents—was determined never to allow an event like the Holocaust to be perpetrated against any group of human beings.

We had fun while in Israel as well. Lyle swam—or rather floated—in the Dead Sea. He rappelled down a 100-foot cliff—as his sister had earlier done—scaring the heck out of his grandfather. We drove through barren deserts, mountain roads, archeological sites and ordinary cities and towns. Lyle was enthralled by the diversity of life in Israel, ranging from the most religious to the most secular, the whitest northern Europeans, blackest Ethiopian Africans, brownest Arabs and swarthiest Persians, as well as multiethnic survivors of Soviet oppression.

Experiencing the difference between religious, traditional, ancient Jerusalem and modern, super-secular, high-tech Tel Aviv is like being in two very different countries. Both of us love architecture, and we admired the Bauhaus district of Tel Aviv as well as the ancient walls and edifices of Jerusalem.

This trip to Israel with my grandson closed a circle for me. This circle began in 1948 with the establishment of the country, my summer in Zionist Hebrew Camp and my support for the new nation-state of the Jewish people. The circle closed with me, as an 80-year-old elder statesman, seeing the love—albeit mixed with skepticism—that my grandson showed toward the same nation 70 years later and nearly 50 years after I first set foot on its soil. This visit coincided with the completion of the first draft of this memoir reflecting on 70 years of passionate, if sometimes critical, support of Israel. It was a fitting end—a trip I will never forget. But Israel's circle of life is never closed. Every year brings new, often unpredictable, challenges. The Talmud says that prophecy ended with the destruction of the Second Temple, and anyone who tries to predict the future is either a knave or a fool. With that caution in mind, I will end this volume by asking what can be done to secure Israel's future, and by suggesting some answers.

The world has benefited in countless ways from the establishment of Israel. I take enormous pride in the indisputable reality that no nation in history, certainly none as tiny as Israel, has contributed more to humankind in so short a period of time as Israel has since its birth only seven decades ago. It has saved countless lives though its medical, pharmaceutical, genetic, agricultural, environmental and other scientific and technological innovations. As the "startup nation," it has contributed disproportionately to the communications revolution. It has revived a dormant language of prayer, turning it into a vibrant spoken and written modern language and literature. It has shown the world how to integrate, though of course not perfectly, immigrants and refugees from Morocco, Algeria, Tunisia, Yemen, Egypt, Iraq, Iran, Syria, Ethiopia, the former Soviet Union and countries in other far-flung corners of the world. It has taught democracies how to fight terrorism while upholding the rule of law. It has prevented Iraq and Syria from developing nuclear arsenals that would have endangered the Middle East and beyond. It has transitioned from a local agrarian subsistence economy into a world-class economic superpower, without reliance on vast natural resources. It has also transitioned its military from a small civilian self-defense force that relied on primitive weapons to one of the world's most powerful and technologically sophisticated armed forces.

Along the way, it has made its share of mistakes, as have all other democracies, especially those facing existential threats.[1] But on balance, Israel has been the most successful new nation that has been born—really reborn—during the past century.[2] Moreover, its "birth certificate" has been more "legitimate" than other nations, which were born of violence, the drawing of colonial maps or coups d'état. Perhaps because so many of Israel's founders were trained in the law, they made sure, like the patriarch Abraham before them, that they secured legal title to the land that became Israel. This legal title was composed of both private and public contracts, treaties, declarations, resolutions and recognitions. Much of the land that the United Nations allocated to a Jewish state in 1947 had already been purchased from absentee landlords at fair market value by the Jewish National Fund and other groups and individuals.

Israel was founded by the pen, though it had to be defended by the sword. Imagine how much more good it could accomplish if its enemies allowed it to turn its swords into plowshares, its nuclear weapons into nuclear medicine.

And yet, despite its lawful birth certificate, and its unparalleled contributions to humankind since its birth, and its successful efforts to defend itself within the rule of law,[3] it is the *only* nation in the world whose legitimacy as a nation is questioned—by other nations, by academicians, by international organizations and even by some "religious" leaders. One powerful nation in particular, Iran, has called for its physical annihilation by military force. This call has been echoed by numerous terrorist organizations, such as Hamas, Hezbollah and ISIS. More than 30 other nations refuse to recognize Israel or establish diplomatic relations with it. Until 1993, this included the Vatican, which only recently changed its view. Several

Protestant denominations, whose leaders routinely demonize the nation-state of the Jewish people, have supported BDS.

Why? Certainly it cannot be because every other nation of the world is more deserving of recognition or diplomatic relations than Israel. Certainly it cannot be because the Palestinians have a more compelling case for statehood than, say, the Kurds. But even if they did, the Palestinians rejected numerous deals that would have accorded them statehood. Even more compelling, recognizing statehood for the Palestinians is not incompatible with recognizing statehood for the Israelis.

Neither is it because Israel receives U.S. aid. So does Egypt, Jordan, the Palestinian Authority, Pakistan and many other nations with horrendous human rights records that are not subjected to the opprobrium to which Israel is regularly subjected.

There is no doubt in my mind that if Israel were not the nation-state of the Jewish people, its actions—indeed is very existence—would not be challenged by the double standards for which it has been judged from even before its birth. In the first place, the Arabs and Muslims would not be as opposed to a non-Jewish state in its midst as they are to a Jewish state. When Lebanon was a hybrid state—divided between Muslim and Christian Arabs—there was far less opposition to the Christian components, one of which was even a Christian president. Even if Lebanon had been divided into two states, one Christian and one Muslim, there would not have been as much opposition to a small Christian state as to a small Jewish one. Nor is it only because both states would have been Arab. Morocco has a substantial non-Arab population, and neither Iran nor Turkey is Arab. According to some Islamic "scholars," even an inch of Muslim land is prohibited from becoming a Jewish state.

Moreover, the world at large, outside of the Muslim Middle East, has always applied a double standard to all matters Jewish. They demand more of a Jewish state than they would of a non-Jewish state. As the bigoted Bishop Tutu acknowledged, Jews are a "peculiar people" who "can't ever hope to be judged by the same standards which are used for other people."[4] Whether this is a theological mandate or simply a cover for anti-Semitism, it is a widespread view among some Christians. How else can the Vatican's long delay in recognizing Israel be explained? The Holy See, which traditionally has more diplomatic relations than most Western countries, refused to recognize the nation-state of the Jewish people until 1993, claiming that the existence of a Jewish state would create a backlash for Christians in Arab countries.

Then there is the role that intersectionality currently plays in the double standard applied to Israel, especially by hard-left academics, students and activists.

Zionism and Jews are accused of being universal oppressors, and the oppressed must stick together to struggle against the oppressors.[5] It's a zero-sum game. So if you are among the oppressed, you can't also be an oppressor. And if you are an oppressor, you cannot be regarded as an ally of the oppressed, even if you are trying to help them. Thus, you cannot be both a Zionist (oppressor) and a feminist (oppressed) or a supporter of gay rights (oppressed) or civil rights (oppressed activist). But if you are a feminist leader of the Women's March or a black supporter of Black Lives Matter, then you get a pass for also supporting an anti-Semite like Louis Farrakhan or the anti-Semitic platform of Black Lives Matter.

It is important not to overstate (or understate) the role that Israel's Jewish character plays in the way it is treated. Criticism of Israel's actions or policies is not anti-Semitic. If it were, the greatest concentration of anti-Semites would be in Tel Aviv! But focusing only on imperfections of the nation-state of the Jewish people is bigotry, pure and simple. As Thomas Friedman has aptly put it:

> *Criticizing Israel is not anti-Semitic, and saying so is vile. But singling out Israel for opprobrium and international sanction— out of all proportion to any other party in the Middle East—is anti-Semitic, and not saying so is dishonest.*

Criticism of Israel is not only *not* anti-Semitic, it is healthy, as long as it doesn't violate my friend Anatoly Sharansky's "three Ds":

> *The first "D" is the test of demonization. When the Jewish state is being demonized; when Israel's actions are blown out of all sensible proportion; when comparisons are made between Israelis and Nazis and between Palestinian refugee camps and Auschwitz—this is anti-Semitism, not legitimate criticism of Israel.*
>
> *The second "D" is the test of double standards. When criticism of Israel is applied selectively; when Israel is singled out by the United Nations for human rights abuses while the behavior of known and major abusers, such as China, Iran, Cuba, and Syria, is ignored; when Israel's Magen David Adom, alone among the world's ambulance services, is denied admission to the International Red Cross—this too is anti-Semitism.*
>
> *The third D is the test of delegitimization: when Israel's fundamental right to exist is denied—alone among all peoples of the world—this, too, is anti-Semitism.*

As it begins its eighth decade, Israel remains in a complex situation, its future unpredictable. It has never been stronger—militarily, economically and even diplomatically. But the potential threats it faces from growing anti-Israel sentiment among young left-wingers has rarely been greater. There are also military threats, especially from Iran, which has sworn to wipe Israel off the face of the earth.[6] Its leaders have said that if they were to acquire a nuclear arsenal and bomb Tel Aviv then that would be the end of Israel, because "Israel is a one-bomb state," requiring only a single nuclear bomb to defeat.[7] In 2004, it was reported that the former president of Iran, Hashemi Rafsanjani, a supposed moderate, had "boast[ed] to an American journalist that] if Iran were to develop nuclear weapons and use them to attack Israel, they "would kill as many as five million Jews."

He estimated that even if Israel retaliated by dropping its own nuclear bombs, Iran would probably lose only 15 million people, which he said would be a small "sacrifice" from among the billion Muslims in the world. The journalist said that Rafsanjani seemed pleased with his formulations. He later elaborated on his boast by stating, "The dropping of one atomic bomb would not leave anything in Israel"; however, an Israeli nuclear retaliation would just produce damages in the Muslim world. This "moderate" former present of Iran continued, "It is not irrational to contemplate such an eventuality."[8]

In other worlds, the "not irrational" calculation being contemplated by at least some Iranian leaders is that since Israel is a "one-bomb country," most of whose population (presumably including its 20 percent Arab population) would be killed by one bomb, and since Iran is a far larger country and part of the enormous "Muslim world," the tradeoff might be worth it, especially to an apocalyptic regime that was prepared to sacrifice hundreds of thousands of its citizens—including thousands of child "soldiers"—in a futile war with Iraq. Would not such a regime equally be willing to sacrifice millions of its citizens to achieve its major political and religious imperative, namely the annihilation of the nation-state of the Jewish people, and with it nearly half the world's Jewish population?

For those who believe the United States would never let such a new Holocaust occur, remember the one important lesson Elie Wiesel learned from the Holocaust: "Always believe the threats of your enemies more than the promises of your friends."

Israel lives by that historic reality. Its leaders will almost certainly act to prevent Iran from acquiring nuclear weapons, even if it has to act alone and with great risk to its armed forces. Moreover, the risk would extend to its civilian population as well, since Hezbollah, which is controlled by Iran, has tens of thousands of sophisticated rockets aimed at Israeli cities, towns, airports and military facilities. A war with Iran—even one in which Israel managed to destroy Iran's nuclear capacity—would be catastrophic, but it may be necessary if Iran seeks to develop a nuclear arsenal after the current deal expires.

Containment of a nuclear Iran is not an option Israel can accept. A preventive war, with all the consequences that entails, would be the only option if Israel's intelligence concluded that Iran was close to developing a nuclear arsenal, since Iran already has the capacity to deliver nuclear-tipped rockets to Israeli targets.

Such a cataclysmic confrontation may be unlikely, but it is certainly possible, and Israel is planning for this contingency now.

Were Israel to engage in a preventive war against Iran's nuclear facilities, it would be condemned by the international community, as it has been in the past. It would be condemned—as it always has been—because the world would never see the number of lives saved by such an action, as it will never see the lives saved by Israel's destruction of the nuclear facilities that were being constructed by Iraq and Syria.

While analogies are always imperfect, it may be instructive to imagine how the world would have reacted if Great Britain and France had waged a preventive war against Nazi Germany in the mid-1930s, when the Nazis were building the war machine with which they soon were to conquer much of continental Europe and kill 50 million people, including tens of millions of civilians. Assume that a preventive war directed against the German military would have cost 10,000—or even 100,000—lives. The world would have seen those dead bodies and would have condemned the "aggressors" for the costs in human lives they incurred in order to prevent the possibility that Hitler might carry out the threats he had made in *Mein Kampf* and in his speeches. Had a preventive war stopped Hitler from carrying out those threats, the world would never have seen the lives saved by the preventive war carried out by Britain and France.

History is dumb as to future probabilities or possibilities. It knows only what did happen, not what might have happened if a different course had been followed. Any leaders of Britain and France who had engaged in a preventive war that cost thousands of lives then and saved millions in the future would have been condemned by the verdict of dumb history because the costs would have been visible, but the savings would have been invisible.

The same would be true of any Israeli (or American) leader who engaged in a costly preventive war to avert Iran from securing a nuclear arsenal. The world would see the visible costs but not the invisible benefits. Great statesmen and stateswomen must be prepared to incur condemnation for making bold, lifesaving decisions whose benefits may never become visible to history. I told this to Benjamin Netanyahu during one of our many dinner conversations. He looked at me soberly and said, "I only hope I never have to make that decision."

Another threat faced by Israel, this one in the longer term, is the diminishing support for the nation-state of the Jewish people by young Americans, especially on the left. Until recently, this diminution of support could be seen primarily on the extreme hard left, especially among university faculty, some students and radical activists. This was not terribly concerning, since these fringe groups have little direct impact on American policy. This tactic of seeking universities and corporations to divest from or boycott Israel was failing. Not a single major university or major corporation had divested or boycotted. (When the Hampshire College faculty voted to divest from Israel, I began a campaign among alumni donors to divest—to stop contributing to Hampshire. The president immediately rescinded the faculty vote.) But the tactic succeeded in alienating some on the center left from Israel. It also succeeded in making it "politically incorrect" to be a Zionist. The result has been a diminution of support for Israel among young centrists. This does not always take the form of overt opposition to Israel; more often, it reflects itself in a lack of concern regarding Israel. It is simply easier not to take sides on the Israeli–Palestinian issue, because taking either side incurs a cost in popularity, acceptability and, some believe, even academic standing.

The result has been a hardening of sides: the anti-Israel groups have become more strident and extreme, causing the pro-Israel groups to become more defensive. The large middle of students and others for whom Israel is not a priority has expanded. One reason for this is the shrill demands of "intersectionalists," who say that one cannot be a Zionist and a feminist, gay rights activist, civil rights advocate, environmentalist or other "do-gooder." So those who wish to be accepted as do-gooders by the intersectionalists are coerced or persuaded to abandon their Zionism, or at least make it less visible.

I am proud that my children and grandchildren do not adhere to either extreme. Their support of Israel is critical, nuanced, calibrated and issue-oriented. They may be less passionate than I am and less committed, but they are equally dedicated to justice, fairness and truth. No one could ask for more.

This diminution of support for Israel among current students threatens the bipartisan support for Israel that has long been a staple of American politics. Recent polls suggest a growing disparity between Republicans and Democrats in their support of Israel. This is especially apparent among young Democrats. The electoral victories of three overtly anti-Israel congressional candidates may not be representative of Democratic voters, but it surely is a sign of the changing times.[9]

Today's students and young people are our future leaders, and the current diminution in support for Israel among young Democrats and "progressives" poses dangers to the future of bipartisan support for the nation-state of the Jewish people. These young people did not experience the Holocaust, the difficult birth of Israel, its wars for survival and its heroic actions to defend itself from genocidal threats. What they have seen is the long occupation, the growth in settlement activities, wars of choice, civilian deaths repeatedly shown on television, and a wealthy and powerful Israel confronted by weak Palestinians.

Whenever I speak about Israel—whether in the United States, Israel, Europe, New Zealand, Australia, Qatar or South Africa—I am asked whether I am pessimistic or optimistic about the prospects for peace in the Middle East. I respond by illustrating the difference between an Israeli pessimist and an Israeli optimist. A pessimist says, "Oy, things are so bad, they can't possibly get worse." An optimist replies, "Yes, they can!"

No supporter of Israel, especially a Jew, can ever be a total optimist. There are too many contingencies, too many uncertainties, too many variables, too much history, too much optimism followed by tragedy.

Consider Weimar Germany or socialist France in the 1920s. Life was generally good for the Jews, especially secular and assimilated Jews. To be sure, residual anti-Semitism did exist, but not like in prior decades when German writer Wilhelm Marr had coined the term anti-Semitism as a positive political program, or when the Dreyfus Affair in France, beginning in 1894 and culminating in 1906, uncovered massive anti-Semitism among artists, priests, military leaders and ordinary French citizens. But middle-class and professional Jews—lawyers, professors, politicians, businessmen, doctors, scientists—in the 1920s were overcoming the exclusionary bigotry of the past and rising to the top of their callings.

Then a series of extremely unpredictable contingencies occurred, beginning with the First World War in 1914. No one wanted that war, but an isolated event in an obscure part of the Balkans knocked down a domino that led to an all-out conflict that changed the world forever. Its impact on Jewish life, though unpredictable at the time, was the most profound in two millennia: the destruction of European Jewry and the creation of the modern state of Israel. Neither is likely to have occurred without the First World War.

The defeat of Germany, the humiliation of the Versailles Treaty and massive inflation and unemployment led directly to the rise of Hitler. The destruction of the Ottoman Empire and the defeat of the Turks by the British in Palestine led—at least indirectly—to the Balfour Declaration, the British Mandate over Palestine and the division of that mandate by the United Nations into proposed Jewish and Arab states.

No one during the first quarter of the twentieth century could have predicted (Theodor Herzl came close) these and other unlikely contingencies that led to the Holocaust and the creation of Israel—the two most dramatic events in modern Jewish history. Yet these events occurred. We are now in the first quarter of the twenty-first century. Once again, the future looks bright for the Jewish people and their nation-state. But once again, there are too many contingencies that make optimistic predictions too uncertain to count on. Cautious optimism, coupled with thoughtful preparation for pessimistic outcomes, is the best we can do.

The existence of Israel, with its powerful armed forces that include a nuclear arsenal, makes a repetition of the tragic events of 1939–1945 unlikely. History never repeats itself, because we generally learn its lessons and take steps to prevent precise repetition. But variations on the past are common, as Hitler noted when he said that no one remembers the Turkish genocide of the Armenians.

Jews and supporters of Israel must be prepared for all contingencies, all variations on the past, and all future threats, no matter how unlikely they seem today.

The best way to prepare for an unpredictable contingency is to be ready for the worst while trying to achieve the best. The Jewish people and their nation-state must be strong—materially, morally and psychologically. National strength includes an Israeli armed forces qualitatively superior to all the combined Arab and Muslim armed forces. It also includes political power disproportionate to our numbers. The Israeli lobby in the United States—AIPAC—is accused of being too strong. I think it is not strong enough. Jewish supporters of Israel are accused of being too wealthy and spending too much money to influence American support for Israel. I think they spend too little money to support Israel. Jews are accused of having disproportionate influence in newspapers, television, Hollywood, the news media and other forms of communication. Yet we are losing the communications war. We must do better.

Another tragic lesson of the Holocaust is that Jews and Jewish institutions need disproportionate power to survive. We are small in number, but the hatred against us looms large. Having morality on our side is essential, but it is not sufficient.

The Jews who died in the Holocaust had morality on their side, but it was not enough to protect them against the overwhelming material forces arrayed against them. History has demonstrated that Jews must be prepared to defend themselves—militarily, politically, economically and in every other way. We should try to make and maintain alliances with friends, without ever counting on those friends to come through in the crunch.

Millennia ago, the psalmist wrote, "God will give the Jewish People strength." He then continued, "God will bless the Jewish people with peace."

I interpret that verse to mean that for the Jewish people and their state, strength must precede peace. Without overwhelming strength, they will never experience peace, because they have too many enemies threatening their destruction. The Jews of Europe lacked strength. They relied on governments—some openly hostile, others promising support to prevent the threat of their enemies from materializing. The threats materialized but the promises did not. The lesson must be learned, lest deadly variations on the tragic past become the future.

Back in 1948, no one could have imagined, and certainly could not have accurately predicted, what Israel would be like seven decades in the future. Nor would it have been possible to predict who Israel's most dangerous enemies would be. Early in its history, Israel had good relations with Iran and Turkey and terrible relations with Egypt, the Gulf States and Jordan. Today the situation is somewhat reversed.

Back in 1948, the Democratic Party and the left were the strongest supporters. The Republican Party and the right were far less so. Today the situation is reversed.

Back in 1948, Israel was a socialist, agrarian, Ashkenazi (European heritage), secular society. The right, the religious and the Sephardim were relegated to the margins, both politically and socially. Today the situation is reversed.

Back in 1948, Soviet Jews were the "Jews of Silence," as Elie Wiesel had called them, living under communist repression. Today, they are among Israel's most productive citizens—initiators of the "startup nation."

The future of the Jewish people and its state is promising, but success—indeed survival—is not assured in a world in which enmity toward Jews and their state has been one of the few historical constants. History is not destiny. History is past. Destiny is future. The future is largely, though not exclusively, in our hands. We must determine our destiny, write our future history, and assure the survival of the Jewish people and their nation-state forever.

Acknowledgments

This book could not have been completed without the assistance of my associates and assistants Aaron Voloj and Hannah Dodson, who were primarily responsible for the end notes and research. Thanks to Adam Bellow for his excellent editorial suggestions; to my agent, Karen Gantz, for making it happen; to my assistant Maura Kelley for managing the manuscript; to Alan Rothfeld for proofreading; to other friends and family for their gentle criticisms; and to my wife, Carolyn, for her loving encouragement of everything I do.

Notes

Introduction

1. Patrick Kingsley, "Anti-Semitism Is Back, from the Left, Right, and Islamist Extremes. Why?" *New York Times*, April 4, 2019, https://www.nytimes.com /2019/04/04/world/europe/antisemitism-europe-united-states.html.

2. Brian Klug, "The Myth of the New Anti-Semitism," *The Nation,* June 29, 2015, https://www.thenation.com/article/myth-new-anti-semitism/.

3. "Behold the people, the children of Israel, are more numerous and stronger than we. Come, let us outsmart it lest it become numerous, and it may be that if a war will occur, it, too, may join our enemies . . ." (Exodus 1:9–10). So the pharaoh ordered the Jewish people enslaved and every male baby killed.

4. "There is a certain people scattered abroad and dispersed among the people . . . , and their laws are diverse . . . therefore, it is not for the king's profit to suffer them" (Esther 3:8).

5. Rabbi Lionel Blue, interview, BBC Radio 4.

6. Quoted in Alan Dershowitz, *The Case Against BDS: Why Singling Out Israel for Boycott Is Anti-Semitic and Anti-Peace* (e-book; New York: Post Hill Press, 2018), 57.

7. Alan Dershowitz, *The Case Against Israel's Enemies: Exposing Jimmy Carter and Others Who Stand in the Way of Peace* (e-book; Hoboken, NJ: John Wiley & Sons), 4.

8. "Is BDS Wrong?" Oxford Union debate, November 2015.

9. Dershowitz, *Case Against Israel's Enemies*, 11.

10. C-SPAN, "Cornel West and Alan Dershowitz Mideast Debate," December 1, 2017, https://www.c-span.org/video/?437547-1/cornel-west-alan-dershowitz -mideast-debate.

11. Dershowitz, *Case Against BDS*, 5.

12. Dershowitz, *Case Against BDS*, 5–6.

13. "Activism," *Forward*, November 14, 2003.

Chapter 1

1. Much of the land was bought from distant land speculators in Syria and other locations. "For dozens of years, the Blue Box served as a fundraiser in every Diaspora home and every Jewish institution in Israel and abroad: A cherished, popular means to realize the Zionist vision of establishing a state for the Jewish people." "The Blue Box," Keren Kayemeth LeIsrael Jewish National Fund, http://www.kkl-jnf.org/about-kkl-jnf/the-blue-box/ (accessed February 15, 2019).

2. Land was purchased, primarily, from absentee landlords and real estate speculators at fair or exorbitant prices. See Alan Dershowitz, *The Case for Israel* (New York: John Wiley and Sons, 2003), 25.

3. Ben-Gurion instructed the Jewish refugees never to buy land belonging to local "fellahs or worked by them." Shabtai Teveth, *David Ben-Gurion and the Palestinian Arabs* (New York: Oxford University Press, 1985), 32.

4. There were some Jewish anti-Zionists, even back then. They were primarily aristocratic German Jews who rejected the concept of Judaism as nationalism in addition to religion. There were also some ultraorthodox rabbis and their followers who opposed the secular Jewish state on religious grounds, but both of these groups constituted a small minority within the Jewish community.

5. Dershowitz, *The Case for Israel*, 76.

6. The initial strategy of the Arab armies was the targeting of civilians via "major urban terrorist attacks." The Arab armies also repeatedly and deliberately dropped bombs on civilian population centers near no legitimate military targets. See Dershowitz, *The Case for Israel*, 76.

7. CSPAN, "Cornel West and Alan Dershowitz Mideast Debate," December 1, 2017.

8. See, e.g., Eric Fripp, *Nationality and Statelessness in the International Law and Refugee Status* (Oxford: Hart Publishing, 2016). "Population transfers used to be accepted as a means to settle ethnic conflict."

9. Dershowitz, *The Case for Israel*, 86–87.

10. "To be a colonial country you have to be working on someone's behalf. The Jews who came to Palestine to join their brothers and sisters who had been there for 3000 years came from Russia. . . . The word *colonial* simply doesn't fit an indigenous movement that started with people who lived in countries around the world but who had relatives and coreligionists living in Tzvat," C-SPAN, "Cornel West and Alan Dershowitz Mideast Debate," December 1, 2017.

11. Shibley Telhami, "Americans Are Increasingly Critical of Israel," *Foreign Policy*, December 11, 2018, https://foreignpolicy.com/2018/12/11/americans-are-increasingly-critical-of-israel/.

12. Immanuel Kant, *Anthropology from a Pragmatic Point of View*. Trans. by Victor Lyle Dowdell (Carbondale: Southern Illinois University Press, 1978), paragraph 46.

13. Dershowitz, *The Case for Israel*, 41.

14. "British Palestine Mandate: History & Overview," Jewish Virtual Library, https://www.jewishvirtuallibrary.org/history-and-overview-of-the-british -palestine-mandate (accessed April 13, 2019).

15. Dershowitz, *The Case for Israel*, 65.

16. Several years ago, I wrote to the president of Holy Cross University, urging him to consider changing the name of the University's athletic teams from the "Crusaders," because the actual crusaders were genocidal murderers. I received a curt denial. Dershowitz, *The Case Against Israel's Enemies*, 158.

17. United Nations, "Chapter 2: The Plan of Partition and End of the British Mandate," in *The Question of Palestine and the United Nations*, 2003, https://www .un.org/Depts/dpi/palestine/ch2.pdf.

18. Today there are upward of two million Arabs living in Israel. Bernard Wasserstein, "The Partition of Palestine," Foreign Policy Research Institute, December 9, 2014, https://www.fpri.org/article/2014/12/the-partition-of-palestine/; "Israeli Arabs: Status of Arabs in Israel," Jewish Virtual Library, https://www .jewishvirtuallibrary.org/the-status-of-arabs-in-israel (accessed April 13, 2019).

19. Some Israelis argue that Jordan is the Palestinian state, since it was originally part of the Palestine Mandate and its population is predominantly Palestinian. This doesn't account for the rights of Palestinian Arabs who now live on the West Bank, which Jordan formally ceded to the Palestinian Authority in 1988. United Nations, "Chapter 2: The Plan of Partition and End of the British Mandate."

20. Sari Nusseibeh, "What Next?" *Haaretz*, January 10, 2018, https://www.haaretz .com/1.5346415.

21. Nusseibeh, "What Next?"

22. See Benny Morris, *1948 and After: Israel and the Palestinians* (Oxford: Clarendon Press, 2003); Avi Shlaim, "The War of the Israeli Historians," *Annales* 59, no. 1 (Jan./Feb. 2004): 161–167.

Chapter 2

1. Shortly after the establishment of Israel, hundreds of thousands of Sephardic and Mizrahi Jews left their homes in the Muslim world. Many were forced or pressured to leave. Dershowitz, *The Case for Israel*, 59. 140,000 Holocaust survivors from Europe immigrated to Israel as well. United States Holocaust Memorial Museum, "Jewish Refugees During and After the Holocaust," My

Jewish Learning, February 10, 2017, https://www.myjewishlearning.com /article/jewish-refugees-during-and-after-the-holocaust/.

2. P. R. Brahmananda, "The Impact on India of Population Transfers in 1947 and After," in *Economics of International Migration*, B. Thomas, ed. (London: Macmillan, 1958).

3. The end of World War II marked the largest population transfers in the history of Europe. Huge numbers of people fled communist regimes while millions of Germans were forced out of Eastern Europe. Bernard Wasserstein, "History: World Wars: European Refugee Movements After World War Two," BBC, February 17, 2011. http://www.bbc.co.uk/history/worldwars/wwtwo/refugees_01 .shtml.

4. In a 2011 interview with Israel's Channel 2 News, Palestinian president Mahmoud Abbas said in reference to the Palestinian rejection of the UN Partition plan, "I know, I know. It was our mistake. It was our mistake. It was an Arab mistake as a whole." Dan Williams, "Abbas Faults Arab Refusal of 1947 U.N. Palestine Plan," Reuters, October 28, 2011, https://www.reuters.com/article /us-palestinians-israel-abbas/abbas-faults-arab-refusal-of-1947-u-n-palestine -plan-idUSTRE79R64320111028.

5. Eliezer Ben Yehuda is largely credited with the revival and modernization of Hebrew in the late nineteenth and early twentieth centuries. He created a modern Hebrew vocabulary and dictionary and was largely responsible for introducing Hebrew into the Israeli school systems. Melissa Weininger, "No. 2882: Eliezer Ben Yehuda," *Engines of Our Ingenuity*, May 10, 2013, https://www.uh .edu/engines/epi2882.htm.

6. Dershowitz, *The Case for Israel*, 156.

7. In response to the question of how many Jews should be admitted to Canada, this official said, "None is too many." Irving Abella and Harold Troper, *None Is Too Many: Canada and the Jews of Europe, 1933–1948* (Toronto: University of Toronto Press, 2012); Ellen Umansky, "Closing Our Doors," *Slate*, March 8, 2017.

8. "West Bank," *Encyclopedia Britannica*, https://www.britannica.com/place /West-Bank (accessed April 13, 2019).

9. "Palestine Liberation Organization," *Encyclopedia Britannica*, https://www .britannica.com/topic/Palestine-Liberation-Organization.Goal of PLO (accessed April 15, 2019).

10. Guy Ziv, "Shimon Peres and the French-Israeli Alliance, 1954–1959," *Journal of Contemporary History* 45, no. 2 (2010): 406–429, http://www.jstor.org/stable /20753593.

11. Alan M. Dershowitz, *Preemption: A Knife That Cuts Both Ways* (New York: W. W. Norton, 2007), chapter 3.

12. Dershowitz, *Preemption*, chapter 3.

13. "As Egyptian President Nasser himself boasted, 'We knew the closing of the Gulf of Aqaba meant war with Israel . . . the objective will be Israel's destruct.'" Dershowitz, *The Case for Israel*, 91–92.

14. Dershowitz, *The Case for Israel*, 91.

15. John R. Crook, "Dean Acheson and International Law," *Proceedings of the Annual Meeting, American Society of International Law* 95 (2001): 118–121, http://www.jstor.org/stable/25659468.

16. "Middle East: Timeline: The Suez Crisis," BBC News, July 19, 2006, http://news.bbc.co.uk/2/hi/middle_east/5194576.stm.

17. John Misachi, "What Was the Suez Crisis?" World Atlas, March 20, 2017, https://www.worldatlas.com/articles/what-was-the-suez-crisis.html.

18. Recently, my cousin Idan Dershowitz, who is a junior fellow at Harvard, wrote a brilliant op-ed in the *New York Times* demonstrating that the prohibition against gay sex in Leviticus may not be as absolute as widely believed. This led some anti-Israel conspiracy theorists to argue that I had put my "son" up to writing a pro-gay article as part of Israel's pinkwashing project.

19. Deborah E. Lipstadt, *The Eichmann Trial* (New York: Schocken, 2011), 179–181.

20. Judy Maltz, "Bobby Kennedy's Little-Known Visit to Israel That Led to His Assassination," *Haaretz*, June 8, 2018, https://www.haaretz.com/us-news/bobby-kennedy-s-israel-visit-that-led-to-his-assassination-1.6153324.

21. Joseph Kennedy Sr. was a staunch isolationist at the outset of World War II and backed Chamberlain's appeasement policy. He also had a strong relationship with Joseph McCarthy and was one of his major financial supporters.

22. Felix Frankfurter met warnings from Polish diplomat Jan Karski about Nazi brutality throughout Poland with disbelief. See Alan Dershowitz, *Chutzpah* (New York: Touchstone, 1991), 279–283.

Chapter 3

1. "Why Do Criminal Attempts Fail? A New Defense," *Yale Law Journal* 70, no. 1 (1960): https://digitalcommons.law.yale.edu/cgi/viewcontent.cgi?article=8810&context=ylj; "Increasing Community Control over Corporate Crime: A Problem in the Law of Sanctions," *Yale Law Journal* 71, no. 35 (1961); Jay Katz, Joseph Goldstein and Alan Dershowitz, *Psychoanalysis, Psychiatry and the Law* (New York: Free Press, 1967).

2. Michael Oren, "The Revelations of 1967: New Research on the Six-Day War and Its Lessons for the Contemporary Middle East," *Israel Studies* 10, no. 2 (2005): 1–14.

3. Simon Dunstan and Peter Dennis, *The Six-Day War, 1967: Jordan and Syria* (London: Osprey Publishing, 2013), 19.

4. Michael B. Oren, *Six Days of War* (London: Penguin, 2003), 132.

5. It is estimated that around 15,000 Palestinians, many of whom were civilians, were killed by Jordan during Black September, when Arafat and the PLO were expelled from Jordan. Rafael Reuveny, "Black September," *Encyclopedia Britannica,* https://www.britannica.com/topic/Black-September-political-organization-Palestine (accessed August 9, 2018).

6. See, e.g., Uri Friedman, "What Obama Meant By '1967 Lines' and Why It Irked Netanyahu," *The Atlantic,* October 30, 2013, https://www.theatlantic.com/international/archive/2011/05/what-obama-meant-1967-lines-why-irked-netanyahu/350925/.

7. See, for example, "About Israel," Israel Ministry of Foreign Affairs, https://mfa.gov.il/MFA/AboutIsrael/Spotlight/Pages/50-years-ago-The-Six-Day-War-and-the-historic-reunification-of-Jerusalem.aspx (accessed April 16, 2019).

8. Dershowitz, *The Case for Israel,* 205.

9. There was a dispute over a small area near Eilat. Both parties agreed to arbitration. Egypt won, and Israel turned over that land. Alan Cowell, "Israel Gives Disputed Resort to Egypt," *New York Times,* March 16, 1989, https://www.nytimes.com/1989/03/16/world/israel-gives-disputed-resort-to-egypt.html.

10. *Security Interests,* April 2002; Arthur Goldberg, "What Resolution 242 Really Said," *American Foreign Policy Interests* (vol. 1, February 1988).

Chapter 4

1. Daniel S. Levy, "Behind the Protests Against the Vietnam War in 1968," *Time,* January 19, 2018, http://time.com/5106608/protest-1968/.

2. Alan Dershowitz, *Taking the Stand* (New York: Crown Press, 2013), 144.

3. Dershowitz, *Taking the Stand,* 144

4. *Rudolph v. Alabama*, 375 U.S. 889 (1963).

5. Evan Mandery, *A Wild Justice: The Death and Resurrection of Capital Punishment in America* (New York: W. W. Norton Company, 2014).

6. Arthur J. Goldberg and Alan M. Dershowitz, "Declaring the Death Penalty Unconstitutional," *Harvard Law Review* 83 (1970).

7. Dershowitz, *Taking the Stand,* 5.

8. *Newsweek,* June 1978.

9. Shimon Peres, *David's Sling: The Arming of Israel* (Great Britain: Weidenfeld and Nicolson, 1970).

10. Marketwired, "Alan Dershowitz Presents a Powerful Case for Israel's Just War on Terrorism in New Book Terror Tunnels," *Yahoo! Finance,* September 15, 2014, https://finance.yahoo.com/news/alan-dershowitz-presents-powerful-case-172030723.html.

Chapter 5

1. Under the U.S. Initial Post-Surrender Policy in Japan, Allied forces were focused on promoting democracy in Japan and de-militarizing the country. In the Allied-occupied West Germany, the U.S. undertook a project of de-Nazification, as well as an economic/aid plan known as the Marshall Plan.

2. Mary G. Gotschall, "Berrigan, Chomsky Discuss Activism During Open Panel," *Harvard Crimson*, April 26, 1976. For Chomsky's assessment of me, see Noam Chomsky and David Barsamian, *Chronicles of Dissent, Interviews of Noam Chomsky by David Barsamian* (Monroe, ME: Common Courage Press, 2002).

3. I then discussed Shahak's charge that Israel was a racist country:

   > Shahak's approach is well illustrated by the content of his interview. He calls Israel "racist" because it designates its residents by their religion. Most countries in the world, of course, do the same thing. Every Arab country draws distinctions between Moslems and non-Moslems. Indeed, even Lebanon, probably the most liberal of Arab countries, explicitly requires certain of its high officials to be Moslems and others to be Christian (Jews—even anti-Zionist Jews like Dr. Shahak—are excluded from attaining these offices). Other Arab countries exclude all non-Moslems from office, and from other important privileges and rights. There are no such exclusions under Israeli law. A Muslim, a Druze, or a Christian could, theoretically, become prime minister of Israel; and many non-Jews do, in fact, hold high office nationally as well as locally. Most countries in the world—and every single Arab country—could learn a great deal from Israel's handling of its minority population.
   >
   > Of course, Israel is a Jewish country. In a world with numerous Moslem, Catholic and Protestant countries, why should there not be one country where Jewish values and culture predominates? As long as there is no discrimination against other minorities, Israel's Jewishness is to be applauded not condemned.

   Alan Dershowitz, "Shahak, Best Proof of Freedom of Speech," *Boston Globe*, April 29, 1973, 5; Noam Chomsky, "In Defense of Shahak," *Boston Globe*, June 5, 1973, 18.

4. Chomsky, "In Defense of Shahak," *Boston Globe*, June 5, 1973.

5. Robert Faurisson, *The "Problem of the Gas Chambers," Or, "The Rumor of Auschwitz"* (Reedy, WV: Liberty Bell Publications, 1979).

6. I did an extensive critique of Faurisson's "findings" in *Chutzpah* (New York: Touchstone, 1991), 174–176.

7. Robert Faurisson and Noam Chomsky, *Memoire en Defense: Contre Ceux Qui Maccusent De Falsifier L'histoire: La Question Des Chambres a Gaz* (Paris: Vieille Taupe, 1980).

8. Alan Dershowitz, "Chomsky Defends Vicious Lie as Free Speech," *Boston Globe*, June 13, 1989.

9. Faurisson and Chomsky, *Memoire en Defense*.

10. The last of our debates can be viewed on YouTube: "Dershowitz vs. Chomsky Debate Israel at Harvard," YouTube, posted January 4, 2012, https://www.youtube.com/watch?v=3ux4JU_sbB0.

11. I tell the story of this case in detail in *The Best Defense* (New York: Vintage, 1982). See also, *U.S. v. Huss*, 482 F2d 38 (2d. Cir. 1973).

12. Telford Taylor, *Courts of Terror: Soviet Criminal Justice and Jewish Emigration* (New York: Knopf, 1976).

13. Dershowitz, *Chutzpah*.

14. David M. Halbfinger, "From Jewish Saint, to Israeli Politician, to Diaspora's Ally," *New York Times*, June 29, 2018, https://www.nytimes.com/2018/06/29/world/middleeast/natan-sharansky-interview.html.

15. I tell the story of my work in this movement more fully in my books *The Best Defense* and *Chuztpah*.

Chapter 6

1. David B. Green, "The Day in Jewish History, 1973: Moshe Dayan Allegedly Suggests Israel Demonstrate Its Nuclear Capacity," *Haaretz*, October 7, 2016.

2. Ralph Blumenthal, "Daniel Berrigan's Speech to Arabs Stirs a Furor over Award," *New York Times*, December 16, 1973.

3. For a discussion of my role in criticizing the Lawyers Guild, see Dershowitz, *Taking the Stand*, 435.

4. It would be 16 years before this bigoted resolution was rescinded.

Chapter 7

1. Quoted in Dershowitz, *Preemption*.

2. Benn, Aluf, "Where First Strikes Are Far From the last Resort," *Washington Post*, November 10, 2002.

3. David Lauterborn, "1983 Beirut Barracks Bombing: The BLT Building Is Gone!" HistoryNet, February 13, 2019, https://www.historynet.com/1983-beirut-bombing-the-blt-building-is-gone.htm.

4. Aharon Barak, Yitzhak Kahan, and Yona Efrat, *The Beirut Massacre: The Complete Kahan Commission Report* (New York: Karz-Cohl Publishing, 1983).

5. Alan M. Dershowitz, "For A P.L.O. Inquiry," *New York Times*, October 17, 1982.

6. Alan M Dershowitz, *Why Terrorism Works: Understanding the Threat, Responding to the Challenge* (Carlton North, Vic.: Scribe, 2003).

7. I was also threatened by a Polish extremist who was angry that I was suing Cardinal Józef Glemp of Poland (see *Chutzpah*). He drove to my house with a baseball bat intending to bash in my head.

Chapter 8

1. I wrote about Vanessa Redgrave in Dershowitz, *Taking the Stand*, 170–176.
2. "Redgrave Is At It Again," *Jewish Telegraph*, November 4, 1980. In more recent years, Redgrave has apparently changed her stance to supporting a two-state solution.
3. Margaretmirren1, "Vanessa Redgrave," YouTube, January 12, 2009 (accessed April 24, 2019. https://www.youtube.com/watch?v=4yKQSMIrGQk).
4. "Redgrave Defends P.L.O. Film," *New York Times*, November 11, 1977 (accessed April 24, 2019. https://www.nytimes.com/1977/11/11/archives/new-jersey-weekly-redgrave-defends-plo-film.html).
5. In recent months, I have defended President Donald Trump's civil liberties, despite accusations that he has denied civil liberties to immigrant families. I have been criticized for this, but I have been doing it since I was a college student, defending the right of communists to speak.
6. The debate can be viewed on YouTube: "Rabbi Kahane Debates Alan Dershowitz Part 1," YouTube, posted May 27, 2015, https://www.youtube.com/watch?v=gAY6vdGV2_4.
7. Paul Hofmann, "Protests from U.S. Jews Stir Controversy in Israel," *New York Times*, June 21, 1979.
8. Hofmann, "Protests from U.S. Stir Controversy in Israel."

Chapter 9

1. Dershowitz, *The Case for Israel*, 72
2. Jonathan A. Greenblatt, "It's Time to Call Out Campus Anti-Semitism by Both the Left and the Right," *Washington Post*, October 26, 2018, https://www.washingtonpost.com/opinions/its-time-to-call-out-campus-anti-semitism-by-both-the-left-and-the-right/2018/10/26/344f0de8-d89b-11e8-a10f-b51546b10756_story.html?utm_term=.5cd6c864a8d4.
3. Haim Shapira, "The Law of Pursuer (Rodef) in Talmudic Sources," Academia.edu, https://www.academia.edu/6228030/The_Law_of_Pursuer_Rodef_in_Talmudic_Sources (accessed April 14, 2019).

Chapter 10

1. Dershowitz, *The Case for Peace*, 36.
2. Elaine Sciolino, "Self-Appointed Israeli and Palestinian Negotiators Offer a Plan for Middle East Peace," *New York Times*, December 2, 2003.

3. Quoted in Dershowitz, *The Case for Peace*, 29.

4. See Dershowitz, *The Case Against Israel's Enemies*, 69.

5. Dershowitz, *The Case for Israel*, 207.

6. Dershowitz, *The Case Against Israel's Enemies*, 39.

7. Stuart E. Eizenstat, *President Carter: The White House Years* (New York: St. Martin's Press, 2018).

8. U.S. Congress, H. Res. 1361, Congress.gov, September 23, 2008, https://www .congress.gov/110/bills/hres1361/BILLS-110hres1361eh.pdf.

9. "Leading International Voices on the 2001 Durban NGO Forum," UN Watch, October 27, 2008, http://blog.unwatch.org/index.php/2008/10/27/leading -international-voices-on-the-2001-durban-ngo-forum/.

10. "Palestinian Campaign for the Academic and Cultural Boycott of Israel," BDS Movement, July 28, 2017, https://bdsmovement.net/pacbi.

11. Dershowitz, *The Case Against BDS*, 8.

12. Maureen Clare Murphy, "Boycotts Work: An Interview with Omar Barghouti," The Electronic Intifada, February 12, 2017, https://electronicintifada.net/content /boycotts-work-interview-omar-barghouti/8263.

13. Dershowitz, *The Case Against Israel's Enemies*, 44–46.

14. Zack Beauchamp, "The Matisyahu Israel Boycott Controversy, Explained," *Vox*, August 19, 2015, https://www.vox.com/2015/8/18/9173239/matisyahu-bds.

15. Maureen Clare Murphy, "Boycotting Israeli Settlement Products: Tactic vs. Strategy," The Electronic Intifada, February 12, 2017, https://electronicintifada .net/content/boycotting-israeli-settlement-products-tactic-vs-strategy/7801.

16. Dershowitz, *The Case for Israel*, 56.

17. Dershowitz, *The Case Against BDS*.

18. Alan Dershowitz, "Ten Reasons Why BDS Is Immoral and Hinders Peace," *Haaretz*, February 12, 2014.

Chapter 11

1. "Kadima," *Encyclopedia Britannica*, https://www.britannica.com/topic/Kadima (accessed April 14, 2019).

2. Charles Krauthammer, "Moral Clarity in Gaza," *Washington Post*, July 17, 2014, https://www.washingtonpost.com/opinions/charles-krauthammer-moral -clarity-in-gaza/2014/07/17/0adabe0c-0de4-11e4-8c9a-923ecc0c7d23_story .html?utm_term=.bc9072b9a0d9.

3. Alan Dershowitz, *Terror Tunnels: The Case for Israel's War Against Hamas* (New York: Rosetta Books, 2014); Alan Dershowitz, *The Case for Moral Clarity: Israel, Hamas and Gaza* (Camera, 2009).

4. "Honorary Doctorate Recipients," Bar Ilan University, https://www1.biu.ac.il /en-about_doctorate (accessed April 14, 2019).

Chapter 12

1. Alex Lockie, "Israel Admits It Took Out a Syrian Reactor in 2007—and It May Have Prevented a Nuclear ISIS," *Business Insider*, March 21, 2018, https://www.businessinsider.com/israel-2007-syria-reactor-strike-prevented-nuclear-isis-2018-.

2. Jack Khoury, Noa Landau, and Ruth Schuster, "Hezbollah Reveals New Details on Kidnapping That Sparked Lebanon War with Israel," *Haaretz*, January 10, 2018, https://www.haaretz.com/israel-news/hezbollah-reveals-new-details-on-kidnapping-that-sparked-lebanon-war-with-israel-1.5418293.

3. As the result of material obtained by Grossman, the *New York Times* presented a much fairer assessment of Hezbollah's use of civilian shields.

4. Alan Dershowitz, "The Case Against the Goldstone Report: A Study in Evidentiary Bias," Harvard Law School, January 27, 2010.

5. Much of that rebuttal appears in my book *The Case Against Israel's Enemies*.

6. See, for example, Steven Erlanger, "A Gaza War Full of Traps and Trickery," *New York Times*, January 10, 2009; Yaakov Katz, "Hamas Used Almost 100 Mosques for Military Purposes," *Jerusalem Post*, March 15, 2010; and "Evidence of the Use of the Civilian Population as Human Shields," Intelligence and Terrorism Information Center at the Israel Intelligence Heritage and Commemoration Center, February 4, 2009.

7. Dershowitz, "The Case Against the Goldstone Report."

8. "Col. Kemp to UN Gaza Session: 'Hamas Seeks Destruction of Israel and Murder of Jews Everywhere,'" UN Watch, May 20, 2018, https://www.unwatch.org/col-kemp-un-gaza-session-hamas-seeks-destruction-israel-murder-jews-everywhere/.

9. "Ehud Olmert Fast Facts," CNN, October 3, 2018, https://www.cnn.com/2013/09/19/world/meast/ehud-olmert-fast-facts/index.html.

10. Josef Federman, "Abbas Admits He Rejected 2008 Peace Offer from Olmert," *Times of Israel*, November 19, 2015, https://www.timesofisrael.com/abbas-admits-he-rejected-2008-peace-offer-from-olmert/.

Chapter 13

1. Alan Dershowitz, "Why I Support Israel and Obama," *Huffington Post*, November 17, 2008.

2. See Dershowitz, *Taking the Stand*, 460.

3. Israel is testing new technologies that could help locate the tunnel routes and exit points. See, for example, Inna Lazareva, "Israel Tests Hi-Tech Tunnel Detection System to Fight Threat from Underground," *Jaffa Telegraph*, July 23, 2014.

4. "Iron Dome: How Israel's Missile Defense System Works," *This Week*, August 1, 2014.

5. "Report: Hamas Planned Rosh Hashanah Attack Through Gaza Tunnels," Jewish Telegraphic Agency, July 28, 2014, citing the newspaper *Maariv* and "security sources."

6. Melanie Lidman, "They Thought It Was Rockets They Had to Be Scared Of," *Times of Israel*, August 6, 2014.

7. Alan M. Dershowitz, "The Case for President's Obama Reelection," *Jerusalem Post*, October 30, 2012.

8. Alan M. Dershowitz, "Obama's Legacy and the Iranian Bomb," *Wall Street Journal*, March 23, 2010, https://www.wsj.com/articles/SB100014240527487 04869304575110042827617582.

9. Cristina Marcos, "House Rejects Obama's Iran Deal," *The Hill*, February 1, 2016. https://thehill.com/blogs/floor-action/house/253370-house-rejects-iran -deal.

10. Alan M. Dershowitz, *The Case Against the Iran Deal: How Can We Now Stop Iran from Getting Nukes?* (New York: Rosetta Press, 2015).

11. Alan M. Dershowitz, "The Consequences of Not Vetoing the Israel Resolution," *Boston Globe*, December 27, 2016.

Chapter 14

1. Jacqueline Thomsen, "Dershowitz to Trump: End Policy Separating Immigrant Families at Border," *The Hill*, June 18, 2018, https://thehill.com/blogs/blog -briefing-room/news/392749-dershowitz-to-trump-end-policy-separating -immigrant-families-at.

2. "Alan Dershowitz Publishes Letter Defending Netanyahu," *Jerusalem Post*, February 28, 2019, https://www.jpost.com/Israel-News/Alan-Dershowitz -publishes-open-letter-to-A-G-defending-Netanyahu-581888.

Chapter 15

1. Florian Eder, "Anti-Semitism in EU Worse over Last 5 Years, Survey," *Politico*, December 10, 2018; "Anti-Semitism in EU Worse over Last 5 years," ADL Global 100, https://global100.adl.org/#map (accessed May 20, 2019).

2. It is impossible to know the precise number of Palestinian civilians killed, because many were "civilians" who engaged in terrorist acts.

3. Josef Federman, "Pro-Palestinian Groups at CUNY Blame 'Zionists' for High Tuition," *Times of Israel*, November 12, 2015, https://www.timesofisrael.com /pro-palestinian-groups-at-cuny-blame-zionists-for-high-tuition/.

4. @HamidDabashi (Hamid Dabashi), "Every dirty treacherous ugly and pernicious act . . ." Twitter, May 8, 2018, 2:02 a.m., https://twitter.com /hamiddabashi/status/993778247799361536?lang=en. These tweets have since been deleted.

5. "War on Nature: How Zionist Colonialism Has Destroyed the Environment in Palestine," *Middle East Monitor*, February 11, 2019, https://www.middleeastmonitor.com/20190211-war-on-nature-how-zionist-colonialism-has-destroyed-the-environment-in-palestine/.

6. Alan M. Dershowitz, "Bishop Tutu Is No Saint When It Comes to Jews," Gatestone Institute, December 20, 2010.

7. "War on Nature," *Middle East Monitor*.

8. Alan M. Dershowitz, "The Torture Warrant: A Response to Professor Strauss," Heinonline, 2003, https://heinonline.org/HOL/LandingPage?handle=hein.journals/nyls48÷=17&id=&page=.

9. Alan Dershowitz, "The Newest Abuse Excuse for Violence Against Women," *Huffington Post*, September 19, 2005.

10. Alan Dershowitz, "How Amnesty International Suppresses Free Speech," *Jerusalem Post*, November 11, 2014.

11. See Alan Dershowitz, *The Case for Peace*, "Chapter 16: A Case Study in Intimidation."

12. Anthony Julius, "The Poetry of Prejudice," *The Guardian*, June 6, 2003.

13. Norman Finkelstein, "Should Alan Dershowitz Target Himself for Assassination?" Counter Punch, January 26, 2016, https://www.counterpunch.org/2006/08/12/should-alan-dershowitz-target-himself-for-assassination/. For the sources of Finkelstein's quotations, see Dershowitz, *The Case Against Israel's Enemies*.

14. See Alan Dershowitz, "Why Are John Mearsheimer and Richard Falk Endorsing a Blatantly Anti-Semitic Book?" *New Republic*, November 4, 2011. See also, "No Place for Atzmon at SW.org," SocialistWorker:org (accessed, May 21, 2019); "Mearsheimer Responds to the Latest Smears on Him . . ." Leiter Reports: A Philosophy Blog, https://leiterreports.type.pad.com/blog/2011/09/mearsheimer-reponds-to-the-latest-right-wing-smears-on-him.html.

15. Alyssa Fisher, "David Duke Defends Ilhan Omar from Anti-Semitism Accusations," *The Forward*, February 11, 2019, https://forward.com/fast-forward/419150/ilhan-omar-david-duke-aipac-zionist-antisemitic-kkk/.

16. I even threatened to leave the Democratic Party if Keith Ellison, the darling of this so-called progressive wing, were elected to head the Democratic Party. He lost in a close vote. See, e.g., Alan Dershowitz, "I Will Leave Democratic Party, If Keith Ellison Is Elected DNC Chairman," *Newsmax*, February 24, 2017.

17. Jonathan Martin, "Prominent Democrats Form Pro-Israel Group to Counter Skepticism on the Left," *New York Times*, January 29, 2019, https://www.nytimes.com/2019/01/28/us/politics/democrats-israel-palestine.html.

Conclusion

1. Dershowitz, *The Case for Israel*, 172.

2. Shoshanna Solomon, "From 1950s Rationing to Modern High-Tech Boom: Israel's Economic Success Story," *Times of Israel*, April 18, 2019, https://www.timesofisrael.com/from-1950s-rationing-to-21st-century-high-tech-boom-an-economic-success-story/.

3. Larry D. Thompson, "Fighting Terrorism, Preserving the Rule of Law," Brookings, July 29, 2016, https://www.brookings.edu/on-the-record/fighting-terrorism-preserving-the-rule-of-law/.

4. Barry Shaw, "Archbishop Tutu, Revisit Israel," *Jerusalem Post*, April 11, 2013.

5. Thus the tolerance for Louis Farrakhan's blatant anti-Semitism, homophobia, antifeminism and overall bigotry and hate by so many on the hard left.

6. Chris McGreal and Ewen MacAskill, "Israel Should Be Wiped Off Map, Says Iran's President," *The Guardian*, October 26, 2005, https://www.theguardian.com/world/2005/oct/27/israel.iran.

7. Jonathan Easley, "GOP Lawmaker Warns Iran Must Be Stopped, Israel Is 'One-Bomb Country,'" *The Hill*, February 3, 2016, https://thehill.com/policy/defense/204311-gop-lawmaker-warns-israel-is-a-one-bomb-country.

8. Dershowitz, *The Case Against the Iran Deal*, 2.

9. John Bresnahan and Andrew Restuccia, "Israel, Anti-Semitism and 2020 Fight on Display as AIPAC Gathers," *Politico*, March 22, 2019, https://www.politico.com/story/2019/03/21/israel-anti-semitism-aipac-2020-1231570.

Index

LITTLE GIRL BLUE

The Life of
KAREN CARPENTER

RANDY L. SCHMIDT

Foreword by Dionne Warwick

An A Cappella Book

The Library of Congress has cataloged the hardcover edition as follows:

Schmidt, Randy (Randy L.)

    Little girl blue : the life of Karen Carpenter / Randy L. Schmidt ; foreword
by Dionne Warwick. — 1st ed.

       p. cm.

    Includes bibliographical references and index.

    ISBN 978-1-55652-976-4 (hardcover)

    1. Carpenter, Karen, 1950-1983. 2. Singers—United States—Biography.
I. Title.

    ML420.C2564S36 2010

    782.42164092—dc22

    [B]

                                        2009049044

COVER AND INTERIOR DESIGN: Monica Baziuk
COVER LAYOUT: Jonathan Hahn
FRONT COVER IMAGE: The Carpenters, Paris, France, September 1971
© Shepard Sherbell / CORBIS SABA
ILLUSTRATION ON PAGE II: Copyright © 2010 by Chris Tassin

Copyright © 2010 by Randy L. Schmidt
All rights reserved
Foreword copyright © 2010 by Dionne Warwick
All rights reserved
First hardcover edition published 2010
First paperback edition published 2011
Published by Chicago Review Press, Incorporated
814 North Franklin Street
Chicago, Illinois 60610
ISBN 978-1-56976-818-1
Printed in the United States of America

For Camryn and Kaylee

In loving memory
Lindeigh Scotte (1956–2001)
&
Cynthia G. Ward (1975–2005)

Never lose an opportunity of seeing anything that is beautiful;

for beauty is God's handwriting—a wayside sacrament.

Welcome it in every fair face, in every fair sky, in every fair flower

and thank God for it as a cup of blessing.

—RALPH WALDO EMERSON

CONTENTS

———— ⚭ ————

FOREWORD

———————

KAREN CARPENTER was and still is the voice that I listen to with a smile on my face. Her clarity, her approach to the lyric being sung, and the smile I could hear in her voice just fascinated me.

We all are familiar with the hits and the performances, but I was privy to the person. She was a sweet, innocent young lady who had so much to give—and she wanted to give. She and her brother gave us *music*—music that reached the innermost parts of our being; and that music is truly missed.

When I first heard her sing a song that I had recorded some years ago ("Knowing When to Leave" from the Broadway show *Promises, Promises*), I felt quite surprised that anyone would attempt this song, simply because of the complex time signature and range required to sing it. She seemed to have no trouble riding the notes as they were supposed to be ridden, and I was impressed!

I felt a need to get to know this young lady, and fortunately it appeared she desired to meet me. I first met her at A&M just after their recording of "Close to You." Years later I happened to be staying in the same hotel as Karen in New York when I ran into her; she was there going through therapy for anorexia nervosa. Since I had not seen her in quite a while, I must say it was shocking to see how very thin she was.

I invited her to my suite the following day for lunch, not knowing that eating was the last thing on her mind, but she graciously accepted the invitation and showed up not really ready to eat but to talk. Little did I know that I succeeded in doing something no one else had been able to do. I was able to get her to eat a cup of soup with a few saltine crackers. We spent the afternoon talking about many things, and she finally told me why she was in New York. It was apparent that anorexia was something she was at odds with and trying to combat, and I felt compelled to let her know I was in her corner and gave her as much encouragement as I could for her to continue her fight. We exchanged phone numbers and promised to keep in touch.

The last time I saw her was at a Grammy photo shoot in January 1983. It was a joyous reunion, and the first thing out of her mouth when she saw me was, "Look at me, I've got an ass!" We laughed so hard and loud that the rest of the group took great notice, to say the least. We both agreed that she had a lot of living to do.

To hear of her untimely transition hurt me as if I had lost a family member. She had so much to live for. Being at her funeral was as difficult for me as it was for her immediate family and host of friends. Yes, I will always remember the day we met and that day in New York, and I cherish the continuing friendship I have with her brother, Richard.

—DIONNE WARWICK

AUTHOR'S NOTE

"WE START out with the answers, and we end up with the questions." Karen Carpenter treasured this quotation, which fellow singer Petula Clark first shared with her, and recited it to close friends in difficult times. Indeed, no matter how many ways Karen's story has been told, the "answers" always seem to prompt more questions.

On New Year's Day 1989, I sat spellbound as *The Karen Carpenter Story* unfolded. The CBS biopic, which opened with the disturbing reenactment of the events of February 4, 1983, the day of Karen's death, made an immediate and enduring impression on this teenage viewer. In the weeks following the airing, Karen Carpenter haunted me. There was something about the way that film presented the pathos of her story atop the soundtrack of her sometimes optimistic but often mournful voice that drew me in. Perhaps it had to do with the movie's slightly sensationalistic nature. More likely it was the depth and density of Karen's voice. Whatever the reason, I could not get her out of my mind. The filmmakers had provided many answers, but I still had questions—about Karen's life, about her death, and certainly about her music. I wanted to know more. And I have spent many years searching for those answers.

I look upon *Little Girl Blue* as a continuation of similar efforts. Barry Morrow's struggles to write a screenplay for *The Karen Carpenter Story* that would offend no one are detailed in this book's prologue. The baton was then passed to Ray Coleman, who had the arduous task of writing the family's authorized biography. It is my understanding that both men became frustrated (and even furious at times) with the unavoidable confines of their respective assignments. Both were strongly cautioned by several inside the Carpenters camp against taking on the assignments in the first place. According to Karen "Itchie" Ramone, wife of legendary record producer Phil Ramone, "Ray Coleman *really* had a rough time in terms of editing. And Barry Morrow, *forget it!* I felt so bad for him. After a while, Ray threw his arms up. As for Barry, he just had his arms tied."

In the face of these admonitions I approached Richard Carpenter with some trepidation. I first met Richard and his wife, Mary, at their Downey home in August 1996 and since that time have been fortunate to visit with him on a number of occasions. Although he has always been genial and accommodating, Richard has rarely lent support to outside ventures without insisting upon editorial control. As expected, he declined to be interviewed for this project. David Alley (his manager at the time) explained that Richard has "said all he wishes to say" in regard to Karen's personal life. But Alley wished me the best with the project and even declared that he and Richard would not discourage others from contributing, which is as close to an endorsement as anyone could hope for.

I believe the lack of collaboration with the Carpenter family, however, has proved to open rather than close important avenues of information. In conducting interviews for this book, it became obvious to me that many details of Karen's life story had never been allowed to see the light of day. In fact, a number of those I interviewed expressed their frustration with the heavy-handed editing that has kept her story concealed this long. I have made every effort to keep this book, unlike the previous, authorized accounts, free of an agenda and the Carpenter family's editorial control. This lack of censorship has permitted me to dig deeper, explore the story beneath the surface, and give people outside the family who were close to Karen ample opportunity to express themselves.

Terry Ellis, Karen's boyfriend and the cofounder of Chrysalis Records, had previously spoken only with biographer Ray Coleman, refusing all other requests to talk about his relationship with Karen. "I could never see the point in helping somebody do a book or a film or a TV show about Karen," Ellis told me. "I always say to myself, 'It's not going to do *her* any good.' That's all I care about. Her." He agreed to speak with me but questioned me at length prior to our interview: "What story do you think you're going to tell?" he asked. How would I address the relationship between her and Richard? How did I plan to deal with her illness? Or her relationship with her mother? It was only after I answered these questions—with honesty and sincerity—that we were able to proceed.

Further important aspects of Karen's life—the ones that traditional means of research could never divulge—were revealed to me during an afternoon I spent in the Beverly Hills home of Frenda Franklin, Karen's longtime best friend and closest confidant. "I want you to know and understand the many layers of Karen," Franklin told me. "She was such an *unusual* human being. . . . You were better for having known her. I don't know one person who knew her who doesn't feel that way. . . . She changed your life."

Franklin, more than anyone, was vocal about wanting someone to finally do justice to her best friend's life story, and as our interview drew to a close, she gave me a quick hug and kiss, patted me on the back, and whispered, "Do good for Karen." Needless to say, this was a very special commandment coming from someone who knew Karen so intimately and loved her so deeply. I hope that I have succeeded.

LITTLE GIRL BLUE

RAINY DAYS AND *RAIN MAN*

———

"I WANT YOU to know I did not kill my daughter."

Agnes Carpenter's first words to Barry Morrow were piercing. Set to interview the Carpenter family matriarch, he was thunderstruck as the woman suddenly jumped in front of the family's housekeeper, who had answered his knock at the door. This startling and awkward occurrence interrupted Morrow's introduction. "Yes, ma'am," he replied with caution. "May I come in?"

———

THE YEAR was 1984. Hollywood producer Jerry Weintraub had called a meeting with Barry Morrow, a screenwriter whose resume included two recent popular television movies starring Mickey Rooney and Dennis Quaid: the Emmy award winner *Bill* (1981) and *Bill: On His Own* (1983). Both were based on the writer's real-life friendship with Bill Sackter, a mentally challenged man he befriended and saved from the institution where Sackter spent forty-four years of his life.

On Thursday, October 18, Weintraub asked Morrow to write the screenplay for an upcoming television movie with the working title *A Song for You: The Karen Carpenter Story*. "You know, I am just not a fan of the Carpenters," Morrow told Weintraub, who had managed the duo's career since 1976.

Morrow knew of the Carpenters' music and recalled news reports of Karen's untimely death the previous year, but he didn't particularly like their music. "It was considered elevator music," he recalls. "I was listening to acid rock, Dylan, and Crosby, Stills and Nash."

Determined, Weintraub began to cajole Morrow. "All right, listen," he said. "Here's what you have to do. I am going to give you three or four albums and a great bottle of wine. I want you to go to a room, turn off the lights, drink this wine and listen to these albums."

Morrow, who admits he had never enjoyed a good bottle of wine at that point in his life, much less a great one, followed Weintraub's orders. "I had never heard her before; I had never stopped to listen," he says. "I had never heard the sadness and the sorrow and the pain in her voice. I thought when she sang 'I'm on the top of the world' she was serious. I never heard the undertones to it, the layers. When I heard the guitar solo in the middle of 'Goodbye to Love,' I thought, wait a second, I never even knew the Carpenters!"

Finishing the bottle of wine, Morrow phoned Weintraub. "I'm in," he said, "if you still want me."

⸎

BARRY MORROW knew very little of the story he was hired to write. Naturally, one of his first interviews was with Karen's brother, Richard Carpenter, who was ambivalent about lending his name to a film about his sister. He saw the potential for pain in such a production, not only for himself but for his elderly, still-grieving parents, devastated by the loss of their daughter. Morrow found Richard to be extremely guarded during their first meetings. More than anything, he saw the surviving Carpenter as highly protective, not only of his sister's but also his own image and, even more so, that of his family. The interviews were frustrating and at times proved futile. This confused Morrow because he knew the Carpenter circle had initiated and endorsed the project. Even so, he was determined to ask tough and direct questions like "Why did Karen die?"

With little to go on, Morrow relied on hopes that others would offer more information. He prepared to interview Karen's parents, who still lived in the house where their daughter collapsed. Immediately sensing the dynamics of the Carpenter family, Morrow knew he would have to take things slowly and cautiously. "I want you to know I did not kill my daughter" was the last thing he expected to hear from Agnes Carpenter. "I felt sorry for her that she would have to say something so shockingly direct and have it be the first thing out of her mouth. I realized this woman was very defensive and may have good reason to be. Agnes was still in denial. These were very commonplace stages that families go through or hide from. They didn't invent that level of dysfunction, but it was certainly there." After an hour spent interviewing Agnes in the living room that day, they were joined by Harold Carpenter, Karen's father, who had little to add.

Morrow began to realize he might never get the story of Karen Carpenter from the Carpenter family themselves. Maybe there was something to what longtime friend and business associate of the Carpenters Ed Leffler had said when he warned him against writing the screenplay for this highly anticipated TV movie of the week. "You have no idea what you're getting into," Leffler said. "*Good luck!*"

It was Leffler's ex-wife, Frenda Franklin, who became Morrow's primary source for reconstructing the events of Karen's life for the screenplay. After their initial meetings, the two spoke often by phone, sometimes for hours at a time. Richard was not pleased to learn this. For years Frenda had been viewed as a threat to Karen's reliance on her family. "Richard started having really strong feelings about what he knew I was going to write," Morrow says.

Morrow submitted the initial draft of the screenplay for review in the spring of 1986. "The first draft just hung this on my mother," Richard said in 1988. "I said, 'I will not have this. I won't, because it's not true.' My mom, she is possessive. A lot of moms are, but she was never what this first draft implied. Forget it."

Carpenter and Morrow met again to look over the second draft. In exchange for modifications to the script, which included the omission of some scenes in their entirety, Richard negotiated with Morrow. He offered to tell more of his personal story, including an addiction to quaaludes and a brief stay in Topeka's Menninger Clinic in 1979. In return, Morrow was to soften some of Agnes's "sharp edges."

By July 1987, CBS gave the green light to Morrow's third draft of the screenplay, which meant a picture commitment was in order. *A Song for You: The Karen Carpenter Story* entered the pre-production stage, and Weintraub hired Emmy winner Joseph Sargent as director. Richard Carpenter, by then named the film's executive producer, was still unhappy with the script. "It put his family under a microscope," Barry Morrow believes. "But that was inevitable." Yet another revision, dated September 30, 1987, did little to soothe Richard's concerns. Harsh and hurtful words from Agnes were still present. "You don't know the first thing about drums," the character tells her daughter. "Karen, sweetheart, Richard is a musician . . . a serious musician. Don't you see the difference?"

Morrow was adamant that the screenplay's scenes were built on solid facts revealed during the interviews he had conducted, all of which the Weintraub Entertainment Group approved and coordinated. "People in the touring group called Agnes the 'dragon lady,'" he says, so he was disinclined to further water down her character.

By December 1988, four drafts of the screenplay existed. When a fifth was requested, Morrow refused, and within a matter of days network executives informed him that writer Cynthia Cherbak had been hired to overhaul his script. Morrow was indifferent. "I was busy and happy to do other things," he says. "Those were heady times for me!" (The screenwriter had also penned *Rain Man*, starring Tom Cruise and Dustin Hoffman, for which he won the Oscar for Best Original Screenplay at the Sixty-first Academy Awards in 1989.)

Even Cherbak's changes could do little to alter Agnes Carpenter's hard-edged character once the director cast Academy Award winner Louise Fletcher in the role. Known for her 1975 role in *One Flew Over the Cuckoo's Nest*, Fletcher brought a passive-aggressive slant to every line of dialogue. "I had nothing to do with the casting," Morrow explains. "Sargent comes in and casts 'Nurse Ratched!' Louise Fletcher could say a nursery rhyme and give you the creeps."

Additionally Joseph Sargent fought to convince the network that a virtual unknown, twenty-seven-year-old Mitchell Anderson, was their "Richard." The choice for "Karen" was twenty-four-year-old Cynthia

Gibb, an attractive character actress who had appeared for three seasons in the original *Fame* TV series. The actress came into the project knowing very little about the story, aside from general facts. "I knew she and her brother were a music team, that they were enormously successful around the world, and I knew their hit singles," she says. "I also knew she had an eating disorder and that she died of it. Beyond that I knew nothing."

When filming began in February 1988, Gibb was dismayed by the number of script revisions occurring on the set each day. "On a daily basis we would go to work prepared to do certain scenes," she says. "We would always have cuts or rewrites. Anything that was controversial at all was either diluted or removed. Because the family was so attached to the project, there was some whitewashing that went on in the telling of the story."

Working so closely with Richard, filming in the parents' home, wearing the Carpenters' clothing, and driving their cars, the cast and crew quickly came to their own conclusions about Karen's story. "If you looked from the outside in, you saw exactly what happened to that family," Mitchell Anderson says. "But from Richard's perspective and his mother's perspective, it was completely different."

Gibb agrees the family's intricate involvement made it even more difficult to portray the complex characters they were attempting to channel. "There were some aspects of Karen's upbringing that I felt had contributed to her illness," she says, "however, the family never felt that she had an emotional disorder. The family did not believe that anorexia was an emotional disorder that becomes a physiological disorder. Therefore, they didn't believe that Karen had anything other than a weight problem. It was difficult to portray certain emotional challenges that Karen had, because the family did not agree that they existed."

Richard has always held firm in his belief that the stress of showbiz and an overprotective family had nothing to do with Karen's anorexia. "What would possess a woman like her to starve herself?" he asked in his 1988 essay for *TV Guide*. "Some people blame it on career pressures or a need to take more control over her life. I don't think so. I think she would have suffered from the same problem even if she had been a homemaker." Richard felt anorexia nervosa was something "genetic, the same way talent is," as he explained to Susan Littwin in a piece for the same publication. "I have no answers. People have been trying to get that out of me. If I had it, I'd give it."

The filming of a watered-down version of one of Barry Morrow's original scenes, set in 1982 in the New York office of Karen Carpenter's therapist Steven Levenkron, remains vivid in the minds of the cast and crew, even today. "Have you told her that you love her?" the therapist asks the family.

The father starts to respond, but his nervous voice is overpowered by the mother's. "We don't do things that way. You show a person, you don't tell them all the time. . . . I don't think you understand our family."

This pivotal scene, Gibb feels, sheds light on the family's level of denial and unwillingness to fully support Karen's mission to get well. "She was making progress, and her family came to see her," she observes. "There was no support for the work that she was doing what-soever. The family was more old-fashioned in their beliefs that 'normal' families don't need therapy, only 'crazy' people do."

"Mrs. Carpenter, go ahead," the therapist says, prompting Agnes to voice her love for her daughter.

"For heaven's sake," she exclaims. "This is ridiculous! We came three thousand miles for this nonsense?" Gibb's head drops slowly to the side, her character seemingly ashamed, having burdened the parents with her personal problems. Missing the point, the mother retorts, "We don't need to prove anything to Karen. She knows we love her."

Heartbroken and horrified by the scene's content, the cast was forced to remain neutral, not voicing their opinions or reacting to their emotions. So many revisions had taken place prior to shooting that Richard was unaware of the reactions on the set and seemed pleased with the outcome. "The response from the family and from Richard himself was as if he were in the *Twilight Zone*," recalls Mitchell Anderson. "When we were doing that scene we were like, 'Oh my god, Agnes was such an asshole!' But after we finished shooting, Richard was so proud of it because he thought the doctor looked like an asshole."

No matter the amount of dilution, Morrow's screenplay spoke between the lines and was ultimately as close to the actual series of events in Karen Carpenter's life as anyone could ask of a biopic. "If there's an arch-villain of the story, it's probably Agnes Carpenter," wrote Ron Miller in a review for the *San Jose Mercury News*. He illustrated her character as "an imposing woman who found it almost impossible to show her love to her troubled daughter, even after her illness had been diagnosed and the threat to her life was clear."

In the final scene of *The Karen Carpenter Story*, however, Agnes Carpenter's character does soften. She almost repents. For a moment the viewer might forgive and forget her sins of the previous ninety minutes. Louise Fletcher's "Agnes" gazes affectionately up the staircase at her grown-up little girl for the last time.

"And Karen," she says with a tender hesitation, "I love you."

"I love you, too, Mom," Karen replies. "Goodnight."

Sadly, the mother's "I love you" on the eve of her daughter's untimely death was a fabrication—creative license justified by CBS Standards and Practices for the purpose of dramatic effect.

1

CALIFORNIA DREAMIN'

───────

HAROLD BERTRAM Carpenter had a rather peripatetic childhood and even more itinerant adolescence. The eldest son of missionaries George and Nellie Carpenter, he was born November 8, 1908, in Wuzhou, a city in southern China where the Gui and Xi rivers meet. Siblings Esther and Richard were born several years later. The Carpenter parents were both fine pianists and often played and sang for guests at their frequent formal dinner parties. Although he greatly enjoyed their performances, Harold was not as interested in making music. Against his will he took piano lessons for a while but loathed practicing. More an appreciator of good music than a musician himself, Harold began listening to records on the family's beautiful Victrola. He especially loved the classics.

Harold's mother was greatly concerned about the limited education her children received in China, where they had no formal education, only tutors. In 1917 Nellie took the children and headed for England where the children were enrolled in boarding schools. Their father joined them four years later when granted a leave of absence. Harold's younger sisters Geraldine and Guinevere were born shortly before their mother moved with the children to the United States. There they stayed on Ellis Island for several months before settling with relatives in Wellsville, New York.

Waking each morning at 5:00 A.M., Harold delivered newspapers before going to Wellsville High School. After two years he was forced to drop out and go to work when his mother became ill with a lung ailment. His uncle Frank Stoddard, a night superintendent at a paper box company in Middletown, Ohio, offered him a job, and he moved in with his uncle and aunt Gertrude. Harold moved several times with the Stoddards, finally settling in Catonsville, Maryland, a small community just west of Baltimore, where the men found work in a printing firm. Harold's mother and father separated shortly before Nellie succumbed to pleurisy in 1927 at the age of forty-four.

⌘

AGNES REUWER Tatum's childhood was somewhat less eventful than that of Harold Carpenter, or perhaps only less documented. She was born on March 5, 1915, in Baltimore, where she spent her youth. Her father, George Arthur Tatum, was part owner in Tatum, Fritz, and Goldsmith, a wholesale undergarment business. He and his wife, Annie May, were the parents of four girls: Jenny, Agnes, Audrey, and Bernice.

Agnes was athletic and played several sports, notably basketball, during her years at Baltimore's Western High School, the nation's oldest public all-girls school. She enjoyed sewing and became a fine seamstress. She made many of the Tatum girls' dresses and coats, in addition to the heavy, pleated, velour drapes that hung in the windows of the family home at 1317 Mulberry Street in Baltimore.

In 1932 George and Annie moved to nearby Catonsville, seeking a quieter existence for their daughters. Agnes's older sister Jenny was no longer living at home, but the other three girls were present when a neighbor introduced them to twenty-three-year-old Harold Carpenter. Agnes was smitten upon meeting the handsome young man and was surprised to see him again just a few days later driving up the street in his shiny Chevrolet. Noticing Agnes and Audrey waiting for a bus, Harold stopped to say hello and offered them a ride.

Agnes and Harold soon began dating, and a four-year courtship ensued. The two were married at Catonsville Methodist Church on

April 9, 1935. Times were tough, and there was little pomp and circumstance. There was no wedding cake, and Agnes sewed her own wedding gown. The only gift was a General Electric iron from the bride's aunt Myrtle and uncle Arthur, who happened to work for GE. Instead of a honeymoon, the newlyweds went for a night out at the movies.

For the next three weeks the couple lived with Agnes's parents in the Tatum home. Following Harold's uncle Frank to yet another box printing company, the couple relocated to Richmond, Virginia, where their first home together was a five-dollar-a-week furnished efficiency apartment. After a year they moved into a larger furnished apartment on Fendall Avenue in Richmond's Highland Park area.

When Agnes's older sister Jenny separated from husband George Tyrell, she felt her sister and brother-in-law would offer a more stable future for the Tyrells' eighteen-month-old baby girl, Joanie. Agnes and Harold became surrogate parents and soon moved to Mechanicsville on the northeast side of Richmond, securing a larger home for the growing family. The Carpenters were Richmond residents for five years before returning to Baltimore for a few months and in 1940 finally settling in an apartment on Sidney Street in New Haven, Connecticut. Jenny reunited with her daughter and moved in with Agnes and Harold, where she remained until 1943.

Working for the New Haven Pulp and Board Company, Harold became skilled at running the company's color printing equipment. Agnes began working, too. She worked eight-hour shifts either six or seven days a week, operating a thread mill machine for Mettler Brothers, a subcontractor of Pratt-Whitney Motor Mounts. Agnes stayed with Mettler's until World War II came to an end in 1945.

———— ᘛ⁐̤ᕐᐷ ————

AFTER MORE than ten years of marriage, Agnes Carpenter became pregnant. With their first child on the way, she and Harold began house hunting and settled on a new construction going up on Hall Street in New Haven's conservative, suburban East Shore Annex neighborhood. Hall Street was cozy and inviting, an almost fairy-tale lane for young families looking to build homes after World War II. Its string of modest, colonial-style homes was just a few miles from Lighthouse Point, a popular beach and amusement park across New Haven Harbor.

The Carpenters and their live-in niece, by then ten years old, moved into the new $8,900 home at 55 Hall Street on August 27, 1946. In less than two months they welcomed a son, born October 15 at Grace-New Haven Hospital. He was named Richard Lynn for Harold's only brother.

As he grew, Richard became interested in his father's extensive record collection. The selections were varied and eclectic to say the least, encompassing everything from Rachmaninoff, Tchaikovsky, and Borodin to Lannie McEntire, Red Nichols, and Spike Jones and his City Slickers. Even before he could read, young Richard would go through the records and listen for hours. He was able to distinguish the records by feeling the edges and grooves of each 78. At the age of three Richard asked for his own record of "Mule Train," a popular novelty cowboy song. His first 45 was Theresa Brewer's Dixieland-tinged "Music, Music, Music," and shortly after that he asked for "How Much Is That Doggy in the Window?" by Patti Page.

At 11:45 A.M. on Thursday, March 2, 1950, just three days shy of her thirty-fifth birthday, Agnes gave birth to a little girl, Karen Anne. Her first words were "bye-bye" and "stop it," the latter a natural response to the antics of an older brother.

Numbering five, the family shared the tidy little 1,500-square-foot, two-story home and its three bedrooms and two bathrooms. "They had nice furniture, everything was neat, everything matched, and everything was clean and shiny," recalls neighbor Debbie Cuticello, daughter of Carl and Teresa Vaiuso. "It had a finished basement, a garage, a beautiful front yard and backyard we all played in. They had a screen porch in the back and neatly manicured lawns and landscaping. Everybody took pride in their neighborhood. There were always shiny cars in the front yards."

In a tradition that continues to the present day, the houses on Hall Street came to be identified by the names of the families that lived there in the 1950s and 1960s. Number 55 is the Carpenter house, across the street is the Catalde house, and so on. "The LeVasseurs were on one side, and they're still there," Cuticello explains. "The Catanias were across the street, and they're still there. The Jones family was next door. The Shanahans were a couple of doors down. It was just a wonderful 1950s neighborhood."

According to Frank Bonito, whose parents bought 83 Hall Street in 1960, "It was a middle-class neighborhood with a lot of working folks. My father was a butcher and owned a grocery store. The Vaiusos, Debbie's parents, owned a farm. He was a wholesale farmer in Branford, which is one town over. I was at 83. Debbie lived at 77. On the other side were the DeMayos. Mr. DeMayo had worked in the post office. Across the street was a family whose father was a professor at Yale. Millstone was their name. Next to them were the DeVitas. They were an older couple with no children, and the husband was a dentist."

The New Haven area was settled by a number of Italian immigrants, providing residents with some remarkable pizza parlors in the area. Nearby Fort Nathan Hale Park was the site of many family picnics and play dates. There the children could swim, fish, and fly kites. In winter the fun turned to sledding and snowballing.

The Bonito, Vaiuso, and Carpenter children spent a great deal of time in one another's homes. Debbie and her brother thought of Agnes and Harold more as aunt and uncle figures, an extended family of sorts. "My brother Joey played with Rich, and I played with Karen," she says. "Our parents shared the same values and seemed to enjoy the hardworking American ethics. As children, we watched very little television and were outside as long as we could stay . . . playing basketball, baseball, roller-skating, hula-hooping, and playing in the yards. Everybody got along. . . . We didn't have a lot of money, and they didn't have a lot of money."

For extra income, Agnes and Harold started their own car washing business, and the two took great pride in their work. Their pickup and delivery service became popular among the neighborhood families and proved to be a success for the frugal couple, who wanted to give their children a comfortable existence. It was the perfect job for Agnes. She was known to be so persnickety in regard to keeping a clean house that she was often seen standing in the front windows scrubbing the locks with a toothbrush. "Mom was known for having the cleanest garage in Connecticut," Karen recalled in 1971. "My God, if you mopped, the mop didn't get dirty!"

According to Frank Bonito, Agnes was "compulsively clean, almost to the point of having some kind of psychiatric issues.... The woman made sure everything was immaculate. I can remember her going next door one time and cleaning the next-door neighbors' windows on her side of the house because they upset her. She was a very nice woman but very uptight. She seemed to be very stressed all the time."

Harold Carpenter hung swings from the rafters in the basement of the Carpenters' home, a favorite hang-out spot for neighborhood kids when it was too cold to play outside. It was a music haven for Richard, who even designated the area with a sign that read RICHIE'S MUSIC CORNER, his version of the family's favorite local record shop. The children would swing in the basement and listen to the music Richard selected from his library, which was categorized, alphabetized, and documented. "Richard had a beautiful sound system," Bonito recalls. "In those days they were called hi-fi's. He would have music on, and Karen and I would be swinging and doing our homework."

As she would do for much of her life, Karen took on Richard's interests. Music became their shared passion, and the two would swing to the music for hours. "I did everything that Richard did," she said in a 1981 interview. "If he listened to music, I listened to music. It was unconscious, but because I idolized him so much... every record that we've ever listened to is embedded in my mind." They enjoyed the sounds of Nat "King" Cole, Guy Mitchell, and Perry Como, and both sat spellbound listening to the overdubbed sounds of Les Paul and Mary Ford, particularly on the duo's masterpiece "How High the Moon." According to Richard, Karen could sing every Les Paul solo. The first record she asked for was "I Need You Now" by Eddie Fisher on RCA-Victor. The two also enjoyed listening to the radio, notably WMGM and Alan Freed's Top 40 show on WINS, "1010 on Your Dial," out of New York.

Karen liked to dance and by the age of four was enrolled in ballet and tap classes. Prior to recitals she could be found singing and dancing on the sidewalk in front of the house in a full costume of sequins, satin, tap shoes, and a huge bonnet. Karen was a short, stocky little girl with her dark blond hair cut in a Dutch-boy style. Debbie Cuticello admits to having looked up to Karen, who was two years her senior: "She was my best buddy. I tried to do everything that she did, basically. She was older than I was, and the two years made a big difference back then. Richard was older. You looked up to him, not necessarily a ringleader but the oldest of the group. He and Karen loved each other. . . . There was sibling rivalry—maybe a little pinching here and there—but it was typical; nothing unusual, nothing different."

While Debbie and Joey Vaiuso attended St. Bernadette School, a Catholic school in the area, Karen was a student at Nathan Hale School, just around the corner from Hall Street on Townsend Avenue. "Karen was a year younger than us," says Frank Bonito. "She was the youngest in the class and one of the best students in the class. We were very close through sixth, seventh, and eighth grades, and we always studied together." Karen and Frank walked to school each morning and returned home at lunchtime. "It was an era when women didn't work outside the house, so we'd come home," Bonito says. "There was no cafeteria or anything, so all the kids just went home for lunch. On the way back I'd stop and pick Karen up, and then we'd walk to school together, picking up other friends as we went along."

Like most little girls who grew up in the 1950s, Karen had the Ideal Toy Company's Betsy Wetsy doll, but she preferred playing with her dog, Snoopy, or her favorite toy machine gun or participating in various sports. A favorite was Wiffleball, a variation on baseball that used a perforated plastic ball invented just thirty miles away by a man in Fairfield, Connecticut. Karen pitched and sometimes played first base. "I was a tremendous baseball fan," she later said. "I memorized all the batting averages long before I knew the first word to a song. The Yankees were my favorites." She also delivered the *New Haven Register* on her paper route each day, sometimes adding weekend routes for extra money.

Teenage Richard was tall, thin, and gangly, somewhat uncoordinated, and not as physically active as Karen. He spent most of his free time indoors with his music. "It was slightly embarrassing," he recalled.

"Karen was a better ballplayer than I was, and when choosing sides for sandlot games, she'd be picked first." The school bullies sometimes teased and picked on him. This left him temperamental, and he could be upset quite easily. Richard's rants were short and usually ended with him storming off and back into the house where he remained the rest of the day. Agnes encouraged him to fight back, but she also relied on Karen to watch over her older brother. "She can take care of herself and Richard," Agnes explained in 1972. "When they were little kids, she always defended him. She'd take on all the roughnecks and make them leave Richard alone."

—◦◦◦—

THE CARPENTERS' dining room was home to the family's piano and therefore one of the highest-traffic areas in the house. The piano was purchased by cousin Joan, by then a teenager, when Richard was eight years old. He grew disinterested after a frustrating year under the direction of the rigid Ms. Florence June, and in a mutual agreement both teacher and parent decided the talent and interest were lacking and the lessons should cease.

Three years later Richard taught himself to play by ear, excelling at flourishes and arpeggios. His parents decided to give it another chance, and he began studying with Henry "Will" Wilczynski, a student from Hartford. This time Richard's interest was sparked and his talent emerged. "During the summer when all the windows were open you would hear Richard play the exercises you have to play," Debbie Cuticello says. "There was always lots of music coming from that house."

Neighbor Bill Catalde saw the Carpenter kids in the same light as any others on Hall Street. "In our world we never thought of them as anything but the wonderful kids that they were. We were just children. With the possible exception of Richard, we never really projected ourselves into the future."

Karen looked up to Richard, his musical talents and intuition, so when he began accordion lessons with Henry Will, she wanted to take lessons as well. Will became a regular around the Carpenter house and soon began courting Joan. Although Karen enjoyed her lessons, she was more interested in exploring her other hobbies, most notably her fascination with drawing. She won a poster contest while attending Nathan Hale and expressed interest in becoming either an artist or perhaps a nurse.

Seeing their son's natural ability and marked progress, Agnes and Harold invested in a new piano, a black Baldwin Acrosonic. By the age of fourteen, Richard was sure his life would be centered on music in some way. His progress reached a point where Henry Will, who by 1959 had received his music degree from the University of Hartford, felt he could no longer challenge the young pianist. He recommended Richard audition at nearby Yale Music School, where he soon began lessons under the direction of professor Seymour Fink.

⸎

HAROLD CARPENTER spent years loathing the cold New England winters, which meant shoveling snow and placing chains on car tires before braving the icy roads. He watched the annually televised Tournament of Roses Parade and longed to be in sunny Southern California with its palm trees and mild climate. As early as 1955, he made tentative plans to relocate after a friend of the family who had previously made the move out West himself offered him a job at the Container Corporation of America in California. Instead, the money he saved for the move went to pay for a much-needed mastoid operation.

By 1960 the family's savings allowed Harold, Agnes, and Richard to vacation in Los Angeles, and they used this opportunity to scout out possible sites for relocation. Karen stayed with her aunt Bernice, uncle Paul, and their children to avoid the lengthy car trip. In addition to their quest for a milder climate, the Carpenter parents saw California—and especially Hollywood—as a place where Richard's dreams of becoming a famous pianist would have a better chance of coming true. Anticipating the expense of the pending relocation, Agnes went back to work in 1962. She became one of the top machine operators at Edal Industries, a New Haven rectifier manufacturer.

By early 1963 it was official. Harold sat the family down one evening and announced they would be leaving Hall Street and New Haven altogether. Richard was ecstatic after having visited Southern California with his parents three years earlier, but Karen was not happy. "She didn't want to leave her friends," says Frank Bonito. "She had even received scholarships to go to one of the local private schools." Before leaving New Haven, Karen graduated with the eighth grade class of Nathan Hale School. "Even though it was just a grammar school graduation, they made a big deal about it," Bonito says. "We had a little dance, and Karen and I made dance cards." In a class prophecy for the year 2000, Frank was predicted to be the mayor of a city on the moon and Karen to be his wife. "I guess they were wrong," he says.

In June 1963 the Carpenters filled their car to the brim with only a sampling of their belongings and said good-bye to their cherished friends and neighbors, leaving behind cousin Joan, who married Henry Will that year. "I remember the day that they left in their shiny car," Debbie Cuticello says. "I remember that day because I was very disappointed. It was a sad day for me. I was very upset. I was losing my best friend, and she was going so far away that I couldn't visit. California was way over on the other side of the world from me. I walked over to say good-bye and brought her a dish filled with macaroni."

Bill Catalde was also there to watch the Carpenters drive away that summer morning. "I remember a secret pact between Karen and I that we would someday marry," he says. "I doubt that Karen would have remembered that vow from long ago, but in retrospect we would have probably fared a lot better than what destiny had in store for the two of us."

2

CHOPSTICKS ON BARSTOOLS

<hr />

U PON MOVING to Downey, California, Harold Carpenter started his job as a lithograph printer in the nearby city of Vernon at the Container Corporation of America, where he worked double shifts to earn extra money for his family. Although Karen was upset to leave her friends in New Haven, the Carpenters never regretted their decision to relocate. California was a land of opportunity in many ways, and just as they had hoped, Richard was busy within two weeks of their arrival. Downey also allowed the Carpenter family to maintain a quiet, middle class, suburban way of life, not unlike their New Haven beginnings.

"Head down the Santa Ana Freeway, turn off on San Gabriel, make a couple of rights, and you're in Downey, a right-wing, unpretentious suburb of the sprawling conurbation that makes up Los Angeles." According to British journalist Chris Charlesworth, "It's where the homes are neat and tidy, where the kids graduate from high school, go to college and [play] football so that bruises will stand them in good stead later in life. It's where the moms and dads go to each other's cocktail parties once a week and where they eat TV dinners during the Million Dollar Movie on Channel 9. It's safe and sound."

Waiting for their New Haven house to sell, the Carpenter family struggled to maintain mortgage payments on the East Coast while renting an apartment in the West. "They were all just struggling like the rest of us and trying to get by," says Veta Dixon, who managed the forty-three-unit Shoji complex, located at 12020 Downey Avenue. "The Carpenters were just wonderful, wonderful people. We loved them immediately, and the kids, too. They lived upstairs on the right in #22."

The family soon moved across the breezeway to #23 when a larger apartment vacated. There they lived directly above a police officer for the City of Downey. When the musical vibrations penetrated the floor, he soon complained to the managers about the sounds coming from upstairs. "Do I have to listen to that piano day and night?" he asked.

"Yes," Dixon claims to have replied, "and if you don't like it you can move out! One of these days you'll be paying big money to see them and hear their music."

Driving around Downey one sunny afternoon, Harold pulled the family car into Furman Park on Rives Avenue to ask for directions. A park groundskeeper by the name of Nip noticed the Connecticut plates and asked if they were new to Downey. Agnes began to tell of her prodigy son and how his talents led them to Southern California. Karen and Richard, embarrassed by their mother's boasting, slumped deep into the backseat of the family car. Nip told the Carpenters that Furman Park's gazebo was the site of a weekly talent show held every Sunday afternoon. At first opportunity, Richard entered the talent show performing "Theme of *Exodus*," Ernest Gold's Grammy for Song of the Year in 1961, and a 1923 Zez Confrey piece called "Dizzy Fingers." He also accompanied Karen singing "The End of the World," a hit for Skeeter Davis in the spring of 1963. Singing with a light, pure, head tone, Karen had an airy quality to her voice, much like other girls her age. There were no signs of the rich, smoky alto register to come.

As he left the stage that day, Richard was approached by Vance Hayes, the choir director at Downey Methodist Church. In need of an interim organist, Hayes felt the young pianist would be well qualified based on the performance he had just witnessed. Having little experience on the organ, Richard was hesitant to accept the offer, but Hayes would not take no for an answer. He began the following Saturday playing for two weddings at fifteen dollars each. Playing for the weekly church services, Richard was responsible for preludes, offertories, and postludes. He often improvised, disguising melodies from his favorite Beatles tunes, even up-tempo numbers, like "From Me to You" or "All My Loving." In his words, he would "church them up." Karen was never far from her brother in those days. She would be in the back of the church or singing in the choir and notice melodies from the Beach Boys, the Beatles, and Burt Bacharach.

A reporter with the local *Downey Live Wire* newspaper heard of the new young organist at Downey Methodist and felt the story would make for a pleasant human interest feature. Along with a photographer, the reporter came to the family's apartment and took Richard's picture next to the family's black Baldwin Acrosonic, one of the few large items they had been sure to move across the country that past summer.

In the fall of 1963, thirteen-year-old Karen entered Downey's South Junior High as Richard, just shy of his seventeenth birthday, began his senior year at Downey High School and enrolled in the school band. "What can you play?" asked Bruce Gifford, the band director.

"Piano," Richard replied.

"Baby or grand?"

The two shared a laugh as Gifford explained he had no need for a pianist in his marching band. Richard went home and unpacked a trumpet he had purchased years earlier for four dollars at an auction. He attempted to play the instrument but to no avail. Luckily, the band director did not require an audition after Richard distracted him with a few impressive piano arpeggios. Outside of his teaching career, Gifford also led a nightclub band with his brother Rex. Richard was recruited and became the group's pianist for a short time, playing at dances, clubs, and weddings. He felt the group's sound was reminiscent of Louis Prima with Sam Butera and the Witnesses.

The Carpenter family's New Haven home finally sold in November 1964. Having tolerated cramped apartment living for a little more than a year, the family packed up and moved to a storybook house located at 13024 Fidler Avenue in Downey. To help offset the purchase of the new home and the higher cost of living in Southern California, Agnes Carpenter took a job running several mimeograph machines in the stockroom at North American Rockwell Corporation. The aircraft assembly plant, Downey's number-one employer, was responsible for manufacturing systems designed for the Apollo spacecraft program.

In the living room of their new home on Fidler, Richard finally had space for a larger piano. With money earned teaching piano lessons and playing the organ at church, in addition to the help of his parents, he traded in the spinet for a Baldwin Model L, a six-foot three-inch parlor grand. For a short period of time he studied piano at the University of Southern California.

∞

ENTERING DOWNEY High School in the fall of 1964, Karen was just fourteen years old, an entire year younger than most of her classmates. Although Karen enjoyed playing sports, she did not like to exercise and detested the idea of running around a track every morning. So she paid a visit to band director Bruce Gifford, by then a family friend, who confirmed her participation in marching band would count toward a physical education credit. Karen also succeeded in opting out of geometry class in favor of joining the school choir.

Gifford presented Karen with a glockenspiel and a set of mallets and put her right to work in his marching band, where she marched in the percussion section alongside the drums. Karen quickly found the glockenspiel cumbersome. Additionally, the tone of the instrument began to bother her. She detected that it played a quarter-step sharp in relation to the rest of the band.

Rehearsing with the percussion section, Karen became increasingly intrigued by what classmate Frankie Chavez and the other drummers were doing. As in the Carpenter home, in the Chavez residence music was part of daily life. "He'd been playing the drums since he was three," Karen said, calling him "a Buddy Rich freak. He even ate the same food as Buddy Rich!" But Chavez denies this allegation. "No," he says, "I didn't eat the same foods as Buddy," but he admits that Buddy Rich certainly influenced his playing.

Karen marched with the glockenspiel for about two months, by which time it became evident to her that Chavez was the only drummer in the band who had a real passion for his music. "I used to march down the street playing these stupid bells, watching Frankie play his tail off on the drums," she later said. "It hit me that I could play drums as good as nine-tenths of those boys in the drum line, outside of Frankie."

Meeting with band director Gifford, Karen informed him of her desire to switch instruments. She wanted to join the drum line. "I finally had to talk him into it," she recalled. "At that time, no girl anywhere was in the drum line of a marching band in any school." This was met with a tepid response from Gifford, to say the least. "Girls don't play drums," he told her. "That's not really normal."

"All I ever heard was 'girls don't play drums,'" Karen later recalled. "That is such an overused line, but I started anyway. I picked up a pair of sticks, and it was the most natural-feeling thing I've ever done."

Karen saw Gifford's cynicism as a challenge. "Well, let me try," she told Gifford.

Although the director was doubtful, he agreed to let Karen transition to the drums. First he assigned her to play a pair of cymbals, which was not her goal but did bring her closer to Frankie and the other drummers. Chavez was in charge of writing and developing drum cadences for the group, and his goal was to have fun and encourage listeners to move or dance. "They were funky and syncopated and kind of infectious," he says. "We were having such a great time that Karen wanted to play the cadences with the drum line, so she left the cymbals and started playing tenor drum." Never one to settle short of her goal, Karen aspired to play the snare drum during parades and the halftime shows at football games. According to Chavez, "the most interesting parts were assigned to the snare drums, so that's where she ultimately ended up. That was the conduit to playing drums."

Immediately at ease with the snare drum, Karen spent countless hours rehearsing before and after school. At home she assembled the kitchen barstools and even a few pots and pans to simulate a drum kit. Her father's chopsticks served as drumsticks. Karen began playing along to LPs like the Dave Brubeck Quartet's *Time Out* and *Time Further Out*, which were filled with difficult time signatures like 9/8 and 5/4. "They liked to play jazz," Chavez recalls. "Richard was a huge Dave Brubeck fan, and Karen and I both loved Joe Morello. They liked everything from Brubeck to Beatles. I remember being at their house and the Beatles' *Rubber Soul* had just come out. I remember sitting around listening to 'Norwegian Wood,' and we were all saying what a great production the album was and how great the songs were. Karen and Richard were good students of the art form."

Karen also sought the guidance of Frankie, with whom she may have been smitten. "There wasn't a romantic interest on my part," Chavez says, "but I always felt there may have been on hers. I had a girlfriend at the time, so Karen and I just became very good friends." Karen's only steady boyfriend during her high school years was a clarinet player by the name of Jerry Vance. Although the two dated for several years, most recall the relationship to have been nothing serious and more of a "buddy" situation than a romance.

As for Karen and Frankie, they too remained "just good buddies," he says. "She had that little tomboy streak to her and used to talk like a beatnik. I loved that she would talk like a jazz player. What developed was a very good friendship and a mutual interest in drums and music. She'd come over after school and we'd talk drums. She always had a ton of questions about playing so we used to talk about the most effective ways to hold the stick, traditional grip versus matched grip, stick control, playing technique, drum styles. We'd talk about different drummers and listen to jazz records and big bands. Karen took to drumming quickly, and it was very natural to her. She showed great ability, had good timing, and kept getting better and better. She ended up being one of the better snare drum players in the drum line in no time."

Given Karen's track record with musical instruments, her parents were skeptical. They were quite sure it was just another passing fancy. Additionally, Agnes and Harold were already struggling to pay for Richard's new Baldwin. But thanks to his urging, their parents agreed to invest in a basic drum kit for Karen. Karen loved the sound of Ludwigs and wanted them because two of her favorite drummers, Joe Morello and Ringo Starr, played Ludwigs exclusively. Agnes wanted Richard's input, and he felt Ludwig drums would be a good investment since they were known to have a higher resale value than most other lines.

On a Sunday afternoon the family drove to the San Fernando Valley with Frankie Chavez in tow to the home of a music teacher who dealt instruments on the side. They settled on an entry-level set that was dark green with a yellow stripe around the center of each piece. Karen contributed some of her own savings to assist with the three-hundred-dollar purchase. "Ludwig makes a great product," Chavez says. "It was a good move." And with that purchase Frankie became Karen's first drum teacher. Although the rudiments of drumming, time signatures, cadences, and fills came naturally to her, she wanted to know more. "A lot of what she picked up early on was influenced by what she heard on recordings," Chavez explains. "As her interest in certain portions of the art of playing came up, I would try to teach her the concepts and answer her questions."

Karen soon began studying drum technique under the tutelage of Bill Douglass at Drum City on Santa Monica Boulevard in Hollywood. Douglass was a well-known jazzer who played with the likes of Benny Goodman and Art Tatum. "Bill was well respected and a great teacher," says Chavez, who also studied with Douglass for eight years. "We used to play on practice pads reading concert music. Bill had Karen reading very complex material and thought she had become quite a reader." The lessons continued for the next year and a half.

After only two months of playing, Karen was convinced she had outgrown her first drum kit and by Christmas persuaded her parents to trade in the entry-level set toward the purchase of a show set identical to one belonging to Joe Morello—a 1965 Ludwig Super Classic in silver sparkle with double floor toms. She also asked for the all-chrome, top-of-the-line Super Sensitive Snare. At first her parents opted for the more economical Supra-phonic 400 but later gave in and purchased the Super Sensitive Snare, too. Bragging to friends about her son's piano talents, Agnes secured him the job of pianist for a local production of the Frank Loesser musical *Guys and Dolls*. Karen packed up her new set of drums and joined Richard for their first instrumental performance together, an unlikely piano-drum duo accompanying the production.

Karen soon became the drummer for Two Plus Two, an all-girl band comprising Downey High School students including Linda Stewart and Eileen Matthews. "We wanted only girls because an all-girl band in those days was very rare," Stewart explains. She and Matthews carried their guitars and amps to school, where they would catch the bus to the Carpenter home for rehearsal each week. Karen recommended friend

Nancy Roubal join to play bass. "Nancy came on board but did not have a bass guitar," Stewart says. "She did what she could on the bass strings of a six-string guitar. It didn't sound as good as we wanted, but we worked through that. The other problem we had was our amps were so small that Karen had to play softly. We were kind of a surf band, but one of Karen's favorite songs to play was 'Ticket to Ride' by the Beatles. None of us sang at that time, so I never heard Karen sing, but I never heard such a good drummer in my young life at that time." After only a few rehearsals Karen approached Linda and the other girls suggesting that Richard join the group. "I said no," Stewart recalls, "because I wanted an all-girl band. Boys were out." The girls were finally booked to play for a local pool party, but when Eileen's mother refused to let her attend, Linda became discouraged. "I was so upset I just broke up the band."

───── ⚭ ─────

HAVING GRADUATED from high school in the spring of 1964, Richard enrolled at nearby California State University at Long Beach. In June of the following year he met Wes Jacobs, a tuba major from Palmdale, California, who was also a skillful upright bassist. "We met in theory class," Jacobs recalled in a 2009 interview. "It was obvious to me that he was a genius. Right from day one he could take all the dictation that the teacher could dish out; he would just write it out. . . . He wanted to do something jazzy. . . . We played, and it just clicked right away. Since I had considerable keyboard experience, I could look at his hands and read what he was doing. I could almost play along with him as if I were reading music. We really locked in stylistically. Within a short time, it was apparent that we had to do something musically, but we didn't know what. At one point he said, 'I'll tell my sister to learn how to play drums, and we'll have a trio.' Within three weeks she could play drums better than anybody that I heard at the college."

In actuality Karen had been playing a number of months by the time she teamed with Richard and Wes to form what became the Richard Carpenter Trio, an instrumental jazz group with the classic combo of piano, bass, and drums. Richard did all the arrangements, and by the end of the summer they were rehearsing on a daily basis, sometimes playing well into the night.

Financing a piano and drum kit, in addition to paying for music lessons, Agnes and Harold were barely making ends meet. Now the newly formed trio wanted amplifiers and microphones. Plus Richard felt a new electric piano would make their act more portable. Even so, a tape recorder took precedence, as this would allow the group to make demos. For several months Richard saved to make a down payment on a Sony TC-200 Stereo Tapecorder. The first recordings of the trio were made during the summer of 1965 in the Carpenters' living room at the house on Fidler.

Richard met trumpet major Dan Friberg, a junior college transfer, in choir during the fall of 1965. The two had several other classes together including music history and counterpoint, and Richard began to call upon Friberg when he needed a trumpet player for the trio's weekend gigs. "Karen was the drummer and didn't sing at all yet," Friberg recalls. "She was listening to Louie Bellson and Buddy Rich. Those were some of her idols. I remember going into her room at their house, and she had pictures on the wall of all these great drummers. Her goal was to be as good as they were. She was great then, by all I could tell, but not good enough for her." Friberg became a recurring soloist with the Richard Carpenter Trio. "We had a girl vocalist named Margaret Shanor," he recalls. "With Karen strictly drumming at this point, Margaret fronted the group."

⚬⚬⚬

It was not until 1966 that Karen came into her full voice. Although she had always sung in tune, her voice had lacked vibrato and any real depth or presence. It was mostly a light falsetto with a noticeable break between her lower and higher registers. "I can't really remember why I started to sing," Karen said in 1975. "It just kind of happened. But I never really discovered the voice that you know now—the low one— until later, when I was sixteen. I used to sing in this upper voice, and I didn't like it. I was uncomfortable, so I think I would tend to shy away from it because I didn't think I was that good. And I wasn't."

Karen deplored the sound of her tape-recorded voice at first but continued to experiment with her abilities as a singer. "It's kind of corny to listen back," she recalled. "We had an original recording of one of Richard's songs that I'd sung, and the range was too big. I'd be going from the low voice to the high voice, and even though it was all in tune, the top part was feeble and it was different. You wouldn't know it was me. Then suddenly one day out popped this voice, and it was natural."

Richard soon introduced Karen to his college choir director, Frank Pooler, with whom she began taking voice lessons every Saturday morning. This would be the only formal vocal training she would ever receive. "We'd have a half-hour or forty-five-minute voice lesson," Pooler says. "She always had her drums with her in the car. From there Richard would take her over to study with Bill Douglass in Hollywood." The lessons with Pooler focused on both classical voice study and pop music. The first half was devoted to art songs by Beethoven, Schumann, and other composers. During the last half Karen would sing the new songs Richard had written. "Karen was a born pop singer," Pooler says. "She wasn't particularly interested in that other stuff, but she had to do it to get into school."

Unlike Richard, who practiced endlessly, Karen rarely, if ever, rehearsed between her lessons with Pooler. Concerned that their money might be better spent somewhere else, the Carpenter parents met with her teacher to inquire about Karen's progress. "The folks were very supportive of both of them, but they weren't rich. I was getting paid five bucks an hour for those lessons, and they finally came up to see if Karen was getting her money's worth!"

Pooler told Karen her voice was "arty" and "natural" and discouraged the idea of subjecting it to any sort of intense vocal training. "He heard this voice and he wouldn't touch it," Karen said in 1975. "He said I should not train it...and the only thing I did work with him on was developing my upper register so I would have a full three-octave range.... Something else you don't think about is being able to sing in tune. Thank God I was born with it! It's something I never thought about. When I sing, I don't think about putting a pitch in a certain place, I just sing it."

Becoming more confident in Karen's vocals, Richard began to feature her with their act and called less upon Margaret Shanor. The group's set strayed from jazz to Richard's pop-influenced originals and tried-and-true standards like "Ebb Tide," "The Sweetheart Tree," "The Twelfth of Never," and "Yesterday." No matter how much singing she was asked to do, Karen also seemed to consider herself first and foremost a drummer who just happened to sing.

Around this time Agnes Carpenter met Evelyn Wallace, a fellow employee at North American Aviation. The women became close friends when Agnes came to Evelyn in tears following a heated disagreement with another coworker. After Wallace was promoted to the division of laboratory and tests for the Apollo program, Agnes took over her old job. "Why don't you stop in and hear the kids?" Agnes would often ask Evelyn. "They practice after school every day."

But Evelyn always seemed to find some excuse. "I thought she was talking about *little* kids," she recalls. "Then I thought it might be that acid rock, and I couldn't stand to listen to that. Finally I couldn't keep saying no. I had to say yes." Reluctantly Evelyn agreed to join the Carpenters in their home for dinner one evening and to hear Karen and Richard rehearse. Proud to finally find a captive audience, Agnes called out to her daughter seated behind the drums. "Sing it, Karen," she said. "*Sing out!*"

Wallace sat spellbound. "I had never heard a voice like that in all my life," she says. "What a beautiful, beautiful voice she had, and I told her when she finished, 'That was beautiful, Karen.' She thought I was just being nice."

<hr />

LIKE MANY college music majors, trumpeter Dan Friberg directed a church choir on the weekends for extra income. At a church in Hawthorne he met Don Zacklin, a member of the congregation. "I was doing lead sheets for him," Friberg recalls. "He would bring me tapes of different artists that he had recorded on Sunday, and I'd write out lead sheets. He would send them in for copyright purposes." Zacklin encouraged Friberg to share some of his original compositions and recordings with his friend Joe Osborn, a business partner in a small record label called Magic Lamp Records.

Joe Osborn was one of the most prominent and sought-after studio bassists on the West Coast pop music scene in the 1960s. He frequently played in tandem with drummer Hal Blaine and keyboardist Larry Knechtel, an association known as the Wrecking Crew. The three were featured on numerous hits by the Beach Boys, the Mamas and the Papas, and many other popular artists of the late 1960s. "We were a bunch of guys in Levis and T-shirts," says Blaine, who first worked with Joe Osborn on the live *Johnny Rivers at the Whisky a Go Go* album. "The older, established musicians in three-piece suits and blue blazers who had been in Hollywood all their life started saying, 'These kids are going to *wreck* the business,' so I just started calling us the Wrecking Crew."

As the spring semester of 1966 drew to a close, Friberg saw Richard on campus and told him of his upcoming audition with Osborn. "I've got a guy that wants to hear some songs that I wrote, but I need somebody to play piano for me," he said.

Richard agreed to accompany Friberg on the informal try-out. "It all goes back to that fateful night at Joe Osborn's in his garage with egg cartons on the wall," he says. It was April 1966. Both Karen and Richard traveled with Friberg and his young wife to Osborn's house, located at 7935 Ethel Avenue in the San Fernando Valley. The audition and recording session were slated for 1:00 A.M. since Osborn was usually in sessions each night until midnight.

Unbeknownst to Karen and Richard, Don Zacklin had asked Friberg to recommend other talented kids from the college to audition for Magic Lamp. So when Karen and Richard showed up, Zacklin and Osborn assumed they'd come along to audition, too. The brother and sister were befuddled but cooperative. "Karen ended up singing that night," Friberg says. "She sang and that was the end of me! To me, her voice was just like nothing else I'd ever heard before or since. It was just so distinctive. To think of all the times I saw her sitting behind the drums, never knowing that she could even sing. It's really weird the way things worked out because that night was what started the whole thing for them. If Richard had said, 'I'm busy,' I probably would have gotten somebody else, and they never would have met Joe."

Captivated by Karen's raw, husky voice, Osborn asked musician friend and drummer Mickey Jones to travel with him to Downey to see this "chubby little girl" perform. "We went to a small dinner house where we heard Karen sing," Jones recalls. "I was shocked. I had never heard a more pure voice in my life." Hearing Karen again, Osborn was won over. He told Mickey Jones he planned to contact the girl's parents. He wanted to record her. This was surely good news, but it did not sit well with Agnes Carpenter. She was set on the idea of her son becoming the family's famous musician. After all, they'd moved across the country in hopes of Richard getting into the music business, and now he was being disregarded in favor of his kid sister, a musical novice. "I know that Agnes was really, really mad about that," recalls Evelyn Wallace. "There are many piano players that are very, very good. But let's face it, all pianos more or less sound alike. All voices do not."

On May 9, 1966, Osborn signed sixteen-year-old Karen Carpenter to Magic Lamp Records' small roster of artists, which included Johnny Burnette, James Burton, Mickey Jones, Dean Torrence (of Jan and Dean), and Vince Edwards, best known as television's Dr. Ben Casey. Since Karen was not of legal age, Agnes and Harold signed on her behalf. Two days later, Magic Lamp's publishing division, Lightup Music, signed Richard as a songwriter in an effort to help reconcile Agnes's displeasure with Osborn having initially overlooked her son's talents. "Joe thought that Richard was a pain in the ass," Mickey Jones recalls. "Richard not only wanted to play the piano but to run everything. Joe did not want him around when he was working with Karen, so he made Richard wait outside the studio."

Any resentment between the two soon gave way to new friendships as Karen, Richard, and Wes Jacobs began spending hours on end at Osborn's studio. That summer Karen recorded several of Richard's original compositions including "The Parting of Our Ways," "Don't Tell Me," "Looking for Love," and "I'll Be Yours." She also played drums on the recordings, which featured Osborn on electric bass and sometimes Wes Jacobs on upright bass. Richard was on piano and the Chamberlin Music Master, a version of the Mellotron, both of which were popular analog synthesizers that provided taped string and woodwind sounds. Osborn used a Scully 4-track recorder and Neumann U87 condenser microphones to tape the sessions. Playback was done through Altec 604 studio monitors. When four tracks were complete, they were bounced or "ping-ponged" to his Scully 2-track machine, which condensed multiple tracks to two or sometimes even one. This process freed additional tracks for overdubbing and layering voices or instruments.

"Looking for Love / I'll Be Yours" (ML 704) was the first and only single by Karen Carpenter for Magic Lamp Records. Five hundred copies were pressed, and most extras were given to family and friends. "There was no distribution that I am aware of," Mickey Jones says. "It was mainly a tax shelter." Like most small labels, Magic Lamp did not have the means to promote their singles, and by late 1967 the company folded.

———— ∞ ————

THE SUMMER of 1966 brought several milestones in the lives of Karen and Richard Carpenter. Shortly after having joined forces with Magic Lamp Records, the Richard Carpenter Trio made it to the finals of the Seventh Annual Battle of the Bands, a prestigious talent competition held at the Hollywood Bowl. The event was sponsored by the County of Los Angeles Department of Parks and Recreation and dubbed "a musical showdown under the stars." Open to nonprofessionals under the age of twenty-one, the contest began with hundreds of groups competing in five preliminary contests held around Los Angeles County. Acts were quickly narrowed to just three entries in each of the following categories: dance band, school band, combos, vocal soloists, and vocal groups.

On Friday night, June 24, the trio performed Richard's multi-time signature arrangement of Antonio Carlos Jobim's "The Girl from Ipanema" and an original whole-tone-inspired jazz waltz entitled "Iced Tea," an ode to their favorite beverage, featuring Wes Jacobs on tuba. From their introduction by master of ceremonies Jerry Dexter, the trio gained full audience attention before even playing a note. The sight of Karen sitting behind a drum kit with her hair piled high was definitely a novelty. "I remember when we walked into the Bowl there were twenty acts on the show, and I was still new to the drums," Karen later explained to Ray Coleman. "It took me a while to set them up. We'd only been together for like six months, and what was even funnier, I couldn't lift them. I couldn't move them, so I had to have everybody carrying my drums, and then I put them together. All the guy drummers were hysterical."

A lengthy drum solo in the middle of "Iced Tea" gave Karen an opportunity to demonstrate her technique. The enthusiastic audience responded with a roar of applause, cheers, and whistles, which even drowned out the music at one point on a recording of the evening's performance. "By then she had gone from having a good rhythmical sense and steady time—the foundation you want—to being a very good player," Frankie Chavez recalls. "She could make some male drummers stand up and take notice, and she actually could outplay some of them, too. She was that good. I thought she made very good progress for the very short time she'd been playing, and it's a credit to her musicality."

Despite having to play on a dreadful upright piano the night of the contest, Richard won outstanding instrumentalist. In addition to winning best combo, the trio took home the sweepstakes trophy for the highest overall score in the competition, beating out Gentlemen and Trombones, Inc. "They won!" Agnes Carpenter proudly exclaimed to Frank Pooler, phoning him the day after the Battle of the Bands. "It's the biggest trophy I've ever seen in my life. My God, they've *got* to be good!"

Gerald Wilson, Calvin Jackson, Jerry Goldsmith, and Bill Holman joined Leonard Feather, chief jazz critic for the *Los Angeles Times*, as the official judges for the event. "The musical surprise of the evening was the Trio of Richard Carpenter," wrote Feather, describing the group's leader as a "remarkably original soloist who won awards as the best instrumentalist and leader of the best combo. Flanking his piano were Karen Carpenter, his talented sixteen-year-old sister at the drums, and bassist Wes Jacobs who doubled amusingly and confidently on tuba." The competition was later broadcast in color on KNBC Channel 4 in Los Angeles.

"The Hollywood Bowl performance was a great place to get exposure," Chavez says. "People that went there were oftentimes movers and shakers who could make things happen with a career. It was a good move." On the way to their car following the win at the Bowl, Richard was approached by a man who congratulated the trio and asked if they would be interested in cutting some records. Richard told the man they already had a contract but took his business card anyway. Once Richard realized it was Neely Plumb, prominent West Coast A & R (artists and repertoire) man for RCA-Victor Records, he quickly explained the contract was only a solo singing contract for Karen with Magic Lamp. Plumb (whose daughter Eve would go on to star as Jan in the classic TV series *The Brady Bunch*) thought the idea of rock tuba might be the wave of the immediate future and wanted to spotlight Wes Jacobs.

The trio signed to RCA-Victor in September 1966 and soon cut eleven tracks, including instrumentals of the standard "Strangers in the Night" and the Beatles' "Every Little Thing." They also recorded "I've Never Been in Love Before" from the musical *Guys and Dolls* and a Richard original, "Flat Baroque." Although he was excited to see the trio signed to a major record label, Richard shared with Plumb his concerns over the rock tuba approach, which he knew had little potential, and even the powers at RCA agreed. Richard told them of Karen's voice and how she had been signed to a vocal contract earlier that year, but after agreeing to listen, the response was: "Just another folk-rock group. No thank you." RCA decided against releasing the trio's music, and the three soon left the label with a few hundred dollars and no record. They considered themselves to have been an artistic success but a commercial failure. "It was really great playing, but we didn't really have that focus," Wes Jacobs recalled. "Karen wasn't singing, and the tuba wasn't going to sell records. There was a lot of talent, but we didn't have direction."

Back on the campus at Cal State Long Beach, Richard spent many hours in the music department practice rooms, where he was able to focus on his own music. As he did on occasion, Richard consulted Frank Pooler for inspiration, in this case in planning their holiday music set. "We're sure sick of 'White Christmas,' 'Silent Night,' and doing the same songs every night," he told Pooler, asking for suggestions.

"I don't know any *new* Christmas songs," he replied, "but I wrote one a long time ago."

Pooler had written "Merry Christmas, Darling" as a young man. In fact, he composed his original version in 1946, the year Richard was born. Twenty years later, in December 1966, Pooler shared "Merry

Christmas, Darling" with Richard Carpenter. "[Richard] was writing tunes at that time," says Pooler, "and I knew that whatever tune he could write would be better than the one I had already written, so I didn't give him the tune. I just gave him the words." Richard said he would work on a new melody, and about fifteen minutes later he was finished. "Merry Christmas, Darling" was written by two teenagers a generation apart. It was among the earliest songs Karen sang with the trio and would provide them with many successes in the years to come.

———— ✺ ————

UPON GRADUATION from Downey High School in the spring of 1967, Karen was presented with the John Philip Sousa Band Award, the highest achievement for high school band students, recognizing superior musicianship and outstanding dedication. "She didn't strike me as musically talented at first," band director Gifford later recalled, "but I've learned to give people time before judging their talent."

In a farewell message inscribed in mentor Frankie Chavez's yearbook, Karen praised his abilities as a drummer and thanked him for inspiring and guiding her talents.

Frankie,

Listen man, it's hard to believe it, but we made it. Anyway, it's been a gas in every sense of the word. I can honestly say that it wouldn't have been near as crazy without ya. I want to thank you for getting me interested in drums. I learned a great deal from you and I'll always owe it to ya.... Oh well, it's time to split so keep in touch in between gigs.

Love ya,

Karen '67

3

STAND IN LINE, TRY TO CLIMB

A STRUGGLING POLITICAL science student from San Pedro who often slept on campus in his station wagon overnight, John Bettis had given up on his mother's dream for him to become an international attorney. Entering Cal State Long Beach, the long-haired folk singer was known for his sense of humor and creativity. He knew very little about music theory but ended up joining Frank Pooler's college choir as an elective. Still, he had a remarkable talent for writing lyrics.

"John used to slip me little notes," Pooler recalls. "They were little pieces of poetry; his observations of rehearsals and observations he had about me. I thought they were really kind of beautiful and very unusual."

Bettis began to compile his observations for what became "A Cappella Music," a composition that according to Pooler was not even considered a song. "It was a cantata!" he exclaims. John was quite sure he would be kicked out of the choir once they heard the finished product, which introduced the various sections of the choir and proceeded to poke fun at each with a tongue-in-cheek approach. The choir listened as Bettis struggled to premiere "A Cappella Music" with only a sparse guitar accompaniment. "Buddy, you need a pianist!" Richard blurted out before coming to Bettis's rescue. Pooler had a feeling the young men's talents might complement one another. "I thought they were a perfect pair so I said, 'You guys should work together.'"

Richard and John Bettis shared a love of music, cars, and girls and became close friends. Agnes Carpenter was not as quick to welcome new faces into the Carpenter circle, especially someone with the gypsy existence of Bettis. She was infuriated to learn Richard was splitting performance fees equally with Bettis once they began playing various gigs together. She reminded Richard that he carried the musical load, and he was the only musically literate one of the two. In her opinion Bettis did not do enough or have the experience to warrant half of the profits.

Through mutual friend Doug Strawn, Richard and John learned of an opening for a ragtime piano-banjo act at Coke Corner on Disneyland's Main Street U.S.A. The two were hired for the summer season of 1967 and worked eighteen-hour shifts. The musicians' union salary of $180 per week was a fortune to two college students, but they wisely invested their earnings in musical instruments and sound equipment.

Disneyland's entertainment supervisor, Vic Guder, made frequent stops throughout the park, walkie-talkie in hand, overseeing the park's wide range of talent. He made certain all acts were in proper costume and performing in accordance with the park's policies. Stopping by Coke Corner, Guder expected to hear turn-of-the-century ditties, like "A Bicycle Built for Two" and Scott Joplin's "Maple Leaf Rag" and "The Entertainer." Instead he discovered the duo granting requests from thirsty patrons wanting to hear modern tunes like "Light My Fire" and "Yesterday." After months of gentle redirection by Guder, their time with Disneyland came to an end. "They had very strict regimens as to what one could and could not do in the park," Bettis recalled. "Richard and I were fired for combing our hair in the park. Now, I grant you we did a lot of other things that did not please them before that time, but that actually caused us to be fired."

According to Guder, the duo was never fired, the season merely came to an end. "Heck no, they weren't fired," he says. "Richard was hired for the summertime. He went back to school in the fall and didn't plan to work full time. Coke Corner is a spot that is a part-time summer job. They'd come back when we'd use the Coke Corner pianist at night for private parties. It's not a full-time gig."

Seeking musical revenge, so to speak, the two set out to write a song about the incident immediately upon termination. "We got all the way to the bridge and didn't finish it because I wasn't at all sure that it was something that we ought to be doing," Bettis said. "Richard really felt so strongly about it and liked the music well enough that he actually wrote the bridge to that, lyrically, and finished it." Like many of their early musical collaborations, "Mr. Guder" was set aside and would resurface several years later.

⸺⸺ ◦◦◦◦ ⸺⸺

FOLLOWING HER brother's lead, Karen enrolled at Cal State Long Beach as a music major in the fall of 1967. Despite the beauty of her newly discovered chest voice, she was expected to use her head voice as it was better suited to the classical art song repertoire required of private voice students. She was also required to sing before a panel of professors called a jury for evaluation at the end of each semester. Such a critical review proved stressful for even the most accomplished musicians. With Larry Peterson, head of the music department, and several other members of the voice faculty present, Karen performed selections from her repertoire before Pooler interrupted. "Look, this is all so serious," he told his colleagues. "This girl's really versatile. Do you guys want a laugh?" Pooler urged Karen to do one of many impersonations he had witnessed in their lessons. In particular he requested the "spastic, hare-lipped singer."

"They'll kick me out of school," Karen objected.

She was surprised and embarrassed by her teacher's request, especially before such an esteemed gathering. "The thing that really endeared me to Karen," Pooler recalls, "was the sense of humor she had about everything and how she could imitate people. She could do anything with her voice."

Pooler was a bit of a maverick in the choral music world, displaying an eccentric approach to his style and work. He was never predictable— at least not musically. Opening the floor to members of the A Cappella

Choir, Pooler would allow students to suggest music literature and styles. The subject of black spirituals surfaced. "I don't want to do a piece that's foreign to me," Pooler told the choir. Though he was experienced in music sung in foreign languages, spirituals and gospel music were unfamiliar territory.

"Well, if you can't show them, *I'll* show them," a voice said, and out stepped Wanda Freeman, one of the few African Americans in the choir. She faced the choir and began to sing.

"I had never done spirituals or black music," Pooler says. "I just didn't feel it, but she did. She was sensational. She was the start of a whole host of first-class gospel musicians that came out of that choir."

Unlike other college choirs in the area that specialized in one style or another, Pooler's groups tackled a wide range of choral genres. "Frank was very innovative," Freeman recalls. "We were doing avant-garde stuff and things that other choirs had never done before; songs with just sounds and things. He was very open to trying gospel."

Made popular by Blood, Sweat and Tears, "And When I Die" was one of several contemporary hits the choir performed. The gospel-style arrangement called for a duet, and Pooler chose the unlikely pairing of Wanda Freeman and Karen Carpenter. "Karen had a nice alto voice," Freeman recalls. "I never really thought anything of it, but it was a very clear voice. When we did 'And When I Die' she really opened up. She really wanted to do that song."

Pooler often praised Karen's versatility as a singer and even used her as a model for other choir students. "Her range was spectacular," he recalls. "She could sing higher than anybody else but also lower than anybody else. At that time her voice was like most adolescent voices. It was not completely unified from the top to the bottom, but she knew how to do it."

WITH THE departure of bassist Wes Jacobs, who in 1967 left the Richard Carpenter Trio and Los Angeles to study classical tuba at Juilliard, Richard was open to exploring new musical opportunities. He had long been fond of vocal ensembles like the Hi-Lo's, the Four Freshmen, and the Beach Boys. He had also enjoyed the close harmony sounds of overdubbing pioneers Les Paul and Mary Ford since childhood. But it was Frank Pooler's choral influence that left a lasting impression on both him and Karen. His philosophy stressed vocal blend, vowel shaping, and precise attack and release. These fundamentals were the basis for what would ultimately become the trademark Carpenters sound.

Richard's first attempt at forming a vocal group produced a quintet assembled during Karen's senior year of high school. They called themselves Summerchimes but soon renamed the group Spectrum. Their first recruit was John Bettis, who sang and played rhythm guitar. Over a period of several months, he, Karen, and Richard conducted informal auditions to complete the group. Gary Sims lived in Downey and, like Karen, was still attending high school when the group originated. "He used to perform with an acoustic guitar, like a folk singer," recalled Bettis, who went with Richard to catch Sims's act. "He had this great baritone voice and joined the group as a guitar player." The final recruit was Dan Woodhams, a tenor vocalist enlisted to sing and play bass guitar, although he "didn't have a clue how to play the bass," according to Bettis. "He played violin, so Richard actually taught him how to play the bass. Danny was the final member. That was the original Spectrum."

The addition of Leslie "Toots" Johnston in the fall of 1967 made the group a sextet. "Johnny Bettis and Gary Sims were friends of mine," Johnston recalls. "Gary was the Carpenters' neighbor, and they were looking for another girl to add to the group. They listened to me, and I had a good pop voice style. Richard was looking for someone who could blend with Karen, which I did very well." A member of the college choir, Johnston sat next to Karen in the alto section during the daily afternoon rehearsals. "We threw jokes back and forth and got along really well," she says. "Karen was such a great musician but didn't read music as well as I did, so she listened to me for the part. We struck up a friendship. She had a dry sense of humor and was funny. She thought I was funny, too. She didn't have a lot of girlfriends, so I think Karen enjoyed having another female around."

Spectrum rehearsed in the garage at the house on Fidler, where there was never a shortage of Agnes Carpenter's famous iced tea—the perfect blend of Lipton instant tea and frozen lemonade. "There had to be a jug of that on the table for every rehearsal," Johnston recalls. "That was *the drink!*"

KAREN BECAME increasingly mindful of her appearance during her first year of college. She had been chubby as a kid. In fact, Richard often called her Fatso (to which she would reply, "Four eyes!"). It was the type of teasing characteristic of most sibling relationships. But as a seventeen-year-old young woman, Karen was five feet four inches tall and weighed 145 pounds. Her classic hourglass figure was a common trait among family members, including her mother and aunt Bernice. "I was heavier," Karen said in a 1973 interview. "About twenty pounds heavier, to tell you the truth. I was just tired of being fat so I went on a diet. . . . I found this sweater I used to wear in high school. Good Lord, I think I could get into it three times today. I don't know how I ever got through a door."

Frankie Chavez recalls Karen as only slightly overweight in high school, but if she had body image issues at the time, he never noticed. There were no warning signs during the period they were close. "She never gave any indication that it bothered her that she carried a little extra weight," he says. "She always seemed very self-confident, and I don't think she ever even contemplated dieting when I knew her. Karen was a perfectionist as far as her performances were concerned, and she set the bar very high for herself, but there was no indication that she had any problems at all."

During the summer of 1967 Agnes took her to see their family doctor, who recommended the popular Stillman water diet that was introduced that year by Dr. Irwin Maxwell Stillman. The plan promised quick weight loss through limiting intake of carbohydrates and fatty foods while increasing daily water intake to eight glasses. Karen hated water, but after only six weeks she shed twenty-five pounds and was determined to maintain her new figure. When Spectrum's late-night rehearsals ended, everyone in the band was hungry and went for dinner, which was frustrating for Karen. "All the guys would want to go to eat at Coco's," she said, "and I would sit there with my hamburger patty and cottage cheese while the guys ordered forty-seven-layer cheeseburgers and giant sundaes." From the summer of 1967 until early 1973, Karen remained at or around the comfortable weight of 115 to 120 pounds.

In early 1967 Richard had received a call from a local singer named Ed Sulzer, whom he had accompanied during a gig back in 1963. Sulzer heard Spectrum was recording in Joe Osborn's garage and offered to shop their demo to various record labels around Los Angeles. He quickly became acting manager of the group. With rare exceptions, Sulzer's enthusiasm for Spectrum's distinctive sound was not shared by the record labels and venues he approached. "People hear what we accomplished, and it sounds like such a natural now," John Bettis explained. "Back then, what we were recording and what we were writing went completely against the grain of what anyone else was doing. And they told us so."

Leslie Johnston describes Spectrum's sound as rich, thick, tight harmony, but she feels the group's creativity was out of sync with most of their audiences. "Here's this middle-of-the-road group with this great sound," she says. "We were such an in-between kind of group. Back then it was either hard psychedelic rock or it was elevator music. We had this pretty sound; it was nice to listen to us, but we weren't a dance group. Agents that would come to the Troubadour just kept telling our manager, 'They're *terrific*, but where do we put them?' Radio stations were afraid to play us because we were too mild for some and yet we weren't the old style either. We were having a tough time, and we were getting discouraged. We really were and should have been a recording group exclusively."

Sulzer secured Spectrum a block of studio time at United Audio Recording Studio in Santa Ana. The group cut several demos of original songs, including "All I Can Do," "All of My Life," "Another Song," "What's the Use," and "Candy." The latter would later become "One

Love" on the 1971 *Carpenters* album. Positioning microphones in the studio, Glen Pace, United Audio's owner and engineer during the Spectrum sessions, noticed a young girl unpacking a set of Ludwigs. "Gee, your boyfriend has you trained really well," he called out to her across the room.

"What do you mean?" Karen asked.

"He has you trained really well for you to come and set up his drums for him."

With a sheepish grin she replied, "*I'm* the drummer."

"This was the first girl drummer I'd ever come across," Pace explains.

Unable to afford more studio time, Spectrum moved their recording sessions back to the Carpenters' living room. Using Richard's Sony Tapecorder, the group began making recordings at home and employing the bathroom as an echo chamber. A string of live performances arranged by Ed Sulzer found Spectrum at the legendary Troubadour in West Hollywood where every Monday night was Hoot Night. Dozens of acts lined up in the alley in hopes of securing a performance time slot. "You had to wait in this huge line to play," Karen explained to the *Los Angeles Times* in 1972. "I often stood there talking with kids, along with people like Jackson Browne and Brewer and Shipley."

Richard purchased a Wurlitzer 140-B electronic piano from Jeff Hanna of the Nitty Gritty Dirt Band and in keeping with his fascination with automobiles personalized the instrument with a 426 HEMI engine decal. Spectrum members routinely unloaded the station wagon and lugged the new Wurlitzer, drums, and various instruments and amplifiers down the alley and through the crowds to perform for fifteen or twenty minutes. Then they turned around and hauled everything back through the crowds to the car. "You should have seen us with our crew-cuts and blue velvet jackets," says Leslie Johnston.

Randy Sparks, who led a group called the New Christy Minstrels, heard Spectrum at the Troubadour and offered the group a week's engagement at Ledbetter's, his club on Westwood Boulevard. This was one of their first major paid engagements. "They were a bit more like a lounge act than a folk group," Sparks says, "which was my niche in the business of music. But Karen was a wonderful singer, and they had a pleasing—if not exciting—sound. They were much appreciated by my crowd." Sparks believed Karen and Richard each displayed unmistakable talent, far beyond that of the group's other members. "The other folks in their band were essentially invisible, in my estimation." As Spectrum spent several weeks on the stage at Ledbetter's, Sparks witnessed their growth with each successive performance. "That's what my operation was all about. Ledbetter's was a place to perform, to experiment, to rehearse, and to develop skills in dealing with audiences."

Next, Sulzer booked Spectrum at the Whisky a Go-Go, where the group opened for Evergreen Blue Shoes, a band whose bass player, Skip Battin, would later join the Byrds. The Whisky (often misspelled "Whiskey") was a popular nightclub on the Sunset Strip and inspiration for the Loggins and Messina song "Whisky." Its lyric instructs:

> Don't do anything mellow at the Whisky . . .
> Don't sing anything pretty at the Whisky . . .
> 'Cause if you do, your musical insurance better be paid up

For the most part Spectrum was mellow and their music indisputably pretty. They did not stand a chance. "The customers sat and listened to us," Karen said of the engagement. "That wasn't what the club wanted. If you sit, you don't dance. If you don't dance, you don't get thirsty. In that case you don't spend, so we were kicked out."

Karen also recalled opening for Steppenwolf at the Blue Law, a large warehouse-turned-club. "At first, the audience was so restive," she said. "We thought we were going to get killed, but we kept going, and they shut up and listened." Again, not what club management preferred.

"Steppenwolf? Oh my God, I was so embarrassed to be there," says Leslie Johnston. "We're in the dressing room with Steppenwolf, and they couldn't have been any more hard rock. In fact, I liked them, but we were so mad at Eddie for that booking. I think we were there maybe two nights. I was just dying because the people were waiting for some hard rock to dance to. They didn't *boo* us, but they looked at us like we were nuts. We had this great, full sound, but Steppenwolf was probably in the dressing room laughing."

As Sulzer struggled to secure live performance opportunities in venues appropriate for Spectrum, the group's sights were set on securing a recording contract. When two major recording companies, Uni and White Whale, presented contracts on the same night at the Troubadour, the group was encouraged, but Richard declined the offers once he realized the labels were demanding too big a cut. Spectrum's members became disheartened and soon began to scatter. Leslie Johnston was asked to go on the road with another group as lead vocalist. "I agreed," she says, "because nothing else was happening!"

CONTINUING TO record in Joe Osborn's studio, gratis, Karen and Richard worked toward the creation of a new demo tape. They usually recorded on weekends or after midnight when Osborn's other sessions ended. According to Karen, "Since Richard did all the arranging and chose the material, and we did our own playing and singing, Richard said, 'We might as well do it ourselves, just overdub it.'... All of a sudden that sound was born." She marveled over the quality of sound they were able to achieve in Joe's studio. "That garage studio had a sound that I don't think we ever matched. It was big and fat."

For an a cappella arrangement called "Invocation" they began with two-part harmonies, then built to four-part, and finally eight. Their eight-part harmonies were tripled, totaling twenty-four voices in all. "Wow, we couldn't believe the results," Karen later recalled. "All of a sudden this ten-ton thing was born. This *couldn't* miss!" Their demo tape also featured Richard's original "Don't Be Afraid" and another he penned with John Bettis called "Your Wonderful Parade." Although the arrangements were identical to those of Spectrum, there was something special about the familial sound that resulted from the layering of Karen's voice with Richard's. Now officially a duo, Karen and Richard chose the name Carpenters, sans prefix. They thought it was simple but hip, like Buffalo Springfield or Jefferson Airplane.

As recording demanded more and more of their time and energy, Karen and Richard saw their obligations at Cal State Long Beach as less of a priority. They often carried copies of *Billboard* and *Cashbox* with them to class and would read them behind their textbooks, so it is no wonder Karen flunked out of a psychology course twice. And she loathed biology: "What good is biology going to do me?" she asked rhetorically in a 1970 interview. "On the stage it's of no use, right? A biology major doesn't have to take a music course." Frank Pooler went to bat for Karen several times in attempts to justify her continued absences from several classes. "She wasn't showing up for some boring class," he says. "I remember going to talk to the president of the university about her. I said, 'Hey, some people need special consideration. Besides, I wouldn't take the class myself.'"

In the summer of 1968 Richard heard about a new national television program called *Your All-American College Show*. Produced by radio legend Wendell Niles and sponsored by the Colgate-Palmolive Corporation, the program gathered top musical talent from college campuses across the country. Along with new recruit Bill Sissoyev on bass, their act was well received during auditions, and they ultimately advanced to the televised portion of the competition. Wearing showy white go-go boots and a wide white headband, Karen tore through their Mamas and the Papas–inspired "Dancing in the Street" with much energy and gusto. Her drumming was intense and her singing strong and deliberate. They appeared as a trio several times during that year, and the group won $3,500.

The publicity alone was enough to keep the trio excited about *Your All-American College Show*, but Wendell Niles and his organization also expressed interest in representing them. Everyone was surprised when celebrity judge John Wayne wanted Karen to audition for the role of young frontier girl Mattie Ross in his upcoming film *True Grit*. The part ultimately went to actress Kim Darby, and Karen continued to explore various musical opportunities. With Richard's blessing, she auditioned for the girl singer spot in Kenny Rogers's group the First Edition. The position had been vacated after vocalist Thelma Camacho was fired for missing too many rehearsals and performances. Surprisingly, Karen was overlooked, most likely due to the fact that it was not a recording audition, and much of Karen's appeal was facilitated by a microphone. The spot was filled by Camacho's roommate Mary

Arnold, an Iowa-born singer who later married Roger "King of the Road" Miller.

With the ongoing assistance of Ed Sulzer, Karen and Richard continued their mission to get their demo tape around to each and every record label in Hollywood. But Columbia Records had hits with Gary Puckett and the Union Gap's "Young Girl" and Bobbie Gentry's "Ode to Billie Joe" and were looking for soundalike acts. Similarly, Warner Brothers Records asked the Carpenters if they could sound like Harper's Bizarre, but they had no interest in emulating others. Richard was convinced that their overdubbed sound and Karen's vocals were commercially viable and that it would only be a matter of time before they would be recognized. Karen felt strongly that A&M Records, a label known for its attention to artistry, would give their music a fair listen, but even the guard at the gate turned them away. Not to worry, Ed Sulzer assured them. He had a friend who knew a trumpet player named Jack Daugherty who might possibly deliver their demo to A&M's cofounder Herb Alpert. It seemed like a circuitous route, but Karen and Richard gave their approval.

In the meantime, a call came in from brothers John and Tom Bähler, well-known jingle singers in Los Angeles. The Bählers had caught one of the Carpenters' appearances on *Your All-American College Show* and invited the duo to audition for a campaign called "The Going Thing," which was in development by the J. Walter Thompson advertising agency for the Ford Motor Company. The brothers auditioned approximately two hundred acts in New York and another two hundred at Sunset Sound in Hollywood, where Karen and Richard were ultimately selected. Visiting the agency, they signed individual contracts and were informed the group would assist in premiering the new 1970 Ford Maverick. It was not a recording contract as they desired, but the contracts came with the promise of fifty thousand dollars each and a new Ford automobile of their choice.

4

SPRINKLED MOONDUST

A&M RECORDS was unlike any other record label on the West Coast. Capitol, Warner Brothers, and others had undergone numerous reorganizations and were starting to be seen as enormous, impersonal conglomerates. A&M was a "family" label, founded precariously in 1962 by trumpet player Herb Alpert and Jerry Moss, his partner in production and promotion. Each contributed one hundred dollars to start what was first called Carnival Records, but after learning the name belonged to an existing label the two renamed the company with the initials of their surnames. A&M Records' first single was Alpert's "The Lonely Bull" recorded with the Tijuana Brass. Records by the Brass, the Baja Marimba Band, and Sergio Mendes and Brasil '66 helped keep A&M afloat throughout the late 1960s. Other artists signed to the label included Leon Russell, Joe Cocker, and Burt Bacharach. The Bacharach-penned "This Guy's in Love with You" became a #1 hit single for Herb Alpert in 1968, A&M's first chart topper.

The A&M Records lot itself was as unique as the label. The studio opened in November 1966 with a skeleton crew of thirty-two employees. Located at 1416 North La Brea Avenue in Hollywood, just south of Sunset Boulevard, the site once housed Charlie Chaplin's movie studio. Says songwriter Paul Williams, who came to the young and vibrant company in 1967, "There was such a sense of history just because of the location. It was charming in its look, and it reeked of Hollywood history. I showed up in a stolen car. I was an out-of-work actor and stumbled into the songwriting career. They were looking for a lyricist for Roger Nichols, and I wound up with a career. It was one of those great accidents. One door slammed shut, and another one opened."

Roger Nichols remembers A&M as an artist-friendly company and attributes most of the label's early success to the recordings of Herb Alpert and the Tijuana Brass. "Thanks to them, A&M really had money," he says. "They didn't have money to burn but money to do things right. They treated people nicely. It was like the crème de la crème of the record companies at that time and a great place to be. There was a great creative energy to the lot, and the premise of the company was that you could pretty much do whatever you wanted to. When I was asked to record for A&M they said, 'Make whatever kind of record you want to.' That was unique. I don't know where you'd go to find that today. There wasn't so much control of the product."

Nichols and others around A&M were acquainted with Jack Daugherty, a Cincinnati-born musician who worked at North American Aviation in Downey, where he made presentations detailing the company's work with the Apollo program. Daugherty worked part time as a music copyist and in his spare time wrote counterpoint exercises and chorales. It was while working at North American that he received a copy of the Carpenters' demo. "I had it for about two months," he recalled in a feature for *High Fidelity*, "and every once in a while I'd listen again. That's a pretty good test."

Daugherty visited A&M's publishing office almost every week to drop off lead sheets he had prepared for Chuck Kaye, head of Almo/Irving Music, A&M's publishing arm. "You have to hear this group," Daugherty told Roger Nichols. "They're a brother and sister. Call themselves Carpenters." But it was Daugherty's friend, Tijuana Brass guitarist John Pisano, who ultimately handed the Carpenters' demo tape to Herb Alpert. "I put on the tape, and I was really knocked out with the sound of Karen's voice to start with," Alpert said in 1994. "It touched me. It had nothing to do with what was happening in the market at that moment, but that's what touched me even more. I felt like it was time."

Manager Ed Sulzer contacted Richard and let him know that Alpert had heard their demo, loved their sound, and wanted Carpenters on the A&M Records roster. The standard recording contract outlined a 7 percent royalty on all record sales and an advance of ten thousand dollars. Karen and Richard were thrilled, but timing posed a problem. Only days earlier they signed with the J. Walter Thompson agency's "Going Thing" campaign for Ford. Though they were grateful for the opportunity and honor, the two asked for release from the contract, each surrendering the fifty thousand dollars and new car. A recording contract with a major label like A&M had the potential for longevity. John and Tom Bähler understood the dilemma and convinced J. Walter Thompson to let Karen and Richard out of their contracts.

Herb Alpert and Jerry Moss took great pride in their artists, "encouraging them to reach their creative potential," as they wrote years later in *From Brass to Gold*, an exhaustive A&M Records discography. "We looked for artists who had a strong sense of themselves musically and surrounded them with an environment and people who could help them express their unique talents." For Alpert, musical honesty and sincerity took priority over potential sales when considering a new artist. "It doesn't matter if they're a jazz musician, a classical musician, or rap or pop," he explained. "I think the real measure is if you are really doing it from your heart. The music that the Carpenters made was straight from their hearts. Richard was and is a real student of the record business. He knows a good song, he knows where to record it, he knows the musicians. Karen had this extraordinary voice, and they put the right combination together, and it was touching."

It was Jerry Moss who officially signed the Carpenters to A&M, just before noon on Tuesday, April 22, 1969. "You think we could meet Herb?" Ed Sulzer asked. Alpert entered, greeted his new acquisitions, and said, "Let's hope we have some hits!"

———— ∞ ————

A&M DID not micromanage their artists, even the newest and youngest on the roster. They held their artists in such high regard that they would often turn them loose to explore and create. Even so, Alpert suggested

Jack Daugherty be signed to serve as producer for the Carpenters. This meant Daugherty would leave his twenty-thousand-dollar-a-year job at North American Aviation and go to work for A&M in hopes the Carpenters' successes would warrant his stay. According to Ollie Mitchell, who played trumpet in Daugherty's band, "Jack was lucky to be in a position to work with Richard, who seemed to do most of the real producing on the recording dates."

Most agree it was Richard who arranged and artistically produced the Carpenters' albums. Daugherty was more of an A & R person for Karen and Richard. "Jack was very user-friendly as far as Roger Nichols and I were concerned," remembers Paul Williams. "He's the one who introduced all of us to the Carpenters. He was a very detailed man, not shy but very reserved. There was something almost 'country gentleman' about him at times. I liked him."

The Carpenters were immediately given run of the entire studio and its amenities. Recording began just a week after having signed with the label. At the time, eight-track recording equipment was standard, and for the first time Richard had a sophisticated recording studio at his disposal. For their first recording sessions, Richard chose to record a ballad version of Lennon and McCartney's "Ticket to Ride," from the 1965 Beatles' album *Help!* Foreshadowing "Ticket" had been a demo of the Beatles' "Nowhere Man" recorded by Karen in 1967. That recording took the up-tempo song and reworked it as a plaintive piano-accompanied ballad with a lead vocal full of melancholia. "Ticket to Ride" also employed this woeful approach, set atop a series of straightforward, arpeggiated chords from the piano.

Rather than seeking out or writing new material, the Carpenters chose to record much of their existing repertoire, most of which was written during the Spectrum years. The album was finished in Richard's mind long before they ever signed with A&M. Several songs were even lifted from the demos cut in Joe Osborn's studio. "Your Wonderful Parade" was given a new lead vocal and the addition of strings, while "All I Can Do" was the original demo as previously recorded. "Don't Be Afraid," one of the songs Alpert had listened to on their demo, was re-recorded entirely. Osborn was recruited to play his trademark sliding bass on the album as he would continue to do on all future Carpenters albums. It was under his guidance that Karen was able to play bass guitar on two recordings, "All of My Life" and "Eve." (Although Karen's bass work may be heard on the original album mix, recent compilations feature Richard's latest remixes, which have substituted Osborn's more sophisticated bass lines.)

Several elements of what would become the Carpenters' trademark style were already in place on this debut. For instance, "Someday," a collaboration with John Bettis, was one of Richard's finest sweeping melodies. It was also the perfect vehicle for Karen's mournful delivery. Richard sang lead on about half of the songs on the debut album, but his solo vocals became less prominent with each successive release until they disappeared entirely.

Recording sessions for the debut album came to a close in the summer of 1969. An August release was slated but delayed when additional mixing was required. Jim McCrary, A&M staff photographer, took the photo for the record jacket, driving Karen and Richard up Highland Avenue and posing them by the roadside. Richard was never happy with the photo, which depicts the blank-faced duo holding a bundle of sunflowers. But when Herb Alpert picked out the cover photo, they were not about to argue.

Offering was finally released on October 9, 1969. Frank Pooler recalls the night the album became available. "White Front Stores, a series of discount stores, were one of the first in the area that was selling it in their record department," he says. "They played the whole thing that night starting at midnight over some local station, so we all stayed up. We had to hear this whole album being played." *The Southeast News*, Downey's newspaper, reported that the local White Front Store "couldn't keep enough albums on the shelves.... A spot check of other local dealers revealed that the album has been moving well throughout the area."

According to music journalist Tom Nolan, "*Offering* tends toward being the sort of album many rock critics were encouraging at the time: a post-folk, soft-psychedelic, Southern Californian mini-oratorio." The debut album did spark enough interest to be featured as a "Billboard Pick" in *Billboard* magazine, citing "fresh and original concepts... With radio programming support, Carpenters should have a big hit on their hands."

The release of the debut single, "Ticket to Ride / Your Wonderful Parade," followed on November 5, nearly a month after the LP, and became a moderate hit. Covering a previous hit song and changing it up a bit was a way many artists achieved midchart hits. This proved to be true for Karen and Richard as well, and even a minor hit was a huge feat for a new artist. It stayed on the charts for six months, finally peaking at #54 by April 1970.

With the bill for *Offering* coming in around fifty thousand dollars, A&M lost money on the Carpenters' first release. That was not a cheap album to make, and initial sales of only 18,000 units left Karen and Richard somewhat nervous about their future with the label. A&M was going through a rough period in 1969, perhaps the worst year in their history, but despite the urging of others, Alpert was convinced the Carpenters had potential. He had no plans of cutting them from the roster. He felt their audience would "catch up to them" and admired the fact that they were so unique and driven.

Instead of setting forth to record another album, Alpert suggested that the Carpenters record several tracks to be considered for single release. "The first album did exactly what I thought it was going to do," he later recalled. "It takes a while for people to get onto a new artist and the frequency and the message that they are trying to send out. It didn't surprise me that the public didn't take to it. It was just a matter of time before they found the right song at the right moment and things turned around. With 'Ticket to Ride,' the idea that we were accustomed to that melody, and that they presented it in another format, was attractive to people. It wasn't their breakthrough record but it certainly got them a little bit of attention."

The duo next laid down several tracks for possible singles: "Love Is Surrender," a contemporary Christian tune with an altered secular lyric; "I'll Never Fall in Love Again," recorded by Dionne Warwick but not yet released as a single; and a cover of the Beatles' "Help!"

"THE THREE B's." Karen and Richard often cited the Beach Boys, the Beatles, and Burt Bacharach as their major pop music influences. The winding path to what ultimately became their second single began in December 1969 when the group played a benefit concert following the Hollywood premiere of the film *Hello, Dolly!* Opening the show with Burt Bacharach's "I'll Never Fall in Love Again," the group was unaware the esteemed composer was in attendance. As Karen and Richard exited the stage, Bacharach was waiting with congratulations and an invitation for them to join him as his opening act for an upcoming Reiss-Davis Clinic benefit to be held at the Century Plaza Hotel on February 27, 1970. The invitation was extended to include various concert dates at which time Bacharach requested that Richard select, arrange, and perform a medley of Bacharach-David songs.

As the Carpenters rehearsed furiously on A&M's soundstage and the medley began to take shape, Herb Alpert came through with a lead sheet for a lesser-known Bacharach-David song entitled "They Long to Be Close to You," first recorded by Richard "Dr. Kildare" Chamberlain in 1963. The song was also arranged by Bacharach for *Make Way for Dionne Warwick* the following year. Alpert had been given the tune several years earlier as a possible follow up to "This Guy's in Love with You" but disliked the "sprinkled moondust" lyric and set it aside. Richard considered Alpert to be a great A & R man but felt the song would not fit in his plan for the medley, which was ultimately narrowed to include "Any Day Now," "Baby It's You," "Knowing When to Leave," "Make It Easy On Yourself," "There's Always Something There to Remind Me," "I'll Never Fall in Love Again," "Walk On By," and "Do You Know the Way to San Jose."

The lead sheet for "They Long to Be Close to You" remained on Richard's Wurlitzer for several weeks. Though it was not suited for the medley, Richard saw its potential as a stand-alone song and with Alpert's urging began to construct his own arrangement. Alpert owned a copy of Warwick's recording but would not let Richard hear it. Aside from two piano quintuplets at the end of the bridge, he wanted nothing to influence Richard's concept.

Three very distinct arrangements of "They Long to Be Close to You" were put to tape, the first with Karen singing in a style similar to that of Harry Nilsson. The result sounded too contrived and was forcibly accenting the word "you." For the second attempt Alpert suggested Jack Daugherty bring in pianist Larry Knechtel and drummer Hal Blaine. "I was Herb's drummer with the Tijuana Brass," Blaine explains. "He had a lot of faith in me." Alpert felt Karen's drumming lacked the muscle of competitive Top 40 records and knew Blaine would add the desired power for this recording. Agnes Carpenter did not agree. Karen, barely twenty, and Richard, soon to be twenty-four, still lived under her roof, where she kept close tabs on all their activities, both personal and professional. When she got word that Karen had been replaced by Blaine, she let him know of her displeasure. "I've seen so many drummers on television," Agnes told him, "and Karen's as good as any of them."

"Karen is a wonderful drummer," he explained. "The problem is she doesn't have the studio experience that some of us have."

This did little to appease Agnes, who was quick to praise her daughter when put on the defensive, but Blaine was not concerned with the parents. He was confident knowing Karen was happy having him in the studio, and that was all that mattered to him. "She had a lot of respect for me," Blaine says. "We had an instant professional love affair because she knew everything I'd done, and she loved what I was doing on their records."

Although Blaine went on to drum on this and numerous Carpenters records, Knechtel's piano performance proved too forceful for the mood of the song. Richard returned to the keys for a third and final approach. "Hold it, Richard," Blaine interjected during his first Carpenters session. "Where are you going with this tempo?" This stunned Richard, who was accustomed to calling all the shots in the studio.

"What do you mean?" he asked.

"Well, are we going to play the beginning tempo or the middle tempo or the ending tempo? You're kind of running away with it after the intro."

After several attempts with the same result, Jack Daugherty cut in, asking, "Well, what do we do about this?"

Blaine suggested using a click track, which is essentially a metronome marking time in the musicians' headphone mix. Like many artists, the Carpenters considered click tracks to be stifling, often resulting in robotic music. They finally gave in after Blaine explained it to be a reference tempo that need not be followed at every moment of a song. "After that," Blaine says, "they wanted all their songs done with click track."

Herb Alpert was pleased with the third version of "They Long to Be Close to You," and as the recording began to take shape, excitement over the new creation spread throughout A&M. Breaking studio protocol, A&M staffers interrupted sessions and pushed open the doors to studio C to ask, "What is that?" When engineer Ray Gerhardt cranked studio monitors to what he often referred to as "excitement level," the reaction was overwhelming for all involved. "Thank God it didn't fit in the medley," Karen recalled of the song. "That was an instant thing from the minute it hit tape. It was really wild."

Despite the fuss, there was talk of releasing "I Kept on Loving You," a recording with Richard's lead vocal, as the A-side. Sharing both recordings with Frank Pooler's choir, Karen and Richard conducted an informal poll of their college friends. "They played both sides of it for them to see which one they liked best," Pooler says. While "I Kept on Loving You" was radio friendly and consistent with other hit songs of the day, "Close to You" refused to conform to Top 40 trends. As a result, Pooler explains, "The choir applauded more for 'Kept on Loving You.'"

Nichols-Williams compositions like "I Kept on Loving You" were frequently appearing as album cuts and B-sides around this time, but the songwriting duo had been hopeful to get an A-side with this second Carpenters single. "It was almost a joke that we'd die in anonymity and never having a hit single," Williams says. "All I wanted was for 'I Kept on Loving You' to be the single until I heard 'Close to You.' They put ours on the B-side, and it was one of the greatest free rides of all time. They were both really fine records, but 'Close to You' just proved to be magical."

IN EARLY 1970, advertising agent Hal Riney hired Beach Boys' lyricist Tony Asher to write a jingle for the Crocker Bank of California.

After Asher broke his arm in a skiing accident he recommended Roger Nichols and Paul Williams for the job. "It actually turned out to be something very different," Williams recalls. "Almost all commercials up to that point had pitch. They had copy, like 'come to our bank' or whatever. For this one they just wanted to show a little short movie of a young couple getting married and riding off into the sunset. They asked Roger and me to write a one-minute song that would accompany that movie." With a budget of three hundred dollars and less than two weeks to write and record the song, Riney provided the songwriters with a bit of inspiration—his own slogan for the soft-sell campaign: "You've got a long way to go. We'd like to help you get there. The Crocker Bank."

Nichols and Williams were busy with other projects and put this one aside until just before the deadline. "I came in that morning and was working on the tune," Nichols says. "Paul came in a little after that, and within ten minutes he had written the first verse." Williams grabbed an envelope and scribbled on the back:

We've only just begun to live
White lace and promises
A kiss for luck and we're on our way

Within a half hour they had written two one-minute jingles. After the original commercials aired, Crocker Bank executives wished to give copies of the song to their employees and asked the songwriters to make it a complete song. "We finished the complete song as an afterthought," Williams says. "When we put all the copy together and added a bridge we had the song. You can see some imperfection in the rhyme scheme in the third verse. It doesn't rhyme like it's supposed to. 'Grow' and 'begun' don't rhyme like they should because that was actually the first verse of the second commercial."

It was after a late-night recording session that Richard Carpenter caught the Crocker Bank commercial on television. Recognizing Paul Williams's lead vocal he figured it had to be a Nichols-Williams tune. "We got two phone calls right away," Williams says. "The first was from Mark Lindsay and the second from Richard."

Richard immediately went to the publishing offices on the A&M lot and picked up a reference disc of the demo. Playing it in their road manager's office, he was ecstatic to hear the bridge and third verse. He took the lead sheet to their next rehearsal where the group put together their arrangement. "It was about borrowing money, but for Pete's sake it was a great thought," Karen remarked in a 1970 interview. "I compliment the bank for having that much awareness of what's going on."

So taken with "We've Only Just Begun" were the Carpenters that they considered holding back the slated single release of "Close to You." Something about "Begun" stood up and proclaimed itself a hit song, whereas "Close to You" seemed more of a risk. But since "Begun" was still in its embryonic stages and not even put to tape, the single release of "(They Long to Be) Close to You" went as planned for May 1970. Richard felt the title was too wordy and opted for this parenthetical variant. "What do you think it's going to do?" Alpert asked Richard as the two sat on the steps outside A&M Studios.

"As far as I'm concerned," Richard said, "it's either going to be #1 or a monumental stiff. No in-between."

5

YOU PUT US ON THE ROAD

"(THEY LONG to Be) Close to You" entered the Hot 100 at #56, the highest debut of the week ending June 20, 1970. As the record moved up the charts, making stops at #37, #14, #7, and #3, the Carpenters set out to form a permanent "in person" band to travel with and support their live shows. Having recently been appointed principal tuba player with the Detroit Symphony Orchestra, Wes Jacobs weighed two significant opportunities. He could play pop music with the Carpenters or continue pursuing his own dream of playing tuba in a major orchestra. "[Richard] called me, and he basically offered me a lot of money...," Jacobs recalled, "but I realized that I would play the same concert two hundred times a year while touring with the Carpenters instead of two hundred different concerts per year in a symphony. I chose the symphony."

Karen and Richard returned to members of Spectrum in hopes of reassembling the original group to cover additional vocal harmonies. "We can't sing six parts," they explained. "Would you like to come back?"

"No, thanks," said Leslie Johnston, who was still singing lead for another group. "I knew that with the Carpenters I'd just be a backup," she explains. "So they became famous and I didn't!"

Former Spectrum bassist Dan Woodhams did accept the invitation to join the group, as did guitarist Gary Sims following his return from a stint in the Army Reserve. High-spirited college friend Doug Strawn was recruited to play multiple reed instruments. He also sang and had a great musical ear after years of experience fine-tuning chords in various barbershop quartets like the Dapper Dans, who had appeared on *Your All-American College Show* in 1968. Bob Messenger, the introverted and eldest member of the group, was equally adroit on bass guitar, saxophone, and flute. The group assembled was one of multiple talents with a common thread of determination to please Karen and Richard. Each would later learn that was not easy to accomplish, but they remained steadfast in their efforts nonetheless.

John Bettis was managing a club called the Babylon in San Francisco when a patron gave him a copy of *Cashbox* showing "Close to You" at #3 with a bullet. He immediately returned to Los Angeles but did not wish to sing with the group. Instead he signed on as a writer with Almo Publishing for a salary of seventy-five dollars a week. For years he would spend six days a week, fifty-two weeks a year, on the A&M lot. He likened it to Metro-Goldwyn-Mayer in its heyday, only smaller.

The new group spent months rehearsing daily on the A&M soundstage, where they tweaked every nuance and worked to accomplish the optimal mix between microphones and instruments. For the singers, pure, tall, and unified vowel sounds and shapes were of prime importance for the desired blend. Each chord was isolated and tuned. Passages were rehearsed a cappella with each singer trying a different vocal part until the finest balance was achieved. For the earliest gigs, most of which were one-nighters, rented cars and a Ryder truck were the standard means of transportation. Karen, Richard, and the guys in the band would unload, set up, perform, tear down, and reload for each appearance. Family friend Evelyn Wallace was asked to set up a bookkeeping system to keep track of the group's earnings and expenses and began working from the Carpenters' home in order to set up forms, pay bills, and distribute any remaining money between Karen, Richard, and the band.

The Carpenters continued as the opening act in a series of shows for Burt Bacharach, including a run at Westbury Music Fair in New York and a week-long stay at the Greek Theater in Los Angeles. "The five-member group is at its best on whisper-like vocals on their hit and the Beatles' 'Ticket to Ride,'" wrote *Los Angeles Times* music critic Robert Hilburn. "They were far less effective on up-tempo efforts like 'Can't Buy Me Love.' The group received only fair response."

Receiving far more than "fair response" was "Close to You," which was climbing the charts and gaining widespread recognition. As a result the Carpenters were booked to make numerous television appearances as guests of David Frost, Ed Sullivan, and Johnny Carson. Seeing Karen and Richard at the premiere taping of *The Don Knotts Show* during the summer of 1970, college friend Dan Friberg came to understand the magnitude of the duo's newfound stardom. "That was when I knew they were hot stuff," he says. "If I didn't realize it before, I sure did at that point." Following the taping, Friberg went backstage, where Karen called out to him in the hallway, and the two exchanged hugs. "We just found out it went to #1!" she exclaimed.

In just two months the "Close to You" single secured the top spot on the Hot 100, where it stayed for four weeks and quickly sold two million copies. "Everything seems to be going the way we wanted it to be," Karen said in a 1970 interview. "The records are selling like mad, and we're just flipped. It's out of sight, you know. I'm happy.... I think the greatest thing that's happened so far is having the #1 record in the country, having it go over two million records, and having it be the biggest single that A&M Records ever had. I think that's the greatest feeling in the world.... I really don't know what we're going to be doing in five years, but I hope it's the same thing."

———— ∞ ————

SELECTING THE right follow-up single to "Close to You" was of utmost importance. It occurred to Karen and Richard that "Close to You" might be their one and only hit, but they believed strongly in their recording of "We've Only Just Begun," which by then had been completed and was ready for release. An ecstatic Jack Daugherty came to Roger Nichols one afternoon at A&M. "Roger, you've got to hear this song," he said. "I think it's a smash."

Nichols remembers being surprised by his enthusiasm. It was merely a bank commercial. He and Williams certainly never figured it would become a monster hit. "When I heard it I thought I was going to faint," he says. "I still think to this day it's one of the greatest records ever made. I'm not just talking about the song, I'm talking about the record. That record is something else. I just freaked out when I heard it. It was unbelievable."

"Begun" displayed all the great qualities of the Carpenters sound and their capabilities as artists. At only twenty years old, Karen was already showing skill as an instinctive vocalist and a master at phrasing. In one breath she sang, "We've only just begun to live," something most other singers of this song never knew or cared to do. Her delivery was compelling, her interpretation convincing. "The thing about Karen's voice is that it's a strange combination of innocence and sensuality," Williams explains. "She had the sound of a bride when she sang that, so it's innocent and sensual at the same time."

"We've Only Just Begun" was released alongside the *Close to You* album in August 1970 and within eight weeks was at #2 on the Hot 100. The song lingered for four weeks, unable to push the Jackson Five's "I'll Be There" or the Partridge Family's "I Think I Love You" from the top spot. Whether it was #1 or #2 made little difference in the grand scheme of things. "Begun" assured the Carpenters were not one-hit wonders, and it went on to become the wedding song for an entire generation of newlyweds in the 1970s.

Mark Lindsay's recording of "Begun" had been put to tape before the Carpenters', but his remained an album cut. "Mark's was a lovely record," says Paul Williams, "but when people heard Karen sing it, that song belonged to her. It's *her* song."

As the *Close to You* album gained momentum and the group's popularity grew, word of the song "Mr. Guder," written some three years earlier about the Disneyland supervisor of the same name, reached the ears of its inspiration. Victor Guder returned from a hiking trip in the High Sierra to stacks of mail. Picking up a copy of a trade paper he read a review for *Close to You* that mentioned "Mr. Guder" by name. He immediately called his secretary and asked, "Do you guys know anything about this?"

"No, we were waiting for you to read it," she said.

"Well, I'd like to hear the record!"

Obtaining a copy of the LP, Guder shut the door to his office and placed the needle to the vinyl.

Mr. Guder, say, Mr. Guder
Someday soon you may realize
You've blown your life just playing a game
Where no one wins but everyone stays the same

"We were kind of shocked at first," Guder says, "but that's just part of the game we play. When you're working for Disney or working for a public company... you're vulnerable to all that stuff. But you know, it didn't faze us as negative at all. It was done when everybody was kind of anti-establishment, and it was a gimmick they used. They were reflecting the Disney image, 'coat and tie,' 'shine your shoes.' That's what Disney stands for. It was very cleverly written."

Richard later admitted "Mr. Guder" was written out of anger. "Looking back, it's a bit harsh, really...," he explained. "We were a little rebellious and we were finally fired. We wrote this song. But now that the years have gone by and I'm looking back at this, it really wasn't a very nice thing to do because the man was just doing his job."

"Mr. Guder, party of two," a waitress in a Newport Beach restaurant called as Victor Guder and his wife awaited seating. As if on cue, the house band began playing the tune. "We sat there and enjoyed it very much," Guder recalls, "and then had our dinner."

———

HERB ALPERT was mindful of the Carpenters' inexperience with the music industry and made numerous efforts to surround them with his most trusted friends and associates, many of whom he had known and respected since the beginning of his own success. He showed care and concern for all artists on the roster but seemed especially protective of Karen and Richard. He viewed A&M Records as a family label, as perceived by radio host Dick Biondi, who called it the "White Motown" during a 1970 interview with Karen and Richard. "Every direction we could have gone, we didn't go unless Herbie checked it," explained Karen several years later. "All I can say is thank heavens for Herb Alpert, because he protected us in every way. There aren't a lot of people in this world who would do that."

Shortly after the Carpenters' arrival at A&M in 1969, Alpert had forwarded a copy of their *Offering* album to his manager, Sherwin Bash of BNB Management, and suggested he listen and consider representing the act. "The vocal harmonies, the construction, the thoughts, and the songs were all very good," Bash recalled, "but there was one thing that I thought was very, very special. It was a girl's voice that I'd never heard anything like before and I don't think I've ever heard anything like since. There are so many people in the world today who are good.... Good is not good enough in our business anymore. This was an exceptional voice that was totally identifiable. Listening to that voice for the first time, I knew that radio could never submerge it, camouflage it, or confuse [it for] anybody. That voice coming out of that radio would be immediately identified for the ages."

Karen and Richard met with Sherwin, and it was agreed BNB would represent their professional careers. Ed Leffler drew the contract on the Carpenters and was assigned to supervise the act. This especially pleased Karen, who had developed a bit of a crush on the handsome gentleman. Leffler was equally charmed but by Karen's talents. "I hadn't seen him this excited in a long, long time," says Frenda Franklin, Leffler's wife at the time. "Eddie came home and said, 'Oh my God, there's something you've just got to hear. You're just not going to believe this!'"

When the Lefflers drove to Santa Monica one evening to see the Carpenters perform in a small club, Frenda was equally entranced by Karen's vocal abilities. "They got up on this little stage," she recalls, "and all of a sudden this sound came out. I was just dumbfounded. It was unbelievable. She had something that just pulled you in."

But after meeting Karen, Frenda was not as impressed with her personality. "I didn't like her much," she says. "I thought she acted like a spoiled brat. She wasn't particularly friendly to me either, but I was used to that. If you're around show business a lot it is like that. Karen was the only girl in the band, and I remember thinking, 'My God, she's so rough around the edges!' She was very much a tomboy. Actually, 'tomboy' would be putting it mildly. She always had this façade so nobody could get through."

BY THE fall of 1970 the Carpenters were the hottest young act in the recording industry, with two hit singles and a hit album on its way up the charts. Capitalizing on the duo's newfound popularity, A&M Records reissued the Carpenters' debut album, *Offering*, with a new cover and title, *Ticket to Ride*. Sales of that record quickly soared to over 250,000 copies. Between December 1969 and December 1970, the Carpenters' personal appearance fee jumped from two figures to five figures. Additionally, the first royalty check from A&M Records arrived in the amount of fifty thousand dollars. "I'd never seen anything like that check in my life," Karen said. "We stared at it all through dinner. That is when you start noticing a change. You feel the same inside. You're the same person, but when you've been through the sort of financial situation we grew up with, you realize you have an awful lot of money."

Although the Carpenters had three gold records—the "Close to You" single, *Close to You* album, and "We've Only Just Begun"—they still lived on Fidler Street in Downey in a $27,000 house. In search of a new home, Agnes, Evelyn Wallace, and real estate agent Beverly Nogawski spent several days driving around the residential neighborhoods on Downey's northeast side. The only orders from Karen and Richard were that the new house must be big and have a swimming pool. The ladies were especially taken with a newly constructed home situated on a cul-de-sac near the San Gabriel River. With no FOR SALE sign in the yard or anything suggesting the sprawling split-level ranch-style home was on the market, Nogawski knocked on the door and brazenly asked the owners to sell their house. "I've got people interested," she told them. The owner, who happened to be the home's builder, was in the process of separating from his wife, and their divorce was imminent. After much discussion they agreed to sell.

On Thanksgiving Day 1970 Harold, Agnes, Richard, and Karen left their house in south Downey and settled into their new $300,000 real estate investment located at 9828 Newville Avenue. The five-bedroom house was huge compared to their previous residence but still quite modest in relation to the fame that awaited them. Reporting on their investment, *Forbes* magazine called it the duo's "suburban dream home," and the details of "chez Carpenter" were published in a 1971 A&M Records press release.

> The home—which they themselves designed and decorated, with the help of an interior decorator—was made for comfort, relaxation and precisely those leisure-time activities they prefer. The living room is a bastion of tranquil elegance. It's decorated in cool colors— white, blue, green—and lavished with velvet, crystal and glass. The dining room is ideal for California meals: it features a glass-top table elegantly supported by a carved wood base. The Spanish-style den is stunningly fabric'd in black and red and ocelot, and features a pool table over which Richard and Karen spend many hours poking cues. To facilitate another favorite sport of the Carpenters, there's a big swimming pool, and there are plans for the building of a fish pond. For an ace cook like Karen, the kitchen of the new house is a dream come true: there's everything in the way of household conveniences from a trash-masher down to "a refrigerator that shoots ice cubes."

Karen selected one of four upstairs bedrooms but was appalled by the gaudy wallpaper and proceeded to redecorate in shades of yellow and black. The king-sized bed and its black fur bedspread became home to her overflowing collection of stuffed animals. "They all have names," she told *Teen* magazine a year later. "That's Gru-pig and there's Marsh-field," she said, pointing to a checkered pig and oversized pink dog.

Richard claimed the large master bedroom downstairs, but Agnes objected. "No, you bought this for us," she said. "You told us you were going to buy us a house, so it's ours. We get this bedroom." He settled for two of the rooms across the hall from Karen's and tore out a wall to create one large space.

Many of the duo's music industry associates wondered why two budding superstars would choose to stay in Downey and live at home with their parents when they could be on their own enjoying the fruits of their labor somewhere nearer to Hollywood. "We can live a normal life here," Karen explained in 1972. "Roam around, do whatever we like. Everyone knows who we are everywhere we go, but here they don't bother us. Sometimes cars pass slowly by the house and people look in, but we expect that. Our friends are here from school—the kids Rich went to college with and my high school friends."

Karen and Richard justified the decision saying they were on the road so much it would make no sense to leave a house sitting empty. In truth it was easier to stay, and neither wanted to rock the boat. Both felt a great obligation to their parents for their support during their formative years. Agnes had been laid off from North American Aviation several years earlier, and Harold was still working his printing job. He retired only when it became obvious his children's success was enduring. YOU PUT US ON THE ROAD was Karen's needlepoint inscription to her parents in a design that illustrated a yellow brick road leading to an emerald dollar sign.

To keep their new residence tidy, Agnes was encouraged to hire a housekeeper. Beverly Nogawski suggested her own employee, Florine Elie, who lived in nearby Compton. Florine's cleanliness and work ethic won even Agnes's approval, and for the next quarter century Elie spent five days a week working for the family. Even so, she admits she was never a real fan of their music: "I'm a Pentecostal person. I just listened to gospel music."

MANAGERS SHERWIN Bash and Ed Leffler soon discovered numerous red flags within the Carpenters' accounting records. They found that Agnes Carpenter had taken charge of her children's finances and essentially put Karen and Richard on an allowance. According to Bash, "Even though they were making hundreds of thousands of dollars, they were treated by their parents—especially their mother—as if they were still children at home and on an allowance. The allowance part didn't bother me, but not having someone who was sophisticated in the handling of monies, tax consequences, and contracts did. It was an area I knew would become a serious problem for the two of them."

Going through what Sherwin called a "library full of bank books" they realized Agnes had opened numerous savings accounts in banks all over Downey and throughout the surrounding area. She had been careful to see that the accounts never exceeded the maximum amount insured by the government. When one account reached its limit she would move on to another bank and open a new account. Evelyn Wallace was juggling as many as five different checkbooks at a time and all the while trying to reserve adequate funds for taxes, but there was no formula in use. She would simply set aside extra funds in hopes it would suffice at tax time. The job quickly became too much for her to handle, and she asked the Carpenters to hire a professional accountant. But Agnes was paranoid. She had heard too many stories of managers and accountants running off with their stars' money and was confident her children's finances would be safe if left in her control.

Management finally called a meeting with Karen, Richard, and their parents, during which Sherwin and Ed explained the desperate need for sophisticated and scrupulous supervision as far as their finances were concerned. "When you start earning millions of dollars you need professional guidance," they were told.

Enter attorney and financial advisor Werner Wolfen of the Law Offices of Irell and Manella. Wolfen had been in charge of Herb Alpert's investments for years and came highly recommended. "He made himself known as the boss," recalls Wallace. "He assured everyone he was going to make the kids rich, and the rest of us were told to do whatever we were told to do to make it happen." Agnes left the table during that first meeting with Wolfen. She refused to talk to him and communicated through handwritten notes. "It took some doing," Bash recalled, "because Agnes felt it was a personal attack and didn't realize it was for everybody's good. Eventually she allowed professional attorneys and accountants to prevail."

The accounting firm of Gelfand, Rennert, and Feldman had the arduous task of cleaning up the financial mess they inherited. Luckily Evelyn had documented everything in her well-intentioned but amateur bookkeeping practices. She was relieved of her accounting duties but continued to work for the Carpenter family in the capacity of secretary, assisting Harold Carpenter in sifting through and replying to what quickly became a barrage of fan mail. By the end of 1971, the Carpenters Fan Club consisted of more than ten thousand members.

Werner Wolfen went on to make other financial recommendations and helped the Carpenters manage their newfound wealth by investing in real estate. Newville Realty Company, a joint partnership for Karen and Richard, was formed, and with the help of Beverly Nogawski they set out to purchase two apartment houses located at 8353 and 8356 East Fifth Street in Downey, site of the old Downey Hospital. Tex McAlister, the owner and builder, named the apartments the Geneva in honor of his mother, Geneva, who'd died in the hospital some time earlier. "The Carpenters asked if I would mind if they changed the name to 'Close to You' and 'Only Just Begun,'" he recalls. "I said 'No, not at all. They're yours. You can do what you want with them now.'" Tex and his wife, Charlene, became close friends of the Carpenter family after this first business transaction. Shortly thereafter, the McAlisters built their own house on Newville Avenue across from the Carpenter home.

⊶∞⊷

IN NOVEMBER 1970, the search was on for what would become the Carpenters' next single. In Toronto, where the Carpenters were set to open three weeks of shows for Engelbert Humperdinck, Sherwin Bash suggested that the group go out and enjoy their last free evening. "Why don't you just get your minds off your business?" he said. "Go see this movie I saw called *Lovers and Other Strangers*."

While watching the film, a melody in the underscore caught Richard's attention. The song was "For All We Know," written for the movie's wedding scene. Richard immediately called the office at A&M and asked that a lead sheet be waiting for him upon his return to Los Angeles. Although credited to Fred Karlin, Robb Wilson, and Arthur James, Wilson and James were actually pen names for Robb Royer and James Griffen, members of the pop group Bread.

The Carpenters were also offered "(Where Do I Begin) Love Story" from *Love Story* but were hesitant to record two successive movie themes. They passed on "Love Story" and chose to record and release "For All We Know," which went on to win the Oscar for Best Original Song that year. Though the chart performance of the Carpenters' single was responsible for most of the song's popularity, Academy rules prevented the Carpenters from performing on the telecast since they had never appeared in a film, and the song was assigned to Petula Clark.

The offer of yet another movie theme came in March 1971 during a recording session at A&M when engineer Ray Gerhardt pressed the talkback button and said, "Richard, Stanley Kramer's on the phone for you."

"*Sure!*" Richard looked at Karen with a sarcastic expression. He went into the booth, picked up the phone, and realized it truly was the legendary filmmaker (*Judgment at Nuremburg, Guess Who's Coming to Dinner*) calling to offer the Carpenters the opportunity to record the title song on the soundtrack of his upcoming film *Bless the Beasts and Children*. Kramer agreed to meet Karen and Richard in Las Vegas where they were set to open for comedian Don Adams at the Sands in what became their final stint as an opening act. Richard dreaded the idea of meeting with Stanley Kramer because chances were slim the song would be a fit with the Carpenters and their style. Pleasantly surprised by the work of the film's composers, Barry De Vorzon and Perry Botkin Jr., he and Karen accepted the offer and recorded "Bless the Beasts and Children" in a matter of days to meet Kramer's deadline.

The Carpenters' first major recognition within the music industry came on the evening of March 16, 1971, at the Thirteenth Annual Grammy Awards. Filmed at the Hollywood Palladium, the show was the first Grammy ceremony to be broadcast live via television. Karen and Richard won for Best New Artist and were especially thrilled to take home a second Grammy for Best Contemporary Performance by a Duo, Group, or Chorus, a category in which they were nominated alongside the Jackson Five, Simon and Garfunkel, Chicago, and the Beatles.

THE SEARCH for hit songs continued in early 1971 as Richard sat down with a stack of demos from A&M's publishing houses, Almo and Irving.

His attention was captured by another Roger Nichols–Paul Williams tune. In spite of the demo's sparse instrumentation, Richard was taken with the song's lyrical hook.

Hangin' around
Nothin' to do but frown
Rainy days and Mondays always get me down

By second listen Richard was certain it was a perfect song for Karen, especially with its melancholy and plaintive melody. The opening line—"Talking to myself and feeling old"—was inspired by Williams's mother. "She used to talk to herself," he says. "She was a sweet little old lady who smoked cigarettes and had a little drink every night. She used to walk through the room mumbling and would swear under her breath. I would ask, 'What the hell's wrong, Mom?' She'd say, 'Oh, you wouldn't understand. You're too young. I'm just old. I'm feeling old.' That's how far away from the Carpenters that the lyric began. It was something from out of my own past."

Along with Roger Nichols, Williams went into the studio as the Carpenters' recording of "Rainy Days and Mondays" was taking shape. There they listened as Bob Messenger tracked his saxophone solo. "I think my face just fell off my skull," Williams says. "That's the greatest record I've heard of one of my songs. From the harmonica intro to the last notes it just made me crazy. When Karen sang it you heard the sadness and the loneliness. For me, listening to her sing that song is almost like a bridge from what was contemporary to the roots of the emotion, back to a Billie Holiday kind of thing. It's just a classic."

As good as "Rainy Days and Mondays" was, Nichols says Karen preferred another of his and Paul's songs she had recorded. She wanted "Let Me Be the One" to be the next Carpenters single. After hearing their arrangement of "Rainy Days," Nichols pleaded, "'Rainy Days and Mondays,' *please!*" He hoped they would hold off on "Let Me Be the One," at least temporarily.

In the summer of 1971 Paul Williams treated his mother to a European vacation. He remembers she was not impressed with the desolation she saw in Germany and was pleasantly surprised to see beautiful flowers in all the window boxes as they crossed into France. Just then, "Rainy Days and Mondays" played over the car radio. "It was the first time we'd ever heard it on the radio, and my mother started crying," he says. "I was hearing Karen singing 'talking to myself and feeling old,' and the woman who gave me the line—the woman who raised me—was sitting behind me, and she didn't even know. Once I told her she laughed and said, 'Oh, I don't talk to myself. You're crazy!'"

"Rainy Days and Mondays" was held out of the #1 spot by Carole King's double A-side single featuring "It's Too Late" and "I Feel the Earth Move." Perhaps a double A-side featuring both "Rainy Days" and "Let Me Be the One" would have pushed the Carpenters to the top of the chart. Instead, the latter never saw release as a single. According to Williams, "Let Me Be the One" has never been a hit, despite its popularity. "It's one of those songs that everybody's recorded, but it's never been a single. It was used very briefly by ABC-TV in 1976. 'Let us be the one you turn to / Let us be the one you turn to / When you need someone to turn to / Let us be the one.' It evolved through the years to a whole ad campaign."

In hopes of getting another potential hit song recorded by the Carpenters, Williams set out on his own to write a song specifically for Karen and Richard. What resulted was a Top 10 hit, not for the Carpenters but for Three Dog Night. "I wrote 'Old Fashioned Love Song' for the Carpenters," he says. "I'd heard that one of my songs had gotten on the charts again and just went gold, so I said to this girl I was dating, 'The kid did it again with another old-fashioned love song.' I sat down at her piano and in about twenty minutes wrote 'Old Fashioned Love Song.' It's real simple. I ran in and did a demo of it and sent it over to Richard, and I don't think he even listened to it all the way through at the time. They didn't love it as I had figured they would so I sent it to Three Dog Night." Later rethinking their dismissal of the song, Karen and Richard performed it in a medley with Carol Burnett on her television series in 1972.

⠀⠀—∞∞—

ARRIVING HOME relatively early after a recording session at A&M Records, Karen went to bed while Richard sat down to watch *The Tonight Show* with Johnny Carson. The musical guest was newcomer Bette Midler, performing a song about a groupie who longs for one more tryst with her rock star. Originally titled "Groupie," its roots go back to Rita Coolidge, who gave songwriter Leon Russell the basic idea for its theme. Coolidge joined Russell and the song's cowriter, Bonnie Bramlett (of Delaney and Bonnie), on Joe Cocker's *Mad Dogs and Englishmen* tour where she performed it. By tour's end it had been renamed with the simple yet dramatic one-word title: "Superstar."

Although Karen had heard "Superstar" on a promo copy of the *Mad Dogs and Englishmen* live album, Midler's performance was Richard's first exposure, and he immediately heard its potential. It was understated and backed only by piano, a contemporary twist to the classic torch song style. He was especially taken with the song's hook, perhaps even catchier than that of "Rainy Days and Mondays."

Don't you remember you told me you loved me baby
You said you'd be coming back this way again baby
Baby, baby, baby, baby, oh, baby
I love you, I really do

As Midler's "Superstar" came to an end, Richard ran through the house and bounded up the stairs. "I've found *the tune*," he told Karen.

"That's nice," she said after hearing the song.

"*Nice?*"

This was one of only a few times Karen was known to have objected to a song selected for her by Richard. But even in this case, she eventually agreed to record "Superstar," although she did so begrudgingly. It was only after hearing the finished product that she heard what Richard had in mind all along. According to Frank Pooler, "Richard was the brains behind the Carpenters. Karen did what she was told."

Karen's vocal track on "Superstar" was her work lead, the first "take" to familiarize the other musicians with the song. Not only that, she read the words from a paper napkin on which Richard had scribbled the lyric as the session began. Knowing the song would never find a place on Top 40 radio stations with the lyric "I can hardly wait to *sleep* with you again," the Carpenters opted for the more radio friendly "*be* with you again." The song's publishers were delighted with the word change and told Richard how that singular line had kept numerous artists from recording the song.

The intensity and emotion in Karen's voice led many to assume she was an "old soul" and wise beyond her years. In a 1972 interview she explained how she delivered such a convincing performance on a song like "Superstar" though it dealt with subject matter she had never experienced. "I've seen enough groupies hanging around to sense their loneliness, even though they usually don't show it," she explained. "I can't really understand them, but I just tried to feel empathy, and I guess that's what came across in the song."

According to Frank Pooler, "When Karen sang, it sounded like she had experienced all this stuff. She couldn't possibly have experienced all that; she was too young. There's a difference between being a singer and having a fine voice. Good singers can have average voices, but there's something about the word communication. That she had. You felt like she was singing it for the first time and only for you."

It was Rod Stewart's "Maggie May / Reason to Believe" single that held "Superstar" a spot shy of #1 this time. It remained at #2 for two weeks, a frustrating location for Karen and Richard and one they had grown accustomed to. The flip side, "Bless the Beasts and Children," also charted at a respectable #67 and was nominated for a Best Original Song Oscar at the Academy Awards.

It seemed as though Bette Midler might have been miffed by the Carpenters' success with "Superstar," the song she introduced to the duo, as she began to poke fun at Karen's goody-two-shoes image during her live act. "She's so white she's invisible!" she would say, but Karen took it all in stride, claiming that it was a tribute. Besides, as she pointed out, the gold record for "Superstar" was on the Carpenters' wall, not Bette's.

Midler curtsied sarcastically to Karen when the Carpenters presented her with a Grammy for Best New Artist in 1974. "Me and Miss

Karen!" she exclaimed. "What a hoot. I'm surprised she didn't hit me over the head with it!"

The two visited with each other at a Grammy after-party. "We got along fine," Karen recalled in an interview later that year. "Bette said, 'I don't know what I'm gonna do now that we're friends.' She's funny as heck. . . . She likes to pick on me, but I think that's just a good showbiz bit for her."

Returning to the Grammys as presenter the following year, Bette recalled the event in her monologue. "It was only a year ago that Karen Carpenter crowned me the Best New Artist of the year," she told the audience. "If that ain't the kiss of death, honey, I don't know what is."

⸺ ∞ ⸺

THE DAYS of the Carpenters performing as an opening act were over. On May 14, 1971, they headlined a sold-out concert at New York City's legendary Carnegie Hall, where Karen and the group performed an already impressive set of their hits in succession. "Rainy Days and Mondays" and "For All We Know" received immediate and enthusiastic response from the audience, who knew their songs word-for-word. "Karen Carpenter has one of those magical voices," wrote Nancy Erlich for *Billboard* in her review from Carnegie Hall. "There are maybe three of them among all the ladies in pop music that create a direct line of communication with their very tone. Words and music are secondary; there is always that quality that comes through."

The concert was a homecoming of sorts, with family and friends from nearby New Haven in attendance. For most, this was their first reunion with the duo in eight years. Karen and Richard were honored with a party thrown at the home of their cousin Joanie and her husband, Hank Will. Though the guest list was small, the gathering became more of an event as word spread that the Carpenters were in town. Festivities were moved outdoors to accommodate a crowd of more than a hundred attendees. "I never really saw Karen as a celebrity," says Frank Bonito, who visited with her that day. "Even when I attended her concerts, I enjoyed them, but it was the time backstage before the concert or at a party afterwards that I enjoyed most. We would just sit and talk and catch up on each other's lives. Karen never flaunted her wealth and position. She actually downplayed it and was always sincerely interested in what was happening in my life. She wanted to know about old school friends and teachers, and she maintained a wonderful childlike quality about herself."

The Carpenters' eponymous album, often referred to as the *Tan Album* (perhaps a nod to the Beatles' *White Album*), was released the same day as the Carnegie Hall concert. It was the first of a string of Carpenters albums to "ship gold," which at the time indicated presales of more than a million copies. But just as Carole King held "Rainy Days and Mondays" out of the #1 spot on *Billboard*'s Hot 100, her epic *Tapestry* LP shut out *Carpenters* on the album charts, too, where it peaked at #2.

Upon returning to Los Angeles, Karen and Richard began taping a summer replacement series for NBC Television the last week of May 1971. "Make Your Own Kind of Music" was a popular recording by Mama Cass and became the theme for this television variety hour that aired Tuesday nights in the eight o'clock time slot usually occupied by *The Don Knotts Show*. "Karen was a mic singer," recalls Allyn Ferguson, who served as a musical supervisor on the series. He remembers her to be quite shy and says she sang very close to the microphone with a "tiny" voice. "She would have never been OK on a musical stage," he says. "You would not be able to hear her at all if you were thirty or forty feet away because she didn't project at all. She understood how to sing on a microphone, and that brought a sort of intimacy to everything she did."

Ferguson was impressed with the duo's unpretentious demeanor. "You work with a lot of people, like Mama Cass. She was really tough to work with. The Carpenters were very nice to work with. There were no big problems, no egos involved or anything. They just liked to do what they did and were very closely connected in their work." In addition to working with regulars Al Hirt, Patchett and Tarses, Mark Lindsay, and the New Doodletown Pipers, Karen and Richard were introduced to many popular entertainers during the eight days of tapings. Mac Davis, Jose Feliciano, Anne Murray, Helen Reddy,

Dusty Springfield, B. J. Thomas, and the Fifth Dimension were among those booked as guests on the series. The Fifth Dimension and Carpenters traded guest spots, with Karen and Richard performing as part of that group's *Traveling Sunshine Show* television special, which was also broadcast that summer.

A review for *Make Your Own Kind of Music* in *TV Guide* detailed the gimmick that plagued the series: "Each number is introduced by the labored use of a letter of the alphabet. Twenty-six cringes a week. Did they have in mind a *Sesame Street* for adults? Possibly. But no adult over the age of nine will be either entertained or amused. . . . The musicians on this show are genuinely talented. Why didn't they leave them alone?" Another review, this one in the *Village Voice*, denounced the series's producers and detailed their mistakes, "like dressing Karen Carpenter in fashions only a little less sickeningly sweet than those worn by Trisha Nixon. By the second or third show it was beginning to look like a disaster area. The Carpenters, who are both gifted and likeable, deserve something better."

Despite the benefits of new friendships and professional associations, in addition to heavy publicity for their new LP, the duo's first encounter with television left them discouraged with the medium. It would be another five years before they agreed to host another television show. Interviewed for FM100 some years later, Karen recalled the NBC endeavor as a mistake, saying they were "violently mishandled. Our TV exposure was disastrous. We realized it immediately, and we shied away from television."

6

NOTHING TO HIDE BEHIND

—————

AT JUST five feet, four inches tall, Karen Carpenter was barely visible on stage when surrounded by her battery of drums. "The audience was rising out of their seats to see where this voice was coming from," recalls Evelyn Wallace. "There was no one out front so they were asking, 'Where is that beautiful voice coming from?'"

By 1971, Karen's drum kit had grown to include four melodic toms. "They were built on rollers, and you could roll them right into your four-piece or five-piece kit," explains Hal Blaine, who, along with drum tech Rick Faucher, designed the set Karen used in concert. Howie Oliver of Pro Drum in Hollywood built the kit for her after she saw Blaine's setup. "There are only three kits like mine in the world," she explained in a 1974 piece for *Melody Maker*. "The other two belong to Ringo and Hal Blaine."

Blaine's original set was designed in a way that the sound of each drum decayed with its pitch "bending" slightly at the end. "It started out with me using my timbales as tom-toms and tuning them down," Blaine explains. "I loved that sound, and eventually I wanted an octave of them. I put together this drum set that everybody called the Hal Blaine monster because it was humongous. I knew nothing about design patents in those days, but I was a Ludwig drummer so I sent them all the dimensions. I was sure they'd call it the Hal Blaine set—like the Gene Krupa and the Buddy Rich, but they called it the Octa-Plus. Now that's a fine name, but Ludwig didn't even mention me. They did send me a thank-you letter."

One of Karen's worst nightmares began to unfold during the summer of 1971, one that had been mounting since the Carpenters' earliest concert engagements. "There is no balance, no center of attention," wrote Lester Bangs, reviewing an appearance in San Diego for *Rolling Stone.* "Here are six people on a stage singing and playing various instruments, and your eye just keeps shifting from one to another without ever finding a nexus to focus on."

True, the in-person Carpenters were a disjointed group and in need of a focal point. The obvious solution was to bring the group's musical focus out from isolation and into the spotlight. "Hire a drummer," wrote one music critic in Omaha, Nebraska. "Why stick a lovely girl with a tremendous voice behind a set of traps and have her pump high-hat cymbals and shoot an occasional rim shot when by rights she should be out front moving to the music while she sings?"

Taking cues from the critics, Richard and the Carpenters' management decided Karen's drums were in the way and ultimately disconnecting her from the audience. "You can't sing like that and hide behind a drum set," manager Ed Leffler told her.

Leffler and Sherwin Bash agreed Karen could be showcased more effectively at center stage. "Richard and I tried desperately to get her away from the drums," Bash recalled. "She was very reluctant. The drums were kind of a security blanket for her. This was a chubby young lady who could hide some of that chubbiness behind all of these drums. She was kind of a tomboy, and the drums were traditionally a male instrument. She was kind of asserting herself in a certain way. The girl vocalist out front was a role that she wanted to achieve, but she was insecure about getting out there. She wasn't sure she was slim enough, svelte enough, pretty enough, or any of those things."

In early 1971 Karen responded to suggestions that she should abandon her drums for a solo microphone in the spotlight. "A lot of people think that since I'm the lead singer I should be fronting the group," she said. "I disagree because I think we've got enough chick singers fronting groups. I think that as long as I can play, I want to play."

According to fellow drummer Frankie Chavez, "There weren't that many girls playing in the forefront at the time. It was a very unique thing that a girl could play *and* sing at the same time and do it well on both accounts. It wasn't a smokescreen, she could actually play!"

Richard avoided confronting Karen on several occasions, but their setup posed additional challenges when it came to the medium of television. It was difficult for camera angles, and much attention was needed in order to effectively present Karen and her drum kit for each sequence. During the filming of *Make Your Own Kind of Music* it was recommended that she stand to sing some selections. "Oh, no, no, no, no, no," she told them. "I'm the drummer here." But the directors were looking for variety in the sequences and felt watching someone sing from behind the drums was odd and would get old after a few numbers.

"Karen wasn't as concerned that people would be able to see her," explains Evelyn Wallace. "It was that she was absolutely in love with those drums, and she just didn't want to leave them. But she finally gave in. The poor kid didn't know what to do." Having been the group's only drummer, Karen had played exclusively for the first two years of live Carpenters performances. It is no wonder she lacked confidence to step into the spotlight and was reluctant to embrace the role of "star" of the group. Richard had long been the musical prodigy, and she was his tagalong. "Karen was really an *accident*," explains Frenda Franklin. "I don't think the family really understood her talent. Nobody got it. Nobody thought she was a good singer. Nobody nurtured her singing. To them she was backup."

Allyn Ferguson, who worked with Karen on the set of the television series, says her poise and self-assurance took a dive when she was singing center stage without her drums. "Her confidence was sitting behind those drums," he says. "It was a part of her, and she was a damn good drummer. When she was not behind the drums her confidence and her security just disappeared. She didn't seem to care much for her own singing. When she had to do a solo out front she was very uncomfortable and showed no confidence. She didn't know whether she was any good or not. She was not a stand-up singer in any way because she didn't believe in herself that way." For *Make Your Own Kind of Music*

Karen lip-synched the musical numbers without even a prop micro-phone. With her hands free she made awkward attempts at gestures of emphasis and emotion.

With the television series in postproduction, the Carpenters took a brief hiatus and drove the family's Continental Mark III cross-country to visit family and friends on the East Coast in Baltimore and New Haven. It was during this drive that Richard finally spelled out to Karen the need for her to leave the drums. "You've got to get up," he said.

"I said to Richard, 'Oh, no you don't,'" she recalled. "It hurt me that I had to get up and be up front. I didn't want to give up my playing. Singing was an accident. Singing seriously came long after the drums." The two finally reached a compromise in which Karen agreed to step out front to sing ballads like "For All We Know" and "Superstar." In return, she could remain at the drums to play on the more up-tempo, rhythmic numbers like "Mr. Guder." Before leaving New Haven, Richard hired the band's new drummer, longtime friend Jim Squeglia, whom he had once played alongside in a band called the Scepters dur-ing high school. Touring with the Carpenters, Squeglia would take on the stage name of Jim Anthony, his first and middle names.

Appearing on *The Mike Douglas Show* the following month, Karen announced her plans. "In the middle of our in-person show I'm going to go out front and do some tunes," she said. "I'm never going to give up playing, no way.... I love it. I wouldn't be doing it if I didn't. People think it's a gimmick. I don't care what they think; it's not a gimmick. It's my instrument."

Out front, Karen was unsure of herself, to say the least. She was rigid, uncomfortable, and incapable of disguising her fears. "Petrified," she recalled in 1976 of her initial reaction to the switch. "You have no idea. The fear! There was nothing to hold onto, nothing to hide behind. My drums, by this time, I had so many of them all you could see were my bangs. You couldn't see the mouth, you couldn't see the hands, you couldn't see anything. We're out on the road and we're doing all the hits and the dummy is buried behind a full set of drums."

Frankie Chavez feels certain that it was torture for Karen to have been removed from her drum kit. "That broke her heart when she couldn't do both from behind the kit and had to go out front," he says. "It's different being out front. I've done both, and being out front it's as if your tether has been cut. There's a certain joy you get from playing the kit that you'd miss if you were asked to not do it anymore."

"I didn't know what to do," Karen later explained. "My mouth still worked well, but I didn't know what to do with my hands or whether to walk or stand still or sit down or what the heck to do. Before, everything was working. It was a cinch to play and sing and have a good time. But when I got out there, until I got comfortable with that, I just kind of planted myself and didn't really do anything."

With each successive tour, Karen's role as the group's drummer lessened as new drummer Jim Anthony took over on more and more songs. "I understood her reluctance," said Sherwin Bash, "but the moment we were finally able to get her out there it was all part of history. She loved being out front. She was basically the master of ceremonies for every show. She was the one that people watched. Richard never had the charisma to keep the audience's attention. It didn't matter. Even when he was speaking you didn't take your eyes off Karen."

WATCHING TELEVISION late one night in the fall of 1971, Richard came across a 1940 movie called *Rhythm on the River*, in which Bing Crosby played the ghostwriter for a washed-up songwriter named Oliver Courtney. Courtney's most famous song, "Goodbye to Love," was mentioned throughout the film but never heard. Richard was immediately taken with the title and imagined an opening line of it as a potential song: "I'll say goodbye to love / No one ever cared if I should live or die." At that point his lyric stopped.

Handing the song idea over to John Bettis, Richard and the group set off on a brief European tour. Writing of the song continued little by little with the choral ending written in London and additional work being done once they reached Berlin. "Richard didn't have the melody completely finished," Bettis recalled. "He had a verse or two but didn't quite know how he was going to form it. It's an odd melody with very long phrases. The song was tricky because of the phrasing."

Returning to the States with Bettis's contributions, Richard sat down with "Goodbye to Love" and came up with a novel idea. In constructing the arrangement he imagined the unlikely sound of a melodic fuzz guitar solo. Jack Daugherty suggested they bring in an established session guitarist and recommended Louie Shelton or Dean Parks, but Richard was relying on Daugherty less and less by this time and chose to contact a young member of Instant Joy, a band that backed Mark Lindsay's opening act for several Carpenters concerts. Karen phoned guitarist Tony Peluso, explained the project, and asked him to meet her and Richard at A&M's studio B.

Peluso was tall and thin. His hair was long and unkempt, halfway down his back. It seemed a mismatch at first. Even he was apprehensive and unsure the combination would work effectively. He could not read music but was a quick study, and when Richard gave him a chord sheet with instructions to play the melody on the first couple of bars and then improvise, the recording was complete in only two takes. The result was one of the first known uses of a fuzz tone guitar solo on a ballad. "When I got the record I actually cried the first time I heard it," John Bettis recalled. "I had never heard an electric guitar sound like that and have very few times since. Tony had a certain almost cello-sounding guitar growl that worked against that wonderful melancholia of that song. The way it growls at you, especially at the end, is unbelievable. It may be my favorite single I've ever had with anybody."

Within weeks of the radio debut of "Goodbye to Love," the Carpenters began receiving what amounted to hate mail from fans who felt the song desecrated the group's image with the incorporating of a grungy-sounding guitar. "That was the first ballad ever done with any sort of rock and roll sensibility," Bettis explained. "Aggressive electric guitar the way it was beginning to be used. There was a schism in instrumentation. It's a watershed record, sonically, because Richard put two disparate worlds together. There was a legion of Carpenters fans that wasn't ready for that, but I think it also garnered new fans."

By mid-1972, Peluso had accepted an offer to become a full-fledged member of the Carpenters' touring band. As the entourage grew to fourteen, the need for adequate transportation was filled with the acquisition of two Learjets, aptly named *Carpenter 1* and *Carpenter 2*, which were used to travel between one-nighters. It was on one such trip that Bettis came up with the song title "Top of the World." According to the lyricist, "When I got in the plane and took off I thought, 'Are we on top of the world now or what? Look at this!' I saw the visual symbolism. I was at the top of the world. I took the title and wrote it with another guy, Kerry Chater. The song never came to be anything. Somehow Richard came in contact with the title again and remembered it from the airplane experience."

Resuming work with Richard, Bettis came up with what he considered to be "the best rhyme scheme I ever executed with the Carpenters. I don't know whether anybody's ever noticed, but that was a tricky rhyme scheme to keep up: 'In the leaves on the trees / And the touch of the breeze / There's a pleasin' sense of happiness for me.'"

The Carpenters recorded "Goodbye to Love" and "Top of the World" for what became their *A Song for You* album released in June 1972. Richard heard the title song on Leon Russell's debut album and felt it would be well suited to their style. "A Song for You" is considered by many to be a contemporary standard and has since been recorded by a range of artists from Willie Nelson to Michael Bublé. The haunting melody and touching lyric combined for one of Karen's finest performances, but, although figured to be a single, it was overlooked because of its duration; it was considered to be too long for Top 40 radio. Stephen Holden of *Rolling Stone* took notice and called it "far and away the album's finest moment. It is a great song that is rapidly achieving the classic status it deserves, and Karen communicates its poignancy with effortless serenity."

Also on the album was "Hurting Each Other," which Richard first heard on KRLA in 1969. Incidentally, it was an A&M Records release by Ruby and the Romantics and one that he later came across in the stockroom on the lot shortly after having signed with the label. He played it, put it away, and was reminded of it again in 1971 while playing arbitrary chord changes on his electric piano during a sound check. His up-tempo-to-ballad formula (à la "Ticket to Ride") worked again, and "Hurting Each Other" became the Carpenters' next hit single.

Nilsson's "Without You" held the #1 spot this time as "Hurting" tried for two weeks to break through. It was the Carpenters' fourth #2 single but the sixth in a string of #1 hits on the Adult Contemporary chart.

Almost as random a discovery was "It's Going to Take Some Time." Richard first heard the song on a quad test pressing of Carole King's *Music* LP played by the engineers installing the Carpenters' new quadraphonic sound system at Newville in the fall of 1971.

Roger Nichols and Paul Williams considered "I Won't Last a Day Without You" to be a complete song with just two verses and a chorus, just as they submitted it to the Carpenters on a demo in 1971. They struggled to honor Karen's last-minute request for an additional bridge and third verse. "We finally worked it out and went in and did the demo the day before they recorded it," Nichols recalls. "They were screaming at us to get it to them and were upset with us because they were right down to the wire in the studio. What bothered me was that I heard Richard never even listened to the demo. He just looked at the sheet music and started changing it. It was kind of a sore point with me because he changed the melody in the bridge and the chord structure. After that, other people heard our version of the song—like Barbra Streisand and Diana Ross—and they all recorded the version as we had written it. I always felt that if the Carpenters had cut a better bridge it would have been a bigger song for them."

Sadly, the Nichols-Williams partnership came to an end in 1972, shortly after the Carpenters' release of *A Song for You*. "Paul wanted to be a star himself," Nichols recalls. "He was taking off and hired managers and lawyers and left me in the dust there. We stopped writing. It just wasn't happening."

The partnership between the Carpenters and producer Jack Daugherty came to an end around this time as well. Richard was enraged to read a review of their latest album in *Cashbox* magazine praising Daugherty's production abilities. Karen and Richard had remained faithful to Daugherty since he helped get their demo into the hands of Herb Alpert three years earlier, but over time this loyalty began to wane. Despite Daugherty's billing as producer, those were Richard's arrangements and Richard's productions. Some called Daugherty the Glenn Miller of the 1970s, but as far as the Carpenters were concerned he was more of an A & R man than a sound architect. He did offer production advice, but most of his time was spent booking studios and musicians, in addition to searching for potential musical material. "In the beginning Jack was the avenue between us and the Carpenters," says Roger Nichols. "He'd always say, 'Have you got anything new? What's happening? Let me hear your songs,' and so on. Later on Richard and Karen really were on the outs with him. Richard didn't need anybody to do that anymore. He felt that he was producing the records and Jack was just putting his name on them."

By 1972 Daugherty had his own secretary at A&M Records and was earning a $25,000 annual salary as staff producer for the label, in addition to his earnings from the sale of every Carpenters record. According to Allyn Ferguson, who worked with Daugherty and the Carpenters, "Jack just took a ride. He got credit for it, but he was not really a producer. He wasn't even at A&M before them. He was just the liaison between the Carpenters and A&M in the beginning, having initially brought them to Herb."

Hal Blaine claims to have stayed out of such politics, but he witnessed similar conflicts between artists and producers over the years. "I spent years with John Denver, and his 'producer' would be fast asleep in a booth. It was the musicians who made the records, but once a group gets rid of the producer and starts saying 'we can make our own records,' that's usually the beginning of the end of the group."

Asked in a 1973 UK press conference what part Daugherty had played in creating the Carpenters sound, Richard responded firmly: "Nothing. That's why he's no longer with us. We produced all those singles. It's a long story, but Jack had nothing to do with anything. He was responsible for getting Herb Alpert to hear our tape, which was very nice, but he wasn't our producer. You'll notice he hasn't had one record on any chart since he left us."

Once terminated, Jack Daugherty took the matter to court, where he claimed that the firing had destroyed his credibility in the music industry. The battle took some nine years to settle, finally going to trial in 1981. Although the court found in favor of A&M and the Carpenters, their defense cost the record company between $350,000 and $400,000. Three years after Daugherty's 1991 death, Michael Daugherty sought to vindicate his father's contributions to the Carpenters' music. "The man who produced the lion's share of the Carpenters' hits was my late father, Jack Daugherty....," he wrote in a letter to the *Los Angeles Times*. "Richard Carpenter seems intent on trivializing Daugherty's inestimable influence in the creation of the Carpenters' sound....My father would have enjoyed knowing that the sound he fashioned more than twenty years ago continues to be appreciated by so many."

AN UNLIKELY friendship was born when Karen began to reach out more and more to Frenda Franklin. "Can we go shopping sometime?" Karen would ask. Or "Could I go to the hairdresser with you?" Initially Karen had been intimidated by Frenda's affluent lifestyle, fine clothing, and expensive jewelry. She seemed in awe of the woman's sense of style and sophistication. Frenda was five years Karen's senior and over time became her closest confidante and mentor. "Karen became like a baby sister to me," Frenda explains. "We became friends. Slowly."

Karen admitted she had been jealous and apologized to Frenda for having been so impolite when the two first met and begged forgiveness. Frenda was taken aback. She was astonished that someone so supremely gifted and amazingly talented could be jealous of anyone.

"You really don't have any idea, do you?" she said.

"About what?" Karen asked.

"About how good you are. If you did, you wouldn't be jealous of anybody."

Karen refused the compliment, instead reiterating her apologies for having been disrespectful. "Well, you were just *awful*," Frenda confirmed, and the two laughed over what in retrospect seemed insignificant.

Shopping with Frenda on Rodeo Drive and around Beverly Hills, Karen was unsure of the proper etiquette used in such upscale stores and boutiques. She was terribly nervous that she might say or do something inappropriate. "Now Frenny, if I go into a store and I do something wrong you'll tell me, right?" she asked.

"Let's get this straight," Frenda said. "I wouldn't want you to go in there and do a cartwheel, but Karen, they want your *money*!"

As their friendship grew, Frenda became one of the few people in whom Karen placed all confidence. "There were things Karen would never ever tell anyone, but maybe Frenda," recalls Evelyn Wallace. "She talked to Frenda a lot about things that happened with her mother." Around her parents, especially her mother, Karen became nervous about what might be said or done in Frenda's presence. The fact that Franklin came from a large Jewish family did not dissuade Agnes Carpenter from voicing her anti-Semitic opinions around her. Karen would apologize profusely for her mother's words and attempt to explain away the ignorant comments and how they stemmed from Agnes's upbringing.

"On one level, they were very good people," Franklin says of the Carpenter parents. "Harold was the greatest. What a doll. What a sweet, sweet man." Evelyn Wallace agrees, recalling Harold as a quiet man who was nice to everybody. "He was a real sweetheart, and I admired him so much," she says. "Many times I wondered how he could live with that woman the way she used to yell and scream at him. She would jump on him, and he would never ever fight back. He just sat there and took it. He wasn't a sissy but just a real nice guy. Agnes was the speaker, so he wasn't really one to get a word in edgewise."

"Agnes kind of has a mean streak in her sometimes," Harold told Evelyn in the home office one afternoon.

"Yeah, I kind of noticed that!" she said sarcastically.

"Harold wasn't allowed to have an opinion," Frenda says. "Agnes was a bulldozer. In my own way I loved her. She was Karen's mother, and she gave her life. But I was sorry that she had so many prejudices. She used really bad language, too. I'd never known anyone that called somebody the *n*-word. Those things do not go down well with me. I was shocked." The Jackson Five was the target of such talk on several occasions, and Karen was mortified when her mother would make such bigoted comments. She seemed ashamed and wanted very much to dissociate herself from what she saw as dogmatic narrow-mindedness.

"Oh, Frenny, you're still going to be friends with me, right?" she'd ask apprehensively. "You're not going to hold it against me, are you?"

"Kace [a nickname derived from K.C.], of course not," Frenda would tell her again and again. "It's nothing to do with you. Don't be silly."

This reaction from Karen was nothing unusual. She was a people pleaser with a strong desire to keep everyone around her happy, even if it came at her own expense. Her closest friends knew she was sensitive and vulnerable, and neither quality could withstand her mother's brutality. Somewhere along the way Karen had adopted a rugged exterior—an almost masculine facade—to protect herself from her mother's unapologetic harshness. She struggled with femininity, and many who were close to her say Karen always remained childlike, like a little girl who never really grew up or blossomed into a woman. In a 1974 *Rolling Stone* cover story, even Tom Nolan remarked on Karen's perceived immaturity. "Karen is in some ways like a child," he wrote, "which is not surprising. A star since nineteen, a committed musician even longer than that, she probably missed out on one or two normal stages of adaptation to 'the real world.'"

Between the years 1970 and 1975, Sherwin Bash witnessed a gradual transformation in Karen from an immature tomboy to an attractive young woman. He felt it was indeed an effort on her part to break free from the only way of life she had known in hopes of exchanging it for a life she very much desired. In his words, there was "a very strong attempt on Karen's part, whether she was consciously aware of it or not, to find a place for herself in the social strata of young womanhood." This transformation had little to do with her status as an entertainer or celebrity. She was more intent on becoming someone who "had friends, could go out on dates, and have a social life," said Bash. "And I don't believe she ever totally achieved it."

What Bash had sensed was in actuality a concentrated effort on Karen's part to shed her tomboy qualities for a more feminine persona. "She wanted to be a woman," says Frenda, who at Karen's urging assisted in a slow but steady makeover. "She so wanted to be refined. She wanted to be what she called 'uptown.' It sounds so peculiar, but she wanted what she knew she could earn and wanted all the finery that went along with her career. She looked to me for that."

The transformation would not be easy, as Karen had exhibited this tough exterior and guise for most of her life. Having grown up playing baseball with the neighborhood boys, then becoming a drummer and going on tour with an all male band, she walked and talked like one of the guys. "She used to walk across the stage like a Mack truck," Frenda exclaims. "Feminine she wasn't. We had to work on her posture a lot and her walking. . . . I worried about it because I didn't want people to take her the wrong way. That wasn't who she was. That was Karen not wanting to get hurt. I think a lot of it was a cover-up. I really do. If you put up a big, thick wall, and you're kind of a tough guy, you're not going to expose your gentleness."

Karen's makeover from Downey to "uptown" took years. In fact, it was more of a work in progress. "We went from A to Z, as you would with a baby," Frenda explains. "She was such a fast study. It was amazing. I wanted her to put her best foot forward, especially if it was on camera or in an interview. I didn't want her to be afraid and let that 'best offense is a good defense' come right out." Karen respected Frenda and took her directives very seriously. "Sit up straight," she would instruct Karen. "Talk like a lady and act like a lady. Oh, and don't come off like a truck driver!" The two would laugh. Just when Karen seemed to have reached her goal of walking and talking like a lady, according to Frenda, "There were still times the 'Downey' would come back out!"

Karen often borrowed accessories from Frenda's extensive wardrobe to complement her own. Lending her a handbag for an award show appearance, Frenda scrawled with a marker on a small index card and dropped it in the purse. Later that evening, Karen opened the bag and discovered the drawing of two huge eyes and was reminded that her friend was watching her every move and hoping for the best. Also on the card were three letters—G.U.S.—an inside joke between trainer and trainee instructing Karen to "grow up, schmuck!"

⸺⸺⸺∞⸺⸺⸺

"BEING THE only girl makes you the center of attention," Karen explained in a 1971 interview for *Teen* magazine. "Let's face it, any girl likes to get attention, and the guys are all very protective toward me. It's wild, I tell you. I can't make a move. They're always watching out for me." Even so, Karen longed for the companionship of another female while on the road. "Sometimes I feel as if I've got to have another girl to talk to, but that's only natural."

Agnes and friend Beverly Nogawski kept weekly hair appointments every Friday morning at the Magic Mirror, a local beauty shop near the intersection of Firestone and Lakewood boulevards in Downey. "Did you know Karen is looking for somebody to do her hair?" Nogawski asked salon manager Maria Luisa Galeazzi.

"The idea of traveling and going places attracted the wild card in me," says Galeazzi, who accepted an offer from Karen after a brief interview at Newville. "But I didn't know what I was going to get myself into! Karen and I became friends—sort of—but I never really took the initiative to become very personal with her. . . . I didn't stick my nose in anything. If I saw things I just kept quiet. See no evil, hear no evil, speak no evil!"

Richard was immediately attracted to the feisty blond Italian. "He had fallen for Maria before they even left on the tour," recalls Evelyn Wallace. "When she would come to do Karen's hair at the house, the doorbell would ring, and before I had a chance to get up from my desk Richard was down those stairs and at the door."

Galeazzi's first gig was July 7, 1972, at University of Houston, where she went straight to work caring for the group's personal property, from travel clothes to stage outfits and jewelry. "Nothing was out of place, and everything was put away and locked up and ready to go for the next gig," she explains. "I remember the first night. My God, I was scared to death. We were a couple of stories down, way underneath the stadium, and I could barely hear the announcement to get Karen up there." Prior to the concert, an intoxicated fan jumped to the stage and sat down at Karen's drums during the performance by opening act Skiles and Henderson. "Karen, I want to marry you!" he yelled as he pounded on the instruments. The man was apprehended after assaulting a police officer. "Don't touch me!" he shouted as he continued to kick and scream his way off stage. "I'm engaged to Karen Carpenter!" Authorities found wedding rings and airline tickets for the supposed honeymoon once they booked him into the local jail.

Leaving the stadium, Galeazzi was unprepared for the farewell rituals of Carpenters fans, something Karen and Richard were accustomed to by this juncture. "I was not ready for all the fans pulling hair and clothes and trying to get into the car. They were just crazy and making the car jump up and down and everything." Neighbors Tex and Charlene McAlister witnessed the pandemonium as well when they would attend concerts with the Carpenter parents. "It was almost impossible to get out of there after a concert because the kids would go so crazy," Charlene recalls. "We were in a limo with their parents, and the fans all thought that we were Richard and Karen. 'Just raise your hand and wave,' Harold told us. The fans were all over the hood of the car. We ended up being the decoy car, and Richard and Karen were behind. It was just a regular car that nobody even looked at."

One of the more serious scares occurred as the Carpenters prepared for a concert at Oregon State University in Corvallis. As Karen and Maria left their hotel rooms they were attacked by several men and tackled to the ground. "We were walking down the hallway to go to the gig and some gypsies jumped us," Galeazzi recalls. "They came out of another room and jumped us! We were down on the ground. It's a good thing the guys from the band were not far behind us. It was really, really scary."

At times, Frank Bonito and other friends were concerned for Karen's safety and did all they could to preserve her privacy. "We wouldn't let her go to the bathroom alone," he says. "We were always very protective of her. This was around the time Patty Hearst was kidnapped and all that. Richard wasn't noticed as much as Karen was since he wasn't in the forefront." He recalls accompanying Karen to a department store once. "When she had her sunglasses on people would walk on by. Everything was fine until she used her credit card. Then we had to leave the store!"

Most Carpenters fans were kind and respected the duo's space. Others could be almost abusive. Dinner interruptions were frequent, so they would often ask for a private room or at the very least position Karen with her back to the main dining room. "They are quite gracious when asked for autographs," wrote Tom Nolan in *Rolling Stone*, "considering how often they are approached in restaurants, after concerts, while riding in limousines. . . . Approached during breakfast in Richmond, Virginia, by a rotund and particularly nervy fellow bearing five napkins to be individually inscribed, Karen blurted out in disbelief, 'Oh, fuck!'"

Despite the fame and recognition, Karen seemed to remain the simple, unpretentious girl Frank Bonito had walked to and from school with years before. Her trust of such friends seemed to grow with every mounting success. "Karen felt comfortable with us," Bonito says. "She was very down-to-earth and never played the prima donna. She was always interested in what we were doing in our lives. We represented history and security. We also represented how her life would be if she weren't a singer."

7

AMERICA AT ITS VERY BEST?

I N THE nation's capital for a music industry awards dinner, Karen and Richard visited the White House as guests of presidential assistants James Cavanaugh, Ken Cole, and Ronald Ziegler on April 25, 1972. There they met Julie Nixon Eisenhower, the president's daughter and a fan of their music, but President Richard M. Nixon was in a meeting with Henry Kissinger and unavailable at the time of their visit. The Carpenters returned to the White House just months later on August 1, this time meeting briefly and posing for photos with President Nixon in the Oval Office. He thanked Karen for her work as National Youth Chairman for the American Cancer Society, an organization the duo supported with the donation of more than one hundred thousand dollars in proceeds from concert tour program sales. Conversation with Nixon was trite. He was known to be inept at making small talk, and Karen and Richard were quite nervous, too. Nixon asked about the amount of sound equipment the Carpenters carried on tour. "About 10,000 pounds," they told him.

"We can probably hear you all the way here," he replied, referring to their scheduled concert in nearby Columbia, Maryland.

In the spring of 1973 Sherwin Bash was contacted on behalf of President Nixon with a request for the Carpenters to entertain at the White House following a state dinner honoring West German Chancellor Willy Brandt. Bash was quick to accept the invitation on the group's behalf, and on April 30, 1973, during a hectic touring schedule of one-nighters, the exhausted Carpenters entourage flew into Washington, D.C. Unbeknownst to them, the Watergate scandal was on the verge of erupting. In fact, just one day prior the president had met with key advisors Bob Haldeman and John Ehrlichman at Camp David, where he confirmed their suspicions that they would be asked to resign their positions.

As the Carpenters relaxed in a nearby hotel, President Nixon addressed a nationwide television and radio audience from the Oval Office regarding Watergate. "I want to talk to you tonight from my heart on a subject of deep concern to every American...," he began. "Today, in one of the most difficult decisions of my presidency, I accepted the resignations of two of my closest associates in the White House.... In any organization, the man at the top must bear the responsibility.... I accept that. And I pledge to you tonight, from this office, that I will do everything in my power to ensure that the guilty are brought to justice, and that such abuses are purged from our political processes in the years to come, long after I have left office."

As the Carpenters' orchestral director Frank Pooler was transported to the White House for his Tuesday morning rehearsal with the Marine Corps Orchestra, agents from the Federal Bureau of Investigation secured the files of Haldeman and Ehrlichman by placing guards outside their offices. Press Secretary Ronald Ziegler called it a "safeguarding procedure." Nixon was outraged to learn of the guards and quickly arranged for them and the files to be transferred to a less conspicuous location. Unaware of the heightened security issues, Pooler went on rehearsing the group he remembers as the best orchestra he ever worked with while with the Carpenters. "Usually it took me two hours to rehearse an orchestra," he says, "but these guys were so good we were done in about an hour. We finished fast and got a private tour of the rooms of the White House the tourists don't generally get."

That evening after dining at the Jockey Club, the band gathered in their downstairs dressing rooms to prepare for the performance. Frank Pooler realized he was the only one in the group who had yet to meet the president. "I've got to meet him," he told Sherwin Bash. "I'm here, for

God's sake. It'll be something to tell my grandchildren." Bash directed him to the Grand Hall where a receiving line of distinguished guests, many in uniform, waited to meet Nixon. Pooler found the president to be much friendlier and better looking in real life than in pictures or on television. "Nixon was charming," he says. "He told me that his daughters had been fans of the Carpenters for a long time." As Pooler was introduced to Mrs. Nixon, he could hear the band warming up. "I'm sorry," he told the First Lady, realizing he was late, "I don't have time to talk to you!" The three laughed as Pooler rushed to lead the orchestra.

Around 10:30 P.M., the president and Mrs. Nixon entered the East Room. Addressing the crowd, which included then soon-to-be Secretary of State Henry Kissinger and his date, actress Mamie Van Doren, Nixon proclaimed, "The Carpenters are very much alive. They are young America at its very best. Mr. Chancellor," he said, addressing the dignitary, "knowing how you have such affection for young people all over the world and how you, as well as I, are working for the peace that we want for them and their children in years to come, we think that, tonight, having the Carpenters—one of the finest young groups in America—entertain us is most appropriate."

The Carpenters opened their performance with "Close to You," musically tiptoeing in an attempt to please such an esteemed audience. "We were afraid to touch anything," Karen recalled. "I was afraid to even breathe on the drums. I was barely touching them because I didn't want to offend anybody." She drummed on more rhythmic numbers like "Love Is Surrender," "Top of the World," and "Mr. Guder," but returned to center stage on the ballads. The Carpenters' new drummer, former Mickey Mouse Club Mouseketeer Cubby O'Brien, had recently joined the group following the departure of Jim Anthony.

In a variation on her standard end-of-show monologue, Karen thanked Pooler and the orchestra before going on to say, "I know I speak for all the people that are associated with Richard and me when I say that being invited to the White House to perform, or just being invited to the White House *period*, is not only a thrill, but it's indeed an honor." She then addressed Chancellor Brandt directly, saying, "Gute Nacht. Auf Wiedersehen."

President Nixon joined the band onstage as a standing ovation spread across the East Room. "We do have dancing afterward," he announced, "but we can't afford the Carpenters!"

———— ∞∞ ————

DURING THE summer tour of 1972, the Carpenters introduced a medley of oldies, songs from the 1950s and 1960s that were enjoying a renaissance at the time. In fact, entire radio stations were switching to an all oldie format. Working toward their fifth album release, Karen and Richard realized there was only enough new material for one side of an LP. Desperation and a lack of time fueled Richard's visualization of an entire side of an album dedicated to a version of their oldies medley that would be bookended with an anthem with the message conveying "the oldies are back!" He asked John Bettis to come up with a list of possible song titles. The list of at least thirty prospective titles was narrowed to one favorite, "Yesterday Once More." The anthem was born as Richard drove up Highland Avenue on his way to A&M. He heard a melody and the start of a song lyric in his head. Arriving at the studio, he played his ideas for Karen and later came up with a first verse.

When I was young I'd listen to the radio
Waitin' for my favorite songs
When they played I'd sing along
It made me smile

Richard returned to Bettis, who created a temporary or "dummy" lyric for the chorus with every intention of reworking the words at a later time. "Well, are you going to change this now?" Richard asked as the song neared completion.

"You know what," Bettis replied, "I don't think so! I think it sounds great this way."

"Are you kidding?"

"No," Bettis said. "This 'Sha-la-la-wo-wo-wo' stuff sounds pretty good!"

A leftover song title suggested by Agnes Carpenter, "Now and Then," became the name of the new Carpenters album released May 1, 1973, the day of the duo's White House performance. An impressive tri-gatefold cover illustrated Karen and Richard driving past their huge Downey home in Richard's red 1972 Ferrari 365 GTB/4 Daytona. The "Now" side of the LP began with its debut single, which hailed from television's *Sesame Street* and composer Joe Raposo. Karen and Richard first heard "Sing" while taping a television special called *Robert Young with the Young* for NBC-TV. The catchy melodic hook left everyone on the set singing and humming the song.

Richard was so taken with "Sing" that he started arranging their version while on set at NBC studios. The finished product featured the Jimmy Joyce Children's Choir on the sing-along "la-la" sections, but it was hardly the type of single the group needed at the time. "The Munchkin Song," some fans called it. A&M did not want to release "Sing" as a single, but Richard was confident of its commercial potential. He was right, and "Sing" went to #3 on the U.S. charts. When performing the song in concert, the Carpenters often solicited the help of local children's choirs.

The crowning jewel of *Now and Then* came in the form of a Leon Russell tune from his *Carney* album. Overlooked as a single due to its duration, "This Masquerade" was one of the Carpenters' most sophisticated recordings ever, with its haunting melody, Karen's intricate drum track, and an impressive flute solo by Bob Messenger.

Rounding out side A was the Carpenters' 1972 cover of Hank Williams's country classic "Jambalaya (on the Bayou)," completed for this album and released as a single in the United Kingdom. "I Can't Make Music" was penned by occasional opening act Randy Edelman and perfectly suited for the Carpenters treatment. "The Carpenters have gone awry," wrote outspoken rock critic Lester Bangs in his review of *Now and Then*. "Side One's alright, just what you needed; more of that nice, syrupy, ultra commercial pap. 'Sing' is one of their all time best singles, and the essence of the act: 'Sing of good things not bad.' But Karen's reading of 'Jambalaya' is almost as bad as John Fogerty's, and there may be gray clouds passing over Carpenterland because she manages to sound almost *used* in Leon Russell's 'This Masquerade' while 'I Can't Make Music' is the Carpenters' hymn of despair like Traffic's 'Sometimes I Feel So Uninspired.'"

The "Then" side of the *Now and Then* LP began with "Yesterday Once More" and, as planned, the monstrous medley of oldies that Richard crafted to emulate a Top 40 radio show. Each selection segued into the next and was joined by the radio deejay antics of multitalented guitarist Tony Peluso. Narrowing down their favorites, Karen and Richard settled on a list including "Fun, Fun, Fun," "The End of the World," "Da Doo Ron Ron," "Dead Man's Curve," "Johnny Angel," "The Night Has a Thousand Eyes," "Our Day Will Come," and "One Fine Day." Their "Yesterday Once More" single went on to become the duo's fifth #2, placing them in a three-way tie with Creedence Clearwater Revival and Elvis Presley for the most #2 singles in chart history. The song also proved to be the Carpenters' biggest worldwide hit and at one point was #1 in Belgium, England, Hong Kong, Israel, Japan, Malaysia, Singapore, and Venezuela.

<hr />

BY THE time President Richard M. Nixon had declared the Carpenters to be "young America at its very best," Karen and Richard were three years into what became a futile struggle for control over their public image, and an endorsement from Nixon only worked against their cause. Early attempts to establish a true identity with the media were brought to a halt by their publicists and record label. But before they were specifically coached by management on how to handle interviewers and questioning, the Carpenters gave several revealing interviews including one in 1970 with Chicago radio legend Dick Biondi. Religion, politics, and current affairs were discussed, and neither Carpenter held back.

BIONDI: What are your feelings on the United States' involvement in the Vietnam War?
KAREN: Oh, I think I'd better let him steam first.
RICHARD: I'm completely against it.
KAREN: I think it's a complete waste...

RICHARD: First of all, nothing's ever going to be settled. It's like the Korean War. Nothing ever came to a complete end. It's been bubbling over there ever since. That was never won or lost. It just sort of terminated. Nothing was ever settled, and this is never going to be settled because it's not an all-out war. It's an "involvement." They don't even call it a war.

KAREN: They never even *declared* one. It's ridiculous.

RICHARD: And they're over their piddling around. One cat shoots so many one day, and then they shoot back the next day. If you're going to have a war, as much as I am against killing or anything like it, you ought to get in there and *do it*.

On the subject of censorship, Karen explained she felt it could be "very confining. It can be very destructive." Asked about her religious views she told Biondi, "I don't need to go to church and listen to some preacher tell me what to believe in. I don't dig that at all." Richard expressed his disgust with the state of organized religion and called it "hypocrisy personified."

Although the interview was one of the first to allow the Carpenters the opportunity to voice their opinions on important and relevant topics, it would be the last. Their publicist was furious. "Most people were asking them about their songs and stuff, so I went into the drugs and Vietnam," Biondi recalls. "I was very proud of myself because I could see their promotion man getting more and more upset."

According to Richard, following the Biondi interview, they were coached by the publicists to avoid controversial topics and anything not in keeping with the image prescribed for them. "We were told when you go out to do interviews, don't say anything adverse about anything. Everything is groovy. Everything is terrific. Don't say anything bad. Don't say you dislike anything. You like everything. And we went along with it."

Meet the Carpenters—A&M Records' young brother-sister hit-makers whose gentle harmony, wholesome image and natural, unpretentious personalities have virtually crashed through to make them the nation's number one recording team. Their sonorous magic has endeared them to music fans of every age and taste, and may be marking the beginning of a new musical mood for the '70s, bringing back the three H's—hope, happiness and harmony. With soft-pedaled persistence and talent galore, these melodic siblings have revolutionized the music industry.

It was through promotional blurbs such as this 1971 press release that A&M Records crafted their image of the Carpenters, and it quickly caught on. "Real nice American kids—in 1971!" wrote *Stereo Review*, saying they were "friendly people, outgoing, well-mannered, casually but tidily dressed, hard-working—and talented. No protest. No defiance. No porn. No blasphemy. No tripping." And according to the *Washington Post*: "Karen may eat a peanut butter cup for quick energy, but not an amphetamine, and there are no groupies camped out in hotels where the Carpenters stay. Autograph hounds perhaps, but not groupies. 'No,' said Karen. 'We don't seem to attract that crowd.'"

The rock press of the early 1970s in effect bullied the Carpenters, and because their music went against the grain of rock standards, they were often relegated to second-class status. Although they were not a rock band, more often than not they were reviewed by rock critics. "They were not rock," explained journalist Rob Hoerburger in a 2008 documentary, "they were not jazz, they were not country, they were not classical, but they had facets of all of that in their music. When you put all of those facets together what you get is this really amazing pop gem."

According to Paul Williams, "The Carpenters were truly one of the first great alternative bands. 'In-A-Gadda-Da-Vida' was the huge #1 album shortly before 'Close to You' and 'Begun' were hits. I was so different from them, too. I was such a raging hippie. I was pretty much a part of the counterculture yet writing songs for Karen and Richard and a lot of other middle-of-the-road acts." Williams was quite a sight on the A&M lot in those days. Often he wore tie-dyed shirts, round glasses, and work boots, with a black top hat resting atop his shoulder-length hair. Leaning on a railing outside an A&M office one afternoon, he noticed Bing Crosby waiting outside the studios for his driver to arrive. "He looked at me, said something, and pointed, like what is this world coming to?" Williams says. "He didn't know who I was then. That was before I became known as an entertainer and Crosby recorded 'We've Only Just Begun.'"

Writing for *Rolling Stone* in 1971, Lester Bangs was the first of many who found more at fault with the Carpenters' appearance than their brand of music. "I would say that they have the most disconcerting collective stage presence of any band I've ever seen," he wrote of a concert in San Diego, California. "Besides being a motley crew, they are individually peculiar-looking. Here it becomes almost cruel to go on, but there is no getting around it, especially since most of the music was so bland and their demeanor so remarkable that you could spend the entire concert wondering at the latter without once getting bored. I found the band almost like tintypes of themselves. . . . I'll never be able to hear 'We've Only Just Begun' without thinking, not of a sentimental autumn as I used to, but inevitably of that disgruntled collection of faces." Bangs also mentioned their image: "The LP cover and promo pix showed 'em side by side, identical, interchangeable boy-girl faces grinning out at you with all the cheery innocence of some years-past dream of California youth. Almost like a better-scrubbed reincarnation of Sonny and Cher."

Bangs was right, at least as far as their image was concerned. An onslaught of eight-by-ten glossy photos and unimaginative album covers made Karen and Richard appear more conservative and square than they really were. For the *Close to You* album cover they were cheek to cheek in formal wear and positioned on a rock next to the ocean. It was a rush job and one that angered Richard. Even so, management did nothing. As simple and classy as their *Tan Album* was, the inside photo looked like every engagement portrait snapped in 1971. Next was *A Song for You*, which resembled a huge Valentine card. The Carpenters' sophisticated musicianship deserved equally sophisticated packaging and promotion. In a 1993 interview, surprisingly, Herb Alpert claimed to have been pleased with the way the Carpenters were marketed by his company. "It's not enough just to have a hit record," he said. "It's to be able to promote it properly and to merchandise it properly with good taste. I think the company did a wonderful job and continues to, because we try to reflect the dignity that they both had as artists."

Despite Alpert's good intentions, early publicity attempts by the label backfired. A&M Records and their publicists succeeded only in frustrating Karen and Richard and creating a stigma for fans of their music, as detailed by journalist John Tobler in a 1974 article: "A number of people, myself included, could be seen stealing away surreptitiously into our favorite record shops and whispering our requirements to an astonished assistant, who probably thought we'd lost our minds. Shades of prohibition!" And Tom Smucker of the *Village Voice* called it "the worst case of consumer stage fright since I first bought rubbers years ago. What would the man behind the counter say when I walked up with my Carpenters record?"

In an article written some twenty years after both Tobler's and Smucker's, Rob Hoerburger explained in a *New York Times Magazine* article the wide appeal of the Carpenters, despite the stigma: "When 'We've Only Just Begun' or 'Rainy Days and Mondays' came on the car radio, kids *and* parents would turn it up. . . . This was musical white bread, to be sure, but it was feeding masses of a biblical proportion."

⎯⎯ ⨯⨯⨯ ⎯⎯

LIVING AT home with her parents and spending a significant amount of time on tour, Karen had little time to devote to romantic relationships. Since her only real interaction with men came in the form of friendships with band members and roadies, it was inevitable that she would eventually meet and fall for someone within the Carpenters' entourage. She was linked to Carpenters guitarist Gary Sims in the early days and later drummer Jim Anthony, but these were what Frenda Franklin recalls as "lightweight relationships," dismissing them as mere puppy love. "They weren't anything Karen wasn't in control of," she says.

Karen dated Alan Osmond for a brief spell, but the Osmonds and the Carpenters were in such demand during that period that the two rarely spent enough time together for a serious relationship to ensue. "She really liked Alan," recalls Franklin. "That was kind of sad because Mrs. Osmond would not allow it. . . . Everything was controlled by these powerful families, and trust me, the Carpenters were little leaguers next to the Osmonds. And they had the big Mormon church in back of them."

Karen downplayed the relationship with Alan in 1974 when she explained to the *Los Angeles Times*, "Contrary to what they write, Alan and I are not married. We've seen each other maybe five times. How can you date someone when you finish work at 3:00 A.M.? If you go to a lounge or coffee shop people stare. So you end up sitting in cars and talking for hours."

Karen expressed to Frank Bonito and other close friends her frustration with finding love and trying to build a relationship on the road. "It's not unusual for people in that kind of situation to have romances with the people they're working with," Bonito says. "They live a very bizarre, confined life because they are constantly traveling. Who do you meet? Even if you wanted to date someone, who do you see?"

In a 1981 BBC radio interview, Karen elaborated: "At one point, there were thirty-two of us on the road. It's a big bunch. You tend to travel in the same circles with the same people, meet the same people, and hang out with the same people. Even when you come home you never really meet anybody new. Being the only girl, outside of my hairdresser, it's not easy having thirty brothers on the road. Everybody, including management, is extremely protective. You get to the point where you don't want to go outside the hotel room because it's more difficult. You really don't meet anybody."

In 1973 Karen grew fond of another member of their entourage. Texan David Alley was close to her age and assigned to the Carpenters' tour by his employer, Showco, a Dallas-based sound equipment outfit. As a high school junior, Alley had been first chair trumpeter in the Texas All-State Band and went on to march with the Mustang Band while attending Southern Methodist University. On tour with the Carpenters, Sherwin Bash mentioned to Alley that Karen liked him. He was stunned by the news and wasted no time in asking her on a date. In no time at all he fell madly in love with Karen, and the two began spending a great deal of time together outside of rehearsals, sound checks, and shows.

"David was always a very, very nice fellow and a real gentleman," remembers Evelyn Wallace. "I had a feeling that Karen was really quite fond of him and he of her, but there was Richard in between. I think they knew that if they started dating or showed their fondness for each other that David would be gone. Karen didn't want him gone, and David didn't want to be gone from Karen either, so he didn't give her that much attention whenever he was at the house since Richard was always there."

Although Karen enjoyed David's company and felt comfortable when they were together, she did not see a future with him and seemed to distance herself at times. "Karen liked to be entertained," Maria Galeazzi recalls. "David was very serious, almost sourpusslike. He wasn't a fun guy. I am not saying he wasn't a nice guy, he just wasn't a barrel of laughs, by any means."

Also working against Alley's chances with Karen was the fact that he was dependent upon his job with the Carpenters. Karen was essentially his boss, in some respects. In fact, she and Richard hired David to manage Morsound, their own sound equipment company formed in 1974. One of Karen's crucial requirements in a potential husband was that he be independently wealthy and not reliant on her income. According to Galeazzi, Karen felt she needed her man to be of a certain status. "The person had to be somebody way up there," she explains. "Her standards were high. Some regular dude was just not going to do. I am not saying that David was a regular dude. He was successful in his own right, but she would have admired somebody that was talented in music and good looking and all that. And I think even that wouldn't have done." As Karen told the *Los Angeles Times* that same year, "It's no good when the chick is bigger than the guy."

Frenda Franklin concurs. "In the very beginning she had a huge crush on my husband, Eddie," she says. "You see, Karen had a propensity to fall in love with people that could change her life in big ways. She certainly had a giant crush on Herbie. She was like a little starstruck girl. These guys were not only handsome, they were powerful, they dressed great, they smelled great, and they were wealthy. She saw it as a way out, definitely. No question about it, it was freedom. But David Alley *wasn't* enough."

8

MOVING OUT

―――――――――

"**H**AROLD AND Karen were both sweethearts," remembers Evelyn Wallace. "Richard, on the other hand, was just like his mother. They could be bitchy. They *were* bitchy, even to each other once in a while. Yet Richard was still her baby."

One such exchange between Agnes and Richard occurred in Acapulco, Mexico, where the Carpenters were invited to perform two twenty-minute shows on consecutive Saturdays for the IBM Corporation's Gold Key Club, June 2–9, 1973. Outside of the performance times, the group was free to enjoy the beautiful secluded villa provided for them at Las Brisas overlooking the Bay of Acapulco. Sharing the spacious house with Karen was boyfriend David Alley. Maria Galeazzi accompanied Richard, while manager Sherwin Bash and his wife, Bobby, also stayed at the villa. Agnes and Harold were invited to Acapulco as well but were upset to learn they had been booked into the nearby Princess Hotel with the IBM executives. With their love interests on the trip, Karen and Richard sought some semblance of privacy, but this did not sit well with Agnes, who felt she and Harold were deliberately excluded. "Why are *we* in the hotel while the *strangers* are in the house?" she demanded.

"I'm not ten years old anymore!" Richard shouted back. The other houseguests looked on as the two bellowed back and forth. Once each had said their piece, everyone did their best to relax and enjoy the luxurious accommodations. They took great advantage of the private swimming pool and made several trips to Pie de la Cuesta, a long, narrow strip of beach north of Las Brisas.

By the time the group returned from Mexico, it was apparent to Agnes that Richard was in love with Maria, but their relationship threatened the family's living situation. Agnes had succeeded in keeping Richard at home with her for twenty-seven years and was not about to lose him to her hairdresser. From a parental standpoint, Galeazzi now recognizes Agnes's desire to be protective of her children, although not to the point of suffocation. "She didn't want anybody taking advantage of them," Galeazzi says. "I can understand that. If I had been their mother I would have been a junkyard dog, too. But I wasn't just a girl that came along and hooked up with him because he was Richard Carpenter. I was just a nice Italian girl who happened to be working for them, and we got together. It wasn't like I was a groupie and fell into his bed or anything." Regardless, Agnes made it her mission to excommunicate Galeazzi from the Carpenter clan, and Karen became the medium. "You *fire* her," Agnes insisted.

"Mom, she does my hair the best of anyone I've ever been to," Karen explained. "And she doesn't do just my hair, she cuts Richard's hair and the guys', too. She does our fingernails, and she always presses our costumes before we go on stage. We didn't expect her to do all that!"

"You can find someone else," Agnes said. "You get rid of her!"

Evelyn Wallace recalls this episode in the kitchen at Newville and how devastated Karen was to be given these orders. "If I heard the words 'you get rid of her' once, I must have heard them a hundred times," she says. "Karen was so nice. I think her mother weakened her."

The months that followed were very tense for Galeazzi. She made every effort to do her job and tend to Karen's needs, but she also wanted to spend her free time alone with Richard. The two enjoyed racing his Ferrari at Riverside, but Karen did her best to monopolize Maria's time with girls-only outings such as shopping trips to Beverly Hills or visits to their favorite needlepoint store. "I was always like her little shadow and supposed to be there for her twenty-four hours a day, seven days a week," she recalls. "It's not like I wasn't doing my job. When I got together with Richard I became even more conscientious about it because I didn't want to screw up."

At Agnes's urging, Karen became more demanding and impatient, and Galeazzi began to sense something was brewing. Alone time for her and Richard was scarce. "If we went anywhere it was the three of us," she says. "Every place we went it was like Karen and Richard and I, and it got old for me, let me tell you. Even the hotel rooms were always Richard's room, Karen's room, and then my room. Most of the time they'd make sure there was a door that opened up from mine into hers so that I was always there ready to assist her."

Things came to a head one evening as the three prepared to go out on the town. As always, Galeazzi stopped by Newville to do Karen's hair and makeup. When she finished, Galeazzi excused herself to return to her apartment. There she would get herself ready for the outing, but Karen stopped her. "No. Bring your stuff and get ready here," she said.

"It's just easier for me to go two miles away and get ready and then come back," Galeazzi explained.

Karen felt challenged and quickly turned to Richard. "You see? This is not working," she told him. "This is just *not working*!"

Next, Karen presented Galeazzi with an iniquitous ultimatum: forget about Richard and go back out on the road as her stylist or remain a couple and resign her position. But Galeazzi refused to conform to either suggestion. "Well, I can do both," Galeazzi replied, shocked at the nerve of Karen's challenge. "I don't understand why I have to make this choice. Be with him and, what, twiddle my thumbs and do needlepoint? If I go on the road, I am going to watch Richard dating other girls. I don't think I could stand that."

Richard visited Maria at her apartment, where the two sat at the edge of her bed and discussed Karen's demands. Both in tears, they agreed the relationship must come to an end. "He had to do what he had to do," Galeazzi recalls. "He made it understood that it was not in his power or in his best interest. I would have never pushed it, and that's why I left. I could have chosen one or the other, but I didn't because it would have been difficult for all three of us. I couldn't see myself just being his girlfriend either, so that's how it came to an end." Galeazzi returned to her job at the Magic Mirror in Downey, weighing in at a skeletal eighty-six pounds due to stress. "I lost so much weight because I was so nervous about it all."

Replacing Galeazzi was Sandy Holland. According to Evelyn Wallace, Karen spelled out her expectations in no uncertain terms, instructing the new employee to keep her distance and stay out of her brother's bed. "If Richard wants his hair cut, cut it. But whatever you do, *don't* play around with him!"

To THE outside world, Agnes Carpenter was an overprotective mother to both her children, but it was apparent to those within the Carpenter enclave that she played favorites. Evelyn Wallace recalls that when speaking of the two, Agnes always made reference to Richard before Karen. "From the time Karen was little, everything was 'Richard, Richard, Richard.' It was always 'Richard and Karen' and 'if it wasn't for *Richard*, there wouldn't be a Karen,' so to speak. He was more important to Agnes than Karen."

According to Wallace, Karen was well aware of her second-place ranking in the home and perhaps even felt it was justified. Agnes's adoration for her firstborn—to the point of idolization, according to some—was emulated and even proliferated by Karen. "She thought Richard was God," Frenda Franklin recalls, "just like her mother thought he was God." Tangible proof of Karen's adulation of her brother remains today in a poignant needlepoint message she crafted for him: THERE IS NO K.C. WITHOUT R.C.

As Frenda explains, Agnes' inability to nurture and nourish her daughter with affection, as she did Richard, led to Karen's own inability to love herself. "[Karen's] relationship with her mother was so stilted that it caused such a great hurt inside her," Franklin says. Of Agnes she laments, "I wanted her to be different with Karen. She just couldn't love her. It was not possible. I think in her own crazy way she did love her, but not like she loved Richard. If your own parent doesn't love you, you're going to walk around with a giant hole that's not ever going to get filled."

In a 1973 concert review that criticized Richard's long hairstyle, a University of Montana columnist wrote, "Whereas Richard may not appear to be every father's favorite son, Karen is the kind of girl every mother could love." This casual remark takes on a most ironic twist when paired with Sherwin Bash's observations of the real mother-daughter relationship he witnessed within the Carpenter family: "I'm sure in her own way Agnes loved Karen, but it wasn't something she was able to express," he recalled. "I think eventually that was one of the most serious problems that Karen had. . . . Over the years, Karen Carpenter became beloved in the world as a very special artist, a very special voice, who reminded everybody of the daughter they wished they had. In her own home she never was told or maybe never even felt that existed from her own parents, especially her mother."

<hr>

KAREN WAS twenty-four and Richard approaching the age of twenty-eight when the two decided it was time to leave home. The dilemma was how to proceed without hurting their mother's feelings. They asked Sherwin Bash for advice. Bash had worked with hundreds of music artists, and in his opinion these siblings were immature. They lacked sophistication—not musically but in their personal lives. He wanted to see them take control of their lives, move out of their parents' house, and seek the independence of two millionaires in their twenties. "Their inability to develop," said Bash, "was created by their inability to separate themselves from a dominating mother who they never wanted to offend and never wanted to hurt. . . . I think that severely stunted and damaged their growth."

According to Evelyn Wallace, this was not the kids' first attempt at independence. The two had rented an apartment together in Bellflower for a brief spell. "That didn't last too long," she explains. "Richard was expecting Karen to do all the cooking and the stuff his mother had done." But Karen claimed to enjoy inventing new recipes and perfecting others. "Cooking is an art and a pleasure for me; I've always loved to cook, ever since I was a child," she said in a 1971 press release entitled "Karen in the Kitchen: Who Says a Young Female Superstar Can't Be a Top-Notch Cook?" She listed her favorite creations, which included pies, cookies, shrimp dishes, and "veal and eggplant concoctions."

Sherwin offered Karen and Richard his advice for officially moving out, but instead of confronting their mother and relocating, the two came up with a way they might evade the issue entirely. They bought their parents a modest 3,000-square-foot home with four bedrooms and three baths at 8341 Lubec Street in Downey, less than two miles from Newville. "The expectation was that their mother and father would move into this new house," Bash said. "When they explained this to the mother, she absolutely refused to move out of this house. Not only did she refuse to move out, she couldn't understand why they would want to separate and be living in two different houses."

Richard was never particularly fond of the Newville house and agreed that he and Karen would move to Lubec Street, while Agnes and Harold stayed at Newville. The decision to move in together seemed natural for Karen and Richard, whose careers came first. They were first and foremost a team and at this point saw no reason to live separately. "If we don't see each other, we talk at least twice a day," Karen said in 1981. "We always have to know what the other one is doing. We're very nosy!"

To many on the outside looking in, siblings living together as adults seemed odd and prompted allegations of incest. Brian Southall, who joined A&M Records' London team in 1973, fought off reporters' questions about this brother-sister relationship that sometimes appeared a little too close. They were, after all, a duo that sang love songs. "There were lots of suggestions about their relationship," Southall said in a 2004 interview. "There was always a worry about the questions that would come out. There were suggestions of an incestuous relationship and stuff like that, which was utter nonsense. But they *were* an odd couple."

According to Karen, over the years and especially near the beginning of their careers, many people thought she and Richard were married. "I remember once when we were looking for an apartment in California, and the landlady asked if we had any kids. 'No,' we said, telling the truth. 'That's good,' she replied, 'and I hope you haven't got any pets either.' And the photographers were always asking us to kiss! Well, you might hold your brother's hand, but you don't kiss him unless it's a family reunion."

Richard said, "Maybe it would have been easier if we *had* been man and wife," with Karen adding, "It's been a hell of a battle. We were mistaken for a married couple for so long. How could anyone fail to recognize us as brother and sister? We're so alike. When we smile we could be Siamese twins."

Unfortunately for the Carpenters, Southall was not present to screen a disastrous phone interview broadcast live on Toronto radio. "We might as well bring it out," the deejay told Richard. "I've listened to the lyrics of your songs. I know that Karen's singing them to you. I know they're about incest. You want to talk about this?" Richard was so caught off guard that he tried to explain how that was untrue. "Absolutely not," he said. "I don't even write all of those songs. They just happen to be love songs. Karen sings them. I sing and arrange. We happen to be brother and sister." Surprisingly, Richard finished the interview, at which time he slammed down the receiver, vowing to never do another phone interview.

"WE'VE MADE it a rule that whoever we go out with must not interfere with our professional lives," Karen explained in a 1976 interview. "I feel if Richard is going out with the wrong girl, I tell him. He needs someone who will give him a good home, security, and children—someone who will understand him because he's a special guy."

Shortly after moving to Lubec Street, Richard began dating Randy Bash, Sherwin's twenty-one-year-old daughter. Some felt she was pushed by her father into dating Richard, but even Karen was fond of her at first and seemed to approve of the burgeoning relationship. But just three weeks in, Agnes chimed in with her critique, and Richard carelessly told Randy of his mother's dislike for her. By the time Randy joined the Carpenters on their European tour in February 1974, Richard was well aware that both his mother and sister had it in for her. Despite the young girl's attempts to be friendly and have lunch or go shopping, Karen ignored and avoided Randy for the duration of the tour. "Richard can have his girl travel with him—she has no career," Karen told the *Los Angeles Times* that year, her antipathy apparent. "But what about me? Is my guy supposed to lay around all day while we're on the road?"

Returning to Los Angeles, Karen was up in arms when Richard invited Randy to move in with them. "Randy came into the picture, and then all hell broke loose," says Maria Galeazzi. "Then Karen didn't mind me as much as she did her because she picked up her bags and moved right in! It came back to bite her." Karen told Richard she would not move the rest of her belongings out of Newville until "that girl" was no longer living under their roof.

After only a week of intense pressure from Karen, Richard told Randy she could not stay. Technically, it was both his and his sister's house, and they were obviously not going to agree on the matter. Although she packed her things and left, Randy continued to sleep there most every night. "She wasn't that particular in what, if anything, she ran around the house in," recalls Evelyn Wallace. After failing to successfully evict Randy from Lubec Street, Karen made it clear to Richard she no longer wanted to wake up in her own house only to find his naked girlfriend had slept over again. She was moving back home to Newville.

⚬⚬⚬

WHEN KAREN began dating tall, handsome record executive Mike Curb, the new love interest became a much-needed distraction from her brother's personal affairs. "It evolved," Curb recalls of his relationship with Karen. "Richard and I both had sisters, and I think we were all very comfortable together." The sibling friendships began when Mike and his sister Carole joined Karen and Richard for dinners in the home of mutual friends Ed and Frenda Leffler. The couples also enjoyed evenings of conversation over food and wine at Jack's at the Beach, a favorite restaurant on the Ocean Park Pier in Santa Monica.

Mike was taken with Karen's love of life, music, and children. In return, she was impressed by his kindhearted personality, his confident nature, and his good looks. In contrast with Karen's history of sabotaging her brother's relationships, Richard was thrilled with her choice of mate this time. "I think Richard was happy that she was dating someone, and I think he liked me," Curb says. "I liked him." Richard and Mike started a tradition of music trivia matches. "He was certainly a much better musician than I, but at the time I was a successful record producer." In addition to the Osmonds, Curb produced Donny Osmond as a solo artist and was just beginning to work with the sibling duo of Donny and Marie. He was named *Billboard* Producer of the Year for 1972 in recognition of his production of both Sammy Davis Jr.'s "The Candy Man" and Donny Osmond's "Puppy Love." He would later produce Debby Boone's "You Light Up My Life," the biggest selling record of the decade.

Visiting the Carpenters at A&M Records was a treat for Curb, who enjoyed watching other artists work and the various production techniques employed. "Being a producer, I marveled at the way Richard and Karen worked together," he says. "Neither one of them ever made small talk. It was always music, records, or something she'd heard on the radio. I have never seen any two people more committed to their careers. Their records never sounded overproduced. They were perfectly produced, but they had just enough edge that they were really right for the moment and the radio."

Karen and Mike found it taxing to juggle their busy careers and still make time for dates and other opportunities to be together. "I was running MGM Records and producing records at that time, and she was constantly recording and traveling," Curb explains. "She would go away on international tours for quite a while, so we were unable to spend as much time together as we wanted to." When openings in their schedules did coincide, Karen and Mike would drive to Newport Beach or San Diego for a boat ride around the harbor.

For their dinner dates, Curb would often drive to Newville to pick up his girlfriend. "I could have been picking up the girl next door," he says, recalling her unaffected personality. "She never ever got caught up in the trappings of being a successful artist. Aside from maybe a gold record on the wall or a Grammy award on the table, it was just like you were going to your next-door neighbor's home. It was such a pleasure to be with her because she just loved music, loved life, loved her family, and was so unaffected. I never remember her going out and buying clothes or talking about trendy things. To her, her whole world was her brother, her family, the parents."

Although they sometimes went for dinner at Knott's Berry Farm in Buena Park, both Karen and Mike favored intimate surroundings. "Both of us preferred something more private," he says. "Not something where fifty people would come up to us. But I went to the Grammys with her and the American Music Awards, too, so we did some public things." One of the couple's first public outings was a double date with Richard and Randy Bash to the Grammy Awards on March 2, 1974, Karen's twenty-fourth birthday.

From the start of their relationship, Curb recalls Karen was always on a diet. "She was always concerned that when she ate her weight went to her hips, so she wouldn't eat," he says. "She always worried about her hips, and that's one of the reasons she wanted to stay at the drums." On May 22, 1974, the Carpenters were photographed at home by Annie Leibovitz for an upcoming *Rolling Stone* cover story. Karen was pleased to have lost some excess weight around her arms and buttocks, and to show off her new figure she wore a new pair of jeans and a tank top. It was a casual and laid-back approach, in contrast with the years of posing cheek to cheek with Richard, wearing matching formalwear. Karen looked radiant and was the picture of good health. Friends were noticing and telling her how great she looked, but no one saw it as obsessive in the beginning, just normal dieting.

Initially, Curb was not alarmed either, but as time went on he started to recognize Karen was establishing the eating patterns and rituals that would proliferate over the coming years. "I noticed very definitely that she was trying to lose weight by just not eating. She would order a meal and maybe eat 25 percent of her food. She was just sort of moving the food around her plate. My sister Carole had the same problem. She and Karen would just *not eat*."

During their dinners, Karen reminded Mike her diet was such a success she could not stop and risk gaining the weight back. "You look *great*," he affirmed. "Now let's eat!" Or he would say, "You only ate a third of your plate. Let's stay until you eat it all." With his urging, she would usually eat her entire meal. Even Richard noticed that Karen seemed to behave differently and eat more sensibly in Mike's presence. "How are you getting her to eat?" he asked.

"I would actually *insist* that she eat," Curb says. "I would tell her that she looked great and that she should eat. And she would eat!"

After dinner, Mike would sometimes drive Karen to A&M, where she would meet Richard for a recording session. "She liked to record at night," Curb says. "I stayed enough to see how incredibly talented Richard was. He was amazing, and she had such respect for him. I remember just being stunned." Curb was even more amazed when he first heard Karen's voice up close and unaccompanied while driving with her to A&M. "She was rehearsing a song and looking at a piece of sheet music," he says. "When she sang in a car you could barely hear her voice, but when she got on a microphone it was like velvet. It was a very, very amazing thing. So many singers think they always have to belt out a song. Karen had one of the softest voices in the world, but when you put that voice on a *microphone*?!"

Despite the couple's commonalities and mutual admiration, dates between Karen and Mike Curb became more and more sporadic due to their career obligations, and they grew apart. "She went on a long tour, and we started seeing each other less and less," Curb recalls. "It was really two people that were just so busy. It never really broke up."

———— ∞∞∞ ————

DESPITE THE fact that the Carpenters' greatest successes stemmed from their recordings, they spent the majority of their professional time on tour. The average Carpenters record took between four and five months to produce. The remainder of the year was spent playing night after night across the country and around the world, in addition to making various personal and television appearances. In 1971 the Carpenters played upward of 150 shows. During 1972 and 1973 they did 174 concerts each year. After six weeks of one-nighters—which was common during those seasons—Karen and Richard were exhausted. While they enjoyed performing, it became a never-ending succession of plane trips, motels, hotels, rehearsals, and sound checks that got them down.

The year 1974 began with the Carpenters greatest hits album, *The Singles 1969–1973*, topping the *Billboard* album charts in the United States. The collection was the duo's first and only #1 album, fueled by nine previous million-sellers, and sales would eventually top twelve million units in the United States alone. It also topped the UK album chart for seventeen weeks between February and July.

The promotional push for the *Singles* album came in the form of the duo's second #1 single, "Top of the World." The Carpenters and A&M Records had certainly underestimated the song's potential when recorded for 1972's *A Song for You*. All involved felt it was a nice album cut but never considered it for single release. Some Top 40 stations had programmed the song based solely upon requests, and in Japan it was culled as a single and quickly went to #1. Carpenters audiences had broken into applause at just the mention of the song once they added it to their live set in the summer of 1972. "All of a sudden people were standing up and cheering," John Bettis recalled. "Richard was kind of scratching his head and saying, 'What *is* all this?'"

When it came around to the *Singles* album, Richard decided "Top of the World" simply must be the next Carpenters single. "A&M took a little bit of convincing," Bettis said. "We're talking about the group that did 'Superstar,' "We've Only Just Begun,' and 'Goodbye to Love' coming along with a country number." Karen re-recorded her lead vocal, and other alterations were made to the recording before the new "Top of the World" was remixed and readied for release. "Then Richard had to hold the release of our single," Bettis said. Country crooner Lynn Anderson released her version of the song—a virtual clone of Richard's arrangement—which quickly climbed to #2 on the country music chart. "We didn't want to make anybody mad because we killed their record," explained Bettis. "We actually had to wait to release that record until Lynn Anderson's had died off the charts."

Additionally, the Carpenters' debut single, "Ticket to Ride," got a facelift for *The Singles*. The original 1969 version was a rare instance where tape captured Karen singing consistently under pitch. Drums were re-recorded, Tony Peluso added a guitar track, and Karen cut a much-improved lead vocal for the new release.

Following the hits album's success came a year of 203 concerts with sold-out tours across Europe, Japan, and the United States. A weeklong stop at New York's Westbury Music Fair was followed by two separate four-week stints in Las Vegas at the Riviera and two weeks at the Sahara in Lake Tahoe. The October run at the Riviera was recorded for an intended live album release that never came to fruition. They also participated in a televised concert with Arthur Fiedler and the Boston Pops and, as they had done in 1971, sold out 18,000 seats to fill the Hollywood Bowl.

Leaving Los Angeles on May 27, the Carpenters headed to Japan, where their shows were enjoyed by 85,000 fans. Tickets to their three weeks of concerts had sold out in less than an hour. "It was during their golden years when they were bigger than the Beatles," says Denny Brooks, a Cal State Long Beach alumnus who frequently toured as the Carpenters' opening act. "I'm an old folkie from the sixties. I really never had any great record success. I was just a good, working act. They were touring all these different countries, and instead of taking a comedian like a lot of these acts did during that time, they took me, just a guy and his guitar."

The Carpenters likened their 1974 touchdown in Japan to the Beatles on *The Ed Sullivan Show*, a mob scene of screaming fans rocking the limousines and pulling at their clothes. "It was outrageous," Brooks says. "Five thousand people at the Tokyo airport was really crazy, but it was a good time. I remember us doing one-nighters all over Japan, something like twenty-eight nights in thirty days in every single town."

Surprisingly, no one in the Carpenters' entourage ever complained to management about the grueling touring schedule the group was subjected to. Richard felt they were not so much overworked but overbooked. "I don't think he was ever truly happy on the road," Sherwin Bash recalled. But Bash continued to book them, filling each and every open date in their already bulging itineraries. "They were always huffing and puffing about having such a grueling schedule," Maria Galeazzi recalls. "These managers don't have any mind for the long run. They want to get the most of them—get it and get it now. . . . Sometimes you wake up in the middle of the night and you don't know where you are. The schedule was usually six weeks in a row, which takes its toll, not so much on the other people but on Karen."

Signs of Karen's stress would surface from time to time, as A&M Records' UK press officer Brian Southall remembers. He received a warning from others at the label in advance of the Carpenters' arrival in London that year. "Karen's the one you don't cross," he was told. "Karen was on an edge," Southall later recalled. "You crossed her at your peril. That was sort of the warning we were given before we started." One evening during a sold-out charity show at the Talk of the Town nightclub, the band was having fun and enjoying some spontaneity in their performance during the last night of the show. "But that was not allowed to happen," Southall observed. "[Karen] was on them like a ton of bricks. The show had to be *exactly* the same as every other show they had done. It was the first time that I had realized that the ad-libs were actually not ad-libs, they were the same ad-libs from the night before. . . . The guys in the band weren't drunk, they weren't falling about. They just wanted to have a little bit of spontaneity. It was frightening to watch when these guys got torn apart."

Maria Galeazzi witnessed the reprimands during her time on the road with the group, too. "Richard was very intense and very dedicated," she says. "He was more methodical and would explain, 'We have to do this the next show or that the next show.' Karen would be more like, 'You screwed up!'"

By 1974 everyone needed a break. Richard and Sherwin have both claimed they never saw the Carpenters as a trendy act that would come and go, but their career appears to have been handled in such a way that someone felt exploitation was the necessary means to success, even if it only proved to be in the form of short-term financial success. But even the financial successes were not of great substance. Their attorney, Werner Wolfen, put pen to paper and later informed the Carpenters they would not see a cent of profit until they had performed a minimum of 150 shows in any given year.

Concert reviews from this period agreed that the Carpenters needed time to relax and regroup. One such review for a show at the Sahara Tahoe appeared in *Variety*: "Not much showmanship... they sorely need advice on stage presentation and pace.... Attending a show is no more than listening to an album." It was true. A Carpenters concert was almost more of a recital of hit songs. From Karen and Richard came rigid directives to their band that every note must sound exactly as it did on the LP. "They were consummate musicians," says Denny Brooks. "There wasn't a lot of patter between songs, they just kept knocking out hit after hit after hit."

Although little time remained for recording, Karen and Richard managed to release three singles in 1974: "I Won't Last a Day Without You" (by then two years old and the fifth single culled from their mammoth hit album *A Song for You*), "Santa Claus Is Comin' to Town" (a track they put to tape in 1972), and one new recording, "Please Mr. Postman." Following closely on the heels of the success of their *Now and Then* album and its side of oldies, the Carpenters decided to record "Postman" as a stand-alone oldie. When the Carpenters' version became their third #1 single, it also marked the second time the song reached the top position on the Hot 100. In 1961 the original recording by the Marvelettes was the first #1 record to come out of Motown Records. It was also a popular album track on the Beatles' 1963 *With the Beatles* album.

<hr>

"Ev, WOULD you do me a favor?"

As she would often do, Karen came to Evelyn Wallace asking for assistance, but she usually prefaced her requests with this polite inquiry. "It kind of tickled me," Wallace recalls.

"Karen, you're my *boss*," she would respond. "All you have to do is say, 'Ev, do this,' or 'Ev, do that.' I'd be happy to. You don't have to ask me, just tell me what you want done, and I'll do it.'" Both women laughed at these exchanges.

It was Halloween 1974. Although Karen had moved back in with Agnes and Harold, it was only to be a short-term stay and a temporary solution. She asked Werner Wolfen to start searching for real estate, preferably a nice condominium and one situated away from Downey. "She wanted me to tell her mother that she wanted to look around for an apartment," Wallace explains. "Karen really wanted to move out of the house. I think her mother was getting her down to the point where she wanted out."

"Will you ask her for me?" Karen pleaded.

"Karen, I'd do anything you asked me, and I will ask her. It would be best for everybody if you can, but I don't think you're going to have much luck."

"OK," Karen said. "Just wait until I am gone."

After Karen left the house, Evelyn approached Agnes as she sat at the kitchen table. "The kids are at that age now, you know," she began cautiously. "They've kind of, well, really got it made. You know?" Agnes's brow raised in anticipation of the next words. "Karen would kind of like to find a place and move into a little apartment by herself. A lot of the kids her age have been doing it for a while now."

Agnes jumped from the table, leaving Evelyn midsentence. "Well, you'd think that I had hit her over the head with a brick," Wallace says. "She jumped out of her chair and she ran to that phone and she called Karen, and she was screaming at her and calling her a traitor and asking how she could think such a thing." Evelyn quietly picked up her purse, slipped out the door, and headed home. "I didn't want to slam the door and let her know I was going because I thought she'd come running after me," she says. "She'd think that I gave that idea to Karen to move out, but I didn't. It was a surprise when Karen asked me to do that. That was the worst thing she ever asked me to do, but I would have died for that girl. She was such a lovely person."

9

THE COLLAPSE

I N 1996, Rob Hoerburger concisely and powerfully summed up
Karen Carpenter's tribulations in a *New York Times Magazine* feature: "If anorexia has classically been defined as a young woman's
struggle for control, then Karen was a prime candidate, for the two
things she valued most in the world—her voice and her mother's love—
were exclusively the property of Richard. At least she would control
the size of her own body." And control it she did. By September 1975
her weight dropped to ninety-one pounds.

Karen's quest to be thin seems to have begun innocently enough
just after high school graduation when she started the Stillman water
diet. Although she was never obese, she was what most would consider
a chubby seventeen-year-old at 145 pounds. She leveled off around 120
pounds and maintained her weight by eating sensibly but not starving
herself. Even so, eating while on tour was problematic for Karen, as she
described in 1973: "When you're on the road it's kind of hard to eat.
Period. On top of that, it's really rough to eat *well*. We don't like to eat
before a show because I can't stand singing with a full stomach.... You
never get to dinner until like midnight or one o'clock, and at that time
if you eat heavy you're not going to sleep, and if you eat heavy you're
going to be a balloon."

Maria Galeazzi never witnessed any eating habits she considered to
be compulsive or irrational during her years on tour with Karen. "When

I was with her she didn't have an eating problem," Galeazzi says. "She always watched her weight because she had a problem with her hips. She was a little bit heavier around there, but she wasn't fat. She never made any comments but always watched what she ate. For instance, she would have two strips of bacon instead of four, or one egg instead of two, but not anything obsessive. I never saw her look in the mirror and say, 'Oh, I'm so fat.' Not ever. I have no idea what triggered it."

Karen was shocked when she saw photos taken during an August 1973 Lake Tahoe concert where an unflattering outfit accentuated her paunch. This prompted her to seek the assistance of a personal trainer, who made visits to her home and recommended a diet low in calories but high in carbohydrates. Instead of slimming down as she had hoped, Karen started to put on muscle and bulk up following this new regimen. Watching the Carpenters' appearance on a Bob Hope television special that fall, she remarked that she had put on some extra weight. Richard agreed she looked a bit heavier. She was quite discouraged and vowed she was going to "do something about it."

Karen's first order of business was to fire her trainer, and she immediately set out on a mission to shed the unwanted pounds on her own. She purchased a hip cycle, which she used each morning on her bed, and because it was portable the equipment was packed and taken with her on tour. "She was working on it," remembers Denny Brooks, who was along for several Carpenters tours during the mid-1970s. "She was a little thick through the hips and thighs and middle. I know that concerned her," he says.

"She lost around twenty pounds and she looked fabulous," recalls Carole Curb. "She weighed about 110 or so, and she looked amazing. . . . If she'd just been able to stop there then life would have been beautiful. A lot of us girls in that era went through moments of that. Everybody wanted to be Twiggy. Just about everybody in the world has some sort of eating disorder—they eat too much or they eat too little. Karen's just got carried away. She just couldn't stop."

Having witnessed Karen's meticulous routine of counting calories and planning food intake for every meal, Richard complimented her initial weight loss during a break from recording as the two dined at the

Au Petit Café, a favorite French bistro on Vine Street near the A&M studios. "You look *great*," he told her.

"Well, I'm just going to get down to around 105."

"A hundred and *five*? You look great now."

Karen's response worried Richard. In fact, this was the first time he paused to consider that she might be taking the diet too far.

"With their success and being up on stage, she attempted to slim down and look a little better in a feminine sort of way," said Sherwin Bash, recalling her as a stocky tomboy prior to 1974. "Karen lost probably twenty pounds and looked terrific.... This didn't satisfy her because she needed more. She needed attention, love, care, and all the things that go with the success of losing that weight. Failing to get it, she continued to lose weight and became painfully thin.... Obviously she was looking at herself and seeing somebody that no one else saw; someone who was unattractive and overweight."

As Mike Curb had witnessed a year earlier, friends and family began to notice extreme changes in Karen's eating habits, despite her attempts at subtlety. She rearranged and pushed her food around the plate with a fork as she talked, which gave the appearance of eating. Another of her strategies involved offering samples of her food to others around the table. She would rave on and on about her delicious meal and then insist that everyone at the table try it for themselves. "Here, *you* have some," she would say as she enthusiastically scooped heaps of her own meal onto others' plates. "Would you like to taste this?" By the time dinner was over, Karen's plate was clean, but she had dispersed her entire meal to everyone else. Agnes caught on to this ploy and began to do the same in return. "Well, *this* is good, too," she would say as she put more food onto her daughter's plate. This infuriated Karen, who realized she would have to find other ways to successfully avoid eating.

⸺⸙⸺

THUMBING THROUGH a copy of *Reader's Digest*, Evelyn Wallace discovered an article detailing a teen girl's obsession with dieting. "She was doing the same things that Karen was doing, like playing with her food or leaving it," Wallace says. "She was somehow always getting away with not eating." The following is excerpted from the January 1975 issue of the *Digest*.

> The young high school sophomore weighed 135 pounds—about five pounds more than average for her height—and decided to diet. But when she reached her proper weight, she went right on depriving herself of food. Eight months later she entered a hospital weighing seventy-four pounds, the victim of self-inflicted starvation. Her bizarre affliction is known as anorexia nervosa.
>
> An emotional disorder that affects thousands of young women during high school and college years, the disturbance appears to be increasing rapidly. Dr. Hilde Bruch, professor of psychiatry at Baylor College of Medicine in Houston, believes that the national preoccupation with slimness plays a part in anorexia nervosa but that the condition is too complex to be defined simply as diet consciousness. The patient's refusal to eat, followed by grotesque emaciation, is the physical symptom of a deep-seated psychological disturbance. Most psychiatrists agree that the cure is twofold: putting back the weight to get the patient out of immediate danger and reaching the underlying emotional problems through psychotherapy.

Although she usually tried to steer clear of personal matters involving her employers, Wallace immediately recognized the parallels between this girl's story and Karen's, and she was alarmed. She went to Agnes with the magazine and read the article aloud. "I think Karen has what this little girl did," she told her. "Really, someone should be *doing* something about it or she'll end up the same way."

Evelyn did not feel it was her place to confront Karen on the matter but suggested to Agnes that Karen might need to see a doctor before the matter worsened. "I didn't want [Karen] to be angry with me and get the idea that I was trying to play doctor, and so I never mentioned the article to her. I showed it to Agnes and told her it was up to her." The magazine remained on the parents' bedside table for several weeks. "I don't think she ever showed it to Karen."

Cherry Boone O'Neill, oldest daughter of entertainer Pat Boone and member of the singing Boone Family, was suffering in a manner very similar to Karen. "I had never heard the term 'anorexia' or even the phrase 'eating disorder' until I was twenty years old in 1974," she says. "When I was seventeen, our pediatrician said he had seen people with my condition before and would have to hospitalize me if I didn't gain weight, but he never mentioned the name of the condition at that point. Finally, after struggling with both anorexia and bulimia for years and thinking that I was an isolated freak, I read an article in a news magazine that described anorexia and bulimia, and it made me realize I was not the only one struggling with these problems. The article didn't really tell me how to overcome my challenges, but it made me feel less alone, and it gave my condition a name. It identified the enemy."

By the time Karen's weight dropped to near ninety pounds, she looked for ways to disguise the weight loss, especially around those she knew would make comments or pester her to eat more. She began to layer her clothing, a strategy Sherwin Bash noticed in the early part of 1975. "She would start with a long-sleeved shirt and then put a blouse over that," he explained, "and a sweater over that and a jacket over that. . . . With all of it you had no idea of what she had become." But Evelyn Wallace was shocked when she caught a glimpse of Karen's gaunt figure as she sunbathed topless in back of the Newville house one afternoon. "They put this screen around her so nobody else could see her," Wallace explains. "She *loved* to go lay out in the sunshine. I don't know whether it was to get a tan or get away from her mother. Anyhow, I happened to go out to the kitchen for something and I saw her out there. She just had on her little bathing suit shorts. You couldn't tell whether it was a girl or a boy. She had absolutely no breasts."

———— ∞∞ ————

IN FEBRUARY 1975 Karen met Terry Ellis, a friend of Ed and Frenda Leffler. Ellis had formed the British record label Chrysalis in 1969. Although he was based in London, where he helped guide the careers of Jethro Tull, Leo Sayer, and others, Ellis had recently bought a home in Los Angeles and was working to expand his label's presence in America. With the intent of matchmaking, Frenda introduced the two over dinner. As Ellis recalls, "I was a single guy, she was a single girl. Frenda

said, 'You two lovely people should meet!' I liked Karen a lot on that
first meeting. It was very difficult *not* to like Karen."

Karen was equally enthralled. Thirty-two-year-old Ellis was tall,
with long, sandy blond hair to his shoulders and striking facial features.
"He was *very* handsome," recalls Frenda. "He was a bon vivant. He
drove a Bentley and was a man about town. He was just private jets
all the way."

The dinner date with the Lefflers became the first of many, and a
new relationship soon blossomed. According to Ellis, "We liked each
other, made contact later, and started to see each other." Ellis observed
that, unlike the rest of the Carpenter family, Karen was quite demonstrative and seemed to thrive on physical touch. "She was very loving
and tactile, and she *loved* to be hugged." Those close to the couple
sensed a strong chemistry between the two. Most important to Karen
was that Richard approve of the man in her life, and he did. He and
Terry Ellis quickly became friends.

Early in their relationship, Ellis encouraged Karen to take some time
off to rest and relax with him on vacation in the south of France and
on Tortola in the Virgin Islands. Arriving at Ellis's island home, Karen
was horrified by a lack of creature comforts. With Terry out of earshot
she phoned Frenda to rant about her surroundings. "Frenny, it's hard to
believe they've even got *phones* over here," she said. "There's not even
a television set!"

Frenda worried Karen would board the next plane back to Los Angeles. "You could never put Karen anywhere where there wasn't television," she explains. "She was regimented. Most people would adapt.
Not Karen."

With Ellis's experience and expertise in the field of entertainment
management and the record industry in general, it was only a matter of
time before he became a part of Karen's professional as well as personal
life. "I was an outsider, and it really wasn't my business," he says, but
when he attended his first Carpenters concert he was flabbergasted by
the lack of professionalism he witnessed in their stage show. "I watched
them perform, and my mouth dropped because she was a terrible performer," he says. "She hadn't the slightest idea about how to use a stage.

She did everything wrong. She wasn't using her vivacious personality or her wonderful smile. She wasn't using the fact that the audiences absolutely worshiped her. She'd sing a song, and when the guitar player or drummer played a little solo she'd turn her back on the audience and sort of click her fingers and had no interrelation with the audience. Anybody who goes near stage when they're six years old learns that you never, ever, ever turn your back on an audience. I just simply couldn't believe they had so-called top-class management and nobody had taken her by the hand and said, 'Karen, let's work on your stage show.' They could have hired somebody to produce their show."

Terry could not hold back. He was an expert in concert construction and was accustomed to evaluating his artists after every show in an effort to continuously better their performances. Back at the hotel, Karen was shocked by his blunt analysis. "Karen, I'm sorry to say this, but you were *terrible*," he said. "Now, that's the bad news. But the good news is that you're never going to be that terrible again! Tomorrow I'm taking you onto the stage, and I am going to teach you some fundamentals."

The two walked the stage as Ellis explained that Karen should never stand in front of Cubby O'Brien or Tony Peluso with her back to the audience during their solos. She should face the audience, walk toward them, and interact.

"What do you mean?" she asked.

"Go to the front of the stage and reach your hand out," he instructed.

"Well, why should I do that?"

"Well, the audience will like it!"

"Well, what will they do?"

"Well, they'll jump up and they'll hold your hand."

"No they won't!"

"Yes, Karen, they will. And they will absolutely love it!"

Ellis continued, explaining to Karen that she had ignored the audience members seated in the balcony the night before. "Walk out to the edge of the stage and look up to the people in the balcony and wave at them," he said.

"Oh, I can't do *that!*"

"Well, yes you can, Karen. They'll love it."

"And what will they do?"

"They'll *wave back*, Karen!"

"No they won't," she said. "They won't!"

She argued, but Karen took the stage that night and took command in a way she had never done before. The interaction with the audience was a natural for her, but for some reason she had avoided such communication in the past. "She was like a kid in a candy store," recalls Ellis. "She discovered something that made life more exciting and more fulfilling."

As Evelyn Wallace recalls, "All of a sudden, here she was moving her arms and walking from one side of the stage to the other so that everybody could see her. It didn't take her long to realize she had to move around and interact more."

Karen's sudden on-stage blossoming took Richard by surprise. According to Terry Ellis, he reacted badly to the change in the dynamic, which was curious since it was at his urging that Karen left the drums for the forefront in the first place. "Richard had been so used to being the focus of everybody's attention that it came as something of a shock to him and something he found difficult to handle. It upset him. He couldn't understand why she was getting attention and he wasn't. At one point in Las Vegas, he was having a bit of a rant about how unappreciated he was and that nobody knew what he did—and he wasn't wrong about that. He was the musical genius behind the Carpenters, but nobody was taking any trouble to ensure that he got the credit he deserved. Karen was the focus of attention. She was the girl with the golden voice; the voice of an angel."

When Ellis arrived in Las Vegas for a series of shows, he discovered Richard was furious after having been introduced as 'the piano player with the Carpenters' during a panel discussion for *Billboard* magazine. "Have you discussed this with your managers?" Ellis asked. "Are they *doing* anything about it?"

"Well," Richard said, "no."

In Las Vegas the Carpenters were augmented by a large orchestra backing their own group. At the beginning of every show the conductor would lead the orchestra in playing an overture just prior to Karen and Richard's entrance. Ellis made one suggestion to Richard. "Rather than you just shambling onto the stage playing the piano, let's let the audiences know who and what you are. Let's have you come out at the first on the stage and *you* conduct the overture!" In Ellis's opinion, an orchestral conductor was a position of command, responsibility, and authority. "That immediately establishes you as someone who is a bit special and not just the piano player." Ellis was happy to help but felt he might have overstepped some boundaries in coaching Karen and Richard. He blamed management—particularly Sherwin Bash—for not having addressed these issues much earlier. "Basically, you're both being held back by your manager," he told them.

"Karen and Richard were kids from Downey, and the show business world was a bit overpowering to them," Ellis explains. "They were excited and felt very lucky that they seemed to have had some breaks. They had a fairly well-known manager, and they felt they were very fortunate to have him, but he did a terrible, terrible job. There was no career plan. There was no one thinking about the long term prospects for the Carpenters or for Richard or for Karen. I don't think anybody was sitting down with them and saying, 'Let's talk about your career and work out how we're going to make this last until you're fifty, sixty, or seventy years old.'"

BY THE time *Horizon* saw release in June 1975, two years had passed since the Carpenters' previous studio album. Disappointing to some was its brevity, clocking in at just under thirty-five minutes in duration, but the tremendous advances in sound quality due to new and improved recording techniques prevailed. The debut *Offering* album was completed using only eight tracks, while the Carpenters' next four LPs were recorded on sixteen. *Horizon* was the first to take advantage of A&M's graduation to twenty-four-track recording, and it did not go unnoticed. Stephen Holden of *Rolling Stone* called it their "most musically sophisticated album to date," saying it "smoothly adapts the spirit of mainstream Fifties pop to contemporary taste. . . . Karen Carpenter has developed into a fine vocal technician, whose mellow interpretation of the Eagles' 'Desperado' and Neil Sedaka's 'Solitaire' evidence professionalism on a par with such Fifties stars as Jo Stafford and Rosemary Clooney.... Richard Carpenter has imposed more elaborately orchestrated textures than before and wisely mixed them at a level that doesn't distract attention from Karen's intimately mixed singing."

Within two weeks of its release, *Horizon* was certified gold. Although it reached the top of the charts in the United Kingdom and Japan, the album missed the U.S. Top 10 when it peaked at #13. According to Richard, the single "Only Yesterday" was one of their better technical achievements, in which he employed a Phil Spector "wall of sound" approach. Even so, the song's success cost him and John Bettis the thousand dollars they bet a studio engineer that it would not be a hit. According to Bettis, sitting down to write "Only Yesterday" he thought to himself, "Oh boy, here we go again—another *yesterday* song." He was able to avoid the sad and somewhat melancholy approach taken in "Goodbye to Love" and "Yesterday Once More," turning this song into an upbeat, optimistic love song and one about "being in love *now*," he explained. "And yesterday was not so good because you weren't here."

In 1991, while remixing various tracks for a Japanese karaoke compilation, Richard discovered an unmarked, forgotten *Horizon* outtake on a multitrack tape for "Only Yesterday." It was Karen's work lead with piano, bass, and drums for the David Pomeranz tune, "Trying to Get the Feeling Again," recorded in 1975. It became the title track for a Barry Manilow album released four months after *Horizon* and a hit single for him in 1976. The Carpenters' version was abandoned when Richard decided the album had plenty of strong ballads. It remained unfinished and was somehow never cataloged into A&M's tape library. Adding a twenty-four-piece string section, acoustic guitar, electric guitar, and synthesizer, Richard completed their version of "Trying to Get the Feeling Again" for *Interpretations: A 25th Anniversary Celebration* released in 1994.

Legendary arranger Billy May's lush treatment of the Andrews Sisters' "I Can Dream, Can't I?" was one of several big band ballads Karen recorded during her career, and according to Holden of *Rolling Stone*, "such a gem of updated schmaltz, it makes me wish that veteran masters of the studio like Gordon Jenkins, Ray Ellis, Nelson Riddle and Percy Faith would be encouraged to collaborate with other best selling middle of the road acts of the Seventies."

Jazz critic Dave Gelly agreed and took notice of Karen's careful attention to microphone technique. "She sings very close to the microphone, starting at around Julie London or Peggy Lee volume, that's to say, not much more than a whisper. Then, she gradually opens up to about Jo Stafford level. No tears, no dramatics—just plain, unfussy and beautifully done."

Ken Barnes's review for *Phonograph Record* called *Horizon* "soft-rock Nirvana," going on to say, "It's certainly less than revolutionary to admit you like the Carpenters these days (in rock circles, if you recall, it formerly bordered on heresy). Everybody must be won over by now. . . . If all MOR were this good, one might not resent its all-out appropriation of the airwaves. . . . As for the Carpenters, they've transcended the genre and stand in a class by themselves."

KAREN'S NEW slim figure required that she purchase a new stage wardrobe, and she opted for a number of low-cut silky gowns, some strapless or even backless. Sherwin Bash was horrified to see her bony shoulders and ribs. Even her hip bones were visible through the thin layers of fabric. He asked Karen to rethink the wardrobe choices before going on stage. "I talked her into putting a jacket on over the bare back and bare arms," he said, "but the audience saw it."

There was often a collective gasp from the audience when Karen would take the stage. In fact, after a few shows, Bash was approached by concerned fans who knew something was terribly wrong but assumed she had cancer or some other disease. Even critics took note of her gaunt appearance. A review for *Variety* praised Karen's exit from the drums but commented on her deteriorating appearance. "She is terribly thin, almost a wraith, and should be gowned more becomingly."

It became increasingly obvious to Terry Ellis that his girlfriend's dieting was far more complex than a simple attempt to shed a few pounds. Even in the few months since the two had met, Karen had withered before Terry's eyes. "When she went onstage she usually had some backless outfit on," he recalls. "You could see her shoulder blades and ribs sticking out. You could tell that she was much thinner than she ought to be."

Five days of shows at Connecticut's Oakdale Theater in Wallingford were attended by many of the duo's childhood friends. Agnes and Harold flew in for the week and were met at their hotel by Carl and Teresa Vaiuso, who drove them to the show. The Oakdale was just fifteen miles north of New Haven's Hall Street, where the couples had first met and raised their families nearly twenty years earlier. "[Harold] was beside himself," Teresa recalled. "As soon as we picked them up, that was the first thing he said. He said, 'She's not fooling me, I know what's wrong with Karen. She has anorexia nervosa.' That was the first time I ever really heard that. I thought, 'What is he saying? Could this be true?' And sure enough, when we went to see her, that's exactly what she had. The father was right."

According to John Bettis, no one really understood why Karen wasn't eating. To those around her the solution seemed simple: *eat.* "Anorexia nervosa was so new to me that I didn't even know how to pronounce it until 1980," he said. "From the outside the solution looks so simple. All a person has to do is eat. So we were constantly trying to shove food at Karen. . . . My opinion about anorexia is it's an attempt to have control; something in your life that you can do something about, that you can regiment. I think that just got out of control with her."

Cherry O'Neill confirms that control was most definitely a factor in her own struggles. "When you start denying yourself food and begin feeling you have control over a life that has been pretty much controlled for you, it's exhilarating. The anorexic feels that while she may not be able to control anything else, she will, by God, control every morsel that goes in her mouth."

In contrast with Karen's dieting rituals, Terry Ellis was a connoisseur of both wine and fine dining. He enjoyed participating in long, leisurely dinners at many of the top restaurants across Europe. Karen would order her usual salad and push the greens around the plate while drinking water with dozens of lemons.

It was not long before Ellis witnessed the habits the rest of Karen's friends and family had observed for many months. She pretended to eat a lot, when in reality she was allocating the food to those around her. On one particular instance, out to dinner with the band, Karen ordered a huge slice of cake at the end of meal. "She made a big deal out of telling everybody how she'd ordered this cake, how it looked amazing, and how she was really looking forward to it," Ellis recalls. "It was like, 'Look at me, I'm eating this big piece of cake!' When it arrived, she nibbled a corner of it and said, 'Wow, this is fantastic,' and started working her way around the room, going to the band saying, 'Boy, this cake is delicious! You've got to try a piece.' By the time she'd finished there was very little left on the plate."

Band members and others made aware of her condition agreed that Karen fit the description of anorexia to a T. Backstage they witnessed her exhaustion. She was lying down between shows, something she had rarely, if ever, done before. They were shocked to see how she could be flat on her back one minute and on stage singing the next. Even when doing back-to-back shows, Karen displayed "a tremendous amount of nervous energy," said Sherwin Bash. He was a no-nonsense kind of man who freely spoke his mind and had no qualms confronting Karen on the issue of anorexia, even calling it by name, and he did not back down. "The fact that she was anorexic was discussed innumerable times. . . . There was every attempt to get her to seek professional help, but I believe her family was the kind of family that the mother would say, 'We can take care of ourselves. We don't need to have someone. This is a family matter.'"

According to Ellis, at times Karen seemed to seek the attention of her family and did not mind it coming at the expense of their frustrations with her disorder. When she dieted, or "overdieted" as he explains, there was a rush of attention from the family, especially Agnes. "Karen had never had attention before, so she liked it. The experts say that one of the things that seems to drive young girls to diet and overdiet is that they were oftentimes the kids that never got attention. It's a way of getting the love from their family that they never got before."

FOR THE summer tour of 1975, manager Sherwin Bash paired Karen and Richard with veteran pop singer Neil Sedaka, who was also managed by BNB Associates. Sedaka, experiencing a comeback and the success of his new single "Laughter in the Rain," would be their opening act. His unbridled energy and onstage antics made him popular with audiences but also made the Carpenters' portion of the show seem a bit dull and disappointing to some. They were pros at presenting their impeccable musicianship in concerts, but there was very little focus on theatrics.

During their first shows together at the Riviera Hotel and Casino in Las Vegas, it was already apparent to the Carpenters that Sedaka's portion of the show was better received by the audiences than their own. "In contrast to my thirty-five minutes, their act was quiet and subdued," Sedaka wrote in his 1982 autobiography *Laughter in the Rain: My Own Story.* "While I was obviously thrilled to be on stage, the Carpenters seemed to walk through the act."

As the tour continued on to New England, the press seemed to agree. "Sedaka Steals Show from Carpenters," read a *New York Daily News* headline. Management began hiding the reviews from Karen and Richard, but Sedaka immediately felt resentment coming from the duo. "I don't know what happened," said Bash. "From the very beginning there wasn't a good feeling between Karen, Richard, and Neil. He was doing things or saying things which they were not comfortable with. . . . I could not soothe all the ruffled feathers."

By summer's end the Carpenters' latest single—their version of Sedaka's own "Solitaire"—was climbing the charts, and the tour returned to the Riviera for another two-week run. On the second night, Richard announced to the band that, due to time constraints, he was pulling the finale, in which Sedaka joined Karen and Richard onstage. All hell broke loose the following night during Sedaka's opening act when he took a moment to nonchalantly introduce and welcome guests Tom Jones and Dick Clark, who were seated in the audience. It was an unwritten rule that this sort of introduction was to be left to the headliner. For Richard, this was the last straw. He was already upset to have learned Sedaka was using the Carpenters' orchestra. And several keys had been broken on Richard's piano during Sedaka's act. Now he was breaking protocol by introducing celebrities in the audience. "When I left the stage," Sedaka recalled, "I heard Richard Carpenter screaming, 'Get that son of a bitch out!'"

Karen was crying, "Neil, I'm so sorry about this."

Sherwin Bash was in Germany making arrangements with promoters for the upcoming European tour when the call came in from the Riviera. "I got a phone call one night from Richard absolutely hysterical." Bash agreed it was a huge blunder and asked Richard if he wanted to fire Sedaka. "You *bet* I want to fire him," Richard retorted.

"I was in Berlin, not exactly around the corner from the Riviera Hotel in Las Vegas," recalled Bash. "I called and had half of the people in my office in Los Angeles fly up there to no avail. Richard would not agree that this was not the end of the world. He just totally lost it over this." The next day Sedaka was informed that Richard wanted him to leave the tour immediately. His remaining days would be paid off.

By the time Terry Ellis reached Richard by phone it was too late. "We fired Neil Sedaka," he said.

"*Excuse me?*" Ellis roared. He was certain the backlash would be terribly damaging for the Carpenters.

"Neil Sedaka was and is a very talented guy and a very seasoned veteran in show business," Ellis says. "He'd been writing hit songs for twenty years at that point; he'd been around show business for a long time, and he knew what he was doing. The poor guy was just doing his job! He was going onstage and doing his absolute best. He had a real show he'd put together, and they didn't. He brought the house down every night because he knew how to do it—and they didn't. This upset Richard, and he decided that Sedaka was getting out of place—he wasn't supposed to do that—he was supposed to support, not upstage. The guy was doing his job! He was being paid to be the very best that he could."

Following the advice of several fellow entertainers, Sedaka held a press conference telling those present he was "in a state of shock. It was Richard who first suggested I tour with them. It was a wonderful trip. Every performance was filled with ovations.... They felt I was too strong. I guess I was going over better than they had expected." He justified the introduction of Tom Jones and Dick Clark saying, "They are both close friends of mine, and I've written songs for Tom. It's the first time I've ever been asked to leave because of *good* performances. I feel badly that such talented people would have such insecurity. Ironically, they have a current hit record, 'Solitaire,' which is my composition."

Sedaka stressed there was no resentment or bitterness, only sorrow. "I don't want to bad-mouth the Carpenters," he said, refusing the invitation of fellow performers Steve Lawrence and Eydie Gorme to tell their Caesar's Palace audience exactly what happened. Before leaving Las Vegas, Elliott Abbott rebooked Sedaka at the Riviera as a headliner, making it obvious which side he took in this battle. Sedaka parted ways with Sherwin Bash and BNB Associates, forming his own management agency with Abbott. Werner Wolfen flew to Las Vegas in an attempt to pacify Richard, who was by then upset with the manner in which Bash had handled the situation. He blamed Sherwin for planting the seed to fire Sedaka during their phone conversation. Richard's solution was to fire Sherwin and hire Terry Ellis as the Carpenters' new manager, but Wolfen was hesitant to do so. He felt there was a possible conflict of interest since Karen was dating Ellis. Even so, Richard insisted Bash be terminated immediately. "It wasn't Karen, it was Richard," Bash recalled. "He arranged with an attorney to have me discharged. And Neil Sedaka, feeling that nobody was representing him in all of this, arranged with his attorney and had me discharged as well. So over introducing Tom Jones and Dick Clark, I was fired by both artists."

Upon returning to home base in Downey, an overwhelmed Richard Carpenter was caught off guard when Terry Ellis refused his offer to manage the Carpenters. He explained he would do so only on a temporary basis, agreeing to stay until a replacement was found. As Ellis predicted, the story of the firing spread like wildfire through newspaper and radio reports. "The Carpenters 'Nail' Neil Sedaka!" "Sedaka Fired for Being Too Strong." Music critics and deejays began to poke fun at the Carpenters when playing or reviewing their music. Joel McNally wrote in the *Milwaukee Journal* that the Sedaka incident was "the first time in recorded history that the Carpenters have been heard to utter a curse—even if it was only 'Grimy Gumdrops.'"

The Carpenters Fan Club worked to respond to hundreds of letters following the Sedaka episode. Evelyn Wallace kept quiet but was embarrassed to learn Richard had lost his temper and caused such a scene. "I didn't think much of him at the time for doing what he did," she says. "I'm sure Richard wanted to introduce those guys, but he could have said something like, 'I'd like to thank Neil for introducing so-and-so,' and that would have shown he was the bigger man."

In a statement to fan club members, Richard offered the following explanation:

> It often happens in our business, not only with the Carpenters, but also with other headliners, that the choice of the opening act proves to be unsuitable for personal or other reasons. Under those circumstances, the headliner has no option but to terminate the engagement of the opener. This was the situation with Neil. Please be assured that we *did not* fire Neil Sedaka for doing too well. In fact we were delighted that he was receiving a nice response from the audience. It was a result of other circumstances of which he is totally aware that made it necessary for us to terminate his engagement. . . . It is a disappointment to us that he found it necessary to make statements concerning same to the press. Personally, the Las Vegas/Sedaka issue is an old matter, and right now I am much more concerned with Karen's health and writing new songs.

Reviews for the Riviera shows continued to come in, most written before the pandemonium ensued. According to *Variety*, "Current fortnight with Neil Sedaka is the best combination for them so far. . . . Audience reaction is overwhelming at times." It went on to praise Sedaka's performance, saying it "generates enough excitement in his opening forty minutes to indicate future headline status . . . prompting a standing ovation opening show." Another reviewer referred to opening night at the Riviera as "Sedaka's night."

COMPOUNDED BY the stress of the Riviera engagement, Karen's failing health could no longer be ignored. In addition to her skeletal appearance, she was mentally and physically exhausted. Fall tours set for Europe and Japan only promised further deterioration for her weakened body and spirit. "I kept telling myself, 'I'm not really sick. I'll be better tomorrow,'" she explained to Ray Coleman in an article for *Melody Maker* entitled "Karen: Why I Collapsed." "When you have a show to do you just bear on through it. But it kept getting worse, and the last two days [in Vegas], I don't know how I got through. . . . It's annoying to feel that I couldn't withstand what I was doing to myself. You tend to say, 'Hey, no sweat. I can handle it,' but this time I couldn't."

Although she made it through the Vegas shows without a major incident, upon returning to Los Angeles Karen checked into Cedars-Sinai Medical Center, where she spent five days while doctors ran tests and worked to strengthen her severely weakened immune system. Upon discharge she was ordered to eat, rest, and refrain from working until the end of October. This would be the first of several hospital stays. Most were concealed, some even from her family. "There were so many hospitalizations," Frenda Franklin recalls. "There were so many near misses."

In this case the doctors declared Karen was in no shape to tour overseas as planned. The concerts would have to be rescheduled to allow her additional time to rest at home where she could attempt to recover and put on some weight. "She is suffering a severe case of physical and nervous exhaustion," said Dr. Robert Koblin in a statement to the press. "She had a hectic four-week schedule lined up in Europe, but I could not allow her to go through with it. In my opinion it would have been highly dangerous to her long term health."

Melody Maker reported that the Carpenters' tour would have been the highest-grossing tour in Britain and that approximately 150,000 people were set to see them during the planned twenty-eight day European trek. Ticket sales for the fifty shows, which sold out in a matter of hours, were refunded. It was reported that the Carpenters may have easily lost upward of $250,000 due to the cancelled concerts. In Japan, promoter Tats Nagashima said the tour would have grossed upward of $1.2 million and set numerous records in that country. On behalf of A&M Records, a concerned Jerry Moss phoned overseas tour promoters and guaranteed whatever losses such concert cancellations would incur.

Karen took the losses quite personally, apologizing profusely to management, those at A&M, and especially Richard. "I felt bad for Richard because my illness held him back," she said the following year. "And he felt bad for me, too, because he considered that it was his fault in driving me so hard. Then we both got mad because we had not put on the brakes earlier and stopped all the pressures that eventually led to my exhaustion."

Terry Ellis accompanied Richard to London and Tokyo where the two held press conferences explaining the cancellations. Richard addressed the UK media with the following statement.

> Karen is really in a state of exhaustion, both mental and physical, but mostly physical. We had a tour in April and a tour in May, a five-week summer tour, two two-week engagements in Las Vegas, and it really left us no time to get much rest. The last week in Vegas she was down to eighty-six pounds.... The whole European tour in all was fifty concerts in twenty-eight days and I wouldn't have wanted her to do it even if through a miracle she got through it.... Karen's really upset at not being able to do this, and I am too, of course. I just wanted to come over in person and apologize.... We will be back as soon as is possible.

"Girls just can't take that life without something going wrong," Terry Ellis added.

Reflecting on this remark, Ellis says he never noticed that women find the touring life physically more demanding than men. "It sounds as though I was complicit in the 'anorexia cover-up' for Karen."

Gossip and rumors greeted the men when they arrived in Europe and Japan, with some reports saying Karen was battling cancer, others hinting she was suicidal. "When Richard returned he didn't want to tell me of the whispers that were circulating," Karen recalled. "It was all so much crap. Not once had suicide entered my head. I was depressed, yes, but my God, not enough to commit suicide. I value life too much for that. No, the real alarm was over my frightening loss of weight. At first I lost the weight I intended to lose, but it went on even though I began eating like mad to counteract it."

Under Agnes Carpenter's close watch, Karen slept fourteen to sixteen hours a day. "My mother thought I was dead," she told Ray Coleman. "I normally manage on four to six hours. It was obvious that for the past two years I'd been running on nervous energy." Her weight eventually climbed to 104 pounds.

Hearing of Karen's illness and ordered bed rest, Frank Pooler went to Newville and spent the afternoon with her. "She was very sick and said it was something with her colon," he says. Per Karen, the diagnosis was spastic colitis, sometimes referred to as irritable bowel syndrome. "I had no idea that she was having eating problems," says Pooler.

Karen confessed to Pooler during his visit that she was depressed because of the situation with Neil Sedaka. "I just think that kind of made her heart sick," he remembers. "She just didn't want to do anything else."

Karen was surprised when letters from worried fans poured in to Carpenters headquarters. "People never think of entertainers as being human," Karen observed. "When you walk out on stage the audience thinks nothing can go wrong with them. They see you as idols, not as ordinary human beings. We get sick and we have headaches just like they do. When we are cut, we bleed. My breakdown was caused by a combination of troubles that came as thick as the layers of a sandwich cake. Everything happened at once."

The fan club commented on Karen's condition in their December 1975 newsletter.

> Please be assured there is no truth in the rumor that Karen is a victim of cancer. Coupled with severe physical and mental exhaustion, due to overwork, dieting and lack of rest, she developed Colitis (i.e.

inflammation of the colon.) Her collapse was inevitable after the rigorous schedule of the past summer months, and her willing spirit was eventually dominated by Mother Nature who compelled her to take a well deserved rest. Thank God she exudes her vivacious, happy personality once again.

10

I NEED TO BE IN LOVE

"TERRY AND I, we're in love," Karen told Evelyn Wallace as the two stepped into the office at Newville one afternoon.

"That's great, Karen!" Ev exclaimed. "I'm glad to hear that you've found somebody."

Karen surprised everyone in late 1975 when she moved into Terry's Beverly Hills home. "Her moving out of Newville nearly knocked me over," Wallace recalls. "Mainly because I didn't think Agnes would let her out the front door."

Richard claimed to have no qualms with Karen's decision to move in with Terry. Even so, it was Karen's wish to remain discreet. "I didn't even know they lived together," says Carole Curb. "In those times, if girls did it they didn't talk about it." But Karen's mother was indeed upset. "Agnes was furious," says Frenda Franklin. "Furious!" Not only was her daughter living with a man out of wedlock, which went against her strong, traditional belief system, she was leaving Downey for the first time. "I suggested that she should come and live with me," Ellis says, "which I suppose was a big mistake on my part. Her mother just freaked out. It wasn't part of her plan."

It was soon obvious to Ellis that Agnes considered him to be a threat to the family's authority over Karen. In fact, the biggest threat was the possibility that he might persuade Karen to go solo and perhaps even move to England, disbanding the duo and leaving Richard on his own. According to Frenda, Terry did want to make Karen a solo artist and had the capability to do so. "Since he owned Chrysalis Records he could have made that happen. They all just freaked so they started their hatchet job on him." Ellis disagrees with the idea that he would have encouraged Karen to go solo but agrees that Agnes was on guard. "The family—and by 'the family' I mean her mother—saw me as a threat to her relationship with Karen and her control over Karen," he says. "My reading of the situation was that her mother saw me as such a threat that she more or less made Karen choose between me and her."

Whether or not Agnes sabotaged the love affair was of little relevance. Within no time it became apparent that the social gap between the couple was far too wide. Karen was "in love with being in love," Frenda claims, "but then when there were demands, like 'I want you to come live in England,' it just freaked her out. Terry was very continental, and he would have taken her away. That would have been good in the end, but it was too soon for her to jump ship like that. She couldn't have lived in England on his level. It was a world of private jets and islands of Tortola. . . . It was the world she wanted but was not even close to being ready for."

As much as Karen wanted to be "uptown" she was still very much a middle-class American girl who liked to relax at home in the evening and watch television with her snack on a TV tray. "There were no televisions in that house," Frenda explains. "You laugh? It was not funny with her." Within a matter of only a few weeks, Karen became restless in Ellis's palatial Beverly Hills home. "I can't go on like this," she told Frenda. "I have to get out of here!"

As they would do periodically, the Lefflers came to Karen's rescue, bailing her out in times of great despair. With Ellis out of town, Karen packed her things and left without warning. "She didn't even have the maturity to end that the right way," Frenda says. "She wanted to have it, but she just didn't have it in her. She just left. She was afraid. We had to go get her. She was pretty broken when she left." The relationship with Terry Ellis ended as quickly as it had begun, but Karen was too ashamed to face him. Instead, she phoned him shortly after moving out.

"This just can't work," she told him. "We aren't right for each other, and it's too difficult. We just have to stop seeing each other."

Ellis sensed this was the work of Agnes and the hypnotic hold she seemed to have over her daughter. "Her mother gave her such hell that she just moved straight back," he says. "It's difficult to know if that's what Karen wanted or if that's what Karen had to have or what was forced on her by her mother and her family." He disagrees that Karen was ill prepared for or ill suited to his lifestyle. "When Karen was with me, we traveled somewhat and went to France, and she really enjoyed it," he says. "When I was with her away from her family she would *come alive*! There was a lot of depth to Karen that you could see privately, but as soon as she got back into the family situation she would change.

"Very early on Harold and Agnes found that Richard had this extraordinary talent. He was a musical genius—no question about that—he was and is, but from the point they realized he had this talent, the whole family's energy was devoted to Richard's career. They moved coasts in order to give him more opportunities, and everybody in the family was told, 'We have this unique talent in the family,' 'Richard is a genius,' and 'We all have to sacrifice in order to ensure that he gets the best opportunities to expose his talents.' So at a very early age Karen was told that her job in life was to support Richard. That continued all the way up through their careers until they became huge stars and beyond. If you were to go into the family environment, where I was a lot, there was that same dynamic of 'Everybody's here for Richard' and 'It's really Richard who's the star.' Even when Karen had become the star, that dynamic still existed, and she would fall in line."

Frenda feels certain that Karen was content not being the star of the family. "That wasn't what made her ill, I am positive of that," she says. "It was just being ignored. That's different. You don't have to be the star, but you can't just be pushed to the side and have no value."

Karen spoke briefly of her relationship with Terry Ellis in an interview for the *Daily Mirror*. "We had a thing going for a while, but we weren't exactly matched. We are still good friends," she said, but confessed, "I don't think I have ever really been in love," a comment she would later regret. "Everyone keeps saying that I'll know when it happens. Well, I'm waiting. Love is something I want very badly to feel. There is nothing more I want out of life right now than to be married and have children. That would be wonderful. But it must happen naturally and, I hope, in the next couple of years."

As Evelyn Wallace recalls, Agnes relished in welcoming Karen back to Newville with a bit of an "I told you so" attitude. "It's a good thing you came back home," she told her. But Karen was unhappy. The breakup with Ellis was terribly painful; it was the closest thing to a long-term relationship she had experienced. Not only was it the end of romance, it was the end of the Carpenters' professional relationship with Ellis, and—perhaps most crushing—it was another botched attempt by Karen at breaking free and leaving home. She was twenty-five years old and returning home to live with her parents in Downey, but Karen vowed that this return to Newville would be short-lived. "She really wanted to move out of that house," Wallace recalls. "I think her mother was getting her down to the point where she wanted out. She wanted to get her own apartment."

———— ∞ ————

KAREN SOON announced plans to move to Century City, where she had purchased her own condominium back in July 1975. The twin twenty-eight-story Century Towers at 2222 Avenue of the Stars overlooked the Hillcrest Country Club and the golf course at Rancho Park. Designed by world-renowned architect I.M. Pei, the gated Century Towers complex was built in 1964 as Century City was being developed out of the backlot of Twentieth Century Fox Studios. Karen bought two adjacent corner units, numbers 2202 and 2203, on the twenty-second floor of the east tower. The first six notes of "We've Only Just Begun" chimed to welcome guests to the luxurious three-thousand-square-foot residence. "It was amazing," says Carole Curb. "She had one of the top decorators redo it. It was beautiful and reflected the new Karen once she'd made the transition and had the successes and everything."

"Well, what do you like?" decorator John Cottrell had asked Karen.

"You better sit down," she cautioned. Karen's decorating tastes were eclectic and a fusion of contemporary, country, and French styles. "I want it to look classy, in a funky kind of way," she told him. "I want it to be top-notch, top class, yet I want people to feel like they can put their feet up on anything. I don't want it to look [stuffy], yet I want it to be beautiful."

"Oh dear," Cottrell said.

In the end, the Lucite- and chrome-accented living room was offset by a country style kitchen. Personalizing Karen's new uptown residence were the many stuffed animals she positioned neatly across the huge bed. The bedroom was designed around an Advent VideoBeam home theater system with a seven-foot-wide screen, just like the one Richard had installed at Lubec Street. Carole Curb recalls that Karen's bedroom closet was a fine example of her friend's quest for perfectionism. "Karen was very, very meticulous," she says. "The clothes hangers were all the same and a quarter-inch apart. The pants were all together, the blouses all together. It was like an amazing boutique with everything arranged in order."

Another frequent visitor was fellow singer Olivia Newton-John. She and Karen first met in 1971 at Annabel's, a nightclub in London's Berkeley Square, and over the succeeding years developed a close friendship. "Karen was a very friendly, outgoing girl," Olivia says. "We hit it off since we are both down-to-earth people. We connected on that level, and we both liked the other's voice. We talked about doing a duet for fun, but it never eventuated because we were both so busy with our own things. We both had such crazy lives that we understood each other. Usually our schedules were so crazy that we just managed to meet for lunch, or I'd go to her place in Century City. Her place was *immaculate*. It was really a very beautiful apartment with the most amazing view. I remember thinking, 'Oh, she's so lucky. She's got this amazing pad all to herself.' She was very clean, very tidy. Obviously she had issues and probably could have had obsessive-compulsive disorder."

Interspersed among the chic and stylish decor was Karen's collection of Mickey Mouse and Disney memorabilia. "She had a lot of child in her," Olivia recalls. "She loved childhood things, she was funny and

she was quirky." As Karen would often do, she invented several nicknames for each of her closest friends. Olivia was affectionately referred
to as Livvy or ONJ (which Karen pronounced Ahhnj). According to
Frenda, Karen had nicknames for everything. "The whole *world* was
a nickname," she says. "It was like she actually had her own language.
She'd say, 'Did you talk to the 'rents?' Those were my parents. If you
didn't know what she was thinking about, you'd think she was from
another country. She'd be fantastic at text messaging!"

Karen's new residence was only a few miles from the Leffler home
on Tower Road, and Frenda welcomed her to the neighborhood and
helped her establish a new sense of community. At Century Towers
there were doormen who took a liking to Karen and made her feel
at home. Just around the corner on Pico Boulevard was Owen's, her
favorite market. "She made it a little neighborhood," Frenda says, "like
her own little Downey. She loved to go on little errands with me or
wherever I went, and she wanted to learn all the nice places for the
locals and things that were native to Beverly Hills and Los Angeles."

When the two entered Edelweiss Candy on Canon Drive, Karen
was thrilled to see the candy being hand dipped and made on the premises. She rarely enjoyed such confectionery delights but was fascinated
with the preparation and presentation of all types of food. "Oh my
God," she told Frenda. "Now *this* is a candy store!"

JANUARY 1, 1976, brought a new contract with A&M Records and the
naming of Jerry Weintraub of Management III as the Carpenters' new
manager. Weintraub was an entertainment powerhouse whose career
began as a talent agent for MCA Records in the 1950s. By the time he
came to manage Karen and Richard he had worked with such clients
as Elvis Presley, Frank Sinatra, and Judy Garland, in addition to having
helped guide John Denver to the enormous success he was seeing by
the mid-1970s.

Weintraub's first order of Carpenters business was to map out a plan
for the duo with longevity as the foundation. They were primarily a
recording group, but prior to 1976 their schedule had left them with

very little time to spend in the studio. Five years of incessant touring had left Karen and Richard burned out, exhausted, and without
personal lives. When not on endless tours of one-nighters across the
United States they could be found in Europe or Japan for even more
concerts, television appearances, and interviews. "It was sickening,"
Karen told *People Weekly* in a cover story for the magazine. "Suddenly
it wasn't fun anymore."

As the Carpenters' new manager, Weintraub vowed to change the
group's direction by limiting the number of concerts they would perform each year and making certain there was plenty of time in the
recording studio. Despite these attempts, their next studio album, *A
Kind of Hush*, did little to mask the poor health and fatigue that had
plagued the duo the year prior. Failing to break into the Top 30 in the
United States, it marked the beginning of a descent in their popularity. The title track and debut single was an insubstantial cover of the
Herman's Hermits hit and one of two castanet-heavy oldies, the other
being Neil Sedaka's "Breaking Up Is Hard to Do." Giving a new meaning to the word "oldie" was "Goofus," written in 1931 and previously
recorded by Les Paul, the Dinning Sisters, and Chet Atkins. Calling the
album "an overdose of pretty," music critic Joel McNally felt *Hush* was
an appropriate title for an album that displayed such little dynamic contrast. "At this point it is the odds-on favorite to win the Grammy," he
joked, "the Nobel Peace Prize and the *Reader's Digest* Sweepstakes."

The album's savior came in the form of a Carpenter-Bettis original
and what John Bettis considered to be "Goodbye to Love: Part Two."
"I Need to Be in Love" began as only a song title and a few bars of
melody by Albert Hammond, who was writing songs with Bettis in
England. Although their version of the song was never completed, the
title was presented to Richard Carpenter, and it came to life in a way
Bettis likened to "a little ball of twine" the duo "unrolled and knitted
into a sweater."

Karen declared "I Need to Be in Love" to be her autobiographical
anthem from first listen. "When he wrote the lyrics to that thing I was
just flabbergasted," she said. "The first verse of that says, 'The hardest
thing I've ever done is keep believing / there's someone in this crazy

world for me / the way that people come and go through temporary lives / my chance could come and I might never know.' I said, 'Oh my God, it's so true.'" Bettis felt the lyric told not only Karen's story but his own and Richard's as well. It was penned during a phase when all three were looking for love with no success. "'I Need to Be in Love' is probably the most autobiographical and my favorite lyric ever written for Karen," he explained. "If there was ever anything that came out of my heart straight to Karen's I would say that was it. I was very proud of it for that."

Karen enjoyed making lists: to-do lists, shopping lists, and even lists of lists. She would often lie awake in bed with a notepad and pencil, planning every detail of the coming day, as she explained to Ray Coleman in 1975. "My mind starts going, 'This has gotta be done, that's gotta be done, you've gotta call this.' Then I find myself with a flashlight in bed writing down about fifty things that have to be done by 10:00 the next morning. It's not the best way to be. It's better to hang loose, but I'm just not that type of person." According to friends, she also made tangible lists of attributes she was looking for in a prospective husband and was not willing to settle for anything less than her own preconceived ideal. "It's really hard to meet people in this business," she told *People* magazine. "But I'll be damned if I'll marry somebody just to be married."

"What are the requirements you're looking for today, Karen?" she was asked during a 1976 interview.

"Well, I have my list here," she joked, "but I'll have to stand just in case it hits the floor!" Little did the interviewer know she had actually put pen to paper to list her requirements in a man. She valued independence and desired a relationship with someone who would understand and appreciate the challenges of her career. "Obviously I would want to cut down on the work," she said, "but you don't have to get married and sit in the house. I couldn't. There's no way I would ever stop singing or performing or doing whatever I want to do. But I want to do it with somebody and share it. I want somebody to share my joy with."

She answered the same question for another journalist later that year: "I want a husband who can accept my success, because I could not give it up and stay at home all day. He must also be pretty well off. I don't want to fight the fear of a man having to live with my money. I've seen that ruin too many marriages. And it's got to be somebody dominant because I am far too domineering myself. I'm a bulldozer. . . . So far nine out of ten of them haven't lasted. I know instantly whether it's going to work out. Most of the men I go out with panic on sight. They become scared to death of me. They're envious of my car or they get upset if we go into a restaurant where I might be recognized. . . . So where is the right guy? Still, I'll say one thing: When I marry it will be for good."

From 1976 on, Karen named "I Need to Be in Love" as her favorite Carpenters song. "It really hits me right at home," she said. "Certain nights on the stage it really upsets me. I sing it and I'm almost putting myself into tears." Despite its beauty, the single fell short of the Top 20, coming in at #25. An obvious choice for its follow-up was "Can't Smile Without You," which went on to become a smash hit for Barry Manilow in 1978. Instead it was overlooked in favor of "Goofus," the final single culled from *A Kind of Hush*. Peaking at #56, it was the Carpenters' lowest-charting single of their career to that point.

⎯⎯ ⌾⌾⌾ ⎯⎯

BUILDING ON changes established by Terry Ellis during his brief stint as interim manager, Jerry Weintraub set out to completely revamp the Carpenters' stage show, which had followed roughly the same format since 1974. "When we first went on the road, all we really cared about was reproducing our record sound," Karen said. "We got that; it sounded just like the record. We didn't care or we didn't know it was also important to perform or be in this showbiz thing."

In addition to the writing and directing team of Ken and Mitzi Welch, Weintraub brought in famed Broadway choreographer Joe Layton, who felt that the Carpenters had played the role of good musicians for too long. There was no need to replicate the recordings in concert for the same fans that had their records at home. "Layton was a genius," explains Michael Lansing, who joined the Carpenters as a roadie in 1976. "With Ken and Mitzi, Joe produced a new show under Weintraub's creative hand, and they threw everything out the door."

Karen's drumming became more of a novelty than ever before with the addition of a lengthy drum spectacular. "She would run from one drum to the other without missing a beat," recalls Evelyn Wallace. "The people would just scream!" The addition of a portable raked stage allowed the entire setup to be angled toward the audience. "It is just drums," Karen explained. "I don't sing a note. We end up with twenty-three drums on the stage. I love to play and I love to sing, but I wouldn't want to give either one of them up." For this percussion feature Karen often donned a pair of blue jeans and a T-shirt with the words LEAD SISTER across the front. She'd earned this nickname in 1974, after a Japanese journalist mistakenly referred to her as the "lead sister" rather than "lead singer."

Despite her love of drumming, Karen had without a doubt emerged as the voice and face of the Carpenters. Most who witnessed the professional relationship between her and Richard recall it as more of an artist-producer relationship than a duo. This might have been the appropriate juncture in their careers for Karen to have received solo billing with Richard maintaining his behind-the-scenes role as producer. Instead, the campaign to establish an equality of importance between the two continued, most notably on stage. "Ladies and gentlemen," said the emcee, "Mr. Richard Carpenter." As Terry Ellis had suggested a year before, Richard opened the show alone, entering to a roll of timpani and an orchestral overture in which he took the baton at center stage as conductor. In addition, a large mirror was hung just above his piano and angled so that the audience could watch as his hands move up and down the keys. "You want to make sure you watch that mirror," Agnes instructed Evelyn Wallace as the family awaited the start of a show in Las Vegas.

"What mirror?" Evelyn asked.

Wallace would never admit it to Agnes, but she saw absolutely no need for the mirror and, in fact, found it to be narcissistic. "People went to see *Karen*," she says. "The audience went to hear *Karen's voice*, not to watch Richard play some song he had written."

But even Karen strongly disagreed. Second only to her mother, she was Richard's biggest fan. "He's so talented that it makes me weep that everybody just walks right by him," she told Ray Coleman in 1975, by which time she was part of the latest effort to establish Richard as the genius behind the Carpenters' sound. "They never give him any credit, but he does everything. He's the brain behind it and yet I get cracks like 'What does the brother do?' Or I get the impression that it's really nice that I've brought my brother on the road. . . . I really get upset for him because he's so good and he never opens his mouth. He just sits back and because I'm the lead singer I get all the credit. They think I did it, and all I do is sing. He's the one that does all the work. There isn't anything I wouldn't do for him to give him the perfection that we both want."

Regardless of the overwhelming love and mutual respect between the siblings, Richard could not help but become jealous of the fuss the record-buying public and concertgoers made over his sister. "Karen is the star," he had explained in 1973. "She's the one who gets the letters and requests for autographs. I don't get much attention. Everyone's mostly interested in Karen. She's the lead singer and the featured part of the act. My end is selecting material, arranging, orchestrating, production, names of the albums, selecting personnel for the group, the order of the show, and how to improve the show. The audience doesn't realize what I do. They don't know I've written several hit songs. It's always Karen, which is fine. It's the same way with Donny and the Osmonds. But to me, I know what I've done. Even though a lot of people and critics don't like it, the fact is it's very commercial. It's well produced and it feels nice to me that I selected an unknown song and made it a hit. That makes me feel good, and sure, it feeds my ego."

The habitual tribute to the oldies remained a part of the new stage show, although it was sometimes exchanged in favor of a medley of songs from the popular Broadway musical *Grease*. In this sequence, Richard tore onto the stage on a motorcycle, and Karen entered wearing pink spandex, a bouffant wig, and an overstated fake bust. New to the show was a grandiloquent Spike Jones–inspired parody of "Close to You," complete with kazoos and pot and pans. Karen loved the dramatics added to their new show. "We're hams," she told Ray Coleman while in Germany in 1976. "We enjoy dressing up and the production. Have we gone over the top? Well, the answer's in the audience; it's been well received so far. Ask me next year."

Most shocking was the finale of "We've Only Just Begun," in which Richard left his fixed stance behind the piano to join Karen at center stage, an effort on the part of the writers to, again, balance his importance with hers. "They pretend for a split second to be lovers, looking straight into each other's eyes," explained Ray Coleman in his review of one of their German concerts. "A rarely seen moment of near passion from a brother-sister act not noted for warmth, in spite of the romantic beauty of their songs. . . . I felt the flesh creep uncomfortably at the sight of grownup brother and sister acting out this slightly incestuous scene as just 'part of the act.'" The positive side to their "mindboggling" performance, according to Coleman, was that the duo finally seemed to have "planted the kiss of life on a two year old corpse and that their audacity has won. Their 1974 show was boring. The 1976 show is over-ambitious. . . . The new show forces a reaction. Nobody sleeps during this concert. The Carpenters are alive and well—and working hard, as always. They know no other way."

Calling the music "polite plastic pop," British critic Mike Evans was also unmoved by all the over-the-top attempts at entertaining. "The curtain went up on a tinseled shrine to American kitsch, a mini Las Vegas, all red lights and glitter," he wrote. The songs were "flawlessly sung and expertly performed with hardly a trace of emotion in the whole performance."

Perhaps Karen and Richard were working too hard. The new show had been scripted by the Welch duo, and every word and gesture—even the ad libs—were written out and rehearsed to robotic perfection. "Theatrics Overshadow Carpenters' Music" was the headline following a concert at Oklahoma University's Homecoming. "They were not only tied down by a script, they were bound and gagged by it. . . . It is unfortunate that they got saddled with the Pollyanna image early in their careers and have decided to cater to it."

———— ⚭ ————

ON TOUR, both Karen and Richard kept to themselves. While the band members were sightseeing in various cities and bowling down hotel hallways, as they were known to do, the siblings were usually secluded in their own hotel rooms. "They were an odd pair," recalls frequent opening act Denny Brooks. "I didn't think they felt comfortable in their own skin. I loved the band, but Karen and Richard just weren't the type of folks that I would really hang out with."

Roadie Michael Lansing, however, found himself quite taken with Karen and made it his mission to make her as comfortable on tour as possible. He brought in carpeting for her dressing room and always made sure her television reception was adequate, even if it meant running wires from the TV set to various metal objects around the space. "I saw her in every kind of conceivable fashion," Lansing says, "from bra and panties in the dressing room to stage outfits ready to walk on." He and roadies Jackie Hylen and Dave Connley would retrieve Karen's huge wardrobe case, which she nicknamed Blackula, from her upstairs bedroom at Newville, slide it down the stairs, and load it into the brown Dodge van marked with the gold-lettered "Carpenters" logo. From there they would transport the wardrobe to the Carpenters' Morsound warehouse in Studio City, where it was loaded into one of two semi trucks that followed the group from city to city.

In Karen, Lansing sensed a depth of character he feels many others looked past. "I think she was misunderstood by so many people," he says. "Karen was much more sensitive than she let on. She really enjoyed just being normal and was so down-to-earth. Talking to Karen was like talking to anybody else. She didn't have airs about her. She was really a fun girl, but I think she wanted to have a lot more fun in life than she did."

To pass time on tour Karen would work on various needlepoint projects and watch videocassettes of her favorite television programs, such as *I Love Lucy* and *Marcus Welby, M.D.*, while stylist Sandy Holland put her hair in rollers. Unlike many other singers, she spent very little time preparing her voice for concerts. "I've discussed this with a lot of singers," she said in 1978. "They say, 'How do you prepare for a show?' I say, 'I get dressed and walk downstairs. What do *you* do?' 'Oh, I do pushups, and I exercise my tonal thingies.' I'm saying, 'My Lord, you wear yourself out before you go on!'"

As the Carpenters rescheduled European tour was underway in the fall of 1976, Agnes and Harold Carpenter joined the group in England for the Palladium engagement and enjoyed sightseeing during rehearsals and sound checks. "The mom ran the show," recalls Denny Brooks. "I mean she ran the whole show. They had management and they had agents, but basically all the big decisions were made by Agnes when she was along. I liked Harold a lot. He enjoyed being along on the road. He was a very charming guy and a hoot to have around. In his distinctive slow drawl he would say, 'Well, boys, where are we gonna hang the feed bag tonight?' The parents didn't have an itinerary. They just followed the yellow brick road and got on the planes with us and went wherever their kids went."

Also along on this tour was Richard's eighteen-year-old girlfriend, first cousin Mary Rudolph, daughter of Agnes's sister Bernice. "I'd stayed at their family's house in Baltimore when Mary was just a teenager," recalls Maria Galeazzi, who lived next door to Mary's older brother and Carpenters roadie Mark Rudolph. "Her brother and I were very close, and from what Mark said, Mary pursued Richard quite a bit. It was like nonstop." Michael Lansing recalls that Mary joined the group as wardrobe and prop assistant and to the press was known as "Mary Pickford," an effort to deter attention from the couple's common roots. "We'd all go bowling or to the movies or just hang out. Mary was dating Richard at the time, but nobody said anything. Nobody ever said a word!"

According to friends, Karen was "livid" and "furious" about her brother's relationship with the girl she had only known as their kid cousin. She was especially upset by the amount of time Richard was spending with Mary on tour. "I never had a boyfriend on the road," Karen had told Ray Coleman in 1975, avoiding mention of then boyfriend Terry Ellis. "Not only didn't I agree with it, but I never met anybody I wanted to have on the road. It's the same thing with the guys bringing wives or women on the road. We tend to think when you go out [on tour] you go to work."

While in England, Karen did her best to distance herself from Richard and Mary and found herself surreptitiously meeting with John

"Softly" Adrian, head of press and promotion at A&M in London. Assigned by the label's regional chief Derek Green, Softly was asked to personally assist the Carpenters for the duration of their London stay. "You'll need to look after Karen when she gets here," Green told him. The handsome, suave thirty-three-year-old former model, who acquired his nickname after appearing in a television series called *Softly, Softly*, was already a fan of the Carpenters. In what he explains as having been an attempt to familiarize himself with the Carpenters and their show, Softly had flown to Germany prior to the group's arrival in London. "We always did that with our artists," Softly recalls. "You couldn't be working with them and not know who they were."

"Why are you sitting there all alone and being so snobby?" Karen's flirtatious handwritten note became an invitation for Softly to join her for breakfast at the Albany Hotel in Glasgow. He smiled from across the room before joining her and recalls being surprised by Karen's normality. Captivated by her sweet disposition, he made a silent vow that the two would become romantically involved. "The attraction was instant, and I would like to think it was mutual," he says, "but we were kind of shy of each other a bit, to be honest."

Softly soon realized it would be more difficult to infiltrate the Carpenters' circle than he imagined. "She was always surrounded by people—family managers and record executives," he recalls. "She had several moats, and you were going to have to cross them to get anywhere near her. She was like a little girl to me, really. A little girl who happened to have an extraordinary voice. Karen was very kind and very sweet, but she lived in a glass bowl. She had sixty-five people telling her what to do and fifty-seven hangers-on and managers and submanagers, and it was like a bloody fiasco."

Softly admits his position with the record label was his only way past the moats. "I had to pick her up at the hotel and take her to interviews and look after her, so I was very close to her during that time. You get to know people rather quickly when you're working that closely with them, and I think she trusted me to take care of her." As he had hoped, a brief interlude of puppy love ensued, and he and Karen began to see more of one another as time allowed. "It was one of those short, very enjoyable, very lovely romances," he says. "Hardly anybody knew about it, really. It was very sweet. That's all, really. It was just very sweet."

Despite their affection for each other, concealing their feelings was imperative. No one would have approved of a relationship between a Carpenter and an A&M staff member. Despite their precautions, word of Karen's involvement with Softly ultimately reached A&M executives and the Carpenters' management. Frenda Leffler was along for this leg of the tour and became concerned about the intentions of this man who seemed to have showed up out of nowhere. "What would you do with all that money?" she asked him.

"I'm doing just fine without it now, actually," he responded. "I could care less about her money."

Despite Softly's claims of truly loving Karen, Frenda and others in the entourage saw him as a bit of a playboy and did not take him seriously. It was not until Karen invited him to join her in Los Angeles for Christmas that everyone became disturbed. In their opinions she was simply infatuated and not thinking this through. "It was a momentary thing, and Karen didn't really see the reality of it," Frenda recalls. "He showed her a lot of attention, and he was a cute guy, but it just wasn't right for her. He was put out of commission rather quickly. The powers that be jumped on it, and Karen didn't have anything to say about it."

Back at A&M headquarters in London, Derek Green was alerted of the budding romance between Karen and his employee. Softly's character and intentions were being scrutinized, but Green assured those who questioned his character that he was indeed a fine man and anything but a gigolo. But after much urging, Green called Softly into his office, where he explained that if he were to go through with his plans to visit Karen in Los Angeles, he would no longer have a job at A&M. With the offer of plane tickets for a Caribbean vacation, Softly was told to go away, relax, and forget all about the fantasy of ever being with Karen Carpenter. "Basically our relationship was sabotaged by many of the people surrounding us," Softly says. "It was nipped in the bud, and I was threatened with my job. I went off to the Caribbean and got married after three months. It was what you might call a rebound."

At the time, Softly figured this was most likely some sort of scheme by Karen to secretly end their impending relationship. It seemed too good to be true anyway. His pride was hurt, and he quietly disappeared from the final leg of the tour. When Karen learned he had left the tour for a tropical vacation, she was sure he had run off with some other woman. In the end, both were persuaded to believe that the other had lost interest, and the relationship came to an end. "They were a controlling bunch," Softly says of A&M and the Carpenters in general. "She was the golden goose, and people protected her. They didn't want anybody, particularly an outsider she might be fond of, to take her away from the family. I think it was that people got scared that I might become her manager or something, which was totally ridiculous. I was not qualified to do that anyway."

Upon her return to Los Angeles, Karen sent a handwritten greeting card to Softly saying, "Thanks for looking after me." He doubts she ever learned how their relationship had been disrupted. In fact, the two never spoke of the fling again. Softly was only told of the conspiracy some fifteen years later when Derek Green broke his silence. Softly was upset to learn of the control Karen seemed to have been subjected to all those years ago. "She was a sad little girl, basically. She couldn't seem to do anything for herself or make any decisions. Everything was done for her. She had her mom and dad and brother and managers, and she was lost in this whole thing."

⸺ ⥁ ⸺

WITH NO serious romantic interests in sight, Karen enjoyed a few sporadic dates with musician friend Tom Bähler and several entertainers including Barry Manilow, actor Mark Harmon, and comedian Steve Martin. "Steve really liked Karen, and of course she thought he was an absolute scream," says Evelyn Wallace. "They were going out, and Karen had picked out what she was going to wear. Then word got around to Richard that Karen was going to go out that night with *the* Steve Martin. It wasn't long before he got in touch with Karen and said, 'Oh, I just got the studio, so we're going to be recording tonight.' Knowing that Karen had a date, he somehow all of a sudden got the studio and they were going to go up and record. See, even when she was on her own and living in the condo, Richard had a string on her. She was never ever her own boss."

Like the celebrities she dated casually, Karen found it extremely difficult in her situation not only to meet people but to find somebody "real," as she would often say. "I want desperately to find the right man," she said in 1976, "but it really has to be someone who is understanding and extremely strong. The average guy could never live under the pressure and all the other absurdities that go along with being in the limelight. You can't force these things. When you do, it always turns into a nightmare. I know a lot of people who have, and they always ended up the loser. I'll go on doing what I'm doing, and if I meet someone who turns me on, we'll go from there....I'm not afraid of being an old maid. The idea doesn't scare me a bit. Happiness shouldn't be contingent on another human being. We've been programmed for so long that your value goes down if you don't end up with a husband or a wife. That's a sickness that has sprouted many unhappy people."

As former manager Sherwin Bash explained, it's extremely difficult for a successful female artist to find a man who can deal with her celebrity status. "I don't know anyone who wants to be Mr. Diana Ross," he said. "Do you want to be Mr. Barbra Streisand? I don't think our male egos work that way, so to find that person is not that easy."

Karen shared with friends her desire for life as a wife and mother. "You see, I so much want to start a family," she told an interviewer in 1976. "I really want kids. Maybe I'm old fashioned, but I could not have children without first being married. I believe in the institution of marriage very strongly. I'm family oriented and I'm proud of it. I had a happy childhood, and I would like to do the kind of job my parents did."

Carole Curb affirms that having children seemed to be her ultimate goal in life. "Even though she had an amazing voice and was very driven, I think ultimately she just wanted to have a husband and kids and the white picket fence." Childhood friend Debbie Cuticello agrees. "She wanted children desperately. She wanted a family, the little white picket fence, the dog, and the two-car garage."

Until that time came, Karen lived vicariously through best friend Frenda Leffler, even climbing atop Frenda's hospital gurney on her way into the delivery room. Unbeknownst to everyone, Frenda was carrying twins. With the arrival of the second baby, Karen looked up toward the ceiling and exclaimed, "Thank you God! You sent one for *me*!" She settled for the title of godmother to babies Ashley and Andrew—the "kidlets" she would call them—and Ashley soon acquired the nickname Ashley Famous. She presented each with a silver dish that she had hand engraved with the message: WHEN I COUNT MY BLESSINGS I COUNT YOU TWICE. LOVE, AUNTIE KAREN.

In anticipation of starting her own family, Karen mulled over names for her future children. It was decided that a son would be named for Richard but that everyone would call him Rick or Richie. For a daughter she chose the name Kristi.

11

JUST LET US KNOW WHAT
THE PROBLEM IS!

———

ROM "(THEY Long to Be) Close to You" in 1970 through
"I Need to Be in Love" in 1976, every Carpenters single (not
including B-sides) reached #1 or #2 on the Adult Contemporary
chart, "a streak that nobody has come close to beating," according to
Christopher Feldman's *Billboard Book of #2 Singles*. On the pop charts
the duo racked up a string of sixteen consecutive Top 20 hit singles
and five Top 10 albums. They won three Grammy Awards in these six
years and were presented with an American Music Award. But these
amazing feats would do little to soothe the pains of the decline in record
sales and popularity the Carpenters would experience in the latter half
of the decade. The slope—particularly steep at home in the United
States—was most upsetting to Karen, who seemed to take each success or failure personally. "Each time you get a hit record you have to
work twice as hard to get another one," she said in 1977. "This business
changes every minute. If you don't spend all your time staying on top
of it or thinking you're staying on top of it, you're going to be gone.
And that's a full-time job."

Though Karen and Richard were still very well known, and their
concerts were a huge draw, record sales began to fall. *A Kind of Hush*
eventually went gold but was not the commercial success of previous

Carpenters albums. Herb Alpert had hinted to Karen and Richard that the album was not on par with their earlier releases. Although Alpert could have held up production in favor of better material, the Carpenters were satisfied enough and pushed for its release.

Allyn Ferguson, who worked with the Carpenters in the early 1970s, witnessed the downhill slide of many artists, even legends like Elvis Presley and Frank Sinatra. "It happens to everybody," he says. "It has nothing to do with the people themselves. They're doing the same thing they always did. The public gets tired of them. It's a strange thing how the American public is not only fickle, but they respond to a lot of different things that are not musical at all, like the publicity and the attention that everybody's giving them. It's like a mob mentality. When the idol starts to have the image disappear, American fans just move on to the next one. That's a part of show business. We have a great term in showbiz—everybody's a 'star fucker,' which means if you're not a star anymore everybody just turns their back. It's very fleeting, and there are tragedies. I think Karen was one of those tragedies, and I could name dozens of other people who can't deal with the fact that it's not like it used to be."

The Carpenters largely blamed their wholesome image for the decline in interest in their music. The image issues that plagued the duo from their debut would likely have faded if allowed to do so, but the fact that both Karen and Richard were vocal about their frustrations only seemed to draw attention to their "Goody Four Shoes" personas. They had been called "milk-fed," "squeaky-clean," "vitamin-swallow-ing," "sticky-sweet," and "Pepsodent-smiling" ad nauseum. The 1974 *Rolling Stone* cover story was one of their first determined efforts to add some grit to their public perception and shed the myth that they were perfect angels. "The image we have," Karen said, "would be impossible for Mickey Mouse to maintain. We're just normal people."

Their quest for acceptance continued with a 1976 cover story for *People Weekly* in which they admitted neither was a virgin and both voted in favor of legalizing marijuana. "It's no worse than alcohol," Karen said. In *Melody Maker* she told Ray Coleman the story of a jour-nalist who asked Richard if he agreed with premarital sex. "When he said 'yes,' the woman wouldn't print it! We were labeled as don't-do-anything! Just smile, scrub your teeth, take a shower, go to sleep. Mom's apple pie. We're normal! I get up in the morning, eat breakfast in front of the TV, and watch game shows. I don't smoke. If I wanted to smoke I would smoke. I just don't like smoking, not because of my image."

What came next was a backlash not unlike that against Tony Peluso's fuzz guitar solo on "Goodbye to Love" in 1972. But they were prepared for the reaction and defended themselves accordingly. "It had to be done," Karen told London's *Daily Mirror*. "We had to shed the goody two shoes image. It was too much. We're normal, healthy people. We believe people should be free to do what they want to do. Richard is thirty, and I am twenty-six. But the letters we got when we said we weren't virgins read as though we had committed a crime. People must have been dumb to have believed that we were that good. I don't drink because I don't enjoy it much, but when Richard and some of the band boys cooled down with beers on stage there was an outcry. And when Richard was seen smoking an ordinary cigarette, the reaction was terrific. And when we said we thought pot ought to be legalized, in came a shoal of letters saying we were drug addicts. . . . We had to speak out and tell the truth about us as it is. It's hell living like a pair of angels."

Like Karen, Olivia Newton-John had her share of image-related issues in the mid-1970s. "That 'white bread' image was something else Karen and I had in common," Olivia says. "We never felt we were taken seriously as singers." Newton-John was the occasional sounding board for Karen's dismay and disappointment concerning the Carpenters' decline in sales and popularity. "They'd had incredible success and then they were going through that slack period we all do," she explains. "It's part of life."

AFTER *A Kind of Hush* it seemed that both Karen and Richard lacked the energy and determination that had shined through on their earlier efforts. It also became more difficult to write and select material radio programmers and audiences wanted. "For the last three years there has been a definite resistance to our product, and I don't know why,"

Karen explained to *Radio Report* in 1978. "We've been doing our best to turn out the finest product we can. Richard keeps changing direction. We've covered practically every aspect that is capable of being put to disc with the exception of classical. We haven't done that yet."

Experimentation, diversity, and perhaps even desperation birthed the Carpenters' next studio album, *Passage*, released September 23, 1977. *Billboard* called it their "most boldly innovative and sophisticated undertaking yet," pointing out that "the material constantly shifts gears from calypso, lushly orchestrated complex pop rhythms, jazz flavored ballads, reggae and melodic, upbeat numbers."

Passage opened with the daring "B'wana She No Home," a Michael Franks tune with a vocal arrangement by jazz great Gene Puerling, the sound architect of vocal groups including the Hi-Lo's and the Singers Unlimited. "B'wana" was one of several songs on the album that were essentially live recordings. "When recording, we usually begin with bass, drums, piano, and build from there," Richard explained in the album's liner notes. "But on several of these tracks, almost the whole thing was recorded live all at once. Certain pieces call for that."

Passage spawned the debut single "All You Get from Love Is a Love Song," one Karen felt was a surefire hit. "We thought it was really going to make it," she said, "but it got hardly any airplay at all." It was a strong album cut but not nearly as strong a single as they needed at this stage. Monitoring airplay became a focus for the Carpenters more with this album than any previous. Some at A&M even began resorting to payola, meaning that payments or incentives were given in exchange for placement on playlists and prominent airplay during a given interval. Even Carpenters fans were enlisted to assist and sent gifts as tokens of appreciation for helping monitor the number of spins a particular song was seeing on a particular station.

Richard first listened to "Calling Occupants of Interplanetary Craft" at the urging of Tony Peluso on a 1976 album by the Canadian group Klaatu. "[He] wanted to do that more than anything in the world," Karen recalled. "When we got done with it, it had turned into an epic. We figured out that we spent more time on 'Occupants' than we did our third album. That was a job. It was a masterpiece when

Richard got done with it." In addition to introducing the song to the Carpenters, Peluso reprised his role of a bemused deejay during the recording's opening dialogue segment.

For their endeavor, Karen and Richard brought in sixty-year-old Englishman Peter Knight, whose work on the Moody Blues' *Days of Future Passed* album had impressed the Carpenters nearly ten years earlier. According to harpist Gayle Levant, working with Knight was a thrill for her and the other studio musicians. "He was a phenomenal arranger," she says. "It was absolutely a joy to play his charts. Those magic moments happen when you hear a chart and you just know that you're working with a man who is magic." It was also Knight who arranged and conducted the orchestra on the *Passage* album's other epic, the sweeping anthem from Andrew Lloyd Webber's *Evita*, "Don't Cry for Me, Argentina." A&M's Jerry Moss disagreed with the Carpenters' decision to record "Argentina," saying it was a socialist anthem, but Richard believed strongly that it was well suited for Karen and in no way meant to be a political statement. For many years, copies of the album produced and sold in Argentina omitted the selection.

Contractual agreements precluded the Los Angeles Philharmonic from being credited as such, so liner notes humorously credit the "Over-budget Philharmonic" instead. With more than a hundred instrumentalists and an additional fifty in the chorus, the recording was done on A&M's Chaplin Stage (and wired into studio D) before an audience of representatives from Los Angeles–area press and media. College friend and tubist Wes Jacobs was visiting Los Angeles and sat in on the colossal recording session.

Although rarely complimentary of the Carpenters' product or live performances, Robert Hilburn, rock critic with the *Los Angeles Times*, praised *Passage* for its "experimental touches that added refreshing character to their musical foundation. On their version of 'Don't Cry for Me, Argentina' there's a maturity to Karen's vocal that was far beyond anything in the early years." Hilburn obviously overlooked "Superstar," "Rainy Days and Mondays," "This Masquerade," and countless others, but his admiration was better late than never. But on "Argentina," there was a sense of depth and understanding. Like many of her recordings, the lyric was autobiographical when placed in context with the personal struggles she faced over the years.

> *And as for fortune and as for fame*
> *I never invited them in*
> *Though it seemed to the world they were all I desired*
> *They are illusions; they're not the solutions they promised to be*

"Sweet, Sweet Smile" was the album's final single and one that took aim at the country music market. "This is the first time we've gone all out after a country hit," said A&M's assistant national promotion director Lenny Bronstein in an interview with Paul Grein. The song was also issued with "Reason to Believe," "Jambalaya," and "Top of the World" in a four-song promotional *Country Collection* EP sent to country stations and regional promoters. "We always try to get one country song on our albums," Karen told *Country Music* magazine in 1978. "Not for any specific purpose but because we like it. We don't go in and say we've got to record a song that will get on the country charts. We always just go in with what we like." Although "Sweet, Sweet Smile" reached only #44 on the pop chart, it went Top 10 on the country chart and peaked at #8. The crossover success and interest from country radio led Karen and Richard to consider recording an all-country album for 1978, but the plan never made it past Jerry Moss, who reminded them that a hit pop album was their priority.

"I Just Fall In Love Again" was an obvious choice for single release from *Passage*, but it was too much in the vein of the traditional Carpenters love song formula, complete with oboe interludes and a fuzz guitar solo. They seemed to consciously move away from such predictability with this album, which incidentally contained no original material. Canadian singer Anne Murray, herself a pop-country crossover, had a Top 20 hit with "I Just Fall in Love Again" the following year.

Passage was the first Carpenters album to be released without any photographs of Karen and Richard, a stark change from their usual smiling portraits. Even the trademark "Carpenters" logo appeared only on the lower portion of the back panel. Popular Los Angeles illustrator

Lou Beach, commissioned to do the *Passage* artwork, was given the title and free reign. "I was exploring the limits of the new color Xerox machines," recalls Beach. "That art came out of a session at the copy center. It was the best-paying record cover job I'd ever had."

While the Carpenters considered *Passage* to be a creative success, commercially it flopped, becoming their first album to fall short of gold status. Ardent Carpenters follower Ray Coleman had felt the duo's two previous albums were inferior, but he proclaimed that *Passage* was an "indecisive" career low. "After all these years of admiring their excellence, we have come to expect something special from Carpenters albums," Coleman wrote in his review for *Melody Maker*. "This one just will not do.... Karen's melting vocals—always their most powerful asset—are lost when they tackle "Man Smart, Woman Smarter" and "Don't Cry For Me, Argentina."... It's a tragic comment on such talent, but Carpenters fans can safely ignore this release; let's wish them a speedy return to musical decisiveness."

Often accused of not allowing the Carpenters the necessary studio time to produce a quality album, former manager Sherwin Bash explained the duo's need for patience once their records sales took a downturn. "Too many artists forget that you don't have to do everything in five years," he said. "But you can space it out and take your time. Take time to recharge those batteries and sit down and think about the next album. If you're going to write it, you're lucky to come out with an album every one or two years. In today's life, even if it isn't for three years the world won't forget. The world doesn't need another album, they only need *great* albums. I could never convince Richard of this."

Karen was fiercely proud of the material she and Richard recorded and was troubled by discouraging reviews, especially from those who had long been on their side. "In this business you've not only got to prove yourself but you've also got to prove them wrong," she had declared in 1976.

Luckily, the Carpenters' presence on the international music scene was strong, with "Calling Occupants of Interplanetary Craft" becoming a huge hit in Japan and "Sweet, Sweet Smile" a smash in Germany. But the fickle American audiences left Karen and Richard scrambling to produce something they would buy. "We just don't know what Top 40 radio is looking for," Karen told *Radio Report*. "One minute they say they're looking for a traditional Carpenters record. We give them one of those and they don't want it. They say they want something different, so we give them 'Occupants' and they don't want that either. We give them country and Top 40 again resists. If somebody would just let us know what the problem is, then we could take it from there. Everybody has a different answer."

Karen was unable to separate these professional discouragements from her personal life. She was so focused on achieving and succeeding in the outside world that her inner world and inner beauties were not valued. Although she claimed to want nothing more than a traditional family life with a husband and children, business came first. In fact, when interviewed in 1975, she told Ray Coleman that if it came to a choice between private life and fame, hers would be fame. "We're very dedicated to our business," she said. "Our life is our music, creating it. We try to do everything with as much perfection as we can. We have certain beliefs, certain loyalties to ways of doing things."

"She was very, very career conscious," recalls Olivia Newton-John. "It was very important to her, she took it very seriously and she took it personally. I'd always had relationships and boyfriends. To me, my career wasn't the be-all and end-all of life, but for her it pretty much was at that point."

"YOU ARE the Perry Comos of today," Jerry Weintraub told the Carpenters. Yet another aspect of Weintraub's visions involved bringing the duo into American living rooms via television. He felt this was a sure way to guarantee permanence for their careers. From specials featuring performers such as Como, Frank Sinatra, Barbra Streisand, and Petula Clark to regular series starring performers such as Judy Garland, Tom Jones, Sonny and Cher, and Glen Campbell, musical variety shows were a staple of American television in the 1960s and 1970s.

At first, Karen and Richard were unconvinced. Their 1971 summer series *Make Your Own Kind of Music* had been a disaster in their opin-

(above) Nathan Hale eighth grade class of 1963: Karen is in row 3, fifth from right.
Frank Bonito

(left) Karen with classmates. From left: Frank Bonito, Anthony Viollano, Debra Cusack, and Karen. Frank Bonito

Eighth grade graduation day, June 1963: Mitchell Porylo, Karen, Carol DeFilippo, Frank Bonito, and Sophie DeFilippo.
Frank Bonito

Class pictures, 1965 (left) and 1967 (right). Downey Historical Society

(above) Concert choir, 1966–67. Karen in second row, middle.
Downey Historical Society

(above right) Singing in the annual Viking Varieties talent show at Downey High School, March 1965. Downey Historical Society

1965–66 Downey High School drum line: Randy Malquist, Karen, Nancy Roubal, John Higgins, and Frankie Chavez.
Downey Historical Society

With Wes Jacobs at Viking Varieties, March 1966.
(below) Early Carpenters promotional photo, 1969.

In rehearsal (above) and in concert (below), Long Beach, California, December 1970.

Frank Pooler

Karen as the American Cancer Society's national youth chairman. The Carpenters donated proceeds from concert tour book sales to the ACS.

American Cancer Society

At home on Newville Avenue with Agnes, Harold, and Richard, early 1971. Robert Trendler/Globe Photos

A serious pose from a duo usually known for their "toothy twosome" personas. A&M Records

Karen at age twenty-one.

A&M Records

On location for Tom Jones's *London Bridge Special*, Lake Havasu, Arizona, February 1972.

A&M Records

With Frank Pooler backstage at the Chevron Hotel, Sydney, Australia, May 1972.

Frank Pooler

The Carpenters during their second visit to the White House and first time visiting with President Richard M. Nixon, August 1972.

Nixon Library/National Archives

The Carpenters softball team comprised band members, roadies, and opening act Skiles and Henderson. A&M Records

Photographed in director's chairs the duo received as gifts from an appearance on *The Carol Burnett Show*, 1972.

A&M Records

Hollywood Bowl, 1974. Sher

On the lot at A&M Records, 1975.

A&M Records

(right) On stage at the Westchester Premier Theater in Tarrytown, New York, May 22, 1975.

Norma Segarra

The "lead sister" in her
element at Toronto's
O'Keefe Centre,
August 1976.

Bob Olsen/Toronto Star/GetStock.com

(above) With guest star John Denver in a "Pocahontas"
skit, later deleted, from *The Carpenters' Very First
Television Special.* ABC-TV

(left) A casual look for a 1976 photo session. A&M Records

Filming a Suntory Pop soft drink commercial for Japanese television, 1977. Suntory

Singing "White Christmas" on *The Carpenters at Christmas* TV special, 1977. ABC-TV

Karen at age twenty-seven.

Harry Langdon

December 3, 1978: Joining the choirs and orchestra from California State University, Long Beach, Karen performs at the *Winter Festival Concert* in the newly completed Pacific Terrace Theater in Long Beach, California. This would be the Carpenters' final American concert appearance. Leo Hetzel

Concert program.

Karen photographed during one of several West Coast sessions for the solo album. Here she is listening to playbacks in studio A on the A&M Records lot in Hollywood, early 1980.

Bonnie Schiffman

At A&M Records.

Bonnie Schiffman

Dancing and drumming in "I Got Rhythm," a production number from the Carpenters' final television special, *Music, Music, Music,* filmed March 1980. ABC-TV

One of several *Made in America* photo sessions, 1981. A&M Records

Dressed to the nines, a confident Karen poses for famed celebrity photographer
Harry Langdon, 1977. Harry Langdon

ions, primarily due to a lack of control over the sketch material. "We stayed away from television for quite a few years until we signed with Jerry Weintraub, at which point he got us our own shows," Karen said. "That's really what we needed. We needed to have full control of what we wanted to put and present on television."

After negotiating a deal with ABC-TV program director Fred Silverman in 1976, Weintraub formed Downey-Bronx Productions with the Carpenters to produce their television specials and remained actively involved throughout the production. He attended most rehearsals and tapings, offered feedback, and made suggestions to director Bob Henry. "Jerry was always an extra set of eyes and ears looking out for Karen and Richard," remembers Jerry Jaskulski, associate producer for several of the Carpenters' specials. "Bob Henry was in charge overall, and they trusted him when it came to the visual presentation of the show. They were always kept aware of all planning and did have veto power if they didn't like something. Richard was certainly in charge of making the musical decisions. Karen could be demanding when it came to her own performances, as she should have been. She also had a great sense of humor. The mere fact that she chose to play the drums shows that she enjoyed letting loose."

After three weeks of intense rehearsals with guest stars John Denver and Victor Borge, *The Carpenters' Very First Television Special* was taped September 30–October 2, 1976. The December 8 airing came in at #6 for the week in the Nielsen ratings and garnered an offer from ABC-TV for additional specials on the network. For their 1978 holiday television special, *The Carpenters: A Christmas Portrait*, Karen and Richard were joined by legendary song and dance man Gene Kelly and other guests. "By the time we did that special they were certainly more relaxed and familiar with the routine," says associate producer Jerry Jaskulski.

Karen agreed, saying, "Each one, in our opinion, has gotten better because you grow. You learn very quickly in television how to do certain things and what you do and what you can pull off and what you can't pull off. There are a lot of things that time doesn't permit you to do the way you want to. If it were up to us we'd spend a week just recording, but you can't do that with television. Luckily, we've come off as close to perfection as we have attempted. Some things we had to let go against our judgment. On the whole we've been real, real happy. We've had the opportunity to work with so many, many good people."

Guest stars on the television specials ran the gamut from legends like Ella Fitzgerald and Gene Kelly to Grade B stars including Jimmy and Kristy McNichol, Suzanne Somers, and John Davidson. While the comedic efforts were entertaining in moderation, the writing was poor to say the least. "The Carpenters should have demanded better scripts, guest stars, sketch ideas, and staging concepts," wrote Paul Grein in a 1991 reassessment of the duo's work. "If they didn't have the power to make those demands, they should have."

Hindsight reveals a number of poor choices in terms of scripts and scenarios. Given Karen's history with an eating disorder, it was a bizarre decision by producers to stage one of her song sequences in a kitchen wearing an apron. "I've found over the years the best way to get a party going is to make sure that people have enough food to eat!" From there Karen went from appliance to appliance, all the while singing and dancing—and baking. "The reason we chose to have Karen in a kitchen environment was to present her to be more like one of the girls," Jerry Jaskulski says. "We wanted to show her as a typical family member and make it easier for the women in the audience to relate to her. Prior to that they had only seen her singing and playing the drums. We all knew Karen had an eating problem, but no one ever thought it would end so tragically."

Unfortunately the producers' narrow-mindedness meant Karen usually portrayed one-dimensional caricatures during their television specials. Her dialogue lacked depth, and as a result she often came across as gullible or naive, at times even a little ditzy. Richard loathed the attempts at comedy and later regretted the emphasis on those sketches and their canned laughter over higher-caliber musical routines. But Karen was the star, and she seemed to enjoy these productions, which gave her the opportunity to sing, dance, drum, and even try her hand at acting, which sparked her interest in starring in a movie. "It's something I would really like to do," she said in 1978. "I love to act and sing. I'm not sure how or when but I'd like to do a musical." In fact, Karen had hinted at this idea as early as 1971, evidenced by this A&M Records press release.

> As for Karen, the far-flung future ("at least five years from 'now'") holds possibilities of singing and acting in a musical comedy. "I've always loved Broadway-type musicals like *Camelot, Finian's Rainbow* and *The King and I.* I'd like to do something like that, eventually." With her vibrant beauty, her electric stage appeal and her voice— which definitely blends pure sweetness with a hunt of sophisticated sultriness—this seems like another dream that could well be gloriously realized. For the Carpenters, dreams seem to turn to reality with the snap of their magical fingers.

Karen loved female comedians like Lucille Ball, Carol Burnett, Phyllis Diller, and even more dramatic actresses like Barbra Streisand, who had seen much success with musicals like *Funny Girl* and *Hello, Dolly!* "Streisand just floors me," she said in 1976, just two months prior to the release of Streisand's *A Star Is Born.* "She's so good. I would like to do something like that."

The natural comedian in Karen was evident to all who knew her. "She was really droll," says Carole Curb. "She made everybody laugh with this amazingly witty and sarcastic sense of humor." According to Frenda Franklin, "Karen did the best Barbra Streisand imitation you've ever heard in your life. She really, really could have been an actress. She wanted to act. She even wanted to study acting. Today it seems as though everybody wants to do everything in the business, but in those days if you sang, you sang. You were lucky that you got the opportunity to sing. But Karen wasn't looking at it like, 'Oh, I want to be a movie star.' She just knew that she had something else to offer."

———— ✦✦✦ ————

IN THE fall of 1956 during a visit to the Music Corner, one of New Haven's popular record shops, Harold Carpenter had purchased Spike Jones's *Xmas Spectacular* album for his children. It was an odd and varied mix of trademark Spike Jones novelty songs and serious choral music arranged by Jud Conlon. A progressive vocal arranger at the time, Conlon came onto the scene in the 1940s and is often credited with pioneering the tight, close harmony sounds used in popular music at the time. He and his "Rhythmaires" backed Bing Crosby, Judy Garland, and others on a number of popular recordings.

"There was one album that I remember from the day I was born," Karen said. "It was Spike Jones's Christmas album. There are some zany things on there.... Spike Jones was a master at zany stuff. A lot of people don't know that it takes more talent and more perfection to pull off crackpot things than it does to do a lot of serious things.... This album was a combination of nutty and serious. We grew up with that album and just loved it to death."

Since signing with A&M Records in 1969, Karen and Richard had wanted to record a Christmas album of their own. They both loved the Christmas season and the abundance of great holiday music, but due to touring and recording schedules they had only been able to fit in two seasonal offerings over the years, "Merry Christmas, Darling" in 1970 and "Santa Claus Is Comin' to Town" in 1974. In preparation for *The Carpenters at Christmas*, their second special for ABC-TV, recording sessions commenced in August 1977. It was quickly decided that these recordings would serve as the foundation for an entire album of Christmas music to be released in conjunction with the television special's airing.

The early Spike Jones recordings proved to be the inspiration for Richard, who admittedly patterned much of this project after the *Xmas Spectacular* LP both he and Karen had enjoyed so much as children. They immediately set out to hire Jud Conlon to do their arrangements, only to find that he'd died in 1966. Their next call went to Peter Knight. It was Knight, along with veteran arranger Billy May, who helped bring the concept to life with the help of an eighty-piece orchestra and seventy-voice choir. A five-minute overture of nine selections was orchestrated with the strings, making way for the grand entrance by Karen's voice.

Frosted window panes, candles gleaming inside
Painted candy canes on the tree

Santa's on his way, he's filled his sleigh with things
Things for you and for me

Sammy Cahn's festive lyric for "The Christmas Waltz" was the perfect match for Karen's warm delivery, which melted into a creative rendition of "Sleigh Ride." Lesser-known titles like "It's Christmas Time," "Sleep Well, Little Children," and "The First Snowfall" were culled from the Spike Jones album. Arranger Billy May, who had previously lent his talents to the Carpenters' *Horizon* in 1975, was responsible for helping re-create the Spike Jones charts in a way best suited to Karen's vocal range. This included the pairing of songs like "Winter Wonderland" and "Silver Bells" in an unforgettable medley with "White Christmas."

It became obvious that there was not time to complete and release the album prior to the airing of the 1977 television special. As a consolation, A&M released "The Christmas Song (Chestnuts Roasting on an Open Fire)" as a special holiday single that year. Karen's is one of the only performances of the tune that truly rivals the warmth and presence of Nat "King" Cole's classic recording. In the same vein were "Have Yourself a Merry Little Christmas" and "I'll Be Home for Christmas," two songs so identified with Judy Garland and Bing Crosby, respectively. Surrounded with the choral and orchestral sounds of a glorious 1940s MGM musical, Karen was as natural and at home with these songs as either a Judy or a Bing. The songs took on new ownership in the capable, worthy hands of Karen Carpenter.

Recording continued off and on between other sessions, tours, and television tapings, and the Carpenters spent a total of fourteen months producing what became *Christmas Portrait*. Midway through the process they took their Christmas selections to the Las Vegas stage at the MGM Grand, complete with a huge tree and nearly eighty musicians. Their usual Vegas orchestra was augmented with a twenty-four-voice choir.

Construction of the album continued in the New Year. "Merry Christmas, Darling" was by then a recurrent holiday favorite on the radio, but Karen was never pleased with the huskier sound from the lead vocal recorded when she was only twenty years old. Her voice had matured and developed immensely, so she opted to re-record "Darling" in 1978, as she had done with "Ticket to Ride" in 1973. The Carpenters also took time to record several nonfestive songs amid the Christmas sessions, including "When I Fall in Love" and "Little Girl Blue" for their 1978 ABC-TV special *The Carpenters—Space Encounters*. The tunes were so similar in style that only the latter was included. "When I Fall in Love" was later included in their 1980 special, *Music, Music, Music.*

The sacred selections intermingled with the secular on *Christmas Portrait* included "Christ Is Born," a lovely musical setting Richard first heard on *The Perry Como Christmas Album* in 1968, the traditional carol "Silent Night," and the vocally demanding Bach-Gounod version of "Ave Maria." Karen's love for the Christmas season and its music was always evident when asked about the album, which was planned for a double LP set at one point. "To sing these songs is something that gives me more pleasure than I can really put into words," she said. "I think we came out with something like twenty-nine songs. We've got at least another twelve in the can that we couldn't finish.... We were dying because we couldn't stuff them on the record. We'd have had to leave the label off!"

In contrast with *A Kind of Hush* and *Passage*, reviews for *Christmas Portrait* were overwhelmingly positive. "They've synthesized everything to ever come out of Sunset Boulevard at Yuletide into two sides of a perfect piece of plastic," wrote James Parade of *Record Mirror*. "[I]t will bring you Disney, Snow White and her snow, whiteness whiter than white, sleighbells...shimmering strings, snowflakes scurrying, ring-ting-tingling, jingling and lots more besides.... Buy this record for instant atmosphere and have yourself a merry little Christmas."

Christmas music was the ideal showcase for Karen Carpenter, and in many ways her renditions were the perfect union of songs and singer. "*Christmas Portrait* is really Karen's first solo album, and it should have been released as such," explained Richard in 2004. "But I don't believe A&M would have been too keen on that, especially since no conventional album had been released by us that year."

12

THE BIRD HAS FINALLY FLOWN THE COOP

AGNES CARPENTER was a worrier. She had trouble getting to sleep each night and had sought the help of a doctor in the early 1970s. "When she'd go to bed, she'd think about what she had to do or things that had been done that shouldn't have been done," explains Evelyn Wallace. "She'd always have something on her mind. She couldn't get to sleep, so they had to give her something strong."

Agnes first noticed Richard's state of exhaustion and inability to sleep in the fall of 1971 after the group returned home from their European tour. He was worried about completing their next album, *A Song for You*, in the allotted time. "I was up just about every night," he recalled in 1988. "I wasn't getting any sleep, and I did not look too hot when I stepped off the plane. I'd never had a pill before or since except for this. I was really in need of some sleep and quite nervous and concerned."

Quaaludes were prescription sedatives commonly used to treat insomnia at the time, and Richard did not hesitate when his mother offered them to help him sleep. "Taken properly they were a very good pill," he later explained. "She took them until they discontinued them—one a night the way you're supposed to. She never had any problem with them."

For a number of years, Richard took the quaaludes as directed. "It was very difficult to sleep on the road," recalls Maria Galeazzi, who began taking quaaludes with Richard during their romance. "I just sort of bummed off of him. It wasn't every night. It was now and then when he couldn't sleep."

According to Evelyn Wallace, "If Richard didn't go to sleep the minute he hit the pillow, he'd get up, and he'd end up fooling around at the piano or get something to eat in the kitchen. Those wear off after a while if you keep busy enough. He'd go up to bed, but he still wasn't sleepy. He'd take another one and sometimes a third one. He was just taking too darn many of them." Richard found that he enjoyed the high the quaaludes gave him—a convenient but risky side effect of sorts—but he was never much of a party animal. For some time he knew nothing about the use of quaaludes as a recreational drug, but the more he took, the longer it would take for the drug's effects to wear off.

Gradually Richard became more and more severely addicted. As his condition worsened his playing began to suffer, and he lost all confidence in his abilities as a pianist. By late 1978 the addiction had taken hold. Disguising the problem became more difficult for Richard because his speech was slurred, and he could barely sign his name because he was unable to hold a pen in his trembling hands. This meant that playing certain intricate piano parts was out of the question. "One side of me was saying, 'You fool! You're killing yourself, you can't function and you're letting your sister and parents down,'" he wrote a decade later in *TV Guide*. "But the other side convinced me I couldn't get by without those pills. . . . I tried a couple of detox programs, but even if you get the stuff out of your system, it's hard to lick the problem. By 1978 I was in trouble, no two ways about it."

Richard hit rock bottom in September when they played the MGM Grand in Las Vegas. He spent most days in bed or dealing with anxiety issues and panic attacks. He would emerge early in the evenings, just long enough to do the show. All he could think about was getting off the stage and going back to bed, where the vicious cycle continued. It was between performances on Monday, September 4, that Richard abruptly informed the band and their crew that he was quitting.

"That's it," he said. "I'm not playing another night." Although it was never Richard's intention, this run at the MGM Grand would prove to be the Carpenters' last professional engagement, save a few public appearances in 1981. Even then, the band reunited only to mime their instrument playing while Karen and Richard lip-synched to their studio recordings.

Los Angeles session singer Walt Harrah, who was brought in to fill in for band member Dan Woodhams after a serious automobile accident, was disappointed to see his stint with the Carpenters end prematurely. "I did their last MGM show where Richard just quit," he recalls. "It was a two-week engagement of something like twenty-eight shows, and he quit after four or five days. I guess he was sick of it. He was very private. He was very aloof and alone and kind of depressed, but so was Karen. It could have had to do with her physical condition. She looked like a Holocaust victim."

With Richard dealing with his addiction and the aftershocks felt from his swift termination of the group's Vegas gig, the last thing he wanted to do was prepare for another appearance. Yet the Carpenters were on the bill for a concert with Frank Pooler, his choir, and the university orchestra. The show was to be held December 3, 1978, in the Pacific Terrace Theater at the Long Beach Convention Center with proceeds benefitting the Carpenters Choral Scholarship Fund at California State University Long Beach. As the date approached, Richard began removing songs from the program when he realized he was unable to perform them. "My hands were shaking too much," he explained some years later. "I told Karen I was dropping 'It's Christmas Time' because I didn't think it would go over well. And I told her I was dropping 'The Nutcracker' because I didn't think the university orchestra could cut it. I pared that damn program down to almost nothing because I couldn't play most of it. Poor Karen. She was buying all of this, even though she knew I had a problem."

The Carpenters took the stage late in the show that Sunday afternoon with guest conductor Doug Strawn leading the choir and orchestra. Karen's entrance on "Sleep Well, Little Children" was uneventful, and Richard was incapacitated. He did manage to fulfill his promised rendition of themes from *Close Encounters of a Third Kind* and *Star Wars*, a medley somewhat out of place in the context of a Christmas performance.

"The Carpenters finally arrived on the stage far too late in the show to make much difference, and stayed for too short a time," wrote Charles Carney in his review for the *49er*, a student newspaper. "Their presence should either have been established during the early portion of the show and woven throughout, or extended for a longer time at the end. As it was, their arrival broke the carefully designed momentum that had been building during the first two-thirds of the show and catapulted it into the predictability of a Las Vegas lounge act." The Carpenters' lackluster appearance in Long Beach was saved only by Karen's rich and warm tones on "Merry Christmas, Darling" and "Silent Night" and a performance of "Ave Maria" rivaling that of the album version.

During the following week, Karen and Richard were scheduled to depart for London, where they were set to appear on *Bruce Forsyth's Big Night* on BBC rival ITV. Richard was in no condition to perform, much less travel overseas. He was practically bedridden and tried to convince Karen that these promotional appearances in London could wait, even though two new albums, *The Singles 1974–1978* and *Christmas Portrait*, had just hit the UK market. "We're going!" she told Richard, determined to follow through with the engagement.

Arriving at the group's rehearsal space in North Hollywood, Karen was met by the band members but not Richard. She called him immediately and discovered he was still in bed and refusing to make the trip. When she visited him later that day, Richard explained how his addiction had gone too far. Although she was aware of his condition, he had always made excuses and she'd usually believed him. "You get pretty devious," he later recalled. "The same way anorexics do. But it finally got so bad that I couldn't get out of bed, and I had to say, 'Karen, I've got a problem here.'"

Due to her tenacious spirit—or perhaps just out of sheer stubbornness—Karen flew to London with the band to make good on their promise to perform. Covering for Richard, she told Bruce Forsyth's audience that he was under the weather. "Two days before we were going to come over, he caught himself a real nice case of the flu," she said through a nervous smile. "So he's flat on his back in Los Angeles, and he's really upset that he couldn't come."

Musically, the show went off without a hitch, thanks to the support of friend Peter Knight and Jeff Wesley, the latter filling in for Richard on keyboards. Taking liberties with the melody, Karen's performance of "I Need to Be in Love" was perhaps the most tender and intimate reading of the song ever. She also performed "Please Mr. Postman," "Merry Christmas, Darling," and the ambitious grouping of "Winter Wonderland," "Silver Bells," and "White Christmas" as a duet with Forsyth.

Word of a possible split between the Carpenters spread across Europe with the airing of the Forsyth show, but Karen did her best to dispel such rumors. "Karen wants everyone to know that she is not going solo," Tim Ewbank wrote in the *Sun*, with Karen explaining that "Brucie's show is setting a sort of unfortunate record for us. It is the first time that the Carpenters have been billed to appear anywhere without both of us going on." Ewbank inquired about her health, to which she replied, "I'm fine now. I've got my energy back and I'm raring to go!"

Indeed, this was one of the first occasions in her entire career that Karen had been away from home without Richard by her side. From her hotel suite at the Inn on the Park in central London, Karen sent her brother a postcard of encouragement, postmarked December 12, 1978: "It's all coming off like clockwork—the album is getting hotter by the minute. The music end is tops. Miss you—Love, KAC1." (Karen's abbreviated signature referred to the personalized California license plate attached to her 1972 Mercedes 350.)

While in London, Karen requested that John "Softly" Adrian assist her. Softly was by then a married man and maintained a safe distance from Karen. Their conversations consisted mostly of small talk. "You haven't said 'thank you' for your wedding present, Softly," Karen said playfully.

"What present?" he asked.

"The present I sent you," she said. "I sent you a crystal punch bowl with glasses!"

Softly was puzzled. The only contact he was aware of came in 1976 when Karen sent him a note saying "The bird has finally flown the coop"—this after her move from Downey to Century City.

"Karen, I didn't get any present from you," he said.

"Hmm," Karen pondered. "Well, I gave it to someone at A&M. Obviously they didn't send it to you." The mystery surrounding the orchestrated ending of their relationship some two years earlier seemed to continue but without their knowledge. The two shared one last hug at London's airport as Karen boarded a plane bound for home.

* * *

SOARING RECORD sales in Europe did little to cheer Karen. The reality of her personal problems and those of her brother hit home once she returned to Los Angeles just in time for Christmas. A year earlier they were celebrating on stage in Las Vegas, but in 1978 the holidays were anything but happy in the Carpenter household. Heated arguments ensued with Richard becoming increasingly dismayed by Karen's withering figure. "He was not all that kind to Karen," recalls Evelyn Wallace. "But at times he'd even argue with his mother, which was taking his life in his hands!" Karen would retort with comments about the consequences of his addiction. To Richard, these were not welcome observations from someone on a similar path of self-destruction. "She was so concerned," Frenda Franklin explains. "You see, Karen was very sensible about everybody else. In the case of Richard, there was nothing to debate. It was terrible. She just couldn't wait any longer to get him help. He wasn't happy with her, but she took the strong role and did what she had to do as a sister."

Richard was called to a meeting at the office of Jerry Weintraub with Werner Wolfen and others present. "Before you know it, in the middle of the meeting Richard was sound asleep in the chair," recalls Wallace. "They knew Richard was on something even then."

On the morning of January 10, 1979, Richard popped ten pills before boarding a plane bound for Topeka, Kansas. "Karen forced him," Frenda says. "She took him on an air ambulance to Menninger's." There Richard checked into the chemical dependency unit with Karen and Wolfen at his side. Both Richard and Werner felt this would be a great opportunity for Karen to address her issues as well, but she was not serious enough about her eating disorder to do anything significant about it. Instead she returned to Los Angeles—full of nervous energy—and began looking for projects to occupy her time while Richard was in rehab. "It was OK for a little bit," she told the *Los Angeles Times*, "but then I was anxious to go back to work."

During her first return visit to see Richard at Menninger, Karen hesitantly shared her plans to go into the studio to begin recording a solo album. Just two weeks into the six-week program, he was in no condition to hear this sort of news and was understandably livid. "He was madder than hell," recalls Evelyn Wallace. "He did *not* want her to go to New York and record on her own. I think that he realized that Karen could sell more records than he could."

By this time, Richard was certain Karen was battling the disorder brought to his family's attention by Wallace three years earlier, and he confronted her about her own well-being and deteriorating physical appearance. "What the hell are you talking about? Going and doing a solo album?! Why don't *you* go and check into something like this that is meant for anorexics!" He reminded Karen of their upcoming tenth anniversary in the music industry. "We can go into the eighties the same way we went into the seventies. We have our talent. We have our record contract."

Karen shut down. She adamantly denied her own issues. "No," she insisted, "there's nothing wrong with me. I don't have anorexia nervosa; I have colitis." In her diary entry for January 24, 1979, Karen wrote: "Confrontation about album."

In public, Karen refused to admit that her physical state was due to anything more than exhaustion from years of overwork. In private, however, Karen took her illness seriously enough to seek professional help—but not without Frenda Leffler by her side. "I had known for a while that she had some sort of a mental illness," Frenda explains. "I knew it wasn't just that she didn't want to eat because she didn't want to eat. She just couldn't conquer this. We were somewhat aware of what it could be, but they just didn't know how to treat it. We didn't have a

Menninger type of thing for her. If we had the great centers for eating disorders they have today, everything could have been different. " With Karen's blessing, Frenda had researched and made appointments with several Los Angeles–based psychiatrists, several of whom dealt with food issues. During each visit, Karen insisted Frenda remain with her while she met with the doctors. "Let me just go in the other room," Frenda said, sensing one doctor's exasperation during a consultation.

"No, Frenny," Karen exclaimed in a panic. "Take me, too!"

"I'm just going to the outer office," she said, assuring Karen she would be fine. "I'll be right out there. You don't have to worry."

"I'm going with you," Karen said, jumping from the couch and heading for the door, leaving Frenda to apologize.

Another cry for help went out to singer Cherry O'Neill when Karen phoned her for advice. "She didn't sound panicked, but she felt that she really needed some help," O'Neill says. "Karen was having particular problems with laxatives, and she didn't believe she could ever get to a point where she was not dependent upon them." O'Neill felt Karen needed a change of scenery. She understood the benefits of getting away from family and the obligations of work. "You need to get away from the pressures of L.A. and show business and concentrate on your own life and survival," she said.

"I'm going to do it," Karen told her. "I'll get well. It's just so damn hard." Evelyn Wallace entered the office during one of the calls in time to overhear Karen say, "Well, I don't want to *die*." Wallace quickly grabbed her things and exited once she realized the serious tone of Karen's conversation.

Cherry sent Karen a copy of a typewritten manuscript for her forth-coming book, which made its way to Ev's desk. *Starving for Attention* was O'Neill's autobiographical look at her battle with anorexia and her eventual recovery. "Whether Karen read the whole thing or not, I don't know," Wallace says. "I think she left it on my desk purposely. Otherwise she would have gotten rid of it or she would have hid it in some of her stuff. Why would she leave that on my desk? I think she wanted me to read it."

BY 1979 Karen's voice had dominated the airwaves for nearly a decade alongside other great pop female vocalists, including Barbra Streisand, Anne Murray, Helen Reddy, and Olivia Newton-John. These singers maintained individual identities as solo artists, garnering a great deal of attention to their personal strengths and abilities, but the public identified Karen as part of a duo. Year after year she was overlooked when Grammy and American Music Awards nominations were announced in categories recognizing female vocalists. Although she rarely voiced disappointment, Karen had yet to receive accolades for her talents as an individual singer.

Karen would mention from time to time that she would like to record a solo album and receive recognition as a solo artist. She had received numerous requests to guest on albums by other artists but always declined out of respect for Richard. In fact, just months earlier she had turned down an invitation from KISS member Gene Simmons, who asked her to sing on his self-titled solo album (which ultimately featured appearances by Helen Reddy and Donna Summer). But Karen had gradually reached a point in her career where she wanted to be known as Karen Carpenter, not just the lead singer from the Carpenters. "That is the ultimate compliment," she had told Ray Coleman back in 1975, "to have respect not only from your fans but also your peers and other singers. To have that kind of reputation and have it stay, it would be fantastic. And it's really nice to know that other people think that something you have is that special."

There was no doubt in Frenda's mind that Karen knew she was good. She was always confident in her talent and abilities. "I think she knew that she had an ability to really touch people," she recalls. "I also think she wanted to do her own thing, and that was a big, big problem. She had talked about it for a long time. It wasn't about hurting anybody. It was about exploring her talents." Frenda encouraged Karen, seeing a solo project as a huge step toward the independence and autonomy Karen so desperately needed. "It was her Emancipation Proclamation," she says. "There's no question, it was her coming out party. That's exactly what it was. But she had no idea the price she was going to pay."

Karen seemed optimistic about her musical options, despite Richard's debilitated state. "Everybody is trying new things," she said in a radio interview during her visit to England in December. "Needless to say, the disco thing is so hot right now. Even a lot of the disco things are pretty, you know. Donna Summer has done some beautiful songs." She also expressed a love for the music of the Bee Gees, whose *Saturday Night Fever* album became one of the best-selling soundtracks of all time.

When asked about future projects and the possibility of both she and Richard working separately, Karen spoke of her brother's interest in scoring a film and hinted of a possible solo project for herself. "We have often thought about it," she said in 1978. "We have discussed it—not necessarily interrupting the Carpenters as a unit but to add on to that. One of the things that Richard's wanted to do for years is produce other people, and if he did something like that I might do a solo album or get into acting, but at the same time keep the Carpenters going because we don't ever want to let that go. We've been discussing a lot of things. There's so much to do, and it's a lot of fun to keep changing."

To the Carpenter family, a solo venture for Karen threatened the Carpenters as a duo. This was especially difficult for Agnes Carpenter, who saw the idea as her daughter tampering with the established formula she had devised. She was fearful a temporary split might lead to a permanent separation and the end of her son's career. "You have to remember, these were uneducated, unsophisticated people," says Frenda of the senior Carpenters. "They were going to stay with the tried and the true. Agnes had washed those cars so that Richard could perform. That was her vision and her goal. That was it! And you stayed with the plan. Anything that deviated or threatened was bad. So Karen was bad."

Initially, Herb Alpert and Jerry Moss supported the idea of a solo project for Karen, as did manager Jerry Weintraub. It was Alpert who recommended producer Phil Ramone, "the Quincy Jones of the East Coast," according to Rob Hoerburger for *Rolling Stone*. Ramone's career with such artists as Billy Joel, Bob Dylan, and Paul Simon was thriving. His recent production of Joel's *52nd Street* album won the Grammy for

Album of the Year for 1979. Karen was hopeful the producer would consent. Ramone, too, had a great deal of respect for Karen as a vocalist and was a self-professed fan of the hits she created with Richard earlier in the decade. "The greatness of her is that within five seconds of hearing that voice on the air you know it is Karen," Ramone says. "Hers is still one of the most instantly identified sounds in the world."

Ramone first met the Carpenters in 1970 when working on an album with Burt Bacharach on the A&M lot. "Herb asked me to come in his office," he recalls. "He said, 'Oh, you've got to hear these two young people we signed recently.' I went crazy. The next time that I heard about them, Burt said they had covered 'Close to You.' Fast-forward a little bit, Burt goes out on a tour and the opening act was the Carpenters. That's when I saw them in New York at Westbury Music Fair."

Jerry Weintraub made the call to Ramone proposing he work with Karen and explained that Richard was taking a year off due to overwork and exhaustion. Phil agreed enthusiastically but was unaware of Richard's bout with quaaludes and his stay at Menninger. "I knew nothing," he says, although he sensed something might be going on beneath the surface. The call from Weintraub was followed by calls from both Alpert and Moss, with both men expressing their support but reminding Phil they were not looking to replace the Carpenters.

Karen's initial meeting with Ramone was a short and informal one that took place at the producer's duplex on Burton Way in Beverly Hills. "Karen didn't want anybody to know that she was even thinking about doing a solo album," recalls Karen Ramone, then Karen Ichiuji and Phil's girlfriend. "She was so hard on herself. She was basically hyperactive, and she really wanted to continue her music. She didn't know whether or not Richard would come out of Menninger's and say he wanted to work again. I think she was really trying to prepare herself for any scenario that might happen. She got all thumbs up by everybody—Herbie, Jerry Moss, and Jerry Weintraub—everybody. She had a huge support system when she started this thing."

Arriving at Karen's Century City condo for the first time, Ramone was caught off guard when the doorbell chimed the first six notes of "We've Only Just Begun." "Isn't that an amazing bell?" Karen said as she answered the door. "I had a guy make it for me, and it's *exactly* as I sang it!"

Phil was puzzled by Karen. He knew her only as the naive girl he had seen in publicity photos and on album covers. He was familiar with the duo's biggest hits and was well aware of their reputation for attention to intricate details in the music, but Ramone's goal was never to achieve the Carpenters' echelon of perfection with Karen. In fact, his plan for her was to follow no set plan at all. "It was a lot of experimenting," he recalls. "We were trying to make an artist's complete dream."

Karen flew to New York on February 16, 1979, for further meetings with her producer, just a week prior to his receiving the Record of the Year Grammy for Billy Joel's "Just the Way You Are." Ramone interrupted Karen when she began talking about recording tracks in Los Angeles at A&M and how she planned to record with all the musicians and engineers she and Richard had known and trusted for years. "No, no," he told her. "You have got to come back to New York. A&M's a great studio to cut in, but it will confuse the issue."

After much consideration, it was agreed that Karen would fly to New York to record with Ramone at his own A&R Recording Studios in Manhattan. "Coming to New York was a big thing for her and for me," he says. "We talked about what the approach should be. How do you make a record when your whole reputation is built on your life as a Carpenter? I personally didn't want to touch anything in that world. I thought of her as an actor who had been typecast, like Judy Garland was typecast after *The Wizard of Oz*. She made all those *Andy Hardy* movies. Recording artists get typed, too. I said to Karen, 'It is like comedians who want to do a serious role as a singer and singers who want to be comedians. You must be cautious here.'"

<hr />

DESPITE HAVING put his stamp of approval on a solo project for Karen, Jerry Weintraub's concern for her health and well-being remained. He was intrigued when he came across a television interview with Steven Levenkron, a psychotherapist specializing in eating disorders, promoting *The Best Little Girl in the World*, his new novel about "the obsession that kills." Weintraub was immediately impressed with the therapist's convincing tone and perceived knowledge of the subject matter, and felt Karen would surely benefit from meeting with Levenkron. Little did he know, Karen was already familiar with Levenkron after having become engrossed with the book at first reading. Weintraub's call to the therapist was returned after several days, at which time he explained his concern for Karen and the struggle that had become apparent some four years prior.

With Richard present, Karen phoned Steven Levenkron in New York from Weintraub's office on March 27, 1979. She purposely moved away from the men and spoke softly in an attempt to keep the conversation private. During their brief exchange Karen felt she had been able to convince the therapist that she was not suffering with anorexia nervosa but a gastrointestinal problem, specifically colitis. Levenkron urged her to find a qualified gastrointestinal specialist and wished her good luck. Returning to Richard and Weintraub, Karen lied, saying that Levenkron could tell she did not have anorexia from their conversation. They were skeptical but pleased to know she had made a significant step in just making the call, an act that hushed the two, if only temporarily.

To further appease Richard and Weintraub, Karen checked into Cedars-Sinai in Los Angeles for a few days of diagnostics. Exhausted and, of course, underweight, she must have thought that going to these lengths would calm the fears of those around her—or at least appear to be an effort on her part to get well.

The April 1979 fan club newsletter told of Karen's solo venture, sparking concern from fans afraid this meant an end to the duo. At that time, no one really knew for certain, not even Karen and Richard themselves. In an attempt to calm fears, the club's next issue included the following statement.

To dispel any rumors that the group has split up, Karen wishes to assure you this is not so. The reason for the temporary lapse in their recordings is that after ten arduous years of concentrating on perfecting music to the Carpenters standards we expect, Richard felt the need for a long vacation which probably will extend into the

New Year. Karen reaffirms they will resume work on their album whenever Richard feels ready. He is really enjoying the freedom from pressures, and we must not be selfish in denying him the time off he deserves.

According to Evelyn Wallace, "It was stuff like that we just kind of skirted around. A person's always allowed to take time off. You don't have to tell people what it's for."

Phil Ramone recalls that Karen was very frustrated once rumors of a Carpenters breakup began to spread. "That was the thing that drove her crazy," he says. "The 1970s saw the breakup of Peter, Paul and Mary, Crosby, Stills and Nash. They were all going out on solo careers. People thought if you left a group you never came back or would never work together again. They could never leave the roost. Not in that family."

In a 1981 interview with Paul Grein, Karen expressed in no uncertain terms that her solo album was never meant to signal an end to the Carpenters as a duo. "It was never planned for me to drop the Carpenters and go cut a solo—that would never happen, ever! If Richard hadn't gone on vacation, I never would have done the solo album."

With flights and studio time booked, Karen's loyalty to Richard still weighed heavily on the eve of her departure for New York. Having completed Menninger's six-week program, Richard spent much of 1979 visiting friends around the country, relaxing, and putting on some of the weight lost during the crisis. He avoided the stress of the business and even his home life, taking up residence in the Long Beach home of Gary Sims and Dennis Strawn, brother of Doug. On the evening of April 30, Karen phoned Richard at Sims's house, hoping to get his blessing before embarking on the project. She knew very well he did not and would not approve, but she made the call regardless. Distraught and in tears, she told him, "I can't go do this unless I know that you're behind it."

In an attempt to pacify Karen, Richard offered his blessing. But before their conversation ended he asked that she promise him one thing: "Do me one favor. Do *not* do disco!"

13

POCKETS FULL OF
GOOD INTENTIONS

WITH GREAT anticipation and a mix of emotions, Karen boarded a plane bound for New York on the morning of May 1, 1979. Production meetings commenced the following day with Phil Ramone asking, "Ideally, what would you like to do?"

"Well, I *love* Donna Summer," Karen replied, explaining how Summer's latest single "Hot Stuff" was her current favorite. "I'd give *anything* if we could do a song like that!" This certainly surprised Ramone. Disregarding her brother's plea, she went on to explain that, in addition to singers like Aretha Franklin and Barbra Streisand, she loved just about anything of the disco genre.

Karen took up residence in a posh suite at the Plaza Hotel on Fifth Avenue. She was fascinated by the panoramic views of the New York skyline and the idea that there were butlers assigned to every floor, but within weeks the novelty of the revered Central Park address wore thin. "We were talking about stupid expenses and the hotel," Ramone recalls. "I said to Karen, 'Why would you want to do that? If we're going to work together, why don't you come live at my house? We've got plenty of room.'"

Ramone proceeded to move Karen into the master suite of the relaxing estate he shared with girlfriend Karen Ichiuji in Pound Ridge, a small town on the New York and Connecticut border. The quaint surroundings of this rural community were much like Hall Street from Karen's childhood. The two Karens quickly became close friends. Ichiuji was a singer herself who recorded under the name Karen Kamon and would later contribute the song "Manhunt" to the popular motion picture soundtrack for *Flashdance*. Phil called her K.K., but Karen preferred her own silly nickname of Itchie. Living together allowed producer and artist to discuss plans for the solo project around the clock. "She was a workaholic," Ramone says. "That house was a very creative house for me, and it was for her, too."

Karen and Phil set out to establish a common vision. Their hourlong commute from Pound Ridge to Manhattan's A&R Studios, located at 322 West Forty-Eighth, allowed the two to peruse demos for the project. "The laughs and silliness we shared on those trips forever made us friends," Ramone recalled in his book, *Making Records: The Scenes Behind the Music*. "While we were driving, Karen would be the DJ, playing all the songs that had been submitted for her consideration. She'd sit with a legal pad, listen intently and rate them. 'Should this be on the A list, or the B?' she'd ask."

During these initial stages, Ramone extended an invitation to friend Rod Temperton to come to New York to write for Karen. The former keyboardist for the funk/disco band Heatwave accepted and moved into Ramone's guest house with only a keyboard and a set of headphones in tow. "All you had to do was make coffee and give him cigarettes," says Itchie. "Our house became this big musical commune." Temperton offered Karen several of his own compositions, including "Off the Wall" and "Rock with You," but at that point the songs were just grooves at the piano, still in their most raw form. She declined both charts, saying they were too funky. According to Itchie, "Everyone else loved the idea," but the project was young and lacked direction. Within a few months, Ramone introduced Temperton to Quincy Jones when the two attended a barbecue held at the home of the pop music titan, and the songs were soon pitched to Michael Jackson.

Karen visited Jackson in the studio during his 1979 solo sessions while he laid down tracks for "Get on the Floor," a song he had cowritten with bassist Louis Johnson. "Phil wanted to show her what Michael's album was like," recalls Itchie. "He was so upset that Karen didn't want to do any of Rod's material at first." Ultimately she chose two Temperton originals for her project, "Lovelines" and "If We Try," the latter being a particularly satisfying match for her smooth and flirtatious vocals. "Once Rod started arranging for her, they got along so well," Itchie adds. "She loved the harmonies they created, and they were so right for each other musically. She felt comfortable working with him, and it was kind of like being with Richard in a sense, artistically."

The two Temperton songs Karen passed on became huge hits for Michael Jackson on his *Off the Wall* solo album. Also featured on the album was his recording of "She's Out of My Life," a song by Tom Bähler long rumored to have been written in response to the end of the composer's own brief relationship with Karen Carpenter in 1978. "Some believe that I had written that as a result of mine and Karen's breakup," Bähler says. "The fact is, I had already written that song by the time Karen and I became romantic. That song was written more about Rhonda Rivera, who later married my friend John Davidson. Rhonda and I had been together for two years, and it was after we broke up that I started dating Karen."

Over time, Karen developed a great sense of security as she recorded with Phil Ramone. It was not the same as working with her brother, but she felt comforted and protected by him in the studio. "If he hadn't been as gentle and sensitive as he is, I couldn't have done it," Karen said. "He knows how close Richard and I are." Aside from the early contract with Joe Osborn's Magic Lamp Records, Karen had worked exclusively for A&M Records and under Richard's guidance. "I was scared to death beforehand," she said. "I basically knew one producer, one arranger, one studio, one record company, and that was it. It was a different surrounding, working with different people with different habits. I didn't know how they worked; they didn't know how I worked. I'm used to blinking an eye and an engineer knows what I want or Richard knows what I'm thinking. . . . I'm used to being part of a duo. Richard's like a third arm to me."

For Karen's sessions, Ramone recruited members of Billy Joel's band. At the time the men were in the middle of recording *Glass Houses*, their fourth album together with Joel and one that produced his first #1 single, "It's Still Rock and Roll to Me." Unlike many of the polished studio musicians Karen was accustomed to working with in Los Angeles, this band was raw—likened to a garage band—and chosen by Ramone for their boundless energy. "Was Billy's group perfect?" Ramone wrote in 2007. "No—but that's what I loved. They were a real band that worked together night after night, playing his music with passion."

At the age of seventeen, drummer Liberty DeVitto and fellow Long Island teens Russell Javors and Doug Stegmeyer formed the band Topper, which eventually evolved to become Billy Joel's band. "Phil thought we'd be an interesting core group of musicians to work with her because of the relationship we had with him and Billy as an artist," recalls Russell Javors. "We were the kinds of musicians that would push the envelope when we worked with an artist, too. I'm sure it was a different kind of atmosphere than Karen was used to working in. We were very vocal about what we thought and what we did. It was a bunch of guys rather than a group of session musicians."

For Karen's album, the band was tracked at A&R's studio A1, located at 799 Seventh Avenue. "It was kind of a family situation," Javors says, "but this was a whole different kind of family than she was used to. We were kind of 'New York' and Karen was nothing like that. We were a rowdy bunch of bar band guys. Karen became part of the fold, and we didn't hold anything back. She certainly got into it, and it felt like she was one of the guys. I think she had fun."

Bob James, renowned smooth-jazz artist, keyboardist, and former musical director for Sarah Vaughan, was enlisted by Ramone to arrange, orchestrate, and play keyboards for the project. "Karen was an arranger's dream," says James, who admits he found himself a bit starstruck at times in the studio. "It was a flattering but also very intimidating assignment. That sound coming through my headphones in the studio was very inspiring and exciting. I remember thinking, 'Wow, I'm actually in the studio playing the piano for Karen Carpenter!'"

Javors was surprised by the tiny sound he heard coming from Karen in the booth. "When you hear her voice on a record it's so big and so full. In the studio it was kind of like a whisper. She didn't really belt it out. She was up close to the mic, and it wasn't this tremendous voice that you'd hear. It was just a very intimate, focused voice. I was amazed at the ease and how softly she really sang." DeVitto concurs "She almost whispered into the mic, but Phil was able to capture that and have it sit on top of the music. He never lost sight of Karen."

In one of their daily phone calls, Karen told Frenda Franklin that she was in awe of this diverse assembly of musicians. "They treated her like an equal in the studio, and she loved the process," Franklin says. "She had the best time!"

At times the band members saw evidence of Karen's sheltered Downey life and would even poke fun at her, which she seemed to enjoy, given her own knack for humor. "She'd never been on an airplane by herself before," Javors recalls. "Then she had these road cases with different sweat suits and Nike sneakers, and they were all the same color and all lined up in a row. She came from a different world." Even Phil would join in and tease Karen, especially when she would show up to a session wearing pressed and starched blue jeans. "This girl loved to be fussy and get it done right," he laughs. "Karen was fastidious, and I would tease her ruthlessly. She had every satin jacket given out by the record company—and a matching pair of sneakers for each one!"

—⊗⊗⊗—

AFTER NEARLY a decade of having tried unsuccessfully to shed the Carpenters' image, Karen realized this break from the confines of the duo might be the perfect opportunity to explore and push the envelope with her music—not in the same manner that *Passage* pushed the envelope with "Calling Occupants," but perhaps by establishing herself as an independent twenty-nine-year-old woman. "She didn't want to do anything totally left field from the Carpenters," Itchie says, "but she wanted to say that she was an independent artist. The Carpenters had their image, and she didn't want to present an image that clashed with that, but she did want an image that set her apart. I saw what Phil was doing. Basically he was trying to help her grow up a bit, gain the confidence to be a woman, and state what she felt and what she thought."

Olivia Newton-John sensed that Karen was torn between following this desire and staying loyal to her family. "She was incredibly ensconced by or tied into her family and Richard and the whole situation," she says. "She wanted to break out as a human being and as a woman and live an independent life. She also wanted to feel her way musically into other areas. . . . I think it was really important for her to feel that it wasn't just Richard or just the production that had made the Carpenters a success. She was just as important and needed to find her own feet and find her own style."

According to Ramone, "Karen was twenty-nine, but she couldn't be a woman who could think like a woman and express herself. . . . Some people still thought that I was taking her down a street she didn't want to travel. We weren't out to shock people. I was not interested in putting out a shock record on her behalf. That would be so wrong for me. But some people were shocked. You can't make a record in fear of what everyone's going to say. You can't make a record that doesn't speak from your heart."

The environment was one of "admiration and appreciation for Karen and her talents," says Russell Javors. "People had such strong feelings about their legacy and what they'd done and the way they did it, but this was *Karen*, and it should complement anything that she'd already done. Nobody was doing it in the spirit of 'we'll show you, Richard,' or anything. Phil was trying to push the envelope a little bit but let her do it naturally."

Song titles like "Remember When Lovin' Took All Night," "Make Believe It's Your First Time," and "Making Love in the Afternoon" led to accusations that Ramone was force-feeding Karen sexual lyrics and themes to create a new persona, but according to those closely involved, he gave Karen complete choice and control. "Phil was trying to pick material that would allow her to push the envelope, but it was never forced on her," says Javors. "He's a nurturer. He kind of opens the road up to you, and you either take it or you don't; but he's not somebody who says, 'You go down this road.' . . . She was very intimately involved in everything that was going on, and this was 100 percent her project."

A number of Karen's song choices contained lyrics with overtones of sexuality, some less subtle than others. "I Love Makin' Love to You" was written by Evie Sands, formerly with A&M Records, and recorded for her *Estate of Mind* album on the Capital/Haven label in 1975. "When I heard Karen was going to cover it," Sands recalls, "I imagined her take on it would be similar to mine or closer to the mellow Barbra Streisand version. It turned out to be a perfect blend of both." Although Karen and Phil finished the ambitious arrangement of Sands's tune, complete with lush background vocals and an outstanding brass section, it was ultimately set aside. The risqué lyric is likely to blame.

> *There's no lightnin' or thunder, any seventh wonder*
> *Mightier than what you've got*
> *Keep it up forever, no one does it better*
> *Baby, get it while it's hot*

For the infectious "Making Love in the Afternoon," Chicago front man Peter Cetera joined Karen in the studio on the song he had written. "Peter was a fan of Karen's voice," recalls Ramone, who produced the *Chicago 13* album around that time. "Cetera wrote the song for her." Billed as a duet, Cetera's role was more of a backup singer to Karen's lead. According to Itchie, "A true duet would have stepped over the line by stepping on Richard. Harmonizing is one thing, but a duet? No. That would have been trespassing."

According to Itchie, "Everybody had input as far as the album was concerned. . . . I remember Billy Joel coming in the studio and saying, 'Uh, excuse me, but why am I not doing keyboards?'" Paul Simon stopped in as well. "They treated her like a major mega artist," Itchie says. "I think she really needed that in becoming her own self. It really got her started building a backbone. It was her environment, and everybody was there to support her, and she absolutely loved it."

Paul Simon recommended to Karen his own "Still Crazy After All These Years," a song originally produced by Phil Ramone on the Grammy Album of the Year for 1976. "It expressed a lot of what she wanted to say," Ramone recalls. "But she had Paul rewrite a line. It used to be 'crapped out, yawning' and she did 'crashed out, yawning.' We talked about how that song wouldn't be a Carpenters song!" Karen's vocal on the mellow, jazz-inflected "Still Crazy" was self-assured, relaxed, and alluring. She also recorded Simon's "I Do It for Your Love" and, in true Carpenters fashion, the oldie "Jimmy Mack," a Motown hit for Martha and the Vandellas in 1967. The initial rhythm tracks and work leads for these two showed little promise, and both went unfinished. Another outtake, a real diamond in the rough, was "Something's Missing in My Life," a stunning ballad by Jay Asher and Paul Jabara and recorded by Jabara as a duet with Donna Summer on his 1978 album *Keeping Time*.

Karen felt challenged by the intricate background vocal arrangements, many of which took on a brass-influenced instrumental feel. Bob James was responsible for several arrangements, including "If I Had You," the most funky, demanding, and ambitious of all. Like Ramone, he felt obligated to move Karen out of the Carpenters mold. "I wanted to give her something different and challenging," James explains. "I was very intrigued to find out how she would react to an arrangement that was deliberately moving away from the Carpenters sound." Karen's inimitable style on the sophisticated "If I Had You" resulted in an original and captivating piece of ear candy with a complex, multilayered call-and-response ending, the brainchild of Rod Temperton.

Although Karen had conveyed to her brother the vocal challenges she faced when singing Bob James's arrangements, she spoke very little about Richard to the guys in the studio. "I don't recall Karen *ever* mentioning him," Russell Javors says. According to Frenda, despite having given Karen the go-ahead, Richard was "not supportive" of the project after it got underway. "I don't want to pick on him," she says. "He wasn't exactly in good shape. His and Karen's timing was always off, but I know during that whole time when Karen did the album and stayed with Phil and Itchie, he was never supportive.... We were all hoping that because she finally was able to do this that it could be the catalyst to really turn everything around. Nothing else was doing it."

Sitting down at the drums next to Lib (as she and others referred to Liberty DeVitto), Karen joked, "Let me show you what I got," before tearing into the kit. A second-generation Italian-American, DeVitto taught himself to play drums after having seen the Beatles on *The Ed Sullivan Show*. He claims to have been a closet Carpenters fan even prior to meeting Karen. "I never bought a record but knew all their songs," he says. DeVitto was attracted to Karen from the start, and his feelings grew the more time the two were together. "To be honest with you, I fell in love with Karen," he says. "I was married at the time, but I felt like I wanted to be with her. Silly, I know. I had no idea how she would have felt about that so I just kept it to myself." When asked his views on Karen as a drummer, the comic emerged: "Is this the part where I am supposed to get in trouble by saying, 'She was all right for a girl'?"

Karen was drawn to the drums as if by some gravitational pull. Occasionally she would go to the studio before the others arrived and sit down behind the battery of drums. "Those days are over," she told Ramone. "I'm not sitting behind the drums and singing anymore."

Sensitive to this downhearted moment he replied, "Well, you never know."

"It doesn't help my rear end," she told him.

Ramone thought Karen looked good during the first recording sessions and did not sense any unusual eating habits. Even so, her comment at the drums that day stuck out in his mind. He had been cautioned about her eating disorder by others. "But there were no clues at all at first," he says. "If there were dead giveaways they came later. Everything seemed logical and fine. Sitting down at a meal was to sit down to have a meal. I know a lot of nitpickers. She wasn't a fusspot."

In her free time, Karen enjoyed going with Itchie to Serendipity, a favorite Manhattan restaurant, and out to the Bottom Line, a popular Greenwich Village music club. She also liked eating seafood but only with an abundance of lemons. "She had a little bit of fish with her lemons!" Itchie laughs. "Then we would eat stone crab claws

at Joe's Pier Fifty-Two across from A&R Studios every night until
the stone crab season was over." The trio of Karen, Phil, and Itchie
also attended a baseball game at Shea Stadium in Queens where Karen
immediately noticed the initials "K.C." on the scoreboard. "Look, it's
for me—K.C.!"

"Come on, Karen," Ramone chuckled. "That's Kansas City, the
team!" A few minutes later Karen was thrilled to hear the announcer
say, "Please welcome Karen Carpenter from the Carpenters," as strains
of "We've Only Just Begun" echoed across the park.

"Oh, here comes Lucy and Ethel," the guys in the band would tease
when Karen and Itchie would arrive at the studio together. According
to Itchie, she was the Ethel to Karen's Lucy in almost every scenario.
Karen's collection of *I Love Lucy* videotapes often traveled with her. A
favorite episode was "The Ballet," in which Lucy trained with Madame
LeMond, an authoritarian ballet teacher. "I think we should go to the
barre," LeMond said.

"Oh good," Lucy replied, "'cause I'm awful thirsty!"

After becoming entangled in the barre, Lucy cried out "Ahh-ba,
Ahh-ba," in hopes of freeing her leg. Watching this, Karen and Itchie
would laugh until they cried. The "Ahh-ba" exclamation became a part
of the twosome's banter with one another. "Sometimes Karen was *really*
tired and *really* had to be 'on' for a performance or whatever," Itchie
explains. "She'd yell out 'Ahh-ba!'" In observance of their inside joke,
Karen bought Itchie a wristwatch. On the underside was engraved
AHH-BA!

Karen sometimes phoned childhood friend Debbie Cuticello asking to spend the weekend at her home in Guilford, Connecticut, an
hour from Phil's estate. "She wanted the chance to get away and enjoy
some good Italian home-cooked meals," Cuticello recalled in 1983. "I
remember the big limo driving down my driveway, and I wondered
what her thoughts would be about the quiet little town of Guilford. She
loved the quiet and the comfort."

Some weeks later, Debbie and her husband, C.J., made the two-
hour drive into Manhattan to visit Karen at A&R Recording Studios,
where she and Ramone played several songs for the couple. Debbie was

especially taken with the contemporary sound of the recordings. "It was wonderful, like an angel's voice," she says. "I was impressed."

The reception at home on the West Coast was less enthusiastic. With a handful of songs completed, Karen flew home to Los Angeles, excited to play the new recordings for her family and friends. This was one of several returns to Southern California during the solo project, each of which proved to be a setback as far as her energy and progress in the studio with Ramone was concerned. Friend Carole Curb felt Karen was torn between these two lives. The decision to move to New York and record a solo album was actually a huge weight on Karen's shoulders. "I just heard that she had decided to go off on her own," Curb says. "It was a big decision to make, and I think all these things contributed to a lot of anxiety. It's hard to leave the nest."

Needless to say, the nest was thrilled to have Karen back but not as excited once they heard the material she had been recording. "Agnes did not like the idea that Karen came out and did this project at all," Itchie says. "She was a very rough person as it was, but then she didn't particularly care for me. Whenever I would go to their house I would speak to Harold, not Agnes. Karen was much closer to her dad, but there wasn't really a whole lot of communication, but he would be loose with me, whereas Agnes was a Gestapo agent. With Agnes there was not a list of dos and don'ts. It was just don'ts."

Although Agnes was disappointed in Karen for attempting an album without Richard, overall she put very little stock in the solo endeavor. According to Evelyn Wallace, "As far as Agnes was concerned, regardless of how many records Karen would have made, to her mother they'd never be as good as Richard's."

Phil Ramone was surprised by the negative response from the family and, in time, those at A&M as well. "I feel like I've taken your daughter out on a date and was supposed to be home by midnight but came in at 12:01 A.M.," he told Jerry Moss. "It's like you met me at the door saying 'I hope you didn't change my daughter.'"

"What could I change?" Ramone asks now. "There are accusations that come at you, like when I worked with Julian Lennon they said, 'You made him sound like his dad.' Man, if I am that good then why couldn't I do it for me? You cannot do something for somebody unless they want it done. We weren't out to change the world, but we were certainly representing her coming of age. And I mean that in the best possible way."

———— ∞∞∞ ————

RICHARD'S SUMMATION that Karen was not well enough to have embarked on such a grand plan was confirmed as she became weaker and thinner over the course of the project. Additionally, signs began to point to the possibility that she was resorting to bulimic practices, ridding her body of food she would ingest to give the appearance she was eating healthily. "She was very thin," Russell Javors recalls. "My wife and I had dinner with her one night, and she ate a hell of a lot then excused herself. That was the first person we'd seen go through that ritual."

Itchie witnessed the same. "At one point she started to gorge herself," she says. "It was amazing. She ate twice as much as me. She said that she had colitis, and I said, 'Oh, so do I.' I would go to the bathroom every single time she did. She would be so pissed because she was very uncomfortable having all this food in her."

In the spring of 1980, sitting at home with Phil and watching a video of herself on Olivia Newton-John's recent *Hollywood Nights* TV special, Karen's warped sense of body image surfaced. Dancing and singing alongside Olivia, Linda "Peaches" Greene (of Peaches and Herb), Toni Tennille, and Tina Turner, Karen looked radiant but too thin. "Oh, God, look how *heavy* I am," she said. Ramone, baffled by what he'd just heard, jumped up from the couch, paused the videotape, and grabbed a nearby crayon. He proceeded to draw lines around each of the ladies' bodies and observed that hers was like a pencil. "You're just two lines," he told her. "You don't *see* that?"

"No, look how fat I am. Look how big my hips are!"

Ramone was incredulous and unable to convince Karen she was by far the thinnest of all the women on stage. Things took a turn for the worse one evening when Phil heard a loud "thump" sound come from his kitchen. Alarmed, he ran in to discover Karen passed out on the floor. She was so thin and frail he worried she might have broken a bone. He carefully moved her to the couch and phoned paramedics.

By the time they arrived, Karen was lightheaded but alert. She refused to go in the ambulance and was concerned when she realized the paramedics were aware of her identity. On her behalf, Phil pleaded that they not release her name. Karen said the collapse was most likely due to her having taken half a quaalude earlier in the evening. It was unfathomable that she would have the pills in her possession after having dealt with Richard's addiction.

Following this scare, Karen attempted to ease the Ramones' worries by promising to start eating properly, but just days later Itchie found laxatives hidden around the house. She found them in Karen's room—in her luggage, her pillowcase, and even her shoes—and throughout the house behind cupboards and in a fruit bowl. Karen assured her that she wasn't using them and just needed them there for security. Phil, Itchie, and their friends were extremely concerned. They knew something was very wrong but admit no one knew what they were dealing with. "The clues were there," he says. "The treatment wasn't."

As friendly and warm as Karen was to those involved in the project, Russell Javors sensed what he calls "a tinge of sadness about her. You could kind of sense that there was something going on. All the clues were there. . . . But the project was about music and not eating disorders. When you're involved in a situation like that, first and foremost, you're there to make a record. You're there to make music."

———⊗⊗⊗———

RECORDING FOR the solo album wrapped in January 1980, by which time Karen had spent the customary $100,000 allotted by A&M Records, plus an additional $400,000 of her own. With the album in the mixing phase, A&M Records began a promotional campaign and assigned the album a catalog number, readying for a spring 1980 release. Several on the A&M lot recall the record was being talked up as a smash hit, and Phil Ramone noticed a renewed sense of optimism in Karen, who was finally exhibiting self-assurance in her work. "She was getting more and more confident," he says.

"So Kace, do you like the way Liv looks here?" Itchie asked, showing Karen the record jacket for Olivia Newton-John's recently released *Totally Hot* LP.

"Oh, look at ONJ!" Karen exclaimed, smiling at the cover photo shot by French glamour photographer Claude Mougin. While she was fond of the look, Karen had trouble picturing herself made up like Olivia, who had been photographed wearing black leather and intense eye makeup. Phil felt Karen's photos should make a statement in congruence with the album's sensual lyrical content. He contacted Mougin to shoot Karen's album cover and promotional photos, which were captured during a two-hour session on February 2, 1980. Karen was accustomed to doing her own hair and makeup or having an assistant along with her on the road, but she rarely received a glamour treatment such as this. Being made up for this *Vogue*-style photo shoot was exciting, but Karen seemed nervous and panicky. "Maybe we should get you some herbal tea, Karen," Itchie suggested.

Unbeknownst to Karen, Itchie crushed up a Valium tablet and added it to her cup of tea. "I spiked her chamomile tea," Itchie recalls. "I put honey and five milligrams of Valium, and she never even knew! She calmed down and was absolutely gorgeous."

When the photo proofs were delivered, Karen was amazed by the transformation; she looked sexy and provocative. She was ecstatic when she showed them to Itchie. "Itch, will you *look* at these?" she said, her eyes wide and mouth open in astonishment.

"Yeah, so how do you feel about them?" Itchie asked.

"I look *pretty*," Karen said in astonishment. "I actually look pretty."

"But Kace, you've always looked pretty," she was assured.

Having selected eleven songs from more than twenty they recorded, Karen and Phil arranged a series of meetings to present the new album to those at the label. The first playbacks were held at A&R Studios in New York with London's Derek Green representing the A&M label at the request of Jerry Moss. Champagne toasts and cheers of "congratulations" flowed freely as everyone celebrated the exquisite and sophisticated sounds Karen and Phil had succeeded in crafting. "It was the coming of a great new artist," says Itchie. "In New York, everybody had their arms open and was excited—the whole nine yards!"

All that remained was a West Coast playback at A&M in Hollywood for Alpert and Moss. At Karen's request, Richard was asked to be present for the unveiling. According to Ramone, "The hardest thing in the world is to have to play back a record to your company that has known you and thinks of you in only one world. Karen certainly had confidence in what we were about to play, but she was nervous as hell. Overall, I think her deepest fear was Richard. He definitely did not like the record."

Song after song, Herb, Jerry, and Richard sat pokerfaced. It was a "den of silence," according to Ramone, who began to bite his nails. He grew increasingly troubled with the passing of each song and sensed Karen's mounting disillusionment, too. She expected cheers and hugs to celebrate each new track, as she had received in New York, but the three men remained impervious. "It's easier when you have ten or twelve people in the room," Ramone says. "My life has been made up of listening and watching and feeling an audience, even if it's just four people. There was much discomfort, and they really had a hard time finding something to love."

"How could you do a *disco* record?" one asked following the play-back. "Why would you attempt a song like that?" another wondered. "Well, somehow you've got to omit something," they said. "We're not happy." Karen was ill prepared to defend the album and was disillusioned by the requests to do so.

"Was this the wrong album for her? No," Ramone says. "Was it not what the expectancy was? Yes. But I think if we'd made an album that was like what the Carpenters were doing at that time, then that would have been shot down even more. Richard decided that he wanted to get going with the Carpenters again—and the label got behind him on that. I think we were in a situation where people did not want to break up this team that was about to re-sign with the label."

Karen had previously played tracks from the album for Frenda, who was ecstatic—but mostly for Karen's sake. "I liked it," she tepidly summons up. "It was *different*. I can't say it was the perfect album, but when you have the Carpenters sound in your ear, you have to kind of divorce yourself from that and go on with it."

When Karen played the album for Mike Curb, he was struck by her noticeable anxiety. "She was back in Los Angeles and called wanting me to hear the album," he recalls. "I went over, and she played it for me, but she seemed very reticent to do the album and reticent to release it—reticent in terms of the effect it might have on her family."

According to Olivia Newton-John, "It's very hard to follow a Carpenters record. The Carpenters' sound and productions were exquisite. She would have gone through criticisms, no doubt." Karen played the album for Newton-John with Richard present. "I remember Richard said, 'You've stolen the Carpenters sound.' That was kind of ironic because she *was* the sound of the Carpenters. Her *voice* was 'the Carpenters.'"

From the project's beginning, Frenda was certain there would be disapproval from A&M and especially Richard. According to her, his negative opinion of Karen's solo work signaled a turning point in the siblings' relationship and one that Karen never seemed to get over. "He told her it was *shit*," Frenda says. "All Karen ever wanted was his approval. It could have turned everything in her life around, but it wasn't there. What's sad is that he has to live with that, and I don't think it even fazes him. I *do* think he should be excused to some extent because he had his own problems, but God Almighty, what does it take to just be kind? They could see she was melting away like a snowman in front of their faces, but they couldn't do it. It was brutal."

Karen's hopes and dreams for the solo album were shattered. After an exhilarating year of creativity, exploration, and hard work, the entire project was rejected by those she loved and respected most in her family and professional life. "We came in with all these high hopes, and then nobody actually liked it," Ramone says. "Of course, they had the right to not like it, but it was never in our minds that this could fail. But it was over. The game was over! There wasn't going to be a part two or attempts to try and figure it out. This wasn't going to be something we could add a few more songs to and make it OK. Sometimes a mix can change things or save the day, but they didn't think that would help. The whole thing was a flop. Karen was completely down in the dumps, and so was I. There was nothing that could cheer us up. What was there to say? At the time we didn't see it as them against us. For us it was all about what *we* did wrong. '*What* did we miss?' '*How* did we miss?'"

Karen and Phil left the A&M lot that day under a veil of disillusionment. "She was absolutely destroyed by the rejection," Itchie says. "You have to understand she was soul searching. She had always felt inferior. She was trying to grow up and start focusing on herself as an artist, a person, a human, and a woman with needs, and it all just went to pieces. It was like somebody just stepped on her and just erased everything she'd worked for."

14

WHITE LACE
AND PROMISES BROKEN

RETURNING TO Los Angeles and no longer juggling the demands of a bicoastal existence, Karen found time to reunite with friends like Olivia Newton-John, who suggested a relaxing getaway to the Golden Door health spa in San Diego. There they were joined by mutual friend Christina Ferrare, an actress and wife of auto industry executive John DeLorean. During their stay at the spa, Karen told the women how she finally felt ready to find a husband and settle down, and spelled out her ever-growing list of requirements in a man. This was met with laughs from the other women, who told her she would be extremely lucky to find someone possessing even half of those prerequisites.

It was around this same time that Karen was astonished to learn that ex-boyfriend Terry Ellis had become engaged. She had always regretted the way she ended their relationship and had even hoped they might one day rekindle their romance. After weeks of introspection and the continued urging of Itchie, Karen decided to call and invite Terry to lunch. After all, in her mind he was only engaged. He was not yet married, so perhaps there was still a chance to renew his interest in her. "Listen, I've made a big mistake," she began. "I really made a big mistake in ending our relationship. Can we get back together again?"

"Well, Karen, I'm engaged," he told her. "I'm going to be married."

Along with Olivia Newton-John and Christina Ferrare, Carole Curb was one in a small group of trusted girlfriends who always kept their eyes and ears open in hopes of finding "Mister Right" for Karen. "I have somebody I think you'd like to meet," she said.

"Yeah, *sure* Carole," she replied, the sarcastic rolling of her eyes perceived across the phone line.

Though Karen valued Carole's good taste and sensitive discretion, she felt as though she had heard it a thousand times before. Moreover, she wasn't thrilled by the idea of a blind date, even one arranged by a well-meaning cupid. "But he's nice, good looking, and he's philanthropic," Curb urged reassuringly.

This latest prospect was Thomas James Burris of Newport Beach, whom Carole had met while attending a dinner with her brother, Mike Curb, whose career path had made several unexpected turns coinciding with the dissolution of his own relationship with Karen. Following the 1974 sale of Metro-Goldwyn-Mayer and the MGM Records label by Las Vegas resort mogul Kirk Kerkorian, Curb's work in the record industry was only part time, and he eventually became involved in government. In 1977 he married Linda Dunphy, daughter of popular Southern California news anchor Jerry Dunphy, and by 1980 Curb was lieutenant governor of California and national vice chairman of the Ronald Reagan presidential campaign. The Curbs knew Tom Burris as an enthusiastic Reagan supporter and active member of another organization overseen by Mike Curb, the Commission of Californias, which promoted relations between California and Baja California. "My sister Carole played a role in the matchmaking," he recalls, "but I did not. It was the busiest time of my life back then. But I did know Tom, and he sure seemed like a nice guy."

Thirty-nine-year-old Burris met a number of Karen's requirements in a potential husband. "He was very attractive, very nice, and he seemed very generous," Carole says. "He had just donated some ambulances to some of the hospitals in Baja California." Burris was not in the music business. A native of Long Beach, Tom had dropped out of school at the age of thirteen and went to work as a mechanic's assistant. In 1958 he joined the Marine Corps and after being discharged worked in a Long Beach welding shop. He later worked as a steel contractor and general housing contractor before becoming the self-proclaimed "industrial developer" who founded Burris Corp. in Long Beach in 1964. In 1975 he moved the business to Corona, California, where he built the city's first planned industrial complex on Pomona Road. An avid NASCAR fan, Burris was a handsome man with blond hair and blue eyes, seemingly affluent and successful, but he was not single. In fact, Burris was the married father of an eighteen-year-old son. He clarified to Carole that he and his wife were separated and their divorce was underway.

Karen first met Tom Burris on a double date with Carole and then husband Tony Scotti on Saturday, April 12, 1980. The couples enjoyed dinner at Ma Maison, the West Hollywood bistro that launched the career of celebrity chef Wolfgang Puck. Having just returned from the East Coast, Karen was a bit jet-lagged. In fact, she wanted to cancel the date, but Agnes Carpenter urged her to attend. Over dinner, Burris told Karen that he was not familiar with the Carpenters or their music. "He really didn't know who I was," she said. "I hadn't known him an hour, but I said to him on the first date, 'What, have you been under a rock for ten years?'" Even so, Karen bought Tom's story and found herself instantly attracted. "I automatically liked him. I liked his way, his look, his style, and his *car*," she laughed. "It was the first time I had actually been attracted on the first date."

At the end of the evening, Karen phoned Frenda Leffler, who had helped ready her hair and makeup that afternoon. "So, how did it go?" Leffler asked.

"Oh, Frenny," she exclaimed, "he reminds me of Chard!" (In addition to "R.C.," "Chard" was one of Karen's many nicknames for her brother.)

After the first date Tom Burris mysteriously disappeared. Karen was disappointed when she did not hear from him right away and blamed herself for running him off. "She told us all about this guy she met and how she really liked him, but she hadn't heard from him" says Frank

Bonito. "What he did was he went off to Las Vegas or somewhere and got a divorce." But Tom soon returned to the scene with gusto, at which time he and Karen embarked upon a whirlwind romance. "It seemed to go really quickly," Carole Curb recalls. She was pleased to see the new couple having a great time together. "What was not to like?" she says. "He had a silver Rolls-Royce, and he was very charming. They got along well and seemed to kind of bond. He seemed really nice."

Best friends Frenda and Itchie did not share Carole's optimism. "I disliked him from the second I met him," Frenda says. "I thought he was a phony and a blowhard. He was egotistical and arrogant."

Itchie tried to remain positive despite some suspicions. She had heard from friends that Tom's background had checked out, and Karen seemed excited. Reportedly, he was not a gold digger. "I liked him at first—sort of," she says. "But I didn't really believe him. He was blond and he was cute but overly manicured and a little too good to be true. He always had a plastic smile and would never look me in the eye." Itchie was shocked when Karen told her, "I think he's going to pop the question," just one day after Tom met her and Phil.

"Now, wait a minute, Kace," she replied. "I just met him. And so did *you* for that matter! Does he know about the anorexia? Does he know what to look for? Does he know the signs?"

"No, no, no, I'm over it," Karen assured her. "I'm eating and I'm really, really happy!"

Itchie was panicked but backed off, not wanting to discourage Karen. "She had searched so long for the perfect guy. I really didn't want to rain on her parade."

Phil Ramone concurred with his wife and Karen's other friends. "It was like he was *too* perfect," he says, "but that was an attractive thing for her."

"So what did you think?" Karen asked Phil after he joined the couple for dinner.

"I don't like his hair," he said teasingly. "He's too perfect. It's *Tom Terrific!*"

Karen soon took Tom to meet the Carpenter family at home at Newville. "She brought him into the office and introduced us all,"

Evelyn Wallace recalls. "He was a really nice looking man, and he was very, very polite. I could see nothing wrong with him. I think she really loved Tom. Maybe it was just a crush, I don't know, but she *seemed* to be in love with him." Like Evelyn, the Carpenter family was initially charmed by Tom. "He gets along fabulously with my family," Karen told *People Weekly.*

Whether it was his good looks, personality, or what Karen told them about his career and real estate successes, the family seemed to be won over by Burris—even Richard at first. "Tom instinctively knew what to do," recalls Itchie. "He started palling around with Richard, although even Richard seemed a little apprehensive at the time."

Tom laughed when he told the family how he had been unfamiliar with the Carpenters and their music before having met Karen. "I didn't know *anything* about the Carpenters," he said.

This left Evelyn Wallace skeptical. "You mean you've never *heard* them?" she asked. "They're on the radio a lot. You haven't heard them on the radio?"

"Oh, I am too busy," he replied.

Recalling the conversation with Burris, Wallace is angry she did not see through what she now recalls as an act. "I know in my heart that he knew darn well who Karen Carpenter was...and that there would be a lot of money there." Friends agreed and cautioned Karen that Tom could possibly be an opportunist. "Is he deaf or something?" Itchie asked. "Has he never turned on a radio or a television? I mean, *come on!*"

———⟨∞⟩———

AFTER MONTHS of disappointment and disillusionment in her professional life, it was no wonder Karen's focus turned to her budding romance with Tom Burris. Undoubtedly their relationship took her mind off the snubbed solo album, which was officially shelved on May 5, 1980. "Duo Takes Precedence," *Billboard* announced, claiming that the album was "shelved at her request, to avoid interfering with a Carpenters LP." A&M Records' president Gil Friesen was quoted saying, "Karen thought about it long and hard and decided that the duo takes precedence; that was the priority in her life, and there was no way she wanted the solo project to interfere."

According to Evelyn Wallace, Phil and Itchie wanted more than anything to see Karen's album through to completion for Karen's sake. "They would have done anything to get it done for her, but Richard wasn't willing to give up one minute." In fact, he had returned to work and even booked studios for various Carpenters-related projects, including their impending "comeback" album. Their *Music, Music, Music* special, which became their final for ABC-TV, was set to air in a matter of weeks, and Karen's album was low on the list of priorities.

According to Phil Ramone, "Once Richard didn't like the album, the traditional response in that family was, 'We're not going to like it either.' Nobody would jump forward to say, 'Now wait a minute, this is what Karen wanted to say, and we should accept that.' And once you've put it on the shelf, you've put it on the shelf." He and Itchie wanted the album on record store shelves and to see Karen singing in clubs and performing concerts to promote her new music. According to Itchie, "The artists who had come forward and supported her thought it was really a strange deal considering who they were and who she was. Once again the attention got focused on Richard, what Richard wanted and what Richard needed."

Musician Russell Javors was worried to hear of the unenthusiastic response from Richard and A&M. "Poor Karen," he says. "She was an artist, and she was just trying to work and to explore her craft, and she had every right as an artist to do that. Collaboration is only as good as the sum of its parts, and you have to let each one of those pieces explore what it is that they do. There have to be equal parts. Nobody can be controlling. Karen was every bit as important to those records—if not more so—than the other part. She had the right to explore it. Richard had his own issues at the time. I am sure that he was not thrilled about this project, but if he were in good enough shape to work they would have been working together. Not her with us."

In a 1993 interview Richard explained how he often felt wrongly accused in the case of the solo album and reaffirmed it was Karen's choice and not his urging that put a stop to the album's release. "I get the blame for this, you know," he said. "People who are 'anti-Richard/pro-Karen' seem to take everything that was wrong with Karen and blame it on me. They say that I talked her out of releasing this record because I was ready to start our new album. It was sheer nonsense. All you have to do if you don't believe me is talk to Herb, talk to Jerry, or talk to Derek.... They believed that it didn't have any hits on it, and they weren't going to release it. It had nothing to do with me."

A&M officials agreed unanimously with the album's cancellation. Despite his enthusiasm at the New York playbacks, Derek Green felt the album was "a dog" from a commercial standpoint. "To everybody's credit, the record was stopped," he told Ray Coleman. "The responsibility to the greatest extent with an artist like that would rest with the producer. And it was a mismatch."

Asked over the years about the album's shelving, Herb Alpert almost always answered with nervous hesitation, choosing his words carefully. According to him, the album did not have an effect on him in the same way that a Carpenters album would. He also described Karen as being indecisive and explained how she would go back and forth between loving and hating the album. Other times he conveniently forgot the details. "I don't *exactly* remember why, but I'm sure she wasn't real comfortable with it."

According to Jerry Moss, the men were simply thinking of Karen's best interests. "We didn't think it would get a really great reaction," he said. "We didn't want to have Karen go through that, you know."

In public and to the press, Karen put on her game face, nonchalantly glossing over the project's demise. "It's a good album," she said in 1981. "It just dragged on so long. It seemed all of a sudden to be getting in the way of us going back to work again.... It got to a point where I had to make up my mind because Richard wanted to go back to work and... I wanted to go back to work, too, as the Carpenters.... I'm sure there would have been people who would have been shocked, and a lot of people who would have loved it. I didn't put it away because I was dissatisfied. We ran out of time."

———— ∞ ————

"I WANT to spend the rest of my life with you," Tom Burris told Karen two months into their relationship. She was unsure how to interpret such a declaration so she phoned Karen Ichiuji for advice. Already hesitant to support her friend's blind faith in Tom, Itchie was shocked to learn of the couple's quickly progressing love affair. "I think Tom proposed," Karen said.

"You don't just *think*," Itchie said, explaining that a proposal of marriage should never be a vague or indefinite statement.

Karen's uncertainty was resolved a few days later on Monday, June 16, when Tom officially asked her to marry him and presented her with a ten karat pear-shaped diamond ring. Although she had been anticipating the proposal, she did not accept right away. Tom was still married, and his divorce would not be final for another two days. Seeking her mother's advice, she asked, "Should I marry him?"

Agnes offered little assistance, telling her daughter she was old enough to know what she was doing. "That's all up to you," she said. But Karen knew what she wanted all along. She was under Tom's spell and not about to let this opportunity pass her by. She returned to Tom, accepting his proposal on June 19, the day after his divorce became final. To celebrate their engagement, Burris presented his fiancée with a new Rolls-Royce Corniche convertible to match his own. "Hey Itch!" Karen said, waking her friend with an early morning phone call. "You wanna be a B.M.?"

"A *what*?"

"Tom proposed! We're getting married next year. Do you wanna be a B.M.? You know—a bridesmaid!"

Interestingly, syndicated astrologer Joyce Jillson forecasted Karen's engagement several weeks prior. "Pisceans have marriage on their minds...," she wrote in the "Celebrity Trends" portion of her May 21, 1980, column. "Karen Carpenter could announce her engagement under these lucky Piscean aspects."

The couple's plan for a year-long engagement hastily narrowed when they announced in July their plans for an August ceremony. "They just seemed to want to move quickly," Carole Curb says. She was shocked but says she felt they were surely old enough to know what they were doing. "I just hoped for the best."

The push to be married alarmed Karen's friends. According to Itchie, "That's when everybody's antennas went up." Despite Karen's excitement over the engagement and fast-approaching wedding, Tom was a stranger to them and one who seemed to be on the fast track to marrying their close friend. Karen assured them of his successes in the world of commercial real estate development and talked about his multiple homes, racecars, yachts, and even an eleven-passenger Learjet, but they sensed something was awry. According to Frenda, "It was like, 'I-met-you-will-you-marry-me?' Karen was just all caught up with this. Never ever could any of us have anticipated that it was going to be what it really was.... What I didn't know was that he didn't have a nickel. I believed the stories she told me. Why wouldn't I? It was coming through reliable sources, Mike and Carole, who are certainly not fly-by-nights." Frenda doesn't blame the two, however: "Had they known the truth, would they ever have introduced her to this horrendous person? No!"

By this time Karen was determined to be married at any cost, regardless of warnings from loved ones. Without her knowledge, the family hired a private investigator to look into Burris's background. "If only we'd done a better job checking him out," Frenda says. "His intentions were very clear right in the beginning. This was a plan, but who could have possibly known? Don't think all of us didn't tell her, but when somebody's not listening, they're not listening."

CASTING HER strong personal opinions of Tom Burris aside, Frenda Leffler set out to assist her best friend in coordinating all things wedding related. Karen wanted her big day to be exactly like those of Frenda and her sister Alana Megdal, who both wed in huge Beverly Hills society events with armies of bridesmaids and groomsmen and every tiny detail executed in the grandest of styles. But with only weeks to organize this magnificent event there was no time to waste.

"Frenda took over right away," Evelyn Wallace recalls. "She took care of everything." Agnes Carpenter was upset to discover many of the big decisions had been made without her input. She claimed to have wanted to spend mother-daughter time assisting Karen, but plans were already underway by the time she volunteered. "Usually, when your daughter gets married, you want to be with her and help her," explains Wallace.

"Agnes did absolutely nothing. Frenda did everything. She helped her get the dress, pick out the cake, and even did the invitations."

"Showering Karen with Love and Affection" was the theme of a wedding shower thrown by Frenda, by then named as Karen's matron of honor, and bridesmaid Carole Curb. The event took place on Sunday, August 3, and gathered more than a hundred women at the exclusive Hillcrest Country Club bordering Karen's residence at the Century Towers. Olivia Newton-John was in attendance, as was Itchie, who flew in for the weekend with fiancé Phil Ramone. Ramone treated Karen and Tom to a Billy Joel concert that weekend at the Forum in Inglewood, California.

The Hillcrest's clubhouse garden room was decorated in shades of lavender and peach with an abundance of lilies and orchids flown in from Hawaii. "Karen loved a good party," recalls Frenda. "She was a vision in yellow organdy that day. Like a spring daffodil." Her two-piece yellow outfit and sun hat were designed by Bill Belew, who was also commissioned to create her wedding gown. Belew had been the costume designer for a number of television specials, including the Carpenters' recent *Music, Music, Music,* for which he would later receive an Emmy nomination.

Maria Galeazzi, Karen's former stylist and Richard's ex-girlfriend, was among the guests at the Hillcrest. She was invited a few weeks earlier when she happened upon Karen as they both were shopping in Beverly Hills. "When I saw her I was shocked," Maria says, recalling that day on Rodeo Drive. "People said she had lost weight, but I had not seen her. She looked so thin."

Agnes seemed happy to recognize Maria among the sea of unfamiliar faces at the country club. "Oh, Maria Luisa," she said. "You have no idea what Richard's been through!"

Agnes was referring to her son's addiction to quaaludes, a problem that Maria witnessed during her time with Richard in the early 1970s. "I didn't go nuts with those pills," she says. "When I got off the road I didn't take them anymore. I guess he just kept on going. I was shocked to hear that part." Maria was not nearly as surprised to hear that Richard was still dating his cousin Mary Rudolph. "What do you expect?"

she says. "They'd thrown daggers at everybody he'd hooked up with. Now he had resorted to staying within the family."

According to friends, Karen was mortified by her brother's involvement with their cousin. Itchie had noticed early on that she was strongly against the relationship. "I thought it was because of the gene thing, but after many confrontations Richard finally just screamed out, 'For God's sake, we had the tests! They were *fine*. We can have wonderful, healthy children!' Karen just did *not* want Richard to marry her."

Karen asked Itchie to play matchmaker for Richard on numerous occasions. "It didn't matter what country or what city we were in, she was scrambling for someone for him. I didn't even know Richard when I had to start coming up with these dates for him. Even I was thrown into that mix. She tried to fix Richard and *me* up!"

"Now I *know* you're out of you mind!" Itchie told Karen, laughing uncomfortably at the mere suggestion she date Richard.

"But I want a sister," she answered back.

"Well, we can still be sisters, but quite frankly, Kace, there is no way I would ever get involved with Richard."

Olivia Newton-John was always near the top of Karen's list of potential dates for Richard. In fact, some recall she considered her to be the "dream match" for her brother. "I always had a boyfriend," Olivia says. "But for Karen to think that I was perfect for Richard was probably the biggest compliment that she could pay to me because she *adored* him."

<hr />

ON AUGUST 7, Karen and Tom applied for their marriage license at the Los Angeles County Clerk's office. With less than a month until the ceremony, many details remained unfinished. In the meantime, Carpenters Fan Club secretary Rosina Sullivan relayed the information via newsletter.

Mr. and Mrs. Harold Carpenter of Downey, California, are very happy to announce the forthcoming marriage of their only daughter KAREN ANNE to THOMAS JAMES BURRIS, eldest son of Mr. and

Mrs. James Burris of Orange County, California, on Sunday, August 31, 1980, in Beverly Hills, California. . . . As emotions run high and excitement reaches fever pitch, the heart strings take an extra tug as we learn of Richard's intention to compose a very personal message for the bride to sing to her bridegroom during the marriage ceremony. . . . What a poignant moment that will be.

As Burris explained to the members of the press, "Richard is writing a special song for us. She'll say 'I do' then come out singing. It's going to be interesting." Calling on longtime collaborator and friend John Bettis, Richard wasted no time churning out a big Broadway-style show tune. He then commissioned Peter Knight, who flew in from England to finish the arrangement and orchestration. This was much more of a task than Knight anticipated, as the song was an epic, jumping moods and octaves. Needless to say, it did not lend itself to the rush order Knight was given when he signed on. Initially, Karen intended to sing in person during the ceremony, but she and Richard ultimately chose to pre-record the song, including her lead vocal. "We were planning on doing it live, but it would have required a huge orchestra," Karen recalled. "When I really thought about it . . . I said no, I don't want to do it live. . . . I don't really think I could have focused. And it's a very difficult song to sing. . . . I was having trouble standing up."

Karen undoubtedly lost her footing when just days before the wedding rehearsal Tom dropped a bombshell—one significant enough to end their relationship. The couple had made every plan to start a family as soon as they were married, and Karen was thrilled at the idea of finally becoming a mother. But it was not until the last minute that Tom shared with her how he had undergone a vasectomy procedure prior to their meeting. Her plan of carrying his children was simply not going to happen. Karen was dumbfounded. Tom offered to reverse the procedure, but their chances at a family would be significantly lessened. Regardless, Karen felt betrayed. Tom had lied to her; he had withheld this information for the duration of their courtship and engagement, knowing full well that starting a family was at the top of Karen's list of priorities. This was the deal breaker. The wedding was off.

Karen was in hysterics when she called Frenda. The matron of honor ran to her side and did her best to comfort her. As much as friends hated to see her in such horrific pain, they silently felt relieved that this nightmare seemed to be coming to an end. With Frenda at her side, Karen picked up the phone and called her mother. She cried to Agnes as she explained the deceit that left her with no choice but to cancel the ceremony. But her mother's power over her was never stronger. Agnes told her she would do no such thing. Family and friends were traveling from all over the country to attend the event, and Harold's brother and sister-in-law were even flying in from London. Moreover, the wedding expenses had already cost what Agnes considered to be a small fortune. "We'll deal with it later," she said. "The invitations have gone out. There are reporters and photographers coming. *People* magazine is going to be there. The wedding is *on*, and you *will* walk down that aisle." Karen was in disbelief. Surely deception of this magnitude justified an end to her plans of marriage to Tom? But Agnes remained firm. "You made your bed, Karen," she told her. "Now you'll have to lay in it."

⸺⚬⚬⚬⸺

THE LUXURIOUS five-star Beverly Hills Hotel on Sunset Boulevard was the site of what promised to be the society wedding of the decade on Sunday, August 31, 1980. For Karen it promised little. Evelyn Wallace was upset to learn of Karen's turmoil some time later. "As she was walking down the aisle, she knew that Tom was not the person he said he was," she explains, "but she carried on. She wasn't marrying the guy she thought Tom was, but she didn't stop the wedding. She carried on like she was really, really happy that day."

Although photographs from that day show a seemingly radiant and glowing bride, few knew of Karen's inner conflict. She had adopted her mother's position and resolved to deal with the problems later. She had long been a master at concealing her true feelings, and this was perhaps her finest performance. "I don't know how she's doing it," Itchie told a friend as the women observed Karen smiling for the cameras. "Kace, are you playacting or are you really happy?" Itchie asked, but Karen's only response was her silent stare.

"She was the typical bride, a little nervous," recalls Debbie Cuticello, who was not privy to news of the previous week. "She was very excited, very beautiful, and just beaming. The wedding was like a fairy tale. It was a Cinderella event for me. There were lots of things we had to do beforehand, like getting fitted, getting the dresses, and doing the rehearsal." Bill Belew's design team, consisting of members of both the ABC-TV and NBC-TV wardrobe departments, oversaw the fittings. "We all had these amazing lavender dresses with these big sun hats," Carole Curb recalls. "It was just sumptuous."

Frank Bonito and his wife were in attendance as well. "Karen let all the girls try on her ring. My wife had a pear-shaped diamond, too, which was of course much smaller." Still, Bonito feels Karen was unaffected by her fame and fortune, regardless of diamonds and other luxuries. On her wedding day she came to him saying, "Frank, this diamond around my neck's not falling right. Would you just knot the chain behind my neck?" As he recalls, Karen was often quite casual about things. "Then she took her ring off to wash her hands, and this ring almost went down the sink drain! I said to her, 'Oh my God, Karen, if that thing goes down the drain we'll be pulling the pipes apart!'"

Greeted with the fragrance of thousands of sweet-smelling gardenias, the five hundred wedding guests began arriving shortly after noon in preparation for the 1:00 P.M. ceremony. "I invited everybody in the city, and everybody in the city showed up," Karen said.

Named for its elegant chandeliers, the Crystal Ballroom's art deco theme was concealed by a facade of silver trellises. Adorned with white orchids, gardenias, violets, and lemon leaves, the framed lattice displays helped simulate a 1930s old English garden setting. The room's chandeliers were interspersed with huge baskets of orchids suspended from the ceiling.

The Who's Who list of celebrities included many of those attending the wedding shower a month earlier, in addition to Casey Kasem, John Davidson, JoJo Starbuck, Dionne Warwick, Burt Bacharach, Herb Alpert, Dorothy Hamill, and Toni Tennille and husband, Daryl Dragon. Head usher Mike Curb arrived in Beverly Hills with an entourage of state police escorts. In addition to his role as lieutenant governor of California, Curb was acting governor of California during Jerry Brown's campaign for president in 1980.

Phil Ramone arrived wearing a tuxedo. "Karen told me it was absolutely formal," he explains. "'I expect you to wear a tux,' she said. The only guys wearing tuxes were me and the waiters. That's how she got back at me for saying I didn't like Tom's hair. Now that's what I consider great humor!"

Organist Frank Brownstead offered Johann Sebastian Bach's "Sheep May Safely Graze" as members of the wedding party took their places. The mother of the bride, escorted by her son Richard, was outfitted in a lavender chiffon gown and picture hat similar to that of the groom's mother. Then, sweeping strings and a most familiar voice came seemingly out of nowhere. As the crowd shifted in their seats in hopes of seeing the bride as she sang, most soon realized the song was pre-recorded. The production was surprisingly polished for a rush job. Even a hasty Carpenters recording was perfection. Down to the wire, the recording was done three days earlier, with the master delivered just hours before the wedding rehearsal. Karen's singing conveyed John Bettis's lyric to great effect and with a soaring sense of optimism and determination.

Because we are in love we reach for our tomorrows
And know we won't be lonely in laughter and in sorrow
Where love abides there is the place we'll keep our home forever
You and I, because we are in love

Frenda's three-year-old twins, Ashley and Andrew, along with their cousin Brooke Megdal, led the seemingly endless trail of bridesmaids and groomsmen down the red-carpeted aisleway to the tune of Wagner's "Bridal Chorus." The bride's attendants, wearing waltz-length lavender chiffon gowns with green sashes, included close friends Connie Chapman, Linda Curb, Debbie Cuticello, Sandy Holland, Karen Ichiuji, Alana Megdal, Carole Curb Scotti, Elizabeth Van Ness, and Karen's cousins Mary Rudolph and Joan Will. Noticeably absent from the bridal party was Olivia Newton-John, who attended the ceremony with *Xanadu* choreographer Kenny Ortega. The film had been released just weeks earlier, and a trip to its Australian premiere prevented Olivia from accepting Karen's invitation to be a bridesmaid. "I wanted the attention to be on Karen anyway," she says.

Richard Burris served as his brother's best man. Other groomsmen and ushers, dressed in traditional morning coats, included Mark Armbruster, Effie Beard, Tom's son Mike Burris, his brothers James Burris and Vern Burris, Jolyn Gissell, Casey Kasem, Ed Leffler, Tony Scotti, and Jerry Van Ness. The ring bearer's pillow was created by Bill Belew from remnants of all the gowns the designer had made over the years for the Carpenters' television specials.

After placing a kiss on his daughter's extended hand, Harold Carpenter escorted Karen down a path of white gardenia topiaries and baskets filled with pink chrysanthemums to the altar, where she was met by the groom. Karen's wedding gown was made from fifteen yards of crisp, white mousseline de soie and modeled after an eighteenth-century English riding ensemble. The long-sleeved dress and jacket with its stand-up collar displayed a sparkling floral design of seashells and sequins. Her silk veil was affixed to a classic-style picture hat made up of a beaded Juliet cap and detachable white chiffon brim. She carried a bouquet of lilies of the valley, white orchids, and white pikake.

Accompanied by the forty-voice Tom Bähler Chorale, under the direction of Peter Knight, Richard sang David Williams's "The Wedding Prayer." Behind Karen's veil, her eyes were closed and her head bowed in silence as if in her own solemn moment of prayer.

> *Bless thou the ring, bless thou the promise*
> *Strengthen our love throughout each day*
> *All happy moments, all times of sadness*
> *Teach us to trust and share them all with Thee*

Well-known television evangelist Dr. Robert H. Schuller, pastor of Garden Grove Community Church, officiated the ceremony, just two weeks before the dedication of his famed Crystal Cathedral, the first-ever all-glass church facility.

"Tom made fun of Schuller during the ceremony," recalls Walt Harrah, who sang in Bähler's chorus. He and others were unnerved by the groom's behavior. Speaking out in his distinctive, commanding voice, Reverend Schuller asked Burris, "Do you take this woman?" In response, the groom proceeded to mimic the pastor. "When he said, 'I do,' he just *mocked* him, and the whole place laughed," Harrah says. "It was really bizarre."

Evelyn Wallace felt Tom was not taking the vows seriously. "He probably knew exactly what was going to happen once he got Karen. All he was in for was the money. He wasn't thinking of her; he was thinking of her money. That's all."

In contrast, Karen delivered her vows in a very solemn and serious manner—almost stern. "So help us God," she repeated, giving a long, firm glare and nod to her groom. "Amen."

Following the ceremony, guests sipped cocktails as they mingled in the Maisonette Room, while Karen and Tom met with the media for a press conference in the Persian Room. Richard was also present and photographed in somewhat of an awkward trio with the newlyweds. According to one reporter, he looked "more like a father giving away his daughter."

The Crystal Ballroom was transformed into a giant banquet hall and the site of the $25,000 wedding luncheon, which began around 3:00 P.M. "The big attraction was Olivia Newton-John," recalls Frank Bonito. "That was not long after the time when *Grease* was big, so there was lots of discussion about where Livvy would sit. We all told Karen, 'Oh, Olivia can sit at *our* table!'" At one point during the reception a security officer approached Bonito as he snapped photos with his camera. "Kindly stop taking pictures of Miss Newton-John," he cautioned when Frank was unable to produce press credentials.

"I am a guest of the bride, and she asked me to take them for her," he fibbed.

The elegant banquet tables were decorated with lavender tablecloths and arrangements of purple orchids, Alba lilies, and African violets. The menu included Karen's favorite, shrimp salad, and a main course of chicken chasseur with broccoli polonaise, rice pilaf, strawberries

Romanoff, and Parducci Chablis wine. Karen and Tom cut the five-tiered chocolate and mocha cream wedding cake, adorned with traditional bride and groom figures on top, and Mike Curb proposed the first toast to the couple. "Excuse me, waiter!" Jerry Weintraub called out to Phil Ramone periodically throughout the meal, poking fun at his tuxedo predicament. Providing the live dance music was the Michael Paige Big Band, inviting the newlyweds to lead the first dance, which was of course to "We've Only Just Begun."

15

BEGINNING OF THE END

FOLLOWING A brief stop in Baja California, the honeymooners flew to the Tahitian island of Bora Bora, where they planned to spend ten days on what promised to be "the most romantic island in the world." Known for its white sand, dazzling turquoise waters, and unique overwater bungalows, Bora Bora had all the ingredients for the perfect romantic getaway for two. But instead of two, these travelers numbered four. Considering that Karen Carpenter's marriage to Tom Burris was essentially over before it began, it is understandable that she might not have had any qualms inviting her husband's brother Rick and his wife to join them on their honeymoon. She had extended the same bizarre invitation to her aunt Bernice and other family members as well, but all declined.

Arriving on Bora Bora, a location chosen by Tom, Karen immediately began to complain about the setting, which she likened to a forsaken, deserted island. She called it Boring, Boring and blamed her loathing on having grown accustomed to hotels with room service and twenty-four-hour concierge service while on tour. True, there were no phones, radios, or televisions in the resort guest rooms, but when Karen rescheduled their return flights and ended the honeymoon early, it had little to do with her dislike for the accommodations. She wanted to get back home to Los Angeles as fast as she could.

Karen and Tom made their home at 61 Linda Isle in Newport Beach, just across the Lido Channel from another of their residences at 117 Via Yella. In addition to Karen's Century Towers condo, the couple also kept a large house in Bel Air and even one in Mexico—a vacation getaway situated in the gated celebrity enclave El Pedregal, the first residential community in Cabo San Lucas. "Karen bought their house in Newport Beach, and she was paying for *all* of these homes," Itchie Ramone recalls. "All the antennas were starting to go up between Frenda, Livvy, Carole, and myself. We knew what was going on."

For a period of time Karen played the part of the happy newlywed, at least to anyone she thought she could fool. "I love it," she said of her marriage during a phone interview broadcast to Japanese radio audiences. "I'm having a wonderful time. I'm very, very happy."

The couple's time in Newport Beach was short lived. Karen preferred to stay at their two-and-a-half-acre rented estate in Bel Air, where Frenda Leffler was close by. From the time Karen moved to Century City she had established a small circle of friends and acquaintances. "She made friends in Century City," Frenda explains, "but she still had never really been on her own. This was Bel Air now, and she was a married lady and on her own."

—⋙⋘—

"NOBODY'S BEING stolen," Karen assured the press during a public appearance in the fall of 1980. Richard and Tom did their best to uphold smiles for the cameras but were ill at ease. Work on the Carpenters' next album had ceased with the couple's engagement and wedding plans, but Richard had stayed busy making preparations for Karen's return to the recording studio. Jerry Moss suggested that the duo stick with their tried-and-true Carpenters formula, which they had abandoned in some ways for the mishmash selections on 1977's *Passage* album.

Perhaps in an attempt to recapture the 1973 success of Joe Raposo's "Sing," the Carpenters told Paul Williams they wished to record his and Kenny Ascher's "The Rainbow Connection" from the highly successful 1979 film *The Muppet Movie*. "I saw Karen after I won the Oscar for *A Star is Born*," Williams says. "She was really sweet about that and also said that 'Evergreen' was a great song. Then the same thing happened with *The Muppet Movie*. They loved the songs from that movie and wanted to record 'Rainbow Connection.'" But Richard was bothered by the syllabification of the song, notably the opening phrases written for Muppet character Kermit the Frog to sing. "Richard wanted me to change some of it," Williams recalls, "but this song was nominated for an Academy Award! The song is written in Kermit's speaking rhythm, and I wouldn't change it. It was written for Kermit; it should be recorded the way that Kermit recorded it."

Although the Carpenters went on to record "The Rainbow Connection," they took artistic license and altered the rhythm and melody to suit their wishes. Even so, Karen was displeased with the outcome, and her work lead was filed away with the album's other outtakes. It was not until 1999 that Richard completed the recording, which ultimately saw release on the *As Time Goes By* collection. "I really wanted them to do 'Rainbow Connection,'" Williams says, "but I didn't like the changes they made in it. Still, it's always a treasure to hear her sing my words."

A surprise call came in November 1980 from legendary guitarist Les Paul. He wanted to meet Karen and Richard, who were busy working in A&M's studio D. Like Lester William Polsfuss, his given name, Evelyn Wallace grew up in Waukesha, Wisconsin. "He was a neighbor of ours when I was a kid," she says. "He went to the same school as we did and lived just down the street." Wallace phoned Richard at A&M and explained Les Paul would like to sit in on a Carpenters recording session. Karen and Richard had often cited Les Paul and Mary Ford among their earliest musical inspirations, making this meeting especially meaningful. They discussed with him their recording techniques and the evolution of the overdubbing process, which Les Paul essentially pioneered.

A few months later on January 20, 1981, Karen arrived at A&M Studios wearing a new patriotic-themed running suit with large block letters across the chest: MADE IN AMERICA. Although the Carpenters had Republican ties, neither was known to be political. But this was Inauguration Day, and Ronald Reagan was sworn in as the fortieth president of the United States. Richard noticed the suit and immediately said, "Well, there it is!" He felt "Made in America" was a perfect name for the duo's forthcoming album. Karen agreed.

Released June 16, 1981, *Made in America* was the Carpenters' first traditional studio album in nearly four years. Although the inner photograph showed Karen looking comfortable and seemingly fit, it had been heavily retouched by A&M's art department. The original, untouched photo reveals her bloodshot eyes and drawn appearance. In just the few short months between that John Engstead photo session and the album's release, Karen had lost even more weight.

The standout track on *Made in America* was "Touch Me When We're Dancing," the obvious choice for debut single. When the demo for "Touch Me" arrived from Welk Publishing, Karen and Richard needed only one listen to know it was the right song to launch their return to Top 40 radio. And it did. The debut single was released a week prior to the album's release and soon peaked at #16. "Touch Me" had all the ingredients of a 1971 Carpenters hit packaged neatly in a 1981 production. "When all the ingredients gelled, the result was irresistible," wrote John Tobler in a review. "That's what we have here, a perfect Carpenters confection, reminiscent of the classic days of the early Seventies."

"(Want You) Back in My Life Again" was one of the most 1980s-influenced recordings in the Carpenters catalog. Incidentally, the synthesizers were manned by two well-known artists in their own right—Daryl Dragon, the "Captain" of Captain and Tennille, and Ian Underwood of the Mothers of Invention. With its strong, melodic, singable hook, "Back in My Life Again" seemed a wise choice for the second single, but it did not fare as well as "Touch Me." Reminiscent of "Top of the World" was "Those Good Old Dreams," a country-tinged collaboration by Richard and John Bettis released as the album's third single. "When It's Gone (It's Just Gone)" was another tune with a country ballad feel, sounding a bit like "Two Sides" from *Passage*. Randy Handley's poetic lyric tells of an aching, unrequited love. Judging from the effectiveness of Karen's interpretation, it sounds as if she penned it herself.

Where's the word for the sadness
Where's the poetry in the pain
Where's the color in the stain where the tears have fallen
It's gone, it's just gone

Karen still loved oldies, and somehow an "oldie-but-goodie" seemed to find its way onto every Carpenters album after 1973's *Now and Then* medley. *Horizon* had "Please Mr. Postman." *A Kind of Hush* opened with the title track and closed with Sedaka's "Breaking Up Is Hard to Do." Then "Man Smart, Woman Smarter" from *Passage* reached all the way back to a 1956 Harry Belafonte album, and Karen even cut a work lead of "Jimmy Mack" by Martha and the Vandellas during her 1979 solo sessions. "Richard and I always talked about bringing back songs," says Mike Curb, who was treated to a preview of the Carpenters' next oldie. "I've gotta play a song for you," Karen told him. "You'll get a kick out of it. It is really fun! It'll bring back memories." After playing the recording of "Beechwood 4-5789" down the phone line she asked, "So, what do you think of this as a single?"

Curb was encouraging and unable to bring himself to tell her it lacked Top 40 potential. "That was the last song she played for me," he says. Whereas "Postman" was a case of the right song at the right time, "There's a Kind of Hush" was overkill, and remaking the Marvelettes' "Beechwood 4-5789" was a waste. A promotional video for "Beechwood," shot on A&M's Chaplin Stage, further relegated the song to the most syrupy sweet category of bubblegum pop. Karen looked ill at ease—to say the least—as a thirty-one-year old woman sporting a poodle skirt and swaying her way around a faux malt shop. "Beechwood" was released on Karen's birthday, March 2, 1982, and became the Carpenters' lowest-charting single at #74 and their final appearance on the U.S. singles chart during Karen's lifetime.

From listening to demos and writing new material through to the mastering process, *Made in America* took over a year to create, twice as long as the average Carpenters record. Considering the wealth of quality leftovers and outtakes from their 1980–1981 sessions, namely "The Uninvited Guest" and "Kiss Me the Way You Did Last Night," both of which saw posthumous release, *Made in America* could have fared much stronger. In his review for *Billboard*, Paul Grein explains: "Innocuous ditties like 'Postman' and 'Beechwood' don't begin to tap the depths of Karen's voice. She needs a meaningful lyric to really show her stuff."

The Carpenters' new album and their contributions to A&M Records were celebrated by Herb Alpert and the entire label on the evening of June 29, 1981, at a party in their honor on the grounds of the Bel Air Hotel. An audience of more than two hundred guests watched as Alpert welcomed Karen and Richard back to the music scene, presenting two matching plaques that displayed their eleven studio albums for A&M. He also announced that the Carpenters' record sales as of March that year had topped seventy-nine million units.

MADE IN America concluded with "Because We Are in Love (The Wedding Song)," written for Karen's wedding, but by the time the album hit shelves, Karen's marriage was already on its last leg. "She thought she'd married the right guy," Maria Galeazzi says, "but this one took her for a ride." Friends of the couple, including Carole Curb, began to hear "bits and pieces that didn't feel good and didn't sound right. I heard that there were some monetary things that popped up with Tom that none of us knew about. That didn't sit right with her. All that glitters isn't gold."

According to Itchie, Karen had learned the truth of Tom's financial status the morning of their wedding. "They were all in the process of investigating, but there wasn't enough time," she says. But Karen was more upset to learn of her family's probing and refused to heed the warnings from Werner Wolfen and others. "Artists are prone to fall in love with somebody who can spend their money without them knowing it," explains Phil Ramone. "Karen was pretty frugal, to say the least. Some of the older-thinking artists watched every penny. The Carpenters had a pretty good money advisor, so I am surprised that Tom got through that fence."

Most had assumed Burris's lifestyle and net worth were comparable to that of Karen's. The expensive cars and other possessions gave him the appearance of a multimillionaire, but what others did not realize was that he was living well beyond his means. On several occasions he treated the Carpenter parents and their friends to a short yacht trip around Newport Harbor, even instructing Evelyn Wallace on steering technique. "Oh, I have six boats," he boasted to her.

"Tom had wanted Karen to think that he was Mr. Money Guy, but it wasn't long after they got married that he started asking her for money," recalls Wallace. "He'd give her some excuse, and she'd give him the money. He'd ask for $35,000 and $50,000 at a time. Finally it got down to the point where all she had left was stocks and bonds."

As Itchie recalls, "Tom couldn't afford the houses, the cars, her wedding ring; he couldn't pay for *anything*." Karen began to share with friends her growing misgivings about Tom, not only concerning his finances but also his lack of feelings for her. He was often impatient, and she admitted being fearful when he would occasionally lose his temper. "He could be very cruel to her," says Itchie. But Karen's longing to be a mother proved to be stronger than her desire to leave her husband. At the house in Newport Beach Karen expressed to Tom her desire to get pregnant and start a family. Of course a vasectomy reversal would be required, and he had promised to go through with the procedure, but in this particular moment Karen just wanted to be intimate with her husband. She never could have dreamed that his response would be so brutal. She was still crying hysterically when she called Itchie for support. According to Karen, Tom had told her he wouldn't even consider having children with her and called her "a bag of bones." Karen was well aware that her weight had plummeted since her wedding to Tom the previous year, but hearing such callous words in response to a physical advance toward her husband was unbearable.

Karen and Tom saw their first anniversary come and go with little merriment. During the last week of August the two set out on a journey taking them more than six thousand miles round-trip in Tom's cumbersome four-wheel-drive Dodge Ramcharger, equipped with CB radio and refrigerator. Although the Carpenters rarely toured or traveled in what would be considered excessive luxury, this trip found the Burris couple roughing it, to say the least. Following a stay in the San Juan

Mountains near Durango, Colorado, Karen and Tom schlepped north-ward. They stopped at Canada's hiking capital, Lake Louise in Banff National Park, before visiting the city of Vancouver. Relieved to return to Los Angeles, Karen recovered from what she considered to have been a disaster of a vacation.

Itchie flew to Los Angeles to find out for herself what was happen-ing in her friend's marriage and offer her love and support to Karen. They met for lunch at their normal hangout, Hamburger Hamlet, but Karen asked the host for a different table than their usual. "We didn't sit at our regular table, which was odd," Itchie recalls. "We sat in the dark, and she wore huge, dark sunglasses."

"OK, what do you want me to do, Kace?" she asked, realizing things had gone too far. "You can't go on living like this."

According to Itchie, this marriage was "the straw that broke the camel's back. It was absolutely the worst thing that could have ever happened to her. She was just so loving and so wonderful, and then the next thing you know you're sitting there across the table from your best friend all bruised up. How do you do that? She was pretty much wrecked." Karen initially passed it off, but she then could not make it through the meal. "She couldn't eat, she was crying, and we had to leave. We didn't want anyone to recognize her."

At the urging of friends and family, Karen met with legal counsel to revise her will on September 1, 1981. She could not yet bring her-self to file for divorce but was obviously moving in that direction. "I give all household furniture and furnishings, household equipment and appliances, and silverware located in the residence occupied by my hus-band and myself to my husband," she stated in the codicil. "I give any residence occupied by my husband and myself as our home at the time of my death to my husband." Karen willed everything else to Harold, Agnes, and Richard, listing estimated assets totaling between five and ten million dollars.

Friends suggested she and Tom seek marital counseling. Instead, the Carpenters prepared to leave for Europe and South America. Itchie went along to keep Karen company on this series of Carpenters pro-motional tours, which began in Paris, France, where Karen's laxative addiction became an issue. "Laxatives were her major companion," Itchie says. "When we were in Paris we made quite a scene in a pharmacy across the street from our hotel about her needing to buy more laxatives. I suggested natural food groups that might relieve her 'constipation,' but she always won those arguments."

Following a brief stop in Amsterdam, the Carpenters arrived at London's Heathrow Airport on Wednesday, October 21, 1981. They made numerous promotional appearances while in London, both in person and on television. On Thursday they taped an interview for *Nationwide*, a popular news magazine on BBC television. Barely one minute into their visit, host Sue Lawley surprised Karen by casting light on her darkest secret. "There were rumors that you were suffering from the slimmer's disease anorexia nervosa," Lawley said. "Is that right?"

"No, I was just pooped," Karen said with an intense frown. "I was tired out."

"You went down to about six stone in weight, I think, didn't you?" Lawley asked.

"I have no idea what 'six stone in weight' is," Karen replied, becoming noticeably uncomfortable and increasingly agitated. She struggled to fake a laugh, rolling her eyes at the interviewer, who quickly converted the amount to approximately eighty-four pounds. "No," she said, shaking her head adamantly. "No."

In actuality her weight was hovering around eighty pounds even then. The interviewer's continued efforts to pinpoint a reason for Karen's skeletal appearance prompted Richard to come to his sister's defense. "I don't really feel that we should be talking about the weight loss," he told Lawley and producers. "Maybe it's better to take a pass on the whole thing. It's really not what we're here for."

"I am just asking you the questions people want to know the answers to," she replied.

All involved regrouped, and the interviewer offered to pursue a new line of questioning geared toward Karen's marriage, an almost equally unpleasant topic but one that Karen could fake her way through. Richard agreed to allow the questioning to continue. A labored exhalation was captured by Karen's lapel microphone as Lawley instructed the

Carpenters to relax. "Now, we have to pretend all that didn't happen," she joked.

"Yeah, I feel *terrific*," Karen chuckled with heavy sarcasm. And the interview continued. By this point Karen had become what author Ray Coleman called a "professional anorexic," perfecting the deceit while assuring all those around her she was just fine. While she was considered by those who knew and loved her to be one of the most honest and open individuals they ever met, she was rarely truthful when it came to anorexia nervosa.

❦

RETURNING TO Los Angeles, Karen and Richard joined the Carpenter family to celebrate Harold Carpenter's seventy-third birthday. Family and friends gathered on the evening of November 9, 1981, for dinner at Sambi of Tokyo, a favorite Downey restaurant. After dinner, the party continued at Newville, where Karen and Tom went upstairs and, as Richard recalled, "had it out."

Evelyn Wallace recalls no sign of tension during dinner but explains, "In the restaurant, Karen wouldn't do that. She would be a lady in a restaurant." After some time, an exasperated Tom barreled down the stairs exclaiming, "You can keep her!" As he raced away from the house in his car, cousin Joanie ran upstairs to comfort Karen, hugging her and telling her how much she loved and cared for her. The guests downstairs were speechless. Karen was humiliated and inconsolable.

Although the family cites this episode at Newville as the last time Karen saw her husband, Frenda visited Karen back in Bel Air around this time and was shocked to find the couple in the process of making a twenty-thousand-dollar upgrade to a house they did not even own. This was oddly uncharacteristic of Karen, who had a reputation for being thrifty, a trait passed down from her parents. With Tom away, Frenda expressed concern to Karen over the unnecessary expense of home improvements. After all, it was a rented house, and the couple was on the verge of separating. "Karen was very frugal," Frenda recalls. "She wasn't frugal if she bought you a gift or something, but she earned her own money, and she paid a price for that money. She wasn't cavalier about it, which I respected. I thought that was a wonderful way to be. She had some areas in which she didn't have much sense, but she *did* have sense in the area of finances. If it had been five hundred dollars I wouldn't have said anything, but this was a lot of money."

Arriving back home, Frenda was not surprised when the phone rang and it was Karen. It had not even been twenty minutes, but the two talked "fifty million times a day," she says. But this call was different. Karen was in a panic. "Oh my God, Frenda! Oh my God, oh my God," she said, her voice quivering in fear.

"Kace, what is it?"

"There was a man that came to the door and I let him in and he said something about the Corniche."

"Don't tell me it was a burglar," Frenda scolded. "Kace, you should never have let anybody in!"

"No, no, no. They really *were* from the car agency," Karen explained.

"Well, what's the problem then?"

"Well, Tom never even bought me the car! It's leased. And he hasn't paid the lease in two months, and they were here to repossess the car. They offered to let me make restitution, and I said, 'No, just take it!'"

"Kace! Oh my God. I'm coming to get you."

"No, no, no," Karen told her. "I want to talk to Tom about it when he comes home."

"All right," Frenda said, "but I am going to get a hold of Eddie."

When Tom returned home Karen confronted him about the leased car. He became furious when he learned it had been repossessed by the dealership. Additionally, he wanted more money and her signature on yet another loan. Mustering up all the strength she could, Karen looked her husband in the eye and said, "Tommy, I am not a bank. I am *not* a bank."

Ed Leffler was on the golf course with friends that day and not easy to reach. As Frenda tried to contact her husband she heard three tiny taps from her brass door knocker. She opened the door to find Karen, who had driven across town after a falling-out with Tom. "She was in a hump, slumped over," Frenda recalls. "Oh my God, I was hysterical.

I tried so hard to be calm because I had two babies there, but I had to help her in the house. I will never forget that day as long as I live. I said, 'That's it. It's over!' She never went back to that house again. We cleaned it out. That was the end of it."

Karen moved in with Frenda for a short time and then back to her condo at Century Towers, telling friends and family she was afraid to return to the Bel Air estate due to recent burglaries in the neighborhood. "She wouldn't go back," Frenda explains. "She couldn't go back. We wouldn't *let* her go back. That was the end, and I know she never saw him again after that. That really was the beginning of the end of her life."

KAREN'S DISASTER of a marriage only served to exacerbate her mental illness and physical descent. "You expect a marriage to go through its ups and downs," says Phil Ramone. "Unfortunately hers read exactly like the solo album, but it was her life. Its failure was exactly the same. That's too much for any human being to take. Any way you look at it, that disaster was the final nail." According to Itchie, "Karen tried to put a smile on her face all the time. No one wants to own up to having been deceived, especially with her life in the spotlight. Her wedding had been the centerfold of *People*. In truth, her marriage didn't really last more than about three months."

Too embarrassed and ashamed to return home to Downey, Karen relied on Frenda and her parents, Ben and Melba, for support during this time of deep depression. "She would sit and my mother would cradle her like she was an infant," Frenda recalls. Mealtime at the Leffler house became a dreaded and terribly painful experience for all involved. "I'd make everything that she liked. Everything. She loved white fish, and she loved the way I made it. Then I made peas. I made everything that I knew she'd like, and she ate one pea!" Adding to the Lefflers' frustration was the fact that Karen would carefully divide, sort, and compartmentalize the food on her plate. "I couldn't help but notice," Frenda says. "She'd make little patterns out of it. I'd watch it. Even that was artistic. Even in the mania she was an artist."

Frenda would sit patiently at the table with Karen long after the rest of the family had finished their meals and left the dining room. She tried every approach she could think of to encourage her friend to eat. "Now Kace, we can't do this," she would say. "Don't make me feed you like a baby!" But Karen just sat quietly. "OK, then open your mouth. Here comes the choo-choo!"

When Karen did manage to eat a few bites she would immediately say she felt sick and quickly disappear to the nearest bathroom. "She couldn't keep food down," Frenda says. "It was a serious depression, no question. I knew she was severely depressed when singing was the last thing on her mind. When you have a passion for music like she had, and all at once you can't even think about it, something is definitely wrong. It was not about music anymore. It was not about fun anymore. It was about trying to eat something. Survival." The absence of food and nutrients left Karen very weak, and she tired easily. This worried Frenda, but there was an underlying determination that showed through at times. "It was frightening," she recalls, "but as sick as Karen was, she'd still want to give the twins their baths. She'd rub their little backs in circles. See, she still tried to do some of the things she loved doing."

While many around Karen felt her obsession with dieting had taken over, those who knew her intimately say that was not the case. There came a time when she did not want to lose more weight, but by then she knew the disorder was out of her control. She wanted to stop and was even ashamed of how she looked. As she had done years before, Karen began layering her clothes to disguise her skeletal frame. She would tell others she was cold and then add a sweatshirt to a turtleneck sweater. "She'd put on so many layers of clothing because she didn't want people to know she was *that* thin," Frenda says. "My feeling always was that she wanted to disappear. I certainly know that's not a medical diagnosis, but that is what it seemed like."

———— ✺ ————

"RICHARD, I realize I'm sick and I need help." As 1981 came to an end, Karen was more freely expressing this realization to family and friends.

She went to her brother and finally admitted things had gone too far. Something had to be done—and soon.

"How do I get over this?" she asked a group of girlfriends who gathered for lunch at the Beverly Hills Hotel. She expressed to them how she felt a great deal of responsibility on her shoulders. In addition to her efforts to maintain a successful career, she spent a lot of time worrying about family issues. Her friends sensed that Karen was constantly trying to keep all members of her family happy, with no time left to take care of herself. She wanted to get help but felt guilty even considering the idea of putting everything on hold to address her personal problems. "Maybe I should just wait for the perfect time," she said.

"Life can't always be that perfect, Kace," Frenda told her from time to time. "It just can't be. You can't be all things to all people all the time. You're just one little girl!"

"Her face was all eyes," Carole Curb recalls. "She looked like she weighed somewhere between eighty and ninety pounds. As I look back I can tell she was reaching out. She'd succeeded in everything else, and she wanted a scientific formula for how she could get over this. I think that she just couldn't quite pull it together. In retrospect, she was pleading for help, which we all wish we'd given more of." Over the years, Curb struggled with her own weight issues and an ongoing battle with anorexia. "In that era we all had little bouts of that. It was really in vogue then. Maybe it's never been out of vogue. Mine wasn't anything like hers. I never got down to eighty pounds. But she would ask me questions about it, and I would try to give her answers."

Karen's food issues had been obvious to Olivia Newton-John for several years by this time, but Newton-John admits it was difficult for her to identify with or comprehend what her friend was experiencing. "Anorexia was not something that was talked about or known about in those days," she says. "People were very thin, but you didn't realize what it was. When I looked at Karen I saw this face with these big, beautiful, soulful brown eyes and this funny, quirky personality. . . . She was a clown on the outside, but you know how clowns are—they are sometimes sad on the inside and funny on the outside—that was Karen."

Karen also reached out once again to Cherry O'Neill. "The fact that I had blazed the trail of recovery before her gave her hope to think she could do the same," O'Neill says. "I think she was looking for encouragement and inspiration along her own journey toward wellness. Karen was acknowledging her own eating disorders and was actively seeking help. I think she knew that she needed to get serious about dealing with her problem, but she didn't want to talk with just any-body. As a public figure, she knew that she was dealing with pressures and expectations that were much different than most people struggling with eating disorders. Perhaps she thought I could identify with those pressures and expectations better than most other people."

O'Neill sensed that Karen sincerely wanted to get better. "She was very blunt and straightforward in the way she spoke about it, and she knew she could do it." What fascinated Karen was that Cherry had seemingly recovered by that time. She was also happily married with a young child, the life Karen still longed for, even though deep down she knew it could never be with Tom Burris. She spoke little of her marital issues or her separation from Tom. Instead Karen remained focused on the matter at hand. "What was behind her was in the past, and she was trying to focus on her future and on moving forward," O'Neill says. "She just felt like she had tried her best and was sorry the marriage failed. She didn't like failure and probably felt it reflected on her personally. That is another hard pill to swallow for perfectionists, and almost all anorexics are."

As she had told Karen several years earlier, Cherry O'Neill believed Karen needed to make some radical changes to her surroundings and suggested she leave Los Angeles for a quieter, more sedate environ-ment where she could work through her issues and take plenty of time to properly heal. "I actually recommended she consider coming to the Northwest and seeing the doctor who helped me," she says. "The pace was so much slower, the values less superficial, and the natural beauty absolutely awe-inspiring and invigorating."

But in Karen's world, one name was synonymous with anorexia treatment, and that name was Steven Levenkron. Since the time she spoke with the therapist by phone from Jerry Weintraub's office several

years earlier, his successful book *The Best Little Girl in the World* had
become a highly acclaimed television movie, which aired in May 1981.
Levenkron's high profile was a huge factor in helping make this decision. Plus, a move from Los Angeles to the Big Apple sure seemed
radical enough in terms of distance. In reality, the two cities could not
have been more similar as far as pace and environmental pressures were
concerned.

With Karen's consent, Itchie Ramone phoned Steven Levenkron,
telling him of an anonymous celebrity she represented. He considered
his extensive list of clients to be held under the strictest confidence
and was annoyed to talk around a situation such as this. He refused to
discuss the possibility of someone in need of his help and demanded
this "unnamed famous person" call him directly. "Well, it's Karen Carpenter," Itchie finally revealed. Levenkron immediately recalled the
brief conversation with Karen two and a half years earlier, when she'd
assured him she was fine and did not have anorexia. Itchie told him that
was simply not the case and that Karen had lied to him, but she was very
sorry and desired very much to meet with him.

The following day, Karen called Levenkron herself from Los Angeles, informed him she had purchased a plane ticket to New York, and
began detailing her plan for recovery—she would be arriving that Saturday and would see him for three hours. When the therapist explained
that he was a family man who did not keep hours on weekends, Karen
broke down. "This will only take you a couple of hours," she promised.
Taking back control of the conversation, Levenkron firmly explained
that Karen was entirely wrong to think she would be cured after one
quick consultation. Enumerating the minimum requirements for treatment, he told her to sit down and really think about whether or not she
was ready to fight. If her answer was an honest "yes" then he would be
willing to help her. But she would need to move to New York, at least
temporarily.

Karen immediately phoned Itchie, tattling on Levenkron for upsetting her. But Itchie supported the therapist's suggestions and affirmed
that she should consider relocating to New York. Like Cherry O'Neill,
she felt Karen would greatly benefit from time away from Los Angeles

and the strict schedule of work and life there. Itchie's encouragement prompted a return call from Karen to Levenkron, just three hours after the first. Her new plan was to move to New York and see him an hour a day, five days a week. He agreed.

Sharing the news with family and friends, Karen was met with much support and without questions, although Evelyn Wallace did her best to talk Karen out of relocating to New York. "Karen, there are wonderful doctors right here in L.A. that could help you," she said, "and they have lovely hospitals here, too." Wallace's attempts proved futile. "She wanted to get as far away from her mother as she could," she explains. "New York was a place she figured her mother couldn't be running up to all the time."

Although Karen confided in Evelyn regarding her illness, the two never spoke specifically of anorexia. Despite her attempts at honesty, Karen refrained from using the words "anorexia nervosa." Frenda Franklin recalls, "She just didn't like those words."

16

DANCING IN THE DARK

L EAVING BEHIND the pieces of her broken marriage, Karen set forth on a year-long recovery mission, relocating to New York City's Regency Hotel in January 1982. Manager Jerry Weintraub was acquainted with the owners of the hotel and arranged for Karen and Itchie Ramone (by then married to Phil) to share a two-bedroom suite with a living room and kitchenette. Itchie secured a private telephone line, in addition to a big screen television with video machine. Karen's weekly TV appointment was every Friday night with prime-time soap opera *Dallas*, while Itchie's must-see was *Dynasty*.

Monthly hotel bills were upward of six thousand dollars, not including room service tabs and phone bills. Although Karen was known to be a penny-pincher, she felt that these expenditures were for the most part justified. Therapist Steven Levenkron received one hundred dollars for each hour-long session five days a week, totaling two thousand dollars month. "I liked Levenkron, at least in the beginning," Itchie says. "He was the new kid on the block, but he did have some answers. No one really knew why someone would get the disorder or how to treat it. We didn't have answers to any of our questions about the disorder, so we were really looking to him to quote 'save' her."

Arriving at Levenkron's office at 16 East Seventy-Ninth in Manhattan, Karen weighed in at an alarming seventy-eight pounds. Although her family cited 1975 as the onset of anorexia nervosa, she felt its inception was a more recent occurrence. From her therapist's brown leather sofa, Karen explained how her anorexic behaviors began "the day she walked away from Menninger's after leaving Richard there." In a 1993 interview the therapist explained, "She had to take this brother who she loved and lock him up in a psychiatric hospital.... That's where she equated the beginning of her anorexia."

A week into their daily sessions, Karen admitted to Levenkron she was taking an unfathomable number of laxative tablets—eighty to ninety Dulcolax a night. The ingestion of large quantities of laxatives did not surprise Levenkron. In fact, it was a common practice for many anorexics. "For quite some time, I was taking sixty laxatives at once," admits Cherry O'Neill. "Mainly because that was how many came in the box.... I would ingest the entire contents so as not to leave any evidence."

What did stun Levenkron was Karen's next casual disclosure. She was also taking thyroid medication—ten pills a day. He was shocked, especially when she explained that she had a normal thyroid. He demanded she bring him the bottle, which she did during the following session. Dated August 17, 1981, the prescription for Synthroid had been dispensed by Newport Center Pharmacy and issued in the name of Karen Burris. Realizing she was using the medication to speed her metabolism, Levenkron immediately confiscated the vial and remaining pills. Of all the terrible forms of self-abuse he had witnessed with his patients, this was the first case of thyroid medication abuse he had seen in his dozen years in the field.

KAREN AND Itchie enjoyed this time together at the Regency Hotel and took advantage of what oftentimes seemed like a recurring sleepover between teenage girlfriends. "OK, so who would your perfect guy be?" Itchie asked.

"Mark Harmon," Karen answered, referring to the actor with whom she enjoyed a couple of dates in the late 1970s.

Although Harmon was in show business, he was not a "Hollywood hoo-ha" as Karen referred to some men. According to Itchie, "Mark would have been the absolute perfect guy with all the qualifications on her list. He was a star in his own right but really down-to-earth, and he was basically a family guy, which was exactly what she was looking for. But to tell you the truth, I don't know that Mark could have ever survived the sharks around her."

With notebook paper and pen in hand, Itchie jotted down a list of the qualities Karen desired in a man. "We were writing down every single little thing that she wanted in a guy as a mate or as a partner," Itchie recalls. Obviously Karen was somewhat separating herself emotionally from Tom Burris, and rightfully so. Her requirements were similar to those she had expressed before her marriage to Burris, but she was determined to never be taken advantage of again. She still desired a man who was articulate, bright, intelligent, and witty. He had to be good looking and be a spiffy dresser. She wanted someone who hailed from a good family and preferred someone who was not in show business. He could be a celebrity but only if he was unpretentious. But above all she wanted someone who would love her unreservedly and unconditionally.

As she settled into her new surroundings, Karen again phoned Cherry O'Neill, who was relieved to hear she had finally taken the first step toward seeking professional help. She was also pleasantly surprised to learn Karen went so far as to remove herself from Los Angeles and what she calls "the ever-present pressures of the music and entertainment business, as well as the expectations of family, agents, managers, and record company executives." But O'Neill believed New York City was just as fast-paced as Los Angeles. "I really felt like her being there was not enhancing or complementing the recovery. She would have benefitted from a more pastoral, less urban, more low-key environment where she would have no alternative but to slow down and focus on herself, her health, and her recovery."

Cherry was also concerned with what she knew of Levenkron's therapeutic approach, which she explains as an effort to have his patients "develop something of a dependence on him as they wean themselves from their family of origin or spouse who may have contributed inadvertently to the eating disorder." In Karen's case it seemed that both family and spouse had aggravated her situation.

According to Levenkron's 1982 book, *Treating and Overcoming Anorexia Nervosa*, the patient must become totally dependent upon the therapist. "The therapist must develop a care-taking relationship with someone who views relationships as always competitive." This sort of dependence was not easy for Karen. She was more comfortable offering care and concern to others. Receiving care seemed to leave her feeling helpless and somehow unworthy. O'Neill tried to encourage Karen, even though she knew Levenkron's plan would take much longer than she had allotted. "She had entered therapy with an agenda and time frame in mind that did not allow for that process to run its course. Once the patient has transferred their dependence onto him, he tries to teach them how to create their own sense of identity, and he helps them disengage from their dependence on him with new behaviors, habits, and thought patterns in place. But that takes a lot of time!"

KAREN RETURNED to Los Angeles for two weeks in April 1982. Most who saw her thought she looked dreadful, but despite her haggard appearance she seemed quite energetic. She even took time to cut several tracks with Richard at A&M Studios during the visit. In what became her final recording session, she laid down work leads for a new Carpenter-Bettis tune, "You're Enough," in addition to a Roger Nichols and Dean Pitchford composition entitled "Now." Richard felt Karen sounded as marvelous as ever, despite her ill health and frailty, but hindsight reveals a weakness to her vocals. Her interpretation, phrasing, and enunciation were beautiful—near perfection, in fact—but something was missing from the timbre.

Frenda tried her best to reason with Karen, citing her voice and the need to keep it healthy and vibrant. "Kace, you've been so lucky for so long," she told her. "But you're going to ruin this gift. I don't care for myself. In fact, I wouldn't care if you never sang again. You have enough money to live on for the rest of your life. It's not for any of those reasons. It's for you. I think you'll be lost without it. If you don't eat something, one of these days you're going to open your mouth and nothing's going to come out!"

When she returned to New York Karen took every advantage of the beautiful spring weather and began a new exercise routine—to and from her sessions with Levenkron—a brisk two-mile round-trip walk. This was yet another method to burn extra calories. Occasionally she would stop by a needlepoint store she'd found on Madison Avenue. Sometimes she was recognized on the street and asked for her autograph, but to those who had not seen Karen in a number of years she was nearly unrecognizable. Comedian David Brenner, who worked with the Carpenters in Las Vegas, was enjoying lunch with a friend at an outdoor café on Madison Avenue one afternoon. "Hi, David," he heard from a passerby on the sidewalk near his table. Brenner looked up and smiled, said "hello" to the woman he assumed to be a fan, and returned to his meal. "But, David, it's me," she interrupted. "We worked together!" Bewildered, he looked up again but had no idea what this stranger was talking about. "It's me, Karen," she said with a laugh. Brenner then recognized the voice and smile.

"Karen!" he said as he stood to hug her. "I'm so sorry. I didn't *recognize* you. You've lost a *lot* of weight." She didn't reply to his observation but explained she was visiting friends in New York. "Great, well, let's have lunch sometime," he said.

"That's about as stupid a thing to say to an anorexic as could be said—'let's have lunch,'" Brenner says, "but I had no idea she had this disease. Ironically, it was the last time I ever saw her."

Former Carpenters manager Sherwin Bash saw Karen in New York in mid-1982 as well. He was walking through Central Park South when he heard a familiar voice. "Shermine Bush!"

"She would never call me Sherwin Bash," he explained. "It was always 'Shermine Bush.'"

Bash turned around to see Karen running to meet him. "I took her in my arms and gave her a kiss," he recalled. "She had her sweater and her jacket and everything on, and through it all I could feel the bones. She said she was doing fine and that she was at the point where she was well aware that she was a victim of anorexia. She said she was doing better and she was under a therapist's care."

In her daily calls to both Frenda and Agnes, Karen reported on life in New York City and her recent visitors. Anticipating her daughter's call, Agnes would always answer on the first or second ring. The two talked at length, but Karen rarely spoke with Harold. "Agnes never once asked Harold if he wanted to talk to Karen," Evelyn Wallace recalls. "She just talked and talked and then—bang—she'd hang up the receiver." On one occasion, Harold answered Karen's call from the office. "Well, just a minute, let me get your mother," he said.

"Oh, no, no, no, Dad," she replied. "You're the one I want to talk to. I *never* get to talk to you. Please stay on the line."

Evelyn suggested Harold take the call in the privacy of the music room. She knew if Agnes discovered Karen was on the line she would surely take the phone away for herself. That afternoon, the two were finally able to enjoy a long-overdue conversation between father and daughter. "I think that she really loved her father," Wallace says. "She didn't have to say anything, but you could tell when she was around him. She just had this happy look when she'd talk to him, and it was always with the sweetest voice. I know she thought the world of her dad, but with her mother, that was another story."

According to Frenda, Harold did his best to compensate where Agnes was lacking. "He really, really, really loved her," she says. "If she had never sung a note he loved her. Pudgy or whatever, he loved her."

Being more than two thousand miles from home, Karen relied on a small but close network of relationships on the East Coast. "Please come and stay in New York," she would beg longtime friend Debbie Cuticello. Debbie and husband C.J. went to Karen's suite at the Regency several times before taking her out for dinner but always made the return trip to their Connecticut home the same evening. "I would bring Karen here once every two or three weeks, and she'd spend the weekend with me," Debbie says. "I was much happier to have her here with me in quiet Guilford than being in New York City."

Karen enjoyed weekends with the Cuticello clan, which by this time included the couple's baby son, Jamie. Babysitting while C.J. and Debbie went to church or out to dinner allowed Karen time to play surrogate mom. Like Frenda Leffler's twins, Jamie Cuticello was quite special to her, and she showered him with love and attention, in addition to gifts including her own needlepoint creations. She also seemed to enjoy the domestic aspect of the family's home and assisted in preparing meals, washing dishes, and helping with other household duties. "She absolutely adored children," recalls Itchie Ramone. "She would have been such a wonderful mom. Mothering was totally instinctive. She even taught me how to iron!"

While visiting Guilford, Karen told Debbie the meetings with her therapist were going better than expected. According to her, it was only a one-year process, and she seemed to be "breezing" through. Her therapist felt she could finish in six months—maybe even four. This seemed to be a very self-deceiving declaration. In fact, Karen was well aware that successful treatment would take years, not months. Following her own quick-fix plan, she told friends and family what they wanted to hear and moreover what she wanted to believe.

Outwardly Karen seemed committed to the idea of therapy, but as evidenced by her daily walking regimen, she was not as committed to making important changes that would result in real progress and positive results. Friends including Carole Curb say Karen continued to dabble in—if not delve into—even stricter anorexic practices while under Levenkron's care. "She was still walking a lot, and she was exercising," Curb says. "And then she was into throwing up and taking water pills that make you lose water weight. Debilitating things like that."

Several months into his sessions with Karen, Levenkron began to suspect that she had fallen off the wagon. He phoned Itchie, soliciting her help with a matter she would long regret. "When she leaves the room, go into her bedroom and check under her mattress," Levenkron instructed. "Check underneath her bed, in her bathroom, and anywhere else you can think of." The therapist wanted confirmation that Karen had stopped using and thrown away all laxatives, diuretics, and other medications. Even the half quaalude she was known to take on occasion was too strong for her tiny body. "But it really helps me to sleep," she told Itchie, who insists that Karen was in no way abusing quaaludes.

"I felt so horrible, but it had to be done," Itchie says. "She had been saying to Levenkron that she had stopped the laxatives and stopped the 'ludes. I said, 'There's just no way. She's just too thin!' I called

Levenkron back and said, 'Look, I found all these things. What am I supposed to do?'"

With Karen in tow, Itchie delivered her findings to Levenkron's office the following day. Learning of the conspiracy and that her friend had collected evidence against her, Karen became incensed. "When I told her what I had done, I really felt like I'd betrayed her," Itchie recalls. "All I could say was, 'I really, really want you to get well.'"

Following that meeting, Itchie realized that in cooperating with Levenkron she had lost her best friend's trust. "It caused a major, major upset," she says. "In retrospect it caused a bit of a setback. She really started to have trust issues with me. I said, 'Look, I am really sorry.' And I truly was. I was invading her privacy; I had no idea what I was doing, and I just panicked because I loved her. . . . After that I just felt that she had to do it for herself from that point on."

But Levenkron was right. Karen had done exactly as he predicted. Like many of the women he worked with, she resisted the very treatment she was seeking. He was not fooled by her tactics and let her know, just as he let hundreds of other patients know: "You are the victim of a disease and not the designer of a creative way of being special." A message entitled "For the Afflicted" appeared in his book and remains a revealing look at the language used by the therapist in meeting with his patients. "You suffer," he wrote, "and are condemned to defend that suffering so that you will feel powerful rather than ashamed. If you defend that suffering eloquently enough, you may be regarded as manipulative and deceitful, instead of desperate. Surely words that connote being powerful are more desirable labels than words that suggest helplessness."

Dependence did not come easy for Karen; it suggested incompleteness and vulnerability. Like many with an eating disorder, Karen would oftentimes argue that she was not in need of any care. She felt she was plenty successful the way she was. Levenkron disagreed and did so using language that cut to her core. He told her she was "incompetent" and unable to keep herself alive. Levenkron's goal was for her to relearn dependence and see it as a healthy dependence upon him. "The victims must learn how to become patients," his book reads.

"The patients must risk trusting, and being receptive to support, guidance, care and even affection."

———— ✺ ————

AFTER MANY weeks of exploring the depths of their daughter's psyche, Levenkron invited the Carpenter parents and Richard to a ninety-minute family therapy session at his office. "They did come to New York—finally," Itchie recalls, "and only after a lot of nudging. By then, Karen seemed to be starting to turn the corner a bit emotionally."

The stigma surrounding mental illness and a need for therapy was frightening for the family, especially Agnes, who felt Karen was simply going overboard as far as dieting was concerned. If only she would stop being so stubborn and just eat. Over the years, the family tried every possible approach to get through to her and make her eat. "Everyone around her did everything that they could have humanly done," Richard said in 1993. "I tried everything—the heart-to-heart, the cajole, the holler.... It can just make you crazy. I tried everything. Obviously it wasn't about to work, and I was upset."

Levenkron explained that the family's attempts to threaten or bribe Karen out of her behaviors would never make them go away. According to his book, "Failure of the family to understand this produces division within the family that in turn results in feelings of anger and guilt. The family atmosphere is chaotic, reinforcing the anorexic's belief that she and no one else knows what is best for her."

Agnes was what Levenkron termed an "oppressive-dependent" mother. At first she appeared to be overbearing, but that same domineering presence is oftentimes a cover for her fear of losing her daughter—or at least control over her daughter. Levenkron suggested to the family that Karen was in need of a more tactile, demonstrative kind of love. Karen bawled uncontrollably during the meeting. She told them how terribly sorry she was for having put them in a situation where they felt a need to defend her upbringing, and she went so far as to apologize for ruining their lives.

"I think Karen really needs to hear that you love her," Levenkron told the family.

"Well, of course I love you," Richard told her unreservedly.

"Agnes?" The therapist tapped the mother's shoe with his own.

Rather than address her daughter, Agnes explained how she preferred to be called Mrs. Carpenter. "Well, I'm from the north," she continued. "And we just don't do things that way."

"Agnes couldn't do it," says Itchie Ramone, who discussed the meeting with Karen and Levenkron after the family left. "*She couldn't do it!...* In therapy you're basically stark naked. Then your own mother can't reach out to you? And the way she doted on Richard! Most children would try to dance as fast as they could to make their parents love them, but it was at that point that I think Karen decided it was time to take a step back."

When Levenkron lightheartedly suggested to the family that Karen might come out of treatment and realize she no longer enjoyed singing, that was it for Richard. His distrust of the therapist was forever solidified. In his mind, there was no question of Karen's deep-seated love for singing. She loved performing and recording more than anything in the world. As she explained to Ray Coleman in 1976, "I gotta sing. I love that crowd." Karen had always considered herself fortunate to be able to make a living doing something she loved. "A lot of people don't get the chance to do that," she explained in a 1981 interview. "They spend their whole life doing a job they hate.... We walk in and sing and have a good time and make albums, go all over the world."

After the meeting with Levenkron, Richard became angry with the treatment plan, which he thought to be worthless. "At that point, he didn't have a lot of respect left for Levenkron," Itchie says. "At first everybody was grabbing for any information Levenkron might have that could help Karen. Then all of a sudden in a few months it turned around to where everyone was asking, 'Is this guy for *real?*'"

Richard was upset that Karen had not checked herself into an inpatient facility as one would do to conquer substance abuse, like a Betty Ford Clinic but for eating disorders. According to Levenkron, he also wanted to put Karen in an inpatient facility immediately after she arrived in New York, but she refused to even consider it. The therapist proceeded to work with her in what he called a "less-than-perfect treatment modality," according to his interviews with Ray Coleman. He went on to say the modality ended up being a nonissue, however, because the damage that would eventually kill Karen had already been done. "In the end," he explained, "what killed her was all her behavior previous to coming to New York."

The Carpenter family returned to Downey and, although greatly alarmed, chose to keep their distance after this painful encounter with Levenkron. Wishing to consult exclusively with Karen during this time, they made no further attempts to contact her therapist. "What I find interesting," Levenkron stated in 1993, "is that in the entire time Karen was in New York, I got zero calls from the entire family. I have never treated anyone with anorexia nervosa that their family didn't call somewhat regularly because they were concerned." Likewise, Richard claimed to have never received a call from Levenkron.

Karen and Itchie were surprised to learn that Levenkron was not an actual doctor. "We used to call him 'Dr. Levenkron' all the time," Itchie explains. "Then we found out that he wasn't even a real doctor. Any medical issues she had, we had to go see this other doctor who was a medical doctor at Lenox Hill Hospital."

According to Evelyn Wallace, "She picked the wrong guy to go to. He wasn't even a doctor! It seemed like Levenkron was simply trying to talk Karen out of having anorexia, but she'd talk to him and she'd go back to the same routine. He was some kind of a counselor. I don't know what you'd call him. Call him a liar! That's what he was."

Wallace could only do so much from afar. She wanted to see Karen with her own eyes and be able to hug her and show her love and support. Although she refused to travel by plane, Evelyn called an area train station to inquire about a round-trip ticket from Los Angeles to New York. "I think I'll go visit Karen," she told Agnes one afternoon.

"Oh no, you can't do that," she responded.

"Oh? Well, I wouldn't stay long or bother her or anything," she explained. "Just visit."

But Agnes was adamant that she not try to see Karen. "The doctor said she can't have any more visitors!"

This puzzled and even angered Evelyn. She knew Karen was not in any sort of confinement. "She was alone in a hotel room," Wallace says. "I was so mad! I thought, 'What in the heck has she got, something *catching?*'"

⸎⸎⸎

BY THE fall of 1982, Karen showed no real signs of progress. In fact, her walks to and from sessions with Levenkron kept her body weight dangling beneath the eighty-pound mark. Itchie Ramone called Levenkron and voiced her concerns. "Look, Karen's getting thinner and thinner and thinner," she exclaimed. "Plus, it's obvious she doesn't have her usual energy anymore. When do you expect this turnaround? She's just skin and bone!"

The therapist agreed that Karen seemed extra tired and was not responding as quickly as he had hoped and vowed to try another approach. Leaving her next session with Levenkron, Karen asked Itchie if she could borrow a swimsuit. "What?" Itchie asked. "There's no pool in the hotel. Besides, it's cold out!"

"No, I have to wear it tomorrow for Levenkron," Karen answered.

The two stopped by the Ramones' apartment to pick up a size 2 light green bikini belonging to Itchie. Karen changed into the bikini and emerged smiling. Itchie was mortified and unable to hide her reaction. "What's the matter?" Karen asked. "It fits."

"Uh, yeah, it fits," she said hesitantly. "You can use it tomorrow, I guess."

Returning to Levenkron the following day, Karen was asked to change into the bikini and stand in front of the office mirror. He urged her to survey and evaluate her body. "She didn't really see any problem with how she looked," Itchie recalls. "In fact, she thought she was gaining a little weight. But she was seventy-nine pounds. That was one of the times where I would go home and lock myself in my bathroom and cry."

Karen, too, was growing impatient and discouraged that she was not progressing as quickly as she had hoped. Her impending self-imposed deadline was on the horizon, and she had nothing to show for almost a year of therapy. "My mother is going to kill me if I haven't gained weight," she told Evelyn Wallace and reportedly expressed the same to her therapist.

In mid-September Karen phoned Levenkron and told him her heart was "beating funny." She was quite upset, anxious, and confused. She complained of dizziness to an extent that she was unable to walk. He recognized her symptoms as those of someone suffering extreme dehydration. He knew she needed immediate medical attention but was unable to refer Karen to a hospital based on his own credentials. Instead he asked Dr. Gerald Bernstein to meet him and Karen for an evaluation.

At what might very well have been her lowest point ever, both physically and emotionally, Karen was admitted to New York's Lenox Hill Hospital on September 20, 1982, to begin hyperalimentation, or intravenous feeding. "When they do that they're really seriously worried that you're going to die," Frenda explains. "That's why they do it. It's a last resort."

Two blocks east of Central Park, Lenox Hill Hospital is an intensive care hospital on Manhattan's Upper East Side. "In the beginning she was definitely a Jane Doe," Itchie recalls. Attempting to check in as Karen Burris, she was recognized by the receptionist as the singer from the Carpenters. She was "terrified but determined," according to Dr. Bernstein, who conducted a series of tests that revealed a critically low blood potassium level of 1.8. The normal range is 3.5 to 5.5. Upon admission to the hospital Karen was, in Levenkron's words, "seventy-seven pounds of dehydrated skeleton."

The next morning Karen went into surgery to have a small-bore catheter implanted within the superior vena cava (right atrium of the heart). An unexpected complication was discovered later that day when she complained to the nurse of excruciating chest pain and X-rays revealed the doctors had accidentally punctured one of her lungs in their attempts to insert the tube. She phoned Frenda at the first opportunity. "I could hardly understand her," she recalls. "I went running on the red-eye to New York. It was just a nightmare!"

As Karen recovered, Itchie took on the arduous task of re-creating the suite from the Regency in her hospital room. "Lenox Hill was an absolute nightmare for me," she says. "I turned her hospital room into a multimedia room. I thought the nurses were going to kill me! I had to set up the TV equipment, a refrigerator, and bring in tons of videos, a cassette player, you name it." Listening to piles of cassette tapes and song demos helped Karen pass the time when she was alone and surrounded by four orange walls. "She was always drumming everywhere," Itchie recalls.

Between various needlepoint projects she watched reruns of *I Love Lucy* and even took time to finally read the manuscript for Cherry O'Neill's forthcoming book, in which O'Neill referred to anorexia as a "sophisticated form of suicide that afflicts millions of young women." The parallels between these two women's stories were apparent. Like Karen, Cherry grew up in a musical family with singing siblings and shared similar desires to please everyone around them. Both women grew up in Christian households with what O'Neill refers to as "authoritarian-type parents."

Near the book's conclusion Karen read how Cherry's newfound freedom spurred a long-overdue confrontation with her mother: "When are you going to stop treating me like a child? Why can't you relate to me as an adult? I'm twenty-four years old and even though I'll always be your daughter, I'm *not* a baby anymore!" The words mirrored Karen's own cries for autonomy. She deeply feared the idea of ever having to face up to her mother, and her attempt at confronting Agnes several months earlier in Levenkron's office had ended up being more of a pleading for forgiveness. But now she knew that she would have to confront Agnes in the future to get her attention.

"I did it!" Cherry wrote in triumph. "I actually said what I felt for years but could never reveal. I declared my independence, embraced my adulthood, and confronted my mother with a truth to which both of us had been blind. The little bird who fought so furiously—and belatedly—to learn to fly refused to have her wings clipped." *Starving for Attention* was in many ways Karen's personal story but with an added "happily ever after" ending. It seemed more like a fairy tale than nonfiction.

As her lung began to heal, Karen's body quickly responded to the artificial means of feeding. The hyperalimentation process completely replaced all of her nutritional needs, and a precise daily calorie intake was dispensed through the catheter. This loss of control was known to oftentimes spark fear in patients, but Karen was assured the goal was to *help* her gain weight, not *force* her to gain weight. Doctors who oppose hyperalimentation argue that it does not teach the patient to eat properly and therefore does not personalize their experience. Karen gained twelve pounds in only a few days. This rapid increase alarmed Itchie, who called Frenda, Jerry Weintraub, and Karen's doctors back home in Los Angeles. "*Please* help me," she told them. "Karen's gained twelve pounds in less than a week! Where does it go from here? She's gaining much too much weight too soon. It's just going to be too hard on her heart!"

Debbie Cuticello and her mother, Teresa Vaiuso, visited Karen at Lenox Hill. "They say I have anorexia," she told them. "But look, I have all my teeth, and I have all my hair," she joked, as if suggesting the diagnosis was in need of revision. Both mother and daughter were distraught to see the once vibrant and youthful Karen in such a debilitated state. She looked too old and frail for someone just thirty-two years old.

Mike Curb was disheartened to see the beautiful young girl he had dated in this predicament. Although Karen walked around the room during his visit, she wheeled intravenous drip bags and an infusion pump beside her. "She was so thin that it almost brought tears to my eyes," he says. "I didn't know what to say then. I was more than shocked; I was heartbroken and devastated."

Solid foods were slowly reintroduced as the level of assistance from Karen's IV lessened, and she continued to gain weight steadily. Unlike many other patients she seemed pleased and excited to show visitors her progress. Richard flew in to visit on October 25 and was expecting to see evidence of the improvement she spoke of in her calls. The sounds of the dripping IV and beeping monitors provided the soundtrack for this family reunion. Cards, gifts, Mickey Mouse toys, and various stuffed animals decorated the room but did little to warm the cold and sterile surroundings. Like most who saw her there, Richard was more shocked and saddened. She was still horribly emaciated and barely identifiable by this stage. "You see how much better I look?" she asked.

Richard nodded in agreement but only to appease his sister. In an attempt to divert the attention away from her situation, Karen told him of other patients who were much worse off. But he was not sidetracked, finally breaking his silence. "Karen, this is *crap*," he said. "Don't you understand? This is crap! You're going about this all the wrong way. This guy isn't getting anything accomplished because you're in a *hospital* now!"

Three days later, on October 28, 1982, from her room at Lenox Hill, Karen scrawled her name across a petition for divorce.

———— ✑ ————

BY NOVEMBER Karen was eating three meals a day at Lenox Hill and trying to stay positive about the weight gain, by then approaching the thirty-pound mark. The return of her menstrual cycle, which had ceased during the previous year, seemed to signify an improvement in emotional and physical well-being. "The extent of her bravery has to be stressed," recalled Dr. Bernstein. "These patients have enormous fear as they look at the pounds coming on." Looking at her developing arms she told her therapist, "I'll just have to keep remembering that they're supposed to look like this."

On the phone with Frenda, Karen bragged about her weight gain. "I've gained!" she said. "I'm going to come home for Thanksgiving, and I'm just going to knock everybody's socks off!"

Yeah, but by hyperalimentation, Frenda thought to herself. That's not eating it on, that's a tube. Just because you gain, that means nothing!

Karen was upbeat when discharged from the hospital on November 8, 1982, but as Cherry O'Neill recalls, "It was during a time when Levenkron was out of town that Karen chose to check herself out of the hospital. She terminated her therapy before she should have. She knew that people were depending on her for another album, and she was giving herself an imaginary deadline of Thanksgiving being the time she had to be 'well' so she could meet everyone else's expectations of her." As Dr. Irving George Newman, a Hollywood internist and father of musician Randy Newman, once told Cherry, "There are no contracts when health is concerned." She shared this advice with Karen but was sure it fell on deaf ears. "That is hard medicine to take, in and of itself, especially for those of us who never want to let other people down. Therapy and recovery don't work that way. It takes several years to develop the behaviors and thought patterns involved in eating disorders. It takes a while to untangle them and turn around to start moving in another direction."

Dr. Bernstein signed the paperwork allowing for Karen's release from Lenox Hill in time to return home for Thanksgiving in Downey. He sensed that she was very positive and optimistic as she left the hospital that day. "She was a little anxious about the future," he recalled, "but also very eager to get back to L.A. and sing."

Karen remained in New York for two weeks after checking out of the hospital. She returned to the Regency Hotel, this time with the aid of a personal nurse and explicit instructions against walking to and from Levenkron's office. It was during this time that Richard phoned Phil Ramone, concerned his sister might overdo things following the release from the hospital. "Promise me that you won't go into the studio," he said. "I am telling her I won't either. You've got to stand alongside me, and she's got to eat. She looks like a skeleton."

Ramone agreed he and Itchie would watch over Karen and was puzzled that Richard would think they would even consider recording together at this juncture. "He asked me not to record, but why would that happen? We'd shelved the album!"

Karen's return to hotel life left her homesick again, and she called Werner Wolfen to arrange her return trip to Los Angeles. He strongly advised her against abruptly ending the treatment, but she would not be swayed. She had checked out both mentally and physically. "I don't care," she told him. "I'm going home. I'm cured. That's it."

On November 16 Karen visited Steven Levenkron for the last time and presented him with a farewell gift, a framed personal message in needlepoint. The large green-threaded words YOU WIN—I GAIN served as tangible proof of the long hours Karen had spent alone in the hospital. Learning of her plan to leave, Levenkron reminded Karen she was abandoning the program much too soon and that treatment takes at least three years. He even suggested a therapist in Los Angeles so that she might continue a routine of some sort upon her return home, but she declined. She promised to call him and swore she would not take any more laxatives or diuretics. Agnes and Harold met up with Karen at Levenkron's office that day. The couple had flown to New York City to bring their daughter and her twenty-two pieces of luggage home.

It was obvious to most that Karen's treatment was inadequate and ending too soon. Frenda felt the timing was one of the biggest hindrances. "She tried to get help," she says. "She went to New York to try. It just wasn't the right way to do it. If this had happened in today's world I think Karen would have lived. I think we would have had a good shot. They know so much more. We were dancing in the dark."

17

TOO LITTLE, TOO LATE, TOO SOON

ROM THE office window, Evelyn Wallace caught a glimpse of the limousine as it pulled up in front of Newville. She ran to meet Karen as she approached the door, and the two embraced. Even though Karen's weight was above one hundred pounds, Ev was shocked to see she looked as frail as ever. "She didn't look one ounce over what she did when she left," she recalls. "I knew not to squeeze her too hard, and I didn't. I just put my arms around her. I could feel every bone in her back."

Karen ate heartily on Thanksgiving Day, much to the delight of her family, and she even called Itchie Ramone that night to tell her of all she had eaten. "She said to me, 'I ate this and that and all my favorite things,'" she recalls. "She was very proud of herself then. We were all very proud of her. It seemed like progress."

In the weeks following her return to Los Angeles, Karen went back to shopping and socializing without delay. Although she spoke with Steven Levenkron regularly by phone, most of her friends believed she had no real intention of returning to his care. At home, she ate very little and slept a lot. This worried Agnes, but she had been cautioned to "keep quiet," says Wallace. "She had been warned by Levenkron to not be jumping all over Karen. Agnes was told that Karen was trying her best to get healthy again and that she should just leave her alone and not be yelling at her and reminding her that she was sick. 'Just leave her alone,' he said."

On December 17, 1982, Karen gave what became her last public performance, singing for Frenda Leffler's twins Ashley and Andrew, their cousin Brooke Megdal, and the children's classmates at the esteemed Buckley School in Sherman Oaks, California. "I never dreamed it would turn out to be the last time—never, never, never," Frenda says. "How could that be possible? But it was. She was so thin. There was just nothing left of her." Ed Leffler was worried about Karen, given her recent traumatic hospital stay in New York, and tried talking her out of making the appearance. "But she wanted to do it for the little children," Frenda explains. "Except for our kids, these children had no idea who she was. To them she was just a nice lady who came to sing."

Wearing a festive cardigan over a turtleneck with red slacks and matching shoes, Karen sat on a platform at one end of a small auditorium before the audience of forty or fifty children watching attentively with their chins on their fists. As Frenda recalls, Karen's joy was palpable that day. "She loved singing more than anything in the world," she says. "Who better to sing for children? She was a natural mother. If life had been different and kinder I know she would have had a wonderful family. It meant so much to her, and she would have excelled at loving her family with the same love she gave to every performance she ever gave. Even that would have been perfection. She didn't know any other way."

Although others felt she was still quite fragile and thin, Herb Alpert saw Karen shortly after the New Year and recalled her looking terrific and healthy. She bounced into his office saying, "Hey, look at me, Herbie! What do you think? How do I look?" She was excited and twirled around to show off her new figure. Alpert agreed that she looked happier and healthier than he had seen her in some time and felt she appeared to have won the battle. "I am so happy," she told him. "I'm ready to record again, and Richard and I have been talking about getting the group together and performing."

On the evening of January 11, 1983, publicist Paul Bloch drove Karen to CBS Television City, where they met Richard for a special photo session celebrating the twenty-fifth anniversary of the Grammy Awards. They posed for group portraits alongside other past Grammy winners, including Glen Campbell, Dionne Warwick, and Helen Reddy. Karen spoke to reporters and mingled with friends including Debby Boone, Johnny Rivers, and Toni Tennille during what became her last public appearance. She looked tired, worn, and much older than a woman of thirty-two. Afterward she and Richard stopped for dinner at St. Germain on Melrose in Los Angeles, where Karen had an appetizer, entrée, French bread, and wine.

On January 14, Karen met Richard and former college friend Dennis Heath for dinner, again at St. Germain. She startled the two when she stopped eating, put down the knife and fork, and looked at them as if frightened or in pain. She struggled to speak but couldn't. After a lengthy visit to the ladies' room, Karen returned and assured Dennis and Richard she was fine. After dinner the three drove to nearby A&M Studios, where they listened to playbacks from the April 1982 sessions.

Debbie Cuticello called Karen on the evening of January 25 after having watched an Olivia Newton-John concert special on HBO. Incidentally, Karen had joined Olivia on the road for several stops during that 1982 *Physical* tour. The two had even discussed the possibility of Karen drumming during a few concerts, but because of her deteriorating health that idea was never realized. In 1982 she was far too weak for such an endeavor, but by 1983, Debbie Cuticello thought she sounded great—at least over the phone. "She was full of energy, vigor, and excitement and seemed to have pulled herself together and was ready to start a new lease on life. I asked her to send me some new photographs, and she said she would."

Despite Karen's efforts to convince friends and family she was cured, her eyes told a more truthful story. The usual rich, warm, twinkling brown eyes were shadowed by a lifeless black. Even her nervous energy seemed stifled. She was taking more naps than usual and sometimes lying down by 7:00 in the evening. When Richard reported to Werner Wolfen that he did not think she looked well, word got back to

Karen, and she was furious. She tracked Richard down and found his Jaguar parked outside the Broadway, a department store in Downey's Stonewood Center. Richard exited the store to find Karen's Jaguar XJS parked next to his XJS. Reluctantly he approached Karen, who was visibly incensed, and with great articulation and eloquence she chastised her brother in the parking lot that evening. "I want you to know that I am doing my best here," she insisted, reminding Richard he did not recover overnight when he came home from Menninger. He responded that, although he may have acted a little strangely, he was most certainly well. He did not believe she was well, and he told her so.

The confrontation continued when Karen demanded another meeting with Richard, this time with Werner present. There she explained that she felt unfairly attacked and that she had not been given the chance to fully recover. Questioning their belief in her ability to do so, she began to cry. "It's not that I don't believe in you," Richard told her, "it's just that I love you so much."

On Thursday, January 27, Florine Elie drove to Century City for her weekly cleaning of Karen's condo at Century Towers. There the housekeeper made an unnerving discovery. "When I was working up there, I found Karen," Elie says. "She was lying on the floor of her closet." She gently shook Karen and rubbed her back. She awoke but was groggy. "Karen, is there something wrong?" she asked.

"No, I am just so tired," she replied, looking up in a daze at Florine.

"Maybe you better go lie on your bed," she said, helping Karen up and tucking her into bed. "You'll be more comfortable this way." Florine checked on Karen again before leaving. By then she was awake and was adamant that she was OK. Even so, this worried Florine, so she called Karen to check on her the next morning before reporting to work at Newville.

Tuesday, February 1, found Karen once again dining with her brother, this time at Scandia on Sunset Boulevard. They were joined by stage producer Joe Layton, and the trio discussed plans for the Carpenters' return to touring. Karen ate with enthusiasm and after dinner returned to Century Towers. This was the last time Richard would see his sister alive.

At the Thirteenth Annual
Grammy Awards, March 16, 1971.
Author's Collection

(right) Carpenter family Christmas card
sent to fan club members, 1972.
Author's Collection

(below) Newville at Christmas, 1972. Ken Bertwell

Between shows in
Acapulco, June 1973.
Maria Luisa Galeazzi

(below) At a softball game
with Richard in Valley Forge,
Pennsylvania, July 1973.
Maria Luisa Galeazzi

(left) At Pie de la Questa with Richard and
Maria Galeazzi. "If we went anywhere it was
the three of us," Maria says. "Every place we
went it was like she and I and Richard. It got
old for me, let me tell you." Maria Luisa Galeazzi

With boyfriend Mike Curb on a boat in San Diego Harbor, 1974. Mike Curb

Striking a comedic pose on stage for a fan at the MGM Grand, Las Vegas, 1976.

Rhonda Martinez

1975 tour program.

(below) With the Leffler "kidlets," Ashley and Andrew, Karen's godchildren.

(above) Karen shows off her diamond ring to wedding guest Olivia Newton-John. Frank Bonito

(right) The beautiful bride on her wedding day, August 31, 1980.

Frank Bonito

Agnes Carpenter and son share a dance as the Michael Paige Big Band entertains at the Beverly Hills Hotel wedding reception.

Frank Bonito

With Tom Burris,
fall 1980. Globe Photos

At Radio Cidade, Rio de Janeiro, November, 1981.

Sydney Junior/Brazilian Carpenters Friends Club

(left) Terribly thin and looking exhausted, Karen
prepares to depart Rio's Jobim International
Airport, November 1981.

Vitor Bruno/Brazilian Carpenters Friends Club

(above) Karen's final public appearance came January 11, 1983, at CBS Television City, where she and Richard (fourth row, second and third from left) attended a photo shoot with past Grammy recipients. "Look at me, I've got an ass!" she exclaimed to Dionne Warwick.

The Recording Academy

(right) A month before her death, Karen posed for this photo with personal secretary and friend Evelyn Wallace. C. Arzac

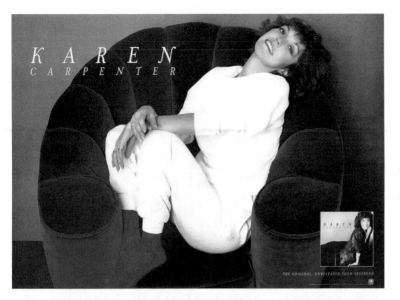

Promotional poster for the 1996 release of *Karen Carpenter*, the original, unreleased solo sessions. A&M Records

The Carpenters' star on the Hollywood Walk of Fame, 6931 Hollywood Boulevard.
Randy Schmidt

(above) The Carpenter Exhibit on display in the foyer of the Richard and Karen Carpenter Performing Arts Center on the campus of California State University at Long Beach. Randy Schmidt

(right) The original Carpenter crypt at Forest Lawn Memorial Park in Cypress, California.
Randy Schmidt

The next day Karen drove to Werner Wolfen's office at Irell and Manella, just a few blocks down Avenue of the Stars. There she and W (her nickname for the attorney) reviewed her final divorce decree. "Well, did you get the better of him?" she asked Wolfen playfully. Further revisions were necessary, so she made another appointment to sign the papers that Friday afternoon, February 4, at 3:00 P.M. Wolfen recalled she wanted desperately to finalize the divorce so that she could begin rebuilding her life without Tom Burris.

Later in the day Karen spoke with Itchie Ramone, who was pregnant with her and Phil's first child. From the time she learned of the pregnancy Karen had begun preparing for the arrival of the baby she called "ours" when talking to the Ramones. "K.C. went crazy buying strollers, a playpen, a swing, a highchair, a car seat, and you name it," Itchie says. "Everything, by the way, was in blue. She was certain the baby would be a boy." Karen shared her plans for the week. She would sign the final divorce papers Friday and then prepare to leave for New York. "That weekend, February 6, she was going to hop on a plane and be there for the birth," Itchie recalls. "But first, she was finally going to sign her divorce papers and pay Tom off. She was ready to pay him the money and send him on his way—one million dollars. That's what she said: 'I'll give you the million dollars, now get lost!'"

On Thursday, February 3, Karen spoke with Richard by phone and asked his advice on videocassette recorders, as she was planning to purchase a new one. He recalled that she yawned a lot during their conversation. That afternoon Karen drove to Downey, where she planned to buy a new stackable washer/dryer for her condo. Hers was in need of repair, but she refused to call a service technician or simply order a replacement. She certainly had the resources to do so, but as she often did, Karen remained loyal to Downey, where she felt she would get the best deal and hometown service. "Both Karen and Agnes shopped at the best stores, and she shopped at the bargain stores," says Debbie Cuticello. "They were never ostentatious. They were always very cautious with their purchases. I'm not saying cheap; I'm just saying they remember their roots. They remembered where they came from."

Stopping by Newville to pick up Agnes, Karen said a quick hello and hugged Evelyn Wallace in the office before setting on a mother-daughter shopping trip. Unable to find stackable units in stock at Gemco, the two postponed their search, and Karen agreed to sleep over and continue the search at the local Sears store first thing Friday morning.

"We're going down to Big Boy. You want to come?" Agnes often invited Evelyn to join the family for dinner. Ev declined the invitation this time but encouraged them to go and have a nice dinner since Karen was visiting. The three drove up Florence Avenue to Bob's Big Boy, where Karen ordered her usual shrimp salad and asked for an extra serving as well. Afterward she told her parents she was still hungry and stopped for a taco. "Boy, that was good," she told them as she finished the snack by the kitchen counter at home.

Settling in, the family gathered in the den to watch a rerun of *Shogun*, the 1980 NBC miniseries starring Richard Chamberlain. At the end of the evening Karen went upstairs to Richard's old room, where she often slept when visiting her parents. She preferred the room to her own since it had a television and videocassette recorder. This particular night she watched a taped episode of *Magnum, P.I.* and then phoned Phil Ramone before bed, finalizing travel plans for her New York trip the following week. Karen mentioned to Ramone that she had recently listened to her solo recordings. Her voice softened in hesitation as she continued. "Can I use the *f*-word?"

"Yeah."

"Well, I think we made a fucking great album!"

Ramone agreed and encouraged Karen to look upon their work together as a positive milestone in her career, regardless of the way it was received by others. "You will make many more records with your brother," Ramone told her, "but don't lose the landmark just because it's not out in the marketplace."

Shortly after midnight, Karen went over her to-do list with Frenda by phone, and the two finalized plans for the next day. "OK, I am going to go try to find a washer/dryer," she said. "Then I'm going to drive in. There shouldn't be a lot of traffic." According to Frenda, Karen enjoyed keeping up with traffic reports. "Then we're going to go get the red fingernail polish!" The two had a noon appointment for a manicure. She was excited and planned to have them finished with bright red polish in celebration of her divorce. "Then we're going to go up to Werner's and sign everything."

Frenda was in agreement. "Honey, I am with ya. It's going to be a *great* day!"

Judging by her voice, Karen was exhausted. "You know, Fren, I am so tired," she said. "I don't know what it is. I just feel like my chest is tired."

The two said their goodnights, but Frenda was worried. She phoned Agnes downstairs. "Do me a favor," she said. "Would you go up and check on her for me?"

Agnes phoned her back a few minutes later. "Well, I think she's all right, Frenny," she reported. "She's going to be OK. I pulled the covers up over her."

Although Agnes and Frenda had their differences, they shared a common concern for Karen's well-being. "We still were all on the same page," Frenda says. "We all wanted to save her. That was our goal."

⚬∞⚬

ON FRIDAY morning, February 4, Karen awoke and went downstairs to the kitchen, where she turned on the coffeepot her mother had prepared the night before. She went back upstairs to get dressed. Around 8:45 A.M. Agnes Carpenter heard the heavy mirrored closet doors slide open above her and Harold's bedroom. "Karen's up," she said, getting up and heading to the kitchen, where she habitually prepared hot cereal and coffee each morning.

On the kitchen counter she saw the percolator Karen had hooked up and the place settings she had prepared—two cups for coffee and two bowls for the cereal. "Before she had always set it for herself, too," Evelyn Wallace says, "along with a bunch of pills the doctor gave her to take. This particular morning it was just a cup for Harold and one for Agnes; nothing for Karen."

Rather than shouting for Karen when the coffee was ready, Agnes picked up the multiline phone and dialed the upstairs bedroom phone, but its ring, heard faintly in the distance, went unanswered. Agnes went to the foot of the stairs and called to her daughter. She continued calling for Karen as she climbed the stairs, but there was no response. Entering the room, Agnes found Karen's motionless, nude body lying facedown on the closet floor. Her eyes were open but rolled back. She was lying in a straight line and did not appear to have fallen. "She had just laid down on the floor and that was it," Agnes recalled. "I picked her up and I called to her and held her." She screamed to Harold to call for help.

"She was out on the floor when I got there," recalls Florine Elie, who arrived just after Agnes discovered Karen unconscious. "It must have been just before 9:00. She was out on the floor, and I am pretty sure she was dead there at the house."

The Downey Fire Department received Harold Carpenter's call at 8:51 A.M. and dispatched Engine Company No. 64 as well as a nearby paramedic unit. "They were there so fast, pulling me off," recalled Agnes, who herself attempted to resuscitate her daughter.

The three firemen from Downey Fire Squad 841 and two paramedics from Adams Ambulance Service in Santa Fe Springs found Karen to be unconscious but detected a slight pulse. "It was a chilling scene," paramedic Bob Gillis recalled to reporters. "Karen looked frail and very thin. She was completely nude." A faint pulse was detected in her neck with her heart beating only every ten seconds. "This is a sure sign of a dying heart," Gillis said. The crew moved her from the closet to the bedroom, where they began performing CPR and finally asked that Harold escort his distressed wife from the room.

Agnes rushed down the stairs and phoned Richard. Like many musicians, Richard was a night owl and still sound asleep when the call came in around 8:55 A.M. So panic-stricken was Agnes that her son had trouble understanding her hysterical cries. Finally realizing Karen was unconscious, Richard threw on a T-shirt and blue jeans and tore out of the house.

Arriving for what she thought to be an ordinary day at work, Evelyn Wallace was startled to see emergency vehicles outside the house and grew worried about Harold Carpenter. "Harold was the first one I thought of," she says. "He had heart trouble and had to take a number of pills for his heart." Hurrying into the house, Evelyn was met with Agnes, sobbing as she held tightly to a railing that separated the entry from the living room. "Agnes, what's the matter?" she asked.

There was no response. "Agnes couldn't talk. She was crying and just waved me up the stairs. I went upstairs and saw they had Karen on a gurney. I could tell they were working on her heart."

Driving frantically from Lubec Street, Richard hoped it was only a collapse, perhaps even one severe enough to persuade Karen to take her condition more seriously. He began to cry as he rounded the corner onto Newville in time to witness paramedics exiting the house with the gurney. With full lights and siren, the ambulance transported Karen's lifeless body and her shaken mother, still in her robe, to Downey Community Hospital. Richard and Harold were instructed to follow cautiously.

Arriving at 9:23 A.M., the unidentified patient was reportedly in full cardiac arrest, not breathing and without a heartbeat. "All we knew was that we were getting a thirty-two-year-old female in full arrest," says Pat Tomlin, RN, who worked in the emergency room. "When she arrived, the first thing that shocked me was her size. She was so frail and fragile looking."

Paramedics told the ER staff, "This is the lady who came from the Carpenter house in north Downey," perhaps a subtle attempt to establish identity without compromising her privacy. In the field the team of paramedics had been unsuccessful in establishing an intravenous line after several attempts, so Tomlin continued the effort. Nurse manager Vivian Carr sat with Richard and Harold, who joined Agnes in a conference room adjacent to the emergency room. Inside, the crew went to work in further attempts at saving Karen. As personnel took their places, Dr. Irv Edwards reached for a laryngoscope and began the intubation process. A young respiratory technician and Carpenter family friend stepped forward with the respirator and began securing the bag and mask. "Oh my God!" she screamed. "It's *Karen*!" The woman's voice cut through the room's intensity, and she began to sob hysterically. The others were quite perplexed by the outburst.

"What's going on? What's wrong with you?" Nurse Tomlin asked her.

"It's Karen," she replied. "It's *Karen Carpenter!*"

Several members of the ER crew, including Tomlin, leaned over the bed for a closer look. "Holy shit," she cried. "It is!" She was shocked to realize this body belonged to the youthful girl she knew only from the Carpenters' album covers. Tomlin knew the words to most of the Carpenters' hit songs, and the lyric to one of them immediately ran through her head: "So much of life ahead . . . And yes, we've just begun." Tomlin sent one of the staff members to notify the hospital manager. "We knew this was going to turn into the nightmare from hell, publicity-wise."

Dr. Edwards was less concerned with the pending media circus and recalls only thinking of the Carpenter family. "This was an incredibly young woman who was too young to die," he says. "What a terrible, terrible, terrible family tragedy this was. They were an extraordinarily popular and much beloved family in Downey, and she was a hometown celebrity."

The medical team at Downey Community spent twenty-eight minutes attempting to resuscitate Karen. "We worked on her for quite a while but then ended up calling the code," Tomlin says. At 9:51 A.M., Karen Anne Carpenter was pronounced dead.

Dr. Edwards emerged from the emergency room and entered the room where Harold, Agnes, and Richard were huddled. The rueful words stumbled from his mouth: "I'm sorry, but Karen is dead." This was a heartrending but not uncommon task the doctor was required to carry out time and time again. "It's never easy to tell a family that someone they love and is dear to them has died," he says. "Richard was fairly composed. Incredulous, but somewhat composed. The parents were absolutely in a state of disbelief."

"Are you *sure* she's gone?" they asked. "Can't you do *anything* to bring her back?"

"We took some time to explain things to the parents," Edwards recalls, "and grieve with the family." Richard was angry. Agnes and Harold were numb. Their faces filled with tears before asking, "May we see her?"

Dispatched to Downey Community Hospital at 9:55 A.M. for a "possible overdose," patrolman J. Rice of the Downey Police Department spoke with Dr. Edwards and his staff, who advised him of Karen's history of anorexia nervosa and depression. "She was extraordinarily thin and what I would describe as gaunt looking," recalls Dr. Edwards. "She did have the appearance or the persona of a person who had anorexia nervosa. In part of my evaluation of Karen we did test her blood sugar, and it was very, very elevated." Tests revealed a blood sugar level of 1,110, which equated to approximately ten times the norm. In Dr. Edwards's opinion, the immediate cause of death was a "hyperosmolar diabetic coma."

Patrolman Rice questioned Karen's parents at the hospital before escorting them home. The family's agony and anguish during the three-mile drive back to Newville without Karen was immeasurable. By the time Harold, Agnes, and Richard returned, the street had been barricaded by local authorities who were stationed at the corner to assist in providing some sort of privacy for the grief-stricken family. National and local media soon swarmed the neighborhood. Heartbroken fans overtaken with sorrow and disbelief gathered behind police lines after hearing the news: "Singer Karen Carpenter, who helped put soft rock at the top of the charts, is dead at the age of thirty-two of a heart attack."

Running errands in anticipation of spending the afternoon with Karen, Frenda Leffler was driving up Palm Drive in Beverly Hills when she caught a special report on the radio. "I almost ran into a tree," she recalls. "Of course I didn't believe it. I went home and I was just in a daze. I opened the back door and I saw Eddie, who was never home early. . . . He looked at me and said, 'She's gone.' Even though we should have known, you don't want to believe that something is really going to happen. You want to think that your loving her was going to make everything all right. But the last blow with this marriage was just more than her little body could take."

Olivia Newton-John also heard the news on her car radio as she traveled down a Los Angeles freeway. "It was a terrible shock," she says.

"I was meeting someone I didn't even know for a business lunch at the Melting Pot on Melrose. I was still in shock, and when I sat down I just burst into tears. . . . It was just horrendous and such a shock. Poor girl, she'd been through a lot. We were supposed to have lunch the next day."

Returning from a business meeting of her own, Itchie Ramone arrived home to the sounds of ringing phones and the voices of a small group of friends crowded around her husband in the middle of the couple's living room. "Have you listened to the radio this morning?" he asked.

"No, I just went to the meeting and came out. Why?" She was alarmed to realize the room had fallen silent. "What's going on?" she asked.

"It's about Karen," Phil said cautiously.

"Oh good God, what has she done now?" she laughed, but Phil remained serious.

"What's wrong? Phil, what's the matter? Is she ill? Is she in the hospital? What's wrong with her?"

"It was her heart," he said.

"It was her *heart*? Is she dead? Did she die?"

As Karen had predicted, Phil and Itchie welcomed their new baby boy, B. J. Ramone, the following week on February 7.

At Cal State Long Beach, Frank Pooler was in a rehearsal when his assistant heard the news reports over the radio. "Come on, let's go over to the office," the assistant told him. "I've got some sad news for you. Karen just died."

Pooler attempted to reach Richard, who proved to be incommunicado. "I went down to the house that night. It was all cordoned off with cops so I just gave them a letter for Richard. I volunteered the choir for anything they might want to have sung at the service."

John Bettis was in a writing session in Nashville. "Those things don't hit you right off," he recalled. "It's almost as if you're watching a TV show or something. It's an out-of-body experience." He immediately called Richard and was surprised to get through. "I don't know how you feel, but I'm mad as hell," he told Richard, later regretting the words he came to feel were egocentric. "The selfishness of my first reaction has haunted me because I actually felt as if Karen had taken something from me that I didn't want to be without. My first reaction was, 'How selfish of you.' Isn't that odd? Since then I've had the other emotions, but that was the first one. I felt cheated."

Richard agreed. "My immediate reaction was anger," he told *People Weekly* in 1983. "Anger at the waste of her life and the loss of her talent. Then the grief set in. The shock was tremendous—I knew she was ill but not that ill." He also admitted to being angry with himself, the therapists, the doctors, and the hospitals.

In Connecticut, C. J. Cuticello raced to get in touch with his wife, Debbie. "Before you turn on the radio or do anything, this is what has happened," he said.

Shaken and stunned by her husband's words, Debbie spent the day recalling her special memories of Karen. "Disbelief," she says. "That was a hard day. That was tough." Bittersweet were her emotions as she went to the mailbox the next day only to find the photos Karen had sent after what proved to be their final phone conversation a few days earlier.

C.J. also broke the news to Frank Bonito, who was employed as a medical social worker at the time. "Channel 8 News has been trying to get you," the receptionist in his office mentioned.

"I had no idea as to why," Bonito says. "C.J. contacted me and he told me. Thankfully he got to me before the TV news. You see this on the news all the time where they call someone up and say, 'Did you hear that so-and-so died?' That is not the way you want to hear about it!"

Songwriter Paul Williams was in Washington D.C. "I was at Wolf Trap with Elizabeth Taylor and doing a big benefit. The news of the day was that Karen had died. Everybody was just stunned. I remember being devastated for everybody, for all of us, for her, and for everyone," he says. "I think that most of us around A&M and those who'd had contact knew what was going on, but the feeling was that she was doing a lot better." At the Cap Centre's Wolf Trap Gala, Williams sang "We've Only Just Begun" as a tribute to Karen. "An angel sang this song for me," he told the crowd of more than twelve thousand. As he tried to hold back his emotions, tears filled his eyes, and the stage lights were brought down.

Also in the nation's capital was Carole Curb, living in Paris at the time but visiting her brother Mike, who'd relocated to D.C. the month prior. "I was on the way to the airport to fly back to L.A. to visit my parents, and I heard it on the radio," she says. "I remember falling to the floor of the limo. I just fell on the floor." Mike Curb was in route to London and heard the news in the airport. "I was so jolted when I heard she'd died that I was just in a state of total shock. I almost fainted. The feeling I had was that she was working her way through it. A lot of people go through a tough time after a bad marriage. . . . I remember how frail she had looked the last time I had seen her, but then my sister had a lot of those same issues. My sister is still alive, so why isn't Karen still alive?"

News reports began hinting that the cause of death was believed to be associated with anorexia nervosa, but this information did little to lessen the astonishment of even those reporting the story. C. P. Smith of the *Orange County Register* wrote: "It's hardly surprising when one of rock's hard-livers dies at an early age. The passing of a Janis Joplin or a Jimi Hendrix is perhaps understandable in a macabre fashion—it's as though the nature of their gut-level music made death into more of an occupational hazard than anything else. But the passing of Karen Carpenter at the age of thirty-two came as a complete shock."

INVESTIGATORS WITH the Downey Police Department drove housekeeper Florine Elie to Karen's Century City residence, where they searched the premises looking for anything unusual or suspicious. "They went through the house and rumbled around," she recalls. "I just sat there and waited on them." They confiscated several bottles of prescription medication and various items unknown to Elie before returning her to Newville, where the mood was somber, to say the least. "They were real sad," Elie remembers. "They didn't talk or do hardly anything."

A bottle of Ativan tablets, commonly used to treat anxiety disorders, was turned over to investigators. The pills were prescribed by

Dr. George Monnet on January 10, 1983, and filled at the local Gemco pharmacy. Monnet later told the investigators he suspected Karen might have also been taking Lasix, a potent diuretic, and not taking the required potassium supplements. In his opinion, this might have caused a cardiac arrhythmia.

On the afternoon of February 4, Los Angeles County medical examiner Dr. Ronald Kornblum conducted autopsy number 83-1611. It began at 2:30 P.M. and lasted two hours. Pending results of further lab tests, the immediate cause of death was marked "deferred." Word from National Medical Services, a Pennsylvania-based clinical toxicology and forensic testing firm, came early in March. The autopsy report became final on March 11, and the certificate of death was amended to list the cause of death as "emetine cardiotoxicity due to or as a consequence of anorexia nervosa." The anatomical summary listed pulmonary edema and congestion (usually caused by heart failure) first and anorexia second. Third was cachexia, which usually indicates extreme weight loss and an apparent lack of nutrition. The finding of emetine cardiotoxicity (ipecac poisoning) revealed that Karen had poisoned herself with ipecac syrup, a well-known emetic commonly recommended to induce vomiting in cases of overdose or poisoning. A letter detailing National Medical Services's lab findings was composed March 23, 1983. After testing both blood and liver, it was determined that 0.48 micrograms/g emetine, "the major alkaloidal constituent of ipecac," was present in the liver. "In the present case," they explained, "the finding of 0.5 micrograms emetine/g, with none detected in the blood, is consistent with residua of the drug after relatively remote cessation of its chronic use."

In a press release detailing Karen's autopsy report and cause of death due to emetine cardiotoxicity, the coroner failed to cite ipecac by name. "It never occurred to me to mention ipecac," Kornblum later told *People Weekly* journalist Gioia Diliberto in her exposé detailing the dangers of the syrup. "In my mind, emetine and ipecac are the same things."

Karen's therapist Steven Levenkron claimed to know nothing of Karen's use or abuse of ipecac. He was reportedly shocked to even hear the word "emetine" as part of the official cause of death. In their phone calls following her return to Downey in November 1982, Levenkron had quizzed Karen about weight maintenance and laxative use. She assured him she was maintaining her new 108-pound figure and had completely suspended use of all laxatives. He never dreamed she was resorting to something much more lethal.

Although she had kept the ipecac secret from Levenkron, Karen had shared with Cherry O'Neill that she was resorting to the syrup on occasion. "She did mention ipecac and admitted to using it to make herself throw up," says O'Neill. "She said she could never make herself throw up so she resorted to using syrup of ipecac to purge. I don't think she knew the dangers of using that substance for more than just emergencies. Not many people knew back then. The combination of self-starvation, the poisoning effect of ipecac over time, and not strengthening her heart and body with regular exercise probably became a lethal combination for her. I remember being concerned that she took ipecac and laxatives to purge, which are probably the most dangerous methods. I was also told that she resumed her use of diuretics upon returning to Los Angeles, and it was obviously more of a drain on her body than she was able to endure."

Itchie Ramone had feared Karen was resorting to ipecac and, after hearing of the autopsy findings, was reminded of a phone conversation the two had the day after Thanksgiving 1982 when Karen's voice sounded weak and raspy. "What's wrong with your voice?" Itchie asked her.

"Oh, I was throwing up a bit," she said. "I think I ate a little too much."

"Oh, no," she thought to herself. "*Please* tell me it's not ipecac!" The Ramones had kept a bottle of ipecac in their kitchen cabinet for years, just in case of emergencies, and it went untouched for the duration of Karen's stay during the recording of the solo album. She believes Karen may have begun using the syrup sporadically in late 1980. "Karen hated to throw up! But I know it started a bit after she met Tom. It was sort of an introduction with ipecac, and it was not a constant. The laxatives were. When she was in New York in 1982 she was not taking ipecac. That habit must have formed after she got home. I was just shocked."

In a radio interview taped shortly after Karen's death, Levenkron discussed the autopsy findings: "According to the L.A. Coroner, she discovered ipecac . . . and she started taking it every day. There are a lot of women out there who are using ipecac for self-induced vomiting. It creates painful cramps, it tastes terrible, and it does another thing that the public isn't aware of. It slowly dissolves the heart muscle. If you take it day after day, every dose is taking another little piece of that heart muscle apart. Karen, after fighting bravely for a year in therapy, went home and apparently decided that she wouldn't *lose* any weight with ipecac, but that she'd make sure she didn't gain any. I'm sure that she thought this was a harmless thing she was doing, but in sixty days she had accidentally killed herself. It was a shocker for all of us who treated her."

In one of Steven Levenkron's most recent books, *Anatomy of Anorexia*, the author boasts of his above-average recovery rate in working with those suffering from eating disorders. "In the last twenty years I have treated nearly 300 anorexics," he wrote. "I am pleased to state that I have had a ninety percent recovery rate, though tragically, one fatality." That was Karen Carpenter.

SADDENED BY the death of his friend and client, hairstylist Arthur Johns recalls being shocked but not all that surprised to learn of her death. "It just seemed like nothing was going right in Karen's life," he says. "From the failed marriage to going to New York and being hospitalized, it seemed like it was one thing after another." Shortly thereafter, Johns received a call from Agnes asking if he would prepare Karen's hair and makeup prior to the public viewing. "Her mother was so pleading and so upset," he recalls. "I found myself saying yes before I even realized how big and how emotional this might be for myself. And it was." Johns called on a good friend to accompany him to the mortuary, where he worked to style Karen's hair one last time. "I was so young myself. Before this I had not done anybody that had died."

Hundreds of friends and fans attended a visitation held Sunday evening, February 6, under the direction of Downey's Utter-McKinley Funeral Home and held at the Forest Lawn Memorial Park Mortuary in Cypress. Guests filed past the white casket adorned with red and white roses to view Karen's body, which was clothed in a rose-colored two-piece suit. A thin, sheer veil draped across the casket's opening, and a barrier of floral arrangements helped keep visitors at a distance in hopes of somehow masking Karen's gaunt form. Agnes, Harold, and Richard, along with other family members, greeted those paying their last respects to Karen throughout the evening. "Most kept their visits short, some chatting quietly about pleasant memories, others bowing their heads in silence," reported the local newspaper.

Among the mourners was Tom Burris, who, according to Karen's closest friends, had come forward saying that he was still Karen's husband (which was legally true, as Karen had never signed the final divorce papers) and threatening against releasing her body to the family. "We had problems with him after Karen passed away," Frenda Franklin recalls. In a statement to *People* magazine Burris claimed he and Karen "always got along" and "always cared about each other. Karen was dealing with her anorexia and her career; I was dealing with my real estate problems. I feel totally guilty, like I'd like to reverse everything. I tried to work with her. I got her in touch with a doctor, but she wouldn't admit she had an eating problem. We both tried, but we just couldn't work it out."

Tom Burris tossed his wedding ring into the casket alongside Karen's body, an act later explained by Ray Coleman to be a sign of affection. Others were unmoved by this display.

Burris later called the Newville house and asked Agnes for Karen's personal wedding album. "Get it wrapped up and send it to him," she told Evelyn Wallace.

"Agnes, why are you sending this to him?" she asked. "I don't think Karen would want him to have that. I wouldn't give it to him!"

But Agnes was "hard-hearted," she says. "She made me wrap that up and mail it to him. I was just fuming to think that she would give him that wedding album. He probably sold it for several thousand dollars."

Itchie Ramone confronted Tom several months later when he surprised her with a phone call shortly after Karen's passing. "I'm *really* sorry I even picked up the phone," she told him. "Tom, the only thing

I have to say to you is if we are ever in the same room at the same time, you'd better make sure you see me first."

———— ❧ ————

LINING UP as early as 10:00 A.M., fans surrounded the gray stone walls of Downey United Methodist Church on the morning of Tuesday, February 8, awaiting the 1:00 P.M. funeral service for Karen Carpenter. Members of the Downey police force, in addition to private guards from Shaw Security, directed dozens of limousines through the crowds of mourners and curiosity seekers lining Downey Avenue. Olivia Newton-John, wearing a black dress and sunglasses, was among a list of celebrities in attendance, which also included John Davidson and Burt Bacharach. "We just missed Dionne Warwick," yelled one spectator as her friend put away her camera. Overflow seating was moved to a large room holding approximately 250 people, and another 400 were led to a courtyard where they were able to hear the service on speakers. "It was simply horrible," remembers Carole Curb, who sat alongside Terry Ellis and his wife. "We just held hands and cried," she says. "We were all heartbroken," Ellis adds.

Karen's New Haven childhood minister Reverend Charles Neal gave the eulogy. "Into every nook and cranny of this global village the sad news travels yet, and the world weeps. For Karen's story is one that has graced this world with life, with love, and with song."

Neal recalled first meeting Karen when she and Richard were part of the Methodist youth ministry that welcomed him when he relocated to New Haven where he attended Yale University. He described her childhood as a balance of "blue jeans, baseballs, and ballet," going on to assess her adulthood and its many ups and downs. "Karen's life has continued to unfold—a unique and beautiful tapestry woven with all the experiences of life: a tapestry at once joyous and furious; a tapestry filled with the joys of time but also the tyranny of time; the joy of success but also the tyranny of success; the joy of life but also the tyranny of life...joy and sorrow, laughter and tears, limelight and loneliness, love and heartache, health and illness, triumph and tragedy, quietness and fury." Neal concluded his tribute with the words of John Bettis.

She sang for the hearts of us all
Too soon and too young
Our Karen is still
But her echo will linger forever

Frank Pooler's Cal State University Choir choir sang "Adoramus Te" by Corsi and backed soloist Dennis Heath on an arrangement of the Bach-Gounod "Ave Maria," transposed from the Carpenters' *Christmas Portrait* album. Pallbearers David Alley, Herb Alpert, Steven Alpert, John Bettis, Ed Leffler, Gary Sims, Ed Sulzer, and Werner Wolfen carried the casket from the church at the close of the service. A small group of close friends and family reconvened for a brief private ceremony at Forest Lawn Cypress. "It's so sad," Harold Carpenter uttered again and again to those gathered. "It's just all so sad."

According to her friends, Karen feared death and especially the idea of being buried in the ground. She pleaded that she never be "planted," a term she used in jest to describe such interment. In keeping with her wishes, Karen's body was entombed above ground in a massive, ornate marble crypt in the Sanctuary of Compassion at Forest Lawn's Ascension Mausoleum. Towering overhead was an elaborate mosaic depicting Madonna and Child by Spanish Renaissance artist El Greco. A lustrous gold epitaph was affixed to the marble shortly thereafter: A STAR ON EARTH—A STAR IN HEAVEN.

EPILOGUE

A SONG FOR YOU

―――――――――

OCTOBER 8, 1996. Karen Carpenter's dream of becoming recognized as a solo artist was realized, albeit too late for her to experience and enjoy. Sixteen years had passed since she and Phil Ramone delivered the solo album to A&M Records, where it was scrutinized and sent to the vaults. It had also been some thirteen years since her untimely passing. Since the album was shelved in 1980, and particularly after her death in 1983, fans had been relentless in pushing for the album's release. They hoped that Karen would find some sort of posthumous vindication once the album made it onto record store shelves.

"People are *really* driving me crazy about the album," Richard had told Ramone several years earlier.

"Well, then why don't you put it out?" he urged.

Aside from Karen's, Ramone had never produced an album deemed unworthy of release, and the rejection weighed heavy on him. "Sixteen years of not having it out on the street made it very frustrating for me," he explains. "There were people who thought it was a disgrace or some crazy, silly album."

Prior to 1996 Richard had remixed several of Karen's solo tracks for a Carpenters album in 1989, then two others on a 1991 box set. The mixes were extremely well done and executed with Ramone's blessing, but he was afraid Karen's vision for the solo recordings might be lost if the entire project were subjected to this form of musical facelift. "We could have easily fixed them up and modernized them and changed some of the parts," Ramone says. "But personally, I like to think of it like a painting. It was done at a particular time, with Karen being the artist. . . . The solo album was something she really, really cared about, and as a friend who cared about her, I thought we should put out everything the way she wanted it."

The resulting eponymous album, *Karen Carpenter*, contained the eleven original recordings as approved by Karen in 1980, plus "Last One Singin' the Blues," an unmixed bonus track. "I have not remixed or done anything to the tapes," Ramone announced in the press release from A&M Records. "These mixes, the material and style, are the way Karen approved them. . . . As years passed, both Richard Carpenter and I wondered when it might be released. Together we stand proud as this was a piece that meant so much to Karen, it was truly a labor of love."

Contributing to the album liner notes, Richard declared, "Karen was with us precious little time. She was a great artist. This album reflects a certain period and change of approach in her career. As such it deserves to be heard, in its entirety, as originally delivered."

Prior to the album's release, Richard had phoned Itchie in hopes that she might unearth the album's original dedication. After consulting the notes she had saved from the project, she called him back: "Dedicated to my brother Richard with all my heart." According to Itchie, he bawled into the phone.

Despite the apparent change of heart, Richard did little to promote the album on Karen's behalf. "When it was released I thought Richard would get behind it," Ramone says. "That was the reason I said 'release it.' He didn't have to *embrace* it, but some of the interviews didn't give you the feeling of he had changed his mind."

Reviews for *Karen Carpenter* were mixed. Some reviewers made unreasonable comparisons to the Carpenters' biggest hits, as illustrated by David Brown in his "C+" review for *Entertainment Weekly*: "For anyone accustomed to hearing her virginal delivery on mope-pop standards like 'Goodbye to Love,' few things will be more disconcerting than the sound of Karen Carpenter loving to love you, baby."

Others reviewed the album without bias or preconception, like Tierney Smith of *Goldmine*, who cited Karen's warm and expressive vocals as the record's saving grace. "She brings a sweetness to the buoyant, gently ringing pop of Peter Cetera's 'Making Love in the Afternoon,' shines on the lovely understated country ballad 'All Because of You' and sounds right at home with the infectious mellow pop of 'Guess I Just Lost My Head.'"

Reviewing Karen's songs for *Rolling Stone*, Rob Hoerburger praised Ramone for recording her in what he called "leaner, decidedly unsaccharine settings . . . her vocals come damn close to soulful. Listening to them, it becomes apparent why singers like Chrissie Hynde, Madonna and Gloria Estefan have 'come out of the closet' and admitted they were Karen fans."

Paul Grein felt the album was not in any way the definitive portrait of Karen Carpenter, "nor was it intended to be," he clarified. "It is a provocative snapshot of her at the age of twenty-nine. Future projects, with Richard or other producers and artists, would have revealed still more facets of this complex woman and multidimensional artist."

Hoerberger agreed that, while it may not have been the album to define Karen Carpenter's career, it was on par with contemporaneous albums. "It holds up with anything that like-minded singers—Barbra Streisand and Olivia Newton-John—were recording at the time, and especially with anything the Carpenters put out immediately before or after. If there is no 'We've Only Just Begun' on the album, it doesn't really matter. Fans typically crave an artist's most personal work—even if it isn't a masterpiece. . . . [It] ends up a cherished souvenir from the collection of a woman who was never allowed more than a vacation from her own image."

———— ∞ ————

THE WORLD in 1983 was not ready for *Karen Carpenter* the album— perhaps in 1980 but not 1983. For a period of several years following her death, appreciation for Karen's music went underground. The mere mention of her name would incite remarks like, "What a waste!" Or even questions like, "Wasn't she that singer who killed herself?" The tragedy appeared to have triumphed over the talent, and it would be years before this injustice would begin to unravel.

Within eight weeks of his sister's death, Richard Carpenter had returned to the recording studios at A&M Records, where he worked meticulously on what would become *Voice of the Heart*, a collection of outtakes and other previously unreleased songs, including several from Karen's last recording session in 1982. "It actually made the time a little bit easier," Richard shared with Paul Grein for *Billboard*. "I think if I'd just stayed home, it would have been that much more difficult. I felt strongly that the material shouldn't be stuck away on a shelf. Putting myself in a fan's position—if I'd never met Karen—I'd want to hear it."

Coinciding with the album's release, the Carpenters' star was unveiled on the Hollywood Walk of Fame on October 12, 1983. "This is a very sad day and at the same time a very special and beautiful day for my family and me," Richard told the 250 or so gathered for the occasion. "My only regret is that Karen is not physically here to share it with us, however I know she is very much alive in our minds and in our hearts." Their star, number 1,769, can be found at 6933 Hollywood Boulevard, just steps away from Grauman's Chinese Theatre.

Fueled by an intense television ad campaign, *Yesterday Once More*, a double-album set featuring twenty-four Carpenters hits, was issued in 1984. Its success prompted a tie-in video released the following year. The fourteen selections were compiled from various television appearances and promotional videos.

Richard released his first solo album, *Time*, in 1987, which featured his own lead vocals on six tracks and guest vocals by Dionne Warwick and Dusty Springfield. "Something in Your Eyes," recorded by Springfield, became a Top 20 hit on the adult contemporary charts. Richard's multitracked, a cappella tribute to Karen, "When Time Was All We Had," featured Herb Alpert on flugelhorn.

That same year, little-known filmmaker Todd Haynes directed and produced *Superstar: The Karen Carpenter Story*, a 16 mm, 43-minute film with a cast of Barbie-type dolls shot against a backdrop of miniature interiors. At first glance the film may have appeared to be a kitschy piece of mockery, but closer examination revealed a serious and sometimes touching and sympathetic account of Karen's life. Shown primarily at film festivals and small theaters throughout the United States, *Superstar*, nicknamed "the Barbie doll movie," garnered a huge underground following and by the year 2000 had earned a place at #45 on the *Entertainment Weekly* list of "Top 50 Cult Films of All Time."

Prior to the film's release, Haynes had attempted to license a number of original Carpenters recordings and other music for the production, but his requests were denied. When he proceeded to use the material for which he was denied permission, legal injunctions from Richard Carpenter ensued, and the film was withdrawn from distribution in 1990. In an open letter to Richard, Owen Gleiberman of *Entertainment Weekly* asked, "Will you please allow people to see Todd Haynes's *Superstar: The Karen Carpenter Story*?" and called it "one of the most startling, audacious and sheerly emotional films of the past decade." Gleiberman asserted that the film was not just a case study but a tribute to the duo's musical legacy. "Todd Haynes has turned Karen Carpenter's life into a singular work of art. Even for those who never cared about the Carpenters' music (but especially for those who did), it deserves to be seen."

In Richard's response, which appeared in the publication the following month, he explained that his issue with the film related not to its content but to the filmmaker's behavior. The fact remained that Haynes had distributed the film to numerous theaters after having been denied permission to utilize the Carpenters' recordings. According to Richard, "His decision to make his movie using this material amounted to a deliberate attack on the rights of those who Gleiberman now suggests ought to give their blessing to Haynes's exhibition of the movie."

The catalyst for a sweeping renaissance of interest in Karen's story and the music of the Carpenters came on January 1, 1989, with the premiere of *The Karen Carpenter Story* on CBS-TV. The revival has continued in varying degrees to this day. The New Year's Day airing took advantage of a captive holiday viewing audience, and the movie finished in first place for its rating week with 41 percent of televisions tuned in. It was the highest-rated television movie licensed by CBS in five years and second most watched for all of 1989, behind *I Know My First Name Is Steven*. "Carpenters Telepic Boosts Record Sales" reported *Variety*. According to their research, sales of the Carpenters' catalog soared some 400 percent in the two weeks immediately following the broadcast on CBS. Absent from record store shelves was a tie-in or soundtrack release. Two previously unreleased recordings debuted in the film, "You're the One" and "Where Do I Go from Here," outtakes from 1977 and 1978 respectively. Both appeared on *Lovelines*, a new Carpenters album released ten months later in October.

There had been more than twenty years of jibes and sneers—two decades of dismissing even Karen's best recordings as bland, homogenized, or saccharine sweet—but with the airing of this low-budget dramatization, prejudice against the Carpenters' recordings began to fade, revealing an extraordinary change in perception. Over time, Karen found her rightful home alongside other timeless vocalists like Frank Sinatra, Nat "King" Cole, and Sarah Vaughan. Not just that, but retro was in. At times it seemed almost cool to like the Carpenters. "Maybe it's just an overdue appreciation of a singer who, despite some terrible material, always had a pure pop voice," wrote Stephen Whitty in an article for the *San Jose Mercury News*. "Or maybe it's simply a twinge of '70s nostalgia. For baby boomers in their twenties, 'Close to You' was part of their AM-radio childhoods. But the Carpenters are back. And it's only just begun. Again."

The revival made its way from the United States to the United Kingdom, where in 1990 a "greatest hits" compilation, *Only Yesterday*, held the #1 spot for a total of seven weeks. Carpenters tribute acts surfaced in the United Kingdom as well. One featuring vocalist Wendy Roberts was even praised by Richard Carpenter, who was amazed to learn the act had sold out the London Palladium, just as the Carpenters had (many times over) in 1976.

Next came *The Carpenters: The Untold Story*, an authorized biography by former *Melody Maker* editor-in-chief Ray Coleman, who previously authored books about Eric Clapton, the Beatles, and others. Bound by restraints similar to those imposed on the writers of the 1989 TV movie, the author skirted around certain subjects and overlooked others altogether in order to craft a book deemed worthy of the Carpenter family's stamp of approval. That same year, it was Coleman who proclaimed the musical duo "too good to be through" in a feature for *The Sunday Times* in London. "There is little doubt that Karen would have enjoyed all the commotion," he wrote. "Fiercely ambitious, professional and proud, she was hurt by the taunts on the way up and would have loved the irony of being considered retro-cool."

That retro-cool acceptance of the Carpenters' product was certainly a long time coming. "It was a transformation in taste that took twenty years," wrote Sue Cummings in *Trouble Girls: The* Rolling Stone *Book of Women in Rock*, calling it a "renewed ironic appreciation. [Listeners] had loved the veneer, then hated it, then found it even more compelling, on a second look, for the complexity in the places where the darkness cracked through."

Also seeing release in 1995 was *If I Were a Carpenter*, a somewhat questionable but highly successful tribute album featuring alternative rock acts including Sonic Youth, Sheryl Crow, and the Cranberries. The collection sparked interest in Carpenters music among yet another generation of listeners, and co-producer David Konjoyan assured the project was honest and in no way done with a tongue-in-cheek approach: "While it's easy to dismiss all of this as just more quirky campiness where the mediocrities of the past are celebrated as masterpieces of the present—'Here's a story of a man named Brady' and all that—there seems to be more to it than that."

Richard approved of the tribute, even making a guest appearance on Matthew Sweet's interpretation of "Let Me Be the One." He felt Karen, too, would have appreciated the sentiments backing the project. "She'd like it for the same reasons I like it," he told *HITS* magazine. "The people involved thought enough of our music or her talent to take time out of their schedules to contribute, and that there continues to be, after all these years, so much interest in our music."

The Carpenters revival wave crested in Japan again in 1996 with the enormous success of *22 Hits of the Carpenters*. The collection included two of the duo's songs that had been featured as opening and closing themes in a popular Japanese teen-oriented television drama called

Miseinen. Interest in "I Need to Be in Love" and "Top of the World" quickly pushed sales of the album over three million copies. "In the U.S., alternative rock and grunge are becoming mainstream, but in Japan, young people really don't want to listen to music that lacks melody," explained Shun Okano, product manager for the Japanese record label, in a feature for *Billboard*. "They like the Carpenters' pleasant melodies and beautiful harmonies. It sounds like something fresh and new to them."

Richard's focus moved back to the United States when in 1998 a twenty-song collection entitled *Love Songs* rode the American album chart for six months. This success was enhanced by the airing of the highly acclaimed *Close to You: Remembering the Carpenters* documentary produced for public television (PBS), as well as other television profiles on A&E's *Biography* and VH1's *Behind the Music*. Additionally, Richard released his second solo album, *Richard Carpenter: Pianist, Arranger, Composer, Conductor*. The album sent him back on tour for a series of shows with orchestras in Japan and several in Southern California. Its only single, "Karen's Theme," received moderate play on easy listening radio stations.

The Carpenters are one of only a few acts that made such an impact on the music scene in the 1970s and do not have a place in the Rock and Roll Hall of Fame. The museum has a reputation for inducting trendy acts based on the tastes of a select few executives, but even record mogul Mike Curb argues that the Carpenters were certainly catalysts for a musical trend during that decade and deserving of such recognition. "Their body of work was really good pop music with an edge," he says. "It was very fresh, pop rock and perfectly produced, but always produced with just enough edge. It didn't sound dated. It sounded fresh. When her voice would come on the radio, there was such a presence to those records that said this is not just a pop record, it's pop rock. They were competing with rock artists right and left."

Whether the duo belongs in the Rock and Roll Hall of Fame or not, interest in their music has never waned. In 2009 the Carpenters' *40/40 The Best Selection*, a forty-track compilation recognizing the duo's fortieth anniversary, debuted in Japan's Top 5. It was the highest debut ever for a Carpenters album in that territory and within a month went to #1. "Karen and Richard are the seventh American act to top Nielsen/SoundScan's Japanese chart in the past five years," revealed Paul Grein in his popular "Chart Watch" column online. "They follow Bon Jovi (*Have a Nice Day* and *Lost Highway*), Britney Spears (*Greatest Hits*), Destiny's Child (*#1's*), Linkin Park (*Minutes to Midnight*), Backstreet Boys (*Unbreakable*), and Madonna (*Hard Candy*)....Japan is the world's #2 music market, behind only the U.S."

"WERE YOU angry about Karen dying and finishing off your career as a superstar?" The question, posed by a reporter working for a 1990 *Daily Mirror* feature, surely caught him off guard, but Richard Carpenter paused only for a moment before answering: "Not angry, I'd say disappointed. There's nothing I'd rather be doing than making records with Karen. You know, when she died I actually had people saying that I should find another Carpenter. They said, 'You own the rights to the name.' I said 'You've got to be kidding.' Not for a split second would I have done that. There could never be another Karen Carpenter."

Richard has spent much of the last quarter century as a family man and patron of the arts in his community. On May 19, 1984, with best man Wes Jacobs at his side, he and Mary Elizabeth Rudolph wed in a private ceremony at Downey United Methodist Church. The couple had dated off and on for eight years. "[Richard] and Mary do not wish to commercialize their marriage," wrote Rosina Sullivan, "so there will be no pictures available through the fan club." On August 17, 1987, they welcomed their first child, a daughter, Kristi Lynn. This was the name chosen years earlier by her aunt Karen, who had hoped to one day have children of her own. The union of Richard and Mary produced four more children: Traci Tatum, born July 25, 1989; Mindi Karen, born July 7, 1992; Colin Paul, born July 20, 1994; and Taylor Mary, born December 5, 1998.

Following a lengthy period of poor health, Harold Carpenter died of heart failure in 1988 on his son's birthday, October 15, at the age of seventy-nine. Agnes Carpenter died November 10, 1996, at Good

Samaritan Hospital in Los Angeles after a lengthy illness and complications following triple-bypass heart surgery. She was laid to rest alongside her husband and daughter in the family crypt at Forest Lawn Cypress.

Tom Burris is remarried and resides with his wife and the couple's son in Lincoln, California, where he manages Aberdeen Burris Contractors. No longer at liberty to speak of his relationship with Karen, he declined to be interviewed for this book. "There's an agreement between me and the Carpenters where I don't reveal anything," he said in 2002. "That is primarily tied to personal information about the Carpenters, their finances, and things like that."

As construction of a new concert hall began on the campus of California State Long Beach, Richard Carpenter stepped forward with a one-million-dollar pledge. As a result, the 1,074-seat venue was named the Richard and Karen Carpenter Performing Arts Center. It was dedicated during a star-studded gala opening on October 1, 1994, which featured performances by Herb Alpert, Rita Coolidge, and Marilyn McCoo. The Carpenter Exhibit, a permanent display of awards and memorabilia, was added to the Center lobby in 2000, and on May 26, 2000, the university honored Richard with an honorary doctorate after his delivery of the commencement speech.

Richard and Mary remained in Downey until 2000, when they relocated their family to Thousand Oaks, California. They soon gained a reputation as generous supporters of the local arts community after pledging three million dollars to the Thousand Oaks Civic Arts Plaza. In exchange for the contribution, a park in front of the plaza was named the Mary and Richard Carpenter Plaza Park. "We weren't thinking about that amount when we had this in mind," Richard told a local reporter, "but we liked the look of where the name would go." In 2007 he and Mary were named Ventura County's Philanthropists of the Year.

In December 2003, Karen Carpenter's body, along with the bodies of her parents, was exhumed from the crypt at Forest Lawn Cypress and reinterred in a new Carpenter family mausoleum in the Tranquility Gardens at Pierce Brothers Valley Oaks Memorial Park in Westlake

Village, California. *Entertainment Tonight* explained that the cemetery in Cypress was more than an hour's drive for Richard, while the Westlake Village location was only minutes from his home in Thousand Oaks. "With room for six," they reported, "the 46,000-pound Partenope-style structure was constructed in Texas over seven months. It is polished sunset red with beautiful warmth and color and lively crystal patterns. Similar structures have a price range of $600,000."

Unaware of the move, a number of visitors arrived in Cypress that Christmas to pay their respects but were shocked to find the empty grave. Forest Lawn employees were unable to disclose any details but offered a rather palpable statement: "Miss Carpenter is no longer with us."

∞∞

"IRREPLACEABLE." ALWAYS a master at crafting words into poetic song lyrics, John Bettis offered this one word recapitulation of Karen Carpenter. "*Irreplaceable.* Not just the voice, but the person.... She was just beginning to blossom as a person. There was so much there that very few people got to see: the sense of humor, the sense of life. There was a certain profundity to Karen. If you believe in all this old soul stuff, there was always a sense that Karen knew more than she had any right to know. She had a sense of feeling and understanding about people that was remarkable."

Olivia Newton-John cherishes her memories of Karen, their friendship, and their admiration for one another as fellow pop singers. She recalls her "perfect pitch, beautiful tone, beautiful interpretation of a lyric, and a very simple, very soothing sound" and says that the feeling in Karen's voice "can't be taught. It's a gift that she had that came from within."

Recalling Karen as an incredibly spirited person, Phil Ramone expresses regret that someone so feisty and vivacious never fully succeeded in breaking free and establishing a singular identity. "Her dreams of what a family and her life could be weren't accomplished," he says. "The top two things in her life—interchangeably—were her music and her family. There's no question how much she cared for her family, but they were a close-knit family with things that frustrated her. At the end of the day, no one really ever understood that she had some kind of an eating disorder. If life were reasonably fair, therapy would have been there for her ten years earlier. It just wasn't there."

Not a day goes by that Itchie Ramone does not think of Karen or is not reminded of her in some way. "What can one say about losing your best friend?" she asks, struggling to articulate the void. "In terms of her voice and her music, I still have her there, but I miss the company. I miss her wit. She was *very* witty! I miss us pulling jokes on each other. What can I say? She will forever remain in my heart. She was Lucy and I was Ethel."

"I feel very, very robbed. We all do," says Frenda Franklin. "Karen touched your life and embraced it with such laughter and fun and happiness. Her take on everything was so left of center, and she was *special*. It's an overused word, no question, but not in her case. She really, really was as unique a person as her voice was unique. I don't know how else to say it. You can't replace that."

ACKNOWLEDGMENTS

I N WRITING this biography I have been assisted by hundreds of people and consider it to be a collaboration between the individuals who agreed to be interviewed and others who contributed to my research in a number of ways. Some shared articles, interviews, concert reviews, audio, and video footage. Others provided important documents, transcripts, photographs, and additional material. All played an important role in the telling of Karen Carpenter's life story.

Several important teachers supported my interest in the Carpenters as a youth and encouraged me to write about their lives and music: Elaine Garvin, Zonelle Rainbolt, Shannon Cunningham, Rebecca Gilchrist, and Billie Goetsch. I also wish to recognize several music educators who shared with me their passion for the art: the late JoAnn Carlson, Jennifer Wedel, Mike Plunkett, Suzanne Aylor, and Charles "Skip" Klingman.

I am grateful to Chicago Review Press for believing in *Little Girl Blue*, and to my meticulous editors, Yuval Taylor and Lisa Reardon, whose passion for this project has remained strong. Their endless support and thorough attention to detail is greatly appreciated.

Special thanks to artist Chris Tassin for his lovely rendering of Karen created exclusively for this book; to Dionne Warwick for her heartfelt foreword; to Petula Clark for her assistance; to Carrie Mitchum for inadvertently introducing me to Karen Carpenter's life story and music; to Barry Morrow, who, in addition to providing files, script revisions, and other important documents, gave this project a much-appreciated change of direction; to Cynthia Gibb and Mitchell Anderson; and to Cynthia Cherbak for sharing additional script revisions and correspondence.

My thanks to Karen's childhood friends Debbie Cuticello and husband C.J. for years of support and for the guided tour of Hall Street and Nathan Hale School in 1996; to Frank Bonito for his encouragement and contribution of previously unseen photos; to Frankie Chavez for sharing his memories of Karen and her inscription in his yearbook; to Leslie Johnston, who recalled the Spectrum era; and to choral music legend Frank Pooler for his contribution of various resources and photos from his personal archives.

Evelyn Wallace deserves a resounding thank-you, due in part to her willingness to recall enough "Karen stories" to fill eight audiotapes. I first met Ev in 1994. Three years later she personally guided me through the Carpenter estate at 9828 Newville Avenue, by then a time capsule akin to Elvis's Graceland. (The property remained in the Carpenter family until June 1997. Sadly, in 2008 a large portion of the home was demolished.) Ev was the personal connection to the Carpenters for fans of their music for nearly three decades. Collectively, her fan club newsletters serve as one of the most comprehensive resources for information about the Carpenters' lives and their music.

Words cannot express my gratitude to two of Karen's closest friends, Frenda Franklin and Karen "Itchie" Ramone. Extremely private and fiercely protective of her memories, Frenda (with rare exception) has not granted interviews regarding her friendship with Karen. As for Itchie, she became a cheerleader for my efforts with this book, just as she had been a cheerleader for Karen since the two first met in 1979. I am indebted to both Frenda and Itchie for their honesty and openness.

My thanks to Carole Curb for years of support and for encouraging Frenda to participate after six or seven years of my subtle but persistent efforts; to Mike Curb for taking time from his busy schedule as head of Curb Records to talk with me; to Maria Luisa Galeazzi, who shared numerous photographs and made herself readily available by phone and e-mail; to Terry Ellis, who surfaced just in time to share his remarkable insight and stories; to Cherry Boone O'Neill for her memories and observations; to Olivia Newton-John, whose initial phone call succeeded in permanently brightening my life; to Phil Ramone for a great interview and several much-appreciated follow-ups; and to Liberty DeVitto, Bob James, Russell Javors, and Rob Mounsey for recalling the 1979–1980 solo sessions.

Thanks to journalist Jon Burlingame, who interviewed Richard Carpenter on November 18, 1988. I appreciate Jon's willingness to dig for the tape and am especially grateful for his permission to transcribe and use the interview in this book. Thanks also to John Tobler for permission to use transcripts of his in-depth interviews with Herb Alpert, Sherwin Bash, and John Bettis.

Grateful acknowledgment is made to the following individuals and their respective institutions and organizations: Bob Garcia, former publicity director at A&M Records, for arranging a tour of A&M offices, studios, and the Chaplin soundstage in 1996; Jim O'Grady for research he conducted at the Downey City Library; Marilynn Hughes for records assistance at the Downey Police Department; Pamela R. Cornell at the Historical Research Center at the Houston Academy of Medicine-Texas Medical Center Library; Marsha Grigsby in the Office of the Los Angeles County Coroner; Michelle Dyson with National Medical Services in Pennsylvania; Bill Hosley of the New Haven Museum and Historical Society; Allen Rice of the Richard Nixon Presidential Library and Museum; David Konjoyan and Paul Madeira of the Recording Academy; Storytech Literary Consulting and Brad Schreiber; Donna Honeycutt, George Redfox, John Vincent, and Frank Williams at the Downey Historical Society; Kristie French with the Frank Pooler Collection at California State University Long Beach; Connie Griffin at the Richard and Karen Carpenter Performing Arts Center; Lauren Buisson with the A&M Records Collection at the University of Southern California Los Angeles; and Brooke Megdal, founder/director of the Loving Heart Center in Brentwood, California, for helping me to better understand anorexia nervosa and other eating disorders.

In 1994 I organized the Newville Avenue Carpenters Mailing List, one of the first and largest online networks devoted to the Carpenters. Much knowledge was shared and many friendships were born during the group's six-year existence. The fans are the experts, and I have learned so much from their willingness to share that expertise. Two generous fans in particular, Lindeigh Scotte and Cindy Ward, left us much too soon and too young. It is in memory of their giving spirits and kindness to all Carpenters fans that I dedicate this book.

Many thanks to my team of experts—Amanda Abbett, Carolyn Allen, Donnie Demers, Sue Gustin, and Chris Tassin—who spent countless hours attentively poring over my drafts, fact checking, and offering insightful comments and suggestions. I consider their knowledge and input to have been invaluable, and their patience is greatly appreciated. Also assisting in the reading of various chapter drafts were Jeffrey de Hart, Robert Ingves, and Paul Steinberg. Photo research assistance was provided by Miranda Bardwell, Donnie Demers, and Jill Anne Matusek, and special thanks to Matusek, Leo Bonaventura, Peter Desmond Dawe, and Chris Tassin for their generosity in sponsoring several important photographs that might not otherwise have been possible. My appreciation also goes to Paul Ashurst, who shared copies of Karen's wedding scrapbook.

I am indebted to Pecan Creek Elementary for providing me with a creative and supportive environment in which to work. In addition to my principal, Aleta Atkinson, and assistant principal, Emily McLarty, the staff, students, and parents have been a cooperative and encouraging captive audience.

Thanks also to Laura Adam, Nancy Alexander, Randy Anglin, Viv Atkinson, Sherry Rayn Barnett, Nick Barraclough, Peter Benjaminson, Jeff Bleiel, Ken Bertwell, Joe Bine, Dana Britten-Stein, Ron Bunt, Chip Cogswell, Bradley Coker, Steve Cox, Mark Crow, Jason Douglas, Patrick Driscoll, Brenda Ehly, Heidi Ewing, Bob Finholm, Julia Foot, Ashley Franklin, Michael J. Glenn, David Grant, Becky Judd, Sydney Junior, Donovan Keogh, Carlos Keyes, Inga Kleinrichert, Jon Konjoyan, Jay Lumbee, Joshua Mahn, Cindy Martin, Rhonda Martinez, Chris May, Doug McComas, Bob McDonald, Bonnie Miller,

Vicki Mitchell, Jena Morrow, Nancy Munoz, Yuka Ogura, Jonathan Owen, Laura Pascoe, Mark Pelzel, Mary Perica, Samantha Peters, Ronald Pledge, Robert Polston, Ying Qin, Pam Quiggle, Matt Ramone, Stephen Richardson, Jaime Rodriguez, Celso Lopes Santos, Victoria Sarinelli, Bonnie Schiffman, Jennifer Schmidt, Norma Segarra, Daniel Selby, Julie Stanfield, Jeffrey Strain, Tiana Galeazzi Taylor, J.B. Thomas, Vickie VanArtsdalen, Pamela Verona, Denise Wagorn, Kimberly Wall, Cindy Williams, and Ron Zurek.

Finally, I wish to thank my family for their love and support: my parents, Linda Schmidt and Ron and Frances Schmidt; my sister, Rhonda Morrison; and my beautiful, talented, and entertaining daughters, Camryn and Kaylee.

SELECTED DISCOGRAPHY

THE CARPENTERS released ten traditional studio albums between the years 1969 and 1981. This selected discography refers to each original conception as first released on A&M Records in the United States. Singles from each album are noted, as are peak U.S. chart positions for both albums and singles. Only the most significant posthumous releases and compilations (notably those containing previously unreleased material) are included. Also listed are Karen's solo releases and other various issues.

CARPENTERS

Offering / Ticket to Ride   (A&M 4205)   1969 (#150)
Invocation / Your Wonderful Parade / Someday / Get Together / All of My Life / Turn Away / Ticket to Ride / Don't Be Afraid / What's the Use / All I Can Do / Eve / Nowadays Clancy Can't Even Sing / Benediction

SINGLES:
Ticket to Ride / Your Wonderful Parade (#54)

Close to You   (A&M 4271)   1970 (#2)
We've Only Just Begun / Love Is Surrender / Maybe It's You / Reason to Believe / Help / (They Long to Be) Close to You / Baby It's You / I'll Never Fall in Love Again / Crescent Noon / Mr. Guder / I Kept on Loving You / Another Song

SINGLES:
(They Long to Be) Close to You / I Kept on Loving You (#1)
We've Only Just Begun / All of My Life (#2)

Carpenters (A&M 3502)   1971 (#2)

Rainy Days and Mondays / Saturday / Let Me Be the One / (A Place to)
Hideaway / For All We Know / Superstar / Druscilla Penny / One Love /
Bacharach-David Medley: Knowing When to Leave, Make It Easy on Your-
self, (There's) Always Something There to Remind Me, I'll Never Fall in
Love Again, Walk On By, Do You Know the Way to San Jose / Sometimes

SINGLES:
For All We Know / Don't Be Afraid (#3)
Rainy Days and Mondays / Saturday (#2)
Superstar / Bless the Beasts and Children (#2 / 67)

A Song for You (A&M 3511)   1972 (#4)

A Song for You / Top of the World / Hurting Each Other / It's Going to
Take Some Time / Goodbye to Love / Intermission / Bless the Beasts and
Children / Flat Baroque / Piano Picker / I Won't Last a Day Without You /
Crystal Lullaby / Road Ode / A Song for You—Reprise

SINGLES:
Hurting Each Other / Maybe It's You (#2)
It's Going to Take Some Time / Flat Baroque (#12)
Goodbye to Love / Crystal Lullaby (#7)
I Won't Last a Day Without You / One Love (#11)

Now & Then (A&M 3519)   1973 (#2)

Sing / This Masquerade / Heather / Jambalaya (On the Bayou) / I Can't
Make Music / Yesterday Once More / Oldies Medley: Fun, Fun, Fun, The
End of the World, Da Doo Ron Ron, Deadman's Curve, Johnny Angel,
The Night Has a Thousand Eyes, Our Day Will Come, One Fine Day /
Yesterday Once More—Reprise

SINGLES:
Sing / Druscilla Penny (#3)
Yesterday Once More / Road Ode (#2)

The Singles: 1969–1973 (A&M 3601)   1973 (#1)

We've Only Just Begun / Top of the World / Ticket to Ride / Superstar /
Rainy Days and Mondays / Goodbye to Love / Yesterday Once More / It's

Going to Take Some Time / Sing / For All We Know / Hurting Each Other / (They Long to Be) Close to You

SINGLES:
Top of the World / Heather (#1)

Horizon (A&M 4530)   1975 (#13)

Aurora / Only Yesterday / Desperado / Please Mr. Postman / I Can Dream, Can't I? / Solitaire / Happy / (I'm Caught Between) Goodbye and I Love You / Love Me for What I Am / Eventide

SINGLES:
Please Mr. Postman / This Masquerade (#1)
Only Yesterday / Happy (#4)
Solitaire / Love Me for What I Am (#17)

A Kind of Hush (A&M 4581)   1976 (#33)

There's a Kind of Hush (All Over the World) / You / Sandy / Goofus / Can't Smile Without You / I Need to Be in Love / One More Time / Boat to Sail / I Have You / Breaking Up Is Hard to Do

SINGLES:
There's a Kind of Hush (All Over the World) / (I'm Caught Between) Goodbye and I Love You (#12)
I Need to Be in Love / Sandy (#25)
Goofus / Boat to Sail (#56)

Passage (A&M 4703)   1977 (#49)

B'wana She No Home / All You Get from Love Is a Love Song / I Just Fall in Love Again / On the Balcony of Casa Rosada / Don't Cry for Me, Argentina / Sweet, Sweet Smile / Two Sides / Man Smart, Woman Smarter / Calling Occupants of Interplanetary Craft (The Recognized Anthem of World Contact Day)

SINGLES:
All You Get from Love Is a Love Song / I Have You (#35)
Calling Occupants of Interplanetary Craft / Can't Smile Without You (#32)
Sweet, Sweet Smile / I Have You (#44)

Christmas Portrait (A&M 4726)   1978 (#145)

O Come, O Come Emmanuel / Overture: Deck the Halls, I Saw Three Ships, Have Yourself a Merry Little Christmas, God Rest Ye Merry

Gentlemen, Away in a Manger, What Child Is This (Greensleeves), Carol of the Bells, O Come All Ye Faithful / The Christmas Waltz / Sleigh Ride / It's Christmas Time / Sleep Well, Little Children / Have Yourself a Merry Little Christmas / Santa Claus Is Coming to Town / The Christmas Song / Silent Night / Jingle Bells / The First Snowfall / Let It Snow / Carol of the Bells / Merry Christmas, Darling / I'll Be Home for Christmas / Christ Is Born / Medley: Winter Wonderland, Silver Bells, White Christmas / Ave Maria

SINGLES:
Christmas Song / Merry Christmas, Darling

Made in America   (A&M 3723)   1981 (#52)
Those Good Old Dreams / Strength of a Woman / (Want You) Back in My Life Again / When You've Got What It Takes / Somebody's Been Lyin' / I Believe You / Touch Me When We're Dancing / When It's Gone (It's Just Gone) / Beechwood 4-5789 / Because We Are in Love (The Wedding Song)

SINGLES:
I Believe You / B'wana She No Home (#68)
Touch Me When We're Dancing / Because We Are in Love (#16)
(Want You) Back in My Life Again / Somebody's Been Lyin' (#72)
Those Good Old Dreams / When It's Gone (It's Just Gone) (#63)
Beechwood 4-5789 / Two Sides (#74)

Voice of the Heart   (A&M 4954)   1983 (#46)
Now / Sailing on the Tide / You're Enough / Make Believe It's Your First Time / Two Lives / At the End of a Song / Ordinary Fool / Prime Time Love / Your Baby Doesn't Love You Anymore / Look to Your Dreams

SINGLES:
Make Believe It's Your First Time / Look to Your Dreams
Your Baby Doesn't Love You Anymore / Sailing on the Tide

An Old-Fashioned Christmas   (A&M 3270)   1984 (#190)
It Came Upon a Midnight Clear / Overture: Happy Holiday, The First Noel, March of the Toys, Little Jesus, I Saw Mommy Kissing Santa Claus, O Little Town of Bethlehem, In Dulci Jubilo, Gesu Bambino, Angels We Have Heard on High / An Old-Fashioned Christmas / O Holy Night / (There's No Place Like) Home for the Holidays / Medley: Here Comes Santa Claus, Frosty the Snowman, Rudolph the Red-Nosed Reindeer, Good King Wenceslas / Little Altar Boy / Do You Hear What I Hear? / My Favorite

Things / He Came Here for Me / Santa Claus Is Comin' to Town / What Are You Doing New Year's Eve? / Selections from "The Nutcracker" / I Heard the Bells on Christmas Day

SINGLES:
Little Altar Boy / Do You Hear What I Hear? (promo)

Lovelines   (A&M 3931)   1989
Lovelines / Where Do I Go from Here? / The Uninvited Guest / If We Try / When I Fall in Love / Kiss Me the Way You Did Last Night / Remember When Lovin' Took All Night / You're the One / Honolulu City Lights / Slow Dance / If I Had You / Little Girl Blue

SINGLES:
Honolulu City Lights / I Just Fall in Love Again
If I Had You / The Uninvited Guest (promo)

Interpretations: A 25th Anniversary Celebration   (A&M 3145403122)
                                                                 1994
Without a Song (a cappella version) / Superstar / Rainy Days and Mondays / Bless the Beasts and Children / This Masquerade / Solitaire / When I Fall in Love / From This Moment On / Tryin' to Get the Feeling Again / When It's Gone / I Believe You / Reason to Believe / (They Long to Be) Close to You / Calling Occupants of Interplanetary Craft / Little Girl Blue / We've Only Just Begun

The Essential Collection: 1965–1997   (A&M 0694934162)   2002
DISC 1: Caravan / The Parting of Our Ways / Looking for Love / I'll Be Yours / Iced Tea / You'll Love Me / All I Can Do / Don't Be Afraid / Invocation / Your Wonderful Parade / All of My Life / Eve / Ticket to Ride / Get Together / Interview / Love Is Surrender / Maybe It's You / (They Long to Be) Close to You / Mr. Guder / We've Only Just Begun / Merry Christmas, Darling / For All We Know

DISC 2: Rainy Days and Mondays / Superstar / Let Me Be the One / Bless the Beasts and Children / Hurting Each Other / It's Going to Take Some Time / I Won't Last a Day Without You / A Song for You / Top of the World / Goodbye to Love / This Masquerade / Sing / Jambalaya (On the Bayou) / Yesterday Once More / Oldies Medley: Fun, Fun, Fun, The End of the World, Da Doo Ron Ron, Deadman's Curve, Johnny Angel, The Night Has a Thousand Eyes, Our Day Will Come, One Fine Day / Yesterday Once More—Reprise / Radio Contest Outtakes

DISC 3: Morinaga Hi-Crown Chocolate Commercial / Please Mr. Postman / Santa Claus Is Coming to Town / Only Yesterday / Solitaire / Tryin' to Get the Feeling Again / Good Friends Are for Keeps / Ordinary Fool / Sandy / There's a Kind Of Hush (All Over the World) / I Need to Be in Love / From This Moment On / Suntory Pop Jingle #1 / Suntory Pop Jingle #2 / All You Get from Love Is a Love Song / Calling Occupants of Interplanetary Craft / Sweet, Sweet Smile / Christ Is Born / White Christmas / Little Altar Boy / Ave Maria

DISC 4: Where Do I Go From Here? / Little Girl Blue / I Believe You / If I Had You / Karen-Ella Medley: This Masquerade, My Funny Valentine, I'll Be Seeing You, Someone to Watch over Me, As Time Goes By, Don't Get Around Much Any More, I Let a Song Go out of My Heart / 1980 Medley: Sing, Knowing When to Leave, Make It Easy on Yourself, Someday, We've Only Just Begun / Make Believe It's Your First Time / Touch Me When We're Dancing / When It's Gone (It's Just Gone) / Because We Are in Love (The Wedding Song) / Those Good Old Dreams / Now / Karen's Theme

As Time Goes By   (A&M 0694931122)   2004
Without a Song / Medley: Superstar, Rainy Days and Mondays / Nowhere Man / I Got Rhythm Medley / Dancing in the Street / Dizzy Fingers / You're Just in Love / Karen-Ella Fitzgerald Medley: This Masquerade, My Funny Valentine, I'll Be Seeing You, Someone to Watch Over Me, As Time Goes By, Don't Get Around Much Anymore, I Let a Song Go Out of My Heart / Medley: Close Encounters, Star Wars / Leave Yesterday Behind / Carpenters-Perry Como Medley: Yesterday Once More, Magic Moments, Sing, Catch a Falling Star, Close to You, It's Impossible, We've Only Just Begun, And I Love You So, Don't Let the Stars Get in Your Eyes, Till the End of Time, No Other Love Have I / California Dreamin' / The Rainbow Connection / '76 Hits Medley: Sing, Close to You, For All We Know, Ticket to Ride, Only Yesterday, I Won't Last a Day Without You, Goodbye to Love / And When He Smiles

KAREN CARPENTER

Looking for Love / I'll Be Yours (single)   (Magic Lamp ML704)   1966

Karen Carpenter   (A&M 3145405882)   1996
Lovelines / All Because of You / If I Had You / Making Love in the After-noon / If We Try / Remember When Lovin' Took All Night / Still in Love

with You / My Body Keeps Changing My Mind / Make Believe It's Your First Time / Guess I Just Lost My Head / Still Crazy After All These Years / Last One Singin' the Blues

RICHARD CARPENTER TRIO

Battle of the Bands　(Custom Fidelity 1533)　　　　1966
Includes: The Girl from Ipanema / Iced Tea

SELECTED TELEVISION APPEARANCES

THIS LIST includes all known appearances by Karen Carpenter on American television during her lifetime. Since many of the programs were syndicated, occasional discrepancies between air dates exist. Other inconsistencies have been found in past publications (notably the Carpenters Fan Club's *Decade* publication from 1979), which have not always distinguished between the taping and broadcast dates. Whenever possible, corrections have been made here to reflect the earliest known air dates.

1966

07/03 *Battle of the Bands! (Richard Carpenter Trio, KNBC-TV, Los Angeles)*

1968

06/22 *Your All-American College Show (Richard Carpenter Trio)*
06/29 *Your All-American College Show (Richard Carpenter Trio)*

1969

09/09 *Your All-American College Show (Karen Carpenter)*

11/23   *Your All-American College Show (Karen Carpenter)*
12/01   *Your All-American College Show (Carpenters)*
12/04   *The Della Reese Show*

1970

01/18   *Lohman & Barkley's Name Droppers*
06/24   *The Virginia Graham Show*
07/20   *The Dating Game*
09/15   *The Don Knotts Show*
09/18   *The Tonight Show*
10/02   *The David Frost Show*
10/18   *The Ed Sullivan Show*
11/08   *The Ed Sullivan Show*
11/13   *The Tonight Show*
11/14   *American Bandstand*

1971

01/24   *Peggy Fleming at Sun Valley*
02/13   *The Andy Williams Show*
02/18   *This Is Your Life*
03/16   *The Grammy Awards*
03/24   *The Johnny Cash Show*
06/30   *The Tonight Show*
07/13   *Make Your Own Kind of Music*
07/20   *Make Your Own Kind of Music*
07/27   *Make Your Own Kind of Music*
07/29   *The Mike Douglas Show*
08/03   *Make Your Own Kind of Music*
08/10   *Make Your Own Kind of Music*
08/17   *Make Your Own Kind of Music*
08/18   *The 5th Dimension Traveling Sunshine Show*
08/24   *Make Your Own Kind of Music*
08/31   *Make Your Own Kind of Music*
09/22   *The Carol Burnett Show*
11/05   *The Tonight Show*

1972

01/14   *The Ed Sullivan Show*
01/19   *The Carol Burnett Show*
02/21   *Jerry Visits (Jerry Dunphy)*
03/14   *The Grammy Awards*
04/10   *The Academy Awards*
05/07   *The Special London Bridge Special*
10/05   *The Bob Hope Special*

1973

06/01   *Robert Young with the Young*
11/05   *The Tonight Show*
11/13   *The Bob Hope Special*

1974

03/02   *The Grammy Awards*
08/04   *Evening at Pops*
12/17   *The Perry Como Christmas Show*

1975

02/18   *The American Music Awards*

1976

05/22   *The Midnight Special*
12/08   *The Carpenters' Very First Television Special*

1977

01/27   *The Tonight Show (Steve Martin, host)*
03/02   *The Dorothy Hamill Special*
12/09   *The Carpenters at Christmas*

1978

02/05	*The ABC Silver Anniversary Celebration*
03/16	*Thank You, Rock and Roll*
05/17	*The Carpenters: Space Encounters*
06/27	*The Tonight Show (John Davidson, host)*
11/19	*Wonderful World of Disney: Mickey's 50*
12/19	*The Carpenters: A Christmas Portrait*

1980

03/13	*20/20*
04/14	*Olivia Newton-John: Hollywood Nights*
05/16	*The Carpenters: Music, Music, Music*

1981

07/11	*America's Top Ten*
10/02	*The Merv Griffin Show*
10/12	*Good Morning America*

1983

01/11	*Entertainment Tonight*

NOTES

THE PRIMARY interviews on which this work is based were conducted by the author between the years 2001 and 2009. Other important interviews were made available by journalists Jon Burlingame (Richard Carpenter) and John Tobler (Herb Alpert, Sherwin Bash, and John Bettis). Numerous interviews with Karen Carpenter and others were culled from diverse publications, as well as television and radio archives, and are identified in the following pages of sources. As a rule, quotations presented in *past* tense are from existing interviews and other secondary sources. Those quotes offered in *present* tense originate from the author's personal interviews, consultations, or correspondence with the following individuals:

John "Softly" Adrian, Mitchell Anderson, Carolyn Arzac, Tom Bähler, Lou Beach, Max Bennett, Ken Bertwell, Dick Biondi, Hal Blaine, Frank Bonito, David Brenner, Denny Brooks, Bill Catalde, Frankie Chavez, Cynthia Cherbak, Petula Clark, Marion Connellan, Carole Curb, Mike Curb, C.J. Cuticello, Debbie Cuticello, Liberty DeVitto, Digby Diehl, Gioia Diliberto, Veta Dixon, Irv Edwards, Florine Elie, Terry Ellis, Allyn Ferguson, Frenda Franklin, Wanda Freeman, Dan Friberg, Maria Luisa Galeazzi, Dave Gelly, Cynthia Gibb, Victor Guder, Walt Harrah, Bill Hosley, Bob James, Jerry Jaskulski, Russell Javors, Leslie Johnston, Mickey Jones, Arthur Johns, Pete Jolly, Michael Lansing, Gayle Levant, Art LeVasseur, Charlene McAlister, Tex McAlister, Brooke Megdal, Ollie Mitchell, Barry Morrow, Claude Mougin, Rob Mounsey, Maxine Mundt, Nancy Naglin, Olivia Newton-John, Roger Nichols, Cherry Boone O'Neill, Glen Pace, John Pisano, David Pomerantz, Frank Pooler, Karen "Itchie" Ramone, Phil Ramone, David Robson, Evie Sands, Bonnie Schiffman, Brad Schreiber, Randy Sparks, Stephanie Spruill, Linda Stewart, John Tobler, Pat Tomlin, Charlie Tuna, Teresa Vaiuso, Evelyn Wallace, Dionne Warwick, Paul Williams

PROLOGUE: RAINY DAYS AND *RAIN MAN*

The first draft just   RC to Burlingame, 1988.
You don't know the first   Morrow, September 30, 1987.
What would possess   Carpenter, 1988.
genetic, the same way   Littwin, 1988.
Have you told her   Morrow and Cherbak, December 24, 1987.
If there's an arch-villain   Miller, 1989.

1. CALIFORNIA DREAMIN'

Mom was known for   Dosti, 1971.
I did everything   KC to Moore, 1981.
I was a tremendous   Oppenheimer, 1972.
It was slightly embarrassing   Gautschy, 1971.
She can take care   Oppenheimer, 1972.

2. CHOPSTICKS ON BARSTOOLS

Head down the Santa Ana   Charlesworth, 1973.
He'd been playing the drums   Hardwick, 1973.
I used to march   Hardwick, 1973.
I finally had to   Hardwick, 1973.
All I ever heard   KC to Tuna, 1976.
We met in theory class   Cameron, 2009.
I can't really remember   Coleman, 1975.
It's kind of corny   Coleman, November 8, 1975.
He heard this voice   Coleman, November 8, 1975.
I remember when   Coleman, November 8, 1975.
The musical surprise   Feather, 1966.

It was really great playing   Cameron, 2009.
She didn't strike me   McGreevy, February 5, 1983.

3. STAND IN LINE, TRY TO CLIMB

They had very strict regiments   Bettis to Tobler, 1993.
We got all the way   Bettis to Tobler, 1993.
He used to perform   Bettis to Tobler, 1993.
I was heavier   Hardwick, 1973.
All the guys   Hardwick, 1973.
People hear what we accomplished   "John Bettis Interview 2007," 2007.
You had to wait   Thegze, 1972.
The customers sat   Tatham, 1976: 12.
At first, the audience   Tatham, 1976: 12.
Since Richard did all   KC to Radio Clyde, 1978.
Wow, we couldn't believe   Diehl, 1971.
What good is biology   KC to Biondi, 1970.

4. SPRINKLED MOONDUST

I had it for about   Lees, 1972.
I put on the tape   Alpert to Tobler, 1994.
encouraging them to reach   Pfenninger, 2001.
It doesn't matter   Alpert to Tobler, 1994.
couldn't keep enough albums   Goldsmith, 1970.
Offering *tends toward*   Nolan, 1975.
fresh and original concepts   Billboard, 1970.
The first album did   Alpert to Tobler, 1994.
Thank God it didn't fit   KC to Roberts.
It was about borrowing money   KC to Biondi, 1970.

5. YOU PUT US ON THE ROAD

[Richard] called me, and   Cameron, 2009.
The five-member group is   Hilburn, 1970.
Everything seems to be going   Kraus, 1970.
Looking back, it's a bit   Tobler, 1998: 26.
Every direction we could have   KC to Nite, 1977.
The vocal harmonies, the construction   Bash to Tobler, 1990.
I'd never seen anything   Nolan, 1974.

suburban dream home   Forbes, 1973.

They all have names   MacDougall, 1971.

We can live   Small, 1972.

library full of bank books   Bash to Tobler, 1990.

It took some doing   Bash to Tobler, 1990.

I've seen enough groupies   Gautschy, 1972.

We got along fine   Haber, 1974.

Karen Carpenter has one of   Erlich, 1971.

Each number is introduced   Miller, 1971.

like dressing Karen Carpenter   Heckman, 1971.

violently mishandled   KC to Goldman, 1978.

6. NOTHING TO HIDE BEHIND

There are only three kits   Henshaw, 1974.

There is no balance   Bangs, 1971.

Hire a drummer   Bresette, 1971.

Richard and I tried desperately   Bash to Tobler, 1990.

A lot of people think   Kraus, 1970.

I said to Richard   Coleman, November 8, 1975.

In the middle of   KC to Douglas, 1971.

Petrified   KC to Tuna, 1976.

I didn't know   KC to Moore, 1981.

I understood her reluctance   Bash to Tobler, 1990.

Richard didn't have   Pogoda, 1994.

When I got the record   Bettis to Tobler, 1993.

That was the first ballad   Bettis to Tobler, 1993.

When I got in   Bettis to Tobler, 1993.

Far and away   Holden, 1972.

Nothing. That's why   Legge, 1974.

The man who produced   Daugherty, 1994.

Karen is in some ways   Nolan, 1974.

a very strong attempt   Bash to Tobler, 1990.

Being the only girl   MacDougall, 1971.

They are quite gracious   Nolan, 1974.

7. AMERICA AT ITS VERY BEST?

About 10,000 pounds   Associated Press, 1972.

I want to talk   Nixon, 1974.

We were afraid   KC to Blackburn, 1974.

Well, are you going to   Bettis to Tobler, 1993.

The Carpenters have gone awry   Bangs, 1973.

We were told   Coleman, November 8, 1975.

Real nice American kids   Pleasants, 1972.

Karen may eat   Rosenfeld, 1973.

They were not rock   Hoerburger, 2008.

I would say   Bangs, 1971.

It's not enough   Alpert to Tobler, 1994.

A number of people   Tobler, 1974.

the worst case of   Smucker, 1975.

When 'We've Only Just Begun'   Hoerburger, 1996.

Contrary to what they write   Haber, 1974.

At one point   KC to Aspel, 1981.

It's no good when   Haber, 1974.

8. MOVING OUT

Whereas Richard may not   Van Valkenburg, 1973.

I'm sure in her own   Bash to Tobler, 1990.

Their inability to develop   Bash to Tobler, 1990.

Cooking is an art   A&M Press Release, 1971.

The expectation was that   Bash to Tobler, 1990.

If we don't see   KC to Aspel, 1981.

There were lots of suggestions   Southall, 2004.

I remember once   Short, 1977.

Maybe it would have been   Short, 1976.

It's been a hell   Short, 1976.

We might as well   Nolan, 1974.

We've made it a rule   Short, 1976.

Richard can have his girl   Haber, 1974.

All of a sudden   Bettis to Tobler, 1993.

A&M took a little   Bettis to Tobler, 1993.

I don't think he   Bash to Tobler, 1990.

Karen was on an edge   Southall, 2004.

Not much showmanship   Variety, 1974.

9. THE COLLAPSE

If anorexia has   Hoerburger, 1996.
When you're on the road   Hardwick, 1973.
With their success   Bash to Tobler, 1990.
most musically sophisticated   Holden, 1975.
Oh boy, here we go   Bettis to Tobler, 1993.
such a gem   Holden, 1975.
She sings very close   Gelly, 1990.
soft-rock Nirvana   Barnes, 1975.
I talked her into   Bash to Tobler, 1990.
She is terribly thin   *Variety*, August 24, 1975.
[Harold] was beside himself   Vaiuso, 2004.
Anorexia nervosa was so new   Bettis to Tobler, 1993.
a tremendous amount of   Bash to Tobler, 1990.
In contrast to my   Sedaka, 1982.
I don't know what happened   Bash to Tobler, 1990.
When I left the stage   Sedaka, 1982.
I got a phone call   Bash to Tobler, 1990.
It wasn't Karen   Bash to Tobler, 1990.
the first time   McNally, 1976.
It often happens   Wallace, October 1975.
Current fortnight with Neil Sedaka   *Variety*, September 3, 1975.
I kept telling myself   Coleman, November 1, 1975.
I felt bad for Richard   Short, 1976.
When Richard returned   Short, 1976.
My mother thought   Coleman, November 1, 1975.
People never think   Coleman, November 1, 1975.

10. I NEED TO BE IN LOVE

We had a thing   Short, 1976.
It was sickening   Windeler, 1976.
an overdose of pretty   McNally, 1976.
a little ball of twine   Bettis to Tobler, 1993.
When he wrote the lyrics   KC to Tuna, 1976.
'I Need to Be in Love'   Bettis to Tobler, 1993.
My mind starts going   Coleman, November 8, 1975.
It's really hard   Windeler, 1976.
Well, I have my list   KC to Tuna, 1976.

I want a husband   Short, 1976.

It really hits me   KC to Tuna, 1976.

When we first   KC to Leonard, 1976.

It is just drums   KC to Tuna, 1976.

He's so talented   Coleman, November 8, 1975.

Karen is the star   Lieberman, 1973.

We're hams   Coleman, 1976.

They pretend for a   Coleman, 1976.

polite plastic pop   Evans, 1976.

They were not only   Sinor, 1976.

I've discussed this   KC to Radio Clyde, 1978.

I never had a boyfriend   Coleman, November 8, 1975.

I want desperately to   St. John, 1977.

I don't know anyone   Bash to Tobler, 1990.

You see, I so much   Short, 1976.

11. JUST LET US KNOW WHAT THE PROBLEM IS!

a streak that nobody   Feldman, 2000: 140.

Each time you get   KC to Nite, 1977.

The image we have   Nolan, 1974.

It's no worse   Windeler, 1976.

When he said 'yes,'   Coleman, November 8, 1975.

It had to be done   Short, 1976.

For the last three years   Moran, 1978.

most boldly innovative   Billboard, 1977.

We thought it was   Theroux, 1978.

[He] wanted to do that   KC to Goldman, 1978.

experimental touches that   Hilburn, February 13, 1983.

This is the first time   Grein, 1978.

We always try   Naglin, 1978.

After all these years   Coleman, 1977.

Too many artists forget   Bash to Tobler, 1990.

In this business   Short, 1977.

We just don't know   Moran, 1978.

We're very dedicated   Coleman, November 8, 1975.

You are the Perry Comos   Coleman, 1994: 214.

We stayed away from television   KC to Goldman, 1978.

Each one, in our opinion   KC to Goldman, 1978.

The Carpenters should have   Grein, March 8, 1991.

It's something I would   Moran, 1978.
Streisand just floors me   KC to Tuna, 1976.
There was one album   KC to Radio Clyde, 1978.
To sing these songs   KC to Sky, 1978.
They've synthesized everything   Parade, 1978.
Christmas Portrait *is really*   "Carpenters Biography," 2005.

12. THE BIRD HAS FINALLY FLOWN THE COOP _____

I was up   RC to Burlingame, 1988.
Taken properly they were   RC to Burlingame, 1988.
One side of me   Carpenter, 1988.
That's it   Coleman, 1994: 239.
My hands were shaking   Carpenter, 1988.
The Carpenters finally arrived   Carney, 1978.
You get pretty devious   Carpenter, 1988.
Karen wants everyone   Ewbank, 1978.
It was OK   Grein, 1981.
Confrontation about album   Coleman, 1994: 244.
That is the ultimate compliment   Coleman, November 8, 1975.
Everybody is trying new things   KC to Radio Clyde, 1978.
We have often thought   KC to Radio Clyde, 1978.
the Quincy Jones of   Hoerburger, 1990.
It was never planned   Grein, 1981.

13. POCKETS FULL OF GOOD INTENTIONS _____

The laughs and silliness   Ramone, 2007.
If he hadn't been   Grein, 1981.
Was Billy's group perfect   Ramone, 2007.

14. WHITE LACE AND PROMISES BROKEN _____

He really didn't know   KC to Moore, 1981.
He gets along fabulously   Mackay, 1980.
shelved at her request   Grein, 1980.
Karen thought about it   Grein, 1980.
I get the blame   Carpenter, 1993.
To everybody's credit   Coleman, 1994: 271.
I don't exactly *remember*   Alpert, 1996.

We didn't think it   Moss, 2007.
It's a good album   Grein, 1981.
Pisceans have marriage   Jillson, 1980.
We were planning on   KC to Aspel, 1981.
I invited everybody   KC to Aspel, 1981.

15. BEGINNING OF THE END

I love it   KC to *Japanese All-American Top 40 Show*, 1981.
When all the ingredients gelled   Tobler, 1998: 94.
Innocuous ditties like   Grein, July 25, 1981.
Richard, I realize   Carpenter, 1983.

16. DANCING IN THE DARK

the day she walked   Levenkron, 1993.
The therapist must develop   Levenkron, 1982: 21.
She would never call me   Bash to Tobler, 1990.
You are the victim   Levenkron, 1982: 191.
The victims must learn   Levenkron, 1982: 193.
I did everything   Carpenter, 1993.
Failure of the family   Levenkron, 1982: 173.
I gotta sing.   Coleman, 1976.
A lot of people   KC to Roberts, 1981.
less-than-perfect treatment   Coleman, 1994: 303.
What I find interesting   Levenkron, 1993.
sophisticated form of suicide   O'Neill, 1982: ix.
When are you going to   O'Neill, 1982: 157.
I did it   O'Neill, 1982: 157.
They say I have anorexia   Vaiuso, 2004.
Karen, this is crap   Carpenter, 2007.
The extent of her bravery   Levin, 1983.
She was a little anxious   Levin, 1983.

17. TOO LITTLE, TOO LATE, TOO SOON

Hey, look at me   Alpert to Tobler, 1994.
She was full of energy   Wallace, July 1983.
I want you to know   Carpenter, 1993.
It's not that I   Carpenter, 1993.

Well, did you Coleman, 1994: 25.
She had just laid down Agnes Carpenter, 1983.
It was a chilling scene National Enquirer, 1983.
Those things don't hit you Bettis to Tobler, 1993.
My immediate reaction Carpenter, 1983.
It's hardly surprising Smith, 1983.
It never occurred to me Diliberto, 1985.
According to the L.A. Coroner Levenkron, 1983.
In the last twenty years Levenkron, 2001: 12.
Most kept their visits short Pickney, 1983.
always got along Levin, 1983.

EPILOGUE: A SONG FOR YOU

For anyone accustomed to Browne, 1996.
She brings a sweetness Smith, 1996.
leaner, decidedly unsaccharine Hoerburger, 1990.
nor was it intended Grein, 1996.
It holds up with Hoerburger, 1996.
It actually made Grein, 1983.
Will you please allow Gleiberman, 1991.
His decision to make Carpenter, 1991.
Maybe it's just Whitty, 1990.
too good to be through Coleman, 1994.
It was a transformation Cummings, 1997.
While it's easy to dismiss Konjoyan, September 11, 1994.
She'd like it Konjoyan, October 3, 1994.
In the U.S., alternative McClure, 1996.
Karen and Richard are Grein, 2009.
Were you angry Appleyard, January 3, 1990.
[Richard] and Mary do not Wallace, July 1984.
We weren't thinking Barlow, 2004.
With room for six Entertainment Tonight/ETonline.com, 2004.
Irreplaceable Bettis to Tobler, 1993.

BIBLIOGRAPHY

Alpert, Herb. Interview by John Tobler. 1994.

————. *Yesterday Once More*. BBC-TV. 1996.

Appleyard, Christena. "How I Learned to Live Without Karen." *Daily Mirror*, January 3, 1990.

————. "My Tragic Karen: Richard Carpenter's Own Story of the Superstar Sister He Couldn't Save." *Daily Mirror*, January 2, 1990.

Armstrong, Dan. "Why They're on Top?" *Southeast News*, December 9, 1971.

Autopsy Report # 83-1611. County of Los Angeles. February 4, 1983.

Bangs, Lester. "Carpenters: *Now and Then*." *Let It Rock*, November 1973.

————. "The Carpenters and the Creeps." *Rolling Stone*, March 4, 1971.

Barlow, Zeke. "Singer Carpenter Donates $3 Million to Thousand Oaks Civic Arts Plaza." *Ventura County Star*, October 24, 2004.

Barnes, Ken. "Carpenters: *Horizon*." *Phonograph Record*, July 1975.

Barrios, Greg. "Carpenter: 'This Album is Karen's.'" *Los Angeles Times*, October 23, 1983.

Bash, Sherwin. Interview by John Tobler. 1990.

Bauer, Stephen. *At Ease in the White House*. Lanham, MD: Taylor Trade Publishing, 2004.

Bego, Mark. *Billy Joel: The Biography*. New York: Thunder's Mouth Press, 2007.

Beller, Miles. "Last Respects Paid to Karen Carpenter." *Herald Examiner*, February 8, 1983.

Bettis, John. Interview by John Tobler. 1993.

"A Billboard Pick: Carpenters—*Offering*." *Billboard*, 1970.

Blanche, Tony and Brad Schreiber. *Death in Paradise: An Illustrated History of the Los Angeles County Department of Coroner.* New York: Running Press, 2001.

Booth, Amy L. "Carpenters: A Song for You." *DISCoveries*, December 1991.

Boskind-White, Marlene and William C. White. *Bulimia/Anorexia: The Binge/Purge Cycle and Self-Starvation.* New York: W.W. Norton, 2000.

Bresette, James. "Bring Karen from Behind Those Drums." *Omaha World-Herald*, May 22, 1971.

————. "Carpenters' Fortune is in Karen's Voice." *Omaha World-Herald*, October 14, 1972.

"Bride-to-Be Karen Carpenter Feted with Pre-Nuptial Party." Unknown Publication, 1980.

Bronson, Fred. *The Billboard Book of Number One Hits.* New York: Billboard Books, 1988.

————. *Billboard's Hottest Hot 100 Hits.* New York: Billboard Books, 2007.

Browne, David. "…And Oh So Far Away." *Entertainment Weekly*, October 11, 1996.

————. "Magic Carpenter Ride." *Entertainment Weekly*, September 16, 1994.

Bruch, Hilde. "Anorexia Nervosa." Manuscript for *Reader's Digest*, 1977.

————. *The Golden Cage: The Enigma of Anorexia Nervosa.* Cambridge, MA: Harvard, 1978.

"Builder Burris to Wed Karen Carpenter." *Corona Independent*, July 8, 1980.

"Burris, Carpenter Have Only Just Begun." *Corona Independent*, July 9, 1980.

Butler, Patricia. *Barry Manilow: The Biography.* London: Omnibus Press, 2002.

Calio, Jim. "Four Years After His Sister Karen's Death, Singer Richard Carpenter Makes His Debut as a Solo Act." *People*, October 26, 1987.

Cameron, Jacob. "Wesley Jacobs: The Career of a Lifetime." *International Tuba Euphonium Association Journal* 36, no. 2 (2009).

Carney, Charles. "Winter Festival Joins Campus Choirs and Orchestra." *The 49er*, December 1978.

"Carpenter Funeral Today." *Associated Press*, February 7, 1983.

Carpenter, Agnes. By David Hartman. *Good Morning America.* ABC-TV, November 3, 1983.

Carpenter, Karen and Richard Carpenter. *Carpenters: Decade.* Downey, CA: Carpenters Fan Club Publication, 1979.

————. By Sue Lawley. *Nationwide.* BBC-TV, October 22, 1981.

Carpenter, Karen. By Bob Sky. KIQQ Radio, December 1978.

————. By Carl Goldman. FM100 Radio, 1978.

————. By Charlie Tuna. October 8, 1976.

————. By Dick Biondi. WCFL Radio, 1970.

————. By Michael Aspel. Capital Radio, 1981.

_____. By Norm Nite. WNBC Radio, February 20, 1977.

_____. By Radio Clyde, December 1978.

_____. By Roy Leonard. WGN Radio, August 1, 1976.

_____. By Tony Blackburn. BBC Radio, 1974.

_____. Interviewer unknown. *Japanese All-American Top 40 Show.* July 11, 1981.

_____. By Mike Douglas. *Mike Douglas Show.* July 29, 1971.

_____. By Dave Roberts. *Music Star Weekend Special.* RKO Radio, 1981.

Carpenter, Richard. "A Brother Remembers." *People*, November 21, 1983.

_____. "Carpenter Responds." *Entertainment Weekly*, May 31, 1991.

_____. "Karen Was Wasting Away... I Had A Drug Problem... And We Couldn't Help Each Other." *TV Guide*, December 31, 1988.

_____. "My Sorrow at Karen's Long Battle with Death." *Mail on Sunday*, November 20, 1983.

_____. Interview by Jon Burlingame. November 18, 1988.

_____. *Only Yesterday: The Carpenters Story.* BBC-TV, 2007.

_____. *Superstar: The Karen Carpenter Story.* BBC Radio, February 4, 1993.

"'Carpenter': No. 1 Hit for CBS." *USA Today*, January 5, 1989.

"The Carpenters: An Interview." *A&M Compendium*, July 1975.

"Carpenters at Greek Theatre." *Southeast News,* July 10, 1970.

"Carpenters Biography." http://www.richardandkarencarpenter.com (accessed 2008).

"Carpenters Coming." *Melody Maker*, December 8, 1973.

"Carpenters Get Their Star: Downey Duo Given Salute." *Downey Herald American*, October 15, 1983.

"The Carpenters 'Nail' Neil Sedaka." *Rona Barrett's Hollywood*, January 1976.

"Carpenters Serenade Brandt at White House." *Variety*, May 9, 1973.

"Carpenters Telepic Boosts Record Sales." *Variety*, February 8, 1989.

"Carpenters Tour Downey, Hospitals." *Southeast News*, December 7, 1971.

"Carpenters: Concerts Off." *Melody Maker*, November 1, 1975.

"Carpenters: *Passage.*" *Billboard*, October 8, 1977.

Certificate of Death: Karen Anne Carpenter. State of California. 1983.

Certificate of Registry of Marriage: Thomas James Burris and Karen Anne Carpenter. County of Los Angeles. Issued August 7, 1980.

Charlesworth, Chris. "Carpenters: It's Plane Sailing!" *Melody Maker*, September 29, 1973.

Coleman, Ray. "Carpenters Über Alles!" *Melody Maker*, November 20, 1976.

_____. "Carpenters: Good, Clean, All-American Aggro!" *Melody Maker*, November 8, 1975.

_____. *The Carpenters: The Untold Story.* New York: HarperCollins, 1994.

_____ . "Karen: Why I Collapsed." *Melody Maker*, November 1, 1975.

_____ . "*Passage.*" *Melody Maker*, October 15, 1977.

_____ . "Too Good to Be Through." *Sunday Times*, September 11, 1994.

Corliss, Richard. "Yesterday Once More." *Time*, November 4, 1996.

Crowe, Jerry. "Karen Carpenter's 'Lost' LP." *Los Angeles Times*, August 31, 1996.

Cummings, Sue. *The* Rolling Stone *Book of Women in Rock: Trouble Girls*, edited by Barbara O'Dair. New York: Random House, 1997.

Daugherty, Michael. "Calendar Desk: Carpenters' Tools." *Los Angeles Times*, October 16, 1994.

Diehl, Digby. "They Put Romance into Rock." *TV Guide*, August 14, 1971.

Diliberto, Gioia. "Karen Carpenter Was Killed by an Over-the-Counter Drug Some Doctors Say May Be Killing Many Others." *People*, May 13, 1985.

Dosti, Rose. "Karen Carpenter Feels Close to Mom, Culinarily Speaking." *Los Angeles Times*, February 11, 1971.

"Downey Youths on 'Your Life.'" *Southeast News*, February 10, 1971.

"Editorial: TV Writers Faked Review." *Billboard*, January 28, 1989.

Erlich, Nancy. "Carpenters: Carnegie Hall, New York." *Billboard*, May 29, 1971.

Evans, Mike. "Carpenters' Tinsel Circus." Unknown Publication, 1976.

Ewbank, Tim. "An Unkind Cut for the Carpenters." *The Sun*, December 1978.

Farber, Sheryl. "Karen Carpenter: Getting to the Bare Bones of Todd Haynes' *Superstar: The Karen Carpenter Story*." *Film Threat #20*. 1989.

Feather, Leonard. "Battle of the Bands." *Los Angeles Times*, June 1966.

Feldman, Christopher G. *The Billboard Book of No. 2 Singles*. New York: Billboard Books, 2000.

First Codicil to Last Will and Testament of Karen A. Carpenter. September 1, 1981.

Flans, Robyn. "In Memoriam: Karen Carpenter." *Modern Drummer*, May 1983.

Fleming, Peggy. *The Long Program: Skating Toward Life's Victories*. New York: Pocket Books, 1999.

Fox-Cumming, Ray. "Carpentry." *Disc*, September 1, 1973.

"Friends, Family Mourn Agnes Reuwer Carpenter." *Downey Eagle*, November 14, 1996.

Gaar, Gillian. *She's a Rebel: The History of Women in Rock & Roll*. New York: Seal Press, 1992.

Gautschy, Dean. "The Carpenters: They've Only Just Begun." *TV/Radio Mirror*, August, 1971.

Gautschy, Jan. "The Carpenters: Two Superstars' Young Dreams Come True." *Words and Music*, March 1972.

Gelly, Dave. *Appraisal of Karen Carpenter's Career*. BBC Radio, June 1990.

Gleiberman, Owen. "Dear Richard Carpenter." *Entertainment Weekly*, April 26, 1991.

Goldsmith, Len. "Carpenters Find Winning Number." *The Southeast News*, January 30, 1970.

Grein, Paul. "Album Recalls Karen Carpenter." *Billboard*, 1983.

_____. "An Essay." *Carpenters International Fan Club Newsletter*, June 1991.

_____. "Carpenters Cracking Country Chart Without Nashville Push." *Billboard*, April 1, 1978.

_____. "Carpenters: Building on Experience." *Los Angeles Times*, August 23, 1981.

_____. "Carpenters' Hits Resurfacing." *Billboard*, May 18, 1985.

_____. "Chart Watch: Week Ending May 17, 2009." http://new.music. yahoo.com/blogs/chart_watch/33675/week-ending-may-17-2009-three-days-is-plenty-for-green-day/ (accessed 2009).

_____. "Closeup: Carpenters—*Made in America*." *Billboard*, July 25, 1981.

_____. "Karen Carpenter Shelves Solo LP." *Billboard*, June 7, 1980.

_____. "Karen Carpenter: She Had Only Just Begun." *Los Angeles Times*, November 7, 1989.

_____. "Karen Carpenter: The Solo Album." A&M Records Press Release. October 1996.

_____. "The Carpenters: Yesterday Once More: A Critical Reassessment of Their Work." *Goldmine*, March 8, 1991.

_____. "Trust Us, This Is Real." *Los Angeles Times*, September 11, 1994.

Haber, Joyce. "Carpenters Nail Down a Spot in Pop Pantheon." *Los Angeles Times*, August 4, 1974.

Haithman, Diane. "A TV Movie He Didn't Want: Brother Guides CBS' *Karen Carpenter Story*." *Los Angeles Times*, July 25, 1988.

Hall, John. "Kids Next Door." *Los Angeles Times*, March 7, 1972.

Hamill, Dorothy. *A Skating Life: My Story*. New York: Hyperion, 2007.

Hardwick, Nancy. "Karen Carpenter: When I Was 16." *Star*, March 1973.

"Hard-Working Carpenters." *Teen*, March 1975.

Harrigan, Brian. "Carpentry." *Melody Maker*, September 6, 1975.

Harrison, Ed. "'Surprise' by the Carpenters." *Billboard*, September 17, 1977.

Haynes, Todd. *Far From Heaven, Safe and Superstar: The Karen Carpenter Story: Three Screenplays*. New York: Grove Press, 2003.

Heckman, Don. "Riffs." *Village Voice*, August 26, 1971.

Henshaw, Laurie and Steve Lake. "Carpenters' Hammer." *Melody Maker*, February 16, 1974.

Hilburn, Robert and Dennis Hunt. "Behind Carpenters' Girl-Next-Door Image." *Los Angeles Times*, February 7, 1983.

Hilburn, Robert. "Bacharach Plays Pop Fare at Greek." *Los Angeles Times*, July 8, 1970.

———. "The Carpenters Come Home." *Los Angeles Times*, August 11, 1972.

———. "A Lesson in Art of Emotion." *Los Angeles Times*, February 13, 1983.

Hinckley, David. "Richard Carpenter Remembers His Sister Karen." *New York Daily News*, November 20, 1983.

Hoerburger, Rob. *Carpenters: Inside the Music: The Ultimate Critical Review*. DVD. 2008.

———. "The Carpenters: *Lovelines*." *Rolling Stone*, February 8, 1990.

———. "Karen Carpenter's Second Life." *New York Times Magazine*, October 6, 1996.

Holden, Stephen. "Carpenters: *A Song for You*." *Rolling Stone*, October 12, 1972.

———. "Carpenters: *Horizon*." *Rolling Stone*, August 28, 1975.

"House Review: London Palladium." *Variety*, December 1, 1976.

"Hundreds Attend Karen Carpenter Rites." *Southeast News*, February 9, 1983.

Hyatt, Wesley. *The Billboard Book of Number One Adult Contemporary Hits*. New York: Watson-Guptill, 1999.

"Inside Track." *Billboard*, October 4, 1975.

Jacobs, Jody. "It Won't Be Your Average Garage Sale." *Los Angeles Times*, July 9, 1981.

Jillson, Joyce. "Astrology." Syndicated Column. May 21, 1980.

"John Bettis Interview 2007." http://www.drownedmadonna.com/modules. php?name=john_bettis (accessed 2008).

Jones, Peter. "Talent in Action: Carpenters: London Palladium." *Billboard*, December 18, 1976.

"Karen Carpenter and Tom Burris Marry." *Beverly Hills People*, September 3, 1980.

"Karen Carpenter Anorexia Death." *National Enquirer*, March 15, 1983.

"Karen Carpenter Wed in Beverly Hills Rites." *Southeast News*, September 3, 1980.

"Karen in the Kitchen: Who Says a Young Female Superstar Can't Be a Top-Notch Cook?" A&M Records Press Release. 1971.

Kinnersley, Simon. "A Death Too Cruel." *Daily Mail*, November 1983.

Knappman, Edward W. *Watergate and the White House: June 1972–July 1973, Volume 1*. New York: Facts on File, 1973.

Konjoyan, David. "That Whitebread Inspiration Came with a Dark Side." *Orange County Register*, September 11, 1994.

———. "Yesterday Once More: An Exclusive *HITS* Interview with Richard Carpenter." *HITS*, October 3, 1994.

Kraus, Bill and Jan Grimm. "Hammer and Nails: A Carpenters Interview." *Rock Spectacular*, Summer 1970.

Landau, John. "Carpenters: *Carpenters.*" *Rolling Stone*, June 24, 1971.

Last Will and Testament of Karen A. Carpenter. May 2, 1972.

Leaf, Earl. "The Carpenters: They Nail a New Sound." *Teen*, January 1971.

Lees, Gene. "Success Comes to Jack Daugherty." *High Fidelity Magazine*, January 1972.

Legge, Beverly. "'I Mean Nobody Could Be That Clean.'" *Disc*, March 2, 1974.

Levenkron, Steven. *Anatomy of Anorexia*. New York: W.W. Norton, 2001.

———. *The Best Little Girl in the World*. New York: Warner Books, 1978.

———. *A Current Affair*, February 5, 1993.

———. Radio interview, source unknown, 1983.

———. *Treating and Understanding Anorexia Nervosa*. New York: Warner Books, 1982.

Levin, Eric. "A Sweet Surface Hid a Troubled Soul in the Late Karen Carpenter, a Victim of Anorexia Nervosa." *People*, February 21, 1983.

Levitin, Daniel. "Pop Charts: How Richard Carpenter's Lush Arrangements Turned Hit Songs into Pop Classics." *Electronic Musician*, May 1995.

Lieberman, Frank H. "The Carpenters: A Talented Brother and Sister Act Which Represents Clean, Wholesome Entertainment." *Billboard*, November 17, 1973.

———. "The Carpenters: Soft Rock and 14 Gold Records." *Saturday Evening Post*. October 1974.

Liebovich, Louis W. *Richard Nixon, Watergate, and the Press*. Westport, CT: Praeger Publishers, 2003.

Littwin, Susan. "Artistic Differences: The Family's Memories vs. Hollywood's Version." *TV Guide*, December 31, 1988.

"Local Coed Performs Sunday." *Southeast News*, November 21, 1969.

MacDougall, Fiona. "The Carpenters: Nailing Down Success." *Teen*, October 1971.

Mackay, Kathy. "A Carpenter Ties the Knot and Finally That Song's for Karen." *People*, September 15, 1980.

McAfee, Paul. "A City in Mourning." *Southeast News*, February 8, 1983.

McCardle, Dorothy. "A Pair of Experts at Coming Back." *Washington Post*, May 2, 1973.

McClure, Steve. "The Carpenters Are a Hit Among Young Japanese." *Billboard*, February 10, 1996.

McFadden, Ian. "Carpenters: It's Only Just Begun." *Melody Maker*, February 23, 1974.

McGreevy, Pat. "Downey is 'Stunned' by Death of Artist." *Southeast News*, February 7, 1983.

_____. "Karen Carpenter Dies in Downey." *Downey Herald American*, February 5, 1983.

_____. "Thirty Minutes with Richard Carpenter." *Southeast News*, October 17, 1983.

_____. "Walk of Fame Star Dedicated to History's Top-Selling Duo." *Southeast News*, October 13, 1983.

McNally, Joel. "It's an Overdose of Pretty." *Milwaukee Journal*, 1976.

McQuay, Dave. "Like TV Dinner for the Ears." *Columbia Flier*, August 1975.

Medigovich, Lori B. "It Still Hurts: Richard Carpenter Remembers His Sister Karen." *Los Angeles Times Syndicate*, April 1988.

Michaels, Ken. "Rainy Days and Carpenters Always Get Me Down." *Chicago Tribune Magazine*, November 21, 1971.

Miller, Merle. "Review: 'Make Your Own Kind of Music.'" *TV Guide*, September 4, 1971.

Miller, Ron. "She'd Only Just Begun: Fine CBS Movie Tells Sad Story of Karen Carpenter." *San Jose Mercury News*, January 1, 1989.

Millman, Joyce. "The Troubled World of Karen Carpenter." *San Francisco Examiner*, January 1, 1989.

Moran, Bill. "'If Somebody Would Just Let Us Know What the Problem Is.'" *Radio Report*, May 29, 1978.

Morgan, Lael. "The Carpenters: They've Only Just Begun." *Los Angeles Times*, January 8, 1971.

Morrow, Barry, and Cynthia A. Cherbak. *A Song for You: The Karen Carpenter Story*. Draft. December 24, 1987.

_____. *A Song for You: The Karen Carpenter Story*. Shooting Draft. February 12, 1988.

Morrow, Barry. *A Song for You: The Karen Carpenter Story*. Draft. September 30, 1987.

Moss, Jerry. *Only Yesterday: The Carpenters Story*. BBC-TV, 2007.

Naglin, Nancy. "The Carpenters Go Country?" *Country Music*, August 1978.

"A New Resting Place for Karen Carpenter?" *Entertainment Tonight/ETonline. com*. http://www.etonline.com/music/2004/02/33452/ (accessed 2004).

"Nixon Thanks Carpenters for Fight Against Cancer." *Associated Press*, August 1972.

Nixon, Richard M. *The Presidential Transcripts*. New York: Dell, 1974.

Nolan, Tom. "The Carpenters: An Appraisal." *A&M Compendium*, July 1975.

_____. "Up from Downey." *Rolling Stone*, July 4, 1974.

O'Brien, Lucy. *She Bop: The Definitive History of Women in Rock, Pop and Soul.* New York: Penguin Books, 1996.

O'Dair, Barbara. *Trouble Girls: The Rolling Stone Book of Women in Rock.* New York: Random House, 1997.

O'Neill, Cherry Boone. *Starving for Attention.* New York: Continuum, 1982.

Oppenheimer, Peer J. "The Carpenters: Our Whole Life Is Caught Between Two Cultures." *Family Weekly,* May 7, 1972.

Parade, James. "Carpenters: *Christmas Portrait.*" *Record Mirror,* 1978.

Paytress, Mark. "The Carpenters." *Record Collector,* January, 1990.

Petition for Dissolution of Marriage: Karen Carpenter Burris (Petitioner) and Thomas J. Burris (Respondent). County of Los Angeles. Filed November 9, 1982.

Pfenninger, Leslie J. *From Brass to Gold, Volume I: Discography of A&M Records and Affiliates in the United States.* Westport, CT: Greenwood Press, 2001.

———. *From Brass to Gold, Volume II: Discography of A&M Records and Affiliates Around the World.* Westport, CT: Greenwood Press, 2001.

Pinckney, Judy. "Friends Bid Farewell to Karen Carpenter." *Southeast News,* February 7, 1983.

Pleasants, Henry. "The Carpenters: Nice Guys Don't Always Finish Last." *Stereo Review,* February 1972.

Pogoda, Gordon. Interview with John Bettis. *SongTalk,* 1994.

Pool, Bob. "Fans Love Carpenters but Not carpenters." *Los Angeles Times,* February 26, 2008.

Pooler, Frank. "The Choral Sound of the Carpenters." *Choral Journal,* April 1973.

President Richard Nixon's Daily Diary. April 29, 1973.

———. April 30, 1973.

———. August 25, 1972.

———. May 1, 1973.

Ragogna, Mike. "The 40th Anniversary of Carpenters: Interview with Richard Carpenter." *Huffington Post,* May 11, 2009. http://www.huffington post.com/mike-ragogna/emhuffpost-exclusiveem-th_b_201408.html.

Ramone, Phil, and Charles L. Granata. *Making Records: The Scenes Behind the Music.* New York: Hyperion, 2007.

Ramone, Phil. CompuServe Chat Transcript. October 18, 1996.

Rees, Dafydd and Luke Crampton. *Rock Movers and Shakers: An A–Z of People Who Made Rock Happen.* Oxford UK: ABC-CLIO, 1991.

Reitwiesner, William Addams, and Robert Battle. "Ancestry of Richard and Karen Carpenter." www.wargs.com/other/carpenter.html (accessed 2008).

"Remembering Karen Carpenter." *Southeast News,* June 24, 1983.

"Richard Carpenter Has Seen 'Every Single Minute of Filming' of 'The Karen Carpenter Story.'" *San Jose Mercury News*, March 6, 1988.

"Riviera-Las Vegas." *Variety*, September 3, 1975.

"The Rockers Are Rolling in It." *Forbes*, April 15, 1973.

Rosenfeld, Megan. "The Carpenters: 'Young America at Its Very Best.'" *Washington Post*, May 6, 1973.

"Sahara-Tahoe." *Variety*, August 21, 1974.

Schmidt, Randy L. *Yesterday Once More: Memories of the Carpenters and Their Music*. Cranberry Township, PA: Tiny Ripple Books, 2000.

Sedaka, Neil. *Laughter in the Rain: My Own Story*. New York: Putnam, 1982.

Seligmann, Jean A. "A Deadly Feast and Famine." *Newsweek*, March 7, 1983.

_____. "Starvation by Intention." *Reader's Digest*, January 1975.

Short, Don. "The Carpenters: 'Too Shocking to Be Untrue.'" *Sunday Mirror*, November 21, 1976.

_____. "I Need to Be Loved." *Woman*, April 16, 1977.

Simmons, Gene. *Kiss and Make-up*. New York: Crown, 2001.

Sinor, Brad, "Theatrics Overshadow Carpenters' Music." *Oklahoma Daily*, October 26, 1976.

Small, Linda. "Carpenters Are Building an Empire." *Free-Lance Star*, April 1, 1972.

Smith, C.P. "Karen Carpenter: Her Serene Voice Sold 60 Million LPs." *Orange County Register*, February 5, 1983.

Smith, Tierney. "Album Review: Karen Carpenter." *Goldmine*, January 31, 1997.

Smucker, Tom. "The Carpenters: Forbidden Fruit." *Village Voice*, June 2, 1975.

Southall, Brian. *The A–Z of Record Labels*. London: Sanctuary, 2000.

_____. *Yesterday Once More: The Karen Carpenter Story*. BBC Radio, 2004.

St. John, Michael. "The Carpenters: Million Dollar Misfits Set the Record Straight." *Super Rock*, June 1977.

Strong, Martin C. *The Great Rock Discography*. Edinburgh, Scotland: Canongate, 2002.

Summons: Karen Carpenter Burris (Petitioner) and Thomas J. Burris (Respondent). County of Los Angeles. Filed November 24, 1982.

Superstar: The Karen Carpenter Story. London: Wallflowers Press, 2008.

Tatham, Dick. *Carpenters: Sweet Sound of Success*. London: Phoebus, 1976.

"Television Reviews: *The Karen Carpenter Story*." *Variety*, January 18, 1989.

Thegze, Chuck. "Carpenters Have Transformed the Laughter into Bravos." *Los Angeles Times*, August 6, 1972.

"Therapist: Anorexia Not Karen Carpenter's Killer." *USA Today*, February 4, 1993.

Theroux, Gary. "The Carpenters Story." *L.A. Music & Art Review*, December 1978.

Tobler, John. "It Happens in the Middle of the Road: Confessions of a Carpenters Fan." Unknown Publication, 1974.

————. *The Complete Guide to the Music of the Carpenters*. London: Omnibus Press, 1998.

Vaiuso, Teresa. *Yesterday Once More: The Karen Carpenter Story*. BBC Radio, 2004.

Van Valkenburg, Carol. "Carpenters Perform for Middle Missoula." *The Missoulian*, May 19. 1973.

Wallace, Evelyn, and Rosina Sullivan. Carpenters Fan Club Newsletters. 1971–1989.

Wallace, Evelyn. "Carpenters—Superstars." 1975.

"Welcome to A&M Records, Former Home of the Charlie Chaplin Movie Lot." A&M Records Map and History. Revised June 20, 1991.

Whitburn, Joel. *Top Adult Contemporary Singles 1961–2001*. Menomonee Falls, WI: Record Research, Inc., 2002.

Whitty, Stephen. "Yesterday, Once More." *San Jose Mercury News*, October 18, 1990.

Wild, David. *And the Grammy Goes To . . . : The Official Story of Music's Most Coveted Award*. Brockport, NY: State Street Press, 2007.

Windeler, Robert. "Karen and Richard Carpenter Aren't at the Top of the World: They Need to Be in Love." *People*, August 2, 1976.

Wyatt, Justin. "Cinematic/Sexual Transgression: An Interview with Todd Haynes." *Film Quarterly* 46, no. 3. (1993).

SUGGESTED READING

THE FOLLOWING books and articles represent some of the best sources for readers interested in learning more about Karen Carpenter and her music. Certain selections are out of print but still in circulation and available at your local library or online. The fan club newsletters are no longer available in hard copy but may be found archived on various Web sites, including www.karencarpenter.com/newsletter_index.html and www.whizzo.ca/carpenter/newsletters.html.

Carpenter, Richard. "A Brother Remembers." *People*, November 21, 1983.
———. "Karen Was Wasting Away.... I Had A Drug Problem.... And We Couldn't Help Each Other." *TV Guide*, December 31, 1988.
Coleman, Ray. "Carpenters: Good, Clean, All-American Aggro!" *Melody Maker*, November 8, 1975.
———. *The Carpenters: The Untold Story*. New York: HarperCollins, 1994.
Grein, Paul. "The Carpenters: Yesterday Once More: A Critical Reassessment of Their Work." *Goldmine*, March 8, 1991.
Hoerburger, Rob. "Karen Carpenter's Second Life." *New York Times Magazine*, October 6, 1996.
Levin, Eric. "A Sweet Surface Hid a Troubled Soul in the Late Karen Carpenter, a Victim of Anorexia Nervosa." *People*, February 21, 1983.
Mackay, Kathy. "A Carpenter Ties the Knot and Finally That Song's for Karen." *People*, September 15, 1980.
Nolan, Tom. "Up from Downey." *Rolling Stone*, July 4, 1974.

Schmidt, Randy L. *Yesterday Once More: Memories of the Carpenters and Their Music*. Cranberry Township, PA: Tiny Ripple Books, 2000.

Tobler, John. *The Complete Guide to the Music of the Carpenters*. London: Omnibus Press, 1998.

Wallace, Evelyn, and Rosina Sullivan. Carpenters Fan Club Newsletters. 1971–1989.

Windeler, Robert. "Karen and Richard Carpenter Aren't at the Top of the World: They Need to Be in Love." *People*, August 2, 1976.

INDEX